Study and Teaching Guide

FOR

THE HISTORY OF THE RENAISSANCE WORLD

By Julia Kaziewicz

A curriculum guide to accompany

Susan Wise Bauer's

The History of the Renaissance World:
From the Rediscovery of Aristotle to the Conquest of Constantinople

WELL-
TRAINED
MIND
PRESS

Charles City, VA

Photocopying and Distribution Policy
Families: you may make as many photocopies of these pages as you need for use within your own family only.
Schools and Co-ops MAY NOT PHOTOCOPY any portion of this book, without a written license from Well-Trained Mind Press. Address requests for permissions to: support@welltrainedmind.com
www.welltrainedmind.com

1.877.322.3445

How To Use This Study Guide

This Study Guide for *The History of the Renaissance World: From the Rediscovery of Aristotle to the Conquest of Constantinople* is designed to be used by tutors, parents, or teachers working with both individual students and groups.

For each chapter of *The History of the Renaissance World,* three sets of exercises are given. Some chapters also include a fourth set—map work.

I. Who, What, Where

This section is designed to check the student's grasp of basic information presented in the chapter: prominent characters, important places, and foundational ideas. The student should explain the significance of each person, place or idea in **one or two complete sentences**.

II. Comprehension

This section requires the student to express, in his own words, the central concepts in each chapter. The student may use two to three complete sentences to answer each question.

III. Critical Thinking

This section requires the student to produce a brief written reflection on the ideas presented in the chapter. Some preliminary exercises are also provided.

IV. Map Work [maps found on pages 791 & following]

This section uses a traditional method to improve the student's geography. In his *Complete Course in Geography* (1875), the geographer William Swinton observed:

"That form is easiest remembered which the hand is taught to trace. The exercise of the mind, needed to teach the hand to trace a form, impresses that form upon the mind. As the study of maps is a study of form, the manner of studying them should be by map-drawing."

Section IV asks the student to go through a carefully structured set of steps with maps (provided on perforated pages in the back of this book): tracing repeatedly, then copying while looking at the original, and finally, where appropriate, reproducing from memory. He will be asked to use a black pencil (one that does not erase easily) as well as a regular pencil with an eraser, as well as colored pencils of various kinds. Large amounts of tracing paper are needed!

On Research and Citations

Many of the critical thinking questions in *The History of the Renaissance World: Study & Teaching Guide* require research. The student may be prompted to use a specific citation style in the question, or he may be given a choice. The most common citation styles for writing in the humanities are MLA (Modern Language Association), The Chicago Manual of Style, and APA (American Psychosocial Association). The most up-to-date versions of these style guides can be purchased through each association's website:

MLA (Modern Language Association) https://www.mla.org/Publications/Bookstore/Nonseries/ MLA-Handbook-Eighth-Edition

The Chicago Manual of Style, and APA (American Psychosocial Association)

http://www.chicagomanualofstyle.org/home.html

APA (American Psychosocial Association)

http://www.apastyle.org/manual/

The most recent version of each style guide should be used, as citation guidelines and rules are constantly changing, especially when it comes to online and digital sources.

You may also consider purchasing a style and citation reference book, like Diana Hacker's *A Writer's Reference* (Bedford/St. Martin's), which includes guidelines for all three style guides listed above. Again, make sure to acquire the most recent edition. Also, Purdue University's Online Writing Lab (OWL) is an excellent, free, web-based resource: https://owl.english.purdue.edu/owl/

Students should be aware that all sources are not made equal. Here is a quick checklist that can be used to test the reliability of a source.

Credibility check:

- Is the source credible?
- Who is the author/publisher/source/sponsor?
- Can you find the author or publisher's credentials?
- What does the web address end in? Sites that end in .edu and .gov are generally credible, but beware of student and employee blog posts.
- Have you heard of the author/website/publishing house before? If not, can you find information about it easily?
- Is the information in the text supported by evidence? If you answered "no," the source you are working with is most likely not reliable.

- Has the information been reviewed? If you are looking at a blog post, is it part of a reviewed publication (like a national newspaper or cable network)? If you answered "no," the source you are working with is most likely not reliable.
- Are there any spelling or grammar mistakes? Are there typos in the writing? If you answered "yes," the source you are working with is most likely not reliable.

Application check:

- Is this source appropriate for the topic you are writing about? Is it relevant to your topic?
- Is the text written for the appropriate audience (not too basic or too advanced for your work)?
- Is the text written to persuade or convince someone of a point? If so, is the text too biased to use as a source in your research? Can you pull objective information from it? If you answered "no," the source you are working with is most likely not reliable.
- Is the source a stated piece of opinion or propaganda? If you answered "yes," the source you are working with is most likely not reliable.
- Are personal biases made clear? Do these biases affect the objective transmission of information? If you answered "yes," the source you are working with is most likely not reliable.
- Is the source trying to sell you something? If you answered "yes," the source you are working with is most likely not reliable.
- Is this the only source you've found? Is limiting your research detrimental to your final writing product?

Timeliness check:

- When was the information posted or published?
- Has the information been updated or revised recently?
- Is the information outdated? Has the information been proven wrong or inaccurate? If you answered "yes," the source you are working with is most likely not reliable.

***Please note that the checklist above is a guideline for considering the reliability of a source, not a hard and fast list of rules. If the student is working on a piece of writing about public relations, for example, and is using an advertisement (trying to sell the reader something) in her work, the article *would* be a good source because it is necessary for the student's essay, even if it does not pass the test above.

Preface

The student may use her text when answering the questions in sections I and II.

Section I: Who, What, Where

Write a one or two-sentence answer explaining the significance of each item listed below.

Age of Enslavement—**Pg. xxv, ¶ 2 & 3**—The Age of Enslavement began in the 1450s when Pope Nicholas V gave the king of Portugal permission to enslave and sell Africans. The Age of Enslavement was a time when all Europeans could profit from slavery without guilt because of the pope's declaration.

Gerard of Cremona—**Pg. xxiii, ¶ 1 & 3**—Gerard of Cremona was an Italian scholar who traveled to the Spanish peninsula in 1140 looking for a rare copy of the thousand-year-old Greek astronomy text known as the Almagest. When Gerard of Cremona got to Toldeo he found the Almagest and more—classical and Arabic studies of dialectic, geometry, philosophy, and medicine; unknown monographs by Euclid, Galen, Ptolemy, and Aristotle; a whole treasury of knowledge.

Petrarch—**Pg. xxiii, ¶ 6**—Petrarch, a poet, was one of the first Italians to give a name to the reawakened interest in Greek and Roman learning when he announced early in the 1340s that poets and scholars were ready to lead the cities of Italy back to the glory days of Rome. Petrarch insisted classical learning had declined and it was time for that learning to be rediscovered; thus the world would have a rebirth or a *Renaissance.*

Pope Nicholas V—**Pg. xxv, ¶ 2**—Pope Nicholas V issued *Dum Diversas* the year before Constantinople fell to the Turks and became Istanbul. *Dum Diversas* was official recognition by the church of the expense and effort that the Portuguese had put into exploring the African coast and approval of enslavement and sale of Africans by the Portuguese crown.

Romanus Pontifex—**Pg. xxv, ¶ 2**—*Romanus Pontifex* confirmed what Pope Nicholas V wrote in the *Dum Diversas* three years prior to its issuance: the enslavement and sale of Africans by the Portuguese was sanctioned by the Holy Roman Empire.

Tursun Bey—**Pg. xxv, ¶ 1**—Tursun Bey, an Ottoman chronicler, was the only Turk to describe the final Ottoman battle in Constantinople. He called the fight a "veritable precipitation and downpouring of calamities from the heavens, as decreed by God Himself."

Section II: **Comprehension**

Write a two or three-sentence answer to each of the following questions.

1. Why did Gerard of Cremona go to the Spanish peninsula in order to find a copy of the Almagest?

A1.—Pg. xxiii, ¶ 2—Gerard of Cremona went to the Spanish peninsula to find the Almagest because Toledo, a city in the center of the peninsula with many libraries, had been recaptured by one of the Christian kingdoms of the north after centuries of Arab rule and he could now travel there safely. The Almagest was likely to be in Toledo because the ruling dynasties of Muslim Spain had brought with them thousands of classical texts which had been long lost to the vernacular languages of the West but had been translated into Arabic. His chances of finding the Almagest in Spain were better than anywhere else in Europe.

2. What did Gerard of Cremona do once he found so many treasured texts in Toldeo? How did he pick what texts to translate?

A2.—Pg. xxiii, ¶ 3—Gerard of Cremona learned Arabic once he found all the treasured texts in Toldeo so that he could read the classic texts and then translate them into Latin. He translated the books he thought were finest.

3. What was Petrarch's personal interest in "a Renaissance"?

A3.—Pg. xxiv, ¶ 1—Petrarch, a poet, wanted to be recognized as an intellectual whose words should be heeded. Advocating for "a Renaissance" would validate and uplift his own work.

4. What is the "Twelfth-Century Renaissance"?

A4.—Pg. xxiv, ¶ 1—The "Twelfth-Century Renaissance" is a term coined by historians to define the intellectual groundwork done by Western scholars, many Italian, that worked through Arabic libraries reacquainting themselves with Greek and Roman thinkers even before Gerard of Cremona arrived in Toledo.

5. When will the history covered in your text end? Why does Susan Wise Bauer choose to end where she does?

A5.—Pg. xxiv, ¶ 4 & 5—The last chapter of *The History of the Renaissance World* will end with the Ottoman attack on Constantinople in May of 1453, when the triumph of the Turks brought a final end to the Roman dream. Though what we call "the Italian Renaissance" continued after 1453, Susan Wise Bauer chooses to end with the Ottoman attack on Constantinople because by the time the city fell the Renaissance had begun to branch out into new eras.

6. What commonly written-about historical periods followed the Renaissance? How did these periods start?

A6.—Pg. xxiv, ¶ 6—The commonly written-about historical periods that followed the Renaissance are the Reformation and the Age of Exploration. The Reformation sprouted out of the followers of the English scholar John Wycliffe and the Bohemian priest Jan Hus who organized against the authority of Rome. The Age of Exploration started when the Portuguese captain Gil Eannes pushed south past Cape Bojador and then a decade later

Prince Henry of Portugal sponsored the first slave market in Europe in the hopes of getting support for further exploration into Africa.

Section III: Critical Thinking

The student may not use her text to answer this question.

The History of the Renaissance World begins with a "Preface." Why? Write a paragraph that defines what a preface is and also explains why Susan Wise Bauer starts her story of the Renaissance with a preface.

The student can look up the definition of "preface" and then write a standard definition of "preface" to begin her paragraph. For example, the Merriam-Webster online dictionary defines "preface" as "an introduction to a book or speech."

On page xxiii, Susan Wise Bauer explains that her history of the world during the period often thought of as "the Renaissance" starts much earlier than the fourteenth century, the time period when historians generally say a rebirth in the interest in classical learning occurred. She continues to explain that by 1340, at the time of Petrarch's declaration that there should be "a Renaissance," the renaissance was already so far advanced that it was visible and able to be named. Further, on page xxiv, it is explained that "The twelfth century saw the real beginnings of the struggle between Church hierarchy and Aristotelian logic. . . . The twelfth century saw the death of the Crusades, the rise of the Plantagenets, the dominance of the Japanese shoguns, and the journey of Islam into central Africa."

The History of the Renaissance World ends with the fall of Constantinople to the Ottomans. The book does not cover what is commonly known as the Italian Renaissance. This is something different from general histories of "the Renaissance," too. Susan Wise Bauer explains that by the time of Constantinople's transformation into Istanbul other historical eras had already begun, namely the Reformation, the Age of Exploration and the Age of Enslavement. She addresses these issues in the preface so that readers of her history understand why she has periodized her work the way that she did.

EXAMPLE ANSWER:

A preface, as defined by the Merriam-Webster online dictionary, is "an introduction to a book or speech." Susan Wise Bauer's *The History of the Renaissance World* starts with a preface in order to introduce readers to her periodization of what is commonly called "the Renaissance." Bauer starts her history in the twelfth century rather than the fourteenth century because work had already begun on re-discovering classical learning. While it was in the fourteenth century that Petrarch declared the world should have a "Renaissance," this was really an observation of work that was already being done. Also, Bauer chooses to end her history with the fall of Constantinople to the Turks in 1453. She explains that she does not dive into what is known as the Italian Renaissance, which continues well past 1453, because what was generally known as the Renaissance was already branching out into what would later be recognized as other historical eras, such as the Reformation, the Age of Exploration and the Age of Enslavement. The preface acts as a way for Bauer to let her

readers know what to expect in the text, and because her periodization differs from the common markers of the Renaissance, tells her readers exactly where she will begin and end her history and why.

Chapter One

Logic and Compromise

The student may use his text when answering the questions in sections I and II.

Section I: Who, What, Where

Write a one or two-sentence answer explaining the significance of each item listed below.

Anselm of Canterbury—**Pg. 5, ¶ 6, Pg. 7, ¶ 5 & 6 and Pg. 8, ¶ 5—Anselm of Canterbury, a believer in Aristotelian logic and fiercely loyal to the pope, disagreed with Henry I's claim of investiture and fought so sharply with Henry I over the issue that he fled to Rome fearing for his life. Anselm of Canterbury returned to England after the Concordat of London, but served only two more years before his death.**

Boethius—**Pg. 5, ¶ 7—Boethius, a sixth-century Roman philosopher, translated some of Aristotle's works into Latin. After getting through the texts on logic, Boethius's translation project was put to an end by Theodoric the Ostrogoth, who had the philosopher beheaded.**

Calixtus II—**Pg. 11, ¶ 2—Calixtus II, pope Paschal II's replacement, was able to get Henry V to renounce the right to investiture in the Concordat of Worms. In exchange newly appointed bishops in Germany only would do homage to Henry V as king before their consecration, assuring their loyalty to the Holy Roman Emperor.**

Domesday Book—**Pg. 4, ¶ 6—The Domesday Book, kept by William the Conqueror's scribes, attempted to record the condition and ownership of every piece of English land. Barely one percent of the names of the feudal lords in the book were Anglo-Saxon.**

Feudalism—**Pg. 4, ¶ 6—Feudalism, a system rooted in tenth-century Francia where the poor served their wealthier neighbors in exchange for protection, was an order in which service and payments (both money and crops) were exchanged for the right to live on, farm, and hold a particular piece of land. William the Conqueror instituted feudalism in England.**

Henry I—**Pg. 3, ¶ 5 & 6, Pg. 4, ¶ 2 and Pg. 8, ¶ 3—Henry I, William II's younger brother, was pronounced Henry king of England on August 5, 1100 even though he was not William II's heir. He then took Normandy from his brother Robert, making him king of England and**

11

Duke of Normandy. After years of fighting, Henry I came to a truce with pope Paschal II over investiture rights called the Concordat of London.

Henry V—Pg. 8, ¶ 6, Pg. 10, ¶ 6 and Pg. 11, ¶ 2—Henry V, son of Henry IV, became the leader of the Holy Roman Empire after his father abdicated in 1105. After forcing Pope Paschal II to grant him the right to investiture and then dealing with ten years of revolts as a result, Henry came to a more firm agreement about investiture with the new pope, Calixtus II, called the Concordat of Worms.

Lanfranc—Pg. 5, ¶ 6 and Pg. 6, ¶ 3—Lanfranc, a teacher at the Bec Abbey in Normandy, studied logic in Italy before entering the abbey and brought the liberal arts with him. Lanfranc taught his students, including a man who would be later be known as Anselm of Canterbury, to use dialectic as a tool for understanding revelation more clearly.

Matilda—Pg. 10, ¶ 1—Matilda, Henry I's daughter, was married off to Henry V of the Holy Roman Empire in 1110 as an assurance of the alliance her father's empire and England against Pope Paschal II.

Paschal II—Pg. 7, ¶ 7 to Pg. 8, ¶ 3 and Pg. 10, ¶ 2 & 6 to Pg. 11, ¶ 1—Paschal II, a believer in the papal right to investiture, threatened Henry I with excommunication if the king did not give up his right to investiture after which they came to an agreement called the Concordat of London. Paschal II also fought with Henry V over investiture and he was eventually forced into an agreement where the pope held on to the right to appoint bishops in exchange for the return of all the lands, political perks and privileges of the papal investiture to Henry V.

Robert—Pg. 3, ¶ 6 to Pg. 4, ¶ 1 & 2—Robert, duke of Normandy and rightful heir to William II's throne, did not have a chance to claim his throne because his brother Henry I was made king before Robert could make it back from the First Crusade. After Henry I invaded Normandy, Robert was taken prisoner in battle and then he lived out the rest of his long life—he died his eighties—under guard.

Trans-substantio—Pg. 6, ¶ 2—Trans-substantio is the assertion that the bread and wine of the Eucharist, while remaining the same in appearance, changes in substance into the body and blood of Christ.

Walter Tyrrell—Pg. 3, ¶ 5—Walter Tyrrell, an experienced hunter, shot King William II with an arrow when they were out hunting and immediately fled the scene. King William II died on the spot.

William II—Pg. 3, ¶ 5—William II, king of the English realm since 1087, was out hunting when he was hit by an arrow by Water Tyrrell. William II collapsed onto the arrow and died on the spot.

Section II: Comprehension

Write a two or three-sentence answer to each of the following questions.

1. What did the first article of Henry I's Charter of Liberties declare? What did the remaining thirteen articles of the Charter of Liberties deal with, and what in particular did the Charter assure English barons?

A1.—Pg. 4, ¶ 3 & 7 to Pg. 5, ¶ 1—The first article of Henry I's Charter of Liberties promised that the "holy church of God" would remain free from royal control and its lands could not be confiscated by the crown. The remaining thirteen articles were all directed towards Henry I's people—particularly towards the barons of England. In particular, the barons were assured that Henry I would not extort additional payments from them, or prevent them from disposing of their own possessions as they wished.

2. How were the *thegns,* or "thanes," of England treated under William the Conqueror?

A2.—Pg. 4, ¶ 4—The *thegns,* or "thanes," of England, Anglo-Saxon nobles, and had once been second only to the royal family in power and influence. However, when William the Conqueror took England, he rewarded his Norman knights by dividing up the newly conquered land into parcels and distributing those parcels to the knights in reward for their service. The number of English thanes grew smaller during the wars of the Conquest and then those that survived the wars lost most of their property to the king's redistribution of English land.

3. What was an English baron's relationship to his land? What was the *servitium debitum?*

A3.—Pg. 4, ¶ 5—An English baron understood that he was a landholder, not a landowner. William the Conqueror introduced a new type of monarchy to England, where the king claimed to own the entire kingdom: all English land, all Norman land, was in his possession. The barons were his "tenants in chief," and in return for their new estates, they owed the king a certain number of armed men for his use: the *servitium debitum.*

4. Though the Charter of Liberties seemed to benefit English barons, how did it really reinforce Henry I's power?

A4.—Pg. 5, ¶ 2—Though the Charter of Liberties seemed to grant English barons the power to dispose of their own goods and ensured that they would not be forced to pay additional payments to the king, it really shored up Henry I's power. Henry I was a usurper and he needed to stay in the barons' favor. By protecting the barons' interests, the Charter guarded Henry I's power by keeping them on his side.

5. What is investiture? Why was having power over investiture so important in the renaissance world?

A5.—Pg. 5, ¶ 4—Investiture is the power to appoint bishops throughout Christendom. Having the power over investiture in the renaissance world was important because the bishop of a city had authority over all of its ecclesiastical resources—land, money, and men— meaning he had as much power as any secular count or nobleman to build, collect revenue,

hire private soldiers, and generally empire-build within the monarch's own land. However, a bishop could not marry and pass his estate to his son; whoever held the right to investiture—the bishop or the king—could then put in place a loyalist which meant access to the new bishop's money and resources.

6. Why was Aristotelian logic frowned upon by most churchmen?

A6.—Pg. 6, ¶ 1—Aristotelian logic was frowned upon by most churchmen because it promised the careful thinker a way to arrive at true conclusions that would apply universally to the whole world, without making any reference to scripture. Aristotle offered the possibility of truth without God, of reason without faith.

7. How did ninth-century Irish theologian Johannes Scotus Erigena and eleventh-century teacher Berengar of Tours use Aristotelian logic in relation to theology? Why were these men excoriated for their use of Aristotle?

A7.—Pg. 6, ¶ 2—Both Johannes Scotus Erigena and Berengar of Tours used Aristotelian logic to argue against the doctrine of trans-substantio. The Bishop of Troyes said Johannes Scotus Erigena was a "master of error" who had dared to come to conclusions about "the truth of God . . . without the utterly faithful authority of the Holy Scripture." Berengar of Tours's writings were condemned by a series of church councils even though he claimed over and over that he was an entirely orthodox son of the Church.

8. What is the pallium? When Anselm was nominated to be Archbishop of Canterbury, why did he refuse to take the pallium from William II's hand?

A8.—Pg. 7, ¶ 5—The pallium is the cloak that symbolized the office of the archbishop. When Anselm agreed to become Archbishop of Canterbury, he refused to take the pallium from William II's hand because he wanted to receive his new authority from the pope, not the king. Anselm insisted that the cloak be placed on the altar so that he could then pick it up; in Anselm's mind this meant that he had been appointed by the pope.

9. What could Henry I lose if he continued to fall out with Paschal II over the right of investiture?

A9.—Pg. 7, ¶ 7 to Pg. 8, ¶ 1—If Henry I continued to fight with Paschal II over the right of investiture the king could lose the possibility of his soul's salvation since Paschal II had the authority to excommunicate Henry, declaring him cut off from the Church, the sacraments, and their saving power. In addition, Paschal II could place the entire country of England under an interdict: churches would be closed, there would be no masses or weddings, crucifixes would be draped with black cloth and the dead would be buried in unconsecrated ground. If the country was placed under interdict, the people of England would surely turn against the king that caused the excommunication.

10. Explain the terms of the Concordat of London, the agreement made in 1107 that signaled a truce between Henry I and Paschal II.

A10.—Pg. 8, ¶ 2 & 3—According to the Concordat of London, only Paschal II could appoint English bishops but each bishop would have to go and pay homage to the king before he could take possession of the physical place in England where he would serve. The agreement

would stand, and bishops would have to carry out the homage part, only until the "rain of prayers" offered by the faithful softened Henry I's heart and caused him to willingly abandon the practice.

11. How did Henry V convince Paschal II to come to a compromise about investiture? What were the terms of their agreement?

A11.—Pg. 10, ¶ 1-3—Henry V married Henry I of England's daughter Matilda, which gave him an alliance and a large dowry which funded the army that Henry V used to march on the Papal States of Italy. With a hostile army waiting just outside his borders, Paschal agreed to a compromise where Henry V would yield his right to appoint bishops, giving the pope the right to decide who would hold spiritual authority, but in return Paschal would give back all of the lands, political perks, and privileges that had gotten entwined, over the centuries, with the bishoprics. The bishops of the empire might be under papal authority, but they would no longer control the vast tracts of land that had made them powerful.

12. What happened when the bishops of Rome heard the details of Paschal II's compromise with Henry V on the morning of Henry V's coronation ceremony? How did Paschal II end up in Henry V's "protective custody"?

A12.—Pg. 10, ¶ 4 & 5—When Paschal II read out the details of his compromise with Henry V the bishops raised so much noise and protest that the reading stopped. Paschal II refused to hold the terms of the agreement when he realized how upset the bishops were, causing Henry to announce that he would not give up the right of investiture, which then made Paschal II declare that he wouldn't crown Henry V emperor after all. After Paschal II refused to make Henry V Holy Roman Emperor, Henry V ordered his men to take the pope into "protective custody," claiming they did this so that the pope wouldn't be harmed by the angry bishops.

13. How did Paschal II get out of Henry V's "protective custody"? What were the effects of the agreement made with Paschal II on Henry V's rule?

A13.—Pg. 10, ¶ 6 to Pg. 11, ¶ 1—Paschal II was let out of "protective custody" only after he issued a new decree that said Henry V had the right to investiture and he was to be crowned Holy Roman Emperor. The deal was widely unpopular with both the churchmen and the German aristocrats in Henry V's own kingdom who feared his growing power. As a result, Henry V spent the next decade putting down territorial revolts in Germany.

14. Explain the terms of the Concordat of Worms, the agreement made in 1112 between Henry V and Calixtus II.

A14.—Pg. 11, ¶ 2 & 3—The Concordat of Worms said that Henry V would renounce the right of investiture. In exchange, Calixtus II agreed that, in Germany only, newly appointed bishops would do homage to Henry V before their consecration. Paying homage to Henry V first assured that the bishops residing in the heartland of the emperor would put their loyalty to Henry V before their loyalty to the pope.

Section III: **Critical Thinking**

The student may not use his text to answer this question.

In this first chapter of *The History of the Renaissance World* we see immediately how the reintroduction of classical thinking affects the players in our story. While Aristotelian logic was seen by some as threatening to the church, it was used by others to prove God is real. Write a paragraphing explaining how Anselm of Canterbury used Aristotelian logic to affirm God's existence. In your answer, make sure to explain how the dialectic and use of ontological argument helped Anselm of Canterbury in his assertion.

In order to successfully answer this question, the student must first understand the terms "dialectic" and "ontological argument." "Dialectic" is defined on page 5, ¶ 7: "the rules of systematic thinking and inquiry laid out by Aristotle." "Ontological argument" is defined on page 7 in the footnote: Anselm defines God as "that of which nothing greater can be conceived" and uses this reasoning to prove that God necessarily exists because we are able to conceive of him.

Aristotelian logic was not seen as a friend to the church. As explained on page 6, ¶ 1, "It promised the careful thinker a way to arrive at true conclusions that would apply, universally, to the whole world, without making any reference to scripture. Aristotle offered the possibility of truth without God, of reason without faith." Anselm was able to turn this thinking around through his use of ontological argument. He asked why God should exist and used only reason to search for the answer. He came to this conclusion: If nothing greater than God can be conceived of, and we conceived of him, that means he must be real because nothing bigger than him can exist. Put in simpler terms, the reason we can think of God is because God made us and he gave us the ability to think. While the logic is circular it abides by the rules of the dialectic—the ontological argument needs no outside proof in order to be considered true. Any rebuttal to the argument can be answered within the argument itself. According to Anselm of Canterbury, the existence of God trumps all else; the reason we can inquire is because God exists and gave us the power of inquiry.

EXAMPLE ANSWER:

Anselm of Canterbury came up with the ontological argument for God's existence. He asked why God should exist and used only reason to search for the answer. He came to this conclusion: If nothing greater that God can be conceived of, and we conceived of him, that means he must be real because nothing bigger than him can exist. Put in simpler terms, the reason we can think of God is because God made us and thus we are able to think. The logic of Anselm's argument abides by the rules of the dialectic—the ontological argument needs no outside proof in order to be considered true. Any rebuttal to the argument can be answered within the argument itself. According to Anselm of Canterbury, the existence of God trumps all else; the reason we can inquire is because God exists and gave us the power of inquiry.

Section IV: **Map Exercise**

1. Using a black pencil, trace the rectangular outline of the frame for Map 1.1.

2. Using a blue pencil, trace the Mediterranean coastline around Italy, Francia, and Africa. Also trace the coastline around Britain/Ireland and up around Germany. You do not need to include small islands. Repeat until the contours are familiar.

3. Using your black pencil, trace the outlines of the Holy Roman Empire. Repeat this also until the contours are familiar.

4. Trace the rectangular outline of the frame in black. Remove your tracing paper from the original. Using a regular pencil with an eraser, draw the coastline around England, Germany, Western Francia, and Italy. Remember to use the distance from the map frame as a guide.

5. When you are pleased with your map, lay it over the original. Erase and redraw any lines which are more than ¼" off of the original.

6. Study carefully the major regions of England, Normandy, Western Francia, Germany and the Holy Roman Empire, Italy, and the Papal States. Then close the book and mark them on your map. After you checked and corrected any misplaced labels, study the locations of London, Canterbury, Tinchebray, Bec Abbey, Worms, and Rome. When you are familiar with them, close the book. Mark each location with your regular pencil. Check your map against the original, and erase and re-draw any misplaced labels.

Chapter Two

The Crusader Enemy

The student may use her text when answering the questions in sections I and II.

Section I: Who, What, Where

Write a one or two-sentence answer explaining the significance of each item listed below.

Alexius Comnenus—**Pg. 13, ¶ 1, Pg. 14, ¶ 4 and Pg. 16, ¶ 3—Alexius Comnenus, the Christian emperor of Constantinople, was able to defeat Bohemund of Antioch in 1108 but he was unable to fight for the city after Bohemund's death because he was too busy fighting the Turks. To make matters worse, he lost Tripoli to Jerusalem and lost the loyalty of the maritime republics to the Crusader Kingdoms.**

Bohemund—**Pg. 13, ¶ 4—Bohemund, a Norman soldier that named himself prince of Antioch after he captured it during the Crusades in 1098, started to plan an attack against Constantinople in 1103. After Bohemund's attack on Constantinople in 1108 failed, he was forced to surrender and pledge to leave Antioch to the emperor after his death.**

Bohemund II—**Pg. 17, ¶ 3 & 7—Bohemund II inherited Antioch when he was an infant; after regents ruled in his name and Bohemund II finally came to power, he decided to extend his rule by taking over the Christian kingdom of Cilician Armenia. Bohemund II pledged his allegiance to John Comnenus after the Byzantine king successfully attacked Cilicia.**

John Comnenus (II)—**Pg. 16, ¶ 4 and Pg. 17, ¶ 5 & 7—John II, Alexius Comnenus's oldest son and successor, started his reign by cancelling his father's deal with Venice. John Comnenus turned away from conflict with the Turkish Sultan of Rum to overtake Cilicia; his shift in attention gained him the loyalty of Bohemund II of Antioch but it also allowed the Turks to grow in power.**

Leo I—**Pg. 17, ¶ 4-6—Leo I, ruler of Cilician Armenia, went to Antioch on the premise of a friendly meeting with Bohemund II, but found himself taken prisoner when he arrived in the foreigner's land; he was released only after he agreed to hand over the south of his country to Antioch. When John Comnenus attacked Cilicia, Leo I allied himself with**

Bohemund II against the Byzantine ruler, but when it became clear John Comnenus would win, Bohemund II abandoned Leo I, and the ruler of Cilicia and his family were taken to prison in Constantinople.

Section II: **Comprehension**

Write a two or three-sentence answer to each of the following questions.

1. Why did Bohemund fake his own death? How did he get people to believe he was dead?

A1.—Pg. 13, ¶ 5 to Pg. 14, ¶ 2—Bohemund's father, Robert Guiscard, conquered the Dukedom of Apulia and Calabria in the south of Italy, and after his father's death Bohemund had technically inherited the dukedom's crown. Bohemund couldn't sail straight to Italy from Antioch because Byzantine ships were waiting in the Mediterranean, so he faked his own death in order to get past Alexius Comnenus. Bohemund spread rumors that he was dead and added believability to the story by hiding in a coffin that was aboard a ship headed for Italy; dead birds accompanied Bohemund in the coffin and the stench of their corpses had people believing it was really Bohemund that was rotting inside.

2. How was Bohemund able to recruit an army of Italians for his fight against Constantinople?

A2.—Pg. 14, ¶ 2—Bohemund's conquest of Antioch in the east had given him hero stature in Italy. After he "came back to life," people swarmed to see him "as if they were going to see Christ himself." Bohemund was able to recruit an army of Italians for his fight against Constantinople by rousing great public enthusiasm via his supposed resurrection.

3. Explain how Crusader power in the east continued to grow after Bohemund's defeat in 1108.

A3.—Pg. 14, ¶ 4—Though Bohemund was defeated in 1108, Crusader power continued to grow in opposition to Alexius Comnenus. In 1109, the king of Jerusalem conquered Tripoli, which gave the Crusaders control of the entire coastline. Two years later, Bohemund died, his heirs refused to hand Antioch over to Byzantine rule, and Alexius Comnenus could do nothing about it because he was busy defending Constantinople against the Turks.

4. Explain Jerusalem's relationship to Tripoli after the city was conquered in 1109. Over what other powerful "lordships" did the king of Jerusalem have authority?

A4. Pg. 14, *—Though Tripoli was conquered by Jerusalem, the city remained its own separate entity, ruled by counts who paid homage to the king of Jerusalem. The king of Jerusalem also had authority over the powerful lordships of the Prince of Galilee, the Count of Jaffa and Ascalon, the Lord of Sidon, and the Lord of Oultrejordain.

5. Describe the division of power in twelfth-century Italy.

A5.—Pg. 16, ¶ 1—In twelfth-century Italy the north of the peninsula was ruled by the Holy Roman Emperor Henry V. The center of Italy was controlled by Pope Paschal II, head of the Christian Church in the west, and the south was controlled by Norman kings. The coast of Italy was ruled by "maritime republics," self-governing Italian cities that controlled coasts

and harbors, and the three most powerful of these were Genoa and Pisa on the western coast, and Venice on the northern end of the Adriatic Sea.

6. What was the relationship between the maritime republics and the Crusader kingdoms?

A6.—Pg. 16, ¶ 2—The three most powerful maritime republics had sent soldiers on crusade and all three were allies of the Crusader kingdoms. Pisan and Venetian and Genoan ships aided the Crusader kings in their territorial struggles against the Turks, supplying naval power and an ongoing supply chain to sieges and battles. In exchange, the Crusader kingdoms allowed merchants from the Italian cities to establish trading posts in the east where they carried on a growing trade in pepper, cinnamon, nutmeg, and saffron, and lived free from interfering outside governments.

7. What deal did Alexius Comnenus make with the Venetians before the First Crusade? What happened after John Comnenus cancelled the deal?

A7.—Pg. 16, ¶ 3 & 4—Before the First Crusade, Alexius Comnenus had given the Venetians their own quarter in Constantinople, complete with churches and the right to carry on trade tax-free. When John Comnenus canceled his father's treaty with Venice he enraged the Venetians. The Venetians retaliated by pillaging and raiding the smaller islands of the Byzantine empire.

8. Why did John Comnenus back down and reinstate Venice's privileges in Constantinople?

A8.—Pg. 16, ¶ 4 & 5—In 1123, a Venetian fleet helped the king of Jerusalem besiege the city of Tyre, which was still in the hands of the Fatimid caliphate, and the next year, the combined forces of Venice and Jerusalem brought Tyre down. In gratitude, the king of Jerusalem gave the Venetians even more privilege in Jerusalem: a street of their own, a church, a bakery, and exemption from all taxes. Realizing the Crusader-Venetian alliance was not good for Constantinople, John Comnenus reaffirmed all of Venice's privileges in Constantinople in 1126.

9. Why did John Comnenus attack Cilicia? How did he come to be allied with Bohemund II of Antioch?

A9.—Pg. 17, ¶ 5 & 6—John Comnenus, seeing that Leo I of Cilicia was distracted by fighting Bohemund II in an effort to retake the south of his kingdom, attacked Cilicia for himself. Bohemund II and Leo I joined forces against John Comnenus, but when it became clear that the Byzantine armies would win, Bohemund II switched sides and allied himself with John Comnenus against Leo I.

Section III: Critical Thinking

The student may not use her text to answer this question.

The Crusades, military campaigns sanctioned by the pope, were meant to restore Christian power in the Holy Land. The land conquered during these Holy Wars was supposed to be handed over to the Christian emperor. However, we know that didn't happen. Write a paragraph explaining why

Alexius Comnenus had the Crusaders that came through Constantinople swear an oath before going off to war. In your answer, explain what was even more motivating to some Crusaders than fighting for God.

The answer to the first part of this Critical Thinking question is clearly spelled out in the first paragraphs on page 13. Alexius Comnenus made all Crusaders that arrived in Constantinople with their own armies swear that whatever "cities, countries or forces he might in future subdue . . . he would hand over to the officer appointed by the emperor." Alexius Comnenus made the Crusaders take this sacred oath because he did not trust them. He feared that after the Crusaders conquered the lands in the name of Christendom that they would then take the lands for themselves rather than turning them over to him, the ruler of Christendom in the east.

The answer to the second part of the Critical Thinking question stems from the motivation behind Alexius Comnenus's oath. What was more powerful to some Crusaders than fighting for God was gaining power for themselves. As stated on page 17, "The Crusaders had broken the unity of the cross for political power, the chance to build their own islands of political power in the east; the Venetians had broken it for the opportunity to build a commercial empire in the same lands." The Crusades were supposed to give all of the power and wealth that came with ruling a kingdom back to the Christian emperor. Fear of crossing the emperor, and theoretically God, was outweighed by the reward of land, loyalty of citizens, personal wealth and political power. In the Crusades, God may have been the fire that lit the match of war, but faith had little power over man's desire for personal glory.

EXAMPLE ANSWER:

Alexius Comnenus knew that the men going off to fight in the Crusades might be tempted to take the land they conquered for themselves. For this reason he had them swear an oath, agreeing to give back to the emperor whatever "cities, countries or forces he might in future subdue." Alexius Comnenus made the Crusaders take this sacred oath because he did not trust them. He was right to question the motivations of the Crusaders; personal glory was worth more to some of the fighters than upholding God's kingdom on earth. Fear of crossing the emperor, and theoretically God, was outweighed by the reward of land, loyalty of citizens, personal wealth and political power. In the Crusades, God may have been the fire that lit the match of war, but faith had little power over man's desire for riches and reign.

Section IV: **Map Exercise**

1. Using a black pencil, trace the rectangular outline of the frame for Map 2.1.

2. Using a blue pencil, trace the coastal outline of the Mediterranean and the Black Sea. It is not necessary to trace any of the multiple small islands around Turkey and Greece, but be sure to include the passageway from the Aegean through to the Black Sea (the Hellespont (opening passage), Propontis (small sea in the middle), and Bosphorus; the Bosphorus Strait is noted on the map).

3. Using contrasting colors, trace the outlines of the Dukedom of Apulia and Calabria, the Papal States, the Holy Roman Empire, the Republic of Venice, Byzantium, Asia Minor, Cilician Armenia, the County of Edessa, the Principality of Antioch, the Kingdom of Jerusalem, and the Fatimid Caliphate in Egypt. Mark the Sultanate of Rum. Repeat until familiar.

4. When you feel confident, trace the rectangular outline of the map onto a new sheet of paper, using your black pencil. Using your blue pencil, draw the outlines of the Mediterannean and the Black Sea (and passage into it). Remove your paper from the original, and draw the lines of the Dukedom of Apulia and Calabria, the Papal States, the Holy Roman Empire, the Republic of Venice, Byzantium, Asia Minor, Cilician Armenia, the County of Edessa, the Principality of Antioch, the Kingdom of Jerusalem, and the Fatimid Caliphate in Egypt. Mark the Sultanate of Rum.

5. When you are happy with your map, lay it over the original. Erase and redraw any lines which are more than ¾" off of the original.

6. Carefully study the locations of the Countship of Sicily, Rome, Pisa, Genoa, Venice, Dyrrachium, the Bosphorus Strait, Constantinople, Antioch, Aleppo, Tyre, and Jerusalem. When you are familiar with them, close the book. Using your regular pencil, label all 12 on your map. Compare with the original, and erase and re-mark your labels as necessary.

Chapter Three

Anarchy

The student may use his text when answering the questions in sections I and II.

Section I: Who, What, Where

Write a one or two-sentence answer explaining the significance of each item listed below.

The Anarchy—**Pg. 22, ¶ 2—The Anarchy was a fifteen-year civil war that destroyed English villages, killed thousands, wrecked the countryside and brought the English people to despair.**

Baldwin II—**Pg. 21, ¶ 2—Baldwin II, king of Jerusalem, befriended Fulk V and gave him the hand of his daughter Melisande. When Baldwin II died, Fulk V and Melisande were crowned king and queen of Jerusalem.**

Fulk V—**Pg. 20, ¶ 5 & 7 to Pg. 21, ¶ 2—Fulk V, the Count of Anjou, was powerful figure in Western Francia that wanted to marry his son Geoffrey the Handsome to Matilda in order to bring his grandchildren into royalty and to gain the protection of the English king. After the marriage between Geoffrey and Matilda was arranged, Fulk V renounced his title as Count of Anjou, married Melisande of Jerusalem and when Baldwin II died, he became king of Jerusalem.**

Geoffrey the Handsome—**Pg. 20, ¶ 3 and Pg. 21, ¶ 5—Geoffrey the Handsome, son of the Count of Anjou, was betrothed to Matilda when he was fifteen and she was twenty-five. Their marriage had a rough start, but by 1133 Matilda bore Geoffrey a son, and then two more followed in the next three years.**

Lothair III—**Pg. 20, ¶ 2—Lothair III was the title given to the Duke of Saxony after he was elected as emperor by the aristocrats of Germany following Henry's death.**

Louis VI—**Pg. 20, *—Louis VI was the ruling Capetian king at the time of Matilda's betrothal to Geoffrey the Handsome. Louis VI was nicknamed "Louis the Fat."**

Melisande—Pg. 21, ¶ 2—Melisande, daughter of Baldwin II of Jerusalem, was married to Fulk V after he renounced his title of Count of Anjou. After her father's death in 1131, Melisande and her husband became queen and king of Jerusalem.

Stephen—Pg. 21, ¶ 7 to Pg. 22, ¶ 2—Stephen, Matilda's cousin and grandson of William the Conqueror, was proclaimed king by the noblemen of England after Henry I died. In 1139 Matilda invaded England and challenged Stephen for the throne; neither Stephen nor Matilda took the crown, but they did succeed in starting fifteen years of anarchy in England.

Section II: Comprehension

Write a two or three-sentence answer to each of the following questions.

1. What were the circumstances of Matilda's younger brother William's death?

A1.—Pg. 19, ¶ 2 & 3—William got drunk with friends and ordered a ship put out to sea for all of them. William was not able to steer the ship properly while he was under the influence of alcohol and ran the ship into a rock not far from the shore. All of the young men on the ship but one drowned and most of the bodies were never recovered.

2. How did Matilda become first in line for the English throne? How did Henry V's status change because of his marriage to Matilda and the death of her brother?

A2.—Pg. 19, ¶ 4 to Pg. 20, ¶ 1—William was Henry's only legitimate son. Though Henry tried to sire another legitimate heir by marrying again after William's death, his efforts were futile. With William out of the picture, Matilda became first in line to the throne of England and Henry V was now in line to become king of England as well as king of Germany, king of Italy, and Holy Roman Emperor.

3. Why did Matilda return to England?

A3.—Pg. 20, ¶ 2—In 1125 Henry died, most likely from some form of cancer. Matilda and Henry produced no heirs and she had no other living children, which meant with Henry's death came the end of the Salian dynasty. With no reason to stay in Germany, Matilda went home to England.

4. Describe the makeup of Western Francia/France at the time of Matilda's betrothal to Geoffrey the Handsome.

A4.—Pg. 20, ¶ 5—Western Francia, a fragment of Charlemagne's eighth-century empire, remained without a national identity through the twelfth century. Only the ring of territories right around Paris was known as France. The rest of Western Francia was governed by local noblemen, held loosely together by personal oaths of loyalty to the king.

5. Who was Fulk the Black? What did he do to become famous, and feared?

A5.—Pg. 20, ¶ 6—Fulk the Black, the great-grandfather of Fulk V, was a psychotically warlike aristocrat who had burned his wife, in her wedding dress, at the stake for adultery, and fought a vicious war against his own son, forcing the defeated youth to put on a bridle and saddle and crawl on the ground in humiliation. Fulk the Black also pillaged and robbed the surrounding lands at will. Fearing damnation in his old age, he made a pilgrimage to Jerusalem, where he was rumored to have bitten off a piece of stone from the Holy Sepulchre with his own teeth so that he would have a relic to bring home.

6. How was it that Matilda had children with Geoffrey the Handsome after she walked out on their marriage?

A6.—Pg. 21, ¶ 4 & 5—Though Matilda walked out on Geoffrey the Handsome after one year of marriage, she was convinced by her father to return to her king. After her return, Matilda bore her young husband a son in 1133, when she was thirty-one and he was twenty, and then gave him two more children in the next three years.

7. How did Henry I of England die?

A7.—Pg. 21, ¶ 6—In 1135, Henry I of England was visiting with his daughter and grandchildren in Anjou. One day he returned from hunting and indulged himself in a dinner of lamprey eels, which disagreed with him. After eating, the king sunk into "a sudden and extreme disturbance" and died.

8. Describe the first four years of Stephen's rule of England.

A8.—Pg. 21, ¶ 8 to Pg. 22, ¶ 1—In the first four years of his reign, Stephen lost land to the Welsh and he struggled against the Scottish High King David I. David I had been an ally of Henry I, but he decided to march against Stephen; Stephen slaughtered eleven thousand Scottish troops and drove back the invasion. After defeating David I of Scotland, Stephen's reign disintegrated into calamity: he arrested two powerful English bishops, confiscated their lands, and then fell out with the Archbishop of Canterbury.

9. What happened to England after Matilda invaded with troops from Anjou and Normandy in 1139?

A9.—Pg. 22, ¶ 2—Matilda's army fought fiercely against Stephen's troops, but neither ruler came out victorious. The barons of England took the lack of leadership as an opportunity to enrich themselves, seizing anyone they imagined had any wealth and put them in prison to get their gold and silver, and tortured them. The chaos that followed Matilda's invasion led to the Anarchy, the fifteen year civil war that brought England to a state of despair.

Section III: Critical Thinking

The student may not use his text to answer this question.

When the noblemen of England heard that Henry I was dead, they panicked. He had no son to succeed him on the throne . . . but he did have a daughter. The noblemen were scared of both the French influence that would come with Matilda's husband were she to take the throne, but perhaps they were even more resistant to her rule because she was a woman. Strong and influential women have often caused waves of fear to ripple through society. Write a paragraph or two about another powerful woman of your choosing that influenced English history.

The student may write about whatever English woman he chooses—the woman does not have to be from the Renaissance era. The student should provide a brief sketch of the period in which the woman lived, the impact she made on English society, and a bit about the opposition the woman faced.

If the student is stuck, here are some women he might want to explore writing about:

> *Boudicca (1st Century)*
> *Queen Elizabeth I (16th Century)*
> *Elizabeth Fry (18th Century)*
> *Millicent Fawcett (19th Century)*
> *Margaret Thatcher (20th Century)*

EXAMPLE ANSWER:

The English suffragette movement—the movement to afford women voting rights equal to that of men—started in the late 18th century and gained momentum over the next 100 years. Regional groups formed all over England in support of the woman's vote. From 1890 to 1919, Millicent Fawcett led the coalition that brought together those regional groups, the National Union of Women's Suffrage Societies. Millicent Fawcett published several articles about women's rights and often spoke out publicly on behalf of a woman's right to vote. She also helped to found Newnham College in Cambridge, England in an effort to help make education accessible to women, and she campaigned for workers' rights and for reforming English laws so that they treated men and women the same. Millicent Fawcett faced opposition from the Liberal government when they refused to grant women the right to vote. She also faced opposition within her own movement: Fawcett encouraged change through constitutional means, but militant suffragettes believed violence would lead to direct action, and thus Fawcett lost the support of a large faction of the movement.

Chapter Four

The Lost Homeland

The student may use her text when answering the questions in sections I and II.

Section I: Who, What, Where

Write a one or two-sentence answer explaining the significance of each item listed below.

Akuta—**Pg. 25, ¶ 3—Akuta, a Jurchen leader of the Wanyan clan, adopted a Chinese dynastic name for himself (the "Jin Emperor"), led the Jurchen towards a national identity, and set out to prove their coherence and power by attempting to conquer the Song empire.**

Annam—**Pg. 27, ¶ 4—Annam was the name given to the Yueh lands around the Gulf of Tonkin that had fallen under Chinese rule. The land was invaded by armies of the Han dynasty and was then controlled as a Chinese province under the control of a Han governor.**

Dai Viet—**Pg. 27, ¶ 5—Dai Viet was formed after the people of Annam broke away from their Chinese overlords and claimed the right to rule themselves. The people of Dai Vet declared themselves an independent kingdom ruled by the Ly dynasty of kings.**

Do Anh Vu—**Pg. 30, ¶ 2—Do Anh Vu, the Dai Viet general facing Khmer invasions under Suryavarman II, scorned the invading Khmer army. He said, "The soldiers of the Son of Heaven quell rebellion; they do not offer battle in contestation as equals," before clobbering the Khmer once again.**

Gaozong—**Pg. 26, ¶ 1, 2 & 6 to Pg. 27, ¶ 2—Gaozong, Qinzong's younger brother, escaped the Jurchen invasion of Kaifeng, reestablished the center of Song rule at Lin'an, and proclaimed himself the next Song ruler. Song Gaozong managed to fight back against the Jurchen by means of the powerful Song navy, but ultimately he had to give up reclaiming the north and agreed to the Shaoxing peace treaty that declared the Jurchen a "superior state," made the Song emperor their vassal, and required a large annual tribute from the Song ruler.**

Jaya Indravarman III—**Pg. 29, ¶ 8 to Pg. 30, ¶ 3—Jaya Indravarman III, the Champa king during the rule of Suryavarman II, agreed to join with Suryavarman as an ally against the Dai Viet in 1132. After being defeated by the Dai Viet, Jaya Indravarman III decided to** switch sides and join with the Dai Viet against the Khmer army, but even this move didn't stop the Champa from being attacked by the Khmer: in 1145 Suryavarman II invaded Champa and added the north of Champa to his own kingdom.

Jayavarman II—**Pg. 30, ¶ 5**—Jayavarman II, Suryavarman's great predecessor, began construction of the Khmer capital city of Angkor shortly after 800.

Li Qingzhao—**Pg. 25, ¶ 1 & 2**—Li Qingzhao, a Chinese poet, was driven from her home in the Song dynasty capital of Kaifeng by the Jurchen in 1127 and was made to settle in Nanjing with her husband as a refugee. Though Li Qingzhao wrote about returning to her home— "The long night passes slowly, with few happy thoughts / Then I dream of the capital and see the road back to it"—she was not able to return because Kaifeng was lost to the Song forever.

Ly Than Tong—**Pg. 29, ¶ 6**—Ly Than Tong was elected ruler of Dai Viet when he was just twelve years old. However, he was gifted with strong generals and was able to keep the invading Khmer at bay.

Ly Thuong Kiet—**Pg. 27, ¶ 6**—Ly Thuong Kiet was a Dai Viet general that earned his fame in 1076 when he repelled invading Song forces from the Dai Viet border. His victory was celebrated with the song *Nam Quoc Son Ho*, meaning "Land of the Southern Kingdom;" the song is remembered as Vietnam's first declaration of independence, though it was written in Chinese.

Qinzong—**Pg. 25, ¶ 1**—Qinzong, the Song emperor in power at the time of the Jurchen invasion in the 12th century, was captured by the aggressors and imprisoned until his death. Quinzong's capture and the fall of Kaifeng marked the end of Song dominance over China.

Shaoxing Treaty—**Pg. 27, ¶ 2**—Shaoxing Treaty, made between the Song and the Jurchen in 1141, stopped the fighting between the two enemies, but it was a humiliation for the Song. It referred to the Jurchen as the "superior state" and the Song as an "insignificant fiefdom," and Gaozong was forced to accept the status of Jurchen vassal, complete with a large annual tribute.

Suryavarman II—**Pg. 29, ¶ 3-5 and Pg. 30, ¶ 3 & 4**—Suryavarman II, king of Khmer, came to the throne in 1113 and immediately used war to increase his power: he put down all internal rebellions and then focused outward on attacks against Champa and Dai Viet. Suryavarman II managed to take the north of Champa for Khmer, but after years and years of attack, he was never able to take any of Dai Viet, and after a final raid in 1150, Suryavarman II disappeared from historical records, his fate unknown.

The Imperial Commissioner's Office for the Control and Organization of the Coastal Areas—**Pg. 26, ¶ 5**—The Imperial Commissioner's Office for the Control and Organization of the Coastal Areas was a new government agency created by Song Gaozong to take charge of the Song warships that were defending the Yangtze against the Jurchen. With the creation of the agency, the Song warships became the world's first permanent, standing, government-run navy.

Yueh—**Pg. 27, ¶ 4—Yueh was the name given by the Chinese to all non-Chinese people living in small kingdoms far south of the Yellow River.**

Section II: **Comprehension**

Write a two or three-sentence answer to each of the following questions.

1. Describe the Jurchen invasion of the Song empire between 1127 and 1130.

A1.—Pg. 25, ¶ 1 and Pg. 26, ¶ 1—The Jurchen first invaded the Song empire in 1127; they successfully captured the Song emperor and took control of the Song capital Kaifeng. The Jurchen horsemen continued further south into the central plains of Song territory, looting and burning the towns they passed. In 1130, the Jurchen crossed the Yangtze and sacked Ningbo, on the southern coast.

2. What factors slowed the invading Jurchen down? How did the Song save themselves from complete destruction by the Jurchen?

A2.—Pg. 26, ¶ 4-6—The northern Jurchen were unfamiliar with southern heat and also with water warfare, but they had to deal with both as they moved further south and faced the Yangtze. The Song were adjusting to their exile and found a way to fight back using their sea power, which had always been in existence to supplement land armies. More and more warcraft were built to patrol the Yangtze and in 1132 the emperor authorized the creation of a new government agency, the Imperial Commissioner's Office for the Control and Organization of the Coastal Areas, to take charge of the fleet.

3. Why did Song Gaozong agree to a peace treaty with the Jurchen in 1141?

A3.—Pg. 26, ¶ 6 to Pg. 27, ¶ 1—By 1141, the war between the Jurchen and the Song had been going on for thirteen years. While the Song were able to fend off the Jurchen from the south, Song Gaozong realized the north was lost. The emperor could no longer afford to mount endless expeditions into the north; the cropland in the south was untilled, the farmers drafted into the army; the only other road for the Song ended in poverty and famine, so he agreed to peace with the barbarians.

4. Though a firm border north of the Dai Viet capital Thang Long was drawn after the defeat of the Song by Ly Thuong Kiet in 1076, how did Chinese culture still manage to infiltrate Dai Viet?

A4.—Pg. 27, ¶ 7 to Pg. 29, ¶ 1—The border between the Chinese and the Dai Viet did not stop the Ly kings, like their Chinese counterparts, from building Buddhist pagodas and funding Buddhist monasteries. Chinese was still used in all court business; would-be officials still had to pass the Chinese civil service examination, based on the teachings of Confucius. The Ly dynasty also adopted the Chinese "Mandate of Heaven": their kings were "Southern Emperors," ruling the "Southern Kingdoms" by virtue of their own, southern, celestial mandate.

STUDY AND TEACHING GUIDE FOR THE HISTORY OF THE RENAISSANCE WORLD

5. Why did Suryavarman II believe it was his duty to subjugate the earth? In your answer, define *Devaraja* and *Chakravartin*.

A5.—Pg. 29, ¶ 4—Suryavarman II followed the Hindu *Devaraja*, which meant the god-king cult. As king of Khmer, he was an incarnation of the divine and was believed to be one with the god. He was *Chakravartin*, which meant he was the earthly ruler of the universe and thus he should subjugate the world to show his divine power.

6. For what reason did Suryavarman II invade Dai Viet?

A6.—Pg. 29, ¶ 5 & 6—After Suryavarman II began to raid Champa, many of the Cham fled north into Dai Viet, which gave them refuge. In 1128, Suryavarman used this as the pretext for an invasion of Dai Viet. Though he marched twenty thousand men into Dai Viet and was driven back, Suryavarman II continued to send regular armies by land and fleets of warships around by water to attack his northern neighbor.

7. Describe the city of Angkor and its water supply during the time of Suryavarman II's rule.

A7.—Pg. 30, ¶ 5—Angkor was a vast, sophisticated metropolis that had no walls and sprawled across swampy ground. It covered perhaps 125 square miles, 320 square kilometers: larger than any other twelfth-century city, and a million people lived within its boundaries, depending on a vast network of canals and reservoirs for drinking water. The largest reservoir, the Western Baray, had been completed in the eleventh century; it was eight kilometers long and two kilometers wide and it held 70 million cubic meters of water, (over 18 billion gallons).

8. Describe the place Suryavarman II had built for himself in which he would live forever.

A8.—Pg. 30, ¶ 6 to Pg. 31, ¶ 2—Suryavarman II built for himself a temple called Angkor Wat, dedicated to Vishnu, the god who dwelt within it, in the great city of Angkor. The temple was the size of a small city, surrounded by its own moat and defensive wall, with carved bas-reliefs showing thousands of scenes of war, court life, religious ritual; scenes from Hindu epics, depictions of the afterlife with the righteous in bliss, the rebellious crushed; and a massive portrait of Suryavarman II himself. Angkor Wat, modeled after the mythical Mount Meru, center of the world of the Hindu gods, was laid out so that at the beginning of the year the sun would fall on the bas-relief scenes of the earth's creation, while closer to the year's end, it would light up scenes of apocalypse, and observation points for future eclipses of the sun and moon were calculated and built into the temple.

9. What happened to Khmer's hold on Champa when Suryavarman II was no longer in power?

A9.—Pg. 31, ¶ 3—Khmer boasted the most glorious temple complex in the world but building that complex drained the kingdom's treasury, as did the constant demands of war. Suryavarman's successors gave up his hard-conquered lands in Champa and retreated, drawing back within Khmer's old borders, unable to continue to afford the extravagant ways of Suryavarman II.

Section III: Critical Thinking

The student may not use her text to answer this question.

It is clear that Jaya Indravarman III was not a great ruler. Sources remember him as "mild and resourceless," and during his reign the north of Champa was conquered by Suryavarman II. But though Suryavarman II was an ambitious leader, that does not mean he did much better than Jaya Indravarman III for the kingdom of Khmer. Write a paragraph describing how Suryavarman II's determination did just as much harm as it did good for Khmer.

It is very clear in the chapter that Suryavarman II was an ambitious ruler. He came to the throne in 1113 after fighting off his relatives and then he secured his rule by putting down all rebellions within Khmer. But Suryavarman II's desire to "subjugate the earth" meant he put all of his kingdom's resources into war. Suryavarman II felt it necessary to "subjugate the earth" because he was Chakravartin, ruler on earth of the universe. For the people of Khmer, that meant that any resources left over from war went into the building of Angkor Wat, the massive and magnificent temple Suryavarman II was building for himself for his eternal afterlife.

Suryavarman II's strength and self-importance was thus his kingdom's downfall. He kept fighting against the Dai Viet and didn't win—the last of his men were wiped out by fever as they crossed the mountains into Thang Long in 1150—and Suryavarman II disappeared from historical record. Suryavarman II's fighting did give him control of the north of Champa in 1145, but after he was no longer in power, his successors were forced to give up their holdings in Champa because they did not have the resources to continue fighting. While Suryavarman II believed he was a great leader when he was alive, his reign caused his people great suffering through constant war and the draining of the kingdom's funds and labor force on the king's grand temple.

EXAMPLE ANSWER:

Suryavarman II came to the Khmer throne in 1113 after fighting off his relatives and then he secured his rule by putting down all rebellions within Khmer. He was a powerful man, but he did not have his people's interests in mind. Suryavarman II's desire to "subjugate the earth" meant he put all of his kingdom's resources into war. Suryavarman II felt it necessary to "subjugate the earth" because he was Chakravartin, ruler on earth of the universe. For the people of Khmer, that meant that any resources left over from war went into the building of Angkor Wat, the massive and magnificent temple Suryavarman II was building for himself for his eternal afterlife. Suryavarman II's strength and self-importance was thus his kingdom's downfall. He kept fighting against the Dai Viet and didn't win—the last of his men were wiped out by fever as they crossed the mountains into Thang Long in 1150—and Suryavarman II disappeared from historical record. Suryavarman II's fighting did give him control of the north of Champa in 1145, but after he was no longer in rule his successors were forced to give up their holdings in Champa because they did not have the resources to continue fighting. While Suryavarman II believed he was a great leader when he was alive, his reign caused his people great suffering through constant war and the draining of the kingdom's funds and labor force on the king's grand temple.

Section IV: **Map Exercise**

1. Using a black pencil, trace the rectangular outline of the frame for Map 4.1: The Kingdoms of China and Southeast Asia.

2. Using a blue pencil, trace the coastline down from the top of the map around the regions of Jin, Southern Song, Dai Viet, Champa, and Khmer to the bottom of the map, around the Bay of Bengal. You do not need to trace the islands to the right of the mainland, though do take note of them. **Do** trace the outline of the island to the right of the Gulf of Tonkin. With your blue pencil, trace the lines of the Yellow, Huai and Yangtze Rivers and also the Bach Dang. Repeat until the contours are familiar.

3. Using pencils in contrasting colors, trace the outlines of the Jin region, the Southern Song region, the Dai Viet region, the Champa region, and the Khmer regions. Repeat until the contours are familiar.

4. Using a new sheet of paper, trace the rectangular frame of the map with your black pencil. Remove your tracing paper from the original. Using your regular pencil with an eraser, draw the coastline down from the top of the map around the regions of Jin, Southern Song, Dai Viet, Champa, and Khmer to the bottom of the map, around the Bay of Bengal. Draw the lines of the Yellow, Huai, and Yangtze Rivers and the Bach Dang. Also draw the outlines of the Jin region, the Southern Song region, the Dai Viet region, the Champa region, and the Khmer regions.

5. When you are pleased with your map, lay it over the original. Erase and redraw any lines which are more than ½″ off of the original. Looking at the map, draw the cluster of islands to the right of the mainland.

6. Now carefully study the locations of Zhongdu, Kaifeng, Yangzhou, Nanjing, Lin'an, Ningbo, Quanzhou, Thang Long, My Son, Vijaya, and Ankora. When you are familiar with them, close the book. Using your regular pencil, mark each location on the map. Check your map against the original, and correct any locations that were misplaced or mislabeled.

Chapter Five

Crusade Resurrected

The student may use his text when answering the questions in sections I and II.

Section I: Who, What, Where

Write a one or two-sentence answer explaining the significance of each item listed below.

Bernard of Clairvaux—**Pg. 36, ¶ 5 and Pg. 40, ¶ 7—Bernard, a Frankish abbot living in the monastery at Clairvaux, was put in charge of the Second Crusade by Pope Eugenius III. When the Second Crusade failed, Bernard of Clairvaux blamed the Crusaders' losses on their lack of holiness and resolve.**

Conrad III—**Pg. 39, ¶ 3 and Pg. 40, ¶ 4—Conrad III, the German king that succeeded Lothair III, led his army to be slaughtered by the Turkish forces at Dorylaeum during the Second Crusade. Conrad III tried another front against the Muslims by attacking Damascus in 1148, but this attempt failed, too, and the only thing Conrad III could do to save face was to stop in Constantinople on his way home to firm up his friendship with the Byzantine emperor.**

Eleanor—**Pg. 37, ¶ 2 and Pg. 40, ¶ 2—Eleanor, wife of Louis VII, had conceived just twice during her seven years of marriage to the king, and her sole living child was a daughter. After Louis VII refused to follow Eleanor's uncle's advice and attack Aleppo, Eleanor announced that she would ask Pope Eugenius III for an annulment; this was less likely to do with Aleppo and more likely to do with Louis VII's chaste attitude.**

Great Seljuk—**Pg. 34, ¶ 4—Great Seljuk was the title of the senior member of the most prominent Turkish clan, direct descendants of Malik Shah himself. The Great Seljuk claimed authority over all the rest but after the Crusades this power was an illusion; the other Turkish rulers and the Muslim soldiers of Damascus and Aleppo were as likely to be loyal to the Crusader kingdoms, against the other sultans, as they were to join together against the Christians.**

Jihad—**Pg. 35, ¶ 6 to Pg. 36, ¶ 1—Jihad is a term in the Muslim faith that means the right and just struggle against an unrighteous enemy.**

Louis VII—Pg. 36, ¶ 6 and Pg. 40, ¶ 5—Louis VII, French king of the Capetian dynasty, joined Bernard on the Crusade for Edessa. After Louis VII's campaign against Edessa failed, he made a pilgrimage to Jerusalem before reluctantly returning to France with his unhappy wife Eleanor.

Manuel—Pg. 35, ¶ 4—Manuel was son and heir to the Byzantine emperor John Comnenus. Manuel was unable to help Edessa fight against Zengi because he was occupied with putting down the usual plots and revolts that accompanied the passing of the Byzantine crown.

Nur ad-Din—Pg. 39, ¶ 2 and Pg. 40, ¶ 6—Nur ad-Din, Zengi's son, followed his father as the Muslim leader of Edessa. After the Second Crusaders left the Muslim world in 1149, Nur ad-Din invaded Antioch where Raymond was killed, his head cut off to be sent to Baghdad as a trophy.

Pope Eugenius III—Pg. 36, ¶ 3—Pope Eugenius III made the papal decree, the *Quantum praedecessores*, which started the Second Crusade, in order to save Edessa.

Quantum praedecessores—Pg. 36. ¶ 3—*Quantum praedecessores* was the papal decree made by Pope Eugenius III that called for a second crusade in order to save Edessa. The decree declared that those who went east to get Edessa back from the Muslims would receive remission of sins, forgiveness of earthly debts, and eternal glory.

Raymond—Pg. 35, ¶ 4, Pg. 39, ¶ 5 to Pg. 40, ¶ 1—Raymond, uncle of Eleanor and a Frankish nobleman who had claimed the title "Prince of Antioch" when he was twenty-two by marrying the ten-year-old daughter of Bohemund II, refused to send help to Edessa when Zengi attacked because he and Edessa's king were on terms of "insatiable hatred." After Louis VII failed to capture Edessa, Raymond tried to convince Louis VII to attack Aleppo, and was rumored to have seduced his niece in an effort to get her to persuade Louis VII to take his advice.

Zengi—Pg. 34, ¶ 2 and Pg. 36, ¶ 1—Zengi, ruler of Aleppo starting in 1128, launched a failed attack against Damascus in 1137 and then, in the name of holy war sparked by the earthquake of 1138, a successful attack against Edessa in 1144. With the fall of Edessa, Zengi took for the first time a royal title and became known by a whole series of honorifics like the ornament of Islam, the help of the believer, and God-helped king.

Section II: Comprehension

Write a two or three-sentence answer to each of the following questions.

1. Describe the state of the Turkish empire after the death of its establishment by the great conqueror Malik Shah.

A1.—Pg. 34, ¶ 3—The Turkish empire broke apart almost immediately after the death of Malik Shah. By the middle of the twelfth century, Turkish sultans ruled from Baghdad, Kirman, Syria, Khorasan, and Rum, and a sixth Turkish kingdom, the Danishmends, had

broken away from Rum. Independent governors called atabegs controlled Damascus and Aleppo.

2. How did the earthquake that occurred in October of 1138 physically affect the Turkish empire?

A2.—Pg. 34, ¶ 6 to Pg. 35, ¶ 1—In October of 1138 an earthquake centered near Aleppo struck, causing the walls of the Crusader castle of Harim to crack, the Muslim fortress of Athareb to collapse killing everyone inside, and the ramparts and walls of Aleppo to buckle. As many as eighty aftershocks went on for two weeks following the big earthquake. Houses fell, stones rained down on panicked crowds in the streets, the ground opened resulting in the deaths of an estimated 230,000 people.

3. Why do earthquakes hold such a sacred place in the Muslim culture? How are they viewed by the Muslim people?

A3.—Pg. 35, ¶ 2—Aleppo sat on a fault, which made earthquakes common, and Muhammad's birth itself was said to have been accompanied by an earthquake that shook the entire world. Earthquakes are commemorated in Sura 99 of the Qur'an: "When the earth convulses in its shock/and the earth unloads its burdens/. . . that day, humanity will go out/separately, to be shown their works. . . ." The Muslim people viewed earthquakes as a divine signal, a judgment, or a promise.

4. Why didn't any Christian armies come to Edessa's aid when Zengi and his Muslim soldiers attacked in 1144?

A4.—Pg. 35, ¶ 4— The king of Jerusalem didn't help Zengi because he was a powerless child. The Byzantine emperor John Comnenus had just died of a lingering hunting wound, and his son and heir, Manuel, was occupied with putting down the usual plots and revolts that accompanied the passing of the Byzantine crown so he was unable to help Edessa. And Raymond, the Prince of Antioch, refused to send help because he and Edessa's king were on terms of "insatiable hatred."

5. Why were Christian soldiers so eager to fight in the Second Crusade?

A5.—Pg. 36, ¶ 4—The First Crusade was legendary and soldiers were eager to participate in that same kind of glory. As the historian Thomas Madden put it, "an entire generation of Europeans had been born and raised on the epic stories of the First Crusade. . . . There was scarcely a Christian knight who did not . . . long for the opportunity to imitate them." The Second Crusade offered knights who had grown up on tales of Christian heroism the opportunity to join their heroes.

6. What happened at the beginning of Louis VII's reign that made him want to join the Second Crusade?

A6.—Pg. 36, ¶ 6 to Pg. 37, ¶ 1—When Louis VII was twenty-one, he attacked the town of Vitry in order to put down the rebellious Count of Champagne. The townspeople— hundreds of unarmed men, women, and children—fled into Vitry's wooden church, and without waiting for the king's orders, Louis VII's officers set it on fire. Louis VII, who had stood helplessly

by and listened to the screams from inside while the church burned, had been eager to make up for the horror he caused at Vitry ever since.

7. How might have Louis VII's religious background affected his ability to produce an heir with his wife, Eleanor?

A7.—Pg. 37, ¶ 3 to Pg. 39, ¶ 1— Louis VII had been educated for the priesthood, but the death of his older brother had unexpectedly put him on the throne. Louis VII learned a life without women in his training, and he was taught that sex, even with a lawful spouse, had the potential to deprive man of judgment and distort his view of God. In the twelfth-century French church, virgins stood at the top of the moral hierarchy, so it was most likely difficult for Louis VII, thrown back into a world where he was expected to father children, to attend to his marital duties.

8. What happened to the German, and then the French and German, armies as they attempted to attack Edessa in 1147 and 1148?

A8.—Pg. 39, ¶ 3 & 4—In 1147, Conrad III's German army decided to march on Edessa without waiting for Louis VII, but it was a grave mistake that led to the slaughter of German men by the Turkish force at Dorylaeum. The Germans retreated to wait for the French at Nicaea, and Conrad III returned to Constantinople to get treatment for a wound he suffered during battle. In 1148, Louis VII led French and German troops up the coast but two months into their campaign they were fatally attacked near Laodicea; Louis VII escaped but the men of the combined armies were not so lucky.

9. What advice did Raymond of Poitiers give to Louis VII regarding his next military move after defeat near Laodicea in the Second Crusade? What did Louis VII want to do instead?

A9.—Pg. 39, ¶ 5—Raymond of Poitiers suggested an assault on Aleppo after Louis VII was defeated near Laodicea. Aleppo was smaller, less fortified, and also happened to be the headquarters of Muslim leader Nur ad-Din. Louis VII did not think the attack was a good idea and instead wanted to finish his pilgrimage to Jerusalem before returning home.

10. How did the Second Crusade end?

A10.—Pg. 40, ¶ 4 & 5—The Crusaders, led by Conrad III, decided to attack Damascus, which was under the control of Nur ad-Din's father-in-law. The siege began on July 24, 1148, and was over in just five days because Nur ad-Din sent troops to relieve the city. The Crusaders were so clearly outarmed that they hastily withdrew.

Section III: Critical Thinking

The student may not use his text to answer this question.

The actual causes of war, while perhaps clear in historical accounts, are often murky. In this chapter we see two very different cases that show us indirect causes (or excuses) for war. Explain the first and second catalysts for Zengi's attack on Edessa and Louis VII's engagement in the Second

Crusade. In your writing, explain how important the secondary cause was in giving legitimacy to each man's first impetus for war.

The first leader we read about in the chapter was Zengi. Zengi, Great Seljuk, claimed authority over the Turks, but his power was an illusion. In order to prove his might, he needed to expand the reach of his power. He started to attack outlying lands near Damascus in 1130, but when he tried to take the city itself in 1137, he failed. In 1138 a giant earthquake hit Aleppo. Zengi was able to use this earthquake as his secondary cause for war. In the Muslim world, earthquakes were seen as signs, and Zengi took the earthquake of 1138 to be a divine sign that he should engage in holy war. As stated on page 35, ¶ 3, holy war transformed "his personal ambitions into an advance for the faith." Fighting in the name of God (the secondary cause) rather than for his own will for power (his first reason to go to war), gave Zengi the strength to attack and conquer Edessa. After the fall of Edessa, Zengi's battles took on the language of jihad, and he was known as "the ornament of Islam, the help of the believer, [and] God-helped king."

The second leader we read about in the chapter was Louis VII. Louis VII was trained for the priesthood and was suddenly made king when his brother died. Fighting in a crusade would be natural for a faithful Christian king. However, Louis VII had another reason to go forward as a leader in the Second Crusade: Vitry. When Louis VII was twenty-one, he attacked the town of Vitry in order to put down the rebellious Count of Champagne. The townspeople—hundreds of unarmed men, women, and children—fled into Vitry's wooden church as Louis VII's troops approached. Instead of waiting for Louis VII to command them, his soldiers set the church on fire. Louis VII was forced to stand outside of the church and listen to the screams of those being burned alive inside. The Second Crusade gave Louis VII an opportunity to do penance for the deaths of those in the church at Vitry. The desire to make up for his sins was made very clear by Louis VII's actions during the Second Crusade. After failing to take Edessa in 1148, Louis VII made a pilgrimage to Jerusalem rather than attacking Aleppo. Louis VII may have been a faithful king, but it seems from his actions that his desire to make up for the horrors at Vitry heavily influenced his decision to join the Second Crusade.

EXAMPLE ANSWER:

In this chapter we read about two great leaders that went to war for reasons other than those that seem most obvious. Zengi, Great Seljuk, wanted to prove his power as leader of the Turks, so he attacked outlying lands near Damascus in 1130. However, when he tried to take the city itself in 1137, he failed. In 1138 a giant earthquake hit Aleppo. Zengi was able to use this earthquake as his secondary cause for war. In the Muslim world, earthquakes were seen as signs, and Zengi took the earthquake of 1138 to be a divine sign that he should engage in holy war. Fighting in the name of God gave Zengi the strength to attack and conquer Edessa. After the fall of Edessa, Zengi's battles took on the language of jihad, and he was known as "the ornament of Islam, the help of the believer, [and] God-helped king." Zengi's primary reason to go to war, to expand his own power, took on new meaning and purpose via his secondary reason to go to war, to fight in the name of God.

For Louis VII, religion was also a strong motivator for his military ambitions. Louis VII was trained for the priesthood and was suddenly made king when his brother died. Fighting in a crusade would be natural for a faithful Christian king. However, Louis VII had another reason to go forward as a leader in the Second Crusade: Vitry. When Louis VII was twenty-one, he attacked the town of Vitry in order to put down the rebellious Count of

Champagne. The townspeople—hundreds of unarmed men, women, and children—fled into Vitry's wooden church as Louis VII's troops approached. Instead of waiting for Louis VII to command them, his soldiers set the church on fire. Louis VII was forced to stand outside of the church and listen to the screams of those being burned alive inside. The desire to make up for his sins was made very clear by Louis VII's actions during the Second Crusade. After failing to take Edessa in 1148, Louis VII made a pilgrimage to Jerusalem rather than attacking Aleppo. Louis VII may have been a faithful king, but it seems from his actions that his desire to make up for the horrors at Vitry heavily influenced his decision to join the Second Crusade.

Section IV: Map Exercise

1. Using a black pencil, trace the rectangular outline of the frame for Map 5.3.

2. Using a blue pencil, trace the coastal outlines of the Mediterranean and the Black Seas including the passage into the Black Sea. Also trace the visible portions of the Caspian Sea (toward the top of the map), the Persian Gulf (into which the Tigris and Euphrates Rivers flow), and the Red Sea. Trace the lines of the Tigris, Euphrates, and Nile. Repeat until the contours are familiar.

3. Now select three contrasting colors to show the territories of Byzantium, the conquests of Zengi, and the conquests of Nur ad-Din. Trace the outlines of each section with the color you choose, as shown by the key on the map. Repeat until the contours are familiar.

4. When you feel confident about the outlines, remove your paper from the original, and close the book. Draw the coastal outlines of the Mediterranean and the Black Seas, including the passage into the Black Sea. Also draw the visible portions of the Caspian Sea, the Persian Gulf, and the Red Sea and the lines of the Tigris, Euphrates, and Nile. Then draw the territories of Byzantium, the conquests of Zengi, and the conquests of Nur ad-Din.

5. When you are pleased with your map, lay it over the original. Erase and redraw any lines which are more than ½" off of the original.

6. Now carefully study the locations of Constantinople, Nicaea, Dorylaeum, Laodicea, Mount Cadmus, Aleppo, Baghdad, Damascus, Acre, Jerusalem, Damietta, Alexandria, Tanis, Cairo, and Fustat. When you are familiar with them, close the book. Using your regular pencil, mark their locations. Check and correct any locations that were misplaced or mislabeled.

7. Looking at the book, mark the various Sultans: the Sultanate of Rum, the Sultan of Baghdad, and the Sultan of Syria. Mark the region of Jerusalem (as opposed to the city), the Principality of Antioch, Fatimid Egypt, Edessa, Cilician Armenia, and the Danishmends.

Chapter Six

Reconquista and Rediscovery

The student may use her text when answering the questions in sections I and II.

Section I: **Who, What, Where**

Write a one or two-sentence answer explaining the significance of each item listed below.

Afonso Henriques—**Pg. 45, ¶ 3-5—Afonso Henriques, Alfonso VII's cousin and governor of the Leonese province known as Portugal, won the Battle of Ourique against the Almoravids. After winning the Battle of Ourique, Afonso Henriques declared himself King of Portugal; Alfonso VII did not recognize the title, but he did not attack Afonso Henriques immediately either.**

Alfonso VII—**Pg. 44, ¶ 2 & *, Pg. 45, ¶ 3 and Pg. 46, ¶ 1—Alfonso VII, son of Urraca and her first husband Raymond of Burgundy, took Urraca's place as leader of León and Castile after her death in 1126 and kept hold of the territory after Alfonso the Battler's death in 1134. Alfonso VII led the Christian forces south of Toledo; he captured the Almoravids' base of operations, Oreja, and then in 1144 destroyed Córdoba and Seville, placing Spain even more firmly in Christian hands.**

Alfonso the Battler—**Pg. 43, ¶ 2, 3 & 5 to Pg. 44, ¶ 1—Alfonso the Battler was the Spanish king that drew together the four Christian kingdoms of Spain—Aragon, Navarre, León and Castile—and fought against the Almoravids until the day he died. He believed Spain was a sacred space where Christianity carried on its undying fight against evil and so he left his kingdom to the Knights Templar, the Hospitallers, and the Knights of the Holy Sepulchre: three of the military orders established to nurture holy warriors.**

Ali ibn Yusuf—**Pg. 43, ¶ 5—Ali ibn Yusuf, the Almoravid ruler, dealt with weakening Almoravid power in Spain in 1134. He was more concerned with Almoravid holdings in North Africa, so he let his grasp on his Spanish territories slip.**

Almohads—**Pg. 44, ¶ 4 & 5—Almohads, the al-muwahhidun, or the Unified Ones, were a group of people that followed the teachings of Ibn Tumart. When al-Mu'min took over, the**

Almohads became a military group that viewed the Almoravids as unpurified Muslims and put them in the same category as the Christians to the north—enemies.

Al-Mu'min—**Pg. 44, ¶ 5**—Al-Mu'min, a follower of Ibn Tumart, built on the prophet's theological groundwork and transformed the religious movement into one of conquest. Al-Mu'min believed the unpurified Muslims in North Africa to be as dangerous as the Christians farther north; they all threatened the beliefs of the Almohads.

Garcia Ramirez—**Pg. 44, ¶ 2**—Garcia Ramirez, a grandson of the legendary Christian warrior El Cid, took control of Navarre after Alfonso the Battler's death and ruled an independent Navarre for sixteen years. Navarre was under the control of Aragon, so Garcia Ramirez earned the title "the Restorer" when he took control of the territory.

Ibn Tumart—**Pg. 44, ¶ 3 & 4**—Ibn Tumart, a devout North African Muslim, preached unceasingly that the end of time was near, that he had been called to purify the practice of Islam and he was called to unite his followers in dedication to Islamic law. Ibn Tumart died prematurely in 1130, but he still managed to gain an enormous following called the al-muwahhidun, or Almohads, the Unified Ones.

Ramiro II—**Pg. 44, ¶ 2**—Ramiro II, Alfonso the Battler's brother, took hold of Aragon after his brother's death. Ramiro II was a monk and gave up his vows in order to be a king because he found the two occupations incompatible.

Reconquista—**Pg. 43, ¶ 3 & 4**—Reconquista was the name for the crusade in Spain between the Christian noblemen and military orders, and the Almoravids. The Reconquista started in 1118 and lasted for centuries.

Urraca—**Pg. 43,¶ 2 and Pg. 44, ***—Urraca, wife of Alfonso the Battler, was part ruler of the four Christian kingdoms of Spain. Urraca, estranged from Alfonso the Battler, ruled over León-Castile until her death in 1126, when the area was taken over by her son Alfonso VII.

Section II: Comprehension

Write a two or three-sentence answer to each of the following questions.

1. Who are the Almoravids, and how did they start a crusade in Spain that lasted for centuries?

A1.—Pg. 43, ¶ 3 & 4—The Almoravids were a North African sect of Muslims that crossed the Strait of Gibraltar into the Spanish peninsula and took over the south of Spain within three years of their arrival. The Christian kingdoms of the north fought back against the Almoravids; the Christian resistance gained energy when a church council at Toulouse in 1118 gave the fight the status of crusade. The battlefield of southern Spain was large and the Almoravids were determined to hold on to the land—thus started a conflict that would be fought for centuries.

2. Why didn't the Almoravids take advantage of the break up of Spain after Alfonso the Battler's death?

A2.—Pg. 44, ¶ 3-5—The Almoravids did not take advantage of the disunion that followed Alfonso the Battler's death because they were busy fighting the Almohads. Though they were of the same religion, the Almohads saw what they believed to be unpurified Muslims, the Almoravids, as enemies.

3. Describe the challenges Alfonso VII faced as he attempted to take Almoravid Oreja. What was the outcome of Alfonso VII's siege on Oreja?

A3.—Pg. 45, ¶ 1-3—Alfonso VII laid siege to the Almoravid castle of Oreja in the spring of 1139, but he quickly found that the castle was strong and well protected. Alfonso VII ordered siege towers built, he made sentries guard the riverbank so he could destroy the Almoravids with thirst, and he built war engines with which to attack the castle. Though an Almoravid army from Marrakesh arrived to help beat Alfonso VII back he persisted, and when no more reinforcements were available, the Almoravids surrendered Oreja to Alfonso VII.

4. Name the Western thinkers described in this chapter that travelled to Toledo before Gerard of Cremona and list their discoveries.

A4.—Pg. 46, ¶ 3—Pope Sylvester II traveled to a monastery near the Muslim-Christian border before he was pope and learned to use the numbering system of the Arabs, generally now known as Hindu-Arabic numerals, in which the place of a number related its value. Robert of Ketton followed, as did Hermann of Carinthia, who first translated the entire Qur'an into Latin. Plato of Tivoli, who also preceded Gerard of Cremona, also translated Arabic texts on astronomy and mathematics into Latin.

5. What did Gerard of Cremona discover in Toledo? How was he able to translate the texts he found?

A5.—Pg. 46, ¶ 4 to Pg. 47, ¶ 1—When Gerard of Cremona arrived in Toledo he discovered a treasure trove of books he had never known existed, including the *Physics* of Aristotle, the *Elements* of Euclid and the *Secrets* of the great Greek physician Galen. While the books had been translated from Greek to Arabic, they had never been translated into Latin, so the books were unknown to the Latin-speaking West. Gerard of Cremona then set himself to learning the Arabic language so that he could spend the rest of his life translating major works on dialectic, astronomy, philosophy, mathematics, and medicine (he translated at least seventy-one books before his death).

Section III: Critical Thinking

The student may not use her text to answer this question.

We may not know what happened at the Battle of Ourique, but we do know that Afonso Henriques was victorious, and that his victory prompted him to declare himself the independent King of Portugal. Write a paragraph explaining how the lost details of the Battle of Ourique turned into an epic Portuguese myth by the sixteenth century. In your paragraph, offer an explanation as to how national pride helped turn the Battle of Ourique into such a grandiose story.

The Battle of Ourique gave Afonso Henriques the opportunity to declare himself King of Portugal, and gave his people the opportunity to understand themselves as an independent nation. The result was that the commonplace Battle of Ourique, probably little more than a large-scale raid into Almoravid-held territory, turned into mythic battle that supposedly involved several kings and a vision of Christ. As described on page 45 in the footnote, "In the years afterward, Ourique loomed larger and larger in Portuguese eyes: the number of Almoravid troops killed increased, the Portuguese valor expanded, and the victory swelled, until by the sixteenth century Afonso Henriques had defeated five Muslim kings after seeing, Constantine-like, a vision of Christ promising victory over the pagans." The belief in the chosenness of a people to rule over themselves translates into national pride. National pride can turn a small event into something larger-than-life, just as the Battle of Ourique transformed from a regular battle into an epic event. As for the inclusion of a vision of Christ, if he appeared to Afonso Henriques, then it was clear that God meant for the Portuguese to be a sovereign people. The Portugese people believed so much in their leader, their faith, and in their existence as a sovereign nation that they needed a story of their fight for independence to match their national pride.

EXAMPLE ANSWER:

The Battle of Ourique turned Portugal into an independent nation and made Afonso Henriques King of Portugal. The result was that, over time, the commonplace Battle of Ourique turned into mythic battle that supposedly involved several kings and a vision of Christ. As time passed, the number of Almoravid troops killed increased, as did the number of Muslim kings taken down by Afonso Henriques. By the sixteenth century a vision of Christ was even said to have appeared before the future Portugese king. Portugese national pride turned the Battle of Ourique from a regular battle into something larger-than-life. As for the inclusion of a vision of Christ, if he appeared to Afonso Henriques, then it was clear that God meant for the Portuguese to be a sovereign people. The Portugese people believed so much in their leader, their faith, and in their existence as a sovereign nation that they needed a story of their fight for independence to match their national pride.

Section IV: Map Exercise

1. Using a black pencil, trace the rectangular outline of the frame for Map 6.1.

2. Using a blue pencil, trace the coastline of the Mediterranean around France and Africa through the Straits of Gibraltar and then the Atlantic up around the coastlines of Portugal, Spain, and France. Then trace the line of the Loire River. Repeat until the contours are familiar.

3. Using pencils with contrasting colors, trace the outlines of Western Francia, Navarre, Aragon, Leon-Castile, and Portugal. Use small peaks to show the mountains around Aragon and Navarre. Repeat until the contours are familiar.

4. Using a new sheet of paper, trace the rectangular outline of the map with your black pencil. Remove your tracing paper from the original. Using a regular pencil with an eraser, draw the coastal outlines around the Mediterranean and Atlantic and the Loire River. Then trace the

outlines of Western Francia, Navarre, Aragon, Leon-Castile, and Portugal. Use small peaks to show the mountains around Aragon and Navarre.

5. When you are pleased with your map, lay it over the original. Erase and redraw any lines that are more than ¼″ off of the original.

6. Now study the locations of Toulouse, Barcelona, Valencia, the Castle of Oreja, Toledo, Cordoba, Seville, the Battle of Ourique, and the Straits of Gibraltar. Also study the mark showing the Almohad Advance. When they are familiar for you, close the book. Using your regular pencil, mark each location. Check your map against the original, and correct any locations that were misplaced or mislabeled.

Chapter Seven

Questions of Authority

The student may use his text when answering the questions in sections I and II.

Section I: Who, What, Where

Write a one or two-sentence answer explaining the significance of each item listed below.

Bernard of Chartres—**Pg. 52, ¶ 9 to Pg. 53, ¶ 1—Bernard of Chartres, a master at the cathedral school of Chartres, made his students become thoroughly familiar with the works of Plato and Aristotle as foundations for their ongoing education in Christian doctrine. He had some unconventional teaching methods—exhortation and flogging—but most importantly he told his students they were dwarves perched on the shoulders of giants, able to see more and farther than their predecessors because they were lifted up by their previous work.**

Collationes—**Pg. 51, ¶ 1—Collationes, written by Peter Abelard, was a series of dialogues about ethics between a Christian, a Jew, and a character called the Ancient Philosopher. In the Collationes the Ancient Philosopher shows a clear understanding of the Highest Good—despite having only natural law to guide him.**

Concordance of Discordant Canons—**Pg. 53, ¶ 2—Concordance of Discordant Canons, written by Gratian, was a vast collection of ecclesiastical pronouncements that contradicted each other with resolutions to the inconsistencies found via the dialectic. The Concordance of Discordant Canons, a core text of the Catholic church tradition until 1918, was a triumph for ancient philosophy because it was a rationalization of spiritual decisions and it brought order by treating Church authority as a simple human system.**

Fulbert—**Pg. 50, 1-3—Fulbert, uncle of Heloise, flew into a rage when he found out his niece was pregnant by Peter Abelard, but made an agreement to let Peter Abelard marry Heloise in secret and continue to let her live at his home in Paris. Fulbert made Heloise's life a misery which resulted in her move to a convent and Fulbert's attack on Peter Abelard, where he sent hired thugs to castrate the theologian.**

Gratian—**Pg. 53, ¶ 2—Gratian was an Italian legal scholar who applied logic to the Church's own proceedings. Gratian created a vast collection of church law where he tried to resolve** inconsistencies in the law through the dialectic; the collection was known as Concordance of Discordant Canons.

Heloise—Pg. 49, ¶ 5 & 6 and Pg. 50, ¶ 4—Heloise, niece of the Parisian priest Fulbert, was the object of Peter Abelard's love and the mother of his child. Heloise was sent to a convent after marrying Peter Abelard in secret, and while she did not see her husband, the two wrote two each other constantly over the next two decades, keeping their marriage alive through their words.

Peter Abelard—Pg. 50, ¶ 4 and Pg. 51, ¶ 1—Peter Abelard, a theologian that believed in applying logic and reason to the scripture, spend most of his adult life in the abbey of St. Denis after impregnating and secretly marrying a woman named Heloise. In 1121, a church council at Soissons ordered Abelard to throw his major work *Theologia Scholarium* into the fire, which he did, but he did not revise his views and he continued to work on the text through its completion in 1135.

Peter Lombard—Pg. 53, ¶ 3 & 4—Peter Lombard, a cleric and teacher at the school of Notre Dame in Paris, wrote the *Sentences*. The *Sentences* provided not just a scheme for organizing theology but also a methodology: discussion, debate, and systemization.

Sentences—Pg. 53, ¶ 3 & 4—*Sentences,* written by Peter Lombard, was the first major attempt by a Western theologian to link every Christian doctrine together into a coherent, logical whole. Using scripture and the Church fathers side by side, applying logic and dialectic to resolve contrary opinions, Peter Lombard created theological categories: Christology, soteriology, ecclesiology, and eschatology.

Sic et Non—Pg. 51, ¶ 1—*Sic et Non,* meaning Yes and No, was the title of one of Peter Abelard's books. *Sic and Non* was a whole collection of quotations from the church fathers that contradicted each other.

Theologia Scholarium—Pg. 49, ¶ 1 and Pg. 51, ¶ 1—*Theologia Scholarium,* finished around 1135, was Peter Abelard's treatise on the nature of God. Peter Abelard had been polishing and revising the *Theologia* for fourteen years, ever since the first version of the book had been condemned by the church council at Soissons.

Section II: Comprehension

Write a two or three-sentence answer to each of the following questions.

1. How did Peter Abelard end up teaching at the cathedral school of Notre Dame, the most prestigious cathedral school in Western Francia?

A1.—Pg. 49, ¶ 4—Peter Abelard spent his teens studying the works of Aristotle in Paris and sharpening his skill with words. In 1102 he set up his own school in the French town of Melun and over time his fame as a master of logic grew. In 1114, his reputation earned him the title of master of the cathedral school at Notre Dame.

2. Why couldn't Peter Abelard publicly marry Heloise?

A2.—Pg. 50, ¶ 1—Peter Abelard could not publicly marry Heloise because the master of a cathedral school was a churchman. Celibacy was increasingly the rule for churchmen and marriage would ruin Abelard's career.

3. What agreement was made between Peter Abelard and Fulbert regarding Heloise and the couple's love child? What did Fulbert do that went against the agreement?

A3.—Pg. 50, ¶ 2—Fulbert agreed to let Peter Abelard have a secret marriage to Heloise, Heloise would come back to her home in Paris, and Abelard would find lodging elsewhere. Heloise left her baby son in the care of Abelard's family and returned to live in her uncle's house, but he made her life a misery, which was not part of the agreement.

4. Why did Peter Abelard send Heloise to live in a convent, and what were the consequences of his decision?

A4.—Pg. 2 & 3—Peter Abelard sent Heloise to live in a convent so that she would no longer have to suffer the abuses of her uncle Fulbert. However, convents were the traditional refuge of wives whose husbands had repudiated them, and Fulbert used the move as an excuse to take revenge on Peter Abelard. He sent hired thugs to Abelard's lodgings in the middle of the night where they pinned him down and castrated him.

5. How did Peter Abelard apply some of Plato's philosophies to the doctrines of the church?

A5.—Pg. 50, ¶ 5—In the first version of *Theologia Scholarium*, Peter Abelard argued that Plato's philosophy of a "world soul" was actually a reference to the Holy Spirit. He wrote that through logic, any man could grasp the essence of the Trinity, and that scripture was *involucrum*, inherently difficult and figurative. In essence, in order to really understand scripture, readers had to use reason and dialectic in order to find its true meaning.

6. Why was Bernard of Clairvaux so against the work of Peter Abelard?

A6.—Pg. 52, ¶ 2 and Pg. 53, ¶ 5—Bernard of Clairvaux held the authority of the church above all, so he found the work of Abelard, which brought logic together with faith, to be offensive. Bernard of Clairvaux had an "abhorrence" for teachers that put their trust in "worldly wisdom" and were invested in "human argument." Unlike Abelard, who questioned everything, Bernard of Clairvaux wrote in his condemnation of Abelard that "The faith of the pious believes. . . . It does not discuss."

7. Why didn't Peter Abelard have to fulfill his sentence of silence? What happened to him after his death?

A7.—Pg. 52, ¶ 6 & 7—Peter Abelard's sentence of silence was never fulfilled because he was already dying from the illness that would kill him. He took shelter at the monastery of Cluny and was in the middle of writing a lengthy self-defense in response to Bernard of Clairvaux when he died. The abbot of Cluny, Peter the Venerable, declared Abelard absolved of all his sins; he then sent Abelard's coffin to Heloise, abbess of the Paraclete convent, and she buried him there.

Section III: Critical Thinking

The student may not use his text to answer this question.

When Peter Abelard started working on the *Theologia Scholarium*, one traditional minded churchman told him, "we recognize only the words of authority." Though couched in terms of religious propriety, the desire for blind faith had more to do with power than it had to do with God. Write a paragraph explaining why traditional churchmen wanted to do away with reason and support only orthodox, accepted understandings of Christianity. In your answer, explain why Peter Abelard's appeal to the Bishop of Sens and to the pope in response to Bernard of Clairvaux's investigation hurt his case rather than helped it.

To believe in God unconditionally was also to take without question the word of His earthly representatives. Traditional churchmen were afraid that rational thinking, though it still came to the same conclusions about God, would disrupt their earthly power—which had nothing to do with God. They didn't want to lose their authority, and the surest way to hold on to it was to say that true faithfulness was unquestioning. If this was true, then no one would challenge the churchmen's authority.

Peter Abelard suggested that practitioners engage with religious texts in a way that put them in charge of their own reasoning. If readers could take their own meaning from a text, they no longer had to agree with all of the churchmen's interpretations, rules and doctrines. Peter Abelard thought Bernard of Clairvaux's problem with him was that he was not faithful enough, where the true problem was that Peter Abelard was not able to be blindly ruled by authority. When Peter Abelard petitioned to the Bishop of Sens and the pope, his skill in argumentation frightened his audience. As written on page 52, "To give Abelard a pass was to accept the categories of Aristotle; and accepting Aristotelian thought might well throw into doubt the entire authority structure of the Christian church. In 1141, the papal court agreed with Bernard. Abelard was to be imprisoned and condemned to perpetual silence." Peter Abelard's voice, which he used to show how logic and faith could work together, was taken away from him completely by the power of the court in an effort to keep that power stable and unquestioned.

EXAMPLE ANSWER:

To believe in God unconditionally was also to take without question the word of His earthly representatives. Traditional churchmen were afraid that rational thinking, though it still came to the same conclusions about God, would disrupt their earthly power—which had nothing to do with God. They supported only orthodox, accepted understandings of Christianity because that traditional view did not question their authority and power. Though Peter Abelard believed he could use logical reasoning to show the Bishop of Sens and the pope that his approach to faith was not hurtful to Christianity, his skills in argumentation confirmed that questioning Christian doctrine could undermine the authority of the church itself. Instead of agreeing with Abelard, the churchmen decided to punish him with silence so he could ask no more questions, and their power would remain intact.

Chapter Eight

The New Song

The student may use her text when answering the questions in sections I and II.

Section I: Who, What, Where

Write a one or two-sentence answer explaining the significance of each item listed below.

Agricultural Treatise—Pg. 56, ¶ 1—*Agricultural Treatise* was the name of Chen Fu's manual on farming. The 1149 text laid out effective rules for land utilization, crop rotation, and systematic fertilization, which helped the Southern Song become more productive farmers.

Hangzhou—Pg. 55, ¶ 1 & *—Hangzhou was the name given to Lin'an in 1276 after the Mongol invasion. Some later accounts use the name Hangzhou for Lin'an when referring to the city in the years prior to the 1276 invasion.

Prince Hailing—Pg. 57, ¶ 4 to Pg. 58, ¶ 2 and ¶ 5—Prince Hailing, one of Akuta's grandsons, led a palace revolt in 1149 and seized the Jin throne for himself. Prince Hailing, a lover of Song culture, abolished Jurchen clan titles, moved the Jin capital to the old Chinese city of Yanjing, and invaded the Song with the intention to possess it; his invasion failed and he was ultimately murdered by his own generals.

Shizong—Pg. 58, ¶ 5 and Pg. 59, ¶ 1—Shizong, Prince Hailing's cousin, took control of the Jin after Prince Hailing's murder and immediately started peace talks with the Song to mend the damage done by his cousin's invasion. Shizong was forced to fight against the Song before finally getting the peace he wanted via the Longxing Peace Accord.

Xiaozong—Pg. 58, ¶ 6 to Pg. 59, ¶ 1—Xiaozong, adopted son of Song Gaozong, became emperor after his adopted father stepped down following the Jin invasion. Though Xiaozong came to power with the intention of warring with the Jin, he was forced to sign the Longxing Peace Accord in 1165 after it became clear that neither empire would make headway against the other.

Zhu Xi—Pg. 57, ¶ 1 & 2—Zhu Xi, a Southern Song philosopher, transformed Confucianism from a tool of the state into a philosophy for every man based on private contemplation and individual education. Zhu Xi turned Confucianism into Neo-Confucianism, the dominant way in which the Song understood the world.

Zhongdu—Pg. 58, ¶ 2—Zhongdu, the "Central Capital," was the name given to the new Jin capital city that sat on the old Chinese city of Yanjing. Prince Hailing moved the capital city to Zhongdu so that Jin culture would be even closer to the Song culture.

Section II: Comprehension

Write a two or three-sentence answer to each of the following questions.

1. Why did the Jin keep Song Qinzong alive?

A1.—Pg. 55, ¶ 2—The Jin kept Song Qinzong alive so that Song Gaozong could never feel fully comfortable with his own authority. Song Qinzong's existence meant that Song Gaozong could easily lose his power. By keeping Song Qinzong alive, the Jin could always send him back home and fatally disrupt the Song chain of command.

2. What did Song Gaozong's court want him to do regarding the Jin? What did Song Gaozong actually do to help the Song during his reign?

A2.—Pg. 55, ¶ 3-5—Some of the advisors in the Song court wanted Song Gaozong to authorize an all-out assault on the Jin while others recommended peace and prudence. Song Gaozong refused to provoke the Jin and instead chose to prioritize the security and stability of the imperial court. The Southern Song flourished without victory: they philosophized, painted, wrote poetry, and cultivated trade that strengthened the Song from within.

3. Where did the French word "satin" come from?

A3.—Pg. 56, ¶ 1—The French word "satin" came from the word "zaituni." "Zaituni" was a word used by merchants from Bagdad for the city Quanzhou, the Southern Song city where satin manufacturing was centered.

4. Described the tenets of traditional Confucianism.

A4.—Pg. 56, ¶ 5—Traditional Confucianism directed its followers towards the orderly performance of duties and rituals as the path to virtue; following rules established character. Confucian academies taught the rules of order, the duties of each man in his place and station, and the importance of ceremony. Confucianism had long been used to train and prepare state officials, and as a tool for conducting government affairs.

5. How did Zhu Xi transform Confucianism? In your answer, make sure to define *li* and *qi*.

A5.—Pg. 57, ¶ 1—Rather than teaching Confucianism as a tool of the state, Zhu Xi taught and spoke of the relationship between the essence of material things, the *li*, and their physical existence, the *qi*. *Li* in itself does not have form that can be touched; *qi* gives shape to *li*, but at the same time obscures it. The essence, the *li*, of every human being is essentially good; that goodness shines through when the *qi* is refined, polished, brought to the place where it is transparent through private contemplation, "quiet sitting," and individual education, "pursuing inquiry and study."

6. In what way is Neo-Confucianism like dialectical inquiry? In what way is the origin of Neo-Confucianism unlike the origin of dialectical inquiry?

A6.—Pg. 57, ¶ 2—Both Neo-Confucianism and dialectical inquiry ask students to read several theories, for example, on truth, and then read them again against one another. Something can be learned from all theories, and by reading theories against one another, what is ultimately true will be revealed and what is useless will fall away. However, Neo-Confucianism's origin is different from the origin of dialectical inquiry: Neo-Confucianism was an adaptation of the state religion to a time when the state was frozen in place while Aristotle's dialectical inquiry was born of an intellectual preoccupation.

7. How did Prince Hailing show his love of Song culture?

A7.—Pg. 58, ¶ 2—Prince Hailing showed his love of Song culture through his studies of the Song lyric poems known as *ci*; he was an aspiring poet himself, an enthusiastic tea drinker and chess player. He wanted the Jin to be like the Song, so he abolished the old honorary titles still held by the heads of the Jurchen clans and moved the capital of the Jin out of the far northern city of Shang-ching to the ancient Chinese city of Yanjing, which he renamed Zhongdu, the "Central Capital." He wrapped up the move and transformation by leveling the old Jurchen tribal headquarters in Shang-ching.

8. How did Prince Hailing prepare for his invasion into Song territory? What did the Song forces do to beat the Jin troops back?

A8.—Pg. 58, ¶ 3 & 4—In preparation for his invasion into Song territory, Prince Hailing lined up half a million horses, drafted both Jurchen and Chinese into new regiments, assembled a fleet of barges to use as warships on the Yangtze and murdered anyone who criticized or questioned his plans. Despite their preparation, the Jin were outmanned and out-fought by the Song navy, with its fleet of small fast attack ships and massive, iron-hulled, paddle-wheel war galleys, propelled by the leg power of scores of Song seamen. The Song terrified the opposition by hurling "thunderclap bombs," gunpowder and metal pellets encased in a paper and bamboo envelope, onto the Jin boats, where they exploded in a shower of projectiles and flame.

9. How did the Song and Jin come to sign the Longxing Peace Accord?

A9.—Pg. 58, ¶ 5 to Pg. 59, ¶ 1—Shizong, Jin leader following Prince Hailing, wanted to make peace with the Song after his cousin's attacks, but the prowar faction of the Song court had strengthened and Song Gaozong purposefully stepped down so his adopted son, Xiaozong, could lead the empire in battle against the northern enemy. The Song counterattack began in 1163, but as the Song divisions began to cross over into Jin territory, Shizong sent a hundred thousand men in response, and the Song were immediately driven back. It became clear that neither empire would make headway against the other so in 1165, the two emperors signed the Longxing Peace Accord, setting the border between the nations at the Huai river.

Section III: **Critical Thinking**

The student may not use her text to answer this question.

No matter what a ruler might do to silence his critics, voices of dissent always manage to be heard. Write a paragraph explaining how Song Gaozong planned to cut off criticism over the way his dynasty handled the Jin invasion and how that criticism was expressed regardless of the emperor's desires. Use some of the poetry found on page 56 of your text as a way to illustrate your explanation; make sure to explain what you think Lu Yu's words mean.

Song Gaozong banned the writing of any private, non-state-sponsored histories in 1144. He created this ban so that he could silence criticism over the way his dynasty had handled the Jin invasion. While the rule stopped criticism written in prose, it did not stop voices of dissent from expressing their opinions in painting and poetry. For example, because landscapes were safe to paint, traditional natural symbols took on new meaning. On page 56 we read that "blossoming plums, once the symbol of spring and new hopes, came to symbolize the southern willingness to go into exile, the misfortune and melancholy of the displaced." Critics of Song Gaozong were able to transform accepted symbols into ways of expressing their dissatisfaction with their leader.

Poetry was also a way for artists to express dissent. The poet Lu Yu was able to write about his frustration with the Song decision to maintain peace with the Jin through his poetry. He writes: "The good sword under the recluse's pillow / Clangs faintly all night long." The sword is hidden under a pillow, useless, but the recluse can hear it clanging faintly, meaning that he can feel the desire to use the sword in a fight against the Jin. The poem continues:

It longs to serve in distant expeditions,

I fetch wine and pour a libation to the sword:
A great treasure should remain obscure;
There are those who know your worth,
When the time comes they will use you.

You have ample scope in your scabbard,
Why voice your complaints?

"It" refers to the sword. The sword, and the desire of the poet, is to fight far away, in Jin land, but in the mean time the treasure, or worth, of the sword is obscured. The sword rests, but the criticism of the poet is vibrant: he believes Song Gaozong should have invaded the Jin. Poetry acts as a loophole in Song Gaozong's law against private histories and as a result the poet Lu Yu is able to make his frustrations known.

EXAMPLE ANSWER:

Song Gaozong banned the writing of any private, non-state-sponsored histories in 1144. He created this ban so that he could silence criticism over the way his dynasty handled the Jin invasion. While the rule stopped criticism written in prose, it did not stop voices of dissent from expressing their opinions in painting and poetry. For example, blossoming plums used to symbolize spring and new hopes. After Song Gaozong made his rule against private histories, Song artists were able to transform their meaning into the southern willingness to go into exile and the resultant melancholy of a people unable to fight against their attackers.

Also, though histories written in prose were banned, private poetry was still permitted. Lu Yu provides us with a good example of how poetry could be used to criticize the emperor. Lu Yu writes, "The good sword under the recluse's pillow / Clangs faintly all night long." The sword is hidden under a pillow, useless, but the recluse can hear it clanging faintly, meaning that he can feel the desire to use the sword in a fight against the Jin. As the poem continues, the sword "longs to serve in distant expeditions" but "remains obscure." However, there are "those who know your worth," meaning there are people just like the poet who were ready and able to fight against the Jin, no matter what Song Gaozong decided for his people.

Chapter Nine

The Heiji Disturbance

The student may use his text when answering the questions in sections I and II.

Section I: Who, What, Where

Write a one or two-sentence answer explaining the significance of each item listed below.

Go-Sanjo—**Pg. 61, ¶ 4 & 5 and Pg. 62, ¶ 5 to Pg. 63, ¶ 1—Go-Sanjo was a Japanese emperor that did not have a Fujiwara mother and as a result he broke the cycle of Fujiwara power in the Japanese court. Go-Sanjo started the tradition of abdicating early so that the emperor could choose his successors and, in an attempt to thwart Fujiwara power, remain an influential advisor behind the scenes.**

Go-Shirakawa—**Pg. 65, ¶ 1 & 4, Pg. 66, ¶ 3 and Pg. 67, ¶ 1—Go-Shirakawa, Toba's son after Konoe, was made emperor following Konoe's death. Go-Shirakawa stayed in power through the Hogen Incident and then abdicated in favor of his son Nijo, and though there was another plot against his family, Go-Shirakawa managed to survive and escape from that rebellion, the Heiji Disturbance, too.**

Horikawa—**Pg. 63, ¶ 2—Horikawa, son of Shirakawa, followed his father as emperor of Japan. Though he was emperor, Horikawa's father continued to rule actively from the monastery during his son's reign.**

Kiyomori—**Pg. 66, ¶ 1 and Pg. 67, ¶ 1 & 3—Kiyomori, a Taira clan member, gained a high position in Go-Shirakawa's court after the Hogen Incident. Kiyomori saved the Emperor Nijo and Cloistered Emperor Go-Shirakawa from the devious Yoshimoto and Nobuyori during the Heiji Disturbance and as a result strengthened the power of the Taira clan in the capital.**

Konoe—**Pg. 64, ¶ 3, 6 & 7—Konoe, son of Toba and Tokuko, became emperor in 1142 at the age of three when Toba forced Sutoku to abdicate in Konoe's favor. Konoe was poisoned thirteen years into his reign.**

Masakiyo—**Pg. 67, ¶ 2—Masakiyo, a faithful friend to Yoshimoto, fled the capital with the Minamoto clan leader after the Heiji Disturbance. After realizing that capture and** execution by the Taira clan leader Kiyomori were inevitable, Masakiyo beheaded Yoshimoto upon his request and then killed himself.

Minamoto—Pg. 62, ¶ 2—Minamoto was the clan name of a noble family in the northeast of Japan. The Minamoto had accumulated large and powerful personal armies and were a threat to the Fujiwara clan.

Nijo—Pg. 66, ¶ 3 and Pg. 67, ¶ 1—Nijo, son of Go-Shirakawa, became emperor after his father abdicated in 1159. Almost immediately after being crowned he was taken off the throne and kidnapped during the Heiji disturbance, though he was rescued by Kiyomori.

Nobuyori—Pg. 66, ¶ 1 and Pg. 67, ¶ 2—Nobuyori, a Fujiwara clansman that felt unappreciated by Go-Shirakawa after the Hogen Incident, aligned himself with Yoshitomo and together they started a rebellion against Nijo. Nobuyori's plan to overthrow the emperor failed and as a result he was beheaded.

Samurai—Pg. 62, ¶ 2 & *—Samurai were local soldiers that were granted land by privately powerful families in exchange for their military service. Samurai were high-ranking warriors in service to their masters and acted as private knights for their landlords.

Shirakawa—Pg. 62, ¶ 5 and Pg. 63, ¶ 2—Shirakawa, Go-Sanjo's oldest son, was married to a Minamoto bride and made emperor by his father at the age of twenty-one. When Shirakawa became emperor, he favored Minamoto and Taira courtiers over the Fujiwara, and at the age of thirty-three he abdicated in favor of his son Horikawa, took monastic vows, and continued to rule actively from his monastery.

Shoshi—Pg. 64, ¶ 4—Shoshi, a ward of Shirakawa, was arranged to be married to Toba by his grandfather. People questioned the relationship between Shoshi and Shirakawa and when she gave birth to a son and heir named Sutoku in 1119, the baby was generally assumed to be Shirakawa's, even though Toba claimed the child as his own.

Sohei—Pg. 62, ¶ 3—Sohei was the name for Japanese warrior monks that protected the wealthy Buddhist monasteries. Sohei were chosen for the monastic life solely because they were good with their weapons.

Sutoku—Pg. 64, ¶ 5-6 and Pg. 65, ¶ 3-5—Sutoku, son of Toba and Shoshi (though probably son of Shirakawa and Shoshi), was made emperor in 1123 at the age of four when his alleged father abdicated in his favor but then in 1139 he was forced by Toba to abdicate in favor of Konoe. When Toba died, Sutoku challenged Go-Shirakawa for the throne in the Hogen Incident and failed.

Taira—Pg. 62, ¶ 2 and Pg. 67, ¶ 3—Taira was the clan name of a noble family in the southwest of Japan. The Taira had accumulated large and powerful personal armies that threated the Fujiwara and helped them to gain more influence in the Japanese government after the Heiji Disturbance.

Tametomo—Pg. 65, ¶ 3—Tametomo, son of Tameyoshi, is written about as a superhero in the fourteenth century account of the Japanese civil struggle called *The Tale of Hogen. The Tale of*

Hogen claimed that "Tametomo had a bow arm that was some six inches longer than the arm with which he held his horse's reins . . . [and he used] a bow that was more than eight and a half feet in length."

Tameyoshi—Pg. 65, ¶ 3 & 5—Tameyoshi was the Minamoto clan leader and Sutoku's right-hand commander during the civil war against Go-Shirakawa. Tameyoshi was put to death by his son Yoshimoto after Go-Shirakawa beat Sutoku.

Toba—Pg. 63, ¶ 2 & * and Pg. 64, ¶ 5—Toba, son of Horikawa, followed his father as emperor of Japan after his father's premature death. Toba was forced by his grandfather to abdicate the throne in favor of his four-year-old son, relegating Toba to a powerless position—junior Cloistered Emperor.

Tokuko—Pg. 64, ¶ 6—Tokuko was the favorite wife of Toba and the mother of his son Konoe.

Yoshitomo—Pg. 65, ¶ 3-5 and Pg. 67, ¶ 1—Yoshitomo, son of Tameyoshi, was, unlike his father and brother Tametomo, a supporter of Go-Shirakawa; when Go-Shirakawa defeated Sutoku's challenge to the throne Yoshimoto had his father put to death and the sinews of his brother's arms cut so that he could no longer use a bow. Then, after failing to overthrow Nijo in what was known as the Heiji Disturbance, Yoshimoto had his friend Masakiyo behead him rather than being killed by Kiyomori.

Section II: **Comprehension**

Write a two or three-sentence answer to each of the following questions.

1. How does the thirteenth-century Japanese history, the *Gukansho*, describe the general feeling towards Fujiwara power during the reign of Go-Sanjo?

A1.—Pg. 61, ¶ 5 to Pg. 62, ¶ 1—The *Gukansho* says that the people of Japan resented Fujiwara power. The Fujiwara clan ruled over Japan as if it was a private estate intended for their pleasure. According to the *Gukansho*, Go-Sanjo believed that the people would not be at peace if Fujiwara Regents and Chancellors continued to dominate the state while the Emperors "concerned themselves only with that which was elegant."

2. What reforms did Go-Sanjo make in Japanese government in an attempt to tamp down Fujiwara power?

A2.—Pg. 62, ¶ 4—Go-Sanjo established a new government department, called the Records Office, that required all landholders to register proof that they owned their land so that the Fujiwara could no longer use public land for the recruitment of private soldiers. Go-Sanjo also promoted a score of Minamoto officials into higher positions at court. Finally, he did his best to organize a line of succession that would place sons of non-Fujiwara mothers on the throne, starting with his own successors: his oldest son was Fujiwara, but from a much less notable branch of the family and his second son was the child of one of his lesser wives, a Minamoto daughter.

3. Explain the Japanese tradition of Cloistered Emperors.

A3.—Pg. 63, ¶ 3—Starting with Go-Sanjo, and continuing on for two hundred years, Japan was ruled by Cloistered Emperors. Cloistered Emperors abdicated at the height of their powers, leaving the throne to child heirs, and then went on ruling from behind the scenes. Though there may have been a new emperor on the throne, everyone knew the retired emperor was in charge.

4. What were the benefits of the Cloistered Emperor tradition?

A4.—Pg. 63, ¶ 4 to Pg. 64, ¶ 1—The Cloistered Emperor tradition was beneficial because it neatly divided time-consuming ritual duties, like ceremonially important but politically pointless duties, from the equally time-consuming duties of actual governance. The sovereign on the throne took care of the first; the ruler in the monastery, the second. It also preserved an appearance of cooperation between the emperor-in-name and his Fujiwara advisor, while the actual power struggle between king and Fujiwara clan went on, more or less, in private.

5. What was the cause for civil war in Japan in 1156? What happened at the Hogen Incident on July 29, 1156?

A5.—Pg. 65, ¶ 2-4—The death of Toba, and the divided support for his son, Go-Shirakawa, or his supposed son Sutoku, for emperor, was the cause of civil war in Japan in 1156. When the two sides finally met Tametomo picked off a number of warriors on the opposing side, but his brother Yoshitomo had the brilliant idea of sending an arsonist in to set Sutoku's headquarters on fire and as the Cloistered Emperor's men scrambled away from the flames, Go-Shirakawa's archers took them down, one at a time. The result, called the Hogen Incident, led to Sutoku's men being shot, burned to death, or crushed by fellow soldiers that were jumping into wells to avoid the flames and Sutoku himself was arrested and exiled.

6. Describe the events of the Heiji Disturbance.

A6.—Pg. 66, ¶ 3 to Pg. 67, ¶ 1—Just after Go-Shirakawa abdicated in favor of his teenaged son, Nijo, Yoshitomo and Nobuyori surrounded the palace of the Cloistered Emperor with five hundred Minamoto samurai, took Go-Shirakawa prisoner, and set his palace on fire while other samurai kidnapped the young emperor. Taira Kiyomori, who was away on a pilgrimage of devotion to Kumano, heard of the attack and came thundering back into Kyoto at the head of a thousand samurai, all loyal to the Taira cause. Young Emperor Nijo was rescued; the Cloistered Emperor escaped; and the troops of Minamoto Yoshitomo and Fujiwara Nobuyori finally scattered in the face of the Taira attack.

7. What happened to power in the capital after the Heiji Disturbance?

A7.—Pg. 67, ¶ 3—After the Heiji Disturbance, Taira Kiyomori executed or exiled almost every important member of both the Yoshimoto and Fujiwara clans. In the span of twenty years, the power of the Fujiwara had collapsed and after the Heiji Disturbance the Taira clan was rising in power. Ultimately, however, the Cloistered Emperor still controlled the palace, and the other clans waited their chance for revenge.

Section III: Critical Thinking

The student may not use his text to answer this question.

Eleventh-century Japan was stifled by the power of the Fujiwara clan. As written on the first page of Chapter Nine, "Generation after generation, imperial princes had married Fujiwara brides. Fujiwara ministers of state, usually close male relations of the reigning empress, dominated weak or young rulers. Emperor after emperor was crowned and then retreated behind the scenes to pursue poetry and luxurious living, political ceremony and religious ritual." Emperors were rendered powerless by the Fujiwara and Emperor Go-Sanjo was sick of it. Write a paragraph explaining how Go-Sanjo got out from under the grasp of the Fujiwara and then explain whether or not you think Japan was better off with Go-Sanjo's new system.

Go-Sanjo was able to get around continuing Fujiwara power by abdicating early and placing his first son as emperor and his second son as Imperial Prince. The student has already explained the Cloistered Emperor tradition in short answer question three. He can paraphrase here. The Cloistered Emperor system worked like this: the current emperor abdicated in favor of his son and then continued to rule behind the scenes. Abdicating early guaranteed the emperor continued power and control over the Fujiwara nobleman in the capital.

*The student may say he is for, or against, the Cloistered Emperor system. Again, the student explained the benefits of the system in short answer question four. The Cloistered Emperor system was beneficial because it divided time-consuming ritual
duties from the equally
time-consuming duties of actual governance. The ruling emperor presided over rituals and the Cloistered Emperor managed the actual running of the government. The system also preserved an appearance of cooperation between the Fujiwara advisor and the emperor while the power struggle continued in private.*

However, these power struggles point to the negative aspects of the Cloistered Emperor system. Like the strong grip of the Fujiwara advisors, the Cloistered Emperor was the one that was truly in charge, and that left the emperor basically powerless and in no better position than he was in during the height of Fujiwara power. Another problem occurred when there were two Cloistered Emperors, as in the case of Toba, Sutoku and Konoe. Cloistered Emperor Toba forced Emperor Sutoku to abdicate in favor of Konoe, leaving Sutoku as a powerless Cloistered Emperor. Sutoku simmered with resentment. When Konoe died, Toba appointed his next son Go-Shirakawa as emperor. As soon as Toba died, Sutoku started a rebellion against Go-Shirakawa. The point here is clear: the Cloistered Emperor system created new power struggles in the Japanese capital that resulted in rivalries, rebellions and battles that did not benefit the country. The system did not fix what was wrong, it merely created new ways for frustration to boil over.

EXAMPLE ANSWER (FOR):

Go-Sanjo was able to get around continuing Fujiwara power by abdicating early and placing his first son as emperor and his second son as Imperial Prince. Go-Sanjo created the tradition of the Cloistered Emperor. The Cloistered Emperor system worked like this: the current emperor abdicated in favor of his son and then continued to rule behind the scenes. Abdicating early guaranteed the emperor continued power and control over the Fujiwara nobleman in the capital.

The Cloistered Emperor system was better than the previous system where the Fujiwara clan ruled because it created a united front for the Japanese people to see: it looked like the Fujiwara advisor and the emperor cooperated with one another while the power struggle continued in private. More importantly, the system allowed the emperor to deal with ritual duties, which were time consuming and took away from the running of the government, while the Cloistered Emperor, who had all the time in the world, actually dealt with the management of the empire. The system created a more efficient running of the Japanese government than under the old Fujiwara power structure.

EXAMPLE ANSWER (AGAINST):

Go-Sanjo was able to get around continuing Fujiwara power by abdicating early and placing his first son as emperor and his second son as Imperial Prince. Go-Sanjo created the tradition of the Cloistered Emperor. The Cloistered Emperor system worked like this: the current emperor abdicated in favor of his son and then continued to rule behind the scenes. Abdicating early guaranteed the emperor continued power and control over the Fujiwara nobleman in the capital.

The system did not solve Japan's problems. Like the strong grip of the Fujiwara advisors, the Cloistered Emperor was the one that was truly in charge, and that left the emperor basically powerless and in no better position than he was in during the height of Fujiwara power. Another problem occurred when there were two Cloistered Emperors, as in the case of Toba, Sutoku and Konoe. Cloistered Emperor Toba forced Emperor Sutoku to abdicate in favor of Konoe, leaving Sutoku as a powerless Cloistered Emperor. Sutoku simmered with resentment. When Konoe died, Toba appointed his next son Go-Shirakawa as emperor. As soon as Toba died, Sutoku started a rebellion against Go-Shirakawa. Sutoku's rebellion exemplifies how the Cloistered Emperor system created new power struggles in the Japanese capital that resulted in conflicts that did not benefit the empire. The system did not fix what was wrong, it merely created new ways for frustration to boil over.

Section IV: Map Exercise

1. Using a black pencil, trace the rectangular outline of the frame for Map 9.1: Japan under the Cloistered Emperors.

2. Trace the coastline around Japan. You need not include the very small unmarked islands around the coastline. Repeat until the contours are familiar.

3. Using a new sheet of paper, trace the rectangular outline of the map in black. Then using a regular pencil with an eraser, draw the Japanese coastline. Erase and redraw as necessary.

4. When you are pleased with your map, lay your paper over the original, and erase and redraw any lines which are more than ½" off of the original.

5. Mark Honshu. Then study carefully the locations of Minamoto, Mt. Hiei, Kamo, Nara, Kumano, and Taira. When you are familiar with them, close the book. Using your regular pencil with an

eraser, label each location. Check your map against the original, and correct any misplaced or mismarked labels.

Chapter Ten

Death of an Army

The student may use her text when answering the questions in sections I and II.

Section I: Who, What, Where

Write a one or two-sentence answer explaining the significance of each item listed below.

Chung-heon—**Pg. 73, ¶ 3 and Pg. 74, 1-3—Chung-heon, a member of the Choe clan, claimed control of the Council of Generals with his brother Chung-su after they had murdered their most powerful rival in 1196. Chung-heon, after becoming sole controller of the throne, transferred most of the power of the government into his own private control and he ruled Goryeo, through his puppet-king, as a private citizen.**

Chung-su—**Pg. 73, ¶ 3 & 7 to Pg. 74, ¶ 1—Chung-su, a member of the Choe clan, claimed control of the Council of Generals with his brother Chung-heon after they had murdered their most powerful rival in 1196. Chung-su quarreled with his brother because Chung-su wanted to marry his daughter off to the crown prince; the quarrel between the brothers escalated into a street fight between their supporters in which Chung-su was killed.**

Chungbang—**pg. 72, ¶ 5—Chungbang was the name of the Council of Generals formed by Jeong Jung-bu, Yi Ko and Yi Uibang after Uijong was taken off of the throne. The Chungbang, made up of a group of officers, took over the job of governing that had once been held by the civilian State Council.**

Han Roe—**Pg. 71, ¶ 8 to Pg. 72, ¶ 2—Han Roe was a civilian official that mocked a losing officer during a staged boxing competition put on by the king. Han Roe's taunting, which included pushing down the officer to demonstrate his weakness, ignited a coup against the king and the civilian officials in which Han Roe himself was killed.**

Heaven-Sent Force of Loyalty and Righteousness—**Pg. 70, ¶ 2—Heaven-Sent Force of Loyalty and Righteousness was the name of an army raised by a rebellious Buddhist monk that revolted against King Injong.**

Injong—**Pg. 70, ¶ 2-5—Injong, king of Goryeo, put down two major rebellions during his reign but did nothing to address the discontent that caused those rebellions. During Injong's reign, old noble families kept their estates apart and filled civil offices, military officers were relegated to the lowest possible appointments, and the great private estates displaced many peasants who then had to turn to banditry to survive.**

Jeong Jung-bu—**Pg. 71, ¶ 3, Pg. 72, ¶ 2 & 5 and Pg. 73, ¶ 2—Jeong Jung-bu, Chief of General Staff to Uijong, was made a mockery of when Kim Ton-jung set his beard on fire for the king's amusement. After Jeong Jung-bu led a rebellion in the palace and killed an entire layer of Goryeo's government, he formed the Chungbang with Yi Ko and Yi Uibang which he ruled until 1179 when he was murdered by a young officer.**

Kim Bo-dang—**Pg. 72, ¶ 7 & 8—Kim Bo-dang, an officer that had been demoted after General Jung-bu's government came to power, rounded up a substantial counterforce of soldiers and civilians who were still loyal to Uijong in 1173. Kim Bo-dang died during his failed attack on the new military government.**

Kim Ton-jung—**Pg. 71, ¶ 4 and Pg. 72, ¶ 2—King Ton-Jung played a practical joke on King Uijong's Chief of Staff, General Jeong Jung-bu, by setting the general's long beard on fire for the king's entertainment. Kim Tom-jung died as a result of Jeong Jung-bu storming the palace and killing civilian officials in protest.**

Kyong—**Pg. 70, ¶ 6 to Pg. 71, ¶ 1—Kyong, the second son of Injong, was preferred by his mother and father to lead Goryeo; his older brother Uijong knew Kyong was the favorite so he stripped Kyong of his titles six years into his reign and then, another six years later, had Kyong banished from the capital city of Kaesong completely.**

Myeongjong—**Pg. 72, ¶ 3 and Pg. 73, ¶ 6—Myeongjong, younger brother of Uijong, was placed on the throne after his brother was put in exile. Myeongjong, already forty when he was crowned, was weak and accommodating, wielded no power, and managed to stay alive and on the throne for twenty-seven years before abdicating to his younger brother Sinjong.**

Sinjong—**Pg. 73, ¶ 6—Sinjong, younger brother of Myeongjong, followed his brother as puppet-king of Goryeo, under the command of Chung-heon.**

Uijong—**Pg. 70, ¶ 6, Pg. 72, ¶ 3 and Pg. 73, ¶ 2—Uijong, oldest son of Injong, took the throne of Goryeo in 1146; he was the eighteenth king of his line but he was not liked for the position by his mother or father, nor the historians of his time. Uijong survived Jeong Jung-bu's rebellion by handing all his power over to the general and going into exile on Koje Island, though ultimately he was killed in his island prison by one of Yi Uibang's men.**

Yi Ko—**Pg. 71, ¶ 5, Pg. 72, ¶ 5 and Pg. 73, ¶ 2 —Yi Ko, a Senior Captain under Jeong Jung-bu's command and member of the same clan as the exiled friends of Prince Kyong, helped Jeong Jung-bu oust Uijong and then form the Chungbang. Power struggles within the Council of Generals led to Yi Ko's assassination by Yi Uibang in 1174.**

Yi Uibang—**Pg. 71, ¶ 5, Pg. 72, ¶ 5 and Pg. 73, ¶ 2 —Yi Uibang, a Senior Captain under Jeong Jung-bu's command and member of the same clan as the exiled friends of Prince Kyong, helped Jeong Jung-bu oust Uijong and then form the Chungbang. In a bid for power, Yi Uibang assassinated Yi Ko in 1174 and then arranged for the marriage of his daughter to King Myeongjong's son, a display of ambitions so bald that Jeong Jung-bu had Yi Uibang murdered.**

Section II: **Comprehension**

Write a two or three-sentence answer to each of the following questions.

1. What are the two major systems for rendering Korean names into the Roman alphabet? What system is used in present day South Korea, and in your textbook? What system is used in present day North Korea?

A1.—Pg. 69, *—There are two major systems for rendering Korean names into the Roman alphabet. The older system, McCune-Reischauer Romanization, uses phonetic symbols and the newer system, Revised Romanization, tries to represent Korean sounds with combinations of vowels and consonants. The current official system of South Korea is Revised Romanization, which is also used in this textbook. Present day North Korea continues to use a slightly altered version of McCune-Reischauer Romanization.

2. What internal divisions did Goryeo face during the Injong's reign?

A2.—Pg. 70, ¶ 3-5—During Injong's reign, the old aristocratic families grew in power, married among themselves, filled civil government positions, and expanded their private estates which resulted in the displacement of Goryeo's peasants and their subsequent turn to banditry. Military officers lost their ability to move up in rank when Injong's officials decided to do away with the exams that allowed them to qualify for important civil posts and thus were relegated to the lowest possible appointments. The army had served the throne loyally in putting down rebellions, and a standing force was needed to protect the northern border against wandering nomadic invaders; but the aristocracy was unwilling to allow soldiers to gain any more power.

3. Explain the relationship between Uijong and Kyong, and how Kyong ended up in exile in 1156.

A3.—Pg. 70, ¶ 6 to Pg. 71, ¶ 1—Uijong and Kyong's parents had a low opinion of Uijong—they thought he was a trifler with no skill for governing—and they preferred Kyong to be king; however, Uijong was still crowned in Injong's place in 1156. Uijong knew Kyong was his family's favorite, so in 1151, after six years on the throne, he seized on a court rumor that Kyong was planning treason and used it as an excuse to strip Prince Kyong of his titles and remove his closest friends from their official positions. Kyong had remained popular, especially with his mother's family, and Uijong was afraid of a coup so after another six years, Uijong banished Kyong and his cronies from the capital city of Kaesong completely.

4. How did Jeong Jung-bu, Yi Ko and Yi Uibang come together in resentment against Uijong? What was the last straw before they decided to go forward with their rebellion?

A4.—Pg. 71, ¶ 7—The setting on fire of Jeong Jung-bu's beard brought together the Chief of General Staff and the two Senior Captains in resentment against Uijong. Three years after the came together, they attended a memorial service where both civilian and military officials had gathered. The civilian officials were drunk and well-fed and the military officials were hungry and upset; with the gap between the ranks made clear, Jeong Jung-bu, Yi Ko and Yi Uibang began to plot a coup.

5. Why did Jeong Jung-bu institute a second purge of civilians after he had already gotten Uijong off the throne? What was the result of the second purge?

A5.—Pg. 72 ¶ 8 to Pg. 73, ¶ 1—Kim Bo-dang, a military man, rounded up a counterforce against Jeong Jung-bu in the name of Uijong, but his attack was a failure and he died, shouting as he slipped away, "The civil bureaucrats all joined in plotting with me!" The accusation set off another purge of civil officials who had not been killed in 1170. As a result of the second purge, civilians who had once been sympathetic to the military's plight now began to turn against the new regime and another army raised in P'yongyang tried to drive the General and his captains out of power.

6. Why didn't Chung-heon want to rule over the Goryeo army? Why didn't he want to put his own sons on the Goryeo throne after he took power?

A6.—Pg. 73, ¶ 4-6—Chung-heon did not want to rule over the Goryeo army because it was unruly and too many men had died trying to wrangle the military. Another strategy Chung-heon used to avoid conflict was not putting his own sons on the Goryeo throne; he did not want to shatter the mystique of the long-lasting Goryeo dynasty. Chung-heon knew that upsetting the image of the Goryeo throne might energize a whole new civilian resistance to the military dictatorship.

7. How did Chung-heon take the rule of Goryeo into his private control?

A7.—Pg. 74, ¶ 2 & 3—Chung-heon made sure that his own personal guards, supplemented by troops who owed loyalty directly to him, became a separate and independent army within the capital, answering only to him. At first, they simply guarded his house but as time went on, they were augmented by mercenaries, deserters from the regular army, and new allies, until Chung-heon controlled thirty-six armed units of well-trained fighters. Then, over time, Chung-heon transferred more and more of the government's powers—including tax collection and the prosecution of lawbreakers—over to his own private control.

8. What was left of the Goryeo government after Chung-heon privatized most the running of the country?

A8.—Pg. 74, ¶ 3—Chung-heon allowed the Goryeo throne, the traditional government offices, and the shell of the army to survive. The Council of Generals was given a handful of ceremonial tasks, the task of carrying out important Buddhist rituals, and the responsibility for making maps. Neither the king, nor the Council of Generals, took any part in actually running the country.

Section III: Critical Thinking

The student may not use her text to answer this question.

Plato's Phaedrus said, "Things are not always what they seem." Write a paragraph explaining one of the following accounts of deceptive appearances that occurred in this chapter. You can write about the appearance of peace Uijong cultivated and why some continued to support him after he was overthrown, or you can write about the true meaning of the king being entertained by Jeong Jung-bu's burning beard. In your answer, explain what the world saw and then explain the truth found beneath.

Uijong's Peaceful Goryeo

Uijong was very clever. Though he fed the power of the aristocrats by allowing them to grow their estates and take up most civil service positions, he made himself look good for the people by posing as a man of culture and peace. He built Buddhist temples and gave them names like "Tranquility" and "Joyful Pleasure." He dug lily ponds, traveled from one beauty spot to another, and gave alms to the poor. Even when Uijong was overthrown by Jeong Jung-bu he still had supporters because he made the people of Goryeo believe he was a faithful observer of Buddhist practices and he tried to lower taxes. The truth is that Uijong, by mistreating the army and by favoring the aristocrats, was not good to his people. The appearance he gave of being a wise and peaceful leader was just that—appearance only.

Jeong Jung-bu's Burning Beard

In 1167, at a royal feast, Kim Ton-jung played a practical joke on the king's Chief of General Staff, Jeong Jung-bu. Kim Ton-jung set the general's long grey beard on fire with a candle. King Uijong found the scene very entertaining. For Jeong Jung-bu, however, the incident was infuriating. In truth, all of the military under Uijong were treated terribly. As written on page 71, Uijong "ordered soldiers to dig ditches and build walls for public projects and forced officers to act as ceremonial bodyguards to civil officials. Enlisted men found their salaries unexpectedly docked, or promised land tracts suddenly reassigned. On royal expeditions, military men were allowed to wait, cold and hungry, until civilians were well fed." On the surface it may have appeared that the fire in Jeong Jung-bu's beard was an accident, or a harmless joke, but underneath it was the symbol of the long smoldering fire of resentment held by the Goryeo military.

EXAMPLE ANSWER (UIJONG'S PEACEFUL GORYEO):

Uijong made himself look good for the people by posing as a man of culture and peace. He built Buddhist temples and gave them names like "Tranquility" and "Joyful Pleasure." He dug lily ponds, traveled from one beauty spot to another, and gave alms to the poor. Even when Uijong was overthrown by Jeong Jung-bu he still had supporters because he made the people of Goryeo believe he was a faithful observer of Buddhist practices and he tried to lower taxes. The truth is the Uijong, by mistreating the army and by favoring the aristocrats, was not good to his people. The appearance he gave of being a wise and peaceful leader was just that—appearance only.

EXAMPLE ANSWER (JEONG JUNG-BU'S BURNING BEARD):

In 1167, at a royal feast, Kim Ton-jung played a practical joke on the king's Chief of General Staff, Jeong Jung-bu. Kim Ton-jung set the general's long grey beard on fire with a candle. King Uijong found the scene very entertaining. For Jeong Jung-bu, however, the incident was infuriating. In truth, all of the military under Uijong were treated terribly. Soldiers were forced to dig ditches, build walls for public projects and act as ceremonial bodyguards to civil officials, but they were not given any respect or proper pay. Military men often found their salaries unexpectedly docked, or tracts of land that were promised to them suddenly

reassigned. On royal expeditions civilians were always fed first while military men were allowed to wait, cold and hungry. On the surface it may have appeared that the fire in Jeong Jung-bu's beard was an accident, or a harmless joke, but underneath it was the symbol of the long smoldering fire of resentment held by the Goryeo military.

Section IV: Map Exercise

1. Using a black pencil, trace the rectangular outline of the frame for Map 10.1: Goryeo.

2. Using a blue pencil, trace the visible coastline around China and Japan. Include Koje Island and the other few distinct islands between the coastlines. Repeat until the contours are familiar.

3. Using a black pencil, trace the Goryeo region, and repeat until the contours are familiar.

4. Using a new sheet of paper, trace the rectangular outline of the frame in black. Using your regular pencil, draw the coastlines of China and Japan, the islands, and then also the specific region of Goryeo.

5. When you are pleased with your map, lay it over the original, and erase and redraw any lines which are more than ¼" off.

6. Now study carefully the locations of P'yongyang, Kaesong, and Koje Island. When they are familiar, close the book, and label each location. Then check them against book, and make any needed corrections.

Chapter Eleven

The First Plantagenet

The student may use his text when answering the questions in sections I and II.

Section I: Who, What, Where

Write a one or two-sentence answer explaining the significance of each item listed below.

Eustace—**Pg. 78, ❡ 4—Eustace, Stephen's son and heir, died of a sudden onset of seizures. Stephen lost the heart to continue fighting against Henry after Eustace died.**

Henry—**Pg. 76, ❡ 5, Pg. 77, ❡ 3 & 4 and Pg. 78, ❡ 7—Henry, Matilda's son, became both Count of Anjou and Duke of Normandy when his father died and gained even more power and land when he married Eleanor of Aquitaine on May 18, 1152. Henry became king of England, too, on December 19, 1154, due to the terms of the Treaty of Wallingford, which both Henry and Stephen signed in January of 1154.**

William of Conches—**Pg. 76, ❡ 3—William of Conches was a well-regarded philosopher and author of a masterwork intended to reconcile Greek natural philosophy with Christian orthodoxy. He was also Henry's tutor in Western Francia.**

Section II: Comprehension

Write a two or three-sentence answer to each of the following questions.

1. What areas of England did Stephen control during the civil war? What areas did Matilda control? What did the land look like in between?

A1.—Pg. 76, ❡ 2—Stephen's armies controlled the southeast of England and the capital city of London. Matilda's soldiers dominated the southwest. The land in between the two strongholds was a wasteland where one could go on a day's journey and not find one person in a village or one piece of farm land that was tilled.

2. Describe Henry's first war adventure in England.

A2.—Pg. 76, ❡ 3 & 4—In 1147 fourteen-year-old Henry left his studies in Western Francia with a small band of soldiers but rumors circulated in England that said Henry had come with an entire army, or perhaps two, possibly with the king of France behind him, and was ready to devastate the opposition. Of course, this wasn't true, and Henry's little group of adventurers lost several initial skirmishes against detachments of Stephen's soldiers. Realizing there was nothing in it for them, Henry's soldiers ditched him, Henry found

himself broke and stranded in enemy territory, and King Stephen of England had to provide Henry with the money to get back home.

3. What happened when Capetian king Louis VII asked the pope for an annulment from Eleanor of Aquitaine?

A3.—Pg. 76, ¶ 7 to Pg. 77, ¶ 1 & 2—When Louis VII asked the pope about annulling his marriage to Eleanor of Aquitaine, the pope refused to discuss it. Instead, he shut the estranged couple into a bedroom furnished with a single bed to encourage their relationship. The result was a disaster: Eleanor gave birth to another girl which made Louis VII resign himself to ending the marriage.

4. What happened the second time Capetian king Louis VII asked the pope for an annulment from Eleanor of Aquitaine?

A4.—Pg. 77, ¶ 2— The second time Louis VII asked the pope for an annulment from Eleanor of Aquitaine he did so with the help of Bernard of Clairvaux and the proof of dissatisfaction with the marriage that came with Eleanor's inability to produce a male heir. The pope now granted the annulment and the decree that their marriage ceased to exist was dated March 11, 1152.

5. Why did Louis VII attack Henry after his marriage to Eleanor? What were the terms of the truce made between the two men?

A5.—Pg. 77, ¶ 5 to Pg. 78, ¶ 1—Louis VII was incensed by Henry's marriage to Eleanor—not only was Eleanor Louis VII's ex-wife but also Louis VII lost half his domain to Eleanor's new husband. Louis mounted a war against Henry, but not only did Henry's troops easily fight off Louis's attacks, they also made their way into royal land, forcing Louis VII to suggest a truce. Peace would be made if Louis VII would recognize Henry's claim to Aquitaine and Henry swore an oath of loyal submission to the French throne.

6. Why did Henry agree to a truce with Louis VII that included being submissive to the French throne?

A6.—Pg. 78, ¶ 2—Henry agreed to a truce with Louis VII that included his submission to the French throne because his power in Western Francia was secure—his lands were more than seven times larger than Louis's royal estates. More importantly, Henry was preparing to fight for England. His mother Matilda had retreated to Normandy and Henry was going to pick up her cause.

7. How did Stephen and Henry come to sign the Treaty of Wallingford? What were the conditions of the treaty?

A7.—Pg. 78, ¶ 3-5—In January of 1153, Henry landed on English shores at the head of three thousand men, immediately took the castle of Malmesbury away from Stephen's forces and reached the Thames by first week of August. When Stephen's son and heir Eustace died, Stephen lost the will to fight and suggested a truce. In January of 1154 the men signed the Treaty of Wallingford which said that Henry would become heir to the crown as long as

Stephen continued to rule as king of England until his death and Henry swore loyalty to Stephen as his lord.

8. What did Henry order on Christmas Day of 1154? Why did he make such an order?

A8.—Pg. 79, ¶ 3—On Christmas Day of 1154, Henry ordered the foreign mercenaries who had flocked into England during the Anarchy expelled. He also ordered all castles built without royal permission to be demolished. He made these orders because he needed to quell the power of the noblemen in England. By demolishing their castles and purging their private armies—made up of mercenaries—Henry took power away from the noblemen and put it back with the throne.

Section III: Critical Thinking

The student may not use his text to answer this question.

At the age of fourteen Matilda's son Henry sailed to England with a small band of soldiers. After losing several small fights, Henry's men deserted him and he was left stranded in England. His mother's treasury was empty, so the King of England himself had to supply the funds to send Henry back to Western Francia and his teenage studies. This was not an auspicious start for young Henry. However, at twenty-one, Henry was Count of Anjou, Duke of Normandy, Ruler of Aquitaine and King of England. Write a paragraph explaining what made Henry a strong ruler. In your answer, explain both political and military decisions Henry made that helped to secure his power.

In this chapter we see two major character traits that helped to propel Henry to such great power: first, he knew when to make a truce and second, he had enormous amounts of energy that kept him on top of the governing of his lands. When Henry's father died he became Count of Anjou and Duke of Normandy at the age of eighteen. When Henry met Eleanor of Aquitaine, he was taken with her, and just months after their meeting (and Eleanor's divorce from Louis VII), they were married. Louis VII attacked Henry soon after his marriage to Eleanor in order to win back some of the land that Henry had inherited in his marriage. But Henry's men were powerful and they not only drove back Louis VII's troops but also started to invade royal land. Henry's military decision to invade Louis VII's land showed his power. When Louis VII suggested a truce, Henry could have said no and kept fighting, but he agreed. The truce firmed up Henry's grip on Aquitaine and ensured no more fighting with Western Francia; it was a politically shrewd move. Similarly, when Henry attacked England, Stephen suggested a truce not even a year into Henry's invasion. Again, Henry could have continued to fight and have Stephen forcibly removed from the throne, but he agreed to a truce. Stephen died ten months after the Treaty of Wallingford was signed and Henry was made King of England rather peacefully. Not only did Henry know when to make a truce, he knew not to rest on his laurels. He used his enormous stores of energy to keep his kingdom in check. For example, only six days after his coronation, Henry ordered the foreign mercenaries living in England during the Anarchy expelled, and he also ordered all castles built without royal permission to be demolished. Those noblemen that resisted were met with force: Henry used his military to lay siege to the rebellious castles and confiscate them for the crown. Henry's quick and fierce military response stopped any more noblemen from defying the king. Getting rid of the personal armies and castles of the noblemen that challenged the English throne secured Henry's power and showed his strength as ruler.

EXAMPLE ANSWER:

Henry was a strong ruler because he made wise political and military decisions. He had a lot of energy that kept him on top of ruling his kingdom. After Henry married Eleanor of Aquitaine, Louis VII attacked. Henry's men were powerful and they not only drove back Louis VII's troops but also started to invade royal land. Henry's military decision to invade Louis VII's land showed his power. When Louis VII suggested a truce, Henry could have said no and kept fighting, but he agreed. The truce firmed up Henry's grip on Aquitaine and ensured no more fighting with Western Francia; it was a politically shrewd move. Similarly, when Henry attacked England, Stephen suggested a truce not even a year into Henry's invasion. Again, Henry could have continued to fight and have Stephen forcibly removed from the throne, but he agreed to a truce. Stephen died ten months after the Treaty of Wallingford was signed and Henry was made King of England rather peacefully. Not only did Henry know when to make a truce, he knew not to rest on his laurels. Only six days after his coronation as King of England, Henry ordered the foreign mercenaries expelled and he also ordered all castles built without royal permission to be demolished. Those noblemen that resisted were met with force: Henry used his military to lay siege to the rebellious castles and confiscate them for the crown. Henry's quick and fierce military response stopped any more noblemen from defying the king. Getting rid of the personal armies and castles of the noblemen that challenged the English throne secured Henry's power and showed his strength as ruler.

Section IV: Map Exercise

1. Using a black pencil, trace the rectangular outline of the frame for Map 11.1, Anjou, Normandy, and England.

2. Using a blue pencil, trace the coastline around England and around the continent. Also trace the line of the Thames. Repeat until the contours are familiar.

3. Now using a black pencil, trace the outlines of the Domains of the King of France. Repeat until the contours are familiar.

4. Using a new sheet of paper, trace the outline of the map's frame in black. Then remove your paper from the original. Using your regular pencil with an eraser, draw the outline of the coast around England and the continent, the line of the Thames, and the Domains of King of France. When you are done with this, check your map against the original, and erase and redraw any lines which are more than ½" off of the original.

5. Mark England, the Domains of the King of France, and Western Francia. Now carefully study the areas of Kent, Normandy, Anjou, and Aquitaine. When you are familiar with them, mark and label their locations. Then study the locations of London, Malmsbury, Paris, and Poitiers. When you are familiar with them, mark them on your map. Check your map against the original, and erase and redraw any marks more than ½" off of the original.

Chapter Twelve

Frederick Barbarossa

The student may use her text when answering the questions in sections I and II.

Section I: Who, What, Where

Write a one or two-sentence answer explaining the significance of each item listed below.

Adrian IV—Pg. 83, ¶ 1, 4 & *—Adrian IV became pope on December 3, 1154 (he was the only Englishman to ever hold the position) and crowned Frederick Barbarossa Holy Roman Emperor in June of 1155. When Adrian IV realized the papal states were against Frederick Barbarossa, he too looked at him unfavorably and made a treaty with the Norman enemy to the south.

Alexander III—Pg. 83, ¶ 4 and Pg. 86, ¶ 1—Alexander III was appointed pope by the cardinals in proper ecclesiastical fashion after the death of Adrian IV. Alexander III fled into Western Francia after Frederick Barbarossa installed the "antipope" Victor IV in Rome, but he was reinstated in 1177 after Frederick Barbarossa made peace with the Lombard League.

Callixtus III—Pg. 86, ¶ 1—Callixtus III followed Paschal III as the Roman antipope. Frederick Barbarossa abandoned the antipope after he made peace with the Lombard League.

Frederick Barbarossa (Frederick of Swabia)—Pg. 82, ¶ 3 & 4, Pg. 83, ¶ 1 and Pg. 85, ¶ 7 to Pg. 86, ¶ 1—Frederick Barbarossa (originally Frederick of Swabia), who got his name because of his auburn colored beard, was elected king of Germany by his cousin Henry the Lion and the council of German electors after the death of Conrad III. Frederick Barbarossa became Holy Roman Emperor in June of 1155 but he could not hold his power over Italy and had to return to Germany in 1177.

Henry the Lion—Pg. 82, ¶ 1, 2 & 4 and Pg. 86, ¶ 2—Henry the Lion, son of the Duke of Bavaria and Saxony, was able to retrieve rule of Bavaria from Conrad III by making an alliance with a powerful Wendish leader and then reclaiming the land as his own; when Frederick Barbarossa was made king of Germany he restored Henry the Lion's title officially. After Frederick Barbarossa returned to Germany in 1177 he took away Henry the Lion's land as punishment for Henry's refusal to accompany him into the final battle against the Lombard League in Italy.

Lombard League—Pg. 85, ¶ 3, 6 & 7—Lombard League, made up of the men of Verona and Parma, Bologna and Venice, was formed in 1167 in opposition to Frederick Barbarossa. The Lombard League defeated Frederick Barbarossa's imperial forces in 1176, after which the German king made peace with the League and with Alexander III.

Paschal III—Pg. 85, ¶ 2—Paschal III followed Victor IV as Frederick Barbarossa's antipope when he died in 1164. Three years into his rule, Paschal III was ordered to canonize Charlemagne which made the founder of the royal office a saint and theoretically further legitimized Frederick Barbarossa's hold on the position.

Roman commune—Pg. 82, ¶ 6—Roman commune was the name for the group of senators who ran the city of Rome's affairs.

Victor IV—Pg. 83, ¶ 4—Victor IV was appointed pope by Frederick Barbarossa after the death of Adrian IV, but Frederick did not have the right to name a pope, so Victor IV was called the "antipope." Frederick Barbarossa's men installed Victor IV in Rome, causing the legitimate pope, Alexander III, to flee to Western Francia.

Wends—Pg. 81, ¶ 2 & *—Wends was the collective name for the Slavic tribes living just north of the German border. The Wends were made up of a federation of five tribes: the Wagrians, Abotrites, Polabians, Rugians, and Liutizians.

Section II: Comprehension

Write a two or three-sentence answer to each of the following questions.

1. Who did the German crusaders want to be the objects of their holy war? How did they convince Bernard of Clairvaux and Pope Eugenius III to approve the target of their crusade?

A1.—Pg. 81, ¶ 2 & 3—The German crusaders wanted to fight the Slavic tribes known collectively as the Wends who were located just north of the German border. Though the Wends were settled farmers, they were not Christians. Bernard of Clairvaux, who had been preaching for months that the purpose of crusade was to submit the heathen to the power of God, agreed that the Wends should be brought into the Christian realm of Germany and subsequently Pope Eugenius III blessed the effort.

2. Why did the Wendish Crusade fail as a holy war?

A2.—Pg. 81, ¶ 4—The Wendish Crusade failed as a holy war because in the fighting and raids, not a single Wend was baptized. The crusaders' inability to convert the Wends was likely because they did not have a clear leader. The Danes split off from the Germans and made their own raids, the Germans couldn't agree on a clear strategy and in a few months the whole effort fizzled out.

3. If Henry the Lion was the son of the Duke of Bavaria and Saxony, why didn't he inherit command of Bavaria and Saxony after his father died?

A3.—Pg. 82, ¶ 1—When the Duke of Bavaria and Saxony was alive, he opposed the election of Conrad III. As soon as Conrad III became the German king he punished the Duke by seizing his lands. After the Duke died, Conrad III returned Saxony to Henry the Lion, but he did not return rule over Bavaria.

4. What deal did Frederick Barbarossa make with Pope Eugenius III that resulted in the German king being crowned Holy Roman Emperor?

A4.—Pg. 82, ¶ 6— Frederick Barbarossa promised Pope Eugenius III that he would help the church official deal with the Norman kingdom of Sicily, which was encroaching on the papal lands from the south, and with the Roman commune that was making trouble by asking for more independence from papal power. In exchange for Frederick Barbarossa's help, Pope Eugenius III promised to crown the German king as Holy Roman Emperor.

5. How did the people of Rome react to Frederick Barbarossa's coronation as Holy Roman Emperor?

A5.—Pg. 83, ¶ 2—The people of Rome did not want to acknowledge Frederick Barbarossa as Holy Roman Emperor. They were infuriated that Frederick Barbarossa had received the crown without their approval. The people rioted and Frederick Barbarossa's men killed over a thousand Romans on their way out of the city back to their camp.

6. Using Genoese and Milan as examples, describe Frederick Barbarossa's reception as Holy Roman Emperor by the papal states.

A6.—Pg. 83, ¶ 3 & 4—The papal states were not welcoming to Frederick Barbarossa as their Holy Roman Emperor. The papal states had developed a system where they were loyal not to a king but to their cities, which meant he had to deal with several rebellions rather than just one. For example, the Genoese built a whole series of new walls and openly defied Frederick Barbarossa, and the consul of Milan persuaded several other cities to join him in a coalition against the Holy Roman emperor.

7. Why did Henry the Lion found the city of Munich on the Isar river and build the port at Lübeck?

A7.—Pg. 83, ¶ 5—Henry the Lion founded the city of Munich on the Isar river so that he could dominate the salt trade that crossed the river there. He built the port at Lübeck to draw merchant ships in. Both projects reflected Henry the Lion's growing strength and his practically independent rule from Frederick Barbarossa in the north and east of Germany.

8. How was Frederick Barbarossa finally able to conquer Milan? What did he do after he took the city?

A8.—Pg. 83, ¶ 6 to Pg. 85, ¶ 1—Frederick Barbarossa was able to finally conquer Milan because he had the help of Henry the Lion and the armies of Pisa. When the city surrendered, Frederick Barbarossa forced hundreds of the city's elite to approach him barefoot, smeared with ashes, and kiss his feet while he allowed his men to sack the city, burn its houses and pillage its churches. When they were done, Milan no longer existed and all of its people were taken away and resettled in other villages.

9. Why didn't Frederick Barbarossa's men attack the Lombard League as soon as it formed? What did the Lombard League do while Frederick Barbarossa's men were tied up?

A9.—Pg. 85, ¶ 4 & 5—Frederick Barbarossa's men did not attack the Lombard League as soon as it was formed because they were attacked by malaria. While the army dealt with the sickness, the Lombard League consolidated its power and began to rebuild Milan. They

also joined together to build a brand new city they called Alessandria, in honor of the exiled pope, that blocked the pass that the German armies needed to use in order to get into Italy.

10. What were the terms of the peace made between the Lombard League and Frederick Barbarossa in 1177?

A10.—Pg. 85, ¶ 7 to Pg. 86, ¶ 1—The terms of the peace made between the Lombard League and Frederick Barbarossa in 1177 were as follows: the cities of the League were given the undisputed right to govern themselves, the antipope Callixtus III was abandoned, and Alexander III was recognized as the sole authority over the Papal States.

11. How did Frederick Barbarossa gain such a strong grasp over Germany after his failure in Rome?

A11.—Pg. 86, ¶ 2—When Frederick Barbarossa returned to Germany after his failures in Rome, he confiscated Henry the Lion's land and drove his cousin into exile. Frederick Barbarossa was punishing his cousin because Henry the Lion refused to accompany the king into Italy for the final confrontation against the Lombard League. Henry's lands were divided up among noblemen who all owed Frederick Barbarossa favors, so he was able to secure their loyalty easily.

Section III: Critical Thinking

The student may not use her text to answer this question.

Frederick Barbarossa knew his power as Holy Roman Emperor was tenuous. He more-or-less forced Pope Eugenius III into giving him the title, and the people of Rome and the papal states were less than pleased with his coronation. Though Frederick Barbarossa ultimately lost power over Rome and the papal states, how did he attempt to use divine right as a way to legitimize his title?

After Frederick Barbarossa became king of Germany he wrote a letter to Pope Eugenius III which for all intents and purposes said the empire had been given to him by God. While Frederick Barbarossa was happy to work with and protect the Church, he demanded that he be the master of his domain. He wrote to the pope, "the catholic church should be adorned by the privileges of its diginity, and the majesty of the Roman Empire should be reformed, by God's help, to the original strength of its excellence." Original excellence here refers to the first Holy Roman Emperor, Charlemagne, who was also King of the Franks and King of Italy at the time of his coronation.

After Frederick Barbarossa defeated Milan he took the bones of the Magi, the three kings who had brought gifts to the baby Jesus after his birth, and installed them in the cathedral in the German city of Cologne. He did this to remind people that God had given him his imperial crown and that the Magi were now the patron saints of the German city in the kingdom over which he ruled; the placement of the bones in Cologne was to suggest there was no greater king than Frederick Barbarossa. Three years later, Frederick Barbarossa directed the antipope Paschal III to make Charlemagne a saint. Making the first Holy Roman Emperor a saint further sanctified the royal office. If Frederick Barbarossa was blessed by the Magi and held a position given to him by God, that was first held by a saint, surely there was no way he would lose his power. Of course, things didn't work out for Frederick Barbarossa in Italy, but he did what he could to hold on to his rule before making peace with the Lombard League, giving up his hold on the papal states, and returning to Germany.

EXAMPLE ANSWER:

Frederick Barbarossa tried to show the people of Rome and the papal states that God gave him the right to rule over them as Holy Roman Emperor, but he failed. After Frederick Barbarossa defeated Milan he took the bones of the Magi from the city and installed them in the cathedral in the German city of Cologne. He did this to remind people that God had given him his imperial crown and that the Magi were now the patron saints of the German city in the kingdom over which he ruled; the placement of the bones in Cologne was to suggest there was no greater king than Frederick Barbarossa. Three years later, Frederick Barbarossa directed the antipope Paschal III to make Charlemagne, the first Holy Roman Emperor, a saint. Making Charlemagne a saint further sanctified the royal office. If Frederick Barbarossa was blessed by the Magi and held a position given to him by God, that was first held by a saint, surely there was no way he would lose his power. Of course, things didn't work out for Frederick Barbarossa in Italy, but he did what he could to hold on to his rule before making peace with the Lombard League, giving up his hold on the papal states, and returning to Germany.

STUDY AND TEACHING GUIDE FOR THE HISTORY OF THE RENAISSANCE WORLD

Chapter Thirteen

The Almohads in Spain

The student may use his text when answering the questions in sections I and II.

Section I: Who, What, Where

Write a one or two-sentence answer explaining the significance of each item listed below.

Alfonso VIII—**Pg. 88, ¶ 5 to Pg. 89, ¶ 1 and Pg. 91, ¶ 8—Alfonso VIII, son of Sancho, inherited rule of Castile at the age of three which meant that Castile was plunged into a struggle between noble families for control of the regency and as a result could not protect its borders. When Alfonso VIII was eighteen he caused the retreat of the Almohads from Huete by leading troops to lift the siege on the city.**

Extremadura—**Pg. 90, ¶ 3—Extremadura was the name of the area outside of Portuguese borders.**

Fernando (Ferdinand II)—**Pg. 88, ¶ 4 and Pg. 91, ¶ 2—Fernando, son of Alfonso VII, inherited rule of León after his father's death in 1157 and became Ferdinand II of León. Ferdinand II banded together with Afonso Henriques to drive Gerald the Fearless out of Spain.**

Gerald the Fearless—**Pg. 90, ¶ 3 to Pg. 91, ¶ 4—Gerald the Fearless, a Portuguese soldier, took advantage of weakened Almohad power on the Spanish peninsula and captured the city of Evora, along with at least four more towns, for himself. After being driven out of Spain by Afonso Henriques and Ferdinand II, Gerald the Fearless aligned himself with Yusuf I, only to turn his back on the caliphate, which resulted in his death.**

Ibn Mardanish—**Pg. 88, ¶ 2 and Pg. 89, ¶ 2—Ibn Mardanish, Muslim ruler of the mini-kingdom made up of Valencia and Murcia after the fall of the Almoravids, agreed to become a vassal of Alfonso VII in exchange for peace. Ibn Mardanish refused to submit to al-Mu'min and instead upheld his alliance with the Christians of Castile.**

Maimonides—**Pg. 89, ¶ 4—Maimonides, older son of Rabbi Maimon ben Joseph, worked as a physician in Egypt. He also started work on a massive, fourteen-volume summary of Jewish law, which he hoped would give the scattered and perplexed Jews a guide for living in troubled times.**

Rabbi Maimon ben Joseph—**Pg. 89, ¶ 3 & 4—Rabbi Maimon ben Joseph took his wife and children and left the oppressive Almohad culture of the Spanish peninsula in 1146 for the more benevolent government of Saladin in Egypt.**

Saladin—Pg. 89, ¶ 4—Saladin was the governor of Egypt. Saladin had a more religiously tolerant government and thus his land became a refuge for those oppressed by the Almohads.

Sancho—Pg. 88, ¶ 4 & 5—Sancho, son of Alfonso VII, inherited rule of Castile after his father's death in 1157, but died after only a single year on the throne.

Yusuf I—Pg. 90, ¶ 2 and Pg. 91, ¶ 7 & 8—Yusuf I, Abd al-Mu-min's successor, spent the first several years of his reign fighting with his fourteen brothers to keep his position as the caliph. After whipping the Muslim cities in Spain in line, Yusuf I attempted to attack the Christian cities, starting with Huete, but he failed and was forced to retreat.

Section II: Comprehension

Write a two or three-sentence answer to each of the following questions.

1. What happened to remnants of the Almoravid empire in Spain after the fall of Almoravid rule?

A1.—Pg. 88, ¶ 2 & 3—After the fall of Almoravid rule, Granada remained in Muslim hands, but without direction from Africa, it began to chart its own political course, making overtures of alliance to Alfonso VII. The cities of Valencia and Murcia formed a mini-kingdom ruled by Ibn Mardanish, who agreed to become a vassal of Christian Alfonso VII in exchange for peace. However, al-Mu'min soon turned his armies toward Spain, forcing Granada to surrender in 1155 and two years later taking Ubeda, Baeza, and Almería for the Almohads.

2. Why did Rabbi Maimon ben Joseph move his family to Egypt?

A2.—Pg. 89, ¶ 3 & 4—In 1146 an Almohad decree was made that said all Jews and Christians living in Muslim areas had to convert to Islam, and Jews who converted had to wear black tunics and black caps to set them apart. As Almohad power in Spain grew, the decree was more and more often enforced, meaning Jews felt humiliated, despised and oppressed. Rabbi Maimon ben Joseph decided to move his family to Egypt because Saladin's government was more religiously tolerant.

3. How did Gerald the Fearless get kicked out of Spain?

A3.—Pg. 89, ¶ 3 to Pg. 91, ¶ 2—Gerald the Fearless campaigned into the Extremadura, took the city of Evora and then took several more small towns for himself. After Gerald the Fearless laid siege to the Almohad city of Badajoz in 1169, Afonso Henriques of Portugal and Ferdinand II of León banded together to drive him out of Spain.

4. Even though Gerald the Fearless was aligned with Yusuf I, how did he come to be killed by the caliphate?

A4.—Pg. 91, ¶ 3 & 4—During his service to Yusuf I in the Moroccan desert, Gerald the Fearless carried on secret negotiations with Afonso Henriques, proposing to hand over his new territory so that the Portuguese would have a base of operations from which to attack the Almohad heartland. Yusuf I found out about Gerald the Fearless's back-door deals and sent soldiers to arrest him. Gerald the Fearless was killed in the process of being arrested.

5. Why did Yusuf I's siege on Huete fail?

A5.—Pg. 91, ¶ 7—Yusuf I didn't seem very engaged in the siege on Huete and instead of appearing on the battlefield, he remained in his tent, carrying on philosophical discussions with his advisors, but his disinterest in the siege wasn't the only reason the attack failed. The twenty thousand Almohad troops were an uneasy mixture of local Spaniards, Arabs, and North Africans, all with their own native commanders, and they did not act as one. The men were forced to look farther and farther for food and they faced a strong defense: the pope promised the defenders of the Christian city of Huete remission from their sins, meaning they fought fiercely for their city, and just when the defenders began to suffer from thirst, they were relieved by a huge rainstorm that refilled the city's reservoirs.

6. What did the battle at Huete between the Almohads and the Christian leaders do for the Christian kingdoms in Spain?

A6.—Pg. 92, ¶ 1—The battle at Huete galvanized the Christian kingdoms in Spain. By 1177, all five of the Christian kings had sworn out treaties or created marriage alliances. Because of Huete, the Christian kingdoms came together and created a strong alliance against the Almohads.

Section III: Critical Thinking

The student may not use his text to answer this question.

In the last chapter we read about Frederick Barbarossa's struggles to quell the many cities in the papal states that were loyal to their own. Cultural and religious allegiances can often outweigh the benefits of gold and glory. Using allegiance as the key, write a paragraph explaining how Rabbi Maimon ben Joseph/Maimonides, Yusuf I's failure to take Huete, and the Christian kingdoms coming together in 1177 are all related.

Religious and cultural allegiances are what relate Rabbi Maimon ben Joseph/Maimonides, Yusuf I's failure to take Huete, and the Christian kingdoms coming together in 1177.

Rabbi Maimon ben Joseph left Almohad territory because of religious persecution. He moved his family to Egypt, where they could live under the more tolerant government of Saladin. Rabbi Maimon ben Joseph's older son Maimonides worked on a fourteen-volume summary of Jewish law so that Jews that were scattered across the world seeking religious freedom could have a united text to turn to. Allegiance to the Jewish faith made Rabbi Maimon ben Joseph move and prompted his son Maimonides to write the summary of Jewish law.

One of the reasons Yusuf I's attack on Huete failed was because his twentythousand troops were a mix of local Spaniards, Arabs and North Africans. When times got tough, the men didn't work together but rather stuck to their own, listening to their native commanders. The men's individual cultural allegiances weakened Yusuf I's overall force and were partly to blame for his inability to take Huete.

The Christian kingdoms in Spain banded together after Yusuf I's attack on Huete. The leaders of these kingdoms realized they had to stick together in the face of their Muslim enemy. Religious allegiance caused them to come together, and by 1177, all five of the Christian kingdoms swore allegiance to each other through treaties or through marriage alliances. The strong religious and political allegiances made between the Christian kingdoms would protect them from the Almohads.

EXAMPLE ANSWER:

Religious and culture allegiances are what relate Rabbi Maimon ben Joseph/Maimonides, Yusuf I's failure to take Huete and the Christian kingdoms coming together in 1177. Allegiance to the Jewish faith made Rabbi Maimon ben Joseph move out of Almohad territory and into religiously tolerant Egypt. Allegiance to the Jewish faith also prompted his son Maimonides to write a fourteen-volume summary of Jewish law so that Jews that were scattered across the world seeking religious freedom could have a united text to turn to. Next, one of the reasons Yusuf I's attack on Huete failed was because his twenty thousand troops were a mix of local Spaniards, Arabs and North Africans. When times got tough, the men didn't work together but rather stuck to their own, listening to their native commanders. The men's individual cultural allegiances weakened Yusuf I's overall force and were partly to blame for his inability to take Huete. Finally, the Christian kingdoms in Spain banded together after Yusuf I's attack on Huete. The leaders of these kingdoms realized they had to stick together in the face of their Muslim enemy. By 1177, all five of the Christian kingdoms swore allegiance to each other through treaties or through marriage alliances. The strong religious and political allegiances made between the Christian kingdoms would protect them from the Almohads.

Section IV: Map Exercise

1. Trace the rectangular outline of the frame for Map 13.1 in black.

2. Using your blue pencil, trace the coastal outline around Western Francia down around the Strait of Gibraltar and the African coastline. Also trace the lines of the Loire and Ebro. Repeat until the contours are familiar.

3. Using your black pencil, trace the lines of the regions of Western Francia, Navarre, Aragon, Castile, Leon, Portugal, Morocco, the Kingdom of Ibn Mardanish, and the Almohads. Repeat until the contours are familiar.

4. Using a new sheet of paper, trace the outline of the frame using your black pencil. Using your regular pencil with the eraser, draw the coastline from Western Francia down around Africa. Then draw the lines of When you are pleased with your map, lay it over the original. Erase and redraw any lines which are more than ½" off of the original.

5. Now study carefully the locations of the regions you traced before: Western Francia, Navarre, Leon, Castile, Aragon, and Portugal, Morocco, the Kingdom of Ibn Mardanish, and the Almohads. When you know them well, close your book. Mark each one on your map with your regular pencil. Then check it against the book, and correct any incorrect labels.

6. Next study carefully the locations of Pamplona, Zaragoza, Barcelona, Toledo, Santiago de Compostela, the Castle of Oreja, Valencia, Badajoz, Lisbon, Evora, Cordoba, Baeza, Seville, Granada, Almeria, and Murcia. Lay your paper over the original, and erase and redraw any marks that are more than ½″ off of the original.

Chapter Fourteen

"Many Nations"

The student may use her text when answering the questions in sections I and II.

Section I: Who, What, Where

Write a one or two-sentence answer explaining the significance of each item listed below.

Abu Abdulluh al-Bakri—**Pg. 99, ¶ 5**—Abu Abdulluh al-Bakri, a Cordoban scholar, combined the work of Arab geographers and travelers' tales into his *Book of Highways and Kingdoms* in 1068. In the *Book of Highways and Kingdoms*, Abu Abdulluh al-Bakri described African Ghana as a kingdom suspended halfway between Islam and native custom, where African Muslims and traditional priests existed side by side.

Ali ibn al-Hassan—**Pg. 97, ¶ 4**—Ali ibn al-Hassan, an Arab prince, was said to have been driven from his home in Shiraz, after which he sailed to Kilwa with his six brothers and father on seven ships. He supposedly bought Kilwa from the Swahili peoples in exchange for cloth and made Kilwa the king's island where he founded the Shirazi dynasty.

Dawud b. Sulayman—**Pg. 97, ¶ 6 to Pg. 98, ¶ 1**—Dawud b. Sulayman was most likely the ruler of Kilwa in 1150. Dawud b. Sulayman was called "Master of the Trade;" he controlled a kingdom that encompassed the islands of Pemba, Zanzibar, Mafia and Kilwa and he created a monopoly on the trading of gold by making all merchants trading for gold do so in Kilwa's port cities.

Diara Kante—**Pg. 100, ¶ 2**—Diara Kante, the Sosso clan leader in 1180, invaded Kumbi-Saleh and drove out the Almoravids.

Dunama—**Pg. 94, ¶ 1, Pg. 95, ¶ 3 and Pg. 97, ¶ 2**—Dunama, the Muslim king of Kanem, was most likely Zaghawa in ancestry and his dynasty, the Saifawa, ruled from the capital city Njimi. Dunama sold slaves in Cairo on his pilgrimages to Mecca, taking advantage of the slow spread of Islam through Kanem to continue to enslave his own people.

Dunama II—**Pg. 95, ¶ 2**—Dunama II is the first king in the *Girgam* to be identified as a black man, unlike the other rules that seem to be identified as Arabs. Dunama II ruled during the thirteenth-century.

Erediauwa I—**Pg. 99, ¶ 3**—Erediauwa I is the present-day Oba of Benin. He was crowned in 1979 and continues Eweka's unbroken dynasty, which started in the twelfth-century.

Eweka—**Pg. 99, ¶ 3**—Eweka, son of Oranmiyan, followed his father as ruler of Benin and began a new royal blood line of the Edo, the Second Dynasty of Benin. Eweka gave himself the title of Oba, king with a link to the divine, and his dynasty and tradition continues to this day.

Girgam—Pg. 95, ¶ 1 & 2—*Girgam*, the royal chronicle of Kanem's rulers, preserves an old oral king list, stretching back at least eleven generations before the conversion of Humai. The *Girgam* includes the biblical patriarch Abraham and it displays a desire to identify the earliest Kanem kings as Arab rather than African.

Hajje—Pg. 95, ¶ 1—Hajje is the word used in the *Girgam* to describe a sacred pilgrimage to Mecca. The Girgam says that Dunama made two successful hajjes.

Humai—Pg. 94, ¶ 3 to Pg. 95, ¶ 1 & 3—Humai, father of Dunama, brought Islam to Kanem. Humai was tutored by a Muslim scholar who mostly likely came to Kanem via the trade routes in North Africa.

Ife—Pg. 98, ¶ 3 & 4—Ife, located east of the Volta river and west of the Niger, was a splendid city founded most likely in 400 BC. By the ninth century AD, Ife was a walled city with a palace and court, paved streets lined with elaborate sculptures of terra-cotta and bronze, and it was known to the Yoruba peoples as both the origin of their civilization and the origin of all peoples of the world.

Ile-Ibinu—Pg. 99, ¶ 2—Ile-Ibinu is a phrase in Yoruba meaning "This is a land of vexation!" that comes from Prince Oranmiyan's frustration with trying to rule the city of Benin. Ile-Ibinu is the phrase from which the name Benin is derived.

Kumbi-Saleh—Pg. 100, ¶ 1—Kumbi-Saleh was the capital of Ghana. In 1076 the Almoravids occupied Kumbi-Saleh so that they could seize control of the lucrative western trade route in North Africa.

Oba—Pg. 99, ¶ 3—Oba is the royal title Eweka gave to himself as ruler of Benin. Oba means king with a link to the divine. Eweka's dynasty is unbroken through the present day, and the Oba of Benin continues to claim to represent all of the Edo people.

Obatala—Pg. 98, ¶ 4—Obatala, an orisha, or a manifestation of the god Ólodùmarè, was given life by Ólodùmarè. According to the Yoruba creation story, Obatala made man and gave him power, and then his sixteen sons spread out among the peoples of the earth and established sixteen kingdoms among them.

Ogiso—Pg. 98, ¶ 6—Ogiso, the title given to the king of Benin, was held by thirty-eight men, with the last Ogiso king, Ogiso Owodo, ruling sometime between 1100 and 1200. The Ogiso was made prosperous by a northward trade in cotton cloth, salt, pottery, and copper.

Ogiso Owodo—Pg. 98, ¶ 6 to Pg. 99, ¶ 1—Ogiso Owodo, the last Ogiso of Benin, ruled Benin sometime between 1100 and 1200. His rule was a disaster, and after forty-one years on the throne he was driven from his country by his own subjects.

Ólodùmarè—Pg. 98, ¶ 4—Ólodùmarè is the Yoruba peoples' creator god. Ólodùmarè created the earth and gave life to Obatala, who subsequently made man and gave him his power.

Oranmiyan—Pg. 99, ¶ 2—Oranmiyan, a prince of the Yoruba, left Ife to help the people of Benin fight against the tyranny of their overlords. Oranmiyan married the daughter of a tyrannical Benin noble, sired a son, and tried to govern the city, but it was so unrewarding that he declared, "This is a land of vexation!"

Salmama I—Pg. 97, ¶ 2—Salmama I would bring Kanem fully into the fold of Islam at the end of the twelfth century.

Soninke People—Pg. 99, ¶ 4 to Pg. 100, ¶ 1—The Soninke people lived in the kingdom of Ghana before the Almoravid invasion in 1076. After the Almoravids occupied Kumbi-Saleh, the Soninke began to migrate outwards from the enemy-controlled center, and Soninke nobles established their own small kingdoms in Ghana's outer reaches.

Sosso—Pg. 100, ¶ 2—Sosso was a clan of the Malinke tribe that controlled one of the kingdoms on the edges of Ghana. The Sosso resisted both Islam and royal control.

Sumanguru Kante—Pg. 100, ¶ 2 & 3—Sumanguru Kante, son of Diara Kante, succeeded his father as the Sosso clan leader in 1200. Sumanguru Kante was a fierce opponent of Islam and of the African slave trade.

Zaghawa—Pg. 94, ¶ 2—Zaghawa was the name for the nomadic people that migrated south from the Sahara Desert, settled near Lake Chad and adopted some of the customs of the villagers there.

Section II: Comprehension

Write a two or three-sentence answer to each of the following questions.

1. What does "people" refer to in Susan Wise Bauer's narrative of African history? What does "tribe" refer to?

A1.—Pg. 94, *—In Susan Wise Bauer's narrative of African history, "people" refers to a linguistic group. For example, the Zaghawa people all spoke the same language. In her narrative of African history, Susan Wise Bauer uses "tribe" to refer to blood ties.

2. What were some typical goods from the west and center of Africa that traveled the North African trade routes? What was life like in Taghaza and Bilma, the desert mining towns that provided salt for the trade routes?

A2.—Pg. 95, ¶ 4—Some typical goods from the west and center of Africa that traveled the North African trade routes were gold, kola nuts, ivory, copper, and salt. Life in the desert towns of Taghaza and Bilma was hard; salt ruled the inhabitants, who were slaves, and even made up the material for their dwellings. The people of these villages dug for salt all day and subsisted only on dates, camels' flesh and millet.

3. Describe early African slave trade. How did Africans find a way around the rule that forbade Muslims from enslaving fellow Muslims?

A3.—Pg. 95, ❡ 5—Since ancient times, the defeated in war were taken captive and sold by their African captors to African purchasers. Slaves were another major African export, sold to Arab merchants along the trade route. African Muslims got around the rule that said they weren't allowed to enslave fellow Muslims by finding tribes outside the Muslim world to capture and use for labor.

4. Where were the three major North African trade routes located?

A4.—Pg. 95, ❡ 6 to Pg. 97, ❡ 1—The furthest west of the African trade routes passed through Taghaza and led down to the Niger river. The central route ran from Tunis down towards the inland bend in the Niger. The easternmost trade route passed by Lake Chad, up through Bilma, and ended in Tripoli.

5. How was Dunama I able to do a brisk trade in slaves in Kanem if Muslims were not allowed to enslave other Muslims?

A5.—Pg. 97, ❡ 2— First, because Dunama I was king, he was able to enslave anyone he wanted to and thus he could create a thriving slave business. Though Dunama I was a Muslim, and theoretically so were the people of Kanem, it took some time for all of Kanem to convert. The peasants were still practicing the old religion and thus Dunama I had plenty of non-Muslims to enslave.

6. What proof do we have of flourishing Kilwa trade during the Renaissance era?

A6.—Pg. 97, ❡ 7 to Pg. 98, ❡ 1—We have proof that Kilwa played an important part in Renaissance world trade via Song pottery. Song pottery shows that sea trade with the southern dynasty of China and ivory from the south passed through Kilwa on its way north. We also know that Dawud b. Sulayman negotiated a monopoly in the trading of gold, where all merchants coming to the eastern coast of Africa for gold had to trade through Kilwa's port cities.

7. Recount the Yoruba creation story.

A7.—Pg. 98, ❡ 4—According the people of Yoruba, the creator god Ólodùmarè looked out from the lower heavens over the endless waters below and decided to create the earth. He descended to the surface of the waters by climbing down a chain, holding a gourd of earth that he piled onto the water and a five-toed chicken that he put on the pile which scratched at it and sent the dirt across the surface of the water to create the earth. Then Ólodùmarè gave life to Obatala, who in turn made man and gave him power, and then his sixteen sons spread out among the peoples of the earth and established sixteen kingdoms among them.

Section III: **Critical Thinking**

The student may not use her text to answer this question.

African history existed in oral tradition for centuries. It was only when Islam came to Africa that written chronicles also appeared. Write a paragraph or two explaining how we can see the influence of Islam in the recorded history of Africa that occurred long before the Islamic religion and culture appeared.

In the chapter there are two very clear instances of the Arab influence on African history. First, on page 95, the student learned about Kanem's king list. The Girgam preserves a king list that stretches back long before the list was actually written, meaning the ancient oral history was preserved at a later time. However, the document is not neutral, and the written history of Kanem's kings was influenced by Islam. As explained in paragraph 2 on page 95, included in the list of kings is the "the biblical patriarch Abraham." The list "also displays a clearly Arab desire to identify the earliest Kanem kings as Arab, rather than as African. The eighth king of Kanem, the list assures us, was 'as white as silk,' and the first king identified as 'a black man, a warrior hotter than fire' is the thirteenth-century ruler Dunama II." We know, however, that there were black rulers before Dunama II, including Dunama I. The Girgam shows us that along with physical writing, Islam brought with it a desire to rewrite the African past as part of Islam.

Similarly, the written history of Kilwa suggests a retelling of the actual past. On page 97, paragraph 5, we learned that "the oldest surviving version of [Kilwa's] Chronicle is a sixteenth-century Portuguese translation done by the explorer João de Barros." The founder of Kilwa, an Arab prince called Ali ibn al-Hassan, was said to have sailed to the island with his brothers and father and to have founded the Shirazi dynasty. However, there is no proof that Ali ibn al-Hassan came from the outside. Again, Ali ibn al-Hassan's Arab past may have been added when the Chronicle was written to reflect Islam in a positive light. As Susan Wise Bauer writes, Ali ibn al-Hassan's tale "might be rooted in the Arab assumption that a civilized, organized Muslim kingdom could not have been founded by native Africans." Archaeological investigations suggest that Ali ibn al-Hassan himself probably lived closer to the twelfth century than to the tenth, which further calls into question the reliability of the story of his founding of Kilwa. Ruins of mosques and prayer rooms do suggest that by the tenth century Arab merchants were trading and settling in Kilwa, so Ali ibn al-Hassan's supposed founding of the city could reflect the Arab culture and interests that had already taken root on the island.

EXAMPLE ANSWER:

When Islam came to Africa it brought with it written chronicles. African history that was preserved via oral tradition was often influenced by Arab interests when it was recorded in writing. One example of this changing of history is seen in the *Girgam* of Kanem. The king list includes the biblical Abraham as a former king of Kanem, and says that the eighth king of Kanem was "as white silk." According to the list, the first black king of Kanem, Dunama II, shows up only in the thirteenth century. We know, however, that Dunama I was most definitely black. The *Girgam* reflects a desire to identify the first kings of the Kanem as Arab instead of African, a clear changing of the past to bolster the power and influence of Islam in Africa. Similarly, the king list of Kilwa, the Chronicle, says that the founder of Kilwa was an Arab prince named Ali ibn al-Hassan that sailed in with his brothers and father and started the Shirazi dynasty. However, there is no proof that Ali ibn al-Hassan came from the

outside. Again, Ali ibn al-Hassan's Arab past may have been added when the Chronicle was written to reflect Islam in a positive light and to strengthen Arab ties in Africa. While ruins of mosques and prayer rooms do show that Arabs were trading and settling in Kilwa by the tenth century, archaeological investigations suggest that Ali ibn al-Hassan himself probably lived closer to the twelfth century, further calling into question the reliability of the story of his founding of Kilwa. Both the king lists of Kanem and Kilwa show the Arab assumption that Africans needed their religion and culture to build thriving civilizations; the rewriting of the king lists offered a way to legitimize the Arab influence in Africa.

Section IV: Map Exercise

1. Trace the rectangular outline of Map 14.1 in black.

2. Using your blue pencil, trace the coastline around the continent of Africa, including the coastline of the Mediterranean and the Red Sea. Trace the lines of the Senegal, the Volta, and the Niger as well. Repeat until the contours are familiar.

3. Using a new sheet of paper, trace the rectangular outline of the map. Remove your tracing paper from the original. Using a regular pencil with an eraser, draw the coastline around Africa, including the Mediterranean and Red Seas. Trace the lines of the Senegal, the Volta, and the Niger as well. When you are happy with your map, lay it over the original. If any of your lines are more than ½" off of the original, erase and redraw them.

4. Now carefully study the locations of Tunis, Tripoli, Cairo, Mecca, Dar'a, Bilma, Njimi, Sijilmasa, Taghaza, Kumbi Saleh, Ife, and Benin. When you are familiar with them, close the book. Mark and label each one with your regular pencil. Lay your paper over the original, and erase and redraw any locations which are more than ½" off of the original.

Chapter Fifteen

The Last Fatimid Caliph

The student may use his text when answering the questions in sections I and II.

Section I: Who, What, Where

Write a one or two-sentence answer explaining the significance of each item listed below.

Al-Adid—**Pg. 106, ¶ 2 & 7—Al-Adid, the Fatimid caliph at the time Shirkuh came into control of Egypt, was the last Fatimid caliph. When Al-Adid became ill it was announced that his name would be dropped from public prayers and he died not knowing he was deposed.**

Amalric I—**Pg. 103, ¶ 7 and Pg. 105, ¶ 1—Amalric I, younger brother of Baldwin III, became king of Jerusalem in 1163 after his brother's death. Though Amalric I tried several times to take control of Egypt, all he ended up getting was control over a spit of land reaching down to the point of the Red Sea.**

Baldwin III—**Pg. 103, ¶ 4, 6 & 7—Baldwin III, successor of Fulk of Anjou as leader of Jerusalem, resisted Nur ad-Din's attempts to take the city. Baldwin made an alliance with Manuel I Comnenus, the Byzantine emperor, and married his thirteen-year-old niece to secure the deal.**

Manuel I Comnenus—**Pg. 103, ¶ 6 and Pg. 105, ¶ 4—Manuel I Comnenus, the Byzantine emperor, married his thirteen-year-old niece to Baldwin III in order to secure an alliance between Byzantium and Jerusalem. Manuel I worked with Amalric I to attempt to take over Egypt, but their joint efforts always failed.**

Shawar—**Pg. 104, ¶ 5 & 7, Pg. 105, ¶ 2 & 6 and Pg. 106, ¶ 1—Shawar, the Fatimid vizier in Egypt, drove Amalric I back from Egypt with the help of troops sent by Nur ad-Din only to make an alliance with Amalric I to drive Shirkuh out of Egypt. Shawar made a temporary peace with Shirkuh after he took Alexandria but on January 18, 1169, when he tried to make plans for the future with Shirkuh, Shawar was murdered by Shirkuh's men.**

Shirkuh—**Pg. 104, ¶ 6, Pg. 105, ¶ 2 and Pg. 106, ¶ 1-3—Shirkuh, captain of Nur ad-Din's Turkish troops, made it his mission to capture Egypt. After taking Alexandria and having Shawar murdered, Shirkuh took control of Egypt, adding it to Nur ad-Din's empire, but he only enjoyed being ruler for two months before dying from overeating fat meat at a banquet.**

STUDY AND TEACHING GUIDE FOR THE HISTORY OF THE RENAISSANCE WORLD

Section II: **Comprehension**

Write a two or three-sentence answer to each of the following questions.

1. Why did Nur ad-Din bathe himself in the Mediterranean if he was not in control of all of Syria?

A1.—Pg. 102, ¶ 2 to Pg. 103, ¶ 1—Nur ad-Din's bath in the Mediterranean acted as a symbolic baptism, reminiscent of the Assyrian conqueror Sargon, that was meant to show his dominance covered the entire land of Syria, all the way to the sea. Nur ad-Din didn't, however, control all of Syria, but he was at the head of the jihad and helped the people's hope for the future of Islam's unity. He may not have controlled all of the land in Syria, but, according to his followers, he was Champion of the Faith, the Pillar of Islam, and the Vanquisher of the Rebels.

2. What stopped Nur ad-Din from taking Jerusalem while Baldwin III was alive?

A2.—Pg. 103, ¶ 5—Nur ad-Din was ready to take Jerusalem after his other conquests in Syria, but then a series of misfortunes stopped him from attacking. Instead of going after the city, Nur ad-Din was forced to use his energies to rebuild Syria after continuous earthquakes and shocks rocked the kingdom. Then, in 1157, Nur ad-Din grew very ill and expected to die, which stopped all plans for conquest.

3. How did Amalric I justify his first attack on Egypt? What did he do to prepare for the assault?

A3.—Pg. 104, ¶ 3—Amalric I justified his first attack on Egypt by saying that the Fatimids had not paid the yearly tribute they agreed to pay Baldwin III in order to get him out of al-Arish. Amalric I prepared for the attack by gathering both land and sea forces. He was able to bolster his navy with ten war galleys from the Pisans in exchange for a merchant outpost in Jerusalem.

4. Though Amalric I was driven out of Egypt by Shawar, how did his troops end up back in Egypt? How was Amalric I able to secure tribute from the Fatimids?

A4.—Pg. 104, ¶ 7—Amalric I was asked by Shawar to return to Egypt to help him drive out Nur ad-Din's officer Shirkuh. Shawar offered alliance and tribute payments to Amalric I if the Jerusalem armies would return to Egypt and help him fight against the Turks. Thus, Amalric I and his troops returned to Egypt and worked with the Muslim Fatimids to drive Shirkuh out.

5. What happened when Shirkuh returned to Egypt with his nephew Saladin in late 1166?

A5.—Pg. 105, ¶ 2—When Shirkuh returned to Egypt with his nephew Saladin, he also came with Nur ad-Din's blessing and a full complement of Turkish troops. Shirkuh and Saladin met Amalric I and Shawar in the Nile valley in March of 1167, defeated them, and then Shirkuh took Alexandria and put Saladin in control of it. The Franks and Fatimids besieged the city, but Saladin held it so a cease-fire was proposed: Amalric I and Shawar handed over a fair amount of cash, and in exchange, the Turkish invasion halted at Alexandria.

6. How did Amalric I come to fight in Egypt for a third time? What was the result of this siege?

A6.—Pg. 105, ¶ 3 & 4—Amalric I and Manuel I combined the armies of Byzantium and Jerusalem and went back to Egypt. Their forces captured the eastern Egyptian city of Tanis

in late 1168, but massive Turkish reinforcements arrived from Nur ad-Din. As a result, the combined Christian army was forced to retreat.

7. Why were so many people against Shawar? Why was Shawar's own son upset with him?

A7.—Pg. 105, ¶ 5—Shawar's initial alliance with Jerusalem had angered many of the Egyptians, particularly those in Cairo, and Shawar's resistance to Shirkuh had turned him into Nur ad-Din's enemy. Shawar even made himself unpopular with his son when he suggested inviting Shirkuh and his officers to a banquet, arresting them, and then recruiting their troops for himself. Shawar's son said that the Franks would surely return to Egypt if they heard that Shirkuh had been arrested, so he threatened to tell Shirkuh of his father's plans, forcing Shawar to abandon them.

8. How did the Fatimid caliphate come to an end?

A8.—Pg. 106, ¶ 6 & 7—In 1171, Nur ad-Din ordered that Al-Adid's name be dropped from public prayers, which was the equivalent of announcing the overthrow of the Fatimid dynasty. Al-Adid grew ill and Saladin announced the change to the Egyptian people, but no one in the caliph's family told him what happened so he died not knowing he had lost his position. With the death of Al-Adid came the end of the Fatimid caliphate.

Section III: Critical Thinking

The student may use his text to answer this question.

In this chapter we read about Amalric I's inability to conquer Egypt. At first he tried to take Egypt on his own, and then he worked with Byzantine emperor Manuel I but they still couldn't shake the Fatimid or Turkish forces. Using your text, write a paragraph in your own words that summarizes the final disastrous attempt of the Crusader-Byzantine armies to take Egypt. After your description, explain why you think the Crusader-Byzantine armies failed (both practically and philosophically).

A description of Amalric I and Manuel I's final attempt to conquer Egypt is given on page 106. The description given is of their attempt to lay siege to the port city of Damietta, found 120 miles north of Cairo: "The Byzantine ships dispatched to support the Crusader land force were underprovisioned, already running low when they arrived, and the Jerusalem army refused to share any of its food. Meanwhile, Saladin had no difficulty resupplying Damietta by sea with money, weapons, and stores. He spent, says Ibn al-Athir, "untold sums of money" on Damietta, knowing that if the city fell, the Christians would have a foothold that he might never undo. Rain soaked the Crusader tents for weeks on end; the Byzantine generals quarreled with the Jerusalem commanders over strategy; a score of the anchored Byzantine vessels were destroyed when the Egyptians sent a fireship into their midst. "The feeling was almost unanimous," writes William of Tyre, "that our toil was being wasted." After fifty days, the Christians gave up and went home, blaming one another for the loss. Once again, crusade had failed."

The student may use the text to summarize the final attack. Practical reasons for the failure are listed in the description: Byzantine forces didn't have enough food and the forces from Jerusalem wouldn't share; no one was getting a good night's sleep because rain soaked the Christian tents for weeks; generals and commanders from Byzantium and Jerusalem couldn't agree on strategy; Saladin's forces were well stocked and well fed; and Saladin dispatched a fireboat that destroyed several Byzantine ships.

Within the practical description we see a greater philosophical reason for the failure of the final crusade: Byzantine and Crusader forces were not working together. They did not help each other and their generals and commanders weren't cooperative with one another. Further, the theoretical idea of the crusades was to fight for God. The Byzantine and Crusader forces were not fighting with God in mind; their own interests came first, as evidenced by their inability to put aside their differences and unite in the name of God.

EXAMPLE ANSWER:

The Byzantine and Crusader forces attempted to lay siege to Damietta and they failed miserably. The Byzantine forces didn't have enough food and the troops from Jerusalem didn't share their provisions. Not only were the forces hungry, they were also miserable because they were soaking wet: rain came down for weeks meaning their tents, and most likely everything else, was sopping wet. Wet and hungry is not a good combination. Most importantly, the commanders from Jerusalem would not listen to the generals from Byzantium, and vice versa. The disjointed troops stood no chance against Saladin's troops. Saladin spent a lot of money on this fight because he knew if the Christians took hold of Damietta he might never drive them out. His men had everything they could ask for. Once the Egyptians sent a fireship through the Byzantine navy and several Christians ships were destroyed, the Christians called it quits, with each Christian faction blaming the other for the failure.

It is clear why the crusade failed practically: Byzantine forces didn't have enough food and the force from Jerusalem wouldn't share; no one was getting a good night's sleep because of the rain; generals and commanders from Byzantium and Jerusalem couldn't agree on strategy; Saladin's forces were well stocked and well fed; and Saladin dispatched a fireboat that destroyed several Byzantine ships. On a deeper level the mission failed because Byzantine and Crusader forces were not working together. They did not help each other and their generals and commanders weren't cooperative with one another. Further, the theoretical idea of the crusades was to fight for God. The Byzantine and Crusader forces were not fighting with God in mind; their own interests came first, as evidenced by their inability to put aside their differences and unite in the name of God.

Chapter Sixteen

Monks and Brahmas

The student may use her text when answering the questions in sections I and II.

Section I: Who, What, Where

Write a one or two-sentence answer explaining the significance of each item listed below.

Baladeva—**Pg. 112, ¶ 7 & 8—Baladeva was Bijjala II's trusted prime minister. Before he died he recommended that Bijjala II recruit Basava, the prime minister's nephew, to take Baladeva's place; Baladeva gave Bijjala II some bad advice and Bijjala II ended up recruiting a zealot.**

Basava—**Pg. 112, ¶ 7 to Pg. 113, ¶ 1 and Pg. 114, ¶ 3—Basava, nephew of Baladeva and his uncle's successor as prime minister for Bijjala II, was a fanatic of Shiva and started the spread of lingayatism in India. Basava short-circuited his own success by getting reckless with the king's treasury, which led to both Bijjala II's death as well as his own.**

Bijjala II—**Pg. 112, ¶ 6 and Pg. 114, ¶ 3—Bijjala II, king of the Kalachuri (formerly a part of the Western Chalukya), captured the Western Chalukya capital Kalyani in 1157 and forced the Western Chalukya king himself to flee. Bijjala II made the mistake of taking on Basava as his prime minster after Baladeva died; not only did Basava introduce the fanatic lingayats to society but he was also the cause of Bijjala II's death.**

Buddha's Tooth—**Pg. 111, ¶ 1—Buddha's tooth, one of the seven unburned relics that was said to have survived Buddha's cremation, was brought to Sri Lanka in the fourth century. Buddha's tooth was enshrined by Parakrama Bahu in a magnificent temple in Polonnaruwa.**

Giant's Tank—**Pg. 109, ¶ 2 to Pg. 110, ¶ 1—Giant's Tank was a massive artificial lake with completely man-made embankments on a sloping plain built by Parakrama Bahu near the northern Sri Lankan town of Mannar. The Giant's Tank turned the dry, salty north of Sri Lanka into an area so fertile that it is still known today as the Rice Bowl.**

Lingam—**Pg. 108, ¶ 2—Lingam was the name for a seamless pillar with no features that represented the all-encompassing, transcendent essence of the Hindu god Shiva.**

Lingayats—**Pg. 113, ¶ 1—Lingayats, zealously devoted to Shiva, dedicated themselves to finding a greater love for God and all of their life's work was worship of Shiva. Lingayats got their name because they all wore a tiny lingam on a cord around their necks or left arms.**

Mahakassapa—**Pg. 111, ❡ 3 & 4**—Mahakassapa, a senior monk in a forest monastery, acted as an advisor to Parakrama Bahu and stayed on in the king's service after he unified the monks in Sri Lanka to help him decide on the correct ways of understanding the canonical laws.

Parakrama Bahu—**Pg. 109, ❡ 1, Pg. 110, ❡ 2, Pg. 111, ❡ 4 and Pg. 112, ❡ 1**—Parakrama Bahu, who united Sri Lanka under his single leadership in 1153, renovated the island's irrigation system, guaranteeing his people fertile land, freedom from famine, and prosperity. Parakrama Bahu transformed the practice of Buddhism in Sri Lanka by getting rid of the three monastic orders, declaring that he himself would act as interpreter of canonical law, and by overseeing the appointment and behavior of the Buddhist monks.

Sankama—**Pg. 115, ❡ 1**—Sankama, son of Bijjala II and brother of Someshvara, kept his father's kingdom going after the death of his brother. However, after Sankama's death, his father's kingdom fell apart because of inexperienced leadership.

Sea of Parakrama—**Pg. 109, ❡ 2**—Sea of Parakrama was a large reservoir built by Parakrama Bahu outside of Polonnaruwa. Parakrama Bahu had an artificial island created in the center of the Sea of Parakrama and on it he built a beautiful three-story palace that overlooked the new waters.

Someshvara—**Pg. 114, ❡ 3**—Someshvara, Bijjala II's son and successor, avenged his father's death by sending troops after Basava, who was responsible for the theft from his father's treasury that led to the conflict that killed Bijjala II, and had him assassinated.

Somesvara IV—**Pg. 115, ❡ 1**—Somesvara IV, the Western Chalukya king, recaptured the old capital of Kalanyi. The Kalachuri kingdom founded by Bijjala II was then reabsorbed into the Western Chalukya.

Vijaya Bahu—**Pg. 108, ❡ 3 & 4 and Pg. 110, ❡ 4**—Vijaya Bahu, a rebel that lived in the late eleventh century, declared himself the Buddhist king of Sri Lanka; while the Chola troops were able to take the north of the island from him, he did hold on to the south until his death. Vijaya Bahu's descendants divided the land among themselves after his death, with the largest Sri Lankan kingdom centered at Vijaya Bahu's own capital city, Polonnaruwa, and other kingdoms found in the Southern Country and Ruhuna.

Virasaivas—**Pg. 114, ❡ 4**—Virasaivas were the disciples of lingayatism. For centuries they would challenge the traditional castes and classes of Hinduism.

Section II: Comprehension

Write a two or three-sentence answer to each of the following questions.

1. How did Parakrama Bahu unify Sri Lanka?

A1.—Pg. 108, ❡ 5 to Pg. 109, ❡ 1—Parakrama Bahu, nephew of the ruling sovereigns of Ruhuna and the Southern Country, and cousin to the king in Polonnaruwa, was going to inherit one of these territories, but ruling one kingdom wasn't enough for him. He had plotted against one uncle, fought against the other and convinced his cousin in Polonnaruwa to make him heir. By 1153, Parakrama Bahu was in control of all three crowns.

2. What practical renovations did Parakrama Bahu bring to Sri Lanka during his reign?

A2.—Pg. 109, ¶ 2 to Pg. 110, ¶ 1—**Parakrama Bahu's practical renovations to Sri Lanka included lowering taxes and channeling remaining government revenues into cleaning up and restoring the irrigation systems that made Sri Lanka fertile. Parakrama Bahu cleaned and restored canals and causeways that had fallen into disrepair, he created a massive reservoir near Polonnaruwa called the Sea of Parakrama, and he built another reservoir in the north near Mannar called the Giant's Tank. The Giant's Tank provided enough water to the dry north to turn it into very fertile ground.**

3. How did Parakrama Bahu balance out the expenses of the restoration and building of dams, reservoirs and canals?

A3.—Pg. 110, ¶ 2—**Parakrama Bahu drained marshes and bogs, channeled the water into paddy fields and grew enough grain to create a surplus. The extra grain balanced out the expenses of restoring and building dams, reservoirs and canals. The new paddy fields created revenue that was more than the revenue that was made from all the old paddy fields and the result was that the people of Sri Lanka were well-fed and prosperous.**

4. In what way were Sri Lankan monks a threat to the unity created by Parakrama Bahu?

A4.—Pg. 111, ¶ 2—**Sri Lanka's monks were divided into three *nikayas*, or monastic orders, and all were struggling for dominance in the capital. They feuded over the rules of monasticism, the interpretation of Buddhist scriptures, and control of the temples. The monks were at the heart of the country's religious practice and if they remained divided they would only drive wedges into Parakrama Bahu's newly unified kingdom.**

5. Describe the character of a Sri Lankan forest monastery during the time of Parakrama Bahu.

A5.—Pg. 111, ¶ 3—**During Parakrama Bahu's time, forest monasteries were known to be more austere than city or village monasteries, with their monks less interested in political wrangling and more strict in their practice. Forest monasteries were places of quiet meditation, not loud conflict. In the forest, removed from the centers of power, the monks were thought to gain a detachment and clarity that was missing from the bustling, wealthy monasteries of the cities.**

6. What was the relationship of the Chalukya with the great twelfth century Chola empire? What happened to that relationship around the time of Vijaya Bahu's rebellion?

A6.—Pg. 112, ¶ 4—**When Chola reached its greatest size, it was bordered on the north and east by two related dynasties known as the Chalukya. The Eastern Chalukya had been conquered and forced into the empire two centuries before while the Western Chalukya had been persuaded and bribed into alliance. The alliance between the Western Chalukya and the Chola empire was broken right around the time of Vijaya Bahu's rebellion when the younger brother of the Western Chalukya king attacked his older sibling, took the throne, and started a war against the Chola.**

7. How did the Hindu temples of central India sustain themselves? How did Brahman priests keep their wealth and power?

A7.—Pg. 114, ❡ 1—The Hindu temples of central India were supported by royal grants of cash and tax-free farmland and in return the Brahman priests who served in the temples supported the king's policies. The Brahmans kept their power by marrying their own kind and keeping their priestly lands inside their own class. They also had power because they presided over a system of Hindu worship that was complicated and inflexible, and yet was the only way to reach the divine presence, meaning that without Brahman guidance, the Hindu worshipper was lost.

8. Why was the philosophy of Basava and the other lingayats a threat to the Brahman priesthood?

A8.—Pg. 114, ❡ 2—The philosophy of Basava and the other lingayats was a threat to the Brahman priesthood because in lingayat worship, each person came to Shiva alone, on their own terms, in a personal encounter that was inward and mysterious and needed no temples, no sacrifices, and no Brahmans. In the worship of Shiva, men and women were equally welcome, there was no class privilege or shame and manual labor was the only service required, meaning the lowest ranks of Indian society—those who worked with their hands—were honored. Lingayatism threatened both the Brahman monopoly on religion and their royal authority.

9. What did Basava's reckless spending of Bijjala II's treasury have to do with both men's deaths?

A9.—Pg. 114, ❡ 3—Basava stole money from Bijjala II's treasury to feed, support, and entertain his fellow lingayats. When Bijjala II found out about this reckless spending in 1167, he retaliated by blinding two of the most prominent lingayats which resulted in his assassination by another indignant lingayat. Basava fled, but Someshvara sent troops to pursue him and Basava was killed either by accident or via execution while he was on the run.

10. How did Somesvara IV die? What happened to the Western Chalukya kingdom ruled by Somesvara IV after his death?

A10.—Pg. 115, ❡ 1—Somesvara IV died in 1187 while he was fighting against the former vassal kingdom of the Hoysala. Within two years of Somesvara IV's death, the Seuna, Hoysala and Kakatiya divided the old Western Chalukya territory between their own small kingdoms.

Section III: Critical Thinking

The student may not use her text to answer this question.

When the Chola were at the height of their power, their king decorated the expanse of Chola land with lingams honoring the power of Shiva. For the Chola king, religious belief tied in with the success of his empire. Religion took on a different role in the kingdom run by Parakrama Bahu. Explain how the Sri Lankan king turned Buddhism not just into Sri Lanka's official religion but also a tool of the state. Begin your answer by explain the reforms Parakrama Bahu made, and then explain the significance of those reforms in terms of Parakrama Bahu's own power and influence.

Parakrama Bahu's list of religious reforms starts in paragraph 4 on page 111 of the textbook. When Parakrama Bahu came to power, there were three monastic orders that struggled for dominance in Polonnaruwa. In order to unify his kingdom, Parakrama Bahu abolished all the monastic orders and declared that there would only be two kinds of monks: gamavasin and arannavasin, village dwellers and forest dwellers. He then said he would act as head of the practice of Buddhism in Sri Lanka and, with the help of his advisor Mahakassapa, Parakrama Bahu would decide on the correct ways of understanding the canonical laws. Under the rules of Parakrama Bahu's reforms, an official katikavata, a royal lawbook laying out exactly how Buddhism should be practiced, was produced, and the katikavata had the same force as divine law. Parakrama Bahu also removed many monks from the monasteries, declaring them laypeople, and he ordered that all new Buddhist priests be ordained in the capital city so that he could supervise them. Monitoring the ordination of new priests meant that Parakrama Bahu could block any too-ambitious candidates from entering the monastery and he could be guaranteed to regulate the behavior of the monks.

Buddhist monarchs have always acted as the protectors and patrons of Buddhist monasteries, giving them grants of land and wealth and looking out for their survival. The king was cakravartin—the king through whom dharma, all that is good and right, will spread across the universe—and bodhisattva—a manifestation of the Buddha himself, an enlightened one who had chosen to remain in the world in order to bring it salvation. A Buddhist monarch always had an important role in the continuation of the religion. But Parakrama Bahu turned that observatory role into a very real and powerful position with his reforms. By unifying the monastic orders he stopped the quarreling that could have pulled apart the kingdom he just put back together. By taking control of the interpretation of the scriptures, he made sure that they aligned with the enforcement of canonical law. By overseeing the monks joining the priesthood, he made sure all religious representatives were on board with his own government. By taking control of the practice of Buddhism in Sri Lanka, Parakrama Bahu turned Buddhism into a tool of the state.

EXAMPLE ANSWER:

When Parakrama Bahu came to power, he unified the Buddhist monastic orders, put himself at their head, and made them a part of state affairs. First, he abolished all the monastic orders and declared there would only be two kinds of monks: gamavasin and arannavasin, village dwellers and forest dwellers. He then said he would act as head of the practice of Buddhism in Sri Lanka and, with the help of his advisor Mahakassapa, Parakrama Bahu would decide on the correct ways of understanding the canonical laws. Under the rules of Parakrama Bahu's reforms, an official katikavata was produced, a royal lawbook laying out exactly how Buddhism should be practiced, and the katikavata had the same force as divine law. Parakrama Bahu also removed many monks from the monasteries, declaring them laypeople, and he ordered that all new Buddhist priests be ordained in the capital city so that he could supervise them. Monitoring the ordination of new priests meant that Parakrama Bahu could block any over-eager or power-seeking candidates from entering the monastery; it also meant he could regulate the behavior of the monks.

Buddhist monarchs have always been involved with the existence of the religion in their realms for they gave money and land to the monks and looked out for their survival. The king was known as cakravartin—the king through whom dharma, all that is good and right, will spread across the universe—and bodhisattva—a manifestation of the Buddha himself,

an enlightened one who had chosen to remain in the world in order to bring it salvation. But Parakrama Bahu turned that observatory role into a very real and practical position of power with his reforms. By unifying the monastic orders he stopped the quarreling that could have split newly reunited Sri Lanka apart. By taking control of the interpretation of the scriptures, he made sure that they aligned with the enforcement of canonical law. By overseeing the monks joining the priesthood, he made sure all religious representatives were on board with his own government. By taking control of the practice of Buddhism in Sri Lanka, Parakrama Bahu turned Buddhism into a tool of the state.

Section IV: Map Exercise

1. Using a rectangular pencil, trace the rectangular outline of the frame for Map 16.1: The Island of Sri Lanka.

2. Using a blue pencil, trace the coastal outline around Sri Lanka and the visible outline of India. Include the small island with Mannar, but you need only draw small circles to show the other islands. Using your black pencil, trace the dotted line across the center. Repeat until the contours are familiar.

3. Using a new sheet of paper, trace the rectangular outline of the map in black. Then using your regular pencil with the eraser, draw the coastline of Sri Lanka and India, including the island with Mannar. When you are happy with your map, lay it over the original, and erase and redraw any lines which are more than ½" off of the original.

4. Study carefully the locations of the areas of Mannar, the "Rice Bowl," the "Giant's Tank," Polonnaruwa, the city of Polonnaruwa, the previous Chola-held Land, the Southern Country, Ruhuna, and the Sea of Parakrama. When you are confident that you know them, close the book. Mark and label each location with your regular pencil. Then check it against the original. Erase and redraw any labels which are more than ¼" off of the original.

Chapter Seventeen

Conquest of the Willing

The student may use his text when answering the questions in sections I and II.

Section I: Who, What, Where

Write a one or two-sentence answer explaining the significance of each item listed below.

Ahmed Sanjar—**Pg. 121, ¶ 5—Ahmed Sanjar was Great Seljuk and the Turkish sultan of Khorasan at the time when Bahram Shah ruled over the Ghaznavid kingdom.**

Al Biruni—**Pg. 121, ¶ 5—Al Biruni was an astronomer that was often found at Bahram Shah's court. Al Biruni wrote 146 books on science and mathematics.**

'Ala' al-Din Husain—**Pg. 122, ¶ 1-3—'Ala' al-Din Husain, Ghurid brother of the son-in-law Bahram Shah had poisoned, led a successful revenge attack on Ghaznavid territory. 'Ala' al-Din Husain's men brought down Ghaznavid elephants, they sacked and destroyed the capital city, and 'Ala' al-Din Husain had the bodies of the previous Ghaznavid rulers dug out of their tombs and burned in the streets; as a result 'Ala' al-Din Husain earned the title of** *Jahan-Suz,* **or World-Burner.**

Atman—**Pg. 119, *— Atman is a term related to the Hindu belief that human beings are made of two parts; atman is the part of the human that consists of the unchanging essence of the divine. The Hindu believer hopes to live by dharma, lose his personality or jivatman, and achieve a being that consists only of atman.**

Bahram Shah—**Pg. 121, ¶ 5 & 6 and Pg. 122, ¶ 3— Bahram Shah, ruler of the Ghaznavid kingdom and vassal of Ahmed Sanjar of Khorasan, was a patron of poets, mathematicians, and philosophers. Though Bahram Shah had a glorious thirty-five year reign, tensions with the Ghurids in the middle of the twelfth-century left Bahram Shah shaken and he died a year after the attack by 'Ala' al-Din Husain on the Ghaznavid capital city.**

Ballal Sen (Ballalsena)—**Pg. 119, ¶ 4 and Pg. 121, ¶ 2—Ballal Sen, son and heir of Vijay Sen, inherited the Sena kingdom in 1158. Ballal Sen wrote several treatises on the subject of the Hindu caste system and passed a law allowing Brahmans to marry more than once, thus increasing the number of Brahman babies and creating more allies to the throne.**

Classical Buddhism—**Pg. 118, *—Classical Buddhism is a shorthand phrase for those elements held in common by Theravada, Mahayana, and most other practitioners of Buddhism.**

Dharma—**Pg. 119, *— Dharma is a Hindu term and belief meaning what is good and right. The Hindu believer strives to live by dharma so that he produces good karma, returns as a** higher being in the next life cycle, and ultimately sheds his jivatman so that he is only atman and will become one with the divine.

Firdausi—Pg. 121, ₵ 5—Firdausi, a poet originally from Khorasan, was often found at Bahram Shah's court. Firdausi wrote the epic history called the *Shahnameh*, which would become the national epic of Iran.

Ghiyas ad-Din Ghuri—Pg. 122, ₵ 4, Pg. 123, ₵ 5 and Pg. 124, ₵ 4—Ghiyas ad-Din Ghuri, a Ghurid clan member, led the Ghurid army in an attack towards Khorasan and with the help of his brother Muhammad, Ghiyas ad-Din Ghuri expanded his borders west of the Himalayas, freeing himself from the domination of the Great Seljuk. Ghiyas ad-Din Ghuri continued his path of conquest into India, defeating the Rajputs and eventually occupying the Sena.

Gopala—Pg. 117, ₵ 4 & 5—Gopala, a devout Buddhist, founded the Pala empire in the eighth century and ruled in the eastern Ganges delta, or Bengal. Gopala was said to have been elected by his fellow commoners to bring peace and justice to the delta but his rule was much more strict; his state was ruled only by "the Law of the Fishes," with the large and powerful devouring the weak in a sea of chaos.

Jivatman—Pg. 119, *—Jivatman is a term related to the Hindu belief that human beings are made of two parts; jivatman is the part of a human being known as personality, which is made up of experience, character, and all those things that differentiate us from one another. The actions of jivatman produce karma and the Hindu believer hopes that through good karma he will live by dharma and ultimately be freed from his jivatman so that he will one day be at one with the divine.

Karma—Pg. 119, *— Karma, part of the Hindu religious belief system, is produced through actions; good actions and intentions produce good karma, bad choices produce bad karma. This Hindu believer hopes to produce good karma by living by dharma so that when the believer is reincarnated he will return in the next cycle of life as a higher and better being.

Khusrau Malik—Pg. 122, ₵ 5 to Pg. 123, ₵ 1—Khusrau Malik, grandson of Bahram Shah, was the last ruler of the Ghaznavid empire. He was executed by Muhammad of the Ghurids in 1187.

Lakshman Sen (Lakshmanasena)—Pg. 119, ₵ 4 and Pg. 123, ₵ 7 to Pg. 124, ₵ 2—Lakshman Sen, grandson of Vijay Sen and one of his chief generals, led Vijay Sen's army in an attack on the Pala city of Gaur and against the Pala king Madanapala in 1150. Lakshman Sen was crowned king of the Sena in 1179 at the age of sixty and, faced with the threat of the Ghurids, fled to Vikrampur where he continued to claim the name of king, even as his realm disappeared.

Mahayana Buddhism—Pg. 118, *—Mahayana Buddhism was a type of Buddhism that elevated compassion, laid great weight on the importance of ritual, and saw enlightenment as accessible to all, even laypeople.

Madanapala—**Pg. 120, ❡ 1—Madanapala was the Pala king at the time of Lakshman Sen's attack on Gaur. Madanapala fled north into the territory known as Bihar and continued to call himself the king of Gaur and to claim rule over the old Pala territory even though most of it lay in Sena hands.**

Muhammad—**Pg. 122, ❡ 4 to Pg. 123, ❡ 1—Muhammad, brother of Ghiyas ad-Din Ghuri, began an eleven-year push into the north Indian lands of the Ghaznavids in 1175 that ended in 1187 with the total occupation of Ghaznavid land and the end of the Ghaznavid empire.**

Prithvi Raj—**Pg. 123, ❡ 3 & 4—Prithvi Raj, ruler of the Rajput kingdom Chauhan, stood in the way of the Ghurids on their march of conquest. Prithvi Raj first beat back Ghurid forces in 1191, but when they attacked again a year later, Prithvi Raj was taken captive and executed.**

Ramapala—**Pg. 117, ❡ 4—Ramapala was king of the Pala empire when Vijay Sen started his campaign of conquest. Ramapala did not realize Vijay Sen meant to take over the Pala empire because Vijay Sen's first conquests were made in the name of Pala domination; it was only after Ramapala's death that Vijay Sen made his intentions clear.**

Theravada Buddhism—**Pg. 118, *—Theravada Buddhism was a type of Buddhism that emphasized reasoning and wisdom, downplayed the importance of rituals in favor of private meditation, and valued monasticism as the highest path.**

Vijay Sen (Vijayasena)—**Pg. 119, ❡ 2-4 and Pg. 121, ❡ 2—Vijay Sen saw Indian Buddhism as an aberration and wanted to change India into Hindu land; as a result he conquered the land around his father's estate and then conquered the Pala king. In addition to forcing Hinduism on his people, Vijay Sen strengthened the hierarchy of the caste system to reinforce his own power and specialness.**

Section II: Comprehension

Write a two or three-sentence answer to each of the following questions.

1. Explain the thousand year cycle of rebellion and conquest in the subcontinent of northeastern India.

A1.—Pg. 117, ❡ 2—The cycle of rebellion and conquest that had been going on for at least a thousand years in the northeastern part of India began when a warrior would conquer himself a kingdom by beating the nearby clan leaders into submission. Then he would found a dynasty, and his sons and grandsons would rule the stitched-together realm by continually persuading, bribing, and bashing the restless chiefs under them to fall back into line. The kingdom would expand, which meant the king would hand over more and more governing power to his deputies in the far-flung areas of his land, and, inevitably, one of those deputies would rebel against his distant overlord and conquer himself a kingdom by beating the nearby clan leaders into submission.

2. Describe the Buddhism of the Palas under Gopala.

A2.—Pg. 118, ❡ 1 and *—The Buddhism of the Palas incorporated the beliefs of classical Buddhism, teaching its followers that all physical things are transient, and that only enlightenment could reveal the physical world as the unreal and passing thing it is. But the Palas also followed teachings and practices from several different strands of Buddhist thought, like Theravada Buddhism, which emphasized reason, wisdom, and private meditation. The Palas also made use of sacred scriptures written in many different languages and drew rituals from Hinduism into the circle of their Buddhist orthodoxy.

3. What was the religious climate like in the Pala realm under the kings that followed Gopala?

A3.—Pg. 118, ❡ 2 to Pg. 119, ❡ 1—Many of the Pala kings that followed Gopala were Hindu, but their Hinduism was flexible and they continued to build Buddhist temples, give lavish gifts of land and money to Buddhist monasteries, and foster a welcoming climate for Indian Buddhism. Monks came from China, from the far southern island of Sri Lanka, and from the mountain kingdom of Nepal to study in the Pala realm. The Odantapuri monastery, built under the patronage of Gopala and his son, had a thousand regular residents and at times would have as many as twelve thousand monks gathered there for special occasions.

4. How did Vijay Sen symbolically represent the ritual of the Great Gift? What meaning did the ritual hold for Vijay Sen?

A4.—Pg. 120, ❡ 3—Vijay Sen symbolically represented the ritual of the Great Gift by giving away a golden horse and chariot, with appropriate prayers and rituals, and also gifting his Brahmans with tracts of land. For Vijay Sen, the symbolic ritual represented his place between heaven and earth. The kingly rituals over which he presided were supposed to show that he brought the divine into the world of men.

5. How did Bahram Shah attempt to deal with the Ghurid threat to his kingdom? What was the result of his plan?

A5.—Pg. 121, ❡ 7 to Pg. 122, ❡ 2—Bahram Shah attempted to deal with the Ghurid threat by marrying his daughter to one of the members of the ruling family of Ghur but when intelligence reached him that his son-in-law was planning an attack, Bahram Shah had him poisoned. The poisoning led to 'Ala' al-Din Husain taking revenge on Bahram Shah for his brother's death by leading an army into Bahram Shah's territory. The Ghurid front destroyed the Ghaznavid army and their elephants. They chased the retreating Ghaznavid army all the way back to Bahram Shah's capital city and then for seven days, Husain and his army sacked, burned, stole, and destroyed everything in their path.

6. Who were the Rajputs, or "sons of kings"? Where did the Rajputs come from?

A6.—Pg. 123, ❡ 3—The Rajputs, or "sons of kings," were warrior clans that ruled their own small kingdoms in the center of northern India. Though the Rajput rulers had invented myths for themselves, claiming to have been created from a cauldron of fire, in ancient times, to replace a warrior race that had grown corrupt and evil, they really grew up from the remnants of empires overthrown by the Ghaznavids on their first advance into India 150

CHAPTER SEVENTEEN: CONQUEST OF THE WILLING

years before. The four most powerful kingdoms of the Rajputs were the Parihars, Ponwars, Solankis, and Chauhans.

7. What are some possible reasons for the great Rajput army's defeat by the smaller Ghurid forces?

A7.—Pg. 123, ¶ 5—There are several reason the Rajput army was defeated by the Ghurids. While Hindu chroniclers blamed Muslim ferocity for the victory, Islamic historians suggested that the rivalry between Rajput kingdoms led the combined army to fight with weakened intensity. Well-trained Ghurid horseman most likely were the reason the Ghurids won; the horsemen overwhelmed the poorly armed and ill-prepared Chauhan foot soldiers.

Section III: Critical Thinking

The student may not use his text to answer this question.

Vijay Sen and his son Ballal Sen attempted to use social and religious reform to strengthen the Hindu ruler's hold over the Sena kingdom. However, these reforms actually ended up pulling the kingdom apart. Describe the caste system in India as it existed before and after Vijay Sen's rule, and explain the religious reforms imposed by Vijay Sen. Then explain how Vijay Sen's policies ended up being the death of the Sena empire.

While the answer to this question is straightforward, some of the information needed for completion is found in the footnote on page 120. If the student did not read the footnotes carefully, suggest that he go back to his text and take another look at the footnotes in the chapter before answering the question.

Though the caste system in twelfth-century India was rigidly structured, it did include some mobility. The king was at the top of the hierarchy, followed by the Brahmans, then aristocratic warriors and landowners and then by those who farmed the land. In between these four major classes were many subdivisions and minor groups. For example, Brahmans were forbidden by religious law to use the plow, so the priests who were given royal gifts of land also became landowners who controlled peasant farmers. Moving between castes was more difficult than moving between classes in European society at the time, but a peasant becoming a landowner was a move similar in difficulty to a peasant becoming a knight in Germany. A king could "upgrade" a local leader into a higher caste so that he would have more authority. Also, new castes could emerge when necessary, as in the case of the kayasthas. The kayasthas were professional scribes that had gained almost as much power as the priests in the fifth century and formed their own caste.

Vijay Sen and Ballal Sen used the caste system to give themselves more power. Marriage between the classes was carefully monitored in order to benefit the crown. When Ballal Sen came to the throne in 1158, he passed a law allowing Brahmans, natural allies of the throne, to marry more than once, meaning more Brahman babies and thus increasing the size of the caste that supported the king.

Firming up the Indian caste system came after Vijay Sen's religious reforms. When Vijay Sen came to power, he celebrated his conquest by symbolically creating the Hindu ceremony of the Great Gift, and building a great Hindu temple to Pradyumnesvara. He then stopped all royal patronage of Buddhism. The people of the old Pala kingdom, now the Sena kingdom, were resentful because they lost their official religion and were stuck in a rigid caste system.

Vijay Sen's triumph of Hinduism was meant to show his power as an earthly ruler, but he only alienated all the people that practiced Buddhism in Sena. Both Vijay Sen and Ballal Sen alienated all those that valued social flexibility by enforcing a caste system that had been ignored by the Pala people. Fed up with such suffocation, the Sena people welcomed a new leader. When the Ghurids came to Sena, the people of the kingdom turned against their own king and the enforcement of Hinduism and the caste system. While they didn't know much about Islam, the people of Sena knew they could no longer take the strict regulations of the Hindu king. Vijay Sen may have thought he was tightening up his kingdom by asserting his preferred religion and shoring up the social hierarchy, but all he did was plant seeds of resentment that led to the Sena people turning on their own king and accepting the invading Muslim army happily.

EXAMPLE ANSWER:

Before Vijay Sen came to power the caste system in India existed as rigidly structured in theory but did allow for some flexibility. Moving between castes was more difficult than moving between classes in European society at the time, but a peasant becoming a landowner was a move similar in difficulty to a peasant becoming a knight in Germany. The king was at the top of the hierarchy, followed by the Brahmans, then aristocratic warriors and landowners and then by those who farmed the land. In between these four major classes were many subdivisions and minor groups. For example, Brahmans given royal gifts of land also became landowners who controlled peasant farmers. A king could "upgrade" a local leader into a higher caste so that he would have more authority. Also, new castes could emerge when necessary, as in the case of the kayasthas. The kayasthas were professional scribes that had gained almost as much power as the priests in the fifth century and formed their own caste.

Vijay Sen and Ballal Sen used the caste system to give themselves more power. Marriage between the classes was carefully monitored in order to benefit the crown. When Ballal Sen came to the throne in 1158, he passed a law allowing Brahmans to marry more than once, thus making more Brahman babies and increasing the size of the caste that supported the king. Firming up the Indian caste system came after Vijay Sen's religious reforms. When Vijay Sen came to power, he celebrated his conquest by symbolically creating the Hindu ceremony of the Great Gift, and building a great Hindu temple to Pradyumnesvara. He then stopped all royal patronage of Buddhism. The people of the old Pala kingdom, now the Sena kingdom, were resentful because they lost their official religion and were stuck in a rigid caste system.

The people of Sena were fed up. When the Ghurids came to Sena, the people of the kingdom turned against their own king and the enforcement of Hinduism and the caste system. While they didn't know much about Islam, the people of Sena knew they could no longer take the strict regulations of the Hindu king. Vijay Sen may have thought he was tightening up his kingdom by asserting his preferred religion and shoring up the social hierarchy, but all he did was plant seeds of resentment that led to the Sena people turning on their own king and accepting the invading Muslim army happily.

Section IV: Map Exercise

1. Using a black pencil, trace the rectangular outline of the frame for Map 17.1.

2. Using a blue pencil, trace the coastline of India and the lines of the Indus and the Ganges. Repeat until the contours are familiar.

3. Using a black pencil, trace the area of the Ghurid advance. Show the mountains with small peaks. Repeat until the lines are familiar.

4. Using a new sheet of paper, trace the rectangular outline of the frame. Remove your tracing paper from the original. Using a regular pencil with an eraser, draw the coastline. Then draw the lines of the Ghurid advance and the peaks of the mountains.

5. When you are happy with your map, lay it over the original. Erase and redraw any lines which are more than ½″ off of the original.

6. Now study the locations of Khorasan, Ghaznavid, Solankis, Parihars, Chauhans, Ponwars, Nepal, Bihar, Sena, Pala, and Bengal. When you are familiar with them, close the book. Label each location. Check your marks against the original map, and erase and redraw any locations which are more than ¼″ off of the original.

7. Now study the locations of Lahore, Delhi, Vikrampur, Gaur, the Second Battle of Taurain, and the Odantapuri Monastery. When you are happy with your map, lay it over the original. Erase and redraw any misplaced or mismarked labels.

Chapter Eighteen

Death of a Priest

The student may use her text when answering the questions in sections I and II.

Section I: Who, What, Where

Write a one or two-sentence answer explaining the significance of each item listed below.

Ranulf de Broc—**Pg. 130, ¶ 4 & 5—Ranulf de Broc, Thomas Becket's archdeacon, took over Thomas Becket's Canterbury estates while the archbishop was in hiding. Ranulf de Broc knew that King Henry II was still upset with Thomas Becket because the archbishop did not want to sign the Constitutions of Clarendon, so before Ranulf de Broc vacated the archbishop's estates, he sent his men to strip the lands of everything useful.**

Theobald of Bec—**Pg. 127, ¶ 2—Theobald of Bec, the archbishop of England at the start of Henry II's reign, died in 1161. Theobald of Bec was chosen by King Stephen in 1138 to be archbishop.**

Thomas Becket—**Pg. 127, ¶ 3, 4 & 6, Pg. 128, ¶ 5 & 6, and Pg.132, ¶ 1—Thomas Becket, Archdeacon of Canterbury, chancellor for King Henry II, and then Archbishop of Canterbury following Theobald Bec, fled to France after not signing the Constitutions of Clarendon because Henry II's wrath made him fear for his life. Thomas Becket's fears were realized when he returned to England five years after fleeing, still refusing to acknowledge the king's reforms; he was murdered by four barons loyal to the king.**

Section II: Comprehension

Write a two or three-sentence answer to each of the following questions.

1. How were English church courts like English secular courts? How were they different?

A1.—Pg. 126, ¶ 2—English church courts were like English secular courts in that they had church officials that acted as judges, scribes, registrars, and summoners. English church courts were different from secular courts in that they dealt internally with all matters involving either clergymen or violations of church laws and, unlike appeals in secular courts, which were heard by the king, appeals in church courts were heard by the pope. In church court, the ultimate penalty was excommunication whereas in secular court, the ultimate penalty was death.

2. What does "the rule of souls" mean, and how did policing the "rule of souls" affect English law enforcement?

A2.—Pg. 126, ¶ 3—"The rule of souls" was a broad phrase that by the end of the Anarchy was used by the church to draw in all cases involving oath breaking and sexual morality, as well as matters of actual church administration. All clergy, whose souls were presumably ruled by the church, were also being tried solely in church court. This meant that if a clergyman committed rape or murder, for which he would be put to death in the king's court, the worst punishment he could face in the church court was imprisonment and excommunication.

3. Why was there a sharp increase in clergymen in England after the Anarchy? How could someone "prove" he was in the clergy?

A3.—Pg. 126, ¶ 4—There was a sharp increase in clergymen in England after the Anarchy because of the benefits of only being able to be tried in church court, meaning you could get away with a crime without facing the death penalty. There was no formal entrance into the English church—no tests, oaths or rituals—so if one could read Latin, one could claim to be a clerk, or if one shaved the top of one's head, one could claim to have taken monastic vows. The loose regulations meant that anyone could claim to be part of the clergy and remove themselves from the reach of the king and his secular court.

4. What was the catalyst for Henry II's church court reforms?

A4.—Pg. 126, ¶ 5 to Pg. 127, ¶ 1—Early in his reign, Henry II was twice thwarted by church courts, once when he tried to convict an archdeacon of blackmail, and again when he attempted to prosecute another archdeacon for poisoning his superior. Both men were acquitted by church courts. Henry was prompted to reform the church courts when he realized that an entire class of Englishmen lay beyond his law's reach.

5. What changes to the church court did the Constitutions of Clarendon propose?

A5.—Pg. 128, ¶ 3 & 4—The Constitutions of Clarendon proposed that clergymen convicted in church trials be automatically stripped of their titles, tried in the king's courts and, if convicted, be punished by secular law. The Constitutions of Clarendon kept bishops out of the affairs of laymen by proposing that no royal official could be excommunicated unless he had first been convicted by a secular court of wrongdoing. In addition, the Constitutions proposed that quarrels between clergy and laymen were to be settled by the secular court and that anyone appealing the decision of a church court should come to the king rather than bypassing him and going to the pope.

6. What was the Assize of Clarendon? How did the Assize of Clarendon change the nature of crime in England?

A6.—Pg. 129, ¶ 3-5—The Assize of Clarendon was an act issued by Henry II in 1166 that said criminals would be tried in the king's courts in front of twelve men—trial by jury. The Assize of Clarendon transformed criminal acts from local, personal insults into offenses against the king's peace and even the king himself; for example, if a criminal were to flee one county for another, the sheriff of the county where the criminal was found had the right to keep him in custody. The Assize of Clarendon became the foundation of English law and influenced the core of Western legislation in that the peace of a realm was an entity that could be offended, making crime into a national problem.

7. Describe what each man, Henry II and Thomas Becket, had to lose when the two met in 1170 outside of Freteval to make peace. What was the outcome of their meeting?

A7.—Pg. 129, ¶ 7 to Pg. 130, ¶ 3—When Henry II and Thomas Becket met to talk after five years of quarreling over church courts, each man had something to lose: Thomas Becket had the permission of the pope to put all of England under interdict if Henry did not allow him to return, and Henry II could stop Thomas Becket from participating in the coronation ceremony of Henry's fifteen-year-old son, once Becket's beloved pupil. When the conversation was finished, Henry declared that Thomas Becket could return safely to England and take up his authority again and Thomas Becket would carry out the coronation ceremony, guaranteeing the younger Henry's claim to the throne. However, nothing was said about the Constitutions of Clarendon, or ultimate court authority, so in the end nothing was resolved.

8. What did Thomas Becket do almost immediately after returning to England from his safe-haven in France? Why was this such an aggressive act?

A8.—Pg. 130, ¶ 6 & 7—Thomas Becket pronounced that two of the king's chief officials and the Archbishop of York were excommunicated from the church almost immediately after returning to England. According to the Constitutions of Clarendon, excommunication of royal officials was expressly forbidden. Thomas Becket's act of excommunication was an open declaration of war against Henry II and his proposed court reforms.

9. How did Thomas Becket die?

A9.—Pg. 131, ¶ 2 to Pg. 132, ¶ 1—After Henry II heard that Thomas Becket had excommunicated two of his chief officials and the Archbishop of York, the king flew into a rage that was interpreted by four prominent Englishmen as an order to kill Thomas Becket. The four men went to the estates of Ranulf de Broc, borrowed a band of armed men from him, and went to Becket's residence at Canterbury. Once there, they followed Thomas Becket into church where he was going to lead the service of vespers; the men tried to drag Thomas Becket out of the church, but ended up brutally murdering him in the church itself.

10. Describe Henry II's reaction to Thomas Becket's death. If the king wanted the archbishop out of the way, why was he so upset?

A10.—Pg. 132, ¶ 1 & 4—Though Henry II wanted Thomas Becket and his refusal to sign the Constitutions of Clarendon out of the way, he was still so upset by the archbishop's death that he shut himself in his rooms for three days, refusing to eat or speak. Thomas Becket's murder not only signaled the end of a friendship but also the end of the church and the state working together. Henry II mourned Thomas Becket and the end of a world where God and the king could coexist in peace.

Section III: **Critical Thinking**

The student may not use her text to answer this question.

Henry II was an energetic king. He had strong ideas about his ruling of England and did everything he could to realize those ideas. He was, in every way, a leader. Thomas Becket, however, was not. While he rose up from a political career to be the Archbishop of Canterbury, he didn't necessarily get there by blazing new paths. Explain how Thomas Becket rode the power of adaptation and conformity to the most powerful position in the English church. Then explain why it isn't surprising that Henry II had a falling out with Thomas Becket after his appointment as archbishop.

In this chapter, Thomas Becket showed us how being a good follower could result in great power. Thomas Becket, son of a merchant, had a political career. When a family friend introduced Becket to Theobald of Bec, Bec was so impressed with him that he asked Becket to come and work for him. Thomas Becket had no church education, but he was quick, reliable and hardworking. These qualities impressed Bec, so he gave Becket more and more responsibility, as well as more church education. In 1154 Thomas Becket became Archdeacon of Canterbury.

The Archdeacon's role was to be the eyes of the bishop—a truly supportive role. Becket's job was to carry out the archbishop's decrees, and to do what the archbishop told him to do. Becket's talent at carrying out someone else's orders caught Henry II's attention, and soon Becket was appointed to the role of chancellor, another executive assistant position. Becket was the king's chaplain, but he primarily acted as chief clerk, overseeing the lesser clerks who drew up the king's decrees and wrote out his charters. He also kept the king's seal, attended all his councils, and was in the king's confidence.

Not one of these jobs required Becket to make his own decisions. He was good at them because he did what he was told to do. As Henry II's chancellor, he was expected to be on Henry II's side . . . and when it came to conversations about the power of the church court, Thomas Becket, in his role as the king's confidant, would provide a sympathetic ear. This is most likely why Henry II thought Becket would make an amenable archbishop, one that would pass Henry II's church court reforms.

But Henry II didn't take into account that as chancellor it was Thomas Becket's job to be sympathetic to the king. When Thomas Becket was made Archbishop, it became his job to uphold the rules of the church. As soon as Becket held the highest office of the church, he changed. He no longer drank and went hunting with Henry II, as he did when it was his job to be the king's friend. As Archbishop, he was restrained, more prayerful and he even wore a monk's hair shirt—a stiff, prickly, vermin-infested garment of goat hair, meant to mortify the flesh—beneath his ecclesiastical robes. He did everything he thought a good Archbishop would do. It is not surprising, then, that Thomas Becket and Henry II had a falling out over church law. Henry II expected an ally in his new Archbishop; Thomas Becket expected to inhabit his new role fully. The two were incompatible.

EXAMPLE ANSWER:

Thomas Becket, son of a merchant, was a politician. When a family friend introduced Becket to Theobald of Bec, Bec was so impressed with him that he asked Becket to come and work for him. Thomas Becket had no church education, but he was quick, reliable and hardworking. These qualities impressed Bec, so he gave Becket more and more responsibility, as well as more church education. In 1154 he became Archdeacon of

Canterbury. The Archdeacon's role was to be the eyes of the bishop—a truly supportive role. Becket's talent at carrying out someone else's orders caught Henry II's attention, and soon Becket was appointed to the role of chancellor. Becket was the king's chaplain, but he primarily acted as chief clerk, overseeing the lesser clerks who drew up the king's decrees and wrote out his charters. He also kept the king's seal, attended all his councils, and was in the king's confidence. Not one of these jobs required Becket to make his own decisions. He was good at them because he did what he was told to do. As Henry II's chancellor, he was expected to be on Henry II's side. When it came to conversations about the power of the church court, Thomas Becket, in his role as the king's confidant, was supposed to provide a sympathetic ear. This is most likely why Henry II thought Becket would make an amenable archbishop, one that would pass Henry II's church court reforms.

But Henry II didn't take into account that as chancellor it was Thomas Becket's job to be sympathetic to the king. When Thomas Becket was made Archbishop, it became his job to uphold the rules of the church. As soon as Becket held the highest office of the church, he changed. He no longer drank and went hunting with Henry II, as he did when it was his job to be the king's friend. As Archbishop, he was restrained, more prayerful and repentant of his previous life of luxury. It is not surprising, then, that Thomas Becket and Henry II had a falling out over church law. Henry II expected an ally in his new Archbishop but Thomas Becket immediately inhabited his new role and supported the rules of the church above all else.

Section IV: Map Exercise

1. Trace the rectangular outline of the frame for Map 18.1 in black.

2. Trace the coastal outline around England and the continent in blue. Repeat until the contours are familiar.

3. Use contrasting colors to trace lands claimed by Henry II and lands claimed by Louis VII. Repeat until the contours are familiar.

4. Using a new sheet of paper, trace the outline of the frame in black. Remove your paper from the original. Using a regular pencil with an eraser, draw the coastal outlines around Britain and by Louis VII. When you are happy with your map, lay it over the original. Erase and redraw any lines which are more than ¼" off.

5. Now study the locations of York, London, Canterbury, Clarendon, Normandy, Paris, Freteval, and Poitiers. When they are familiar, close the book. Mark each location on your map. Then check them against the original, and erase and redraw any marks which are more than ¼" off of the original.

Chapter Nineteen

Foreign Relations

The student may use his text when answering the questions in sections I and II.

Section I: Who, What, Where

Write a one or two-sentence answer explaining the significance of each item listed below.

Aimery of Limoges—**Pg. 135, ¶ 6 to Pg. 136, ¶ 1—Aimery of Limoges, the Patriarch of Antioch, was forced by Raynald of Chatillon to hand over funds that would support the prince's attack on Cyprus. Aimery of Limoges gave Raynald of Chatillon the funds for the attack only after he was beat up and tortured by Raynald of Chatillon's henchmen.**

Andronicus—**Pg. 139, ¶ 3 & 6—Andronicus was the Byzantine general that led a successful attack on a Hungarian force at Semlin in 1167. The win meant control over Croatia, Dalmatia, and Bosnia for Manuel I, but it also resulted in Byzantium losing control over Serbia.**

Béla—**Pg. 139, ¶ 2—Béla, younger brother of Stephen III, was pushed towards the Hungarian throne by the Byzantine army in 1164.**

Constance—**Pg. 135, ¶ 4 & 5 and Pg. 137, ¶ 3—Constance, granddaughter of the original prince of Antioch, was put in charge of Antioch by blood right after her husband Raymond was beheaded by Nur ad-Din. Constance made a mistake when she married Raynald of Chatillon, but she made up for it by arranging for her daughter Mary to marry the Byzantine emperor Manuel I in 1161.**

Géza II—**Pg. 139, ¶ 2—Géza II, the powerful Hungarian king, died in 1161. His successor was his son Stephen III.**

John Ducas—**Pg. 135, ¶ 3—John Ducas, general under Manuel I, led a failing campaign in 1156 against the Normans in southern Italy. John Ducas attempted to force the surrender of the coastal city of Brindisi but he was captured by the Norman navy, as was the rest of the Byzantine fleet.**

STUDY AND TEACHING GUIDE FOR THE HISTORY OF THE RENAISSANCE WORLD

Mary of Antioch—**Pg. 137, ❡ 3—Mary of Antioch, daughter of Constance and Raymond of Antioch, was married to Manuel I on Christmas Eve, 1161. Mary was sixteen at the time of her marriage; Manuel I was forty-three.**

King Colomon of Hungary—**Pg. 137, ❡ 5—King Colomon of Hungary declared that he was also the king of Croatia in 1102. The only commonality between Hungary and Croatia after King Colomon of Hungary's declaration was loyalty to the same king.**

Raynald of Chatillon—**Pg. 135, ❡ 5 and Pg. 137, ❡ 1 & 2—Raynald of Chatillon, husband of Constance of Antioch, led a successful attack on Cyprus but was quickly subdued, forced to beg for mercy, and made to give up control of Antioch by Manuel I. A year after losing control of the city, Raynald of Chatillon was caught and imprisoned for stealing livestock near Edessa and he spent the next sixteen years in an Aleppo prison.**

Stefan Nemanja—**Pg. 139, ❡ 4-6—Stefan Nemanja, Raskan prince and brother of the Byzantine-supported ruler of Raska, deposed his brother with the help of Hungarian troops and declared himself Grand Prince of all Serbia. Stefan Nemanja beat back Byzantine troops in late 1168, became ruler of a newly independent Serbia, and started the Nemanjic dynasty, which would remain on the Serbian throne for two centuries.**

Stephen III—**Pg. 139, ❡ 2 & 3—Stephen III, son of Géza II, was only fifteen when he inherited his father's crown in 1161. Stephen III had to fight a civil war started by Manuel I in order to keep his throne; he was able to stay in power but only after turning over Croatia, Dalmatia and Bosnia to Byzantium.**

Thoros II—**Pg. 136, ❡ 3-5—Thoros II, the exiled prince of Cilician Armenia and sworn enemy of the Byzantine empire, made an alliance with Raynald of Chatillon and worked with the Prince of Antioch to attack and sack Cyprus. Thoros II ended up hiding in a ruined castle from Manuel I and the Byzantine troops after they took the land in Cilicia Thoros II had reclaimed following the attack on Cyprus.**

Section II: Comprehension

Write a two or three-sentence answer to each of the following questions.

1. Review: When and how was the Abbasid caliphate established? Who did the Abbasids have to wipe out in order to come to power, and what tensions related to the caliphate continued on?

A1.—Pg. 134, *—The Abbasid caliphate was established in 750 AD by Abu al-Abbas, a caliph from the clan of the Prophet himself who was elected in opposition to the reigning Umayyad caliph, Marwan II. After his election, Abu al-Abbas had managed to wipe out most of the surviving Umayyad clan members, bringing an end to the era of the "Umayyad caliphates" which had ruled since the Prophet's death, and introducing the Abbasid caliphate in its place. The Fatimid caliph who controlled Egypt and Jerusalem and the Abbasid caliph who still ruled in Baghdad were enemies of each other, as well as enemies of Byzantium and the Crusader kingdoms.

2. Describe the deterioration of the Turkish realm during the reign of Ahmed Sanjar.

A2.—Pg. 134, ¶ 2—The Turkish realm deteriorated during the reign of Ahmed Sanjar. By the end of his life, he had lost the Ghurids, he had been driven out of Transoxania by nomadic Chinese tribes called the Western Liao, and Nur ad-Din was doing as he pleased in the Mediterranean lands. At the very end of his life, Sanjar had tried to put down a native revolt in Khorasan itself and had failed so badly that the rebels had actually taken him captive and pillaged his capital city of Merv.

3. What happened, generally, to the Turkish lands after Ahmed Sanjar's death?

A3.—Pg. 134, ¶ 3—The Turkish lands fell into disunity after Ahmed Sanjar's death. He was the last Great Seljuk. Khorasan became a no-man's-land, and from the Oxus to the Mediterranean shore, each Turkish sultan looked out for his own interests.

4. Where were the borders of Byzantium at the coronation of Manuel I compared to the reaches of the empire under Justinian six hundred years earlier?

A4.—Pg. 135, ¶ 2—Byzantium looked small at the time of the coronation of Manuel I compared to its vast reaches under Justinian. When Justinian ruled, Byzantium had stretched from the tip of the Spanish peninsula, across North Africa and Egypt, up the Mediterranean coast, across Asia Minor, Greece, and all of Italy. When Manuel I became emperor in 1143, he ruled over Greece, half of Asia Minor, and the western and southern coasts of the Black Sea.

5. How did Byzantium grow during the fifteen years of Manuel I's reign?

A5.—Pg. 135, ¶ 3—Byzantium did not grow during the first fifteen years of Manuel I's reign. Manuel I's attack on the Sultan of Rum resulted in no land gains, and though he had forced the princes of Antioch and Jerusalem to swear allegiance to him, he did not control their kingdoms. In addition, in 1156, his yearlong campaign to take southern Italy, the "Dukedom of Apulia and Calabria," away from the Normans had ended with John Ducas and the Byzantine fleet captured by the Norman navy.

6. Why did Constance of Antioch remarry after Raymond's death? Who did she end up marrying?

A6.—Pg. 135, ¶ 4—Constance of Antioch was just twenty-one when she found herself the mother of four, widowed, and in charge of Antioch. While she held the rule of Antioch by blood right, her cousin the king of Jerusalem, the Patriarch of Antioch, and Manuel I himself all insisted that she marry. Instead of marrying a man that would have bent to the will of the male rulers telling her what to do, Constance married the French crusader Raynald of Chatillon, a young opportunist only two years her senior.

7. How did Thoros II end up as the exiled prince of Cilician Armenia? Where was he in his struggle for power at the time Raynald of Chatillon suggested an alliance?

A7.—Pg. 136, ¶ 3—Thoros II's kingdom had been overrun by Manuel I's father twenty years before Raynald of Chatillon suggested an alliance. At the time of the attack the young Thoros II had been taken to Constantinople in chains along with his father the king and his older brother; only Thoros II survived. Thoros II escaped from his prison in 1142 and had

STUDY AND TEACHING GUIDE FOR THE HISTORY OF THE RENAISSANCE WORLD

been fighting a guerrilla war ever since, with its high point in 1152 when he managed to kill the local Byzantine governor.

8. Describe the Antiochene-Armenian attack on Cyprus.

A8.—Pg. 136, ¶ 4—When the Antiochene-Armenian troops landed on Cyprus they scored an easy victory because Cyprus was unaccustomed to war and had only a small garrison. The Antiochene-Armenian troops overwhelmed the garrison and proceeded to murder and sack their way through the island, burning crops, stealing herds, raping women, and slaughtering all who fell in their way. In a gesture of mockery to Manuel I, Raynald of Chatillon had the noses of the priests cut off and sent them back to the emperor in Constantinople.

9. What happened to Raynald of Chatillon, and the leadership of Antioch, after his attack on Cyprus?

A9.—Pg. 136, ¶ 5 to Pg. 137, ¶ 1—After Raynald of Chatillon attacked Cyprus, Manuel I led a massive Byzantine army into Cilicia. Raynald of Chatillon had no choice but to humble himself and beg the king for forgiveness: he put on sackcloth, went to Manuel I's camp barefoot, and once there he threw himself in the dust in front of the emperor and begged for pardon. Manuel I agreed to forgive Raynald, on condition that the Prince of Antioch surrender the citadel of Antioch to imperial control and house a detachment of the Byzantine army in his city indefinitely.

10. How did the kingdom of Croatia change after King Colomon of Hungary declared himself to be Croatia's sovereign? How did it stay the same?

A10.—Pg. 137, ¶ 5—After King Colomon of Hungary declared himself to be Croatia's sovereign, the only thing that changed was that the Croatians were now loyal to Colomon as their king. The Croatians continued to live by their own laws, speak their own language, and serve in their own army.

11. Outside of Croatia, how was the rest of the old Roman province of Illyricum divided in the first half of the twelfth century?

A11.—Pg. 137, ¶ 6 to Pg. 139, ¶ 1—Outside of Croatia, old Illyricum was divided into Dalmatia, with the king of Croatia as its protector and ruler; Bosnia, settled by another wave of Slavic tribes, but under Hungarian control since 1137; and Serbia. The Serbs, sharing a language and an old tribal identity, were divided into two territories under two families of princes who sometimes cooperated with each other, but were more often at odds. The Prince of Duklja, the coastal land, was a Byzantine vassal and Raska, the inland territory, was also more or less under Byzantine control, since Manuel I had sent soldiers to help a younger brother push an elder off the throne.

12. How was Manuel I involved in the fighting over Hungary's throne after Géza II's death?

A12.—Pg. 139, ¶ 2—Manuel I wanted to reduce Hungarian power so he decided to mess with the Hungarian succession in order to weaken his northern neighbor. Manuel I sent weapons and money to heir Stephen III's two uncles, both of whom mounted challenges for the

throne. Then, in 1164 he sent a Byzantine army across the Danube in support of Stephen's younger brother Béla for the throne.

Section III: **Critical Thinking**

The student may not use his text to answer this question.

Manuel I told Andronicus not to attack the Hungarian forces at Semlin because the astrological signs were unfavorable. Andronicus attacked anyway, and the Byzantine army came out on top. Did he make the right choice? Write a paragraph arguing whether or not Andronicus's decision was the right one, using the aftermath of the attack at Semlin as evidence.

There are two ways for the student to answer this question: first, the astrological prediction did not affect the attack at Semlin because Andronicus won; second, the astrological prediction was correct because resentment of the Hungarians after the defeat at Semlin led to the independence of Serbia.

The student may argue for either side as long as he uses examples from the text to support his point. If the student argues that Andronicus made the right decision, he should use the new Byzantine holdings of Croatia, Dalmatia and Bosnia as proof of the mission's success. If he argues that Andronicus should have heeded Manuel I's warning, he should use the independence of Serbia as proof that, in deed, the astrological signs were unfavorable.

EXAMPLE ANSWER (FOR ANDRONICUS'S ATTACK):

Though Manuel I told Andronicus to delay his attack on the Hungarian forces at Semlin because the astrological signs were unfavorable, Andronicus made the right choice to attack because the Byzantine forces won. The result was that Manuel I took control of Croatia, Dalmatia and Bosnia, meaning he was able to expand the borders of the perpetually shrinking Byzantium.

EXAMPLE ANSWER (AGAINST ANDRONICUS'S ATTACK):

Andronicus should have listed to Manuel I when he said the astrological signs were unfavorable for the attack at Semlin and held off on attacking the Hungarians. Though Andronicus won the battle, he set off a chain of events that eventually led to Serbia breaking free of Byzantine control. After their defeat at Semlin, the Hungarians sent troops into Serbia to help the Raskan prince Stefan Nemanja depose his brother, the Byzantine-supported ruler of Raska. Stefan Nemanja then declared himself Grand Prince of all Serbia. Byzantine forces were sent back to Serbia sometime in late 1168 to drive Stefan Nemanja out, but in the fighting that followed, Nemanja's brother died and the Serbs were able to drive out the Byzantine troops, forcing them to give up control of the Serbian lands. Stefan Nemanja then firmly ruled an independent Serbia and started the Nemanjic dynasty, which would remain on the Serbian throne for two centuries. Andronicus made the wrong decision when he ignored the astrological signs because his attack on Semlin cost Byzantium Serbia.

Chapter Twenty

The Venetian Problem

The student may use her text when answering the questions in sections I and II.

Section I: Who, What, Where

Write a one or two-sentence answer explaining the significance of each item listed below.

Alexius—**Pg. 144, ¶ 6 and Pg. 145, ¶ 1—Alexius, Manuel I's nephew, was Mary of Antioch's lazy and very unpopular chief advisor. Alexius was arrested and blinded on the orders of Andronicus Comnenus.**

Alexius II—**Pg. 144, ¶ 5 and Pg. 145, ¶ 2—Alexius II, son of Manuel I, succeeded his father as emperor of Byzantium at just eleven; his mother Mary of Antioch served as his regent. Fourteen-year-old Alexius II, like his mother, was strangled to death by Andronicus Comnenus.**

Andronicus Comnenus—**Pg. 144, ¶ 7 to Pg. 145, ¶ 2 & 5 and Pg. 146, ¶ 1—Andronicus Comnenus, exiled cousin of Manuel I, returned to Constantinople and took over: he had Alexius arrested and blinded, he had Mary strangled to death in order for him to become co-ruler with Alexius, and once he was secure on the throne he had Alexius II strangled as well. Andronicus Comnenus died in 1185 after he was brutally attacked by an angry mob in Constantinople.**

Isaac Angelus—**Pg. 145, ¶ 5 and Pg. 146, ¶ 1—Isaac Angelus was hailed as a hero by the people of Constantinople after he turned and killed a hangman sent to kill him by Andronicus Comnenus. Isaac Angelus became the new ruler of Byzantium after the death of Andronicus Comnenus; his rule marked the end of the Comneni dynasty.**

Vitale Michiel—**Pg. 141, ¶ 4 and Pg. 143, ¶ 1, 3 & 6 to Pg. 144, ¶ 1—Vitale Michiel, the Doge of Venice, the chief magistrate and prince of the city, refused to pay Manuel I for the damage done by the Venetians living in Constantinople on the new Genoese quarter. Vitale Michiel declared war on Manuel I after the Byzantine king jailed all the Venetians in Byzantine territory, but the move was a mistake; Vitale Michiel was not able to free any prisoners, he** lost thousands of men to plague in Chios while waiting for diplomatic talks with Manuel I, and ultimately he was assassinated by his people for his failure.

William the Good—Pg. 141, ¶ 3—William the Good, a young Norman nobleman, ruled over the kingdom of southern Italy (the "Dukedom of Apulia and Calabria") and the kingdom of Sicily. Manuel I's presence as a friend to Venice stopped William the Good from taking over more Italian territory.

Section II: Comprehension

Write a two or three-sentence answer to each of the following questions.

1. Describe the relationship between Venice and Byzantium before the Venetians made a treaty with Hungary.

A1.—Pg. 141, ¶ 2 & 3—Before the Venetians made a treaty with Hungary, they had a working relationship with Byzantium that kept the competing rulers in Italy at bay. The Venetians traded tax-free in some parts of the Byzantine empire and had their own quarter in Constantinople, and in exchange the Venetians sent ships to help out when Manuel I invaded Southern Italy. The Venetians' friendly relationship with Manuel I stopped Frederick Barbarossa and William the Good, both struggling for control in Italy, from taking over.

2. Why did the Venetians want to make a treaty with Hungary, their previous enemy? What were the terms of the treaty?

A2.—Pg. 141, ¶ 4—The Venetians wanted to make a treaty with Hungary to keep Manuel I's growing power in check. Vitale Michiel offered to ratify the treaty with Hungary by marrying both of his sons to Hungarian princesses.

3. How did Manuel I retaliate against the Venetians after they made an alliance with Hungary? What was the response of the Venetians living in Constantinople to Manuel I's countermeasure?

A3.—Pg. 141, ¶ 5 to Pg. 143, ¶ 1—After the Venetians made an alliance with Hungary, Manuel I granted both the Pisans and the Genoans, Venice's rivals, more trading privileges and enlarged quarters within Constantinople itself. The Venetians living in Constantinople, enraged by Manuel I's actions, attacked and sacked the new Genoese quarter, tearing off roofs, knocking over walls, and leaving it uninhabitable.

4. How did all the Venetians living in Byzantium come to be arrested on March 12, 1171?

A4.—Pg. 143, ¶ 1 & 2—After the Venetians living in Constantinople sacked the new Genoese quarter in the city, Manuel I demanded that the Venetians both rebuild the quarter and pay damages to Genoa. Vitale Michiel refused to meet Manuel I's demands, something Manuel I thought was going to happen because he had already sent secret messages all across Byzantium ordering his officials to arrest every Venetian citizen on Byzantine soil at one time. On March 12, 1171, Venetian men, women, and children living in Byzantium were taken into custody and imprisoned; all of their property— houses, shops, ships, land—was confiscated.

5. What happened between the Venetians and the Byzantines after Doge Vitale Michiel declared war on Manuel I?

A5.—Pg. 143, ¶ 3-6—After Doge Vitale Michiel declared war on Byzantium, the Venetians set sail for Byzantine territory, and then were stalled in Chalcis by the Byzantine governor who offered to play mediator between Vitale Michiel and Manuel I if the Venetians would lift the siege on the island. Vitale Michiel agreed and sent two Venetians representatives to Manuel I's court while he led the Venetian troops to the island of Chios to wait for the negotiations to proceed. At the same time that Manuel I was toying with the Venetian ambassadors and making them wait to speak to him, plague struck the Venetian troops at Chios; Doge Vitale Michiel decided to give up and retreat home in order to save what Venetian lives where left.

6. How did Vitale Michiel's failure in Chios affect Serbia? How did it affect the Venetian prisoners that were being held in Constantinople?

A6.—Pg. 144, ¶ 2 & 3—Venice lost power because of Vitale Michiel's failure in Chios and as a result Stefan Nemanja, the Grand Prince of Serbia, lost his strongest ally. Serbia's loss was Manuel I's gain; he marched into Serbia, invaded the capital, and forced Nemanja to swear himself back into vassalhood. In Constantinople, as Manuel I carried on tricky and unsuccessful negotiations with Venice, the Venetian captives seeped out of their prisons a few at a time and limped back home.

7. Describe Andronicus Comnenus's approach to getting and keeping hold of Byzantine power.

A7.—Pg. 145, ¶ 2 & 3—Andronicus Comnenus used violence to get and keep his hold on Byzantine power. He murdered Alexius II's regent, his mother Mary of Antioch, and then he murdered Alexius II once he felt comfortable on the throne. He eliminated anyone that might oppose his rule, and he reminded all who dared threaten him of this fate by leaving the corpses of the men he had hanged suspended and by refusing to let the bodies be cut down for burial.

8. How did Andronicus Comnenus die?

A8.—Pg. 145, ¶ 6 to Pg. 146, ¶ 1—Andronicus Comnenus was on his way back to Constantinople to stop the people from supporting Isaac Angelus as emperor when he was confronted by a mob and his own guards refused to fight to protect him. Isaac Angelus ordered Andronicus's right hand cut off and his right eye gouged out and then he turned Andronicus Comnenus over to the crowd for punishment. Andronicus Comnenus was tortured for hours before he finally died; like the men he had previously killed, his own body was left hanging for several days before it was cut down and tossed into the gutters.

Section III: **Critical Thinking**

The student may not use her text to answer this question.

Manuel I died in 1180. He increased the Byzantine empire's power, but ruined its alliances and friendships. It seems from our reading in this chapter that the people of Constantinople were unperturbed by the foreign hostility Manuel I created. For this critical thinking question, write a paragraph that explains the difference between patriotism and nationalism, and also suggests which sentiment motivated the actions of the mob that revolted against the government run by Alexius II, his regent Mary of Antioch and her chief advisor Alexius. You may look up the definitions of both patriotism and nationalism before composing your answer.

The Merriam-Webster Online Dictionary defines patriotism as "love that people feel for their country," and nationalism as "a feeling that people have of being loyal to and proud of their country often with the belief that it is better and more important than other countries."

In this chapter the student read about some instances of anti-foreigner sentiment in Constantinople. For example, Mary of Antioch was "a westerner herself" and as a result "was inclined to grant too much favor to the Italian merchants in Constantinople and too little to the citizens of the empire itself." Mary's favoring of Italian merchants caused her to be unpopular with her subjects. When Andronicus Comnenus was said to be on his way to Constantinople to take over, the people in Constantinople started rioting and "Pisans, Genoans, and any remaining Venetians in the city were lynched." The Byzantine people got rid of the outsiders in Constantinople. While protesting the rule of Alexius II, Mary of Antioch and her chief official Alexius would have reflected patriotism—an attempt by the people to install a leader that would do better in protecting the interests of their beloved empire. The mass rioting and deaths of hundreds of Italians reflects an extreme nationalist mindset. The people of Constantinople wanted the foreigners out of their city and their empire.

EXAMPLE ANSWER:

Patriotism is defined as love of one's country, whereas nationalism is defined as a feeling of loyalty to one's country that is so strong one believes one's country is better and more important than other countries. The actions of the Byzantine people in Constantinople at the time of Andronicus Comnenus's return to power reflect more nationalistic than patriotic thinking. The people's feeling of superiority was already reflected in their dislike for Mary of Antioch, who favored Italian merchants in the city. Then, when Andronicus Comnenus was approaching the city from his exile in Paphlagonia, the people of Constantinople rioted in excitement. The rioting led to the lynching of hundreds of Pisans, Genoans and Venetians in the city. The Byzantine people got rid of the outsiders in Constantinople. While protesting the rule of Alexius II, Mary of Antioch and her chief official Alexius would have reflected patriotism—an attempt by the people to install a leader that would do better in protecting the interests of their beloved empire—the mass rioting and deaths of hundreds of Italians reflects an extreme nationalist mindset. The people of Constantinople wanted the foreigners out of their city and their empire.

Section IV: Map Exercise

1. Trace the rectangular outline of Map 20.1 in black.

2. Using your blue pencil, trace the coastline of the Mediterranean and the Black Sea. Trace the line of the Danube as well. You do not need to trace all the small islands around Greece and Turkey, but include Chios as it is marked and the entirety of the Kingdom of Sicily. Repeat until the contours are familiar.

3. Using contrasting colors, trace the areas belonging separately to Byzantium and the Holy Roman empire. Using a third contrasting color, trace the outline of the Kingdom of Sicily. Repeat until the contours are familiar.

4. Using a new sheet of paper, trace the rectangular outline of the frame in black. Then remove your paper from the original, and, using your regular pencil, draw the coastline and the outlines of the territories of Byzantium and the Holy Roman Empire. Mark the Kingdom of Sicily as well. When you are happy with your map, lay it over the original, and erase and redraw any lines which are more than ½" off of the original.

5. Now study the locations of Genoa, Pisa, Rome, Venice, Dyrrachium, Chalcis, Euboea, Chios, the Bosphorus Strait, Constantinople, and Bursa. When you are familiar with them, close the book. Mark and label each location on your map. When you are happy with your map, check it against the original. Erase and redraw any marks which are more than ¼" off of the original.

6. Mark the areas of the Republic of Venice, the Papal States, Croatia, Bosnia, Serbia, Byzantium, Asia Minor, Paphlagonia, and Cilician Armenia.

Chapter Twenty-One

Resentments

The student may use his text when answering the questions in sections I and II.

Section I: **Who, What, Where**

Write a one or two-sentence answer explaining the significance of each item listed below.

Adele of Champagne—**Pg. 152, ¶ 5—Adele of Champagne was Louis VII's third wife. She bore Louis VII his only male heir, Philip II Augustus.**

Aoife—Pg. 149, ¶ 1—**Aoife, daughter of Diarmait Mac Murchada, was married to Richard de Clare as part of a deal her father made with the Earl of Pembroke. Richard de Clare agreed to fight on Diarmait Mac Murchada's behalf in exchange for a chance to inherit the throne of Leinster, a deal that was sealed with Richard de Clare's marriage to Aoife.**

Diarmait Mac Murchada—**Pg. 148, ¶ 2 to Pg. 149, ¶ 2—Diarmait Mac Murchada, Irish king of the eastern kingdom of Leinster, had an affair with the king of Meath's wife which resulted in a war between the two Irish kings. After Diarmait Mac Murchada was driven out of Leinster by the king of Meath and Rory O'Connor, Henry II of England helped him to recover his throne in 1171, though he died not long after recovering his power.**

Geoffrey—**Pg. 150, ¶ 2 & 4 to Pg. 151, ¶ 1 & 5 and Pg. 152, ¶ 1— Geoffrey, one of Henry II and Eleanor of Aquitaine's eight children, was given control of Brittany in Western Francia in 1169. Geoffrey joined his brothers and Louis VII in rebellion against Henry II, but was forced to beg his father for forgiveness when the rebellion fell flat.**

Henry the Younger—**Pg. 150, ¶ 2 & 4 to Pg. 151, ¶ 1-3 and Pg. 152, ¶ 3— Henry the Younger, one of Henry II and Eleanor of Aquitaine's eight children, was given control of Anjou and Maine in Western Francia in 1169. When Henry II refused to give Henry the Younger independent control over a small part of Henry II's kingdom, Henry the Younger ran away from home and rebelled against his father with the help of Louis VII; the rebellion failed, however, and Henry the Younger was forced to take a strict oath of homage to his father in order to regain rule over his part of Henry II's kingdom.**

Isabelle—**Pg. 153, ¶ 1—Isabelle was the wife of Philip II Augustus. When the Count of Flanders tried to claim that he had the right to more territory in France because of Isabelle's right to inheritance, Philip went to war with him and fought for the next four years over the debated land.**

John—**Pg. 150, ¶ 2 & 4 to Pg. 151, ¶ 1— John, one of Henry II and Eleanor of Aquitaine's eight children, was not given any land when his father divided up Western Francia between his sons and thus earned the nickname "John Lackland."**

Margaret—**Pg. 153, ¶ 5—Margaret, wife of Henry the Younger and the half sister of Philip II Augustus of France, bore Henry the Younger one child but it died three days after birth. After Henry the Younger's death, Philip II Augustus demanded Margaret's dowry be paid back to France, leading to open conflict in 1186 between France and England.**

Philip II Augustus—**Pg. 152, ¶ 5 and Pg. 153, ¶ 4 & 6—Philip II Augustus, son of Louis VII, succeeded his father as the French king at the age of fifteen. Philip II Augustus expelled the Jews from France in order to raise money for his wars and he showed religious inflexibility by making increasingly strict laws related to swearing, blasphemy, gambling and other church-condemned pastimes.**

Richard—**Pg. 150, ¶ 2 & 4 to Pg. 151, ¶ 1 & 5 and Pg. 152, ¶ 2— Richard, one of Henry II and Eleanor of Aquitaine's eight children (and his mother's favorite), was given control of the Duchy of Aquitaine in Western Francia in 1169. Richard joined his brothers in rebellion against their father but their rebellion fell flat; Richard was the last son to beg for mercy and pardon from his father.**

Richard de Clare—**Pg. 149, ¶ 1 & 3—Richard de Clare, son of the Earl of Pembroke and nicknamed "Strongbow" for his skill, agreed to fight on behalf of Diarmait Mac Murchada in exchange for the chance to inherit the throne of Leinster by way of marrying Mac Murchada's daughter Aoife. After Diarmait Mac Murchada's death, Richard de Clare ruled as king of Leinster with Henry II's permission in exchange for Henry II's control of all the port cities in Ireland.**

Rory O'Connor—**Pg. 148, ¶ 3 and Pg. 149, ¶ 4—Rory O'Connor was both king of Connacht and High King of Ireland. After Henry II and his troops sailed to Ireland to protect Richard de Clare, Rory O'Connor signed the Treaty of Windsor which divided Ireland into two parts: one directly under Henry II's control and the other ruled by the High King of Ireland as Henry II's vassal.**

Rosamund Clifford—**Pg. 151, ¶ 6—Rosamund Clifford was the famously beautiful mistress of Henry II.**

Treaty of Windsor—**Pg. 149, ¶ 4—The Treaty of Windsor, drawn up in 1175, was a formal agreement between Henry II and Rory O'Connor that divided Ireland into two separate spheres: one directly under Henry II's control, the other ruled by the High King as Henry II's vassal.**

Section II: Comprehension

Write a two or three-sentence answer to each of the following questions.

1. Why was the High King of Ireland called "co fresabra"? How did being "co fresabra" influence Rory O'Connor's decision to support the king of Meath in his fight with Diarmait Mac Murchada?

A1.—Pg. 148, ¶ 3—The High King of Ireland was called "co fresabra," meaning "with opposition" because he had to fight for his title and his authority was constantly challenged by his peers. Rory O'Connor was no exception and had already been forced, more than once, to fight to defend his title. If Rory O'Connor supported the king of Meath in his fight against Diarmait Mac Murchada, then the king of Meath would support Rory O'Connor as High King.

2. How did Henry II get control of the port cities in Ireland?

A2.—Pg. 149, ¶ 3—Though Richard de Clare could claim to be king of Leinster after Diarmait Mac Murchada's death, Henry II did not want one of his knights establishing an independent monarchy right across the water, so he assembled an army at the western port city of Gloucester, ready to sail to Ireland. Richard De Clare did not want to fight the King of England, so he pledged his loyalty to the king and proved it by surrendering the port of Dublin, the towns on the sea coast and all the fortresses to Henry II. Richard de Clare would rule as king of Leinster with Henry II's permission and in exchange Henry II took direct control of the port cities.

3. Why did most of the Irish kings pledge loyalty to the king of England after Richard de Clare pledged his loyalty?

A3.—Pg. 149, ¶ 4—Most of the Irish kings pledged loyalty to the king of England after Richard de Clare pledged his loyalty because they did not want to pledge their loyalty to Rory O'Connor, the High King of Ireland, himself. No single Irish kingdom had a force large enough to drive the king of England away and they did not want to submit to the High King. This is how the Irish kings, all except for the king of Ulster, came to be vassals of the king of England.

4. Why couldn't Henry II claim the north of Ireland as his vassal?

A4.—Pg. 149, ¶ 5—The kings that ruled in the north of Ireland were descended from the ancient and contentious clan of the Uí Néill. These kings declined to submit to the English in any form. Even though the rest of Ireland pledged their loyalty to Henry II, the north of Ireland remained entirely out of Henry II's hands.

5. What happened when Louis VII made an act of war with Henry the Younger against Henry II? Why did some of the English barons side with Louis VII? Why might Eleanor of Aquitaine have encouraged her sons to rebel against their father, Henry II?

A5.—Pg. 151, ¶ 5 & 6—When Louis VII made an act of war with Henry the Younger against Henry II, many English barons sided with Louis VII because Henry II was an authoritarian and controlling king that made many enemies. His sons, Gregory and Richard, also rebelled

against their controlling father, as did Eleanor of Aquitaine. Eleanor of Aquitaine, on bad terms with her husband after the death of Thomas Becket, most likely joined with the rebels because she was angry about Henry II's relationship with his mistress Rosamund Clifford.

6. What happened to Eleanor of Aquitaine as she tried to escape to the court of Louis VII?

A6.—Pg. 151, ¶ 6—Eleanor of Aquitaine did not make it safely to the court of Louis VII. As she traveled back to her first husband for safety, Henry II's men caught up with her. Henry II ordered her to be kept under guard in Chinon Castle. Eleanor of Aquitaine would remain under house arrest for the next fifteen years, separated from contact with her sons.

7. Summarize the end of Henry the Younger and Louis VII's rebellion against Henry II.

A7.—Pg. 152, ¶ 1-3—In August of 1174 Louis VII sieged Rouen in Normandy but was defeated by Henry II, who had employed Welsh mercenaries that were excellent at fighting in the woodlands; they descended on supply trains, destroyed them, and then disappeared back into the forest. Louis VII saw there was no more point in fighting on, so he sent a message to Henry II to end the fight, with Geoffrey and Henry the Younger already having surrendered. Richard held out, but with everyone else deserting the cause and having only a handful of men left, he was made to go to his father's camp and beg for forgiveness.

8. How did the French dukes challenge Philip II Augustus at the beginning of his reign? What did he do to show that he would not be taken advantage of by the dukes?

A8.—Pg. 152, ¶ 8 to Pg. 153, ¶ 1—The French dukes tried to take power away from Philip II Augustus at the beginning of his reign but he fought hard to keep the dukes in check. For example, the Duke of Burgundy tried demanding that some of the king's vassals switch allegiance to him but Philip II immediately marched into Burgundy, attacked the fortress of Chatillon, and captured the duke's oldest son who was kept prisoner until the Duke of Burgundy had backed down. Also, when the Count of Flanders tried to claim territory that belonged, by right of inheritance, to Philip's wife Isabelle, Philip went to war with him and fought for the next four years over the debated land.

9. Why did Philip II Augustus expel the Jews from France in 1182?

A9.—Pg. 153, ¶ 2 & 3—Philip II Augustus expelled the Jews from France in 1182 for two reasons: first, he needed to raise money for his wars and second, he had very strict views on religion. He raised money by confiscating Jewish lands, seizing their synagogues, and wiping out all debt owed to them—as long as the debtors paid one-fifth of the outstanding loan into the royal purse. As a European Christian, Philip II Augustus believed that the Jews were complicit in the crucifixion of Christ and as a strict Christian, Philip II Augustus felt the Jewish presence in France was an offense to God.

Section III: **Critical Thinking**

The student may not use his text to answer this question.

We have read about myriad reasons for a country going to war with its neighbor. One of those reasons pops up more often than not: family feuds. Write two or three paragraphs explaining how the family affairs of Henry II caused the conflicts he faced in this chapter with Louis VII and Philip II Augustus.

The student should remember that Henry II's wife, Eleanor of Aquitaine, was previously married to Louis VII, but could not bear him a son. The couple divorced, Eleanor of Aquitaine married Henry II, and then gave him several male heirs. Not only did the marriage produce a secure lineage for Henry II, it also gave the English king control over a large portion of Western Francia, land that Louis VII felt he himself should control.

Louis VII had married the daughter of his second marriage, Margaret, to Henry the Younger, meaning that Louis VII was Henry II's son's father-in-law. When Henry II divided up his land in Western Francia among his sons to help appease the English and French kings, Louis VII saw an opportunity to get back at the husband of his ex-wife and his daughter's father-in-law. He suggested to his son-in-law Henry the Younger that he ask for independent rule of some part of his father's domain, rather than just governorship over Anjou and Maine. Henry II refused his son's request, as Louis VII believed he would, causing Henry the Younger to find refuge with his father-in-law. When Henry II demanded Louis VII send Henry the Younger home, the French king refused. Henry II understood this to be an act of war. Things didn't get better when Geoffrey and Richard joined their brother in France, and when Eleanor of Aquitaine tried to flee and find refuge with her ex-husband. Eleanor of Aquitaine was detained en route and then kept under house arrest for the next fifteen years. Henry II put down the rebellion with the help of Welsh troops, and soon Henry the Younger and Geoffrey begged their father for forgiveness. Louis VII saw there was no more point in fighting against the man who took his wife and land, so he gave up as well. Richard was the last to surrender.

The family feud continued after Louis VII's death. His son, Philip II Augustus, was the half-brother to Margaret, the wife of Henry the Younger. Margaret and Henry the Younger made only one child, and the baby died three days after birth. When Henry the Younger died, there was no heir to his estate. Thus, Philip II Augustus demanded from Henry II that he return Margaret's dowry to the French throne. Again, this family affair caused open war between France and England.

EXAMPLE ANSWER:

Henry II's family feuds as king started, in a way, long before his actual reign. Henry II's wife, Eleanor of Aquitaine, was previously married to Louis VII, but could not bear him a son. The couple divorced, Eleanor of Aquitaine married Henry II, and then gave him several male heirs. Not only did the marriage produce a secure lineage for Henry II, it also gave the English king control over a large portion of Western Francia, land that Louis VII felt he himself should control.

Louis VII had married the daughter of his second marriage, Margaret, to Henry the Younger, meaning that Louis VII was Henry II's son's father-in-law. When Henry II divided up his land in Western Francia among his sons to help appease the English and French kings, Louis VII suggested to his son-in-law that he ask for independent rule of some part of

his father's domain, rather than just governorship over Anjou and Maine. Henry II refused his son's request, as Louis VII believed he would, causing Henry the Younger to find refuge with his father-in-law. When Henry II demanded Louis VII send Henry the Younger home, the French king refused. Henry II understood this to be an act of war. Though Henry II's sons Geoffrey and Richard, and his wife Eleanor of Aquitaine joined Henry the Younger's rebellion, Henry II put down the uprising quickly with the help of Welsh troops. Louis VII saw there was no more point in fighting against the man who took his wife and land, so he gave up as well.

The family feud continued after Louis VII's death. His son, Philip II Augustus, was the half-brother to Margaret, the wife of Henry the Younger. Margaret and Henry the Younger made only one child, and the baby died three days after birth. When Henry the Younger died, there was no heir to his estate. Thus, Philip II Augustus demanded from Henry II that he return Margaret's dowry to the French throne. Again, this family affair caused open war between France and England.

Chapter Twenty-Two

Saladin

The student may use her text when answering the questions in sections I and II.

Section I: Who, What, Where

Write a one or two-sentence answer explaining the significance of each item listed below.

Al-Salih Ismail—**Pg. 156, ¶ 2-5—Al-Salih Ismail, son and heir of Nur ad-Din, begged his subjects to eject Saladin from Damascus. Al-Salih Ismail was still under Saladin's thumb when he died, supposedly of colic, in 1181.**

Guy—**Pg. 157, ¶ 1 and Pg. 158, ¶ 2—Guy, the unpopular husband of Sibylla, was made king of Jerusalem after Baldwin V's death via a plan devised by Raynald of Chatillon. After the Battle of Hattin, King Guy surrendered to Saladin and was well fed and made comfortable in his imprisonment.**

Raymond of Tripoli—**Pg. 156, ¶ 7 to Pg. 157, ¶ 2 and Pg. 157, ¶ 3—Raymond of Tripoli, guardian of Baldwin V, laid claim to Jerusalem after the boy's death. When Sibylla and her husband Guy were crowned queen and king of the city, Raymond asked Saladin for troops to help claim the city in exchange for friendship but Raymond ended up fighting against Saladin outside of Tiberias after Raynald of Chatillon attacked a caravan under Saladin's protection.**

Sibylla—**Pg. 156, ¶ 7 to Pg. 157, ¶ 2—Sibylla, mother of Baldwin V, laid claim to Jerusalem after her son's death and was crowned queen of the city via a plan masterminded by Raynald of Chatillon. Sibylla soon fell out with Raynald of Chatillon; when the troublemaker attacked a caravan under Saladin's protection, Queen Sibylla and King Guy demanded that Raynald make restitution.**

Section II: **Comprehension**

Write a two or three-sentence answer to each of the following questions.

1. Why didn't Saladin complete his attack on the castle of Montreal in October of 1171 and force the Christian enemy to surrender?

A1.—Pg. 155, ¶ 3—Saladin did not complete his attack on Montreal because he did not want to turn the castle over to his master, Nur ad-Din. If Nur ad-Din had taken the castle, then his pathway into Egypt would be clear. If Nur ad-Din made it to Egypt, it may have meant the end of Saladin's autonomy over his land, and perhaps even his dismissal as deputy governor of Egypt.

2. What excuse did Saladin give Nur ad-Din for leaving Montreal in the hands of the Christians? How did Nur ad-Din react?

A2.—Pg. 155, ¶ 4 to Pg. 156, ¶ 1—Saladin told Nur ad-Din that he had to leave Montreal and return to Egypt because he feared a coup was developing in his absence. Nur ad-Din was not fooled. Nur ad-Din no longer valued Saladin's rule and resolved to enter Egypt and kick Saladin out.

3. Describe how Saladin turned on al-Salih Ismail.

A3.—Pg. 156, ¶ 4—Saladin arrived in Damascus after Nur ad-Din's death and claimed to be the protector and guardian of his former master's heir, al-Salih Ismail. However, Saladin decreed that his own name should be substituted for al-Salih Ismail's in the Friday prayers after his army was victorious over a group rebelling under al-Salih Ismail's orders in 1175. He then said no more coins were to be struck in al-Salih Ismail's name and in May of 1175, the Abbasid caliph in Baghdad, which Saladin now controlled, declared Saladin to be Sultan of Egypt and Syria.

4. How did Saladin increase both his own power and the power of the Egypt in his first years as sultan?

A4.—Pg. 156, ¶ 5—Saladin increased his own power at the beginning of his rule by marrying Nur ad-Din's widow and then laying claim to all of his predecessor's lands. He also increased his political strength by fighting rebellious Muslim governors, invading Crusader armies, and when necessary, making treaties with the Crusaders to protect his own power. He increased the strength of Egypt by setting up an Office of the Navy and channeling a good deal of revenue into building additional ships to bulk up the Egyptian fleet.

5. Why did Saladin want Raynald of Chatillon dead?

A5.—Pg. 157, ¶ 2—Raynald of Chatillon attacked a large and wealthy caravan that was traveling from Syria to Egypt under Saladin's protection in early 1187; he took "every last man" prisoner and stole the baggage. Queen Sibylla and King Guy ordered Raynald to make restitution because Saladin threatened to attack if the men were not released and the goods restored. When Raynald refused, Saladin vowed to kill Raynald.

6. Where did the Crusaders gather in an effort to fight off Saladin? What did Saladin do in response, and for what reason?

A6.—Pg. 157, ❡ 4—The Crusader coalition gathered at Sephoria, a well-watered and provisioned city in the north of the Kingdom of Jerusalem from which they could block Saladin's path to Jerusalem itself. But rather than facing them directly, Saladin moved sideways and sacked the city of Tiberias, trapping Raymond's wife in the citadel with the surviving defenders. He attacked Tiberias so that the Crusaders would have to leave their position in Sephoria, forcing them to travel through bare, shelterless, and dry land to face their enemy, land that would surely deplete and weaken their forces.

7. What happened at the Battle of Hattin? How did Saladin treat King Guy of Jerusalem and Raynald of Chatillon after their capture?

A7.—Pg. 157, ❡ 5 to Pg. 158, ❡ 1—The Battle of Hattin was over in just six hours, with the Crusaders, incapacitated by heat and thirst, slaughtered, and Raynald of Chatillon, King Guy, and the commanding officers of both the Templar and the Hospitaller orders taken prisoner. After the battle, Saladin ordered King Guy and Raynald of Chatillon to his tent and there offered King Guy a drink; when Guy offered Raynald the rest of the drink, Saladin beheaded him right there. The code of Muslim hospitality said that only those who were offered food and drink by the host were protected in a host's house, and Saladin himself had not offered Raynald the drink.

8. Why did the citizens of Christian Acre let Saladin into their city without protest?

A8.—Pg. 158, ❡ 3—The citizens of Acre had almost no defenders left because they had all gone out to help the Christian forces at Sephoria. When Saladin approached Acre, the citizens decided to let him in without protest because they had no defenders and they had also heard that Saladin was merciful towards his captives. When the citizens of Acre surrendered to Saladin in return for safe-conduct, he agreed, entered the city through the open gate, and celebrated Friday prayers in the old Acre mosque.

9. How Saladin bring together the king of France, the king of England, the Holy Roman Emperor?

A9.—Pg. 159, ❡ 3-5—Though Saladin had conquered much of the Holy Land, Tyre held out. The Archbishop of Tyre asked Henry II of England and Philip II Augustus of France to take the cross in a third crusade; the crusade was already authorized by Pope Gregory VIII who had issued a call for a seven-year truce all throughout Europe so that kings and armies could pour their energies into recovering Jerusalem. The king of England, the king of France, and even the seventy-year-old Holy Roman Emperor agreed to fight against Saladin in the third crusade.

Section III: **Critical Thinking**

The student may not use her text to answer this question.

At the beginning of the chapter, we read a passage including the words of ibn Shaddad about Saladin's ruling style. Official court biographers sometimes stretch the truth about the traits of their masters. Write a paragraph that analyzes ibn Shaddad's portrayal of Saladin. Do Saladin's actions match Ibn Shaddad's description? Use examples from the chapter to support your answer.

The second paragraph on page 155 gives us ibn Shaddad's portrayal of Saladin: "Saladin's biographer ibn Shaddad, determined to paint his subject as the ideal Muslim ruler, gives us inadvertent glimpses of the real man: a devout believer, but also pragmatic, hardheaded, calculating. He studied his faith, but 'his studies did not dig too deep' or lead him into unpopular theological controversy. He fasted during Ramadan, but his fasts 'fell a little short' when the demands of war called him to be at his strongest. He never made the hajj, the pilgrimage to Mecca that would have taken him away from his restless realm: 'He always intended and planned it,' ibn Shaddad explains, '[but] was prevented because of lack of time.' His desire to see Islam triumph was genuine: 'In his love for the Jihad on the path of God he shunned his womenfolk, his children, his homeland, his home and all his pleasures, and for this world he was content to dwell in the shade of his tent with the winds blowing through it left and right.'"

Ibn Shaddad describes Saladin as a conscientious ruler that loves his religion but does not let his religion get in the way of ruling his people. We see Saladin's quest to be a strong ruler develop in the chapter. When Nur ad-Din died, Saladin arrived in Damascus claiming to be his master's son's caretaker. But soon Saladin took all of al-Salih Ismail's power and had himself declared the Sultan of Egypt and Syria. The actions of the usurper do not match with Ibn Shaddad's description, but the events that follow do line up with what Ibn Shaddad wrote.

As Saladin took his predecessor's lands, built up the Office of the Navy and attacked the Crusader kingdoms, he did so because, as his secretary Qadi al-Fadil explained, his "sole purpose" was to keep the Islamic cause unified. Also, as Saladin took over the Crusader cities, he showed mercy to those who surrendered to him. He even let the Christians in Jerusalem who chose to leave the city take their money and belongings with them. Saladin showed his commitment to Islam by exalting his faith through conquest rather than through the senseless slaughtering of Christians.

The student should recognize in her analysis of the passage and her use of evidence from the chapter that though Saladin did want more power, he made decisions during his conquests that also showed his commitment to spreading the Muslim faith and the values he associated with the Muslim religion and culture.

EXAMPLE ANSWER:

Ibn Shaddad, Saladin's biographer, wanted the world to know that Saladin was the ideal Muslim ruler. He made conquests to spread his faith but he also showed mercy to his enemies. Ibn Shaddad wrote that Saladin avoided religious controversy, and although he fasted during Ramadan, he would cut his fasts short if he had to go to war to protect his people and their faith. Though Saladin always wanted to make the hajj, he was unable to because he was busy tending to his people. Saladin had a genuine desire to see Islam triumph, and we can see in the chapter that he followed through on that goal. Saladin first had to get into power, so when Nur ad-Din died, he arrived in Damascus claiming to be

al-Salih Ismail's, caretaker. But soon Saladin took all of al-Salih Ismail's power and had himself declared the Sultan of Egypt and Syria. The actions of the usurper do not match with Ibn Shaddad's description, but the events that follow do line up with what Ibn Shaddad wrote. As Saladin took his predecessor's lands, built up the Office of the Navy and attacked the Crusader kingdoms, he did so because, as his secretary Qadi al-Fadil explained, his "sole purpose" was to keep the Islamic cause unified. Also, as Saladin took over the Crusader cities, he showed mercy to those who surrendered to him. He even let the Christians in Jerusalem who chose to leave the city take their money and belongings with them. Saladin showed his commitment to Islam by exalting his faith through conquest and showing the goodness of Islam through the merciful treatment of those he conquered.

Section IV: Map Exercise

1. Using your black pencil, trace the rectangular outline of map 22.1.

2. Using your blue pencil, trace the coastline of the Mediterranean and the visible portion of the Red Sea. Also trace the lines of the Nile and of the Tigris and Euphrates. Repeat until the contours are familiar.

3. Using contrasting colors, trace the territory belonging to Byzantium and the conquests of Saladin. Repeat until the contours are familiar.

4. Using a new sheet of paper, trace the rectangular outline of the map. Using a regular pencil with an eraser, draw the coastline of the Mediterranean, the Red Sea, the Nile, and the Tigris and Euphrates. Then draw the lines of the separate territories of Byzantium and the Conquests of Saladin. When you are happy with your map, lay it over the original. Erase and redraw any lines which are more than ½″ off of the original.

5. Now study carefully the locations of Antioch, Aleppo, Edessa, Mosul, Irbil, Tripoli, Baghdad, Damascus, Tyre, Sephoria, the site of the Battle of Hattin, Acre, Tiberias, Jerusalem, Ascalon, Tanis, Danietta, and Fustat. When you are familiar with them, close the book. Mark each location: Antioch, Aleppo, Edessa, Mosul, Irbil, Tripoli, Baghdad, Damascus, Tyre, Sephoria, the site of the Battle of Hattin, Acre, Tiberias, Jerusalem, Ascalon, Tanis, Danietta, and Fustat. Check them over the original map, and erase and redraw any lines which are more than ½″ off of the original.

6. Mark the location of the castle of Montreal.

Chapter Twenty-Three

The Gempei War

The student may use his text when answering the questions in sections I and II.

Section I: Who, What, Where

Write a one or two-sentence answer explaining the significance of each item listed below.

Antoku—**Pg. 161, ¶ 4 and Pg. 163, ¶ 1 & 3—Antoku, son of Emperor Takakura and Tokuko, was made emperor when his grandfather forced Takakura to abdicate in his favor. Antoku fled Kyoto after Taira defeat at the Battle of Kurikara and was later killed at the strait of Dan-no-Ura during the Gempei War when his grandmother jumped with him in her arms off a Taira ship that was being attacked by the Minamoto navy.**

Gempei War—**Pg. 163, ¶ 2-4—The Gempei War, fought between 1180 and 1185, brought the Taira clan's power in Japan to an end. The culminating battle of the Gempei War on April 25, 1185 resulted in the deaths of Antoku, his grandmother, the Taira samurai and a few days later Munemori.**

Go-Toba—**Pg. 163, ¶ 6 to Pg. 164, ¶ 1—Go-Toba, another of Go-Shirakawa's grandsons, was made Emperor at the age of three.**

Minamoto Yoritomo—**Pg. 162, ¶ 3 & 4, Pg. 163, ¶ 6 and Pg. 164, ¶ 2—Minamoto Yoritomo, son of Yoshitomo, exiled at the age of thirteen after the Heiji Disturbance, came out of exile two decades later to fight the Taira clan. After the Taira were crushed in the Gempei War, Minamoto Yoritomo claimed the lordship of Japan under the title utaisho and then, in 1192, he claimed the title of shogun.**

Munemori—**Pg. 162, ¶ 5 to Pg. 163, ¶ 1, 4 & 5—Munemori, son of Taira Kiyomori, gathered Taira supporters in Kyoto after his father's death to fight off the advances of Minamoto Yoritomo. After Munemori lost the Battle of Kurikara and was stuck with the rest of the Taira leaders on a ship trapped at the strait of Dan-no-Ura by the Minamoto navy, he was pushed to his death by a Taira courtier because he was too much of a coward to sacrifice his own life; it was revealed later that this disgraceful behavior was not a surprise because Munemori, supposedly bought from an umbrella seller by his mother, was not a real Taira.**

Shigemori—Pg. 161, ¶ 2—Shigemori, son of Taira Kiyomori, was the military commander of Japan's capital city.

Shogun—Pg. 164, ¶ 2—Shogun was the title of the Military Commander in Chief, the supreme commander of Japan, second only to the sitting emperor. The title was given to Minamoto Yoritomo seven years into his rule, in 1192, by Emperor Go-Toba.

Takakura—Pg. 161, ¶ 2—Takakura, Emperor Nijo's half brother, became emperor himself after Nijo's death and took as his wife Tokuko, daughter of Taira Kiyomori.

Tokuko—Pg.161, ¶ 2—Tokuko, daughter of Taira Kiyomori, was arranged to marry Emperor Takakura after Emperor Nijo's death.

Utaisho—Pg. 163, ¶ 6—Utaisho was the title taken by Minamoto Yoritomo after he took lordship of Japan. Utaisho, meaning Commander of the Inner Palace Guards, a warrior's title, was appropriate for a victorious fighter.

Yorimori—Pg. 161, ¶ 2—Yorimori, brother of Taira Kiyomori, was the Cloistered Emperor Go-Shirakawa's chancellor.

Yoshinaka—Pg. 162, ¶ 5 and Pg. 163, ¶ 2 & 6—Yoshinaka, Minamoto Yoritomo's younger cousin and an ambitious and skilled samurai whose father died the Taira purges of 1159, claimed the western city of Shinano for himself after the death of Taira Kiyomori and accumulated a following even greater than Minamoto Yoritomo's. After the Battle of Kurikara, Yoshinaka pursued and destroyed as many Taira clan leaders as possible but he was not able to claim any power in Japan because his cousin drove him out of Kyoto and named himself utaisho.

Section II: Comprehension

Write a two or three-sentence answer to each of the following questions.

1. How did the Taira clan come to have so much power after the Heiji Disturbance?

A1.—Pg. 161, ¶ 2—Cloistered Emperor Go-Shirakawa needed the support of Taira Kiyomori and his samurai to keep his power over rebellious Emperor Nijo. In exchange for protection, Go-Shirakawa helped Taira Kiyomori become a member of the State Council, Captain of the Palace Guards, Chief of the Central Police, and finally Prime Minister. At the same time clan gained enormous power because Taira Kiyomori's family also rose in rank: his brother became chancellor to the Cloistered Emperor, his son became military commander of his city, and his daughter was married to Emperor Nijo's successor Takakura.

2. How did Go-Shirakawa plan to check Taira power? What happened instead?

A2.—Pg. 161, ¶ 3 & 4—In an effort to check Taira power, Go-Shirakawa confiscated land that Taira Kiyomori had commandeered and returned it to its original Fujiwara and Minamoto rulers. Instead of backing down, Taira Kiyomori raised a large samurai army, put

Go-Shirakawa under house arrest in Tokyo, and then forced Emperor Takakura to abdicate in favor of Takakura's baby son Antoku—Kiyomori's own grandson.

3. Why did Munemori attack Yoshinaka before attacking Minamoto Yoritomo? What was the result of Munemori's military strategy?

A3.—Pg. 162, ¶ 6 to Pg. 163, ¶ 1—Munemori attacked Yoshinaka before Yoritomo because Yoshinaka's army was huge and Munemori wanted to tackle his biggest enemy first. However, Munemori's army was filled with inexperienced peasants, farmers, and woodcutters. When Yoshinaka ordered a herd of oxen, equipped with pine torches lashed onto their horns, driven straight at the enemy, Munemori's men panicked and stampeded into the narrow Kurikara Pass, where the men were pinned down and slaughtered by Yoshinaka's men.

4. Describe the culminating battle of the Gempei War that took place on April 25, 1185. What happened to Antoku, Kiyomori's widow, and Munemori during the battle?

A4.—Pg. 163, ¶ 3 & 4—At the culminating battle of the Gempei War, Kiyomori's widow and her grandson Antoku, along with Munemori and the Taira samurai, were trapped on a ship at the strait of Dan-no-Ura that was being battered by the Minamoto navy. Kiyomori's widow took her grandson in her arms and jumped from the ship, followed by the defeated Samurai, and finally by Munemori, who was pushed because he refused to jump. Munemori survived the fall but one of the Minamoto boats fished him out of the water and took him prisoner; Munemori was beheaded at Kamakura a few days later.

Section III: Critical Thinking

The student may use his text to answer this question.

In this chapter we learn briefly about the war that ended the Taira clan and resulted in the shogunate rule of Japan: the Gempei War. We moved quickly through Japan's 12th century civil war because *The History of the Renaissance World* is such a sweeping volume. In this critical thinking question, take some time to look up a topic from this chapter that interests you. Then, write a paragraph that starts with an explanation of why are you are interested in the topic, how you went about finding more information about the topic, and finally give us some of the details you found out about your topic. Make sure to cite your source(s)!

The student has a lot of freedom in this critical thinking question. The objective is for the student to dig a bit deeper into the biography of one of the chapter's featured players, to find out more about one of the battles mentioned, or to dig deeper into the listed parts of Japanese society. Here are a possible list of topics that the student may want to find out more about:

- *More information on the epic history* Tales of Heike.
- *Minamoto Yoritomo's military strategy after coming out of exile.*
- *Munemori's family history.*
- *The Gempei War (also known as the Genpei War).*

- *The events of the Battle of Kurikara.*
- *The events of the battle at Dan-no-Ura.*
- *The end of Taira rule.*
- *The beginning of the Japanese shogunate.*

As listed in the prompt, the student should write a paragraph that starts with an explanation of why he is interested in the topic. Then he should explain how he found more information about the topic. A great place to start is by looking at the information found in the footnotes to the chapter. Finally, the student should relay some of the information that he discovered in his research. Make sure that the student cites his source(s).

EXAMPLE ANSWER:

I was very interested in the note about Munemori's family history. I was surprised to learn that Munemori was not a true Taira clan member. Susan Wise Bauer writes that "everyone in the clan knew that [Munemori] wasn't a real Taira. His mother had confided to them all, after the debacle of Kurikara, that she'd bought him from an umbrella seller as a baby" (163). A footnote followed the detail. The information in the chapter came from page 96 of James Sequin De Benneville's *Saito Mussashi-bo Benkei (Tales of the Wars of the Gempei)* which was published in 1910. I searched to see if a full text of the book was available online because it is old enough to be in the public domain. I found the full text and then I searched for the passage Susan Wise Bauer used for her text. Looking on the same page that was used as the source for the story in the chapter, I found that Taira Kiyomori's widow confided to those gathered around her before her death at Dan-no-Ura the truth about Munemori. The couple had only one son, Shigemori, and that made Taira Kiyomori uneasy. Taira Kiyomori and his wife conceived another child, but it turned out to be a girl. The wife of Taira Kiyomori then had the baby girl exchanged for the male baby of an umbrella maker in order to ease her husband's worries. The story goes that Taira Kiyomori never knew of the switch.

Section IV: **Map Exercise**

1. Trace the rectangular outline of Map 23.1 in black.

2. Using your black pencil, trace the coastal outline of Japan and the visible outline of the mainland. Repeat until the contours are familiar.

3. Using a new sheet of paper, trace the rectangular outline of the frame in black. Remove your paper from the original, and, using your regular pencil with an eraser, draw the outline of Japan and the mainland.

4. Now study the locations of Shinano, Kamakura, Kyoto, the Battle of Kurikara, the Dan-no-Ura Strait, and Mt. Hiei. When they are familiar to you, close the book. Mark each one on your map with your regular pencil. When you are happy with your map, check it against the original, and erase and redraw any marks which are more than ¼" off of the original.

Chapter Twenty-Four

Kings' Crusade

The student may use her text when answering the questions in sections I and II.

Section I: **Who, What, Where**

Write a one or two-sentence answer explaining the significance of each item listed below.

Alys—**Pg. 167, *—Alys, Philip II's half sister, was betrothed to Richard in 1169, when Alys was eight and Richard eleven, as part of a peace deal with Louis VII, and Alys was sent to live at the English court until she came of age even though Henry had not yet approved the finalization of the marriage. Part of the 1189 treaty between Philip II, Richard and Henry II was that Henry II give consent for the ceremony, though it was never performed and eventually Alys went home and later married a French nobleman in 1195.**

Ban Kulin—**Pg. 168, *—Ban Kulin was the ruler of Bosnia. Ban Kulin had been appointed by Manuel I as a Byzantine vassal ruler, but had then pushed the Byzantine armies out of Bosnia and begun to rule independently.**

Bohemund III—**Pg. 170, ¶ 5—Bohemund III, king of Antioch at the time of the Crusade against Saladin, did not welcome the German army that divided after the death of Frederick Barbarossa into his lands because they were a sickly bunch, and encouraged the troops to join the Franks fighting for Acre.**

Henry VI—**Pg. 170, ¶ 2 & 5 and Pg. 173, ¶ 2—Henry VI, son of Frederick Barbarossa, became king of Germany after his father drowned in the shallow Saleph river. Henry IV made an agreement with Philip II to hassle Richard on his way back to England, and when the king passed through his territory Henry VI imprisoned him until he could raise a fee of seventy thousand marks to get himself out of jail.**

Section II: Comprehension

Write a two or three-sentence answer to each of the following questions.

1. Describe the dynamic between Henry II and his son Richard around 1188. In what way did the relationship between father and son influence Richard's friendship with the French king, Philip II?

A1.—Pg. 166, ❡ 3-5—The dynamic between Henry II and his son Richard was strained because Henry II did not immediately name Richard his heir after Henry the Younger's death. Richard was still very loyal to his mother and hostile to his father, while Henry II had not forgotten Richard's long holdout at Poitiers in 1174. The French king Philip II, friendly with Richard even though France was back at war with England, wanted Richard to inherit the English throne because France would benefit from their friendship; as their mutual desire to have Richard inherit the English throne grew, so did their closeness.

2. Why were both Richard and Philip II threated by Richard's younger brother John? How did they relate their feelings of frustration over John to Henry II?

A2.—Pg. 166, ❡ 5 to Pg. 167, ❡ 2—John was named Lord of Ireland and Henry II intended to give the kingship of Irish lands to his younger son. Richard saw the bestowal of power over Ireland to John as a threat to his inheritance of the throne, which also worried Philip II because he wanted the Western Frankish lands bordering his own to be governed by a sympathetic king of England, not a mere duke subject to a younger brother's decrees. In the fall of 1188, Philip II and Richard together summoned Henry to a conference at Bonsmoulins and demanded that the king name Richard his heir and require the barons of England to swear loyalty to him at once.

3. Explain what happened between Henry II, Richard and Philip II after Richard and Philip II made their demands to the English king.

A3.—Pg. 167, ❡ 3-6—Henry II's refusal to be bullied by his son and the French king made Richard swear homage to the king of France in place of his father. When Henry II sent the English knight William Marshal after Richard, hoping to persuade his son to return to England, he discovered that Richard had sent out around two hundred letters in an effort to raise supporters for his fight, meaning he had never intended to make peace with his father. In response, Henry II abandoned his plans for Crusade and instead began to prepare for all-out war with his son and the French king.

4. Why did Henry II agree to a peace treaty with his son and the French king Philip II? What were Richard and Philip II's final demands, and what great deceit did Henry II discover via the negotiations?

A4.—Pg. 167, ❡ 2 & 6 to Pg. 168, ❡ 2—Henry II agreed to a peace treaty with his son and Philip II because he was very sick; he was so ill that he had to be supported by two of his knights in order to stay on his horse. In the treaty made on July of 1189, Henry II agreed to name Richard his heir, to require the barons of England to swear loyalty to Richard, and to give up any claim to the allegiance of all English knights who had gone over to Richard's side. When

Henry II received the list of knights who had deserted his cause for Richard's, he discovered his son John's name at the top of the list.

5. Why was Richard given the nickname "Lionheart"? What were his first actions as the English king?

A5.—Pg. 168, ¶ 3—Richard was given the nickname "Lionheart" because he was dazzling in person: he was an experienced soldier and politician; he was tall, golden-haired, "of a shapely build" with "straight and flexible limbs;" and he was said to possess the valor of Hector, the greatness of Alexander, and the manhood of Roland. His first actions as king were to release his mother Eleanor from house arrest and to fulfill his father's vow to proceed with the Crusade against Saladin.

6. What obstacles did Frederick Barbarossa face as he tried to get his Crusader army through Constantinople?

A6.—Pg. 168, ¶ 6 to Pg. 170, ¶ 3—Frederick Barbarossa left Germany in April 1189, traveling through Hungary where he picked up two thousand troops led by the king of Hungary's brother, then through Serbia and Bosnia, finally arriving outside of Constantinople where he expected safe passage through Isaac Angelus's lands. However, Isaac Angelus was threated by the huge force Frederick Barbarossa amassed, so instead he sent guerrilla bands to harass the Crusaders. Frederick Barbarossa was only granted passage after he threatened Isaac Angelus with possible permission from the pope to declare a Crusade against Byzantium so that he could attack Constantinople in order to get through to the real Crusade.

7. What stopped the Crusaders from taking Acre for their own before the arrival of Richard?

A7.—Pg. 170, ¶ 6 to Pg. 171, ¶ 2—The Crusaders could not take Acre for their own because they couldn't muster up enough force to beat the city. The German Crusaders that carried on after the death of Frederick Barbarossa met up with King Guy of Jerusalem outside of Acre; he had begun a siege against the city in August of 1189 but the German reinforcements did nothing to help him take the city. The siege was still on when Philip II arrived in April of 1191, but Frankish reinforcements were also unable to bring Acre down.

8. Explain the terms of the truce made at Acre after Richard's arrival. Why did the truce break down so quickly?

A8.—Pg. 171, ¶ 5 to Pg. 172, ¶ 1 & * —The truce made between Saladin and the Crusaders said that the Crusader soldiers would surrender the city, their lives would be spared, and in return Saladin would release all of the prisoners he still held, pay a substantial sum over to the Crusader war effort, and also return the fragment of the True Cross that had been taken from Jerusalem during the conquest. Acre surrendered, but on either Saladin's side or Richard's the deal broke down (Ibn al-Athir and ibn Shaddad said Richard killed the prisoners before Saladin had a chance to fulfill his side of the bargain while William of Tyre's *Continuation* insists that Saladin reneged multiple times first, and Roger of Hoveden accuses him of killing some of his prisoners before Richard killed any of the Acre garrison). In response to the breakdown, Richard marched out nearly three thousand prisoners on August 20 and slaughtered them within sight of Saladin's headquarters, ending the possibility of any more negotiations and causing Saladin to prepare for all-out war.

9. What happened when Saladin met Richard north of Arsuf of September 7, 1191?

A9.—Pg. 172, ¶ 5—When Saladin met Richard outside of Arsuf on September 7, 1191, the Muslim leader was dealt a serious defeat. Richard planned the battle carefully, breaking the opposing line in three places with his cavalry so that his foot soldiers could rush through into the body of the Muslim army. The Muslim front was broken, resulting in a turning point in the war; Saladin would never face Richard in pitched battle again.

10. Why did Saladin and Richard agree to make peace? List the terms of the treaty made between Saladin and Richard on September 3, 1192.

A10.—Pg. 172, ¶ 6 to Pg. 173, ¶ 1—Saladin and Richard agreed to make peace because they both realized that neither one of them would be victorious. Richard also wanted peace so he could go home and deal with reports that Philip II was planning on taking the lands in Western Francia for himself while trying to persuade John to seize Richard's English territories. The terms of the treaty the men agreed were: a three year peace would be imposed; Richard would hand over captured territories to Saladin; Christian-held land on the coast would be left alone; Christian pilgrims would be allowed to visit Jerusalem and other holy sites unmolested; King Guy would rule Cyprus; and Acre was declared the new capital of the Kingdom of Jerusalem, which survived as a tiny Crusader territory on the coast that no longer included the city of Jerusalem itself.

11. How did Richard find himself in trouble and imprisoned after he made peace with Saladin? How did Richard get the money to be released from his captivity?

A11.—Pg. 173, ¶ 2—Richard found himself in greater danger from his fellow Christians than he had been from Saladin. He was captured on his way back through Henry VI's territory and was imprisoned, as per Henry VI's agreement with Philip II to hassle the king, until February 1194. Instead of handing him over to Philip II, Henry VI used the opportunity to raise cash: he ordered that Richard buy his freedom for seventy thousand marks of silver which Richard raised via Eleanor and the English barons by collecting gold and silver from the churches, confiscating the year's crop of wool, and charging a 25 percent tax on the income of all Englishmen.

12. What were the circumstances of Richard's death?

A12.—Pg. 174, ¶ 1-3—Richard died in 1199 after an attack on the Viscount of Limoges, who had discovered a buried stash of gold and silver on his estate and sent Richard a portion of it, but the king demanded the whole thing. When the viscount refused to hand it over, Richard laid siege to the viscount's castle. Richard died after he was hit by an arrow shot from the walls of the castle; the doctor who extracted the arrowhead made a mess of the job, the wound turned gangrenous, and twelve days later Richard was dead.

13. How did John come to pledge allegiance to Philip II? What happened to John after Richard's death?

A13.—Pg. 172, ¶ 6, Pg. 173, ¶ 3 and Pg. 174, ¶ 3—After the failed siege at Acre, Philip II tried to woo John to seize Richard's English territories, most likely in the hopes of taking the English lands in Western Francia for himself. Philip II was successful—John fled England and took refuge in Philip II's court. Richard left England and Western Francia to John, making John the new King of England.

Section III: Critical Thinking

The student may not use her text to answer this question.

On page 173, we read that "The Third Crusade, beginning with yet another burst of religious fervor, had ended with political compromise between the Crusaders and their enemies, and with bloodshed between men of the same faith. Crusade had become simply another name for war; and its participants were more likely than not to die at the hands of their fellow believers." Write a few paragraphs explaining how the relationship between Richard and Philip II clearly exemplifies the breaking down of the values of Crusade. In your answer, explain how personal desires outweighed fighting in the name of God.

Richard and Philip II started out as great friends. At first they had the common enemy of Henry II. Both would benefit from Richard being named heir to the English king. Richard would get his father's kingdom and Philip II would get a sympathetic English king that would be good to the lands that bordered his own. When the two men decided to join the Crusade together, they also had a common enemy: Saladin. However, the tie between the two kings was quickly unraveled by personal interests.

Richard raised money for the Crusade by ransacking the treasury, selling state offices to the highest bidder, and collecting 10 percent of the kingdom's goods and cash as a "tithe Saladin." On August 16, 1190, Richard and Philip II—having sworn an oath to divide all proceeds from their conquests equally between them—departed from Marseille, bound for Jerusalem.

On the way to the Crusade, Richard was shipwrecked in Cyprus. He had paused there to capture the island from its Greek governor and did not meet Philip II until early June. Philip II was angry at Richard because Richard refused to hand over half of Cyprus. In Richard's mind, the spoils of the Crusade started in the Holy Land, so Cyprus was his personal conquest. In Philip II's mind, Richard was a greedy liar. This revelation came at the same time that Richard broke his vow to marry Philip II's half sister Alys. Fed up with Richard, Philip II left the Crusade after the massacre at Acre.

With the Crusade far from his mind, Philip II plotted ways to get revenge on Richard. He stopped in Rome on the way back to France and asked Pope Celestine II to release him from his treaty of friendship with Richard, so that he could attack Richard's lands in the English king's absence. When Celestine refused, Philip II made a deal with the Holy Roman Emperor Henry VI instead. Henry VI agreed "to lay hands upon the king of England, in case he should pass through his territory." Philip II also wooed John over to his side, planning to take the English lands in Western Francia for himself. Philip II got his revenge on Richard as the English king returned home. Henry VI detained him for the sum of seventy thousand marks. Richard managed to pay up and immediately planned war against Philip II and John, who had taken refuge at the French court.

The deterioration of the relationship between the men shows how fighting for God was always secondary to fighting for their own egos. Both men were power hungry at heart. Richard went against his father and joined up with Philip II in order to extort the throne from Henry II. Philip II wanted to make sure the next English king wouldn't get in his way, which would work if Richard, his friend, was the king. But the spoils of war drove the men apart because each wanted the money for his own kingdom. Instead of fighting together against the common enemy in the Crusade, the men turned on each other to further their own personal ambitions.

EXAMPLE ANSWER:

The Third Crusade was supposed to be fought in the name of God. The Crusaders were meant to fight together to drive Saladin out of the Holy Land. Philip II and Richard, already great friends because of their common enemy Henry II, Richard's father, agreed to fight in the Crusade together. After Henry II's death, Richard was made king. He raised the money for the Crusade and then he made an oath with Philip II that they would divide all proceeds from their conquests equally between them.

On the way to the Crusade, Richard was shipwrecked in Cyprus. He had paused there to capture the island from its Greek governor and did not meet Philip II until early June. Philip II was angry at Richard because Richard refused to hand over half of Cyprus. In Richard's mind, the spoils of the Crusade started in the Holy Land, so Cyprus was his personal conquest. In Philip II's mind, Richard was a greedy liar. This revelation came at the same time that Richard broke his vow to marry Philip II's half sister Alys. Fed up with Richard, Philip II left the Crusade after the massacre at Acre.

With the Crusade far from his mind, Philip II plotted ways to get revenge on Richard. He stopped in Rome on the way back to France and asked Pope Celestine II to release him from his treaty of friendship with Richard, so that he could attack Richard's lands in the English king's absence. When Celestine refused, Philip II made a deal with the Holy Roman Emperor Henry VI instead. Henry VI agreed "to lay hands upon the king of England, in case he should pass through his territory." Philip II also wooed John over to his side, planning to take the English lands in Western Francia for himself. Philip II got his revenge on Richard as the English king returned home. Henry VI detained him for the sum of seventy thousand marks. Richard managed to pay up and immediately planned war against Philip II and John, who had taken refuge at the French court.

The deterioration of the relationship between the men shows how fighting for God was always secondary to fighting for their own egos. Both men were power hungry at heart. Richard went against his father and joined up with Philip II in order to extort the throne from Henry II. Philip II wanted to make sure the next English king wouldn't get in his way, which would work if Richard, his friend, was the king. But the spoils of war drove the men apart because each wanted the money for his own kingdom. Instead of fighting together against the common enemy in the Crusade, the men turned on each other to further their own personal ambitions.

Chapter Twenty-Five

The Sack of Constantinople

The student may use his text when answering the questions in sections I and II.

Section I: Who, What, Where

Write a one or two-sentence answer explaining the significance of each item listed below.

Alexius (Older)—**Pg. 176, ¶ 2 and Pg. 179, ¶ 2—Alexius, older brother to Isaac Angelus, kicked Isaac Angelus off the throne in 1195, imprisoned him and then blinded him. Alexius fled Constantinople after Philip and the younger Alexius laid siege to the city with the power of the members of the Fourth Crusade behind them.**

Alexius (Younger)—**Pg. 176, ¶ 2 & 3 and Pg. 179, ¶ 2 & 5—Alexius, son of Isaac Angelus, fled his uncle Alexius's reign at nineteen and sought safety at the German royal court, where his sister was married to the German king Philip. Alexius was crowned co-ruler of Byzantium after he laid siege to Constantinople with the help of his brother-in-law and restored his father Isaac Angelus to power, but it wasn't long before Alexius V Ducas removed Alexius from the throne, put him in prison, and then ordered him strangled.**

Alexius V Ducas—**Pg. 179, ¶ 5 & 7—Alexius V Ducas, the imperial name of Mourtzouphlus, young Alexius's trusted lieutenant, took Alexius prisoner and declared himself emperor. Alexius V Ducas's reign was challenged by the members of the Fourth Crusade causing him to flee Constantinople of April 12, 1204.**

Baldwin I—**Pg. 180, ¶ 3—Baldwin I, the imperial name of the Count of Flanders, was elected by the Fourth Crusaders to rule in Constantinople, the capital of a new Crusader kingdom called the Latin Empire.**

Emeric—**Pg. 177, ¶ 2 & 6—Emeric, king of Hungary, was the sole monarch, in 1201, to answer Pope Innocent III's call to crusade, though he was joined by French noblemen, German barons, and English knights. Emeric's rule extended to Zadar, the first city the Crusaders attacked under the direction of Enrico Dandolo, even though it was a Christian city under the power of a Christian king.**

Enrico Dandolo—**Pg. 177, ₵ 3-5—Enrico Dandolo, the Doge of Venice at the time of the Fourth Crusade, agreed to provide ships and provisions for the Crusaders. When the Crusaders couldn't come up with the money to pay for the ships, Enrico Dandolo made them a deal: if the Crusaders would stop at the port city of Zadar, take it from Hungary and return it to the Doge, then he would give them their fleet.**

Foulques—**Pg. 177, ₵ 2—Foulques, a charismatic French preacher, traveled through the countryside calling on the faithful to take the cross, whipping up a fervor for another crusade.**

Irene—**Pg. 176, ₵ 3 and Pg. 178, ₵ 2—Irene, second daughter of Isaac Angelus, was married to Philip, King of Germany. Irene convinced her husband Philip of Germany to help her brother Alexius regain power in Constantinople.**

Otto—**Pg. 177, ₵ 1 and Pg. 178, ₵ 2—Otto, the second son of Henry the Lion, was elected by a group of German nobles as a rival king to Philip of Germany and was named emperor elect by Pope Innocent III.**

Philip—**Pg. 176, ₵ 3, Pg. 178, ₵ 2 and Pg. 179, ₵ 2—Philip followed Henry VI as German king and married the second daughter of Isaac Angelus, Irene. Philip helped restore the power of Alexius and Isaac Angelus in Constantinople.**

Pope Innocent III—**Pg. 176, ₵ 5 and Pg. 180, ₵ 5—Pope Innocent III started pleading for a renewed crusade effort just eight months after his election in August of 1198. Pope Innocent III's crowning of Otto as Holy Roman Emperor led to the Fourth Crusade turning on Constantinople, causing a bloody ending to his treasured cause.**

Section II: Comprehension

Write a two or three-sentence answer to each of the following questions.

1. How did Pope Innocent III hope to persuade the heads of state in Europe to join in a renewed fight for the Holy Land?

A1.—Pg. 176, ₵ 5 to Pg. 177, ₵ 1—Pope Innocent III offered the usual rewards to those willing to fight in the next crusade for the Holy Land—full pardon for sins and eternal salvation, plus the more immediate promise of debt relief—but he also pointed out the bad behavior of the Europeans and how this distracted them from crusading. England and France were at war; the kings of Christian Spain were fighting each other instead of the Almohads; Philip II of France had shut his wife in a convent so that he could marry again; Philip of Germany was struggling with a splinter group of nobles who had elected the second son of Henry the Lion, Otto, as a rival king. Pope Innocent II knew that there were plenty of sins that needed forgiving.

2. Who were the participants in the Fourth Crusade? What problems did they face even before the Crusade started?

A2.—Pg. 177, ¶ 2-4—The participants in the Fourth Crusade were mostly regular noblemen, barons and knights and not one of them had enough money to fund a crusade. Six French noblemen went to Venice and negotiated with the Doge of Venice, Enrico Dandolo, for a fleet that would transport them to the Holy Land and provisions for the soldiers for a fee of 85,000 marks. But when the Crusaders assembled at Venice in June 1202, less than a third of the expected force showed up, and they collected only about a quarter of the required payment.

3. How did Zadar come to be returned to the Doge of Venice?

A3.—Pg. 177, ¶ 5 & 6—Enrico Dandolo funded the Crusaders' journey to the Holy Land in exchange for their agreement to stop at the Hungarian port city of Zadar with the intention of conquering it and returning it to Venice. Dandolo himself accompanied the Crusaders to Zadar, where a nasty siege followed despite protests from the walls that the Crusaders were attacking a Christian city, held by a Hungarian king who was himself a Crusader. As a last resort, the defenders hung crucifixes from the parapets but, encouraged by Dandolo, the Crusaders carried on with the siege until the city surrendered to Venice.

4. Why was Philip eager to help Alexius, his wife Irene's brother, take back the Byzantine throne? How did Philip and Alexius plan to remove the usurper from Constantinople?

A4.—Pg. 178, ¶ 2 & 3—Philip, denied the title of Holy Roman Emperor by Pope Innocent III in favor of Otto, believed that if he restored a Christian king to his throne he would prove to everyone that he was worthy of being crowned emperor. Philip and his brother-in-law Alexius sent envoys to the Crusaders at Zadar and asked them to help Alexius get the throne back, claiming it was their duty as Crusaders to help restore the possessions of those who had been wrongly dispossessed. To entice the Crusaders further, Alexius promised ten thousand soldiers to aid in the holy war and 200,000 silver marks, which would solve all of the financial troubles of the Fourth Crusade.

5. What did Alexius and Philip expect to happen when they arrived with their Crusader army at Constantinople? What actually happened?

A5.—Pg. 178, ¶ 6 to Pg. 179, ¶ 2—Alexius assured the Crusaders that the people of Constantinople would immediately rally to him, and that any fighting would be brief. Instead, the city closed against him and the Crusader army was forced to lay siege to it. While the siege was brief, it was violent; Venetian warships hurled stones and arrows from the water while scaling ladders were put into place, a din so great was made that it seemed as if the land and sea were crumbling, and when the attackers finally got into the city, they set it on fire to stop the emperor's royal guard.

6. Why did the people of Constantinople turn on young Alexius?

A6.—Pg. 179, ¶ 4—Alexius knew that his uncle Alexius still had partisans in the city so he kept the Crusader army in Constantinople to protect his rule. Alexius, discovering that the royal treasury had been thoroughly raided, could pay his hired troops only by collecting

special taxes and breaking into the tombs of the previous emperors for their jewels, but even the taxes and the looting yielded only a fraction of the amount Alexius said he would pay. In addition, Alexius lost favor with the people because the Crusaders were bored and angry; they began to fight with the natives and destroy the city just because they had nothing else to do.

7. How did the mission of the Fourth Crusade turn into the rescue of Constantinople?

A7.—Pg. 179, ¶ 6—When the Crusaders that had stayed in Constantinople to fight for Alexius realized they were never going to get paid, and never going to make it to Jerusalem or Egypt, they turned their attention on Constantinople itself. Alexius V Ducas was a usurper and a murderer, and it was their duty to seize Constantinople and bring justice to the palace. The clergymen who had accompanied the expedition assured them that bringing Constantinople back under the authority of the Church of Rome, after its long estrangement, was a valid crusading goal and would be rewarded with remission of sins.

Section III: Critical Thinking

The student may not use his text to answer this question.

Throughout Chapter Twenty-five we read about how the boredom of the men in the Fourth Crusade turned into anger. With nothing else to do, the Crusaders got into brawls, harassed the citizens of the cities in which they were settled and set fire to things for fun. The bloody end of the Fourth Crusade, then, should not have been a surprise. Write a description of the end of the Fourth Crusade and explain how it was the appropriate conclusion to this particular holy war.

A vivid description is found on page 180 of the death and destruction in Constantinople caused by the men of the Fourth Crusade. After seizing the throne from Alexius V Ducas, the Crusaders began to strip the city clean: "Gold and silver, table-services and precious stones, satin and silk, mantles of squirrel fur, ermine and miniver, and every choicest thing to be found on this earth. . . . So much booty had never been gained in any city since the creation of the world. Everyone took quarters where he pleased, and there was no lack of fine dwellings in that city. So the troops of the Crusaders and the Venetians were duly housed. They all rejoiced and gave thanks to our Lord . . . that those who had been poor now lived in wealth and luxury." While the greed displayed by the Crusaders was not inline with the goals of holy war, it wasn't as bad as what followed: "Ibn al-Athir writes that, during the three-day sack of the city, the Crusaders killed priests, bishops, and monks, and destroyed churches. The altars were stripped, icons smashed apart, jewels pried out of sacred vessels, relics stolen. The eyewitness Nicholas Mesarites tells us that, in their greed, the Crusaders stripped women to see 'whether a feminine ornament or gold was fastened to the body or hidden in them.' " The violence only increased as the Crusaders grew more lawless: " 'They slaughtered the newborn, killed matrons, stripped elder women and outraged old ladies. They tortured the monks, they hit them with their fists and kicked their bellies, thrashing and rending their reverend bodies with whips. . . . [M]any were dragged like sheep and beheaded, and on the holy tombs, the wretched slew the innocent.' By the second day of the sack, many of the Crusaders were thoroughly drunk from looting Constantinople's luxurious wine cellars. They were, says Nicetas Choniates, braying like salacious asses at the very sight of women, and a sickness of rape swept through the city. No one was spared: virgins, married women, the old, even nuns were violated in the streets. Men who tried to stop the assaults were run through, decapitated, or left to die in the streets with their limbs hacked off." After the city was cleaned of its treasures and the Crusaders had become bored with even rape and murder, they elected one of their own, the Count of Flanders, to be the new emperor: Emperor Baldwin I.

The men of the Fourth Crusade were not rich and fighting in the Crusade offered them a chance at glory and gold. They also seemed to be a violent bunch. Throughout the chapter we saw their restlessness manifest itself through brawls and fires, so it is not surprise that the men, bored and angry that they were not paid as they were promised by Alexius, went berserk.

EXAMPLE ANSWER:

The end of the Fourth Crusade showcased the corruption of holy war. The Crusaders, in control of a city full of riches, could not help themselves and they stripped the city of all its gold, jewels, and precious things. The greed that took hold of the Crusaders caused them to rob even the church, killing priests, bishops, and monks, and destroying churches to get at the treasures and jewels in the altars and sacred relics. The men even made women strip to see if they were hiding gold or jewels beneath their clothes. The treatment of women worsened; babies and matrons were killed, elderly women were stripped, and the Crusaders raped virgins, married women, the old, and even nuns. Men that tried to help the women were beaten, decapitated or left to die with their arms or legs cut off. Monks were also tortured. They were hit, kicked, whipped and beheaded and then dragged around like sheep. After the city was cleaned of its treasures and the Crusaders had become bored with even rape and murder, they elected one of their own, the Count of Flanders, to be the new emperor: Emperor Baldwin I. One can't say that it makes sense that the Fourth Crusade ended this way, but looking back at the corruption at the heart of all the Crusades— the unwillingness of the conquerors to give their spoils to the church—paired with the particular temperament of the men in the Fourth Crusade, the kind of catastrophic end we read about now seems inevitable. It is not surprising that the men, poor, bored, angry and power hungry, went berserk.

Chapter Twenty-Six

Westward

The student may use her text when answering the questions in sections I and II.

Section I: **Who, What, Where**

Write a one or two-sentence answer explaining the significance of each item listed below.

Aconcagua—**Pg. 189, *—Aconcagua, the highest peak in the Andes, has an elevation of 22,841 feet and is the second-highest mountain among the "Seven Summits," the nickname for the highest elevations on the seven continents (only Everest, which reaches 29,092 is higher). Aconcagua is the highest summit outside Asia.**

Chimu—**Pg. 192, ❡ 2-4—Chimu was the name of a people that settled over the old Moche ruins and that made their center at the city of Chan Chan. Chimu oral history credits the beginning of their civilization to Tacaynamo.**

Chan Chan—**Pg. 192, ❡ 3—Chan Chan, the Chimu capital, covered about nine square miles and was home to perhaps thirty thousand people. Ruins suggest that Chan Chan was more a center for pilgrimage than an actual living city.**

Cuzco—**Pg. 192, ❡ 4-6—Cuzco, the most prosperous of the Inca villages, was at first a shabby agricultural outpost, occupied by llama herders and farmers scratching out a living in cold high-altitude fields. When Manco Capac took over Cuzco the previous inhabitants of the city were "utterly destroyed" by the Incan king.**

Hunac Ceel—**Pg. 187, ❡ 2-4—Hunac Ceel, Mayan king, conquered Chichen Itza followed by a good part of the Yucatán Peninsula. He made Mayapan the center of his flourishing empire.**

Inca—**Pg. 192, ❡ 4—Inca was the name of a people that settled on the southern edge of the Chimu border around 1200. They were led by a legendary king named Manco Capac, a king that was driven by the desire for conquest.**

Manco Capac—**Pg. 192, ❡ 5 to Pg. 193, ❡ 1—Manco Capac was the first Inca king, ruling from Cuzco around 1200. Manco Capac was a conqueror; legend has it that Manco Capac and his** family "utterly destroyed" the natives of Cuzco, tearing the villagers into pieces, eating their hearts and lungs, and ripping pregnant women open.

Moche—**Pg. 191, ¶ 3-4—Moche was the name of a people that lived on the northwest coast of South America. They constructed huge mud-brick buildings, had well-designed roads, vast irrigation canals, and made figurines and paintings to preserve the likenesses of the Moche kings and noblemen.**

Nazca—**Pg. 189, ¶ 4 to Pg. 191, ¶ 2—Nazca was the name of a people that lived in the rain shadow of the Andes Mountains in the Atacama Desert. The Nazca people lived near underground rivers that would rise to the surface of the desert and they made huge line drawings on the dry ground by sweeping away the stones and debris from the desert floor to reveal the lighter sands beneath.**

Tacaynamo—**Pg. 192, ¶ 2—Tacaynamo, the subject of a Chimu oral history, was a bearded man who arrived on the South American coast from the sea where he beached his balsa wood raft and settled in the old Moche land. His son and his grandson conquered more and more of the nearby river valleys and established a royal dynasty.**

Section II: Comprehension

Write a two or three-sentence answer to each of the following questions.

1. Describe the way of life in the northern part of the Yucatán peninsula under the descendants of Hunac Ceel.

A1.—Pg. 187, ¶ 4 to Pg. 188, ¶ 1—Hunac Ceel's descendants ruled over the northern Yucatán peninsula from Mayapan, a city that was easy to defend and hard to besiege. The strong central control from Mayapan over the Mayan people was evidenced by the treatment of conquered aristocrats, who were required to live in the capital city, under the eye of the kings, while their estates farther away were administered by stewards on their behalf. In the city of Mayapan, living was civilized; the middle of the town housed the temples, around which lived the lords and priests, and within the walls of the city the people planted wine trees, cotton, pepper and maize.

2. What is a rain shadow? Give an example from the chapter of an area that is in a rain shadow.

A2.—Pg. 189, ¶ 3—A rain shadow is a stretch of desert blocked by the peaks from moisture-bearing winds. The winds, hitting the mountains first, drop all of their water; by the time they flow over the summits and down to the desert, they are entirely dry. An example of an area in a rain shadow is the Atacama Desert, where less than an inch of precipitation falls per year, and in its driest parts, rain falls once every forty or fifty years.

3. How did the Nazca people survive in the Atacama Desert?

A3.—Pg. 189, ⸿ 4—Though the Nazca people lived in a rain shadow, they were able to survive in the Atacama Desert by living near underground rivers that would abruptly rise to the desert surface. Subterranean water gave life to the Nazca people.

4a. What did the center of Moche civilization look like before it disappeared?

A4a.—Pg. 191, ⸿ 3—The Moche civilization was spread out in mud-brick buildings found in the northern valley that served as the center of their empire. The Moche built two gigantic hill complexes of temples, palaces, courtyards, administrative buildings, and cities of the dead: the Place of the Sun, the Huaca del Sol, and the Place of the Moon, the Huaca de la Luna. Their craftsmen produced 143 million adobe bricks for these buildings, each stamped with the symbol of its maker.

4b. What did the areas surrounding the center of the Moche civilization look like before they too disappeared?

A4b.—Pg. 191, ⸿ 4—The hills and valleys that surrounded the center of Moche civilization contained a grid of wide, well-designed roads and a sophisticated system of communication: relay runners traveled the roads, carrying messages marked with cryptic symbols on lima beans. Vast irrigation canals, some running nearly a hundred miles through the Moche state, provided the growing villages with water. At its height, the Moche ruled over fifteen thousand square miles of territory from the Place of the Sun and the Place of the Moon.

5. What brought an end to the Nazca and Moche civilizations?

A5—Pg. 191, ⸿ 5 & 6—Both the Nazca and Moche civilizations were brought down by the ravages of nature. The Nazca suffered from a drought that probably dried up the underground rivers of the Atacama Desert, thus depriving them of a water source. The Moche were at the mercy of drought and then extreme flooding caused by El Niño events; floods and mudslides ravaged the Moche valley while winds and tides drove coastal dunes farther and farther inland, spreading sterile sand across Moche's fertile fields.

6. What did the Moche do in an effort to stop the natural disasters that were ruining their civilization? What evidence do we have of these precautionary actions?

A6.—Pg. 192, ⸿ 1—The Moche tried to stop the natural disasters that were ruining their civilization by sacrificing children to appease the deities they believed governed the wind and the sky. Three small children were found buried in a ceremonial plaza at the Place of the Moon, at the edge of a drastic mudslide. More bones were found, buried in at least two different ceremonies, above and beside the original three skeletons.

7. According to Inca legend, where did Manco Capac come from? What does the legend about Manco Capac tell us about his ruling style and the general character of the Inca?

A7.—Pg. 192, ⸿ 5 to Pg. 193, ⸿ 2— According to legend, Manco Capac, the oldest of eight siblings, "had no father or mother"; instead, the eight brothers and sisters emerged from a hill covered with gold, and immediately embarked on conquest. They said to each other that they should seek out fertile lands and subjugate the people on those lands, and they should

wage war against anyone that did not receive them as lords. The legend about Manco Capac tells us that the Inca had a will to conquer and were not afraid of bloodshed.

Section III: **Critical Thinking**

The student may not use her text to answer this question.

The early history of the South American peoples is, as we read in this chapter, "a puzzle." We have to read the clues left behind and figure out what they mean. However, sometimes that is not possible. Write a paragraph that describes the line drawings at Nazca and explains what some historians have suggested the line drawings might mean. Then write a paragraph explaining what you think the art historian George Kubler meant when he said of the line drawings that "the lines 'inscribe human meaning upon the hostile wastes of nature.'"

The first part of this answer is very straightforward. The student needs to recall what she read in the chapter and write it down. The Nazca people created enormous patterns, hundreds of feet across, on the dry ground by sweeping stones and debris away from the desert floor to reveal the lighter sands beneath. The huge line drawings revealed themselves to be objects, like a spider, a bird, a fish, a monkey, a hummingbird, a parrot, a lizard, or hands. There is no single explanation for the drawings. The archaeologist Maria Reiche, who first mapped out the figures in the 1940s, believed that the lines charted astronomical movements. (The student doesn't necessarily have to recall the name of the archaeologist, but she should know what the archaeologist thought.) However, many of the lines can't be associated with any known movement of the stars. Some of the drawings seem to mark underground water flow, but because not all of them do the explanation of the drawings as paths to waterways doesn't fit. It is possible that the paths were used for sacred walking rituals, a practice carried on in later Andean cultures—but there is no way to know whether the rituals existed as early as the Nazca civilization.

The second part of the question is up for interpretation. Art historian George Kubler said that the only thing we can know for certain about the line drawings is that "the lines 'inscribe human meaning upon the hostile wastes of nature.'" The student should address what she thinks Kubler means. From what we know in the chapter, what were the Nazca looking for? What kind of environment did they live in, and how might that have affected their view of the world? How might leaving a permanent mark on the earth in a formation too big to be viewed as whole or understood unless from afar fit with the Nazca culture? Is that how they saw their world? Maybe they were trying to sort out their place on the earth, an entity too big for them to see from their desert homes but that they were aware of nonetheless. Perhaps the symbols were meant to be as mysterious as the miraculously appearing rivers that surfaced from underneath the desert sands. What Kubler may have meant is that the lines were evidence of the Nazca trying to understand their world. Perhaps the images were the only way the Nazca people could interact with and find meaning in their harsh and ever-changing environment. Your student may have a very different answer than what is offered here. Whatever she writes, make sure she is connecting Kubler's quote to what she learned in the chapter and that she explains her answer clearly.

EXAMPLE ANSWER:

The Nazca people created enormous patterns, hundreds of feet across, on the dry ground by sweeping stones and debris away from the desert floor to reveal the lighter sands beneath. The huge line drawings revealed themselves to be objects, like a spider, a bird, a fish, or a

monkey. There is no single explanation for the drawings. One archaeologist believed that the lines charted astronomical movements. However, many of the lines can't be associated with any known movement of the stars. Some of the drawings seem to mark underground water flow, but because not all of them do the explanation of the drawings as paths to waterways doesn't fit. Later Andean cultures had sacred walking rituals, so it is possible that the paths were used for that purpose. But we don't know if the rituals existed when the Nazca were around so we can't be sure.

The one thing we can be sure about is what art historian George Kubler said, that "the lines 'inscribe human meaning upon the hostile wastes of nature.'" The Nazca people lived in a harsh environment and were reliant upon rivers that appeared out of nowhere for water. They also had to deal with deadly droughts. What Kubler may have meant is that the lines were evidence of the Nazca trying to understand their world. Perhaps the images were the only way the Nazca people could interact with and find meaning in their harsh and ever-changing environment. The images didn't make sense from up close, only from far away. Similarly, the weather might not have made sense to the Nazca, and they were struggling to find the bigger picture. If they could find a way to take a step back, like the viewer of their line drawings, perhaps they would figure out the key to the puzzle of their environment.

Section IV: Map Exercise

1. Trace the rectangular outline of the frame for Map 26.2 in black.

2. Trace the coastline in black. Trace the mountain peaks. Repeat until the contours are familiar.

3. Using a new sheet of paper, trace the rectangular outline of the frame in black. Then using your regular pencil with the eraser, draw the coastline. Show the mountains with small peaks. Check it against the original, and erase and redraw any lines more than ¼″ off of the original.

4. Study the areas of the Andes, the Atacama Desert, and the Equator. Close the book, mark and label them, check them against the original, and correct any mistakes.

5. Then study the locations of the Moche and the Nazca, the Chimu, and of Chan Chan, Cuzco, and the Place of the Sun and Place of the Moon. Close the book, and mark them on your map. Check them against the original, and erase and redraw any that are more than ¼″ off of the original.

Chapter Twenty-Seven

The Mongol School of Warfare

The student may use his text when answering the questions in sections I and II.

Section I: Who, What, Where

Write a one or two-sentence answer explaining the significance of each item listed below.

Borjigid—**Pg. 195, ¶ 3 & 4—Borjigid was the name of the clan of Temujin; the clan was driven from their home by the Taichi'ut clan.**

Borte—**Pg. 195, ¶ 3 & 5—Borte was arranged to marry Temujin when she was just ten years old. Though Temujin ran away from Borte and her clan when his father died, he returned to her when he was sixteen and insisted that her father honor their arrangement.**

Genghis Khan—**Pg. 198, ¶ 3 & 4—Genghis Khan, possibly meaning Khan of All Oceans, or Universal Khan, was the title given to Temujin after he defeated his rivals and became khan of the Mongols. The title, Genghis Khan, differentiated Temujin from Jamuqa, who held the title Gur Khan, or Great Khan.**

Ilah Ahai—**Pg. 197, ¶ 3 and Pg. 198, ¶ 2—Ilah Ahai, Temujin's lieutenant, was sent on an exploratory raid into the Western Xia before Temujin returned to the Mongol heartland and claimed the title of Great Khan. Ilah Ahai returned to Temujin with camels, livestock, and information about how the Western Xia fortified their cities.**

Jamuqa—**Pg. 196, ¶ 3 & 4 and Pg. 197, ¶ 1 & 2—Jamuqa, a childhood friend of Temujin's, joined in the coalition led by Temujin to attack and destroy the Merkit. Jamuqa's friendship with Temujin ended when Jamuqa challenged Temujin for the role of Great Khan; Jamuqa lost and was killed by Temujin for his disloyalty.**

Li Anchaun—**Pg. 198, ¶ 6, Pg. 199, ¶ 4 and Pg. 201, Timeline—Li Anchaun displaced his cousin Weiming Chunyou from the Western Xia throne in 1206. Li Anchaun made peace with Genghis Khan after Weishaowang refused to send Jin men to help the Western Xia leader battle the Mongols.**

Li Renxiao—**Pg. 197, ¶ 4 to Pg. 198, 1**—Li Renxiao built schools for Confucian learning, endowed Buddhist temples, put into place a Song-style examination system for civil servants and created iron coins with which Western Xia merchants could trade with both the Jin and the Song while he was king of the Western Xia. Li Renxiao supervised the editing and revision of hundreds of volumes of Buddhist treatises in Tangut, he ordered the Western Xia law codes written in the Tangut script, and in 1190 his court scholars assembled a Tangut-Chinese dictionary called *A Timely Gem* which contained the earliest complete bilingual glossary in the world.

Merkit—**Pg. 196, ¶ 2 & 3**—Merkit was the name of a three-tribe coalition that attacked Temujin and kidnapped Borte in retaliation for the kidnapping of a Merkit woman years before—Temujin's mother. The Merkit were wiped out by Temujin and his alliance during their mission to rescue Borte.

Taichi'ut—**Pg. 195, ¶ 4**—Taichi'ut is the name of the clan that drove Temujin and the Borjigid clan from their home. Though the Taichi'ut chief captured Temujin, the teen managed to escape.

Temujin—**Pg. 195, ¶ 3, Pg. 196, ¶ 4, and Pg. 198, ¶ 3**—Temujin, member of the Borjigid clan, was a strong leader and great fighter, and he beat out his friend Jamuqa for the leadership of the Mongols. After triumphing over his enemies and exploring the richness of the Western Xia, Temujin returned to his homeland and was hailed as the Mongols' khan with the special title "Genghis Khan."

Toghrul—**Pg. 195, ¶ 5 to Pg. 196, ¶ 2 & 6**—Toghrul, an experienced middle-aged soldier and leader of the Kerait tribe, helped Temujin rescue his wife from the Merkit and subsequently destroy them. Toghrul was killed by a border guard of the Naiman tribe after he hesitated in support for Temujin as Great Khan and was forced to flee westward.

Weiming Chunyou—**Pg. 198, ¶ 2 & 6**—Weiming Chunyou, son of Li Renxiao, followed his father on the Western Xia throne only to be displaced by his cousin Li Anchaun.

Weishaowang—**Pg. 199, ¶ 3**—Weishaowang was made the Jin emperor right around the time that the Mongols were attacking the Western Xia. When Li Anchaun asked Weishaowang for help in the fight against the Mongols he refused, saying it served him well if his enemies attacked each other.

Western Xia—**Pg. 197, ¶ 4 & ***—Western Xia was the name for a group of people that had once been nomads and then settled and aspired to be like the Song. The Western Xia are also known as the Xi Xia or Hsi Hsia and are often called the Tangut, after the dominant ethnic group within the kingdom.

Section II: **Comprehension**

Write a two or three-sentence answer to each of the following questions.

1. Who were the Mongols? Where did they come from and how was their society structured?

A1.—Pg. 195, ¶ 2—The Mongols were a loosely related set of tribes that migrated southward from the *taiga*, the cold northern pine forests, and ranged across the flat northern grasslands north of China known as the steppes. According to the thirteenth-century *The Secret History of the Mongols*, they had descended from the union of a forest doe with a predatory blue-grey wolf. Every Mongol tribe had its own khan to lead it, and the khans and tribes struggled with each other for power, just as the clans and chiefs within each tribe fought constantly among themselves for horses, wives, loot, and the chance to rise to leadership of the tribe.

2. Describe the circumstances of Temujin's childhood that led to his preparation as a great fighter and survivor.

A2.—Pg. 195, ¶ 3 & 4—At the age of nine, Temujin was betrothed to the ten-year-old daughter of a clan leader from another tribe, and was sent to live with the bride's family but he ran away and returned home because his father had died. Then Temujin and his family were driven from their home by the Taichi'ut; they spent the next years scrounging for food in the barren Khentil mountain range and Temujin was even captured by the Taichi'ut clan chief only to escape. The harsh events of his upbringing seasoned Temujin to fight and survive.

3. How did Jamuqa meet his end? What was his final request?

A3.—Pg. 196, ¶ 7 to Pg. 197, ¶ 2—Jamuqa, losing followers and realizing he could not beat Temujin in the battle for Great Khan, escaped into the mountains and lived there as an outcast until he was finally taken prisoner by Temujin's men. Knowing he would be put to death, Jamuqa asked one last favor from his childhood companion: to be put to death swiftly and without bloodshed, the way an honorable warrior would die. Temujin granted the request and as Jamuqa left his presence, two guards broke the prisoner's back.

4. How did Genghis Khan change the role of the Mongol khan?

A4.—Pg. 198, ¶ 4—Genghis Khan changed the role of the Mongol khan by evolving the role into a leadership position that commanded much more than nomadic raiding parties. He organized his personal bodyguard into ranks and offices; his men, more than ten thousand of them, traveled with the khan wherever he went thus creating a moving government, a "state on horseback." Genghis Khan also ordered an educated Turkish man that he held prisoner to create an alphabet capable of reducing the Mongolian language to writing, which was then used to write the first Mongol state records, a book of legal decisions.

5. Why did the Mongols choose to attack the Western Xia?

A5.—Pg. 198, ¶ 5 & 6—The Mongols chose to attack the Western Xia because they could be reached across open land rather than a mountainous peninsula neck. The Western Xia were also the most vulnerable of the three undefeated peoples that surrounded the Mongols.

Li Anchaun had recently displaced Weiming Chunyou on the Western Xia throne which suggested weakness.

6. What tactic did the Mongols use to break past the Western Xia at the mountain pass north of the Chung-hsing?

A5.—Pg. 199, ¶ 1—The Mongols used a familiar tactic to break past the Western Xia troops stationed at the mountain pass north of Chung-hsing. They pretended to withdraw, which drew the Western Xia forces out of their entrenched position, and then the Mongols were able to close around them to fight in the open. By resorting to their old style of warfare, the Mongols were able to drive the Western Xia army from the pass.

7. How did Genghis Khan expect his dam to help him in the fight against the Western Xia? How did it actually help him?

A6.—Pg. 199, ¶ 2-4—Genghis Khan ordered his soldiers to dam the nearby branch of the Yellow river with the intent of flooding the Western Xia capital out. Though the dam didn't actually work, breaking and flooding the Mongol camp instead, the Western Xia were frightened enough by the Mongol forces that Li Anchaun decided to make peace. He bought Genghis Khan off with tribute and a royal marriage to one of his daughters.

8. What happened when Genghis Khan and the Mongols attacked the Jin capital of Zhongdu in 1214?

A7.—Pg. 199, ¶ 7—When Genghis Kahn and the Mongols attacked Zhongdu in 1214 the Jin emperor retreated quickly to his southern headquarters, the old Song capital of Kaifeng, leaving a governor in charge of the city. This was not a popular move and the Jin troops scattered, disgusted by what they saw as a cowardly retreat. Many of the Jin fighters joined the Mongols and brought with them even more knowledge about warring against an empire.

9 . How did the Mongols conduct themselves after the Zhongdu governor took poison and the city's defenses collapsed?

A8.—Pg. 200, ¶ 1 & 2—Once Zhongdu became defenseless, the Mongol besiegers broke into the city and spread through its streets, murdering, looting, and burning. The Mongols treated the city as they would have treated a conquered tribe; though they had become skilled conductors of war, they had no experience as victors over a sedentary people, and they destroyed Zhongdu. Much of the city burned and thousands were killed, their corpses piled in huge heaps outside the walls.

Section III: Critical Thinking

The student may not use his text to answer this question.

In this chapter we read about the rapid growth of the Mongol state. Temujin turned into Genghis Khan and he created a huge mobile government that traveled with him wherever he went. Yet, the increasing sophistication of the Mongols did not outweigh their nomadic and warring background.

In fact, these roots often helped the Mongols in their conquests. Write a paragraph or two explaining how the rough background of the Mongols aided in their quest to build an empire.

Like the Western Xia, the Mongols wanted to grow into a more civilized people. Genghis Kahn adopted a written language, kept state records, and created a centralized government. But the warring roots of the Mongols often helped them in their quest to be a settled and serious people. When Genghis Kahn was attacked by Li Anchaun at the mountain pass north of Chung-hsing, he was stuck. Then, as written on page 199, "Only when they resorted to their traditional mode of fighting—pretending to withdraw, drawing the Western Xia forces out of their entrenched position to follow, and then closing around them to fight in the open—were they able to drive the Xia army away from the pass." The old fighting tactics of the Mongols helped them to beat the Western Xia. When the Mongols got to Chung-hsing, Genghis Khan ordered his soldiers to dam the nearby branch of the Yellow river, hoping to flood the capital out. While the dam didn't work—it broke and flooded the Mongol camp—Li Anchaun was so intimidated by the Mongols that he felt he couldn't fight them alone. When the Jin emperor Weishaowang refused to send help to the Western Xia, Li Anchaun made peace with the Mongols. Using brute intimidation helped the Mongols get an advantage over the Western Xia.

Next, the Mongols attacked the Jin. It took the Mongols four years to reach the northern Jin capital of Zhongdu. The fighting was hard and uncomfortable. Again, the Mongols' background helped them to survive. The Mongols were used to being uncomfortable. They had always lived on the move, so traveling slowly across Jin land, warring their way to the capital, was commonplace to them. Troops made of farmers and bakers led by barons and lords surely would have given up long before reaching their enemy's capital. Not only did the Mongols thrive as they worked their way across the Jin empire, they learned. The learned how to besiege a walled city, how to withstand an attack of heavily armed infantry, and how to drive an entrenched force backward. These new skills, coupled with what the Mongols already knew about the nomadic and warring lifestyle, made it impossible for the Jin to beat them and helped the Mongols build their empire.

EXAMPLE ANSWER:

The warring roots of the Mongols often helped them in their quest to build an empire. When Genghis Kahn was attacked by Li Anchaun at the mountain pass north of Chung-hsing, he was stuck. When he guided his men to their traditional mode of fighting, the Mongols were successful. The Mongols pretended to withdraw, which made the Western Xia follow them, making room for the Mongols to close around their enemy and fight in the open. When the Mongols got to Chung-hsing, Genghis Khan ordered his soldiers to dam the nearby branch of the Yellow river, hoping to flood the capital out. While the dam didn't work—it broke and flooded the Mongol camp—Li Anchaun was so intimidated by the Mongols that he felt he couldn't fight them alone. When the Jin emperor Weishaowang refused to send help to the Western Xia, Li Anchaun made peace with the Mongols. Using brute intimidation helped the Mongols get an advantage over the Western Xia.

Next, the Mongols attacked the Jin. It took the Mongols four years to reach the northern Jin capital of Zhongdu. The fighting was hard and uncomfortable. Again, the Mongols' background helped them to survive. The Mongols were used to being uncomfortable. They had always lived on the move, so traveling slowly across Jin land, warring their way to the capital, was second nature to them. Not only did the Mongols thrive as they worked their way across the Jin empire, they learned how to besiege a walled city, how to withstand an

attack of heavily armed infantry, and how to drive an entrenched force backward. These new skills, coupled with what the Mongols already knew about the nomadic and warring lifestyle, made it impossible for the Jin to beat them and helped the Mongols build their empire.

Section IV: Map Exercise

1. Trace the outline of the rectangular frame of Map 27.1 in black.

2. Trace the coastline in blue (just a little). Also trace the line of the Yellow River. Repeat until the contours are familiar.

3. Trace the areas of the Western Xia, the Jin, and the Southern Song in contrasting colors. Trace mountains with small peaks. Repeat until the contours are familiar.

4. Using a new sheet of paper, trace the rectangular outline of the frame in black. Using your regular pencil with an eraser, draw the coastline. Then draw the line of the Yellow River. Then draw the areas of the Western Xia, the Jin, and the Southern Song. Show the mountains with small peaks. When you are happy with your map, lay it over the original. Erase and redraw any lines that are more than ¼″ off of the original.

5. Now study the Altai, Khentil, and Goryeo areas. Then study the locations of Zhongdu, Chunghsing, Kaifeng, and Yangzhou. When they are familiar for you, close the book, and mark and label them on your map. Check them against the original, and erase and remark any that are more than ¼″ off of the original.

6. Finally, study the movements of Ghangis Khan: the Negotiations 1209, Dominance 1209, Initial invasion 1210, and Initial Invasion 1211. Also study the location of Lake Baikal and Burkhan Khaldun, the birthplace of Genghis Khan. When they are familiar for you, close the book, and mark and label them on your map. Check them against the original, and erase and remark any that are more than ¼″ off of the original.

Chapter Twenty-Eight

John Softsword

The student may use her text when answering the questions in sections I and II.

Section I: Who, What, Where

Write a one or two-sentence answer explaining the significance of each item listed below.

Arthur—**Pg. 202, ❡ 3 and Pg. 203, ❡ 1—Arthur, son of Geoffrey and Constance, claimed by Philip to be the rightful king of England, took refuge in Philip's court. Arthur was captured by the king of England's, his uncle John's, men and then he disappeared, allegedly slain by the king himself.**

Constance—Pg. 202, ❡ 3—**Constance, wife of the late Geoffrey of England, had two daughters and one son, named Arthur, with her husband. Constance took refuge in King Philip of France's court after he insisted Arthur, not John, was the rightful king of England.**

Isabella of Angoulême—**Pg. 202, ❡ 4—Isabella of Angoulême, daughter of the Count of Angoulême, was betrothed to the Count of Marche. John divorced his wife and then negotiated his marriage to the young Isabella with the Count of Angoulême.**

Simon de Montfort—**Pg. 205, ❡ 4—Simon de Montfort, suspected by John of being a vassal of the king of France, inherited the English title Earl of Leicester from his uncle even though he himself was born near Paris, son of the Count of Montfort-l'Amaury. John allowed Simon de Montfort to keep his inherited title but he did not allow him to keep the lands that came with the title, taking them for himself.**

Stephen Langton—**Pg. 204, ❡ 2—Stephen Langton was made the Archbishop of Canterbury by Pope Innocent III without asking King John for approval. John used Langton's appointment as an excuse to seize all of Canterbury's estates, and their revenue, for himself.**

Section II: Comprehension

Write a two or three-sentence answer to each of the following questions.

1. What happened between John and Philip after Richard the Lionheart's death? How did Philip once again disrupt English family affairs?

A1.—Pg. 202, ¶ 2 & 3—Philip ceased to be John's ally after Richard the Lionheart's death; he only allied himself with the Englishman to bother the English king. Philip riled the English family by claiming that Arthur, son born of Geoffrey seven months after his death, was the rightful king of England. Soon the dukes of English-held Anjou, Maine, and Tours joined the French king, Constance, and Arthur, who had taken refuge in Philip's court, in rejecting John's claim to the throne.

2. Why did John want to marry Isabella of Angoulême? What enemy did John make after arranging his marriage to the young French girl?

A2.—Pg. 202, ¶ 4—John recognized that French strength was growing against him, so he divorced his first wife for failure to bear him an heir in 1199, and in 1200 set his sights on Isabella of Angoulême, the young daughter of the Count of Angoulême. Isabella was already betrothed to the son of the Count of Marche, a marriage that would have created a strong, French-loyal enclave right in the middle of the land John wanted for himself. The Count of Angoulême gave Isabella in marriage to John which turned the Count of Marche into another of John's enemies.

3. How did John start to refill the treasury after his coronation and during his war in Western Francia?

A3.—Pg. 203, ¶ 5 & 6—After his coronation John accepted numerous bribes and payments from men who already held royal office and hoped to keep it under the new regime, and from towns and officials that hoped for "goodwill," "peace," and "loving treatment." While John was fighting in Western Francia he collected a fee called "scutage" from the English barons. Instead of going to war, a baron could buy the right to stay at home with a cash payment; John had been collecting the scutage fee since 1199.

4. What strategy did John use to refill his treasury after the war in Western Francia ended?

A4.—Pg. 203, ¶ 7 to Pg. 204, ¶ 1—When the war in Western Francia ended John could no longer collect scutage fees. He switched strategies and went after the church. In 1207 he called the bishops and abbots of England to a council in London and informed them that all of the priests and parsons in England would be required to pay taxes on the revenue from all church-held land.

5. How did John justify seizing the Archbishop of Canterbury's estates and their revenue for himself?

A5.—Pg. 204, ¶ 2 to Pg. 205, ¶ 1—Pope Innocent III, without asking John for approval, had chosen Stephen Langton to fill the role of Archbishop of Canterbury. John did not accept this appointment, telling the pope that he knew nothing of Langton except that the man had

"dwelt much among his enemies," that he was incensed that Innocent had not asked for his consent to the appointment, and that he would stand up for the rights of his crown "even to death." Then, John refused to allow Langton to enter England, and confiscated all of Canterbury's estates and their revenue for himself.

6. What happened after Pope Innocent III put England under interdict?

A6.—Pg. 205, ¶ 2 & 3—After Pope Innocent III put England under interdict John confiscated more church property, under the excuse that the clergy who held the property only did so on condition that they perform their job, which they obviously could not do because they weren't working under the interdict. Though John profited from the interdict, the people suffered. Church services ceased and the bodies of the dead were carried out of cities and towns and buried in roads and ditches without the prayers of the priests.

7. Describe the decision John made about the Jews living in England in 1210. Why did he make this decision? How did John treat other religious clergy?

A7.—Pg. 205, ¶ 5—In 1210 John ordered all the Jews in England imprisoned. He imprisoned the Jews so that he could take all of their money for himself. John continued to exploit other religious clergy, locking up their corn so that he could keep the revenue.

8. How did John respond to the rapidly growing resentment against him?

A8.—Pg. 205, ¶ 6—John responded to the rapidly growing resentment against him not by reforming his financial policies but by creating a personal guard. He grew very paranoid, suspecting everyone around him. He went everywhere armed to fight, protected by men that were also armed and ready to fight.

Section III: Critical Thinking

The student may not use her text to answer this question.

Nicknames can be endearing and they can also be cruel. Often nicknames show us something of our true nature. Explain how the military actions of King John of England earned him the nickname "Johannem Mollegladium," or John Softsword. In your answer, explain what you think the nickname means.

The start of John's reign was rough. As soon as he became king of England, his old friend Philip, king of France, turned against him. Philip was only friendly with John when it upset the sitting king. Now that John was king, Philip had to find a way to mess with his reign. Philip claimed that Geoffrey's son Arthur was the rightful king of England, thus dividing the family and gathering the support of three dukes of English-held land in Western Francia. John could not hold on to his family, nor could he hold on to his allies.

Various battles followed, as did negotiations and temporary truces. John tried a marriage bind as a way to gain more power in France, divorcing his first wife and taking the twelve-year-old (or maybe even younger) Isabella of Angoulême as his wife. Though John broke up a potential French-loyal enclave in the middle of the French land he wanted for himself, he still couldn't regain power. By 1203, he had lost almost every English possession in Western Francia.

John muddled up another opportunity to gain ground against the French king when he captured nearly two hundred French knights in Poitiers; one of those men was his nephew Arthur, the key to Philip's fight against England. Something happened to Arthur after he was captured. He was sent to Rouen where he was to be guarded. But, he disappeared. John was suspected of killing Arthur himself. Public opinion turned against John; Philip may have lost an important part of his strategy against the English, but John did himself more harm than good by losing his nephew. Arthur's disappearance joined with John's inability to finish the sieges he had begun or to relieve English-held castles under French attack made the king a laughingstock. The French had begun to call him "Johannem Mollegladium," or John Softsword. The nickname implied that John was a weak man, unable to defend his land or his people. His sword—his fighting strategy and military prowess—was ineffective. Late in 1203, John deserted Normandy. He had lost all of the land in Western Francia that belonged to his father. His nickname accurately reflected his inability to fight for and keep his land.

EXAMPLE ANSWER:

John fought against king Philip of France from the very beginning of his reign. First, Philip ditched his friendship with John and made an alliance with Arthur, John's nephew. Philip said that Arthur was the rightful heir to the English throne, thus dividing the family and gathering support of three dukes of English-held land in Western Francia. John could not hold on to his family, nor to his allies. The fight between the two men continued for three years. John tried a marriage bind as a way to gain more power in France, divorcing his first wife and taking the twelve-year-old Isabella of Angoulême as his wife. Though John broke up a potential French-loyal enclave in the middle of the French land he wanted for himself, he still couldn't regain power. By 1203, he had lost almost every English possession in Western Francia.

John muddled up another opportunity to gain ground against the French king when he captured his nephew Arthur, the key to Philip's fight against England. Arthur was sent to Rouen where he was to be guarded. But, he disappeared. John was suspected of killing Arthur himself. Public opinion turned against John. Arthur's disappearance joined with John's inability to finish the sieges he had begun or to relieve English-held castles under French attack made the king a laughingstock. The French had begun to call him "Johannem Mollegladium," or John Softsword. The nickname implied that John was a weak man, unable to defend his land or his people. His sword—his fighting strategy and military prowess—was ineffective. Late in 1203, John deserted Normandy. He had lost all of the land in Western Francia that belonged to his father. His nickname accurately reflected his inability to fight for and keep his land.

Chapter Twenty-Nine

Sundiata of the Mali

The student may use his text when answering the questions in sections I and II.

Section I: Who, What, Where

Write a one or two-sentence answer explaining the significance of each item listed below.

Epic of Sundiata—**Pg. 207, ¶ 2 and Pg. 209, ¶ 3—*Epic of Sundiata,* told for centuries by professional bards called griots, is an African oral history that includes the story of how Sosso king Sumanguru overran Kumbi-Saleh and took Ghana for himself. The epic also tells the story of Sundiata as the Islamic hero that was victorious in the war against Sumanguru.**

Griots—**Pg. 207, ¶ 2—Griots were professional African bards. It is through the griots' retelling of the oral history *Epic of Sundiata* that we know of Sumanguru and Sundiata.**

Keita—**Pg. 207, ¶ 3 to Pg. 208, ¶ 2—Keita were a Muslim clan in the Malinke tribe that challenged Sumanguru's power.**

Nare Fa Maghan—**Pg. 208, ¶ 2—Nare Fa Maghan, king of the Keita when Sumanguru took over Ghana, led his people in revolt against the Sosso king. Sometime around 1217, Sumanguru's armies sacked the capital city of the Keita nine separate times and each time the Keita, under Nare Fa Maghan, regathered themselves and again rebelled.**

Sundiata—**Pg. 208, ¶ 6 and Pg. 209, ¶ 1-3—Sundiata was made Keita king in 1230, and after an aggressive campaign against the Sosso, Sundiata seized control of the old Ghana lands, claimed Kumbi-Saleh as his own, and established his own empire, known as Mali. Sundiata continued to conquer outlying territories until Mali stretched past Ghana's old boundaries to unite a new expanse of western African land.**

Section II: **Comprehension**

Write a two or three-sentence answer to each of the following questions.

1. Why was control over Ghana so desired by African leaders?

A1.—Pg. 207, ¶ 3—Control over Ghana was so desired by African leaders because the heartland of Ghana was fertile and abundant. The ground was watered by both rivers and sweet wells, with plenty of fish, elephants, giraffes, rice, and sorghum for all. In addition, the thirteenth-century cosmologist al-Qazwini wrote that the area was so full of gold that it "grows in the sand of this country as carrots do in our land, and the people come out at sunrise to pluck the gold."

2. What brought the Muslim faith to the Keita?

A2.—Pg. 208, ¶ 2—The Keita had traded up the Niger river valley, through the central trade route that led to Tunis, for generations. The northern goods that came back down to Africa were accompanied by Islamic beliefs, thus bringing the Muslim faith to the Keita clan.

3. How did Nare Fa Maghan's successor handle the conflict between the Keita and the Sosso? What did this mean for the reach of Sumanguru's power?

A3.—Pg. 208, ¶ 3—Nare Fa Maghan's successor decided to make peace with the Sosso. In addition to submitting to the Sosso, the Keita king handed over his sister in marriage to Sumanguru. The submission of the Keita meant that, for a time, the Sosso controlled almost all of the old Ghana territory.

4. How did the Keita use the marriage treaty made with the Sosso to undo their rival clan?

A4.—Pg. 208, ¶ 5 & 6—According to the *Epic of Sundiata,* Sumanguru's bride tried to wheedle out of him, on their wedding night, the secret of his invulnerability on the battlefield: "What is it that can kill you?" she said, before allowing him to lay a hand on her. The bride finds out that Sumanguru's secret is witchcraft and that Sumanguru is a practitioner of the dark arts. The bride runs away from Sumanguru and tells her brothers what she has discovered; Sundiata, the king's younger brother, uses the knowledge to destroy Sumanguru.

5. In what way does the *Epic of Sundiata* reflect religious tensions between the Keita and the Sosso? Explain what real world circumstances caused the Keita to view Sumanguru as a religious enemy.

A5.—Pg. 208, ¶ 6 & 7—The *Epic of Sundiata* reflects religious tensions between the Islamic Keita and the non-Muslim Sosso in its depiction as Sumanguru as a practitioner of the dark arts. The sorcery attributed to Sumanguru was a result of his hostility towards Islam, refusing to allow his people to observe Muslim practices and executing Muslims who fell into his hands. In addition, Sumanguru fought against the custom practiced by the Keita of selling slaves into Islamic lands and as a result he drove Muslim merchants from every territory he conquered.

6. Describe the destruction of Sumanguru's kingdom.

A6.—Pg. 208, ¶ 8 to Pg. 209, ¶ 1—Sundiata had little trouble gathering allies to fight against Sumanguru, especially because of Sumanguru's hostility towards Muslims. A long and catastrophic civil war began; by 1235, Sundiata's allies had driven Sumanguru's army backwards to his capital city and by 1240 Sumanguru had fled, his empire in fragments, and his palace burned to the ground by Sundiata's men. Sundiata seized control of the old Ghana lands, claimed Kumbi-Saleh as his own, and established his own empire.

7. In what way was Sundiata's success dependent on the African slave trade?

A7.—Pg. 208, ¶ 7 & 8 and Pg. 209, ¶ 4—Sundiata was able to gather supporters to fight with him against Sumanguru because many African kings supported the custom of selling slaves into Islamic lands. In Kumbi-Saleh, under Sundiata's rule, the slave market grew larger and busier. Slave traders came down the central trade route to Sundiata's new capital city, Niani, and as a result his kingdom, Mali, grew richer and richer.

Section III: Critical Thinking

The student may not use his text to answer this question.

What is a *jinn*? In the excerpt of the *Epic of Sundiata*, Sumanguru's father is called a *jinn*. After looking up the word *jinn*, use what you know from the chapter about how the Keita viewed Sumanguru and write a paragraph explaining why this detail was included in the epic. Also explain how Sumanguru's ruthlessness, as portrayed in the excerpt from the chapter given on page 207, is tied to the word *jinn*.

Excerpt of the Epic of Sundiata *from page 207 of the text:*

He was skilled in warfare . . .
His father was a jinn,
His mother was a human being. . . .
The authority of kingship was given to him;
His power as a king was great;
He used to make hats out of human skin,
He used to make sandals out of human skin.

The student should start by looking up the word jinn. *There are several interpretations of the word, depending on the context in which it is found, so it is important that the student find its meaning as related to African and Muslim cultures. In general, the student should find that* jinn *means "genie." As the student learned in the chapter, the* Epic of Sundiata *claims that Sumanguru was a practitioner of the dark arts, or witchcraft. The epic gives us the lineage of the dark arts in Sumanguru's bloodline by telling us his father was a genie.*

The excerpt of the poem ties Sumanguru's "authority" as a "great" king with both the magic of his father's bloodline and cruel power, telling us he made "hats" and "sandals" out of human skin. In some African myths, jinn are said to want to possess human beings, which would relate to Sumanguru's penchant for human skin. The epic suggests that Sumanguru used humans as accessories because he was more than human; he was part jinn, *a magical creature that looked at the value of human lives as lesser than his own kingly greatness.*

EXAMPLE ANSWER:

In the African heritage the word "jinn" means genie. In the *Epic of Sundiata* we are told that Sumanguru is a practitioner of the dark arts, or witchcraft. It is only after his Keita bride finds out about his secret that the Keita are able to overpower him. The epic gives us the lineage of the dark arts in Sumanguru's bloodline by telling us his father was a genie. The excerpt of the epic we read in the chapter ties Sumanguru's "authority" as a "great" king with both the magic of his father's bloodline and cruel power, telling us he made "hats" and "sandals" out of human skin. The epic also ties Sumanguru's penchant for wearing human skin back to the dark arts because in some African myths jinn are said to want to possess human beings. The epic suggests that Sumanguru used humans as accessories because he was more than human; he was part jinn, a magical creature that looked at the value of human lives as lesser than his own kingly greatness.

Section IV: **Map Exercise**

1. Using your black pencil, trace the rectangular outline of the frame for map 29.1 in black.

2. Using your blue pencil, trace the coastline. Also trace the line of the Niger and the Senegal. Using contrasting colors, trace the outlines of the separate territories of the Sosso, the Mali, and the Old Ghanan Empire. Repeat until the contours are familiar.

3. Using a new sheet of paper, trace the rectangular outline of the frame in black. Using your regular pencil with an eraser, draw the coastline. Also draw the line of the Niger and the Senegal and the outlines of the separate territories of the Sosso, the Mali, and the Old Ghanan Empire.

4. When you are happy with your map, lay it over the original. Erase and redraw any lines that are more than ¼″ off of the original.

5. Now study carefully the locations of Niani, Gao, Kumbi Saleh, and Mani. Study also the Central Trade Route to Tunis. When they are familiar, close the book, and mark and label them on your map. Check them against the original, and erase and remark any that are more than ¼″ off of the original.

Chapter Thirty

The Jokyu War

The student may use her text when answering the questions in sections I and II.

Section I: Who, What, Where

Write a one or two-sentence answer explaining the significance of each item listed below.

Bakufu—Pg. 211, ¶ 5—*Bakufu* was the Japanese word for the system of government run by the shogunate. In particular, *bakufu* was used to describe the shogunate at Kamakura.

Go-Horikawa—Pg. 215, ¶ 1—Go-Horikawa was made emperor and placed on the Chrysanthemum Throne by Masako and Yoshitoki after the Jokyu War.

Go-Takakura—Pg. 214, ¶ 5 to Pg. 215, ¶ 1—Go-Takakura, Go-Toba's half-brother, was made Cloistered Emperor by Masako and Yoshitoki after the Jokyu War.

Goseibai shikimoku (regulation)—Pg. 212, ¶ 4—*Goseibai shikimoku*, one of the first laws issued by the *bakufu* at Kamakura, stated "No person, even one whose family have been hereditary vassals of the shogun for generations, shall be able to mobilize troops for military service without a current writ." Sanctioned violence, as defined in the regulation *Goseibai shikimoku*, would remain the exclusive right of the shogunate for the next century and a half.

Goseibai Shikimoku (book)—Pg. 215, ¶ 3 & 4—*Goseibai Shikimoku* was a single, disorganized lawbook put together by Yasutoki made up of fifty-one unconnected regulations that governed the Kamakura shogunate. The *Goseibai Shikimoku* concluded with the promise that the members of shogunate would disregard family ties and would act based on reason, without fear of retaliation from colleagues or powerful families.

Hojo Masako—Pg. 213, ¶ 2 & 3 and Pg. 215, ¶ 1 & 2—Hojo Masako, Minamoto Yoritomo's widow, rebelled against her father and took over rule of the shogunate with her brother Yoshitoki. Masako and Yoshitoki beat Go-Toba during the Jokyu War and as a result they increased shogunate power in the west.

Hojo Tokimasa—Pg. 212, ¶ 5 and Pg. 213, ¶ 3—Hojo Tokimasa, father of Minamoto Yoritomo's widow and grandfather to Minamoto Yoriie, declared himself *shikken* and then placed his grandson under house arrest. Hojo Tokimasa was exiled to the eastern province of Izu by his children after he had Minamoto Yoriie assassinated and was suspected of plotting the murder of his other grandchild Sanetomo.

Juntoku—Pg. 214, ¶ 4—Juntoku was the son of Go-Toba and was the reigning emperor at the time of the samurai attack on Kyoto. Juntoku was exiled to an island separate from his father after the Jokyu War.

Minamoto Yoriie—Pg. 212, ¶ 5 & 7—Minamoto Yoriie, son of Minamoto Yoritomo, followed his father as shogun in 1202 at the age of twenty, though his grandfather Hojo Tokimasa declared himself Minamoto Yoriie's *shikken* and the young shogun was placed under house arrest. When Minamoto Yoriie refused to fade meekly into the background, Hojo Tokimasa had him assassinated.

Sanetomo—Pg. 213, ¶ 2 & 4—Sanetomo, Minamoto Yoriie's younger brother, was made shogun by Hojo Tokimasa after he had Minamoto Yoriie killed. Sanetomo's life was saved when Yoshitoki became *shikken*, but the young man, who became increasingly paranoid and drowned his fears in wine, was assassinated in 1219 by his own nephew, son of Minamoto Yoriie, for vengeance's sake.

Shikken—Pg. 212, ¶ 5—*Shikken* was the Japanese word for Regent of the Shogun. In 1203, Hojo Tokimasa set up a thirteen-man council to assume the power of the shogunate and the title of *shikken* was created, giving Hojo Tokimasa the ultimate power of the regency.

Yasutoki—Pg. 215, ¶ 3—Yasutoki, son of Yoshitoki, became the third *shikken* after his father died in 1224. He was an experienced solider, well-liked and wise, and he spent his time as *shikken* creating the layers of administration that the shogunate lacked: inventing new positions for secretaries and executives, constructing a hierarchy of councils and committees, and collecting into a single lawbook the laws that would govern the Kamakura shogunate.

Yoshitoki—Pg. 213, ¶ 3 and Pg. 215, ¶ 1 & 2—Yoshitoki, Hojo Masako's older brother, worked with his sister to exile their father Hojo Tokimasa after which Yoshitoki took the title of *shikken*. Yoshitoki and his sister Masako beat Go-Toba during the Jokyu War and as a result they increased shogunate power in the west.

Section II: **Comprehension**

Write a two or three-sentence answer to each of the following questions.

1. Why couldn't the Kamakura *bakufu* replace the ancient authority of the Japanese emperor in Kyoto?

A1.—Pg. 211, ¶ 5 to Pg. 212, ¶ 1—The Kamakura *bakufu*, created by Minamoto Yoritomo, did not command the sort of administrative network needed to run a country. His warriors were still banded together in traditional uneven clusters, owing loyalty to different lords and obligations to different clans. Because there was no accepted military structure and there were no clear lines of command, the Kamakura *bakufu* could not replace the ancient authority of the emperor in Kyoto.

2. How did Minamoto Yoritomo work around the Kamakura bakufu's inability to take all power completely from the emperor?

A2.—Pg. 212, ¶ 3—Minamoto Yoritomo knew that he had to get the emperor to work with the Kamakura *bakufu* in order to establish and keep shogunate power in Japan. Minamoto Yoritomo received official, imperial recognition of his Kamakura-based military government in the east from Go-Shirakawa in 1185. The emperor retained his ritual importance; the cloistered emperor maintained his administrative authority; and the shogun at Kamakura was given the power to use force.

3. After the establishment of the shogunate, what were the official ruling positions in the Japanese imperial government and the Kamakura *bakufu*? Why did the court priest Jien write in the *Gukansho* that it was "strange" for Go-Toba to be in power by himself?

A3.—Pg. 212, ¶ 6 and Pg. 213, ¶ 6—The official ruling positions in the Japanese imperial government were the emperor, who did not exercise actual authority, and the Cloistered Emperor, who administered state affairs. The official ruling offices in the Kamakura *bakufu* were the shogun, who did not actually rule, and the *shikken*, who actually made the decisions for the shogun. Go-Toba ruled for six years as emperor without a Cloistered Emperor, and Jien found that odd, writing that it was "strange" to have "no Retired Emperor" administering the affairs of the state.

4. Why did Go-Toba retire to the role of Cloistered Emperor in 1198?

A4.—Pg. 213, ¶ 7 to Pg. 214, ¶ 1—Go-Toba retired to the role of Cloistered Emperor in 1198 because he wanted real power; he gave the throne to his toddler son and began to conduct state affairs in his own way. As Cloistered Emperor, Go-Toba controlled court appointments, he approved or denied requests for promotions, and he managed domestic crises. Most importantly, he was able to arrange for his own young son, rather than the future heir of the reigning emperor, to become Crown Prince.

5. How did the Japanese emperor's seat acquire the nickname the "Chrysanthemum Throne"?

A5.—Pg. 213, ¶ 7 to Pg. 214, ¶ 1—When Go-Toba became Cloistered Emperor, he arranged for his son to be the Crown Prince, rather than the heir of the reigning emperor. Go-Toba's

personal crest, a double flower with sixteen petals, was later adopted by the Japanese court as a symbol of the imperial right to rule. From this crest, the emperor's seat acquired the nickname the Chrysanthemum Throne.

6. Why did Go-Toba want to go to war against Yoshitoki and Masako?

A6.—Pg. 214, ¶ 2—Go-Toba believed that Yoshitoki and Masako intended to split Japan in half: two countries, one ruled by emperor, the other by shogun. He also heard gossip that the samurai were tired of the dominance of the Hojo, the clan of Yoshitoki and Masako. Go-Toba could take care of his own suspicions about Yoshitoki and Masako's plan to divide Japan by using the support of the samurai who were fed up of their rule.

7. What happened when Go-Toba's plans to attack the shogunate were found out?

A7.— Pg. 214, ¶ 2 & 3—When Go-Toba's plans to attack the shogunate were found out, he ordered his imperial retainers to attack the shogun's representative in Kyoto, an inoffensive deputy who panicked and disemboweled himself when he saw the emperor's men bearing down on him. In retaliation, Yoshitoki ordered a great number of samurai to march on Kyoto. Go-Toba had the bridges destroyed in their way, but the shogunate's attack was short and devastating, quickly defeating the imperial army and causing dismay and confusion among people of all ranks.

Section III: Critical Thinking

The student may not use her text to answer this question.

Minamoto Yoritomo took a great risk when he established shogunate rule of Japan. Explain the gamble Minamoto Yoritomo took and why taking this risk was necessary for the establishment of the shogunate. In your answer, use the Jokyu War as an example of how the skills of the samurai helped them to gain power.

The student can refresh herself on the details of the establishment of shogunate rule in Japan by reading over Chapter 23. An overview of the gamble Minamoto Yoritomo took when he established the power of the shogun can be found in this chapter on page 211.

Samurai were very powerful; their expertise in fighting determined the outcome of wars. But they always worked in service of someone else, like a government minister, a clan leader, or an ambitious official. Minamoto Yoritomo knew that the collective power of the samurai could be stronger than the power of the people telling the samurai what to fight for, but he had to promise the samurai something in return before asking them to fight for him.

Up until Yoritomo's leadership, the samurai had not been able to breach Japanese bureaucratic hierarchy and declare what issues they thought were worth fighting over. In order to get the samurai to fight for him against the reigning power structure of the Japanese government, Minamoto Yoritomo had to promise the samurai something that he did not yet have; he said that if they swore an oath of allegiance to him, he would guarantee them the estates, the titles and the offices of those in power. When he made this promise to the samurai, he did not have the jurisdiction to give away any of these estates or titles. He needed the samurai to fight for him so that he could take these prizes and then give them to the samurai in return. It was a huge gamble.

The samurai were great fighters. As we have seen across history, kings could force their citizens to fight for them, but thousands of farmers and merchants—unskilled at warfare—were often easily defeated by smaller numbers of experienced fighters. In this chapter we see Yoshitoki and Masako fight against Go-Toba's great army in the Jokyu War. Despite Go-Toba's defenses, the shogunate was able to make a quick, devastating attack against the city, take Go-Toba and Juntoku captive, appoint their own Cloistered Emperor, and place their own choice of emperor on the Chrysanthemum Throne. They were also able to install representatives throughout Kyoto so that they could direct the new royal family. The skill of the samurai fighters enabled them to infiltrate the bureaucratic framework of the imperial government. None of this would have been possible without Minamoto Yoritomo's initial gamble: he established shogunate rule, and then the samurai were able to use their skill as fighters to beat the imperial army in the Jokyu War, gain strength in the west, and tip power towards the shogun.

EXAMPLE ANSWER:

Before Minamoto Yoritomo came into power, samurai had not been able to breach Japanese bureaucratic hierarchy and declare what issues they thought were worth fighting over. When he started his rebellion, Minamoto Yoritomo told the samurai that if they swore an oath of allegiance to him, he would guarantee them the estates, the titles and the offices of those in power. When he made this promise to the samurai, he did not have the jurisdiction to give away any of these estates or titles. He needed the samurai to fight for him so that he could take these prizes and then give them to the samurai in return. It was a huge gamble.

The samurai were great fighters and this enabled them to quickly win the Jokyu War. Despite Go-Toba's defenses, the shogunate was able to make a quick, devastating attack against Kyoto, take Go-Toba and Juntoku captive, appoint their own Cloistered Emperor, and place their own choice of emperor on the Chrysanthemum Throne. The leaders of the shogunate were also able to install representatives throughout Kyoto so that they could direct the new royal family. The skill of the samurai fighters enabled them to infiltrate the bureaucratic framework of the imperial government. None of this would have been possible without Minamoto Yoritomo's initial gamble: he established shogunate rule, and then the samurai were able to use their skill as fighters to beat the imperial army in the Jokyu War, gain strength in the west, and tip power towards the shogun.

Chapter Thirty-One

The Unwanted Throne

The student may use his text when answering the questions in sections I and II.

Section I: Who, What, Where

Write a one or two-sentence answer explaining the significance of each item listed below.

Alexius Comnenus—**Pg. 219, ¶ 7—Alexius Comnenus, the twenty-two-year-old grandson of the late Andronicus Comnenus, proclaimed himself emperor at Trebizond, on the shores of the Black Sea, in opposition to Baldwin, the Latin emperor of Constantinople.**

Boril—**Pg. 221, ¶ 4—Boril, Kaloyan's nephew and successor, was driven back from the Latin Empire's holdings in 1208 by Henry. Boril lost the southern Bulgarian city of Philippoupolis, which Henry then made part of the Latin Empire.**

Despot and Despotate—**Pg. 220, *—Despot was the title often given, in Byzantium, to a high official who was also heir presumptive to the imperial throne. A despotate was the land ruled by the despot.**

Henry—**Pg. 221, ¶ 4—Henry, Baldwin's brother, second ruler of the Latin Empire, managed to gain back some of the power that was lost with the death of Baldwin. He forced Theodore Lascaris of Nicaea to sign a temporary truce with Constantinople, he drove back the Bulgarians, capturing the southern Bulgarian city of Philippoupolis and making it part of the Latin Empire, and he forced the Despotate of Epirus to sign a peace treaty with Constantinople.**

John III Vatatzes—**Pg. 222, ¶ 2 to Pg. 223, ¶ 1—John III Vatatzes, Theodore Lascaris's son-in-law, took over rule of the Empire of Nicaea in 1222, after which he captured most of the Latin Empire's land south of the Sea of Marmara in 1224, and then in 1225 made a treaty with Robert that left the ruler of the Latin Empire with nothing but Constantinople. John III Vatatzes fought in the name of the true Constantinople, as evidenced by the coins he had minted for himself: on one side appeared the seated figure of Christ, and on the other, John III and the Virgin Mary clasped their hands over the scepter of Nicaea.**

Kaloyan—**Pg. 220, ❡ 3 & 4 and Pg. 221, ❡ 1 & 2—Kaloyan, one of three brothers that declared Bulgaria free after the death of Andronicus, fought his way into Thrace, and in 1204 had Innocent III crown him** *basileus*, **Emperor of the Bulgarians. Kaloyan chipped away at the Latin Empire after he led his troops in victory over the Crusader army outside of Adrianople in 1205.**

Michael—**Pg. 220, ❡ 1 and Pg. 221, ❡ 4—Michael, Alexius III's cousin, declared himself ruler over the northwestern Greek region known as Epirus in early 1205. Michael was forced by Henry to sign a peace treaty with Constantinople in 1211.**

Partitio Romaniae—**Pg. 217, ❡ 2 & 3—***Partitio Romaniae* **was the official treaty made between the Crusaders and the Venetian doge after the conclusion of the Fourth Crusade. The** *Partitio Romaniae* **divided Byzantium up between the Venetians and Crusaders, and a third realm was created for the French Crusader Boniface, Marquis of Monferrat.**

Peter—**Pg. 221, ❡ 5 & 6—Peter, Henry's brother-in-law, claimed the leadership of the Latin Empire in 1216 but as he journeyed from Western Francia to Constantinople, he was waylaid. Peter was taken prisoner by Theodore Comnenus Ducas and he was never heard from again.**

Philip—**Pg. 221, ❡ 8—Philip, Yolanda and Peter's oldest son, refused to take his father's place as emperor in Constantinople and stayed happily ensconced in Western Francia.**

Robert of Courtenay—**Pg. 221, ❡ 8 and Pg. 222, ❡ 3—Robert of Courtenay, Yolanda and Peter's second son, reluctantly accepted rule of the Latin Empire in 1221 after two years of delaying his decision. Robert had little drive to save the Latin Empire, and in 1225, he made a treaty with John III Vatatzes that left Robert with nothing but the city of Constantinople itself.**

Theodore Comnenus Ducas—**Pg. 221, ❡ 5—Theodore Comnenus Ducas, half-brother of Michael, took over the Despotate of Epirus after Michael's death. Theodore Comnenus Ducas hoped to challenge the Latin Empire for control of the lands near the Black Sea, and when he learned that the new Latin Emperor was attempting to pass through his lands on the way to Constantinople, he ordered him taken prisoner; Peter was never heard from again.**

Theodore Lascaris—**Pg. 219, ❡ 7 to Pg. 220, ❡ 1 and Pg. 222, ❡ 1—Theodore Lascaris, Alexius III's son-in-law, raised a rebellion against the Latin Emperor with the city of Nicaea as his headquarters late in 1204. Theodore Lascaris recentered Greek culture at Nicaea and was hailed by the Greek monk Acominatus as the "savior and universal liberator" of the people and city of Constantine.**

Yolanda—**Pg. 221, ❡ 6—Yolanda, wife of Peter, ruled the Latin Empire as his regent after his disappearance. She was known as the "Latin Empress Consort of Constantinople."**

Section II: Comprehension

Write a two or three-sentence answer to each of the following questions.

1. What were the terms of the *Partitio Romaniae*?

A1.—Pg. 217, ❡ 2 & 3—The *Partitio Romaniae* gave Baldwin I the entire Crusader share of Constantinople itself, which worked out to five-eighths of the city, plus Thrace, the northwest of Asia Minor, and a few outlying islands. The Venetians took three-eighths of the city of Constantinople for their own, plus the scattering of islands between Venice and the Dardanelles. A third realm was created especially for the French Crusader Boniface Marquis of Monferrat which was centered at Thessalonica; though subject to Baldwin of Constantinople, it was essentially Boniface's to run as he pleased.

2. Why was the French Crusader Boniface, Marquis of Monferrat, given his own realm after the sack of Constantinople?

A2.—Pg. 217, ❡ 3—The French Crusader Boniface, Marquis of Monferrat, was given his own realm after the end of the Fourth Crusade because the Crusaders were afraid that he might go home and take his soldiers with him. Boniface had a lot of support and lost the election to be emperor by a slim margin. He was given a realm as a consolation prize so that he might stay put in Byzantium.

3. How did the king killer and traitor Mourtzouphlus (Alexius V Ducas) finally meet his end?

A3.—Pg. 219, ❡ 1-3—Mourtzouphlus attempted to join forces with Alexius III, who welcomed him with deceptive friendship, only to have Mourtzouphlus seized and blinded in the middle of the night. Not long after, Mourtzouphlus escaped and was captured by Baldwin's men as he stumbled sightless through the countryside. Baldwin, wanting to make an example of the man who lifted his hand against God-appointed authority, took Mourtzouphlus to the top of a column and made the traitor leap off so that when his body hit the earth he was "all shattered and broken."

4. Why was it hard for Baldwin to maintain unified control over Byzantium?

A4.—Pg. 219, ❡ 5 & 6— Baldwin may have had control over Constantinople, but the people of the eastern empire of Byzantium saw the western Crusaders as aliens: "Latins" instead of "Greeks," speakers of alien tongues, holding allegiance to a different Church. Since 1054, the Christians in the east had recognized the bishop of Constantinople, the Patriarch, as their head, but the new Latin emperor was loyal to the pope in Rome. At the time of the Crusader takeover, a Venetian "Patriarch" had been appointed by the victors to replace the native head of the eastern church, bringing it back under the authority of the pope; as a result the Greek bishops had been forced to swear obedience to Rome, which deepened the eastern resentment of the western Crusaders.

5. What circumstances brought Emperor Baldwin and the Doge of Venice to work together to save Byzantium?

A5.—Pg. 220, ¶ 2—Emperor Baldwin's power was challenged by three Greek states—the Empire of Trebizond, the Empire of Nicaea, and the Despotate of Epirus—each one ruled by Byzantine royalty, each king claiming to be the rightful successor to the Byzantine crown and the loyal protector of the Greek Orthodox Church. As the Greeks gained more power they acted more aggressively towards the Franks, killing them and then occupying their land. Baldwin and the Doge of Venice came together because they saw that they were losing all of their land to the conflict.

6. What happened to Bulgaria after the death of Andronicus?

A6.—Pg. 220, ¶ 3 & 4—After the death of Andronicus, three Bulgarian brothers that claimed to have descended from the family of the former kings raised a private army and declared Bulgaria free again. Their "empire" consisted only of a small patch of land on the southern banks of the Danube, and within a decade the older two brothers, Peter and Asen, had been assassinated by other Bulgarian rivals. But the third brother, Kaloyan, fought his way into Thrace, and in 1204 had talked Innocent III into crowning him *basileus*, Emperor of the Bulgarians.

7. How did the Latin moment of dominance over Byzantium start to unravel?

A7.—Pg. 220, ¶ 6 to Pg. 221, ¶ 2—In April 1205, Baldwin I met Kaloyan on the plain outside of Adrianople; the Crusaders were badly outmaneuvered by the lightly armed, mobile Bulgarian army. A score of Crusader knights were taken prisoner, many more were killed on the field, and Baldwin I himself was captured, his exact fate unknown (although the rumor was that Kaloyan himself killed Baldwin and turned his skull into a goblet). With its emperor dead and its leaders in chains, the Latin army retreated from Adrianople, beginning the end of the Latin moment of dominance over the old Byzantine empire.

8. How did Greek culture thrive under Theodore Lascaris?

A8.—Pg. 222, ¶ 1—Theodore Lascaris killed the sultan of Rum, added Paphlagonia to his dominions and annexed part of the Empire of Trebizond, enlarging his kingdom of Nicaea further. The senior churchman in his empire, the Patriarch of Nicaea, had begun to act as the head of the Greek church, taking it on himself to consecrate the Archbishop of Serbia with his own hands. Theodore Lascaris's military and religious actions meant that the thriving Empire of Nicaea was the new center of Greek culture, the new city of Constantine.

Section III: Critical Thinking

The student may not use his text to answer this question.

Constantine united his men in battle behind Christ in the 4th century, leading to a unified empire under one God. We are reading now of the failed Crusades and their aftermath. Inspired by Constantine's devotion to God but lacking the true faith the great emperor held, these Crusades created empires that quickly fell apart. Using religious devotion as the common point between the two empires, compare the Latin Empire to the Empire of Nicaea. In your answer, explain why you think one failed and the other succeeded.

As the student learned in Chapter Twenty-Five: The Sack of Constantinople, the motivation of many participants in the Fourth Crusade was not found in their love of God but in their desire for wealth and fame. The Latin Empire was formed out of that corrupt crusade. The Count of Flanders, elected by the crusaders after their rape-and-pillage spree in Constantinople, presided over "great rejoicings" and "feastings and ceremonies" at his coronation over an empire that he and his followers had just utterly destroyed. The Latin Empire was carved out of the old Byzantine empire and was divided from the beginning. The Venetians looked at the Franks warily, and just because Constantinople was under Crusader control did not mean that the rest of Byzantium fell into line behind Baldwin I. There was animosity between the "Latins" and the "Greeks," and most importantly, there was religious tension. The Christians in the east recognized the bishop of Constantinople as the head of their church rather than the pope. Baldwin I was loyal to the pope, so he brought in a Venetian "Patriarch" to act as the head of the church, bringing with him the authority of the pope and displacing the bishop of Constantinople. The Greek bishops had to swear allegiance to the pope, and this only caused more tension on the city. With outside forces attacking the Latin Empire and the inner turmoil caused by religious divisions, Baldwin I could not keep his empire together.

In Nicaea, Theodore Lascaris built a center of Greek culture based on the mission of Constantine. He exalted the Patriarch of Nicaea as the head of the Greek church and unified his people around his authority. The Patriarch of Nicaea then consecrated the Archbishop of Serbia, enacting his power as head of the Greek church by performing a duty reserved for the pope or patriarch. After this, Greek monk Michael Acominatus wrote that Theodore Lascaris should be called "a savior and universal liberator." Theodore Lascaris left Nicaea to John III Vatatzes, who confirmed the city's unity behind God in his leadership of the city. John III Vatatzes captured most of the Latin Empire's land south of the Sea of Marmara, and forced Robert into a peace treaty that left nothing to the Latin Empire but the city of Constantinople itself. John III Vatatzes fought for Nicaea under the name of the true Constantinople, the city dedicated to Constantine, and he showed his dedication to this religious cause through the coins he had minted. On one side of the coins appeared the seated figure of Christ. On the other side of the coins appeared John III Vatatzes and the Virgin Mary, mother of God, with their hands clasped over the scepter of Nicaea. Unlike the Latin Empire, Nicaea was successful as a city and realm because of its unity behind God.

EXAMPLE ANSWER:

The Latin Empire was created out of death and destruction that was supposedly enacted in the name of God—the Fourth Crusade—but was really done out of greed and the desire for power. From the beginning the Latin Empire was divided. The Venetians looked at the Franks warily, and just because Constantinople was under Crusader control did not mean that the rest of Byzantium fell into line behind Baldwin I. There was animosity between the "Latins" and the "Greeks," and most importantly, there was religious tension. The Christians in the east recognized the bishop of Constantinople as the head of their church rather than the pope. Baldwin I was loyal to the pope, so he brought in a Venetian "Patriarch" to act as the head of the church, bringing with him the authority of the pope and displacing the bishop of Constantinople. The Greek bishops had to swear allegiance to the pope, and this only caused more tension on the city. With outside forces attacking the

Latin Empire and the inner turmoil caused by religious divisions, Baldwin I could not keep his empire together.

The Empire of Nicaea was built by Theodore Lascaris as a center of Greek religion and culture based on the mission of Constantine. He exalted the Patriarch of Nicaea as the head of the Greek church and unified his people around his authority. The Patriarch of Nicaea then consecrated the Archbishop of Serbia, enacting his power as head of the Greek church by performing a duty reserved for the pope or patriarch. After this, Greek monk Michael Acominatus wrote that Theodore Lascaris should be called "a savior and universal liberator." Theodore Lascaris left Nicaea to John III Vatatzes, who confirmed the city's unity behind God in his leadership of the city. John III Vatatzes captured most of the Latin Empire's land south of the Sea of Marmara, and forced Robert into a peace treaty that left nothing to the Latin Empire but the city of Constantinople itself. John III Vatatzes fought for Nicaea under the name of the true Constantinople, the city dedicated to Constantine, and he showed his dedication to this religious cause through the coins he had minted. On one side of the coins appeared the seated figure of Christ. On the other side of the coins appeared John III Vatatzes and the Virgin Mary, mother of God, with their hands clasped over the scepter of Nicaea. Unlike the Latin Empire, Nicaea was successful as a city and realm because of its unity behind God.

Chapter Thirty-Two

The First Delhi Sultanate

The student may use her text when answering the questions in sections I and II.

Section I: Who, What, Where

Write a one or two-sentence answer explaining the significance of each item listed below.

Ali Mardan—**Pg. 228, ¶ 4—Ali Mardan, governor of the eastern Bengalese province appointed by Qutb-ud-din, revolted against Aram Shah when he became ruler. He claimed the eastern Bengalese province for himself.**

Aram Shah—**Pg. 228, ¶ 4 to Pg. 229, ¶ 2—Aram Shah, Qutb-ud-din's son, followed his father as ruler of the north Indian kingdom based out of Lahore, though he immediately lost the southern cities of Gwalior and Ranthambore to revolt, and the eastern Bengalese province to Ali Mardan. Aram Shah's leadership was challenged by Iltumish; Iltumish killed Aram Shah in battle outside of Delhi and then took the dead man's throne.**

Dhimmi—**Pg. 230, ¶ 3—Dhimmi was the status Iltumish gave to the Hindus of India: non-Muslim subjects of a Muslim king, allowed to hold property and to claim legal rights but exempt from Islamic requirements, like resident aliens in a modern nation-state.**

Fidaiyan (fidawi)—**Pg. 228, ¶ 1—Fidaiyan (singular fidawi) were young devotees of the Mulahidah (Nizari) cause that carried out strategic murder of prominent Turkish leaders. The fidaiyan, not afraid to sacrifice their lives on their missions, were often successful, and increasingly feared; almost every twelfth-century assassination was chalked up to them by their Turkish and Sunni Muslim enemies.**

Firoz—**Pg. 230, ¶ 6 to Pg. 231, ¶ 1—Firoz, one of Iltumish's sons and known to be a weak and licentious prince, challenged his sister for the title of Sultan of Delhi. Though Raziyya held on to the throne, Firoz's challenge was reflective of the general opposition to a woman holding the Sultanate.**

Ghulams—**Pg. 228, ¶ 4 to 229, ¶ 1—Ghulams were the Turkish slave officers that were loyal to Indian leaders.**

Hasan Sabbah—**Pg. 227, ℂ 1—Hasan Sabbah was a Shi'ite leader who hoped to lead a Muslim opposition against the advancing Turks at the end of the eleventh century. Sabbah seized the mountain castle of Alamut around 1090, where he and his followers, known as the Mulahidah (or by Western historians as the Nizari), strengthened its defenses and then captured other nearby castles as well.**

Iltumish—**Pg. 229, ℂ 1-3 and Pg. 230, ℂ 2—Iltumish, Qutb-ud-din's son-in-law and one of his trusted lieutenants, challenged Aram Shah for the throne and won when he killed his rival in battle outside of Delhi. Halfway through his sultanate, Iltumish was recognized by the caliph in Baghdad with by a robe of honor and the ceremonial title *Sultan-i-azam*, "Great Sultan," legitimate and God-ordained ruler over his conquered lands; this gave Iltumish and his successors the right to use the title "Auxiliary of the Commander of the Faithful" on their coins.**

Jaitra Singh—**Pg. 230, ℂ 1 & 2—Jaitra Singh, Hindu ruler of Mewar, held out against Iltumish's attacks and this resistance was hailed by the Hindus of India as a religious victory. Jaitra Singh's successful defense of his crown was also a defense of the Hindu world against the Muslim invaders.**

Mahmud—**Pg. 225, ℂ 2 and Pg. 228, ℂ 2—Mahmud, son of Ghiyas ad-Din Ghuri, expected to take his father's throne but instead was made deputy ruler of the western territories only by Muhammad Ghuri, Mahumud's uncle and his father's successor; after Muhammad's Ghuri's death Mahmud claimed the western territories as an independent king.**

Mamluks—**Pg. 225, ℂ 2 to Pg. 226, ℂ 1—Mamluks were Turkish warriors who had begun their careers in slavery. The mamluks were treated well when they were slaves; they worked hard for their masters, and after they converted to Islam and could no longer be enslaved, they often moved into important official positions in the Ghurid realm.**

Mulahidah (Nizari)—**Pg. 226, ℂ 4 and Pg. 227, ℂ 1—Mulahidah (known to Western historians as the Nizari) is the Persian name for a particular sect of Shi'ite Muslims that were both feared and admired by the Crusaders (they had another name for them: the Assassins). The Mulahidah were founded by Hasan Sabbah in 1090 and by 1150 the Mulahidah had established itself as a small mountain state firmly opposed to Turkish power.**

Qutb-ud-din—**Pg. 228, ℂ 2 & 3—Qutb-ud-din, a former Turkish slave turned governor, claimed to be an independent king of Lahore and declared himself sultan of the north Indian lands after the death of Muhammad Ghuri. Though Qutb-ud-din only ruled for four years, he created a particularly Indian Muslim land with a sultanate that lasted for over three centuries.**

Raziyya—**Pg. 230, ℂ 5 to Pg. 231, ℂ 1—Raziyya, daughter of Iltumish, was left the title of Sultan of Delhi after her father's death. Raziyya was a competent and clear-thinking ruler, and she even wore male clothing and armor, but the opponents to a woman Sultan threw her rule into a long and violent chaos.**

Section II: **Comprehension**

Write a two or three-sentence answer to each of the following questions.

1. How did Islamic rulers cultivate loyalty in the Turkish slaves they owned?

A1.—Pg. 225, ¶ 3—Young Turkish men bought at slave markets were placed in regiments, trained as soldiers, and separated from their old lives. They were given new names, new identities, and they were cut off from all ties except those between slave and master. This dependence created loyalty; the master was the slave soldier's employer, protector, and champion.

2. What happened to the mamluks after they converted to Islam and were set free?

A2.—Pg. 226, ¶ 1—When the highly skilled mamluks converted to Islam and were set free, they were guaranteed security in the Ghurid realm. Mamluks generally remained on in the service of their ex-masters and they almost always became part of the most elite corps of mounted soldiers. The Turkish soldiers were now fighting for Muhammad Ghuri and in powerful governing positions over his conquered cities.

3. What is the different between a Shi'ite Muslim and a Sunni Muslim?

A3.—Pg. 226, *— When the Prophet Muhammad died in 632, the leadership of the new Muslim community was claimed by the Prophet's old friend Abu Bakr, though others believed that the rightful leader was the Prophet's son-in-law Ali. Supporters of Abu Bakr are called Sunni Muslims while supporters of Ali as the Prophet's rightful successor are called Shi'ite Muslims.

4. What happened to the Ghurid empire after Muhammad Ghuri's murder?

A4.—Pg. 228, ¶ 2—Muhammad Ghuri's death brought an immediate end to the Ghurid empire. Within months, the whole huge expanse had fallen apart under Ghuri's rivaling successors. His nephew Mahmud claimed the western territories as an independent king, and three of his Turkish slaves turned governors did the same over their own lands: one in Ghazni, a second in the Sind, and a third, Qutb-ud-din, in Lahore.

5. How did Qutb-ud-din create a particularly Indian Muslim land?

A5.—Pg. 228, ¶ 3 & 4—After Muhammad Ghuri's death Qutb-ud-din claimed to be an independent king of Lahore and declared himself sultan of the north Indian lands. Qutb-ud-din's rule was built on the previous twenty years of his service to the Ghurids in northern India; and during those decades, he had worked hard to help the two Ghuri brothers transform their realm into a Muslim land. In his hands, it became a particularly Indian Muslim land that was free from domination that came from beyond the mountains, but also a land where the old Hindu religious traditions were done away with.

6. How did Iltumish spend the first twenty-five years of his sultanate?

A6.—Pg. 229, ¶ 3 to Pg. 230, ¶ 1—Iltumish spent all of his time as sultan fighting: it took six years to drive out the other Turkish pretenders in Ghazni and the Sind, finally bringing

both under his control by 1217; the city of Lahore wasn't subdued until 1228; and Bengal was not completely under his control until 1231. At the same time, Iltumish did his best to invade the Hindu lands that had not fallen to Ghurid rule. Iltumish mounted a major assault against the Hindu ruler of Mewar, Jaitra Singh, but although he was able to sack the city of Aghata, Jaitra Singh held out against him.

Section III: Critical Thinking

The student may not use her text to answer this question.

Political conspiracies are often at the heart of murder-mystery novels and television shows. The secretive world of backroom politics is undeniably intriguing. In this chapter we learn about one of these secret societies, the Mulahidah/Nizari. Write a paragraph explaining how this sect emerged. Then write a paragraph that explains how the English word for political killings has its origins in the history of this group.

The Mulahidah, better known to Western historians as the Nizari, were a sect of Shi'ite Muslims that kept themselves well hidden and were considered to be very dangerous. According to twelfth-century travelers' tales, the Mulahidah lived in the impregnable fortress of Alamut, in the mountains south of the Caspian Sea, and swore absolute allegiance to a leader known as the Elder, or the Old Man. If he ordered them to kill his enemies, they went out, dagger in hand, to fulfill the command unquestioningly and without fear, believing that "when a man dies for his lord, or in any good cause, his soul goes into another body, better and more comfortable."

The myth of the "Old Man of the Mountain" came from the history of Hasan Sabbah, a Shi'ite leader who hoped to lead a Muslim opposition against the advancing Turks at the end of the eleventh century. Sabbah seized the mountain castle of Alamut around 1090, where he and his followers, the Mulahidah/Nizari, strengthened its defenses and then captured other nearby castles as well. By 1150, Sabbah had been followed by two successors, each of whom gathered more supporters and captured more castles, until the sect had established itself as a small mountain state that stood firmly opposed to Turkish power.

Sabbah used the political strategy of fidaiyan, strategic murder carried out by young devotees of the Mulahidah/Nizari cause, to fight against the Turkish state. The fidaiyan were not afraid to sacrifice their lives when they were on their missions to kill Turkish leaders, so they were very successful and very feared; as a result, hostile Sunni historians suggested that the fidaiyan were drugged with hashish into willingness to carry out their suicide missions. When Crusaders picked up the word "hashishin" they Latinized it into the word "assassin." This is how the English word for political killings, "assassination," came to be.

EXAMPLE ANSWER:

The Mulahidah, known to Western historians as the Nizari, lived in the impregnable fortress of Alamut, in the mountains south of the Caspian Sea, and swore absolute allegiance to a leader known as the Elder, or the Old Man. If he ordered them to kill his enemies, they fulfilled the command unquestioningly and without fear. The myth of the "Old Man of the Mountain" came from the history of Hasan Sabbah, a Shi'ite leader who hoped to lead a Muslim opposition against the advancing Turks at the end of the eleventh century. Sabbah seized the mountain castle of Alamut around 1090, where he and his

followers strengthened its defenses. By 1150, Sabbah had been followed by two successors, each of whom gathered more supporters and captured more castles, until the sect had established itself as a small mountain state that stood firmly opposed to Turkish power.

Sabbah used the political strategy of fidaiyan, strategic murder carried out by young devotees of the Mulahidah/Nizari cause, to fight against the Turkish state. The English word "assassin" came from the derogatory Sunni word for the fidaiyan, "hashishin." The fidaiyan were not afraid to sacrifice their lives when they were on their missions to kill Turkish leaders, so they were very successful and very feared; as a result, hostile Sunni historians suggested that the fidaiyan were drugged with hashish into willingness to carry out their suicide missions. When Crusaders picked up the word "hashishin" they Latinized it into the word "assassin." This is how the English word for political killings, "assassination," came to be.

Section IV: Map Exercise

1. Trace the outline of the frame for Map 32.2 in black.

2. Trace the coastline in blue, including Sri Lanka. Also trace the lines of the Indus, the Ganges, the Narmada, and the Kaveri. Trace until the contours are familiar.

3. Using a black pencil, trace the area for the Sultanate of Delhi under Iltumish. Trace the mountains with small peaks. Repeat until the contours are familiar.

4. Using a new sheet of paper, trace the rectangular outline of the frame in black. Using your regular pencil with an eraser, draw the lines of the coastline and the Indus, Ganges, Narmada, and Kaveri rivers. Show the Himalaya mountains and the Salt Range with small peaks. Draw the line of the territory of the Sultanate of Delhi under Iltumish. When you are happy with your map, lay it over the original. Erase and redraw any lines which are more than ¼" off of the original.

5. Study the locations of Herat, Ghazni, Lahore, Delhi, Ranthambore, Gwalior, and Aghata. When they are familiar for you, mark and label them on the map. Check them against the original, and erase and redraw any lines which are more than ¼" off of the original.

6. Now study the Makran, Sind, Mewar, Vindhya, Chola, Orissa, Himalaya, Punjab, and Salt Range areas. Label them on the map, check them against the original, and correct any incorrect labels.

7. Label the Arabian Sea and Sri Lanka.

Chapter Thirty-Three

Heresy

The student may use his text when answering the questions in sections I and II.

Section I: **Who, What, Where**

Write a one or two-sentence answer explaining the significance of each item listed below.

Albigensian Crusade—**Pg. 238, ¶ 5—Albigensian Crusade, a name taken from one of the Cathar sects known as Albigenses, was the name given to the crusade that lasted twenty years against all Cathars, all supporters of Cathars, and anyone suspected of Catharism.**

Arnold, the Abbot of Cisteaux—**Pg. 238, ¶ 6 to Pg. 239, ¶ 1—Arnold, the Abbot of Cisteaux, a surviving papal legate, was the first supreme commander of the Albigensian Crusade. The Abbot of Cisteaux gave the command to the crusaders to kill everyone in Béziers, leaving God to tell the heretics from the faithful.**

Bogomilism—**Pg. 236, *—Bogomilism was a belief system preached in Bulgaria by a tenth-century priest named Bogomil that spread from Bulgaria down into Serbia and Bosnia, and eastward as far as Constantinople, surviving into the fourteenth century. Bogomil missionaries traveling to Italy and Western Francia probably provided the seed from which Catharism grew though Bogomilism never posed a serious political threat to the Bulgarian kings, and the patriarch of Constantinople was never in a position to organize a campaign against it.**

Cathars/Catharism—**Pg. 236, ¶ 2 & 3—Cathars, from the Greek *katharos*, meaning "the Pure Ones," were a group of heretics living in southern Francia; though Catharism had already split into more than one sect, all Cathars were dualists, dividing all things in the universe into good and evil, light and dark, pure and good, and the Cathars resisted as much interaction with the material world as possible. They fasted, rejected sex, and suffered through marathons of prayer and meditation, they rejected the orthodox doctrine of the Incarnation, since this required the benevolent God to tie himself to the enslaving, corrupt material world, and they believed "that almost all the Church of Rome was a den of thieves, and that it was the harlot of which we read in the Apocalypse."**

Dominic de Guzman—**Pg. 236, ¶ 5 to Pg. 237, ¶ 2—Dominic de Guzman was a local priest granted the request to teach in Languedoc in 1206 by Pope Innocent II in an effort to evangelize the Cathars back into the orthodox fold. Dominic de Guzman believed that the Cathars could be turned back to orthodoxy if they saw that an orthodox clergyman could also lead an ascetic and pure lifestyle; he himself traveled through Languedoc barefoot, arguing with the Cathars one on one but this humble approach made little headway, and the Cathars continued to flourish.**

Donatists—**Pg. 234, ¶ 2—Donatists were fourth-century heretics that complained that kings at the time of the apostles never claimed the right to punish anyone for what they believed, and so kings of their time should not exercise that right. Augustine countered the Donatists's claims by saying that the kings at the time of the apostles did not believe in Christ, and now a Christian king could serve God "by enforcing with suitable rigor such laws as ordain what is righteous, and punish what is reverse," such as wrong actions and wrong beliefs.**

Peter Waldo—**Pg. 235, ¶ 4—Peter Waldo was a twelfth century wandering preacher that gained an enormous following by preaching that the Church hierarchy was corrupt, that priests ought to give up their positions and work with their hands, and that it was "a bad thing to found and endow churches and monasteries." His followers were known as Waldensians and they traveled through the French countryside preaching a stripped-down, evangelical-style gospel of repentance.**

Pierre de Castelnau—Pg. 237, **¶ 5-7—Pierre de Castelnau, a representative of the pope, excommunicated Raymond VI after the Count of Toulouse refused to take action against the heretics in Languedoc. Pierre de Castelnau was murdered on his way back to Rome by a squire hoping to win Raymond VI's approval.**

Raymond VI—**Pg. 237, ¶ 3-8 and Pg. 238, ¶ 4—Raymond VI, Count of Toulouse, overlord of Languedoc, and an orthodox Christian, refused to take action against the Cathars because he wanted to remain as independent as possible, and as a result he was excommunicated by the legate Pierre de Castelnau. Pope Innocent III then declared Raymond VI the focus of a new crusade (which included the Cathars); when Raymond VI heard of the huge force assembled against him, he sent the pope a message of abject repentance, and joined the Crusade himself.**

Waldensians—**Pg. 235, ¶ 4—Waldensians were followers of the twelfth century wandering preacher Peter Waldo. Waldensians traveled through the French countryside, preaching a stripped-down, evangelical-style gospel of repentance that said "the doctrine of Christ . . . is sufficient for salvation without the statutes of the church."**

Section II: **Comprehension**

Write a two or three-sentence answer to each of the following questions.

1. How did the Nicene Creed give power to claims of heresy?

A1.—Pg. 234, ¶ 1—The Nicene Creed was the first official fence built around the Christian faith to define who was in and who was out, and it also created the ability to punish heresy with the sword. Before Nicaea, Christians could accuse each other of error all they wanted, but argument and excommunication were the punishments allowed. After Nicaea, bishops had much more power: they could ask the emperor to enforce the creed he had sponsored with political might and violent force.

2. How does Augustine rationalize the right for Christian kings to punish wrong actions as well as wrong beliefs?

A2.—Pg. 234, ¶ 2 & 3—Augustine says that a Christian king could serve God "by enforcing with suitable rigor such laws as ordain what is righteous, and punish what is reverse," such as wrong actions and wrong beliefs. For example, he asks why adulterers could be punished by law, but not those that are sacrilegious. Augustine also says that "fear of punishment or pain" is often a proven way of teaching men, so the church should be allowed to compel "her lost sons to return" with force.

3. What happened to religious heretics, generally, in the medieval world?

A3.—Pg. 234, ¶ 4 to Pg. 235, ¶ 2—In the medieval world, heretics were compelled by fear and pain, but they were not, generally speaking, punished with the sword (except for the Gallic bishop Priscillian, who was executed in 385 for teaching magic to his followers and is thought to have been the first Christian heretic to suffer death). The Theodosian Code of 438 made heresy an imperial crime, but most of the penalties deprived the heretics of property and certain rights; heretics could be fined or exiled, and were not allowed to serve in the imperial service. And although heretics who persisted in gathering followers and teaching them were threatened with "the sharp goads of a more severe punishment," the most severe punishment they faced was usually imprisonment and financial loss.

4. While most eleventh- and early twelfth century heretics were threatened with imprisonment or financial loss, what gruesome fate did other heretics of the time suffer?

A4.—Pg. 235, *— An isolated execution of heretics had taken place in 1022, when a handful of men and women in Orléans, claiming secret knowledge that was available only to initiates, had been burned to death with the approval of Robert the Pious, second king of the Capetian dynasty. In 1028, the Archbishop of Milan had offered a handful of ascetics who rejected the Church's authority the choice between recantation and death by fire; several chose fire. Two other burnings of heretics followed, one in 1114 in Soissons and a second in 1143 at Cologne; but in both cases the heretics, after speaking publicly about their anti-orthodox opinions, were tossed into bonfires built by indignant laypeople, without the approval of the local clergy.

5. What was the common point among the twelfth-century charismatic heretics in the south of Francia? Use examples to back up your answer.

A5.—Pg. 235, ¶ 4—The twelfth-century charismatic heretics in the south of Francia had the common belief that the organized Church was fallen and corrupt and had nothing to do with true spiritual life. For example, at Cologne, a small group of rebels against Rome began to preach that "he who sits in the Chair of Peter has lost the power to ordain," because the papacy had been "corrupted through involvement in secular business." In the last quarter of the twelfth century, Peter Waldo gathered an enormous following by preaching that the Church hierarchy was corrupt, that priests ought to give up their positions and work with their hands, and that it was "a bad thing to found and endow churches and monasteries."

6. Why didn't the people of southern Francia rally against the heretics preaching in their lands?

A6.—Pg. 235, ¶ 5 to Pg. 236, ¶ 1—When a priest in southern Francia asked a local knight, "Why do you not expel these people and shun them?" the knight answered "We cannot do that . . . for we were raised with them, and we have relatives among them, and we see that they lead honest and decent lives." The heretics were the friends and families of the local Christians, so a peace was kept among them.

7. Where was the twelfth-century stronghold of Catharism in southern Francia? Why did Catharism take root in this place?

A7.—Pg. 236, ¶ 4—The stronghold of Catharism in twelfth-century southern Francia was in the southern province of Languedoc, bordering the Pyrenees and the Mediterranean Sea. Languedoc was a relatively lawless chunk of Western Francia, where the authority of the local counts was weak and the local priests were poor, uneducated, and superstitious. To the people of Languedoc, Catharism offered a new kind of power: an authority centered only within themselves, a chance to rise through the ranks of the Cathars to the shining elite ranks of the perfected.

8. What did Dominic de Guzman find when he traveled barefoot through Languedoc, trying to bring the Cathars back into the orthodox fold?

A8.—Pg. 237, ¶ 1 & 2—Dominic de Guzman found that the papal representatives were displaying altogether too much pride and pomp. He wrote that the Cathars weren't getting new followers with gorgeous apparel and cavalcades of retainers, but with zealous preaching and apostolic humility. He felt zeal must be met with zeal, and though he traveled barefoot and tried to show he was leading an aesthetic and pure lifestyle, he was able to make little headway with his humble approach.

9. Describe the terms of the crusade declared by Innocent III against the Cathars and Raymond VI.

A9.—Pg. 237, ¶ 8—The terms of the crusade Innocent III declared against the Cathars and Raymond VI were that all of Raymond's subjects were absolved from their obedience to him. Anyone who took up the sword against the Count of Toulouse would be given absolution of sin and would have all the privileges awarded to Crusaders who had made the long, dangerous journey to Jerusalem. Finally, anyone who took wealth or property away from a Cathar could keep it.

10. What happened when the bishop of Béziers told the Catholic citizens of the city to "quit the city and leave the heretics behind"? What was the Abbot of Cisteaux's response?

A10.—Pg. 238, ¶ 6 to Pg. 239, ¶ 1—When the bishop of Béziers told the Catholics of Béziers to "quit the city and leave the heretics behind," the citizens refused to desert their homes, not wanting the greedy crusaders to get a penny of their possessions. When the crusaders asked the Abbot of Cisteaux what to do, because they could not tell the Christians from the heretics when they stormed the city, he replied "Kill them all. . . . The Lord knows which ones belong to him." Béziers was sacked: almost everyone was killed, including women, children and the clergy.

11. How did Simon de Montfort become the leader of the Albigensian Crusade? How did Simon de Montfort treat those that resisted the armies of God?

A11.—Pg. 240, ¶ 1, 4, & 5—Simon de Montfort was elected to be leader of the Albigensian Crusade after the Abbot of Cisteaux went back to his monastery following the siege of Carcassonne. Pope Innocent III confirmed the election by declaring Montfort not only general of the Crusaders but also ruler of all lands "conquered or to be conquered" during the Crusade. Simon de Montfort was cruel and vindictive to those who resisted the armies of God; in Bram he ordered the eyes of the defenders put out and in Minerve he ordered 140 captured "perfected heretics" burned alive, both men and women.

Section III: Critical Thinking

The student may not use his text to answer this question.

What is heresy? Heresy is defined on page 233 as "a departure from orthodoxy that was not merely dangerous, but placed the thinker outside the gates of the kingdom of God. Heresy was more than error. Error was wrong belief; error became heresy when the believer, confronted by the Church's condemnation, refused to give it up." In order for heresy to exist, there had to be a set of rules in place regarding religion and worship. The first boundaries were drawn when the Nicene Creed was approved by Constantine. But how did Raymond VI, an orthodox Christian, come to be the focus of an attack on heresy? Write a paragraph explaining how Raymond VI came to be the focus of a new crusade and then explain how Pope Innocent III changed the meaning of both crusade and heresy.

When Pope Innocent III found himself unable to make headway against the Cathars in Languedoc, he sent some of his representatives to see the Count of Toulouse, overlord of Languedoc, in order to demand that he take action against the heretics in his land. Raymond VI was a powerful nobleman, and his reach restricted the power of the king. He liked to act independently and refused to take the pope's orders. Raymond VI was an orthodox Christian himself, but he did not want to become the subject of someone else's orders. The legate that heard his refusal, Pierre de Castelnau, excommunicated Raymond VI as a result. Then, a squire hoping to win the count's approval murdered Pierre de Castelnau on his way back to Rome. When the pope got wind of everything that happened, he declared a crusade against both the Cathars and the count.

Pope Innocent III's declaration changed the meaning of both crusade and heresy. The pope expanded the idea of crusade from a fight to reclaim the Holy Land, to war against non-Christians living in Christian lands, and with the declaration against the Cathars and Raymond VI, to war against unorthodox Christians and war against a thoroughly orthodox brother whose only offense was his refusal to take political commands from Rome. Pope Innocent III changed the boundaries of heresy to include not just a refusal to give up unorthodox beliefs, but to also include political dissent. Pope Innocent III did not like what Raymond VI was up to, and even though he was an orthodox Christian, Pope Innocent declared him a heretic and led a crusade against him.

EXAMPLE ANSWER:

Raymond VI found himself the target of a crusade when he refused to listen to the pope's demand that he take action against the heretics in his land. Raymond VI was an orthodox Christian himself, but he did not want to become the subject of someone else's orders. Pierre de Castelnau, acting as the pope's representative, excommunicated Raymond VI after he refused to fight the Cathars. Then, a squire hoping to win the count's approval murdered Pierre de Castelnau when he was on his way back to Rome. When the pope got wind of everything that happened, he declared a crusade against both the Cathars and the count.

Pope Innocent III's declaration changed the meaning of both crusade and heresy. The pope expanded the idea of crusade from a fight to reclaim the Holy Land, to war against non-Christians living in Christian lands, and with the declaration against the Cathars and Raymond VI, to war against unorthodox Christians and war against orthodox Christians that didn't follow his orders. Pope Innocent III changed the boundaries of heresy to include not just a refusal to give up unorthodox beliefs, but to also include political dissent. Pope Innocent III did not like what Raymond VI was up to, and even though he was an orthodox Christian, Pope Innocent III declared him a heretic and led a crusade against him.

Section IV: **Map Exercise**

1. Trace the rectangular outline of the frame for Map 33.1 in black.

2. Trace the outline of the coast in blue around England and around the continent, including the visible portion of the Mediterranean Sea. Also trace the line of the Herault from the Mediterranean. Using your black pencil, trace the outline of the kingdom of Philip II. Trace the mountains with simple peaks. Repeat until the contours are familiar.

3. Using a new sheet of paper, trace the outline of the rectangular frame in black. Using your regular pencil with an eraser, draw the coastline around England and the continent, including the Mediterranean and also the line of the Herault. Then draw the line of the territory of the Kingdom of King Philip II. When you are happy with your map, lay it over the original. Erase and redraw any lines more than ½" off of the original.

4. Now study the locations of Brittany, Normandy, the Pyrenees, and Languedoc. Mark each on your map, check the book, and correct any mis-markings.

5. Now study the locations of Tours, Chartres, Melun, Paris, Soissons, Reims, Sens, Cluny, Lyons, Beziers, Termes, Lastours, Minerve, Carcassonne, Toulouse, Bram, and Alaric. When you are

familiar with them, close the book. Mark and label each one on your map. Check your map with the original, and erase and remark any incorrect labels.

6. Finally, carefully study the locations of Argenteuil, St. Denis, Paraclete, Clairvaux, and Cluny. When you are familiar with them, close the book. Mark and label each one on your map. Check your map with the original, and erase and re-mark any incorrect labels.

Chapter Thirty-Four

Reconquest and Failure

The student may use her text when answering the questions in sections I and II.

Section I: Who, What, Where

Write a one or two-sentence answer explaining the significance of each item listed below.

Alfonso IX—**Pg. 242, ¶ 2 and Pg. 244, ¶ 7—Alfonso IX, king of León, was constantly attacking Portugal while also helping the king of Navarre attack Castile. After the battle at Las Navas, the king of León declared a truce with the kings of Portugal and Castile.**

Amicia—**Pg. 243, ¶ 1—Amicia, young daughter of Simon de Montfort, was betrothed to James, the three-year-old son of Pedro the Catholic, as part of a peace treaty made between her father and Raymond of Toulouse.**

James—**Pg. 243, ¶ 1 & 2 and Pg. 246, ¶ 4—James, son of Pedro the Catholic and heir to his throne, was just three years old when he was betrothed to Amicia, daughter of Simon de Montfort, as part of a peace treaty with Raymond of Toulouse. James was sent to live with his prospective bride's family and after his father's death he was returned to Aragon and installed on the throne at the age of five.**

Muhammad al-Nasir—**Pg. 243, ¶ 3 and Pg. 244, ¶ 4 & 5—Muhammad al-Nasir, grandson of Abu Ya'qub Yusuf and Almohad caliph at the time of Pedro the Catholic's rule, had been agitating for war against Aragon since 1207. After a crusade was called against the Almohads in retaliation for their attack on Salvatierra, and the two sides met at Las Navas, al-Nasir fled on horseback to Marrakesh, fell into a depression, and died the next year.**

Pedro II—**Pg. 242, ¶ 3 and Pg. 246, ¶ 3—Pedro II, or Pedro the Catholic, ruler of Aragon and great-grandson of Ramiro the Monk, was crowned by the pope in November of 1204; he reciprocated this honor by promising Innocent III and his successors a perpetual tithe of 250 gold *mazmudins* and by promising to defend the faith and persecute heresy and wickedness whenever it reared its head in Aragon. Pedro II's faithfulness was challenged by his loyalty to his family, and he ultimately died at war with Simon de Montfort while he was trying to protect his brother-in-law's kingdom.**

Sancho I—**Pg. 242, ¶ 2 and Pg. 244, ¶ 7—Sancho I, son of Afonso Henriques, ruled in Portugal and fought off constant attacks against his northern border from Alfonso IX, king of León. After the battle at Las Navas, the king of Portugal declared a truce with the kings of León and Castile.**

Sancho the Strong—**Pg. 242, ¶ 2, Pg. 243, ¶ 9, and Pg. 244, ¶ 3—Sancho the Strong, king of Navarre, spent his time attacking his cousin Alfonso VIII's kingdom of Castile. When he first heard that the king of Aragon was under Almohad attack, Sancho the Strong thought about joining the Muslim forces against his neighbor; however, he joined Castile and Aragon in the fight against the Almohads after Pope Innocent III declared a crusade against the Muslims in Spain in January 1212.**

Yusuf II—**Pg. 244, ¶ 6—Yusuf II, al-Nasir's young successor, lost control of his empire after the Christian victory at the Battle of Las Navas de Tolosa. The Almohads lost their hold on the remaining Muslim lands in Spain and they also lost territory after territory in Africa, with Yusuf II's governors breaking away one at a time to establish their own dynasties.**

Section II: Comprehension

Write a two or three-sentence answer to each of the following questions.

1. Why was the Albigensian Crusade difficult for Pedro the Catholic to navigate?

A1.—Pg. 242, ¶ 3 & 4—The Albigensian Crusade was difficult for Pedro the Catholic to navigate because he pledged allegiance to the pope but he also had to consider his family ties. Pedro the Catholic promised Innocent III that he would persecute heresy and wickedness whenever it reared its head in Aragon. However, Raymond of Toulouse was his brother-in-law; Pedro's older sister Eleanor had married the Count of Toulouse in 1200 and now Raymond was on Simon de Montfort's bad side.

2. How did Pedro the Catholic broker a truce in 1210 between Simon de Montfort and his brother-in-law?

A2.—Pg. 242, ¶ 5 to Pg. 243, ¶ 1—In 1210, Pedro the Catholic traveled to his brother-in-law's lands and met with Simon de Montfort himself, proposing a truce with the Crusader general. As part of the treaty, he offered to betroth his own son and heir, three-year-old James, to Montfort's young daughter Amicia. This would eventually make Montfort the father-in-law of the queen of Aragon, and Montfort agreed.

3. What happened to Pedro the Catholic's fight against Muhammad al-Nasir after Almohad troops had begun to cross the Strait of Gibraltar in May 1211?

A3.—Pg. 243, ¶ 9 to Pg. 244, ¶ 2—As Muhammad al-Nasir approached Aragon, Alfonso VIII of Castile hurried to Pedro's side, but the kings of León, Portugal, and Navarre refused to join the coming fight (in fact, Sancho the Strong contemplated joining with the Muslim forces against his neighbors). Al-Nasir's forces swarmed forward across southern Spain, forcing the surrender of the Castilian fortress of Salvatierra which was Castile's strongest

outpost, a symbol of Christian power, nicknamed the "right hand of the Lord of Castile." Pedro the Catholic then sent a message to Rome, suggesting that once the Muslim advance had finished with him, they would attack Rome, to which Innocent replied with a call for another crusade.

4. Describe the July 16, 1212 battle at Las Navas.

A4.—Pg. 244, ¶ 4 & 5—On July 16, the Muslims and Christians met at Las Navas, where the Crusader force had divided into three, each wing commanded by one of the Spanish kings. In a pincer move, two wings crushed the Muslim center, felling about 100,000 of their opponents, while Sancho the Strong burst through the chains of men protecting al-Nasir's personal tent and raided it himself. Al-Nasir, who had remained at the back of the assault, fled on horseback and his men retreated in his wake.

5. Why did Pedro the Catholic and Raymond of Toulouse decide to mount an attack on Simon de Montfort?

A5.—Pg. 245, ¶ 2 & 3—After Las Navas, Pedro the Catholic attempted to negotiate a peace between Raymond of Toulouse and Simon de Montfort, even sending to Pope Innocent III and asking him to order Montfort to stand down, but nine months passed and no truce had been reached. Simon de Montfort ignored appeals from both sides and Innocent III, getting contradictory reports from Pedro II and his legates, reversed his own position several times. At the same time, the people of Toulouse suffered from hunger and disease, lost crops and slaughtered livestock, burned homes and fields, forcing Pedro the Catholic and Raymond of Toulouse to take matters into their own hands.

6. What happened when the army of knights from Aragon and Toulouse attacked Simon de Montfort's central fortification, the castle at Muret?

A6.—Pg. 246, ¶ 2-4—Though Simon de Montfort had only fifteen hundred men at his disposal, he still managed to inflict severe damage on the invading forces. Pedro the Catholic was killed, Raymond was forced to flee, and Simon de Montfort marched into Toulouse and claimed it as his own, taking control of all of Languedoc. After his victory, Simon de Montfort released James at the pleading requests of the people of Aragon, but with a five-year-old king on the throne, Aragon remained in chaos.

Section III: Critical Thinking

The student may not use her text to answer this question.

In the last chapter we read about Raymond of Toulouse's resistance against the Albigensian Crusade. In this chapter we read about Raymond of Toulouse's dragging feet regarding his penance. We also read about the formation of another crusade, this time declared in January 1212 by Pope Innocent III against the Almohads in Spanish territory. Simon de Montfort continued to lead the fight, but the local nobility in Southern France were growing tired of him. Write a paragraph that explains the similarity between Raymond of Toulouse and Simon de Montfort; though Simon de Montfort despised Raymond of Toulouse, explain how both men wanted the same thing.

Raymond of Toulouse resisted Pope Innocent III's order to attack the Cathars in his territory because he didn't want to take orders from anyone. He liked his independence and power. The result was that Innocent III added Raymond of Toulouse to the list of enemies to be attacked in the Albigensian Crusade. Raymond realized he was outnumbered, so he begged for the pope's forgiveness.

In this chapter we found out that Raymond:

> had not yet finished fulfilling all of the penances that had been laid on him by the pope in 1209 as a condition of his reinstatement in the Church's good favor, and he continued to drag his feet. In early 1211, another letter from Rome arrived for the count, insisting that he make good the penance and join fully in the fight against his heretical vassals. In addition, since his zeal was in question, he was to dismiss his mercenary soldiers, require his knights to dismantle their castles and strongholds, and give the clergy of the orthodox Church supreme authority 'in everything they might require' (Pg. 243, ¶ 6).

In a nutshell, the pope was telling Raymond to give up all authority over his realm. Of course, Raymond refused. He retreated to his own estates in Toulouse. In the summer of 1211, Simon de Montfort laid siege to him, laying waste all of the surrounding countryside. Raymond kept getting into trouble because he did not want to give up his wealth and power.

Simon de Montfort was also power-hungry. He rose to the ranks of the crusaders and was elected leader after the Abbot of Cisteaux decided he had had enough of fighting. In the last chapter, on page 246, he is described as "tall, broad-shouldered, and handsome," and also "totally dedicated to the service of God." This description of Simon de Montfort took on a different tone as we continued reading. We found out the he was sadistic, gouging out people's eyes and burning people to death. And in this chapter we found out that Simon de Montfort's fierce loyalty to God may have been rivalled with his own desire for might. As Pedro the Catholic and Raymond of Toulouse prepared to mount an attack on Simon de Montfort's castle at Muret, they were joined by a "great many men" from the neighboring territories. It turns out that "Simon de Montfort's violent and unceasing campaigning had increasingly seemed less for the church than for himself, and the local nobility wanted him gone, crusade or no crusade" (Pg. 246, ¶ 1).

While Raymond of Toulouse might have wanted to keep his independence, and Simon de Montfort might have been cruel for his own pleasure, both men acted out of personal desires. Raymond of Toulouse was an orthodox Catholic, and Simon de Montfort was the lead crusader, but again, both men put themselves before God.

EXAMPLE ANSWER:

Raymond of Toulouse made it clear that while he was an orthodox Catholic, he put his own personal interest in power and wealth before the demands of the pope. Raymond of Toulouse resisted Pope Innocent III's order to attack the Cathars, only giving in to Rome when there were thousands of crusaders outside his door. Even after he joined the pope, he was slow to finish his penances. He did not want to give up his mercenary soldiers, he did not want to require his knights to dismantle their castles and strongholds, and he certainly

did not want to give the clergy of the orthodox Church supreme authority "in everything they might require." Instead of giving up his authority, Raymond retreated to his own estates in Toulouse. In the summer of 1211, Simon de Montfort laid siege to him, laying waste all of the surrounding countryside. Raymond kept getting into trouble because he did not want to give up his wealth and power. But Simon de Montfort really wasn't any better than Raymond of Toulouse. In fact, they had the same goal: personal power. Montfort fought hard in the Albigensian crusade and was made lead crusader after the Abbot of Cisteaux returned to his monastery. But Montfort's strength soon was used for sadism, and he gouged out the eyes of those he fought, and mercilessly burned his enemies to death. Simon de Montfort's fierce loyalty to God may have been rivalled with his own desire for might. As Pedro the Catholic and Raymond of Toulouse prepared to mount an attack on Simon de Montfort's castle at Muret, they were joined by many men that questioned Montfort's motives. They felt his violence and campaigning were no longer for the church, but for himself. Even though Montfort and Raymond of Toulouse were always fighting, they both had the same goal in mind: power. Both men acted out of personal desires. Raymond of Toulouse was an orthodox Catholic, and Simon de Montfort was the lead crusader, but again, both men put themselves before God.

Chapter Thirty-Five

From Bouvines to Magna Carta

The student may use his text when answering the questions in sections I and II.

Section I: Who, What, Where

Write a one or two-sentence answer explaining the significance of each item listed below.

Articles of the Barons—**Pg. 252, 5 & *—Articles of the Barons was the name of the forty-nine-item list of grievances, like too much taxation, presented to King John in April of 1215 by the earls and barons of England. Articles of the Barons grew out of the Unknown Charter which was based on Henry I's Charter of Liberties, and was a precursor to the Magna Carta.**

Barons' War—**Pg. 254, ¶ 4-6—Barons' War was the war started by John in opposition to the Magna Carta. The resistance was led by the French prince Louis, but as soon as John died William Marshal, Henry's regent, said he would uphold the Magna Carta thus ending the dispute.**

Curia Regis—**Pg. 253, ¶ 3—Curia Regis was the name of the gathering of churchmen, earls, and barons that made the final decision over fines and scutages to be imposed by the king. The Curia Regis, the common counsel of England, was given its name in the time of William the Conqueror, but its power was reaffirmed with the signing of the Magna Carta.**

Frederick II—**Pg. 250, ¶ 2 & 6—Frederick II, formerly king of Sicily, became king of Germany after joining forces with Philip II of France against the Count of Flanders and Otto IV. They beat the combined English and German forces at Bouvines in July of 1214 and Frederick II took hold of Germany.**

Henry III—**Pg. 254, ¶ 6 and Pg. 256, Chart—Henry III was John's son. Henry was nine years old when his father died, and his rule was enforced by his regent William Marshal.**

Hugues de Boves—**Pg. 250, ¶ 3 & 5—Hugues de Boves insisted that the English and German forces fight the French at Bouvines on a Sunday. Once it was clear that the French would win the battle, the English baron fled with his men.**

Louis—Pg. 248, ¶ 5 and Pg. 255, ¶ 2—Louis, Philip II's oldest son, was made head of the crusade against John, king of England, and was promised the crown of England by his father should the crusade succeed. Louis almost became king of England again, after the signing of the Magna Carta, but after John died and the barons turned against the prince, he retreated back to France (albeit with ten thousand silver marks from the royal treasury).

Magna Carta—Pg. 253, ¶ 3 & 4—Magna Carta, the Great Charter confirmed by John at Runnymede on June 15, 1215, provided the barons with multiple layers of protection against the king's whimsy; it protected their goods, their lands, and their inheritances against John's arbitrary decrees; it rested the final decision over fines and scutages in the hands of the Curia Regis; and it said that "no one shall be taken or imprisoned or dispossessed or outlawed or exiled or in any way ruined, nor will we go or send against him, except by the lawful judgment of his peers or by the law of the land." The Magna Carta also appointed a committee of twenty-five barons who had the power to confiscate royal castles, lands, and possessions, should John refuse to abide by its terms.

Unknown Charter—Pg. 252, 3 & *—Unknown Charter was the name of the twelve-item list of grievances, based on the Charter of Liberties first written by Henry I, brought to John by the earls and barons of England in January of 1215. The Unknown Charter was ignored by John and was followed by the Articles of the Barons.

William Longsword—Pg. 250, ¶ 1 and Pg. 254, ¶ 4—William Longsword, the illegitimate brother of John of England, was sent by the king to command the English archers fighting with the Count of Flanders in the attack on Philip II. William Longsword gave support to Louis when he was sent over from France as a replacement for King John after he refused to uphold the Magna Carta.

William Marshal—Pg. 254, ¶ 6—William Marshal was the regent for John's nine-year-old son Henry III. William Marshal told the barons he would uphold the Magna Carta, bringing an end to the Barons' War.

Section II: Comprehension

Write a two or three-sentence answer to each of the following questions.

1. How did Pope Innocent III plan to resolve the quarrel with John, king of England, over Stephen Langton's appointment as Archbishop of Canterbury?

A1.— Pg. 248, ¶ 1-3—At the beginning of 1213, Innocent III decided that the interdict on England was clearly not going to resolve the quarrel over Stephen Langton's appointment as Archbishop of Canterbury so he declared that John should be deposed via crusade. Innocent III wrote to Philip II and told him that if France was able to get the English king off his throne, England would become his possession forever. In addition, anyone who provided either money or his own sword to help overthrow John would receive the benefits of crusade.

STUDY AND TEACHING GUIDE FOR THE HISTORY OF THE RENAISSANCE WORLD

2. What happened after Innocent III made his intentions to start a war against John clear?

A2.—Pg. 249, ¶ 2—After Innocent III declared his intention to start a war against John clear, John decided to get right with God. In May, just before Philip II could launch his fleet towards England, John met with the pope's legate in London, agreed to Stephen Langton's appointment, and publicly acknowledged the pope as his spiritual head (accompanied with a thousand pounds of silver as tribute to Rome). The legate then went straight to Paris and forbade Philip to attack his newly restored brother in Christ.

3. How did Philip II redirect his energies after the pope told him he could not attack John?

A3.—Pg. 249, ¶ 3 & 4—Philip II was greatly put out by the pope's decision to stop the attack on John because he had already spent sixty thousand pounds putting his invasion force together and he had been counting on "the remission of his sins." Unable to attack John, Philip found another object of wrath: the Count of Flanders, who had broken his vassal's oaths by refusing to attack England. French ships and soldiers had already assembled for crusade; Philip decided to use them to firm up his control over Flanders.

4. How did Otto IV become the Holy Roman Emperor? Why did the Count of Flanders turn to Otto IV when Philip II decided to march on Flanders?

A4.—Pg. 249, ¶ 6—Otto IV became the Holy Roman Emperor in 1209 after Philip of Germany was murdered in 1208. After Otto IV was crowned, he promptly fell out both with Philip of France, his rival for power on the continent, and with Innocent III, who excommunicated him the year after his coronation, when Otto refused to hand over the control of Italian lands to the papacy. The Count of Flanders knew the Holy Roman Emperor would help him because they had common enemies.

5. Why did king John of England say "Since I became reconciled to God, woe is me; nothing has gone prosperously with me!" after the battle at Bouvines?

A5.—Pg. 250, ¶ 4-6—The English and German troops that met French forces at Bouvines in July of 1214 were defeated by their enemies, causing John to cry out in agony. The French began the fight with a cavalry charge against the Flemish mounted knights and violent fighting followed, with the experienced French soldiers coming out on top. The English and German allies were slowly driven back; the English baron Hugues de Boves fled with his men as did several Flemish dukes; Otto IV continued to fight, remounting three times after his horses were killed beneath him but soon retreating to his family lands and losing his title; William Longsword was taken prisoner and then exchanged for a French nobleman taken captive by the English; and the Count of Flanders ended up imprisoned in the Louvre, where he remained for the next twelve years.

6. For what main reason did the earls and barons of England want John to confirm the Charter of Liberties first penned by Henry I?

A6.—Pg. 251, ¶ 3 to Pg. 252, ¶ 3—The main reason the earls and barons of England wanted John to confirm the Charter of Liberties penned by Henry I was because of the heavy taxes they had to pay. John made the earls and barons pay for his wars, and upon returning home

from Chinon where he made the five-year truce with Philip II, he demanded another scutage be paid at the sum of three marks of silver for the failed campaign in Western Francia.

7. What was the main desire of the English earls and barons when they attempted to append the Charter of Liberties with a list of "evil customs" to be righted by the king?

A7.—Pg. 252, ¶ 3 & 4—The main desire of the English earls and barons was to be treated fairly by the king. For example, first on the list was a demand that the king concede his right to "take a man without judgment" and eighth on the list was a provision limiting scutage to "one mark of silver" per baron, and the amount could only be raised with the consent of the barons themselves. The earls and barons wanted to limit the king's power to seize and punish and to consent to the taxes imposed upon them; they wanted to be part of the way they were ruled.

8. How did the English noblemen react to John putting off ratifying the Unknown Charter and the Articles of the Barons?

A8.—Pg. 252, ¶ 5—On May 3, 1215, after realizing the king was not going to yield to their requests, the chief barons of England renounced their allegiance to the crown of England. Two weeks later, a group of the rebels seized London on Sunday morning, installed one of their own as the new acting mayor of the city and then they sent letters throughout England to the noblemen still faithful to John and asked them to "stand firm and fight against the king for their rights and for peace." Most of the noblemen that received the letters went to London to join the rebellion against the king.

9. What did John do before signing the Magna Carta to ensure he would be able to get out of its bounds?

A9.—Pg. 253, ¶ 5 to Pg. 254, ¶ 2—Before John signed the Magna Carta he'd written to Innocent III, pointing out that should the barons deprive John of kingly authority, they would also be depriving Innocent III— the papal overlord of England, to whom John had sworn loyalty as a vassal—of his spiritual authority. Innocent III, ever mindful of his own power, announced on April 24 that the Magna Carta was annulled and the pope threatened excommunication for England if the king observed it. After signing the Great Charter, John retreated to the Isle of Wight and then emerged to gather an army of soldiers made up of mercenaries, men from Aquitaine, and papal loyalists in order to start a war.

10. How did Louis, son of Philip the French king, become king of England?

A10.—Pg. 254, ¶ 3 & 4—The earls and barons of England did not want to establish a democracy with the Magna Carta; they merely wanted to find a better king and thus they chose Louis. King Philip agreed and on May 21, 1216, Louis landed in England where he was greeted happily by William Longsword and many others. Louis marched to London unopposed; the barons welcomed him to the city, and proclaimed him king of England there.

11. How did Louis lose the kingship of England?

A11.—Pg. 254, ¶ 5 to Pg. 255, ¶ 2—After John died, William Marshal, Henry's regent, said he would uphold the Magna Carta. Louis's French troops had treated the barons with arrogant disdain and Louis himself had been quick to claim for his own personal possession the castles and lands he had seized in his war against John. The barons no longer supported Louis, and by the following summer, it had become clear to Louis that his hopes of an English crown were doomed so he gave up and went home (with ten thousand silver marks from the royal treasury in his pocket).

Section III: Critical Thinking

The student may not use his text to answer this question.

Magna Carta is a very important document. It has influenced modern government in myriad ways; the American Bar Association even has a monument to honor the document, inscribed "To commemorate Magna Carta, symbol of Freedom Under Law." For this critical thinking question, take some time to explore the Magna Carta. Use the sources listed in the chapter in the footnote on page 253, the sources listed below, and/or sources of your own finding and then write a list of eight things you did not know about the Magna Carta, or things that you found very interesting about the document and its history. Make sure to keep track of the bibliographic information that corresponds to each fact/idea. Then, write three questions about the Magna Carta that you could use for a research project at a later date. Remember: a good research question is open-ended, considers "How?" "What?" or "Why?," and stems from thorough preliminary research (your list of facts).

List of sources from page 253:

- *Magna Carta,* by J.C. Holt (Cambridge University Press, 1965)
- *English Historical Documents*, vol. 3, *1189–1327*, ed. Harry Rothwell (Eyre & Spottiswoode, 1975)
- *1215: The Year of Magna Carta*, by Danny Danziger and John Gillingham (Touchstone, 2005)
- *Three Crises in Early English History,* by Michael Van Cleave Alexander (University Press of America, 1998) **An extensive bibliography of the best-regarded studies can be found on pages 114–120.

Internet sources:

- Magna Carta Exhibition from the British Library: http://www.bl.uk/magna-carta
- Magna Carta at National Archives & Records Administration: http://www.archives.gov/exhibits/featured_documents/magna_carta/
- Magna Carta from the History Channel: http://www.history.com/topics/british-history/magna-carta

- "The Mad King and Magna Carta" by Dan Jones from *Smithsonian Magazine*
  http://www.smithsonianmag.com/history/mad-king-magna-carta-180955745/?no-ist

The student can use as many sources as he likes as long as he keeps track of where his information is coming from. The student can use whatever citation guide works for him. If he does not have a citation preference, consider using MLA style or Chicago style. Each style manual has its own website (https://www.mla.org/MLA-Style, http://www.chicagomanualofstyle.org/home.html), and you can also purchase the style manual in book form. You can also use the Online Writing Lab from Purdue University as a source: https://owl.english.purdue.edu. MLA and Chicago style citations are the most popular citation styles for work in the humanities.

After the student compiles his list of facts and ideas, he can base his research questions off of one fact, or several facts that lead to a compelling question. He should have eight facts and three questions in total.

EXAMPLE ANSWER:

Facts:

1) Some of the ideas behind the constitution of the United States of America came from the Magna Carta. The Founding Fathers saw the Magna Carta as a "cornerstone of traditional liberties."

MLA Citation:

Woolf, Christopher. "The Magna Carta, nearly 800 years old, still influences modern perceptions of civil rights." *PRI's The World.* **PRI International. 26 Aug. 2014. Web. 22 Dec. 2015.**

2) The Magna Carta was not originally written down; it was put on paper only after it was talked about. The result is that there is no single original document.

MLA citation:

Jones, Dan. "The Mad King and Magna Carta." *The Smithsonian Magazine.* **Smithsonian.com. July 2015. Web. 22 Dec. 2015.**

Research Question:

1) How many governing documents of modern nations cite the Magna Carta as a document that influenced their structure? In what ways can we see the Magna Carta's inspiration in these documents?

Section IV: Map Exercise

1. Using your black pencil, trace the rectangular outline for map 35.1.

2. Using your blue pencil, trace the coastline around England, Ireland, the continent, and the visible portion of the Mediterranean. Include the lines of the Thames, the Seine, and the Loire. Using two pencils in contrasting colors, trace the outlines of the English empire and the regions belonging to France.

3. Using a new sheet of paper, trace the rectangular outline of the frame in black. Using a regular pencil with an eraser, draw the coastline around England and the continent, including the visible portion of the Mediterranean. Then draw the lines of the regions belonging to the English Empire and to France. When you are happy with your map, lay it over the original. Erase and redraw any lines which are more than ½″ off of the original.

4. Now mark the areas of Ireland, Wales, and England on your map. Then study carefully the locations of Connacht, Meath, Ulster, Leinster, Flanders, Normandy, Brittany, Poitou, Aquitaine, and Languedoc. When you are familiar with them, close the book. Mark each one and label it on your map. Check it against the original, and erase and remark any mistakes.

5. Now study closely the locations of Waterford, Dublin, St. Edmonds, Rouen, Paris, Tours, Poitiers, and Le Blanc. When you are familiar with them, lay your paper over the original, and erase and remark any marks that are more than ½″ off of the original.

6. Now, with your paper still over the original, trace the rectangular outlines of the small boxes that show the enlargement of the areas in England and in Flanders. Remove your paper from the original. Study closely the locations of Windsor, Runnymede, Staines, London, Canterbury, Dover, Tournai, Lille, Valenciennes, and the Battle of Bouvines. When you are familiar with them, close the book, and show the location of each in the enlarged boxes (you can use dots and lines, as the book does). When you are happy with your marks, check them against the original, and erase and remark any misplaced or mislabeled marks.

7. Finally, study the locations of Chatillon and Chinon. Mark them on your map, check your marks against the original, and make any necessary corrections.

Chapter Thirty-Six

The Birth of the Inquisition

The student may use her text when answering the questions in sections I and II.

Section I: Who, What, Where

Write a one or two-sentence answer explaining the significance of each item listed below.

Amaury—**Pg. 259, ¶ 2 & 5—Amaury, Simon de Montfort's son, was joined by Prince Louis for an attack on the southern province of France that had rebelled against his father. Prince Louis withdrew his support for the war after being unable to take Toulouse, and without Louis's support Amaury had no hope of retaking his father's conquests.**

Dominicans—**Pg. 258, ¶ 4—Dominicans, or Order of Preachers, was a monastic order started by Dominic Guzman in an effort to conquer the Languedoc heresy by converting, rather than murdering, its inhabitants. The order was approved by Honorius III soon after he became pope.**

Fourth Lateran Council—**Pg. 257, ¶ 2 & 3—Fourth Lateran Council was the name of the gathering at Lateran Palace that began on November 11, 1215. More than eight hundred abbots and priors and four hundred bishops and archbishops were in attendance to discuss doctrine and heresy.**

Francis of Assisi—**Pg. 257, ¶ 2—Francis of Assisi was an Italian monk that gathered together a small band of devout men who had followed his call to strictly observe Matthew 19:21 ("If you will be perfect, go, sell all that you have, and give it to the poor"), and in 1210 Innocent III had given him permission to establish his own monastic order. The order was called the Lesser Brothers, or Minor Friars (later called the Franciscans, after their founder).**

Franciscans—**Pg. 257, ¶ 2—Franciscans was the nickname for the monastic order started by Francis of Assisi in order to strictly observe Matthew 19:21. The order was established in 1210 and was originally called the Lesser Brothers, or Minor Friars.**

Honorius III—**Pg. 258, ¶ 4 and Pg. 259, ¶ 2—Honorius III succeeded Innocent III as pope and immediately put his energy into the crusade on the Holy Land proposed during the Fourth**

Lateran Council. When Raymond of Toulouse returned to his home city and defeated Simon de Montfort, Honorius II announced a revival of the Crusade against Languedoc.

Lateran Council—**Pg. 257, *—Lateran councils were held by the pope in Rome, at the hall known as the Lateran Palace.**

Louis IX—**Pg. 259, ¶ 7—Louis IX, son of Louis VIII (Prince Louis), became ruler of France after his father's death, with Blanche of Castile serving as his regent.**

Raymond VII—**Pg. 259, ¶ 5 and Pg. 260, ¶ 3 & 4—Raymond VII, son of Raymond of Toulouse, claimed his father's countship in 1222 after his father's death. In an effort to show his willingness to fight against heresy, Raymond VII establish a method of heretical extermination at the Council of Toulouse that established the Inquisition.**

Section II: Comprehension

Write a two or three-sentence answer to each of the following questions.

1. Why did Pope Innocent III call for the Fourth Lateran Council? What business had to be settled before the pope could follow his original agenda?

A1.—**Pg. 257, ¶ 3 to Pg. 258, ¶ 1—Pope Innocent III intended for the Fourth Lateran Council to address matters of doctrine and heresy, but the exiled Raymond of Toulouse was also present, along with his son and a handful of his supporters, because he had come to plead for the restoration of his lands, currently in the hands of Simon de Montfort. While Innocent III was inclined to give Toulouse back to the count, the majority of the priests present objected, arguing that Raymond would once again give shelter to heretics. Ultimately, Simon de Montfort was given permanent dominion over Toulouse, with only Raymond's family lands in Provence held in reserve for his son.**

2. How did the Fourth Lateran Council proceed after the business with Raymond of Toulouse was taken care of?

A2.—**Pg. 258, ¶ 2—After the matter with Raymond of Toulouse was settled, the Fourth Lateran Council went about its business, confirming seventy articles of doctrine. After all of them were read aloud to the full council, a call for yet another crusade to the Holy Land was made. As far as Innocent was concerned, the Albigensian Crusade was at an end, but the wronged Raymond of Toulouse, simmering with fury, left Rome and made his way to Avignon, in Languedoc, where he began to collect an army.**

3. Describe Raymond of Toulouse's homecoming.

A3.—**Pg. 258, ¶ 3—Simon de Montfort was deeply unpopular in southern France, and Raymond had no trouble assembling a sizable band of supporters. He occupied the lands east of the Rhone without difficulty, with more than one town opening its gates to him willingly, and he continued to advance steadily on his enemy. Simon de Montfort was fighting near the Rhone when the city of Toulouse itself revolted against him and sent**

Raymond an invitation to reenter as count and lord; he marched into Toulouse in triumph on October 1, 1217.

4. What happened to Innocent III's body after he died?

A4.—Pg. 258, ¶ 4—Innocent III died suddenly while visiting the central Italian town of Perugia. The cardinals of Rome went immediately into conclave to elect his successor, neglecting to bury the dead pope's body. Two days later, the theologian Jacques de Vitry found Innocent III's body decomposing in the church of St. Lawrence, stripped of its gold-trimmed robes by thieves.

5. How did Simon de Montfort's siege on Toulouse finally come to an end?

A5.—Pg. 258, ¶ 5 to Pg. 259, ¶ 1—Simon de Montfort continued to attack Toulouse after Raymond was put back in control, but his constant assaults on the city's walls were always driven back by the citizens, who joined Raymond's knights in building new defenses and operating the mangonels, catapults that hurled boulders over the city's walls at the attackers. Nine months into the siege, a stone pitched from a mangonel worked by the women of Toulouse struck Simon de Montfort between the eyes and shattered his skull. A knight nearby hurriedly covered the body with a cape, but word of Montfort's death spread at once, and his men immediately abandoned the siege.

6. How did the attack at Marmande strengthen the resistance against Amaury de Montfort and Prince Louis?

A6.—Pg. 259, ¶ 3-5—When Amaury de Montfort and Prince Louis besieged and captured the small town of Marmande they decided to massacre all of the inhabitants, probably hoping to terrify the rest of Languedoc into surrender. However, the strategy backfired, resistance stiffened, and when Prince Louis took his army on to Toulouse and laid siege to it, he decided the city was far too strong so he went home. With Louis gone, Amaury de Montfort had no hope of retaking his father's conquests.

7. In what way did Philip II Augustus's reign change Western Francia?

A7.— Pg. 259, ¶ 6—When Philip II Augustus died he had been ruler of Western Francia for over forty-two years. During that time he doubled its territory, extended the power of the throne to unheard-of lengths, and reduced the independence of its dukes, counts, and barons. Philip II had turned Western Francia into the nation-state of France.

8. Explain the terms of the deal, the Treaty of Paris, made between Raymond VII and Blanche of Castile.

A8.—Pg. 259, ¶ 7 to Pg. 260, ¶ 2—The Treaty of Paris proclaimed that if Raymond VII would tear down Toulouse's newly constructed defenses, yield several castles, and swear to fight Catharism, the French throne would recognize him as the rightful ruler of Toulouse. In addition, Raymond would have to spend four thousand silver marks to establish a new university in Toulouse where right theology and proper doctrine would be taught. Raymond VII agreed to the deal, which was signed in Paris in 1229.

Section III: Critical Thinking

The student may not use her text to answer this question.

At the end of this chapter we learned about a new way to deal with heretics: inquisition. In your own words, describe the method established at the church council in Toulouse in 1229 that would eliminate heretics from southern France. Then explain how this new method could be used for evil rather than for good.

The last two paragraphs of the chapter explain the new method to find heretics established at the church council in Toulouse in 1229:

> As further proof of his willingness to exterminate heresy, Raymond played host to a church council that met in Toulouse late in 1229. The council affirmed the establishment of the new University of Toulouse and laid out exactly how the extermination should proceed. 'We appoint,' the council's written canons explain, 'that the archbishops and bishops shall swear in one priest, and two or three laymen of good report . . . in every parish . . . who shall diligently, faithfully, and frequently seek out heretics in those parishes.' When heretics were located, their houses were to be burned; if they repented 'through fear of death,' they would merely be exiled and forced to wear crosses of colored cloth sewn onto their garments.

This method of searching out heretics by appointed committee diffused the hunt out among both priests and laypeople: both were now authorized to inquire into the orthodoxy of their neighbors. Young Raymond had brought an end to the Albigensian Crusade; but in doing so, he had allowed the Council of Toulouse to establish the Inquisition.

The first part of the student's answer should recap, in her own words, the decision made at the church council in Toulouse. The second part of the student's answer should consider the bad that could be done if the power to accuse and mark people as "other" fell into corrupt hands. Any personal grudge or prejudice could sway a person to falsely accuse an enemy of heresy. Those accused could be marked, exiled, or killed. The student's answer should explore what could happen when a group of people, especially those whipped into a state of religious frenzy, have the power to condemn those that do not join their hysteria.

EXAMPLE ANSWER:

The church council held in Toulouse in 1229 was a way for Raymond VII to show his willingness to abide by the French king's authority, and the pope's authority, by finding another way to exterminate heresy in the southern region of France. At the church council the plan for the extermination of heresy was laid out as such: the archbishops and bishops would swear in one priest and two or three laymen of good report in every parish to seek out heretics in those parishes. The homes of heretics would be burned, and if the heretics repented they would be exiled and forced to wear crosses of colored cloth on their garments. If they did not, they would die. This style of questioning, what would turn into the Inquisition, made everyone a suspect. If one did not appease those appointed to search out heretics, a false accusation could be made. Personal grudges, long-standing prejudices, and

momentary irrational whims could cause a person to accuse another of heretical actions. With only the word of one against the other, there was no way for a person to defend him/ herself. This could lead to widespread panic and mania, with people being hunted, exiled, and killed for no other reason than that someone accused them of something they didn't do, and there would be no way to prove their innocence.

Chapter Thirty-Seven

Moving Westward

The student may use his text when answering the questions in sections I and II.

Section I: **Who, What, Where**

Write a one or two-sentence answer explaining the significance of each item listed below.

Ala ad-Din Muhammad ibn Tekish—**Pg. 262, ¶ 3 and Pg. 263, ¶ 2 & 7—Ala ad-Din Muhammad ibn Tekish, shah of Khwarezm, hoped to seize control of the caliphate in Baghdad. Ala ad-Din Muhammad ibn Tekish did not trust the diplomatic attempt made by Genghis Khan, murdering the Mongol's ambassadors, and as a result brought war to Khwarezm and his death in exile on an island not long after.**

Chagatai—**Pg. 267, ¶ 4—Chagatai, Genghis Khan's second son, was given his father's lands in Central Asia after his father's death.**

David the Builder—**Pg. 264, ¶ 3—David the Builder was a Christian king that managed to bring the patchwork of native mountain tribes, Turks, refugees from Cilician Armenia, and various Muslim settlers under his rule in Georgia in the beginning of the twelfth century.**

George IV—**Pg. 264, ¶ 4—George IV, son of Tamar and ruler of the Kingdom of Georgia, was badly wounded in a fight against the Mongols and forced to give up the south of his country. Though he was able to field an impressive number of troops to meet the Mongol invasion, Jebe and Subotai crushed the Georgian army near the capital city of Tbilisi, staged a fake withdrawal, and then stormed back to kill the survivors, leading to George IV's surrender.**

Jalal ad-Din—**Pg. 263, ¶ 7 to Pg. 264, ¶ 1 & 6 and Pg. 266, ¶ 1—Jalal ad-Din, Ala ad-Din Muhammad ibn Tekish's son and heir, slipped away from the Mongol attack on Khwarezm and led five thousand men to a safe haven in the north of India. Jalal ad-Din had one victory against a Mongol outpost but soon his men were slaughtered by Genghis Khan on the bank of the Indus river; Jalal ad-Din escaped but his wife and children were taken captive and all of his sons were put to death.**

Jebe and Subotai—**Pg. 263, ¶ 7 to Pg. 264, ¶ 4—Jebe and Subotai, two of Genghis Khan's highest-ranking generals, were sent after Shah Ala ad-Din Muhammad ibn Tekish after he fled from the Mongol attack on Khwarezm but they were unable to catch him. They followed him, nonetheless, with twenty-five thousand soldiers behind them, and they continued into the Kingdom of Georgia where they were able to take the southern part of the Georgia kingdom for the Mongols.**

Jochi—**Pg. 263, ¶ 5, Pg. 266, ¶ 3 & 8 and Pg. 267, ¶ 1—Jochi, Genghis Khan's oldest son, was left in charge of a substantial Mongol army after his father returned to Mongolia following the Battle of the Indus. Jochi beat the coalition of Georgians, Turks and Rus's, chasing the Rus' survivors to the shores of the Dnieper river; he stopped there, his orders carried out.**

Mstislav III—**Pg. 266, ¶ 6 & 7—Mstislav III, Grand Duke of Kiev, joined the coalition of Georgians and Turks that were preparing to fight against the Mongols; he recruited the nearby princes of Galich, Chernigov, and Smolensk, and led a force of eighty thousand Russian warriors south to the Kalka river. Mstislav III's forces were disorganized, fighting began before the Kievans even knew the battle had begun, and Mstislav III was captured and killed by suffocation.**

Muhammad al-Nasawi—**Pg. 262, ¶ 4 and Pg. 263, ¶ 2—Muhammad al-Nasawi was Ala ad-Din Muhammad ibn Tekish's secretary. He recorded the message that came with the gifts of diplomacy sent by Genghis Khan and also explained that the second delegation of Mongol ambassadors were "seized" and "disappeared forever."**

Ogodei—**Pg. 267, ¶ 5 to Pg. 268, ¶ 2—Ogodei, the third son of Genghis Khan, received the title of Great Khan of the Mongols after his father's death. There was some dissension over Ogodei's appointment, but by 1229, the Mongols had agreed to recognize Ogodei as Genghis Khan's rightful successor.**

Tamar—**Pg. 264, ¶ 3—Tamar, granddaughter of David the Builder, governed a Christian Georgia at the end of the twelfth-century that covered almost all of the land bridge between the Caspian Sea and the Black Sea.**

Tolui—**Pg. 267, ¶ 4—Tolui, the youngest son of Genghis Khan, received the Khan's own homeland after his father's death.**

Section II: Comprehension

Write a two or three-sentence answer to each of the following questions.

1. How did Shan Ala ad-Din Muhammad ibn Tekish plan to defend himself against the Mongol front? What actually happened?

A1.—Pg. 263, ¶ 5 & 6—Shah Ala ad-Din Muhammad ibn Tekish believed that the nomadic Mongols would be difficult to defeat on open ground but unable to take fortified cities, so he divided his troops up among his frontier fortresses at Otrar, Khojend, and Bukhara.

In Otrar, the official responsible for the murder of the Mongol ambassadors was taken prisoner and executed by having molten gold poured into his eyes and throat; the garrison at Khojend tried to escape along the riverbank at night, but Jochi's men chased the soldiers away from the river and through the desert until, one by one, they fell to Mongol arrows or exhaustion; and in Bukhara, the townspeople surrendered almost immediately, but a small royal detachment held out in the city's citadel. Genghis Khan ordered the citadel stormed, with Bukhara's civilians driven in front of his own men as a shield and after twelve days of assault and slaughter, the citadel too was taken; the defenders were massacred.

2. Describe Genghis Khan's movement east across Khwarezm.

A2.—Pg. 264, ¶ 5—As Genghis Khan and his sons turned eastward to conquer Samarkand and to continue across Khwarezm, they generally looted cities that surrendered and put them under Mongol governorship, and their citizens were spared. Cities that resisted the Mongols were exterminated: at Tirmidh, Genghis Khan ordered the entire population driven outside the city walls and put to death; at Merv, seven hundred thousand people were massacred (some contemporary chroniclers put the total at more than a million); at Nishapur, four hundred useful artisans were spared and everyone else was beheaded. Two massacres were carried out in Balkh, one when the city first fell, a second after the false withdrawal of Genghis's men lured survivors out of the nooks and crannies where they had hidden, wiping out all traces of the culture from that region.

3. What happened to Jalal ad-Din and his family during the effort to attack the Mongols?

A3.—Pg. 264, ¶ 6 to Pg. 266, ¶ 1—After receiving word that Jalal ad-Din's forces had managed to defeat a Mongol outpost, Genghis Khan turned and began to ride eastward, back towards India. He caught up with Jalal ad-Din on the banks of the Indus river, and drove him and his men steadily backwards into the water where most of the Shah's men were killed by Mongol arrows as they struggled in the water. Jalal ad-Din himself managed to flee into the distance but his wives and children, left behind, were taken captive; all of his male children were put to death.

4. What had the Rus' been doing since their Christian conversion in the tenth century?

A4.—Pg. 266, ¶ 5—Since their conversion to Christianity in the tenth century, the Rus' had been mostly occupied with internal matters. Each major city of the Rus' was ruled by a prince who paid lip service to the overall rule of a Grand Duke, but protected his own power, sometimes viciously. The ruler of Kiev had most often claimed the title Grand Duke, but for the last half century, his authority had been constantly challenged by the rulers of the city of Novgorod.

5. How did Genghis Khan die?

A5.—Pg. 267, ¶ 2—Genghis Khan died while he was directing his campaign to finish destroying the Western Xia. He was out hunting in 1225 when he fell and as a result suffered from recurring fevers and muscle spasms that grew gradually worse. Sometime in 1227, in an unknown camp south of the Li-p'an Mountains, the Universal Khan of the Mongols drew his last breath, but his death was kept secret, by his own wish, until his generals finished demolishing the last Xia strongholds in September of 1227.

Section III: **Critical Thinking**

The student may not use his text to answer this question.

As we know from our history reading, and from hearing contemporary news reports, diplomacy is a tricky thing. Describe, in your own words, the attempt at diplomacy carried out by Genghis Khan towards Shah Ala ad-Din Muhammad ibn Tekish. Then write a paragraph explaining why you think the Shah reacted the way he did. What was the key component missing in the negotiation between Genghis Khan and the Shah?

The chapter opens with a description of Genghis Khan's attempt at diplomatic relations with Khwarezm. When Shah Ala ad-Din Muhammad ibn Tekish heard of the Mongol advance towards Khwarezm he left his attempt to take Baghdad and returned home. The advance turned out not to be an army but three Mongol ambassadors. They carried presents of precious metals and semiprecious stones, rhinoceros horns and white camel wool. The message that accompanied the gifts said:

> I am familiar with the magnificence of your empire and I know that your
> authority is recognized in the majority of the countries of the world. Therefore,
> I consider it my duty to strike up friendly relations with you . . . You know
> better than anyone else that my provinces are nurseries for soldiers, of mines of
> silver, and that may produce an abundance of things. If you would agree that
> we open up, each from our own side, an easy access for negotiations between
> our countries, this will be an advantage for us all.

The Shah's reaction to the gifts and message was one of distrust. He bribed one of the ambassadors to act as a spy. Then, when a second delegation came from the Khan, the Shah had them arrested and murdered. Genghis Khan reacted as one would expect. He rounded up an army of 200,000 soldiers and laid siege to the three cities where the Shah had stationed his troops. The Shah escaped but died less than a year later on the island where he was hiding.

The student should recount the mess between the Mongols and the Turks in his own words. Then he should explain what he thinks went wrong in their negotiations. The Khan had a reputation for ruthlessness, so it seems fair that the Shah would not trust his ambassadors. However, the Khan also had conquered more territory than any other Mongol could have dreamed of, and a partnership with Khwarezm would have opened up brand-new trade routes and the opportunity to gain unheard-of wealth for both leaders. Ultimately the Shah made his decision based on fear rather than trust. He decided to question the intentions of Genghis Khan and take matters into his own hands by bribing one of the ambassadors to spy and murdering the second delegation. The result was that his cities were massacred and he died in hiding.

EXAMPLE ANSWER:

Genghis Khan wanted to pass through Khwarezm in order to open up brand-new trade routes for his Mongol empire. He sent a delegation of ambassadors to see Shah Ala ad-Din Muhammad ibn Tekish. The ambassadors came bearing gifts, like semiprecious stones and white camel wool, and they had a message from the Khan. The message asked for friendly relations between the two leaders and that both would prosper from the relationship. The

Shah did not believe the Khan was sincere, so he bribed one of the ambassadors to be a spy. When a second delegation of Mongol ambassadors came to Khwarezm, the Shah had them murdered. As a result, Genghis Khan formed an army of 200,000 soldiers and attacked. Three major cities in Khwarezm were attacked and the Shah fled, ending up in exile on an island where he died less than a year later.

The Shah did not trust Genghis Khan, and the result of that mistrust was slaughter and ruin. The Khan had a reputation for ruthlessness, so it seems fair that the Shah would not trust his ambassadors. However, the Khan also had conquered more territory than any other Mongol could have dreamed of, and a partnership with Khwarezm would have opened up brand-new trade routes and the opportunity to gain unheard-of wealth for both leaders. Ultimately the Shah made his decision based on fear rather than trust and the diplomatic attempt made by Genghis Khan turned into war.

Section IV: Map Exercise

1. Trace the rectangular outline of the frame around Map 37.1 in black.

2. Using a blue pencil, trace all visible coastline, including the Caspian Sea, the Aral Sea, and Lake Baikal. Also trace the lines of the Oxus and the Indus. Repeat until the contours are familiar.

3. Using contrasting colors, trace the Western Xia, Jin, and Southern Song areas. Also trace the areas of the Kingdom of Georgia and of Goryeo. Repeat until the contours are familiar. Trace the mountains with small peaks. Finally, using your black pencil, trace the outline of the conquests of Ghengis Khan in black. Repeat all until the contours are familiar.

4. Using a new sheet of paper, trace the rectangular outline of the frame in black. Then using your regular pencil with an eraser, draw the visible coastline and the lines of the Caspian Sea, the Aral Sea, Lake Baikal, and the Oxus and the Indus. Draw the lines of the Western Xia, Jin, and Southern Song areas. Draw the lines of the Kingdom of Georgia and of Goryeo. Show the mountains with small peaks. Then draw the outline of the conquests of Ghengis Khan. Erase and redraw as necessary.

5. When you are happy with your map, lay it over the original. Erase and redraw any lines which are more than ½" off of the original.

6. Now study the locations of Tbilisi, Nishapur, Merv, Bukhara, Balkh, Tirmidh, Samarkand, Khojend, Otrar, Otukan, Ordu-Baliq, Zhongdu, Kaifeng, Yangzhou, and Burkhan Khaldun. When they are familiar for you, close the book. Mark and label each on your map. Then lay your map over the original, and erase and remark any which are more than ½" off of the original.

7. Mark the areas of the Hindu Kush and Li'pan.

Chapter Thirty-Eight

South of India

The student may use her text when answering the questions in sections I and II.

Section I: Who, What, Where

Write a one or two-sentence answer explaining the significance of each item listed below.

Chandrabhanu—**Pg. 272, ¶ 1-3—Chandrabhanu, king of the Javakas, was an adventurer who crossed over into Sri Lanka from southeast Asia. Chandrabhanu took control of the north of Sri Lanka with his Javaka army, under the pretext that they were also followers of Buddhism, but he was removed by Jatavarman Sundara in 1263.**

Jatavarman Sundara—**Pg. 272, ¶ 3—Jatavarman Sundara stretched Pandyan power from the central coastal city of Nellore, all the way down to the Indian Ocean. Jatavarman removed Chandrabhanu in 1263 and put the northern part of Sri Lanka entirely under Pandyan domination, thus earning him the name "Emperor of the three worlds:" his lands encompassed the north of the Sri Lanka, his own Pandyan realm, and the west of the Chola.**

Magha—**Pg. 270, ¶ 1 & 4 and Pg. 271, ¶ 4—Magha, a Hindu nobleman, fled south from Orissa with his own private army along the eastern coast of India in 1215 in order to find a new country. Magha took over Sri Lanka, wrecking the island and forcing his captives to convert to Hinduism, and he ruled for four decades from Polonnaruwa.**

Parakrama Bahu II—**Pg. 271, ¶ 3— Parakrama Bahu II, Vijaya Bahu III's son, turned Dambadeniya into a settled place of learning, a refuge for Pali speakers and writers, a center for Sri Lankan Buddhism.**

Sangha—**Pg. 271, ¶ 2—Sangha was the name for a Buddhist house of worshippers.**

Sirisamghabodhi—**Pg. 271, ¶ 1—Sirisamghabodhi was a great fourth-century king that was revered for his moral excellence. Sirisamghabodhi, who had fought off rebels and had sacrificed himself for his people, was an inspiration for Vijaya Bahu III.**

Vijaya Bahu III—**Pg. 271, ❡ 1 & 2—Vijaya Bahu III, a Sri Lankan refugee hiding in the mountains from Magha and purported descendent of Sirisamghabodhi, rallied together the scattered sanghas and united the remaining Sri Lankans behind him. Vijaya Bahu III founded a Buddhist kingdom on Sri Lanka centered at Dambadeniya, where Buddha's tooth was enshrined.**

Section II: Comprehension

Write a two or three-sentence answer to each of the following questions.

1. Why wasn't Magha able to establish his own power in Orissa or Chola? Why was Sri Lanka a good target for his ambitions?

A1.—Pg. 270, ❡ 2 & 3—Orissa was ruled by a string of powerful Hindu kings descended from Chola royalty, and Chola, though shrunken from its twelfth-century greatness, was still strong; neither was suitable for an ambitious soldier looking to establish his own power. Sri Lanka was open to invasion because three years prior to Magha's arrival a newcomer from the south of India had arrived and taken the throne for himself. But the newcomer could not raise enough support to fight back against Magha, who had swelled his private army to over twenty thousand by hiring south Indian mercenaries.

2. What did Magha do once he arrived in Sri Lanka?

A2.—Pg. 270, ❡ 4 to Pg. 271, ❡ 1—When Magha arrived in Sri Lanka, he stormed the island with savagery, wrecking the Buddhist shrines, destroying sacred writings, forcing his captives to convert to Hinduism, confiscating the land that he overran, and seizing crops, livestock, and treasure for his own. He captured the capital city of Polonnaruwa, burned parts of it, took the king captive and put his eyes out, and then he established himself as king, using his standing army of thousands to keep power over the inhabitants. He wasn't able to take the whole island, however, because some natives of Sri Lanka were able to retreat south into the mountains and establish villages there where they were able to protect the Buddhist order.

3. How did Sri Lanka come to be divided between Dambadeniya and Polonnaruwa?

A3.—Pg. 271, ❡ 2—Vijaya Bahu III centered his operations at the mountain settlement of Dambadeniya, which became his capital. When he discovered that several monks had taken the Buddha's Tooth with them in their flight from Polonnaruwa, he ordered the sacred relic brought to him, and mounted a great festival celebrating his re-enthronement as Sri Lanka's true king. His efforts created a boundary between his conquests and those of the Hindu invaders, dividing the island into two realms: the Buddhist kingdom of Dambadeniya, and the Hindu realm of Polonnaruwa.

4. What did Vijaya Bahu III and Parakrama Bahu II do to revive Buddhism in Sri Lanka and ensure its longevity?

A4.—Pg. 271, ¶ 3—When Vijaya Bahu III was ruling over Dambadeniya, he had ordered all of his subjects who had "good memory" and who were "skilled in quick and fair writing" to record everything they could remember of the destroyed Buddhist scriptures, rebuilding a massive library. Parakrama Bahu II had immersed himself in it, earning a reputation for learning. He then weeded out unworthy monks and "purified the Order of the perfectly Enlightened One," he resurrected the great Buddhist religious festivals and rituals, and he built Buddhist temples and monasteries.

5. What happened to Polonnaruwa after Magha's death in 1255?

A5.—Pg. 271, ¶ 4—After Magha died in 1255, the north separated into patches of private power, ruled by chieftains called vanniya. Magha had no known heir, and no one replaced him on the throne at Polonnaruwa, thus his kingdom fell apart.

6. Where did the Chola go after the rule of Jatavarman Sundara?

A6.—Pg. 273, ¶ 1—Jatavarman Sundara reduced Chola rule to a strip of land around the capital city of Thanjavur. Soon after, the Chola disappeared. After 1279, there are no more records of Chola kings; the Pandya had taken their place as lords of south India.

Section III: Critical Thinking

The student may not use her text to answer this question.

In the last chapter we read about the failed diplomatic actions of Genghis Khan and Ala ad-Din Muhammad ibn Tekish. In this chapter we again see an attempt at diplomacy, this time for a small kingdom looking to expand without war. Write a paragraph explaining how Dambadeniya used trade rather than battle as a way to grow their influence in the world.

The Dambadeniya kingdom managed to remain a stronghold of Buddhism in Sri Lanka despite the power struggles felt on the north of the island. An account of Dambadeniya's attempts at international trade is given on page 273. In 1283, an embassy from Dambadeniya arrived in Egypt, hoping to arrange a trade treaty with the sultan in Cairo. The ambassadors arrived at the port of Ormus, went up the Euphrates to Baghdad, and then on to Cairo. Once there:

> A letter from the king was presented to the Sultan, enclosed in a golden box, enveloped in a stuff resembling the bark of a tree. The letter was also written in indigenous characters upon the bark of a tree. As no person in Cairo could read the writing, the ambassador explained its contents verbally, saying that his master possessed a prodigious quantity of pearls, for the fishery formed part of his dominions, also precious stones of all sorts, ships, elephants, muslins and other stuffs, bakam wood, cinnamon, and all the commodities of trade. . .

The successors of Parakrama Bahu II still ruled in Dambadeniya and they were hoping to interact with the rest of the world. They were not using spears or arrows but trade as a way to grow their influence. In this way the Dambadeniya kingdom and the Pali language expanded their reach.

EXAMPLE ANSWER:

When Magha arrived in Sri Lanka, he pushed the natives of the island south into the mountains. From there, a new Buddhist kingdom was formed, centered at the capital of Dambadeniya. Despite other power struggles on the north of island, the Dambadeniya kingdom remained a stronghold of Buddhism. The successors of Parakrama Bahu still ruled in Dambadeniya, and they looked to trade as a way to expand their kingdom's influence, rather than war and territorial expansion. In 1283 an embassy from Dambadeniya went to Cairo in Egypt, hoping to make a trade treaty with the sultan. The ambassadors brought a letter from the king, enclosed in a golden box. The ambassador had to explain the contents of the box because no one could read the Pali language. He told the king that the box was full of pearls, precious stones, muslins and cinnamon—all things that could be traded with the Egyptians. This was the way Dambadeniya was interacting with the rest of the world. They were not using spears or arrows but trade as a way to grow their influence. In this way the Dambadeniya kingdom and the Pali language expanded their reach.

Section IV: Map Exercise

1. Trace the rectangular outline of the frame for Map 38.1 in black.

2. Using your blue pencil, trace the coastline, including around the island. Also trace the line of the Kaveri. Repeat until the contours are familiar.

3. Using a contrasting color, trace the line of the territory of the Pandya. Then using a different color trace the Orissa area. Repeat until the contours are familiar.

4. Using a new sheet of paper, trace the rectangular frame of the map in black. Then using a regular pencil with an eraser, draw the coastline, including the island. Draw the line of the Kaveri. Then draw the line of the Pandyan territory, erasing and redrawing as necessary. When you are happy with your map, lay it over the original. Erase and redraw any lines which are more than ¼" off of the original.

5. Now study carefully the locations of Nellore, Thanjavur, Polannaruwa,and Dambadeniya. When they are familiar to you, close the book. Mark and label each on your map. Then lay your map back over the original, and erase and remark any marks which are more than ¼" off of the original.

6. Finally mark Palk Strait and the Giant's Tank. Also mark the Arabian Sea.

Chapter Thirty-Nine

The Fifth Crusade

The student may use his text when answering the questions in sections I and II.

Section I: Who, What, Where

Write a one or two-sentence answer explaining the significance of each item listed below.

Al-Adil—**Pg. 275, ¶ 2—Al-Adil, Saladin's brother and possessor of the Ayyubid throne, was seventy-two and in poor health when the Fifth Crusade was launched against Egypt.**

Al-Kamil—**Pg. 276, ¶ 2, Pg. 277, ¶ 1 & 4 and Pg. 278, ¶ 4 & 5—Al-Kamil, al-Adil's oldest son and governor of Damietta, had to desert Damietta to protect his claim on the throne after his father's death. After al-Kamil secured his place as Sultan, he stopped the Crusaders from attacking Cairo and was even able to get them to return Damietta to his power in exchange for letting the Crusaders live.**

Al-Mu'azzam—**Pg. 277, ¶ 4—Al-Mu'azzam, al-Kamil's brother and deputy governor in charge of Syria, helped al-Kamil put down the rebellion in Cairo after their father's death.**

Andrew II—**Pg. 275, ¶ 4—Andrew II, king of Hungary, joined the Fifth Crusade reluctantly, and only because he had promised twenty years to go on crusade and had still not fulfilled his vows. After arriving in Acre in the late summer of 1217, he realized that there weren't enough soldiers to do anything effective, so he made a couple of desultory raids into Muslim territories, declared his vow fulfilled, and then went home.**

King John of Jerusalem—**Pg. 275, ¶ 3 & * and Pg. 276, ¶ 2—King John of Jerusalem (more and more known as the kingdom of Acre), actually the regent for his young daughter Yolande, was the most powerful sovereign to join the Fifth Crusade. King John led the Crusaders into the Egyptian port city of Damietta, hoping to conquer the city in order to have a strong base from which to attack Cairo.**

Pelagius—**Pg. 278, ¶ 3-5—Pelagius, the senior papal legate accompanying the Fifth Crusade, talked the bulk of the army into leaving Damietta and marching towards Cairo. When the campaign failed, Pelagius was offered as a hostage to ensure Damietta's return to al-Kamil.**

Yolande—**Pg. 275, ❡ 3 & * and Pg. 276, ❡ 2—Yolande was the ruler of the kingdom of Jerusalem (increasingly known as the kingdom of Acre). Yolande's father John ruled as her regent.**

Section II: Comprehension

Write a two or three-sentence answer to each of the following questions.

1. Why didn't Frederick II of Germany join in the Fifth Crusade?

A1.—Pg. 275, ❡ 5 to Pg. 276, ❡ 1—Frederick II of Germany was still fighting against supporters of the deposed Otto in Germany and used the defense of his crown as an excuse not to join the Fifth Crusade. He did, however, send an army to join the Crusaders in April of 1218.

2. How did the Egyptians protect Damietta from invasion?

A2.—Pg. 276, ❡ 3 & 4—Damietta was protected by three sets of walls, which meant it could not be broken into. Damietta could also not be starved out, as it was supplied with food and water by a branch of the Nile that was protected by a tall, fortified tower; massive iron chains were strung from the tower to the walls of Damietta to prevent ships from travelling up the Nile into Egypt. When Crusader forces finally got into the fortress and cut the chains, al-Kamil immediately sank cargo ships in the Nile in front of the city, creating a reef too shallow for the Crusaders to sail past.

3. What happened to Damietta's defenses after al-Adil's death?

A3.—Pg. 276, ❡ 6 to Pg. 277, ❡ 1—When al-Adil died a Cairo nobleman tried to usurp the throne from his successor al-Kamil, so al-Kamil had to leave Damietta to fight for his own rule. Without its governor, Damietta's defenses weakened. The Crusaders made their way around the reef, back into the Nile, and by February had blocked Damietta from resupply.

4. Why did Francis of Assisi go to Damietta?

A4.—Pg. 277, ❡ 2—Francis of Assisi went to Damietta because he had a burning desire to preach the Gospel and an equally fiery desire to suffer martyrdom for the sake of Christ. He had tried twice before to travel to Muslim lands; his first effort had been derailed by storm and shipwreck, his second by illness. Finally, he had managed to make his way to Egypt, where he hoped to bring peace to the Crusade-wracked country by converting the Sultan.

5. How did al-Kamil react to Francis of Assisi's visit to Cairo?

A5.—Pg. 277, ❡ 4—Al-Kamil received Francis of Assisi politely and listened to his preaching about faith in Christ and the Gospel willingly as long as he did not speak against Mohammed. Al-Kamil was ultimately unconvinced, but he dismissed Francis of Assisi with unfailing courtesy, and had him escorted safely back to the camp at Damietta.

6. What happened when the Crusaders finally stormed into Damietta on November 4, 1218?

A6.—Pg. 277, ¶ 6 to Pg. 278, ¶ 1—When the Crusaders finally stormed into Damietta on November 4, they found a graveyard. Five out of six citizens had died of starvation and plague. Appalled by the scene, the Crusaders did not indulge in any of the violence that had marked the conquest of Constantinople and instead allowed the survivors to leave the city, and even tried to feed (and baptize) the starving children.

7. Describe what happened to the Fifth Crusade after the conquest of Damietta.

A7.—Pg. 278, ¶ 2 & 3—After the conquest of Damietta the Crusaders were stuck in the city because Al-Kamil had beefed up the Ayyubid army with his brother's men while no further Crusader reinforcements arrived. Francis of Assisi, having made no progress either in converting the Egyptians or in attaining martyrdom, left to visit Bethlehem and then returned home; Jacques de Vitry occupied himself in writing a comprehensive history of the Crusades; and Frederick II did not arrive, although he talked Pope Honorius III into crowning him Holy Roman Emperor, in 1220, by promising to embark on crusade immediately afterwards. By June of 1221, the Crusader army was fed up with Damietta and was convinced by Pelagius to attack Cairo.

8. How did the Fifth Crusade end?

A8.—Pg. 278, ¶ 4 & 5—The Crusaders marched slowly towards Cairo, fending off constant attacks from al-Kamil's front lines, and they were eventually cut off from their supply of food by al-Kamil's boats. The Crusaders decided to retreat back towards Damietta, but by this point the Nile was in full flood, and al-Kamil ordered the sluice gates that lined the Crusader path back to Damietta opened, forcing the Crusaders to take a narrow road back to Damietta that was blocked by al-Kamil's army. The Crusaders turned over Damietta in exchange for their lives, and that was the end of the Fifth Crusade.

9. What hope did the Crusaders have for a future defeat of the Muslim army?

A9.—Pg. 279, ¶ 2 & 3—The Crusaders had heard tales from India that a Christian king from deep in the heart of that unknown land was approaching Baghdad, and would sweep the Muslims away in front of him. He was known, variously, as King David or Prester John; this "King David," ruler of a huge Christian realm hitherto undiscovered, had hundreds of thousands of men and he had already defeated Khwarezm and was even now hurrying towards the Holy Land to rescue its sacred sites. But there was no King David, no Christian army from India, no help on the horizon—the reports were garbled tales of the Mongol advance from the east and the Great Khan that was coming was not a rescuer of Christendom.

Section III: Critical Thinking

The student may not use his text to answer this question.

In this chapter we read that the Fifth Crusade, according to Roger of Wendover, "assembled in great force at Acre, under the three kings of Jerusalem,* Hungary, and Cyprus." The asterisk next to Jerusalem leads us to a footnote that reads "By 'Jerusalem,' Roger of Wendover means the remnants of the Kingdom of Jerusalem centered at Acre; increasingly it was known as the kingdom of Acre." The fight over the boundaries and ownership of Jerusalem (now known as a city in the nation of Israel) is one that continues to this day. Using your research skills, answer the following questions:

- What is the Arab-Israeli conflict?
- How does the "Holy Land" play into the Arab-Israeli conflict?
- What is the current state of the Israeli-Palestinian conflict?

The student can use any method of research he would like to answer these questions—internet searches, book research, or research done with the help of a local librarian. The Arab-Israeli conflict is very complicated. The goal here is to engage the student in research that connects Renaissance history to contemporary world events. The example answers offered below reflect a very general overview of the conflict.

- *What is the Arab-Israeli conflict?*

The Arab-Israeli conflict began in the late nineteenth century as a struggle over land between the Palestinian Arabs and the Zionist Jews. The nation of Israel was established on May 14, 1948, by the United Nations; Israel is a Jewish nation in Palestine, a territory inhabited by Palestinian Arabs. Both Israelis and Arabs claim the land in Palestine is theirs via ancestral rights, and war continues to break out between the two groups.

- *How does the "Holy Land" play into the Arab-Israeli conflict?*

The Jewish people believe the land in Israel was promised in the Bible to Abraham and his descendants, including the Jews. The ancient Jewish kingdoms of Israel and Judea are within the borders of the current state of Israel. At the same time, the Palestinians that were displaced when Israel was created say that they have a right to the land based on their longtime residence in the area. Arabs also say that Abraham's son Ishmael is the forefather of the Arabs, and thus the promise God made to Abraham and his descendants extends to the Arabs as well.

- *What is the current state of the Israeli-Palestinian conflict (as of date of publication)?*

Israelis and Palestinians fight over the creation of the Jewish state and the inability for those displaced when the nation was formed to return to their homes. There is also great conflict surrounding Israel's occupation of land in the West Bank, and control over Gaza. Israel's military presence is often oppressive to the Palestinians living in these areas, and Palestinians are have often fought against the occupying force. These lands were supposed

to become a Palestinian state per the Oslo Accord made in 1993, but after years of friction and mutual provocation, the Palestinian people rebelled in the September 2000 uprising called the "Intifada." Israel and Palestine continue to work at peace agreements, but violence between the two peoples goes on. In 2007 most Palestinians and Israelis agreed a two-state solution was the best solution. Peace talks began again in 2013, but were suspended in 2014.

Chapter Forty

From the Golden Bull to the Baltic Crusade

The student may use her text when answering the questions in sections I and II.

Section I: Who, What, Where

Write a one or two-sentence answer explaining the significance of each item listed below.

Béla—**Pg. 282, ¶ 5—Béla, teenaged son of King Andrew of Hungary, was looked at by the noblemen of Hungary as a possible replacement for his father after Andrew announced that all lands gifted by the crown would remain permanently in the hands of their receivers, to be passed down as hereditary estates from father to son into eternity.**

Boleslaw—**Pg. 284, ¶ 1—Boleslaw, a Piast prince, was crowned first king of the Polans in 992 but his coronation brought no unity to his so-called people. Cousins of the Piast fought with each other for the crown, and local tribal leaders resisted the victors.**

Cumans—**Pg. 282, ¶ 3—Cumans were a wandering tribal alliance of Turkish, Mongol, and northern Chinese peoples who had migrated slowly to the west, threatening the border of Hungary. Andrew brought in the Teutonic Knights to fight the Cumans.**

Gertrude—**Pg. 282, ¶ 2—Gertrude, the first wife of Andrew of Hungary, was daughter of the Count of Bavaria and a direct descendant of Charlemagne himself. Andrew's marriage to Gertrude gave him both a connection to German nobility and many new citizens to Hungary via the form of aristocratic retainers and relatives.**

Golden Bull—**Pg. 282, ¶ 5 to Pg. 283, ¶ 3—Golden Bull, named after the golden seal that dangled from the scroll, was the charter signed by Andrew in 1222 that said the rights of the wealthy and powerful would be protected: Hungarian nobility could not be taxed arbitrarily; they could could not be forced to fight in foreign wars; nor could the king create new nobility by giving away his lands. The charter also said that "No man shall be either accused or arrested, sentenced or punished for a crime unless he receive a legal summons,** and until a judicial inquiry into his case shall have taken place" and that, should Andrew refuse to abide by it, "the bishops as well as the other barons and nobles of the realm, singularly and in common . . . [may] resist and speak against us and our successors without incurring the charge of high treason."

Konrad—Pg. 284, ¶ 2 & 5—Konrad, Polans duke of Mazovia, hoped to conquer the lands directly above him, the lands of the Lithuanians. Konrad of Mazovia saw the land of the Lithuanians as fair game, so he offered the Teutonic Knights an opportunity to crusade against their sacrilegious ways in exchange for land in his dukedom.

Lithuanians—Pg. 284, ¶ 2 & 3—Lithuanians were a tribal people living above Polans that were divided into three different people based on dialect: farthest to the north were the Letts, bordered by the Rus' on the east and just below the cold Baltic Sea; Prussians lived in the basin of the Vistula river; and between them lay a larger group who simply claimed the name Lithuanian. Lithuanians were seen as wild pagans because they worshipped mythological creatures, venerated nature, and burned their dead.

Novae Institutiones—Pg. 281, ¶ 4, Pg. 282, ¶ 2 and Pg. 283, ¶ 2—*Novae institutiones*, or "new institution," was the name given by King Andrew of Hungary for the gifts he gave to his loyal supporters after he was crowned king of Hungary. Because *novae institutions* favored those in Andrew's inner circle, like the Germans Andrew allowed to settle in Hungary, the Hungarian knights and counts threated to rebel against Andrew unless he signed the Golden Bull which put limits on the gifts.

Piast—Pg. 283, ¶ 7 to Pg. 284, ¶ 1—Piast was the name of the dynasty that ruled the Polans, though fighting within the dynasty tore the Polans apart. The Piast converted to Christianity sometime in the tenth century.

Polans—Pg. 283, ¶ 7 to Pg. 284, ¶ 2—Polans were a Western Slavic tribe who had, for two centuries, occupied the river-crossed lands between the Carpathian Mountains and the Baltic Sea. The Polans were ruled by a dynasty called the Piast, who had converted to Christianity sometime in the tenth century, but the Piast fought with each other so by the beginning of the thirteenth century the Polans were divided into a series of dukedoms: Little Poland, Mazovia, Kujawy, Greater Poland, Silesia.

Teutonic Knights—Pg. 282, ¶ 3—Teutonic Knights were a military order made up of Germanic Crusaders that were granted papal recognition around 1200. The order's original purpose had been to protect the pilgrim hospital St. Mary's of the Germans, in the city of Jerusalem; but after the hospital had been destroyed by Saladin in 1187, the Teutonic Knights were set adrift, looking for both a purpose and a homeland.

Section II: **Comprehension**

Write a two or three-sentence answer to each of the following questions.

1. What natural occurrence helped King Andrew of Hungary secure his throne? What did Andrew do on his own to safeguard his power?

A1.—Pg. 281, ¶ 2-4—King Andrew of Hungary was supposed to serve as regent to the five-year-old son of his brother King Emeric, the actual heir to the throne, but Andrew had instead seized the throne for himself. His sister-in-law had taken the child and fled to Austria, where the conflict was resolved when the boy died of illness the following year. Three weeks later, Andrew had arranged for the Archbishop of Hungary to crown him as rightful king of Hungary, and then he started to give away royal lands like villages, castles lands and fortresses, gifts called the "new institution," to his supporters.

2. What were the terms of the *novae institutiones*?

A2.—Pg. 281, ¶ 2 to Pg. 282, ¶ 1—There were no terms associated with the *novae institutiones*. The lands Andrew gave away had no strings attached; if you were one of Andrew's partisans and received the gift of a village in exchange for loyalty, you owed the king no further service in return, no tithe of crops or service, no taxes, and no obligation to answer to anyone for the welfare of the villagers, who now were subject to your whims.

3. How did Andrew's marriage to Gertrude affect the social and governmental structure of Hungary?

A3.—Pg. 282, ¶ 2—Gertrude, Andrew's first wife, was daughter of the Count of Bavaria and a direct descendant of Charlemagne himself. She provided Andrew with a direct connection to German nobility and their marriage also opened the door for German nobles and knights to settle in Hungary. As a result, these German knights became the lords of Hungarian castles and the lawmakers of Hungarian villages.

4. Why did the Teutonic Knights settle in Hungary in 1211? What was expected of the knights?

A4.—Pg. 282, ¶ 3—The Teutonic Knights were purposeless after Saladin destroyed the pilgrim hospital St. Mary's of the Germans in 1187, so Andrew invited them into Hungary to help protect his borders from the Cumans. The Teutonic Knights agreed to fight for Andrew in exchange for a home in the eastern part of Hungary known as *Erdö-elve*, meaning "through the woods," or Transylvania. The Teutonic Knights were permitted to live, govern themselves, and crusade against the Cumans; they were expected to remain loyal to Andrew, but were exempt from both taxes and tribute.

5. What did Andrew propose to do with the *novae institutions* when he returned from the Fifth Crusade in 1219? What was the reaction of the Hungarian people?

A5.—Pg. 282, ¶ 4—In 1219, Andrew announced that all lands gifted by the crown would remain permanently in the hands of their receivers, to be passed down as hereditary estates from father to son into eternity. This would have carved Hungary up into an unrecognizable set of principalities, many of them under German control, and it was one step too far for the

Hungarian knights and counts. The Hungarian knights and counts then got the support of Honorius III, who believed that Andrew was not zealous enough in promoting the interests of the Church within his realm, and they drew up a charter protecting their own rights, as well as the rights of the Christian priests under his rule.

6. How did Andrew and the Teutonic Knights come to fight against one another?

A6.—Pg. 283, ¶ 4 & 5—After Andrew signed the Golden Bull, it seemed to the Teutonic Knights that he had lost so much support that he was vulnerable, so they made a play at making their land in Transylvania an independent state. Honorius III backed the Teutonic Knights after they sent a petition asking that they be put directly under the authority of Rome, answerable only to the pope—a request that would have exempted them from obedience to earthly kings. Andrew responded by assembling an army, marching into Transylvania, and driving the Teutonic Knights out.

7. Why was a crusade started against the Lithuanians?

A7.—Pg. 284, ¶ 3-5—A crusade was started against the Lithuanians because they were wild pagans: the Lithuanians venerated nature, worshipped mythological creatures, and burned their dead in hopes of seeing them in the world to come. Honorius III had already tried and failed to convert the Lithuanians via missionary bishops. Konrad of Mazovia saw the land of the Lithuanians as fair game, so he offered the Teutonic Knights an opportunity to crusade against their sacrilegious ways in exchange for land in his dukedom.

8. In what way did the Baltic Crusade change as fighting dragged on?

A8.—Pg. 285, ¶ 1—The Baltic crusade started as a war against the pagan Lithuanians. However, the crusade turned into an ugly, bloody, protracted struggle in which "primitive tribes with no common political organization were obliged hopelessly to protect their lives, farms, tribal independence, and religion against the superior might of the west." Before long, the fighting forked into a double war, one against the pagan Lithuanians, the other against nearby Christians who hoped to seize some of the land east of the Baltic for themselves.

Section III: Critical Thinking

The student may not use her text to answer this question.

The theme of displacement continues from the last chapter in this Critical Thinking question. Write a paragraph or two explaining how both religious beliefs and the desire for a homeland motivated the Teutonic Knights in their crusade against the Lithuanians.

The Teutonic Knights were a German military order created with the purpose of protecting the pilgrim hospital called St. Mary's, but when Saladin captured Jerusalem in 1187, they had nowhere to go. Andrew welcomed the Teutonic Knights into Hungary for two reasons: he was tied to the German nobility and military by his first wife Gertrude, and he also wanted to protect Hungary's border from the Cumans. The Teutonic Knights were given land in his country's eastern reaches, known as Transylvania; they ruled themselves (with the expectation that they remain loyal), and they were exempt from taxes and tribute.

However, after the Teutonic Knights tried to make Transylvania an independent state, they were kicked out of Hungary by Andrew. Konrad of Mazovia then offered the Teutonic Knights another opportunity to crusade and in return gain a homeland: they could come into his dukedom and fight against the enemies of Christ who lived around the Vistula. In exchange, he promised them a northern tract of land in his dukedom for their own "in perpetuity . . . and in addition the lands which they might conquer thereafter with the help of God." Then, in 1226, Honorius III declared the fight against Lithuanian-speakers to be a new crusade, complete with full absolution of sin for those who took part.

If the Teutonic Knights were successful in converting and conquering the Lithuanians, they would also be rewarded with a homeland. The chapter ends with this thought on the Baltic Crusade: " 'It was completely joyless and full of hard fighting,' writes Nicolaus von Jeroschin of the new Crusade, '. . . a land of horrors and wilderness . . . [where] the knightly sword of Christianity greedily devoured the sinners' flesh.' For the next fifty years, the Teutonic Knights would lay waste to the lands of the Lithuanians—fighting, perhaps, for Christ, but hoping to gain themselves a kingdom."

EXAMPLE ANSWER:

The Teutonic Knights were a German military order created with the purpose of protecting the pilgrim hospital called St. Mary's, but when Saladin captured Jerusalem in 1187, they had nowhere to go. Andrew then welcomed the Teutonic Knights into Hungary for two reasons: he was tied to the German nobility and military by his first wife Gertrude, and he also wanted to protect Hungary's border from the Cumans. The Teutonic Knights were given land in Transylvania, they ruled themselves (with the expectation that they remain loyal), and they were exempt from taxes and tribute. However, after the Teutonic Knights tried to make Transylvania an independent state, they were kicked out of Hungary by Andrew. Konrad of Mazovia then offered the Teutonic Knights another opportunity to crusade and in return gain a homeland. If they fought for him again the Lithuanians, then they would be given a piece of his dukedom and any land they gained during the crusade. In 1226 Honorius declared that participants in the Baltic Crusade would be given full absolution of sin. The Teutonic Knights fought against the Lithuanians for Christ, but also for the benefits of crusade and for a chance at their own land.

Section IV: Map Exercise

1. Using your black pencil, trace the rectangular outline of the frame for Map 40.1: The Baltic Crusade.

2. Using your blue pencil, trace the visible coastline of the Baltic Sea and the Black Sea. You do not need to include all the small islands in the Baltic. Also trace the lines of the Danube and the Vistula. Repeat until the contours are familiar.

3. Using contrasting colors, trace the outline of the territories of Rus, Hungary, and the Holy Roman Empire. Show the mountains with small peaks. Repeat until the contours are familiar.

4. Using a new sheet of paper, trace the outline of the frame of Map 40.1 in black. Remove the sheet of paper, and draw the lines of the coast of the Baltic and the Black Seas. Then draw the lines of the territories of Rus, Hungary, and the Holy Roman Empire. Show the mountains with small peaks. Erase and redraw as necessary. When you are happy with your map, lay it over the original. Erase and redraw any lines which are more than ½″ off of the original.

5. Now study carefully the locations of Bavaria, Austria, Silesia, Polans, Little Poland, Kujawy, Mazovia, Greater Poland, Prussians, Lithuanians, Letts, Transylvania, and Cumans. When they are familiar to you, close the book. Using your regular pencil with the eraser, mark and label each one. Then check it against the original, and correct any misplaced or mislabeled marks.

Chapter Forty-One

Lakeshores, Highlands, and Hilltops

The student may use his text when answering the questions in sections I and II.

Section I: Who, What, Where

Write a one or two-sentence answer explaining the significance of each item listed below.

Bulala—**Pg. 290, ¶ 4—Bulala was a clan of African traditionalists who resisted Islam and were aghast by Dibalemi's desecration of the *mune*. Some accounts say that the undercurrent of rebellion faced by Dunama Dibalemi at the end of his reign was caused by the Bulala.**

Dunama Dibalemi—**Pg. 288, ¶ 6 to pg. 289, ¶ 1 and Pg. 290, ¶ 4—Dunama Dibalemi, who ruled from sometime in the 1220s to 1259 and was a direct descendent of the first royal convert to Islam, Dunama, forced his people to convert to Islam and made his insistence clear by destroying the *mune*. Dunama Dibalemi made Kanem very profitable via trade on Lake Chad, but by the end of his reign he was facing rebellion, possibly caused by the Bulala, and possibly caused by the lieutenant governors in the outer reaches of his kingdom, who also happened to be his sons, that were growing independent.**

Ezana—**Pg. 287, ¶ 2—Ezana was an eastern African king that had been converted to Christianity by Constantine himself. Ezana's kingdom, Axum, remained a Christian realm until its disintegration, sometime in the middle of the tenth century.**

Gebra Maskal Lalibela—**Pg. 287, ¶ 5 and Pg. 288, ¶ 2—Gebra Maskal Lalibela, who claimed to be a descendant of Moses and his Ethiopian wife, was the most accomplished of all Zagwe church builders. In the first quarter of the thirteenth century, Lalibela built nearly a dozen churches along the Jordan river.**

Marara—**Pg. 287, ¶ 3—Marara was local chief that lived on the southern edge of the old Axumite land; his people, the Agau, had been forced to submit by the Axumites nearly nine hundred years before. Marara claimed to be the rightful successor to the Axumite throne so he took the small southward town of Adafa as his capital, made the descendants of the bygone Axumites as his subjects, and started his own dynasty, the Zagwe ("of Agau").**

Yekuno Amiak—Pg. 288, ¶ 3—Yekuno Amiak, a highland dweller from the Amhara people, married the daughter of the last Zagwe king and then in 1270 usurped his father-in-law's throne. Yekuno Amiak claimed to be descended from King Solomon.

Section II: Comprehension

Write a two or three-sentence answer to each of the following questions.

1. What happened to Axum after Ezana's death and then the fall of the capital city?

A1.—Pg. 287, 2—After Ezana died, Axum remained a Christian realm until it disintegrated sometime in the middle of the tenth century. After the capital city fell, a ghost of the empire was left behind, including a network of monasteries and nunneries. There was a scattering of conquered and converted peoples who went on living, in peaceful obscurity, between the highland headwaters of the Nile river and the shores of the Red Sea.

2. How did Gebra Maskal Lalibela use the coronation ceremony to show that the Zagwe king was a descendent of Moses and his Ethiopian wife?

A2.—Pg. 288, ¶ 1—The coronation ceremony for the Zagwe king was an elaborate affair that reaffirmed the king's ties to Moses. The king was crowned by a priest, beneath the portrait of the angel Michael in the church that bore the angel's name. He was tonsured to represent his spiritual calling, and he was dressed in priestly clothes rather than a crown.

3. Explain the connection Yekuno Amiak claimed to have to King Solomon. How did the connection help Yekuno Amiak?

A3.—Pg. 288, ¶ 3 & 4—Legend had it that the queen of the western Arabic kingdom Sabea, who had visited Solomon to see his splendor, had returned from her journey pregnant; her son Menelik then stole the Ark of the Covenant from Solomon himself and carried it into Africa. This made Yekuno Amiak both the son of kings and the guardian of the (as yet unseen) Ark, a worthy successor to the Axumite throne, one that had the support of the monasteries and nunneries. With their recognition of his right to rule, Amiak moved the capital to Shewa and from there his descendants, the Solomonid dynasty, would rule for two and a half centuries.

4. What was the *mune* and why was it so powerful? What did Dunama Dibalemi do to the *mune*?

A4.—Pg. 289, ¶ 1 & 2—The *mune* was a religious object believed by the Kanem people to bring them victory in war; it was wrapped and hidden away and no one dared to open it. No one knew the exact nature of the *mune* and that is exactly why it was powerful—its secrecy made it potent. Dunama Dibalemi opened the *mune* and whatever was inside of it flew away, ripping away its secrecy and its power.

5. Why didn't Dunama Dibalemi need the *mune*?

A5.—Pg. 289, ¶ 3—Dunama Dibalemi didn't need the *mune* because he was good at war; he had no need for talismans. Dunama Dibalemi spent the early years of his reign building

up his cavalry units, until he could put forty thousand mounted soldiers on the field at one time. He established a sizable arsenal on the northern shore of Lake Chad and from there he often launched sea raids on the lands of those who were not converted.

6. How do we know that Dunama Dibalemi was a faithful follower of Islam? If he was so devout, why didn't he convert those pagans he captured on his raids of Lake Chad?

A6.—Pg. 290, ¶ 2 & 3—We know that Dunama Dibalemi was a faithful follower of Islam because he refused to abide by the nature of the mune, he lived by the pillars of Islam, he went on *hajj* twice, he gave alms to the poor, and he was known for his religious warfare and charitable acts. However, Dunama Dibalemi used captive non-Muslim slaves as his primary currency, trading them north for horses and goods in short supply in central Africa. By keeping the lands south of Lake Chad non-Islamic, Dunama Dibalemi was able to continue using them as hunting grounds for slaves that did not fall under Islamic prohibition.

7. Why did the Mapungubwe settle near the Limpopo river?

A7.—Pg. 290, ¶ 7—The Mapungubwe were a band of traveling farmers, searching for fertile fields, who had come into the Limpopo river valley in the eleventh century. Settling near the Limpopo allowed the Mapungubwe to create farms of millet, beans, pumpkins, melons, sheepfolds, and cattle herds, and they were able to hunt elephants and to trade ivory down the Limpopo to Arab traders on the coast. The Mapungubwe stayed near the Limpopo because the fertile fields and the ivory trade helped them to grow wealthy.

8. Explain how we know that wealth was unevenly distributed among the Mapungubwe.

A8.—Pg. 290, ¶ 8 to Pg. 291, ¶ 2—Around 1220, in the Mapungubwe kingdom, a new complex was built on top of a nearby hill, accessible through only four guarded paths. The complex included a new palace, new spacious homes, and then thirty years or so after, it included massive stone walls to enclose them, with smaller huts of nearly five thousand people clustered around the hill's base. The judges, tax collectors, cattle, goats and sheep lived outside of the walls of the complex, telling us that the king and his court lived in a special place designated only for the noble and wealthy.

Section III: Critical Thinking

The student may not use his text to answer this question.

Explain how water plays an important role in the histories we read in this chapter. How did water influence/affect the lives of the Zagwe, the Kanem, and the Mapungubwe?

The Zagwe, Kanem, and Mapungubwe all relied on water for their growth and prosperity. For the Zagwe it was religious prosperity, and for the Kanem and Mapungubwe it was material prosperity. All three kingdoms used their proximity to bodies of water to build up their civilizations. In the case of the Mapungubwe, water was also the cause of the end of their greatness.

Though the Zagwe people didn't leave any records behind, they did leave churches that were carved from single massive chunks of volcanic rock. A narrow rocky river cut through Gebra Maskal Lalibela's capital city. The river, which channeled into deeper hand-cut narrows, was renamed Yordanos, the Jordan. The steep rock faces on both sides of the Yordanos were whittled away into huge standing outcrops, enormous lumps of stone on the banks; and then those blocks were chiseled, hollowed, and shaped, by skilled masons of the king, into churches with domes, pillars, and arches. The Mount of Olives church stood to the north, the Mount of Transfiguration to the south. The banks of the Jordan river became a new holy landscape. The way the water cut into the earth allowed for the Zagwe to use its banks to build churches, the marker of their civilization.

Dunama Dibalemi built up Kanem's power by raiding those that were not converted to Islam that lived on the shores of Lake Chad. He would launch sea raids "on the lands of the pagans, on the shores of this lake . . . [he] attacks their ships and kills and takes prisoners." During his thirty years on the throne, Dibalemi used his ships and cavalry to stretch his reach across the entire basin of Lake Chad. This gave him control of the southern part of the Eastern Trade Route, and a guaranteed path to trade in the north. Though Dunama Dibalemi was a devout Muslim, he did not covert those he took prisoner because he relied on slaves and the slave trade for his kingdom's prosperity. When Dunama Dibalemi died, Kanem was the strongest kingdom in central Africa.

South of Zagwe and Kanem, on the Limpopo river, was the Mapungubwe kingdom. The Mapungubwe left no histories or king lists behind, but they did leave gold, ivory, glass beads, and Chinese celadon, all markers of an impressive trade network that was made possible because of the kingdom's proximity to water. Settling near the Limpopo allowed the Mapungubwe to create farms of millet, beans, pumpkins, melons, sheepfolds, and cattle herds, and they were able to hunt elephants and to trade ivory down the Limpopo to Arab traders on the coast. Traces of the Mapungubwe settlement show remnants of trade with Egypt, China, and India. The Mapungubwe stayed near the Limpopo because the fertile fields and the ivory trade helped them to grow wealthy; the king even built a complex on top of a hill to separate himself and his riches from the common people. But then the Limpopo became unreliable, drying up and then flooding. The people outside of the king's complex moved away to Great Zimbabwe, and the trade routes shifted with them. By 1290, with no more farmers, no more taxpayers, and no more trade on the Limpopo, the king also abandoned his palace.

EXAMPLE ANSWER:

The Zagwe, Kanem, and Mapungubwe all relied on water for their growth and prosperity. The Zagwe people didn't leave records behind, but they did leave massive churches. The churches were built out of single chunks of massive volcanic rock on the shores of the Jordan river. The way the water cut into the earth allowed for the Zagwe to use its banks to build churches, the marker of their civilization. The Zagwe created a new holy landscape on the banks of the Jordan river. In Kanem, water gave Dunama Dibalemi material prosperity. He built up Kanem's power by raiding those that were not converted to Islam that lived on the shores of Lake Chad. This gave him control of the southern part of the Eastern Trade Route, and a guaranteed path to trade in the north. Though Dunama Dibalemi was a devout Muslim, he did not covert those he took prisoner because he relied on slaves and the slave trade for his kingdom's prosperity. When Dunama Dibalemi died, Kanem was the strongest kingdom in central Africa.

South of Zagwe and Kanem, on the Limpopo river, was the Mapungubwe kingdom. Settling near the Limpopo allowed the Mapungubwe to create farms of millet, beans, pumpkins,

melons, sheepfolds, and cattle herds, and they were able to hunt elephants and to trade ivory down the Limpopo to Arab traders on the coast. Traces of the Mapungubwe settlement show remnants of trade with Egypt, China, and India. The Mapungubwe stayed near the Limpopo because the fertile fields and the ivory trade helped them to grow wealthy; the king even built a complex on top of a hill to separate himself and his riches from the common people. But then the Limpopo became unreliable, drying up and then flooding. The people outside of the king's complex moved away to Great Zimbabwe, and the trade routes shifted with them. By 1290, with no more farmers, no more taxpayers, and no more trade on the Limpopo, the king also abandoned his palace. Water gave the Mapungubwe great wealth, and it was also the Mapungubwe's downfall.

Section IV: Map Exercise

1. Using your black pencil, trace the rectangular frame of Map 41.1: Zagwe, Kanem, and Mapungubwe.

2. Using your blue pencil, trace the outline of the continent, including the Mediterranean and the Red Seas. Also trace the line of the Senegal, the Niger, the Nile, and the Limpopo. Repeat until the contours are familiar.

3. Now using contrasting colors, trace the outline of the Zagwe, Empire of Ghana, Benin, and Empire of Kanem areas. Repeat until the contours are familiar.

4. Using a new sheet of paper, trace the rectangular outline of Map 41.1 in black. Using your regular pencil with an eraser, draw the coastline around the continent and the Mediterranean. Then draw the Zagwe, Empire of Ghana, Benin, and Empire of Kanem areas, erasing and redrawing as necessary. When you are happy with your map, lay it over the original, and erase and redraw any lines which are more than ½" off of the original.

5. Now study carefully the locations of Malinke, Susu, Owan, Ife, Edo, Igbo, Nri, Kumbi Saleh, Taghaza, Sijilmasa, Tunis, Tripoli, Bilma, Nijimi, Aafa, Shewa, Kilwa, and Mapungubwe. Also study Sakalava. When they are familiar for you, close the book. Then mark and label each one on your map. Check your map against the original, and erase and remark any labels which are more than ½" off of the original.

Chapter Forty-Two

The Sixth Crusade

The student may use her text when answering the questions in sections I and II.

Section I: **Who, What, Where**

Write a one or two-sentence answer explaining the significance of each item listed below.

Balian of Sidon—**Pg. 296, ¶ 4—Balian of Sidon was a Syrian of Frankish descent appointed by Frederick II to act as a regent for the king in Jerusalem. Garnier l'Aleman was also appointed to serve with Balian of Sidon.**

Conrad—**Pg. 295, ¶ 2 & 3—Conrad, born at the end of April 1228, was the son and heir of Yolande and Frederick II. When Yolande died delivering Conrad, Frederick II's claim to be king of Jerusalem was thrown into doubt; Conrad was clearly the next in line for the crown, so by acting as his guardian Frederick II was able to reaffirm his claim on Jerusalem.**

Garnier l'Aleman—**Pg. 296, ¶ 4—Garnier l'Aleman was a Syrian of Frankish descent appointed by Frederick II to act as a regent for the king in Jerusalem. Balian of Sidon was also appointed to serve with Garnier l'Aleman.**

Gregory IX—**Pg. 294, ¶ 2, Pg. 295, ¶ 5 and Pg. 296, ¶ 2—Gregory IX, an Italian cardinal elected to be pope after Honorius III's death, excommunicated Frederick II for failing to keep his vow to go on crusade. Gregory IX excommunicated Frederick II again after the Holy Roman Emperor declared he was going on crusade to Jerusalem, and when Frederick II made a deal with al-Kamil to retake Jerusalem, Gregory IX said that he had arranged a deal "between Christ and Belial."**

STUDY AND TEACHING GUIDE FOR THE HISTORY OF THE RENAISSANCE WORLD

Section II: **Comprehension**

Write a two or three-sentence answer to each of the following questions.

1. How did Holy Roman Emperor Frederick II also become "King of Jerusalem"?

A1.—Pg. 293, ¶ 3, 4 & *—Frederick II was married to Yolande, whose dead mother had been the granddaughter of Amalric, king of Jerusalem from 1163 to 1174, and the great-granddaughter of Fulk of Jerusalem, former count of Anjou and father of Henry Plantagenet. Yolande was the rightful heir to the Jerusalem throne but her father, John, acted as her regent and called himself king. John agreed to let Frederick II marry Yolande in hopes that his new son-in-law would provide him with an army with which to reclaim Jerusalem, but instead, Frederick added the title "King of Jerusalem" to his own string of honorifics, claiming that as Yolande's husband, he was more entitled to the regency than her father.

2. What stopped Frederick II from going on crusade in August 1227? Did he give a good reason to return home?

A2.—Pg. 294, ¶ 1 & *—Frederick II attempted to go on crusade in August of 1227, but after three days on course to the Holy Land, he returned home, claiming to be seized with an illness. The genuineness of Frederick's complaint continues to be a matter of debate. David Abulafia, one of Frederick's most accomplished biographers, points out that one of his companions, the Landgrave of Thuringia, also sickened and actually died at sea but Pope Gregory IX certainly didn't believe in Frederick's illness, and his opinion seems to have been shared by many.

3. How did Frederick II react to his excommunication from the church by Pope Gregory IX?

A3.—Pg. 294, ¶ 3 to Pg. 295, ¶ 1—After being excommunicated Frederick II seized every religious right that had been the subject of negotiation over the past centuries: he appointed bishops and archbishops and other prelates, he drove away those sent by the Pope, and he raised imposts and taxes from the clergy. He claimed the right to rule Italy directly, and instead of negotiating with Gregory IX, he wrote to all the Christian kings and princes in Europe, accusing the Roman church of avarice, advising all emperors, kings and princes to disinherit the pope because what happened to him could happen to them. Frederick II's defiance of the pope was so blatant that he was widely believed to be the Antichrist.

4. Why was Frederick II excommunicated for a second time?

A4.—Pg. 295, ¶ 2-5—After Yolande gave birth to a son and heir, Frederick II was able to say he needed to reclaim Jerusalem for Conrad. In early September 1228, the emperor landed at Acre and began the Sixth Crusade. Unfortunately, as Frederick II was excommunicated, the church could hardly take credit for it, which annoyed Gregory IX so much that he excommunicated Frederick II for a second time.

5. What was Frederick II's plan to take back Jerusalem with only a tiny army to fight against the Muslim occupants? What wrench was thrown into his plan?

A5.—Pg. 295, ¶ 7—Frederick II had made a deal with al-Kamil to get Syria back from his brother al-Mu'azzam in exchange for Jerusalem. However, al-Mu'azzam died and al-Kamil didn't need Frederick II's help any longer.

6. How did al-Kamil and Frederick II treat each other after their original agreement fell apart?

A6.—Pg. 295, ¶ 7 to Pg. 296, ¶ 1— Al-Kamil treated Frederick II with great friendship. Frederick II settled in Acre and messengers came and went between him and al-Kamil until the end of the year, with Frederick refusing to leave without Jerusalem, and with al-Kamil wishing not to start a war. Finally, the two men negotiated the surrender of Jerusalem.

7. What were the terms of the treaty made between al-Kamil and Frederick II?

A7.—Pg. 296, ¶ 1—Al-Kamil and Frederick II made a treaty that gave Jerusalem to Frederick II as long as he followed several conditions. First, he was not to rebuild the walls; second, the nearby villages would remain Muslim; and third, the Temple Mount (including the Dome of the Rock) was to stay in Muslim hands, with the Christians only given visiting rights, and Muslim worship was to continue there uninterrupted.

8. What were the reactions of both the Muslims and the Christians to Frederick II's retaking of Jerusalem?

A8.—Pg. 296, ¶ 2—No one was happy about Frederick II's retaking of Jerusalem. The Arab historian Ibn al-Athir, wrote "the Franks (God curse them) took over Jerusalem by treaty. May God restore it to Islam quickly!" and Ibn Wasil wrote "The news spread swiftly throughout the Muslim world which lamented the loss of Jerusalem, and disapproved strongly of . . . al-Kamil's action as a most dishonorable deed." The Christian reaction was almost as strong; Frederick II had entered into a binding and sacred agreement with an infidel, and this was no way for a Christian emperor to act.

9. Why was Frederick II treated with such disgust as he left Acre, even thought he had just restored the Holy City for Christendom, Jerusalem, to the Christians?

A9.—Pg. 296, ¶ 3 & 4—After the treaty was complete with al-Kamil, Frederick II went to Jerusalem, entered the Church of the Holy Sepulchre, visited the Tomb of the Living God, and "wore the Crown there, to the honour of the Most Highest." He merely meant that he had entered the church as Holy Roman Emperor, but the indignant patriarch loyal to Gregory IX accused him of usurping his infant son's title and crowning himself king of Jerusalem with his own unholy hands, and the rumor spread. On May 1, as he headed down towards the harbor at Acre, ready to board his ship and set off for home, the rumors that he had taken his son's title via self-coronation caused the people of Acre to hurl pig guts and offal at him as he made his way out of the city.

Section III: **Critical Thinking**

The student may not use her text to answer this question.

Once again we see the motivation for crusade mix with desire for personal gain. In this chapter we saw Holy Roman Emperor Frederick II finally go on crusade. What took him so long? Write a paragraph explaining why Frederick finally decided to fulfill his obligation to fight for God, and how that decision had more to do with his own material desires than his piety.

The chapter opens with a reminder that Frederick II was not present at the surrender of Damietta in 1221 because he never participated in the Fifth Crusade. The chapter continues, "Promising again and again to descend on the Crusade in glory, complete with German reinforcements, Frederick II had always found a reason not to leave Germany. Now the Fifth Crusade was over; but Frederick had vowed that he would go on crusade, and the sacred promise still had to be fulfilled. In 1223, he assured Honorius III that he would be ready to go by 1225. In 1225, he postponed the planned trip east another two years."

Frederick II attempted to go on crusade in August of 1227, but after "pretending" to make for the Holy Land for three days, he returned home, claiming to be seized with an illness. Pope Gregory IX would have none of Frederick II's dilly-dallying, so he excommunicated the Holy Roman Emperor. However, Frederick II suddenly had a personal reason to go on crusade: to claim his own power. Yolande gave birth to a girl that died when she was just nine months old. Yolande then gave birth to a boy, Conrad, but this childbirth killed her. When Yolande died, Frederick II's claim to be king of Jerusalem was thrown into doubt. But Frederick II found a way around this uncertainty. Conrad was clearly the next in line for the crown, so by acting as his guardian Frederick II was able to reaffirm his claim on Jerusalem. "Now, at last," as written on page 295, ¶ 4, "Frederick had good reason to go to Jerusalem." Though he was excommunicated, Frederick II wanted to go on crusade to affirm his own power and might.

EXAMPLE ANSWER:

In previous chapters we read about Frederick II's avoidance of going on crusade. This chapter opens with a reminder of Frederick II's dodgy behavior. He wasn't at the surrender of Damietta in 1221 because he didn't show up to the crusade. He vowed to Honorius III that he would go on Crusade in 1225, but in 1225 he postponed his trip again. Honorius III died in March of 1227 and Frederick II still hadn't gone on crusade. In August of 1227 he attempted to go, but after three days turned around because he was sick. The new pope Gregory IX was having none of it, so he excommunicated Frederick II. Soon after, Frederick II's wife had a son, and this son was the claimant of the title "king of Jerusalem." As his son's guardian, Frederick II had the motivation to take back Jerusalem, and finally go on crusade. The religious motivation for this trip is dubious, as Frederick II was excommunicated, and when he did announce that he was going to take back Jerusalem, Gregory IX excommunicated the emperor for a second time. But Frederick II would not be stopped and his personal motivation to take Jerusalem for himself finally led him to start the Sixth Crusade.

Chapter Forty-Three

The Tran Dynasty

The student may use his text when answering the questions in sections I and II.

Section I: Who, What, Where

Write a one or two-sentence answer explaining the significance of each item listed below.

Bang Klang T'ao—**Pg. 300, ¶ 4 & 5—Bang Klang T'ao, a Syam clan leader who had never fallen under Khmer domination, worked with Pha Muong in 1238 to attack Sukhothai and drive out Khmer officials. Bang Klang T'ao was proclaimed by Pha Muong to be the king of the valley, the first king of the independent kingdom of Syam.**

Bo Dala—**Pg. 301, ¶ 3—Bo Dala, daughter of Jaya Paramesvaravarman II and crown princess of the Champa, was taken captive by the Dai Viet after the battle between the Dai Viet and the Champa that took her father's life.**

Cao Tong—**Pg. 298, ¶ 2—Cao Tong, king of the Dai Viet, was driven from his throne by a palace revolt and then he took refuge with the Tran, the wealthiest family in the Nam Dinh Province. King Cao Tong was able to return to his capital city of Thang Long with the help of the Tran family after he married his son to their young daughter.**

Chieu Hoang—**Pg. 298, ¶ 5 to Pg. 299, ¶ 1—Chieu Hoang was given the Dai Viet throne by her father when she was just seven in 1224; she had no say in court because her Tran mother and in-laws acted as her regents. Chieu Hoang married Tran Canh and then handed her right to rule over to him.**

Hue Tong—**Pg. 298, ¶ 2-5 and Pg. 299, ¶ 2—Hue Tong of the Ly Dynasty, son of King Cao Tong, was married to the young daughter of the Tran family while the family was exiled in Nam Dinh Province. Hue Tong became king of the Dai Viet in 1210, but in part because he did not have a son, he became depressed, abdicated the throne to his daughter Chieu Hoang, and retired to a monastery where he committed suicide just months after Tran Canh was made emperor, bringing an end to the Ly dynasty.**

Indravarman II—**Pg. 300, ¶ 4**—Indravarman II was an obscure Khmer king that managed to keep the Syam loyal by granting Pha Muong a royal title and a princess for his wife.

Jaya Paramesvaravarman II—**Pg. 300, ¶ 6 to Pg. 301, ¶ 1**—Jaya Paramesvaravarman II, who inherited Champa rule in 1227, began an extensive rebuilding program that included temples, palaces, dams and ships. He sent Champa ships to raid the Dai Viet coast, carrying off both goods and slaves, he reinstalled the *lingas*, and he reasserted his own rule as a Hindu monarch.

Pha Muong—**Pg. 300, ¶ 4 & 5**—Pha Muong, a Syam chief kept loyal to the Khmer via being granted a royal title, made an alliance with Bang Klang T'ao in 1238 and together the two men led an attack on the Khmer officials in Sukhothai and drove them out. Pha Muong proclaimed Bang Klang T'ao king of the valley and created the first independent kingdom of Syam, the root of the Thai nation.

Syam—**Pg. 300, ¶ 3**—Syam, the people who lived in the fertile western valley of the Chao Phraya river, separated from Khmer in 1238. On the bas-relief scenes of battle carved at Angkor Wat, the Syam march with the armies of the Khmer king, but they march apart, wearing their own battle dress.

Tran Canh (Thai Tong)—**Pg. 298, ¶ 6 to Pg. 299, ¶ 1, 6, & * and Pg. 300, ¶ 1**—Tran Canh, first cousin of Chieu Hoang, married the young queen and then was handed over the right to rule; in December of 1225, Tran Canh (known more often by his posthumous royal name, Thai Tong) was proclaimed emperor of the Dai Viet. Tran Canh, after trying unsuccessfully to escape his throne in 1236 by entering a monastery, spent most of his time composing treatises on Buddhist philosophical topics and acting obediently as the figurehead of the Dai Viet government, biding his time until he could abdicate in favor of his son.

Tran Thu Do—**Pg. 298, ¶ 6 and Pg. 299, ¶ 2 & 3**—Tran Thu Do, chief of the royal guards and uncle to Chieu Hoang, arranged for his niece to marry her first cousin Tran Canh and convinced Hue Tong to commit suicide after Tran Canh's coronation so that there were no possibilities of revolt in favor of the Ly dynasty. Tran Thu Do appointed himself Grand Chancellor after Hue Tong's suicide and until his death in 1264, Tran Thu Do remained de facto ruler of the country, uncrowned king of the Dai Viet and the true founder of the Tran dynasty.

Section II: Comprehension

Write a two or three-sentence answer to each of the following questions.

1. How did Tran Thu Do try and eliminate any possibility of Ly revolt against the Tran family?

A1.—Pg. 299, ¶ 2-4—Tran Thu Do shored up the Tran hold on the Dai Viet crown by first convincing Hue Tong to commit suicide; Hue Tong's death put an end to two hundred years of Ly rule. He also built a temple over a huge pit, invited the Ly clan to come honor their ancestors in it, and then pushed the entire temple with all inside into the pit and buried them alive. Another history says that Tran Thu Do sent out geomancers to scour the entire Dai Viet kingdom for sites on which a future king of the Dai Viet might be born and when those places were located Tran Thu Do ordered them razed, built over, or ruined.

2. What happened to the Dai Viet government and system of law under the direction of Tran Thu Do and Tran Canh?

A2.—Pg. 299, ¶ 5—Under the direction of Tran Thu Do and Tran Canh, the Dai Viet government got a complete overhaul while the system of law remained true to Dai Viet custom. The countryside was divided into twelve administrative provinces; new taxes were introduced to help pay for a larger standing army and a series of dike projects; an accurate census was carried out; and a Chinese-style academy, the National College, was founded to train scholars and future officials in the knowledge of the classic Chinese writings. However, the Tran clan, while paying homage to the importance of Confucian education, remained true to Dai Viet in their ways: a later Tran emperor wrote, "Our forefathers, since the very beginning of the Dynasty, established their own system of law and did not follow the Song laws and institutions."

3. Why didn't Pha Muong try to claim rule over the first independent kingdom of the Syam?

A3.—Pg. 300, ¶ 4 & 5—Pha Muong had a deal with Indravarman II; he was given a royal title and a princess for a wife, and in return the Syam were loyal to the Khmer. But then Pha Muong switched alliances and joined with Bang Klang T'ao to drive the Khmer officials out of Sukhothai, creating the first independent kingdom of Syam. Pha Muong, perhaps realizing that his willingness to violate his oath of loyalty to the Khmer king had weakened his authority, then proclaimed his ally, Bang Klang T'ao, king of the valley.

4. Describe Champa's prosperity under Jaya Paramesvaravarman II.

A4.—Pg. 300, ¶ 7 to Pg. 301, ¶ 2—Jaya Paramesvaravarman II brought Champa back to life through a rebuilding program that included temples, palaces, dams and ships. He sent Champa ships to raid the Dai Viet coast, carrying off both goods and slaves. Champa ships also took aloewood, elephant tusks, and rhinoceros horns north to Chinese ports and brought back silk and porcelain, and Jaya Paramesvaravarman himself laid in stores of jewels and gold, flaunting them in his royal costume to show his power.

5 What were the circumstances of Jaya Paramesvaravarman II's death?

A5.—Pg. 301, ¶ 3— Around 1252, Jaya Paramesvaravarman II demanded that the Dai Viet return three provinces to him that were long ago seized by the Ly dynasty. The provinces were a sore point between the Champa and the Dai Viet, and together Tran Canh and his uncle took the opportunity to strike at Jaya Paramesvaravarman II. A Dai Viet army stormed into the north of Champa and Jaya Paramesvaravarman II died in the battle that followed.

Section III: **Critical Thinking**

The student may not use his text to answer this question.

We don't find out much about Indravarman II in this chapter. Susan Wise Bauer writes that he was "an obscure king almost unknown to the chronicles." What else is out there about Indravarman II? Do some research and find out at least three more things about the little-known Khmer ruler. Make sure to cite your sources in your answers.

This is a relatively short chapter filled with new names and straight-forward strategic power moves. The student can expand on his learning by looking up additional information on Indravarman II. The student can use his research method of choice. Findings should be written out in full sentences with clear citations, either as part of the sentence, as an in-text parenthetical citation, or as a footnote.

EXAMPLE ANSWER (ONE PIECE OF NEW INFORMATION):

Citation as part of sentence—

According to *Adventure Guide to Cambodia* by Janet Arrowood, Indravarman II was the son of Jayavarman II and he ruled over Khmer from 1219 to 1243. The reason we don't know much about Indravarman II is most likely because his successor, who was also his enemy, destroyed historical accounts that recorded the accomplishments of Indravarman II's rule.

In-text citation—

Indravarman II was the son of Jayavarman II and he ruled over Khmer from 1219 to 1243. The reason we don't know much about Indravarman II is most likely because his successor, who was also his enemy, destroyed historical accounts that recorded the accomplishments of Indravarman II's rule (Arrowood, *Adventure Guide to Cambodia*).

Footnote (Chicago-Style)—

Indravarman II was the son of Jayavarman II and he ruled over Khmer from 1219 to 1243. The reason we don't know much about Indravarman II is most likely because his successor, who was also his enemy, destroyed historical accounts that recorded the accomplishments of Indravarman II's rule.[1]

1. Janet Arrowood, *Adventure Guide to Cambodia* (Hunter Publishing, 2010), Kindle edition.

Section IV: **Map Exercise**

1. Trace the rectangular outline of the frame for Map 43.1 in black.

2. Using your blue pencil, trace the coastal outline. You do not need to include the small islands off the coast. Repeat until the contours are familiar.

3. Using contrasting colors, trace the outlines of the Dai Viet, Nam Dinh Province, Syam, Sukhothai, Khmer, and Champa areas. Repeat until the contours are familiar.

4. Using a new sheet of paper, trace the outline of the frame in black. Then using your regular pencil with an eraser, draw all the visible coastline. Then draw the separate areas of the Dai Viet, the Nam Dinh Province, Syam, Sukhothai, Khmer, and Champa areas. Erase and redraw as necessary. When you are happy with your map, lay it over the original. Erase and redraw any lines which are more than ½" off of the original.

5. Study the location of Chao Phraya on your map, and mark it. Check your work, and correct it necessary.

Chapter Forty-Four

Young Kings

The student may use her text when answering the questions in sections I and II.

Section I: Who, What, Where

Write a one or two-sentence answer explaining the significance of each item listed below.

Alhambra—**Pg. 307, ¶ 2**—Alhambra, or the "Red One," was the name of the fortified palace al-Ahmar had constructed for himself after he declared himself king in Granada. The Alhambra was named after the red clay bricks that the builders first used and it would become the official residence of al-Ahmar's descendants, the Nasrid dynasty, and the capital of the Kingdom of Granada.

Blanche of Castile—**Pg. 303, ¶ 2 and Pg. 304, ¶ 2**—Blanche of Castile, Louis IX's regent, refused to bargain with the barons when they wanted more power and also stopped them from kidnapping Louis IX after they elected the Count of Boulogne as their own king. However, Blanche of Castile changed her mind and gave the barons lands and castles after she found out that King Henry III of England was attempting to turn the barons against Louis IX.

Cortes—**Pg. 306, ¶ 4**—Cortes was the name of the lawmaking assembly composed of Aragonese nobility. James of Aragon talked the cortes into passing a tax that would pay for the war on the Muslim-ruled island of Majorca.

Crusade indulgence—**Pg. 306, ***—Crusade indulgence was an official pronouncement, validated by the authority of the pope, that reduced the amount of punishment a sinner would have to undergo in the afterlife.

Ferdinand III—**Pg. 306, ¶ 6 and Pg. 307, ¶ 3**— Ferdinand III, son of the king of León by his second wife, was crowned king of Castile at the age of eighteen, and then in 1230, after the king of León died, Ferdinand beat out his two older half siblings to claim the crown, making him the king of a united León-Castile. Ferdinand III fought to reclaim Spain from the Muslims: he beat Ibn Hud and then took Murcia in 1243, Jaén in 1246, and Seville in 1248.

Hugh de Lusignan—**Pg. 308, ¶ 2-5—Hugh de Lusignan, count of the small province of Marche, pretended to be loyal to Louis IX while he was allied to Henry III, the son of his wife, Isabella of Angoulême. Hugh de Lusignan fought with Henry III against Louis IX in 1242 and lost; after he was taken prisoner he was forced to apologize, he lost most of his land in Marche, and all of his money.**

Ibn al-Ahmar—**Pg. 307, ¶ 1 & 2—Ibn al-Ahmar declared himself to be king of Arjona in 1232, and then the cities of Córdoba and Jaén at once went over to him, though Córdoba was taken by Ferdinand III in 1236. Al-Ahmar took Almería after Ibn Hud's death and then in 1238, he proclaimed himself king in Granada and constructed the Alhambra.**

Ibn Hud—**Pg. 306, ¶ 3 and Pg. 307, ¶ 2—Ibn Hud was an independent governor who had begun as an Almohad official in Murcia and took advantage of the Almohad decay for his own benefit; he swore allegiance to the Abbasid caliph in far-off Baghdad, and in return was awarded the title Commander of the Faithful, and before long he also controlled Seville, Córdoba, and Granada. Ibn Hud was assassinated by the governor of Almería in 1237, five years after he surrendered to Ferdinand III.**

Isabella of Angoulême—**Pg. 308, ¶ 2—Isabella of Angoulême was engaged to Hugh de Lusignan but was taken away by King John of England, was married to him, and had five children with him. In 1220, four years after John's death, Isabella returned home, married Hugh, and between 1221 and 1234 she had nine more children, half siblings to the king of England, with the Count of Marche.**

The Peace of Alcalá—**Pg. 305, ¶ 2 to Pg. 306, ¶ 1—The Peace of Alcalá was a truce negotiated by James of Aragon in 1227, when he was just nineteen. The Peace of Alcalá brought peace between the battling clans and finally gave the towns of Aragon the breathing space to mend their walls and restock their treasuries.**

Section II: Comprehension

Write a two or three-sentence answer to each of the following questions.

1. Why were the French barons against Louis IX, even though France was more prosperous than ever?

A1.—**Pg. 303, ¶ 2 & 3—The French barons were against Louis IX, even though France was more prosperous than ever, because France's strength came at the cost of their own power. Louis IX's grandfather, Philip Augustus, had taken a loose collection of almost-independent noble estates in Western Francia and turned them into France, a country united under a strong-handed king. But the nobles had to give up their own strength in order for the king to rule with that strong hand.**

2. Describe the plan hatched by the French barons to take power away from the king.

A2.—**Pg. 303, ¶ 4 & 5—The French barons saw Louis IX as a child and Blanche of Castile as a foreigner, both unfit to rule France. Thus they made the Count of Boulogne, the uncle of** the King, their own king, and after they crowned him they expected Blanche of Castile to pay tribute. They also planned to kidnap Louis IX on his coronation tour near Corbeil, but Blanche of Castile found out about the plan, surrounded Louis IX with armed men, and got her son back to Paris as quickly as possible.

3. How did Blanche of Castile thwart Henry III's plans to take back the French lands King John had lost?

A3.—Pg. 304, ¶ 1 & 2—Henry III encouraged rebellion by the barons against Louis IX, but his attempts came to nothing. Blanche of Castile had rethought her refusal to meet the baronial demands and was "lavishly distributing amongst them the lands and castles of the royal domain." She managed to bribe and persuade most of the discontented nobility to swear allegiance to her son, and Henry III's messengers went home.

4. How did Henry III manage to find a friendly shore to land on after his first attempt against France failed?

A4.—Pg. 304, ¶ 3—Henry III persuaded the Count of Brittany to break his vows to Louis IX and swear allegiance to the English throne instead, in exchange for the title Earl of Richmond and the opportunity to become Duke of Brittany instead of a mere count. The Count of Brittany gave Henry III a friendly shore to land on. In May of 1230 he sailed from Portsmouth with his army and landed at Saint-Malo, on the Brittany coast.

5. What happened to Henry III's campaign from Brittany against Louis IX?

A5.—Pg. 304, ¶ 4—Nothing happened during Louis IX's campaign against Louis IX. He stayed in Brittany for five months, doing nothing but spending money. Inexperience, empty pockets, and the prospect of fierce French opposition put a halt to the English army's invasion before it ever even happened.

6. How did Hugh de Lusignan and Isabella of Angoulême come to be taken prisoner by Louis IX?

A6.—Pg. 308, ¶ 3 & 4—Hugh de Lusignan and Henry III marched against Louis IX and his thirty thousand men in 1242. Henry III brought his men and Hugh's—barely two thousand in number—to face the French across the Charente river, which could be crossed only by a slender bridge; perhaps Henry III thought that this would narrow the odds. On July 22 the English were easily beaten by the French, Henry III fled, and Hugh de Lusignan and Isabella of Angoulême were taken prisoner, only being released after they apologized and Louis IX took most of Marche, and all of the Count's money, for himself.

Section III: Critical Thinking

The student may not use her text to answer this question.

James of Aragon and Ferdinand III of León-Castile fought against the Muslims that occupied Spain and reclaimed the land for Christianity. This was a crusade in everything but name. Write a paragraph, using the information from the chapter, that explains what the Spaniards did differently from the previous crusaders we read about, and how these differences led to success against the Muslim opposition.

James of Aragon started out his fight against the Muslims by uniting the warlike nobles around him and pointing them all towards a single cause: driving out the Muslim occupants of Spanish land. Simply getting everyone on the same side, and motivated towards the same cause, was very different from the previous crusades we have read about. James of Aragon was strategic in his attack, going after Majorca before attacking the powerful Ibn Hud. He also was prepared with enough men and enough money to move forward. James made sure that he had the nobility and the church on his side: he talked the cortes, the lawmaking assembly of Aragonese nobility, into passing a tax that would pay for the war, and he talked the papal legate in Aragon into offering crusade indulgences to anyone who would fight with him. Unlike Frederick II (who was successful in retrieving Jerusalem, but without actual fighting), for example, James of Aragon had the church on his side. Also, and this wasn't necessarily in James of Aragon's control, he was successful in his first battle; this good fortune fed the rest of his battles with both morale and money. In December of 1230 James of Aragon led his army in sacking the capital city of Palma and claimed the island for himself. It was his first great victory, and it gave Aragon a serious edge in carrying on trade across the Mediterranean Sea. Once James of Aragon was in Muslim territory, he took advantage of the infighting between the Muslim governors; he pushed steadily through the Islamic-held territories, and by 1236 Córdoba was in his hands.

Ferdinand III also had a strong start to his war against the Muslims in Spain. After successfully taking the crown of León from his half siblings, Ferdinand III became the king of a united León-Castile. In 1232, Ferdinand led the armies of his double kingdom south against Ibn Hud and after two years of fighting, Ibn Hud had to sue for peace. Both men fought hard over the next decade. James of Aragon took Valencia in 1245, after thirteen years of fighting. Ferdinand III took Murcia in 1243, Jaén in 1246, and Seville in 1248. Only the Kingdom of Granada survived; it was the last Muslim enclave in Spain.

It is important for the student to note that both James of Aragon and Ferdinand III were supported by their people. They were fighting for God and gave their soldiers crusade indulgences. They did not let petty squabbles and greed get in their way. Working with their people, both men were able to reclaim almost all of Spain for Christianity.

EXAMPLE ANSWER:

James of Aragon and Ferdinand III made sure they had all of their ducks in a row before going off to fight in holy war. James of Aragon started out his fight against the Muslims by uniting the warlike nobles around him and pointing them all towards a single cause: driving out the Muslim occupants of Spanish land. Simply getting everyone on the same side, and motivated towards the same cause, was very different from the previous crusades we have read about. He also was prepared with enough men and enough money to move forward. James made sure that he had the nobility and the church on his side: he talked the cortes into passing a tax that would pay for the war, and he talked the papal legate in Aragon into offering crusade indulgences to anyone who would fight with him. James of Aragon's preparation most likely helped his success in his battle for Majorca in December of 1230, which was a crucial first step in his fight against the Muslims. Controlling Majorca gave James of Aragon a serious edge in carrying on trade across the Mediterranean Sea, which

mean even more prosperity for his kingdom. Once James of Aragon was in Muslim territory, he took advantage of the infighting between the Muslim governors; he pushed steadily through the Islamic-held territories, and by 1236 Córdoba was in his hands.

Ferdinand III also had a strong start to his war against the Muslims in Spain. After successfully taking the crown of León from his half siblings, Ferdinand III became the king of a united León-Castile. In 1232, Ferdinand led the armies of his double kingdom south against Ibn Hud and after two years of fighting, Ibn Hud had to sue for peace. Both men fought hard over the next decade. James of Aragon took Valencia in 1245, after thirteen years of fighting. Ferdinand III took Murcia in 1243, Jaén in 1246, and Seville in 1248. Only the Kingdom of Granada survived; it was the last Muslim enclave in Spain. Both James of Aragon and Ferdinand III were supported by their people. They were fighting for God and gave their soldiers crusade indulgences. They did not let petty squabbles and greed get in their way. Working with their people, both men were able to reclaim almost all of Spain for Christianity.

Section IV: Map Exercise

1. Trace the rectangular outline of the frame for Map 44.1 in black.

2. Using your blue pencil, trace the coastline all around England and the continent. Also trace the line of the Charente river. Repeat until the contours are familiar.

3. Using contrasting colors, trace the lines of the areas of France and of England (be sure to note the difference between contemporary borders and those depicted in this map). Repeat until the contours are familiar. Then using your black pencil, trace the outline of the area of Normandy. Repeat until the contours are familiar.

4. Using a new sheet of paper, trace the rectangular outline of the frame in black. Then using your regular pencil with an eraser, draw the coastline around England and the continent, including the Charente river. Erase and redraw as necessary. Then draw the separate territories of England and of France. When you are happy with your map, place it over the original, and erase and redraw any lines which are more than ½" off of the original.

5. Now study carefully the locations of Portsmouth, Paris, Montlhery, Corbeil, Saint-Malo, Nantes, Taillebourg, and Bourdeax. Also study the broader regions of Normandy, Brittany, Marche, and Aquitaine.

6. When they are familiar for you, close your book. Mark each location on your map. Check your map against the original, and erase and redraw any location which is more than ½" off of the original.

7. Mark the Charente. Mark the directions of the invasions of Henry III, as the map shows.

Chapter Forty-Five

The Mongol Horde

The student may use his text when answering the questions in sections I and II.

Section I: Who, What, Where

Write a one or two-sentence answer explaining the significance of each item listed below.

Aizong—**Pg. 312, ¶ 4 to Pg. 313, ¶ 2—Aizong, Jin emperor at the time of the Mongol approach led by Subotai, tried to get the Song to help him fend off the Mongol attack, but to no avail. The Mongols trapped Aizong and hundreds of thousands of his subjects inside the walls of Kaifeng; the Jin held out for over a month, but as soon as Subotai's men were able to finally get into the city, Aizong killed himself.**

Batu—**Pg. 313, ¶ 4, Pg. 315, ¶ 2 and Pg. 316, ¶ 6—Batu, the younger son of Jochi, had to conquer the land given to him by his grandfather, so he followed Subotai and fought with him across Rus land, making himself the ruler of Riazan', Moscow, Kiev and all of the other Rus' principalities except for Novgorod by 1240. After Ogodei's death, Batu remained in the west, governing his conquered lands from Sarai, his new capital city on the lower Volga; his kingdom became known as the Golden Horde.**

Béla IV—**Pg. 315, ¶ 4 and Pg. 316, ¶ 2—Béla IV, son of Andrew of Hungary and king since his father's death in 1235, met Subotai and the Mongol army at the Sajo river where the Mongols destroyed the Hungarians. Béla IV managed to escape and elude the trail of Kadan, the assassin sent by Subotai to kill him, by crossing the Adriatic and taking refuge on a rocky island.**

Choe-U—**Pg. 311, ¶ 4 & 6—Choe-U, Choe Chung-heon's son, took over for his father as head of the military state in Goryeo in 1231 and eventually had to appeal to the Mongols for peace. When the Mongols retreated, Chloe-U, King Gojong, and all the top Goryeo officials sneaked out of Kaesong and established themselves on the island of Kanghwa where the water kept them safe from the Mongols.**

Chormaghan—Pg. 313, ¶ 6—Chormaghan, a veteran Mongol general, led a breakaway strike force in late 1237 into Georgia where he took the capital city Tbilisi and most of its eastern reaches. The Georgian nobles captured by Chormaghan were pressed into the Mongol ranks.

Gojong—Pg. 311, ¶ 4 & 6—Gojong was Goryeo's king, but he was only a figurehead monarch and did not have any power. After Choe-U appealed for peace at the end of 1231, Gojong joined the military leader on the island of Kanghwa where the water kept them safe from the Mongols.

Henry the Pious—Pg. 315, ¶ 3—Henry the Pious, the Duke of Greater Poland, fought with his own soldiers and the Teutonic Knights against the invading Mongols but when they met the Mongols on April 9, near the town of Liegnitz, Henry's knights were slaughtered, along with the farmers and metalworkers Henry had drafted to fill the ranks. Henry fell with them; when the survivors finally began to clear the field, Henry's stripped and headless body was recognized by his wife only because he had six toes on his left foot.

Kadan—Pg. 316, ¶ 1 & 2—Kadan, a younger son of Ogodei, had helped lead the charge against Henry the Pious of Poland, and after the victory had ridden hard south to be present at the second battle. Kadan was sent by Subotai to kill Béla IV after he escaped from the battle field, but Kadan gave up when Béla crossed into the Adriatic and took refuge on a small rocky island.

Orda—Pg. 313, ¶ 4—Orda, the oldest son of Jochi, received an inheritance from his grandfather that was already-conquered territory, unlike his brother Batu. Orda's territory was on the lower Syr Darya river, south of the Aral Sea.

Pak So—Pg. 311, ¶ 5—Pak So, commander of the Goryeo army, was spared his life by Sartaq after he opened the gates of Kuju because of how hard the Goryeo army fought against the Mongols.

Sartaq—Pg. 310, ¶ 4 and Pg. 311, ¶ 5 & 6—Sartaq, a Mongol general, led a Mongol division towards Goryeo where he spared the life of Pak So, granted Choe-U peace in exchange for an enormous tribute, and then was fooled when Choe-U, King Gojong, and the other top Goryeo officials sneaked off to safety on the island of Kaesong.

Yu-ke-hsia—Pg. 311, ¶ 5—Yu-ke-hsia, a notorious bandit chief that hid out near the Yalu, sent five thousand outlaws to help the Goryeo army in their fight against the Mongols.

Section II: Comprehension

Write a two or three-sentence answer to each of the following questions.

1. How were the lands of the Universal Khan divided after his death?

A1.—Pg. 310, ¶ 1 and Pg. 313, ¶ 4—The lands of the Universal Khan were divided up between his sons and grandsons after his death. Tolui, the youngest, was given the flat grassy Mongol steppes in the heartland; Chagatai, the Universal Khan's second son, found himself in

Central Asia between the Amu Darya river and the northwestern edge of the steppes; and the two sons of his dead oldest son Jochi, Batu and Orda, were in the western lands, beyond the Aral Sea. Ogodei served as the overlord of all of them; he was the Great Khan, presiding over the entire realm from his homeland near the Kherlen river.

2. Where did the Jin go after the north of the empire fell, and what had they been up to since the fall?

A2.—Pg. 310, ¶ 2 & 3—After the north of the Jin empire was taken by the Mongols, the Jin moved their capital from Zhongdu to Kaifeng and there had reestablished their government. Their territory was shrunken and much of their farmland was in the hands of the enemy, so they had been mounting campaigns against the Song land below them. They had also been working hard to fend off the Mongols: in both 1230 and 1231, Ogodei's great general Subotai was beaten back by Jin counterattacks.

3. What happened the first time the Mongols found themselves at the Yalu river in 1218?

A3.—Pg. 310, ¶ 5 to Pg. 311, ¶ 2—In 1218, a Mongol detachment had chased fleeing steppe peoples known as the Khitan into the peninsula near the Yalu river, and they asked military dictator Choe Chung-heon to send them aid when the Khitan holed up at the Goryeo city of Kangdong. Choe Chung-heon agreed and sent troops and provisions: a thousand men and a thousand bags of rice. Once they had defeated the Khitan, the Mongols demanded tribute as payment for delivering Goryeo from the Khitan menace, and then almost all of them left— forty-one men, according to the *Goryeo-sa*, were left at the border town Uiju where they were instructed to practice the language and wait for the Mongol return.

4. How did Choe-U get the Mongols to retreat from their 1231 attack on Goryeo? Where did he go after the Mongol retreat?

A4.—Pg. 311, ¶ 6 to Pg. 312, ¶ 1—Choe-U appealed for peace with the Mongols at the end of 1231 and managed to swap an enormous tribute—twenty thousand horses, ten thousand bolts of silk, and numerous other riches—for a halt in the Mongol progress. Most of the Mongol troops withdrew, leaving military commanders in charge of the captured territory. But feeling unsafe, King Gojong, Choe-U, and all the top officials sneaked out of Kaesong, crossed the strip of water between the Goryeo coast and the nearest island, Kanghwa, and reestablished themselves on the island. The Mongols demanded their return but they refused, able to supply themselves quite well by sending ships farther south to the unconquered coast, and all the Mongol commanders could do about it was shout threats across at the king, fruitlessly ordering him to come back, because they had no experience with water.

5. Who helped the Mongols get to the Jin? What route did Subotai use to get to the Jin capital of Kaifeng?

A5.—Pg. 312, ¶ 3—Subotai and his men had been helped, in their advance through the Jin territory, by the Southern Song. Subotai, knowing that the Jin (still in possession of a strong army) would have their most formidable defenses erected to block an approach from the north, had negotiated passage with the Song through the lands below Kaifeng so that

STUDY AND TEACHING GUIDE FOR THE HISTORY OF THE RENAISSANCE WORLD

he could send part of his attack force around to assault the city from its more vulnerable southern side.

6. What happened when the Mongols reached the Jin capital of Kaifeng?

A6.—Pg. 313, ¶ 1 & 2— Subotai attacked the city from the north and the south, trapping the Jin army, which led to their slaughter and to Aizong getting pinned inside Kaifeng along with hundreds of thousands of his subjects. The siege went on for over a month, in summer heat; inside the city, the Jin ate their horses, then grass, then boiled their saddles and the skins covering the military drums to make soup, and eventually even ate the dead. Weakened by hunger and then by plague, the defenses finally collapsed, Subotai's men poured into the city, and Aizong committed suicide.

7. Describe Subotai and Batu's tear across Rus territory.

A7.—Pg. 313, ¶ 7 to Pg. 315, ¶ 2—Subotai and Batu started by capturing Riazan' on December 21, 1237, just before the Christmas Mass, and they burned everything, and killed or seized everyone. Moscow fell, as did Kiev, after a ten-week siege; so many panicked Kievans crowded into the Church of the Tithe, hoping for safety, that the second floor gave way and the church collapsed inward (six years later, a traveler passing through Kiev made note of the skulls and bones still piled on the deserted streets). By 1240, all of the Rus' principalities except for Novgorod, the most distant, were under Batu's rule.

8. Why were the Hungarians doomed in their fight against the Mongols, even though they were heavily armored and seemingly ready to fight?

A8.—Pg. 315, ¶ 4 to Pg. 316, ¶ 1—First, Subotai's approach trapped the Hungarians: he backed his own men slowly away and then, when the Hungarians advanced, encircled them. Second, in front of the Mongol advance, refugees had fled across the Carpathians into Hungary, and Béla IV had welcomed them, which did not please his noblemen. Summoned by their king, the Hungarian nobility showed up to fight, but they were disgruntled, lacked enthusiasm, and some even hoped the Hungarians would lose, as opposed to the Mongols, who were enthusiastic, vicious, and eager to beat their opponent.

9. How did the Mongols come to be known as the Antichrist?

A9.—Pg. 316, ¶ 3—As the Mongols approached Vienna and the Holy Roman Empire, rumors of their quick moves spread, terrifying all who heard. A Hungarian priest announced that the Mongols were, in fact, the Antichrist. A Polish Franciscan wrote to his brethren that "Tribulation long foreknown and foretold has come upon us . . . with a ferocity already described by the testimony of the Holy Scriptures" and Count Palatine of Saxony, in a letter to a fellow duke wrote that "They are the sword of the Lord's anger for the sins of the Christian people."

Section III: **Critical Thinking**

The student may not use his text to answer this question.

The Mongols were a great and powerful force. But even these fierce fighters were flawed. Write a paragraph explaining the Mongols' weaknesses. In your answer, consider how nature thwarted the Mongols.

In this chapter we read about the damage inflicted by the Mongols on the Renaissance World. But we also saw that two natural phenomena, water and family ties could hold them back.

Choe-U, King Gojong, and the top officials of Goryeo were able to hide from the Mongols after they bought them off by crossing the strip of water between the Goryeo coast and the nearest island, Kanghwa. There, they reestablished themselves and, as written on page 312, the Mongol commanders "had no experience with water; they were reduced to shouting threats across at the king, fruitlessly ordering him to come back." Similarly, when Béla IV was being pursued by Kadan, the pursuit ended when Béla IV crossed into the Adriatic and took refuge on a small rocky island. We find out that, as written on page 316, "the Mongols generally did not like to cross oceans; even when their prey was in sight. Instead Kadan went back to his general." The Mongols were mighty, but if you could put a body of water between yourself and their troops, you just might have a chance of surviving.

Family ties were another natural occurrence that thwarted the Mongols' advances. Just as Subotai was about to organize an attack on the Holy Roman Empire, he received the news that his old friend and master, Ogodei Khan, was dead. Subotai immediately turned around and went home. Not only did family ties stop the Mongol assault on Europe, they also caused infighting. A family feud had broken out over the succession to the title of Great Khan. When Subotai returned to Karakorum, he found the Mongol clans divided in support of Genghis Khan's grandsons. The four years of infighting that followed brought a temporary end to Mongol conquests. Even the Mongols weren't above losing their focus to family feuding and internal power grabs.

EXAMPLE ANSWER:

The Mongols were powerful, but two natural occurrences got in their way: water and family. The Mongols didn't know how to deal with water. They didn't know how to fight in it or travel across it. Because of water, Choe-U, King Gojong, and the top officials of Goryeo were able to hide from the Mongols after they bought them off. They found refuge on the island of Kanghwa and all the Mongols could do was shout at them to come back from the other shore. Similarly, Béla IV of Hungary was able to escape the pursuit of his Mongol assassin by crossing into the Adriatic and taking refuge on a small island. Kadan did not want to cross the ocean, even though Kadan was in sight, so he returned to Subotai empty-handed. The Mongols were mighty, but if you could put a body of water between yourself and their troops, you just might have a chance of surviving.

The natural ties of family also thwarted Mongol conquest. Just as Subotai was about to organize an attack on the Holy Roman Empire, he received the news that his old friend and master, Ogodei Khan, was dead. Subotai immediately turned around and went home. When he got back to Karakorum, he found that a family feud had broken out over the succession to the title of Great Khan. The four years of infighting that followed brought a temporary end

to Mongol conquests. Even the Mongols weren't above losing their focus to family feuding and internal power grabs.

Section IV: **Map Exercise**

1. Trace the outline of the rectangular frame for Map 45.2 in black.

2. Using your blue pencil, trace the coastal outline around northern Europe, the Mediterranean, the Black Sea, the Caspian Sea, and the Aral Sea. Also trace the lines of the Danube, the Vulga, the Amu Darya, and the Syr Darya. Repeat until the contours are familiar.

3. Now using your black pencil, trace the outlines of the Mongol Conquests. Using contrasting colors, show the areas of Hungary and Georgia. Repeat until the contours are familiar.

4. Now using a new sheet of paper, trace the rectangular outline of the map in black. Then using your regular pencil with an eraser, draw the coastline all around the Mediterranean and northern Europe, including the Black Sea and the Caspian Sea. Erase and redraw as necessary. When you are happy with your map, lay it over the original. Erase and redraw any lines which are more than ½" off of the original.

5. Now study carefully the areas of the Holy Roman Empire, Austria, Polans, Greater Poland, the Prussians, the Lithuanians, Hungary, Croatia, Serbia, and Georgia. When they are familiar to you, close the book. Mark each one on the map. Then check your work against the map, and correct any mismarked or misplaced labels.

6. Now study carefully the locations of Vienna, Liegnitz, Budapest, and Tbilisi. Study the locations of Kiev, Moscow, and Riazan as well. When they are familiar for you, close the book and mark each one on your map. When you are happy with it, then place your map over the original. Erase and re-mark any marks that are more than ½" off of the original.

7. Study and mark the location of the Battle of the Sajo River. Mark the Volga and the Danube as well.

Chapter Forty-Six

The Debt of Hatred

The student may use her text when answering the questions in sections I and II.

Section I: Who, What, Where

Write a one or two-sentence answer explaining the significance of each item listed below.

Animadversio debita—**Pg. 320, ¶ 1 & 2**—*Animadversio debita*, **meaning "debt of hatred," was the penalty for those who had rebelled not only against the emperor but against God himself. Pope Gregory IX did not specify the exact nature of the ultimate *animadversio debita*, but repentant heretics were to be imprisoned for life while unrepentant heretics clearly deserved much worse; Frederick II had already decreed the legality of burning at the stake for the Lombard cities within the empire and the first stipulation in the Sicilian Code of 1231 condemned heretics as traitors, subject to the same penalty of death.**

Excommunicamus—**Pg. 320, ¶ 1**—*Excommunicamus* **was Gregory IX's papal decree published in 1231 that said anyone pointed out for heresy by the Dominicans was to be taken into custody by imperial officials, held for examination, and then punished with *animadversio debita*.**

Henry—**Pg. 319, ¶ 2 and Pg. 320, ¶ 7 to Pg. 321, ¶ 1**—**Henry, son of Frederick II and king of the Germans since 1222, rebelled against his father when he was old enough to rule without his regents and then declared open war against his father in December of 1234. Henry was quickly defeated by Frederick II, locked up in prison, and in 1242, unable to take the confinement any longer, he spurred his horse over a steep cliff face and was killed.**

Henry Raspe—**Pg. 323, ¶ 6**—**Henry Raspe, one of Frederick II's German subjects, was declared king of Germany in place of Conrad by Pope Innocent IV. Henry Raspe marched on Conrad's own forces but died on campaign.**

Imperial diet—**Pg. 319, ¶ 3**—**Imperial diet was a general assembly of all the dukes of Germany, presided over by the emperor.**

John of Brienne—**Pg. 318, ¶ 3 & 4**—**John of Brienne, the father of Frederick II's dead wife, was given permission by Pope Gregory IX to attack Sicily. John lost the desire for battle when** he realized that, unlike rumors he heard from Pope Gregory IX, Frederick II was in fact not dead, and he hastily retreated.

Pope Innocent IV—Pg. 323, ¶ 1-3—Pope Innocent IV, the Genoese cardinal Sinibaldo Fieschi, a canon lawyer, followed Gregory IX as pope. Pope Innocent IV created the idea of "absolute papal monarchy," meaning the pope stood above church law, was unbound by it, able to change it, depart from it, or even nullify it as needed.

William of Holland—Pg. 323, ¶ 6 and Pg. 324, ¶ 2—William of Holland was named king of Germany by Pope Innocent IV after Henry Raspe died on campaign against Conrad's forces. William of Holland was still fighting Conrad in German after Frederick II died.

Section II: Comprehension

Write a two or three-sentence answer to each of the following questions.

1. Describe the state of the The Holy Roman Empire as Frederick II returned home from Jerusalem.

A1.—Pg. 318, ¶ 2—The Holy Roman Empire was falling apart as Frederick II returned from Jerusalem. Germany had possessed its own strong national identity since the tenth century; the northern Italian cities, separated from the German duchies by the Alps, had already reassembled the twelfth-century Lombard League that had defied Frederick II's grandfather; and Sicily, part of the empire only because Frederick II had inherited its crown from his mother Constance, was for all practical purposes a separate kingdom. The Holy Roman Empire was held together by the fiction of the Roman resurrection, and that fiction was no longer powerful enough to keep the empire together.

2. How did Pope Gregory IX promote the destruction of the Holy Roman Empire? Was his strategy effective?

A2.—Pg. 318, ¶ 3—Pope Gregory IX promoted the destruction of the Holy Roman Empire by giving John of Brienne permission to attack Sicily, by promising his support to the Lombard League, and by spreading a rumor that Frederick II was dead. Pope Gregory IX's plan was not effective because Frederick II was alive and he returned home to fight for his land. When the Lombards and King John found out Frederick II was alive they lost heart; Gregory IX was forced to agree to a truce which lifted the emperor's excommunication in return for Frederick II not taking revenge on his agitators.

3. What happened when Frederick II sent for Henry to attend the 1231 imperial diet at Ravenna?

A3.—Pg. 319, ¶ 3-5—When Frederick II sent Henry a message ordering him to attend an imperial diet at Ravenna, the Lombard League cities immediately banded together and blocked Henry's pathway through the Alps. Henry, without a great deal of regret, sent his apologies to his father. Frederick, displeased with reports of Henry's lavish lifestyle and his tendency to favor court advisors who were hostile to the emperor, then ordered his son to meet him in the north of Italy in 1232, where Henry took an oath of loyalty to his father.

4. How had Frederick treated heresy since the beginning of his reign?

A4.—Pg. 319, ¶ 7 & 8—Frederick II had always treated heresy as an intensive offense against the empire itself; he said in 1220 that "To offend the divine majesty is a far greater crime than to offend the majesty of the emperor." Heresy deserved at least the same penalty as treason. At the beginning of his reign, he had decreed that heretics within his realm should be banished forever and all of their possessions should be confiscated.

5. Explain how heresy brought Frederick II and Gregory IX to work together.

A5.—Pg. 320, ¶ 4-6—Frederick II wanted the Holy Roman Empire to cooperate under his rule while Gregory IX was also fighting disorder and chaos, though Gregory IX believed that this disorder came from the supernatural world. Between 1231 and 1240, the two men cooperated in a series of decrees that increased the reach of the Inquisition and bound their two purposes closer and closer together. Heretics were burned at the stake in Verona, Milan, Rome, Germany and Trier, aligning Frederick II's interests, however briefly, with those of the pope.

6. What happened after Henry declared war on his father in December of 1234?

A6.—Pg. 321, ¶ 1—When Frederick II heard that his son had declared war against him, he approached his son's camp near Koblenz by avoiding the hostile northern Italian lands altogether, landing on the northern shore of the Adriatic and then marching up through the loyal eastern German duchy of Carinthia. Joined by the Duke of Carinthia and by the equally loyal Duke of Lorraine, he progressed to Worms where his presence in his country, after so many years away, was greeted as a Second Coming by his people. By the time he reached Worms, Henry's supporters had faded away and Frederick II was able to take Henry and two of his sons and imprison them.

7. How did Gregory IX come to excommunicate and depose Frederick II after working together to fight heresy?

A7.—Pg. 321, ¶ 3 to Pg. 322, ¶ 1—Frederick II fought hard to regain his control over Italy by campaigning in Lombardy, Vicenza, Mantua, and Milan, all while Gregory IX pleaded for peace in Italy. It had become increasingly clear to Gregory IX that Frederick's designs on Italy would, eventually, reach down to Rome itself. When, early in 1239, Frederick landed troops on the shores of the island of Sardinia, which the pope claimed as his own territory, Gregory IX rose up in wrath, condemned the emperor's ambitions, and in the Lenten season, Gregory IX pronounced Frederick II not only excommunicated but deposed.

8. Why did Frederick II retreat from his planned attack on Rome in August of 1241? Did this retreat make a difference for Frederick II's ongoing quarrel with the Church?

A8.—Pg. 322, ¶ 2 to Pg. 323, ¶ 1, 4 & 5—Frederick II retreated from his attack on Rome because Pope Gregory IX died and Frederick II wanted to show that his quarrel was not with the Church but with Gregory IX himself. However, when Pope Innocent IV ordered Frederick II to give up all of the territory he had conquered since his excommunication by Gregory IX, Frederick II refused. Innocent IV then traveled to the French city of Lyons and renewed both the excommunication and the call for Frederick's deposition as emperor,

starting a war between the two men and making Frederick II's retreat from Rome in 1241 pointless.

9. What was happening in Italy while Conrad fought William of Holland's forces in Germany?

A9.—Pg. 323, ¶ 6 to Pg. 324, ¶ 1—While Conrad was fighting off William of Holland's forces, Frederick II started to lose his foothold in Italy. Bishops and cardinals loyal to the pope were preaching revolt to the emperor's subjects in Sicily and Lombardy and early in February of 1248, Frederick II's army was unexpectedly defeated while laying siege to the city of Parma; the emperor was forced to flee to Cremona, and most of the gold and treasure he had been using to finance the war fell into Lombard hands. The Milanese, heading the Lombard League, led the recapture of Modena; Como fell; and in 1250, still battling, Frederick II grew ill with dysentery.

10. Where did Frederick II die, and where was he buried?

A10—Pg. 324, ¶ 2—Frederick II died in Apulia, but, according to the Franciscan Salimbene, "because of the very great stench of corruption which came from his body, he could not be carried to Palermo, where the sepulchers of the kings of Sicily are." Salimbene was a northerner, and other northern Italians believed his horror story. In fact, Frederick's body was embalmed, taken by ship to Sicily, paraded through the streets with an honor guard, and buried in Palermo, at the church of Monreale.

Section III: Critical Thinking

The student may not use her text to answer this question.

When Pope Innocent IV came to power, he declared that he had an "absolute papal monarchy." Write a paragraph explaining what "absolute papal monarchy" meant to Pope Innocent IV, and what it means to have "absolute" power. Then explain why this kind of power can be very dangerous.

The first part of the student's answer will be very straightforward. The Genoese cardinal Sinibaldo Fieschi, a canon lawyer, was made Pope Innocent IV after the death of Gregory IX. Absolute papal monarchy is defined in the text on page 323: "Innocent IV had a lawyer's mindset, and before long was combining Roman law with canon principles to come up with a clear articulation of his own power. Church law, he wrote, was above secular law; and since, in Roman jurisprudence, the prince stands above the law, so the pope also stands above church law, unbound by it, able to change it, depart from it, or even nullify it as needed. Absolute papal monarchy: it was a theory that Innocent IV spent much of his papacy elaborating and defending, and it was almost custom-designed to infuriate the emperor."

The student then should consider what is means to have "absolute" power. She may look up the definition if she'd like. For example, according to the American Heritage New Dictionary of Cultural Literacy, 3rd Edition, "power tends to corrupt; absolute power corrupts absolutely," which is "an observation that a person's sense of morality lessens as his or her power increases." Other definitions describe "absolute power" as "unrestricted control" or "freedom from all limitation." Pope Innocent IV did not say he had "absolute power" but the implication of an

CHAPTER FORTY-SIX: THE DEBT OF HATRED

"absolute papal monarchy" is that the pope would be "unrestricted" by the laws of man or the laws of the church, thus he would be able to do whatever he wanted and say that he had the authority to act in that way because his tenure was "absolute."

As per the definition given by the American Heritage New Dictionary of Cultural Literacy, unrestricted power or freedom from limitation can lead to corruption. Doing the right thing would come second to doing the thing that would increase the ruler's power. In the case of the pope, an "absolute papal monarch" combined with the lawlessness of the Inquisition could lead to anyone being accused of heresy if they did not adhere to the pope's rules and regulations. He could declare anyone against the church, and ultimately sentence anyone to death, because of his right to the "absolute papal monarchy." There would be no one to check his power; if they tried to stop him, he could declare them heretics and have them burned at the stake.

EXAMPLE ANSWER:

Pope Innocent IV said that church law was above secular law, and that the pope stood about church law. He was unbound by it, able to change it, depart from it, or even nullify it as needed. This was "absolute papal monarchy," where the pope's ability to do what he wanted was unrestricted. "Absolute papal monarchy" was like having "absolute power" because there was no one that could control the pope. Pope Innocent IV did not say he had "absolute power" but the implication of an "absolute papal monarchy" is that the pope would be unrestricted by the laws of man or the laws of the church; thus he would be able to do whatever he wanted and say that he had the authority to act in that way because his tenure was "absolute." Unrestricted power or freedom from limitation can lead to corruption. Doing the right thing would come second to doing the thing that would increase the ruler's power. In the case of the pope, an "absolute papal monarch" combined with the lawlessness of the Inquisition could lead to anyone being accused of heresy if they did not adhere to the pope's rules and regulations. He could declare anyone against the church, and ultimately sentence anyone to death, because of his right to the "absolute papal monarchy." There would be no one to check his power; if they tried to stop him, he could declare them heretics and have them burned at the stake.

Chapter Forty-Seven

The Shadow of God

The student may use his text when answering the questions in sections I and II.

Section I: Who, What, Where

Write a one or two-sentence answer explaining the significance of each item listed below.

Bahram—**Pg. 327, ¶ 2 & 4**—**Bahram, brother of Raziyya and favorite for the Delhi throne by the Forty, declared himself king after the imprisonment of his sister and the death of Malik Hakut. Bahram only lasted two years before his own soldiers assassinated him.**

Balban—**Pg. 327, ¶ 6 and Pg. 329, ¶ 6**—**Balban, the Turkish Grand Chamberlain, was a slave that worked hard and eventually became Nasiruddin's vizier, the de facto sultan of Delhi. Balban won many battles against outside enemies as vizier, and when Nasiruddin died in 1266, Balban claimed the sultanate of Delhi as his own.**

Malik Altuniah—**Pg. 326, ¶ 4 to Pg. 327, ¶ 3**—**Malik Altuniah, governor of the southern city of Bathinda, was able to turn the Turkish officials in Raziyya's court against her; together they killed Malik Hakut and took Raziyya prisoner. Malik Altuniah wanted to be sultan, so he drew up a contract of marriage with Raziyya but supporters of Bahram took Malik Altuniah and Raziyya captive on October 13, 1240 and they were executed the next morning.**

Malik Hakut—**Pg. 326, ¶ 3 and Pg. 327, ¶ 1**—**Malik Hakut, an African soldier born in the highlands of the southern Nile, was appointed by Raziyya as Master of Stables, a military position that directed the deployment of both horses and elephants. Malik Hakut was accused of being Raziyya's lover and was killed by Malik Altuniah when he rebelled against Raziyya.**

Naramasimha Deva—**Pg. 327, ¶ 7 to Pg. 328, ¶ 1**—**Naramasimha Deva, the Hindu king of Orissa, fought constantly against Muslims. In 1238 he took away parts of Bengal that had once fallen under Islamic rule, then he took the Delhi-controlled city of Laknaur in 1243, and the year after, a massive battle on the shores of the Ganges ended with Orissa armies triumphing.**

Nasiruddin—**Pg. 327, ¶ 4 & 5**—**Nasiruddin, Raziyya's youngest brother, aged twenty when he was elevated to the sultanate of Delhi in 1246, survived on the throne for two decades by not trying to rule. Nasiruddin was devoted to fasting and prayer and the study of the Holy Word, he was a model of all gentle virtues, and he turned the running of the sultanate over to his Turkish officials.**

Section II: Comprehension

Write a two or three-sentence answer to each of the following questions.

1. How did Raziyya handle the rumors that she appointed Malik Hakut to be Master of the Stables because he was her lover?

A1.—Pg. 326, ¶ 3—To stop the rumors that she appointed Malik Hakut to be Master of the Stables because he was her lover, Raziyya abandoned traditional female appearances. Whenever she rode out, she used a war elephant rather than a horse, and wore a man's armor and headdress.

2. Explain Balban's rise from slave to vizier.

A2.—Pg. 327, ¶ 6—Balban was taken captive in a Mongol raid on his tribe as a young man, sold at the Baghdad slave market, and finally bought by Iltumish himself when he was in his early thirties. Balban had spent his entire adult life as a slave; but in Delhi, this was no bar to advancement. He had worked his way into Iltumish's good graces, had served Raziyya herself in the court position of Chief Huntsman, and by 1246 was one of the most experienced soldiers and administrators of the Forty so Nasiruddin chose him to be vizier, making him the de facto sultan of Delhi.

3. What outside threats did Delhi face at the start of Nasiruddin's reign?

A3.—Pg. 328, ¶ 1-2—When Nasiruddin first became the ruler of Delhi he faced threats from the Hindu king of Orissa Naramasimha Deva and from the Mongols. Naramasimha Deva took away parts of Bengal that had once fallen under Islamic rule in 1238, then he took the Delhi-controlled city of Laknaur in 1243, and the year after, a massive battle on the shores of the Ganges ended with Orissa armies triumphing. To the north, the Mongols came into Lahore in 1241, looted the city, slaughtered anyone who resisted, and then withdrew, but more invasions seemed likely.

4. How did Balban deal with the Hindu and Mongol threats?

A4.—Pg. 328, ¶ 3 to Pg. 329, ¶ 2—Balban met the threats by organizing annual military campaigns against both Hindu opponents and Mongol outposts, and he made these excursions yearly military expeditions that buttressed the boundaries of Delhi and beat back the enemies at the sultanate's edges. In 1246, the armies of Delhi crossed into the region of the northern river known as the Sind and launched an attack on the scattering of Mongol forts there, causing the Mongols to flee in fear. The following year, Balban led a

similar campaign against Hindu rebels who had fortified themselves at Talsandah, east of Kannauj, and seized it for Delhi.

5. Why did Balban arrange his daughter to marry Nasiruddin?

A5.—Pg. 329, ¶3—Balban arranged for his daughter to marry Nasiruddin because he hoped to be the grandfather of the next sultan. However, the single son his daughter bore to Nasiruddin died in infancy, and no more heirs appeared.

6. Why did Balban lead troops into war against the hill country of Mewar in 1260? What was the result of the fighting?

A6.—Pg. 329, ¶ 4—Balban led troops against the hill country of Mewar, a Rajput kingdom south of Delhi, because it had caused the sultanate unending headaches by raiding, burning, and pillaging: in the eyes of the mamluks, it was a land of thieves, cattle rustlers, and bandits. Thousands of Mewar soldiers were killed by the sword, or trampled under the feet of Balban's elephants; civilians were slaughtered, captives were skinned alive, then hung over the gates of cities that resisted. And when guerrilla warfare continued from the forests, Balban supplied his army with axes and ordered them to clear a hundred miles of trees away, laying the ground bare so there was nowhere to hide, leading Balban to a spectacular victory.

7. How did Balban justify his place as sultan of Delhi?

A7.—Pg. 330, ¶ 1—Balban worked out a theory that made his strength as ruler identical to the will of God. He was *Zil-i-llahi*, "shadow of God": God's vice-regent on earth. He held his crown from God alone. He was answerable to no man, bound by no legal code, and vulnerable to no challenge.

8. What did Balban do, and what did he have others do, to prove that he was *Zil-i-llahi*?

A8.—Pg. 330, ¶ 2—Balban gave daily demonstrations of his status as divinely appointed representative of God to his people. He gave up drinking in public, remaining always distant, aloof, and solemn; he created an imposing armed guard that surrounded him everywhere he went; he dressed magnificently and sat on a diamond-studded throne; and in his audience chamber he instituted a new ceremony: his courtiers were to prostrate themselves before the throne on their bellies and kiss his feet. They were not to laugh in his presence.

9. What practical things did Balban do to secure his place as *Zil-i-llahi*?

A9.—Pg. 330, ¶ 3—In order to make sure the public supported his place as *Zil-i-llahi*, Balban sent the surviving members of the Forty on missions to distant corners of the sultanate; those who survived were selectively pruned through poisoning. Balban also had a network of spies throughout the empire, sending constant reports back to Delhi about the behavior of far-flung officials. To prove just how serious he was about keeping his subjects in line, he had one of his spies that failed to provide an update on the doings of a provincial governor publicly executed and hung up on the city gate of his target.

10. How did Balban go from being a slave to turning his people, for all intents and purposes, into slaves themselves?

A10.—Pg. 330, ¶ 4—Balban rose from being a slave to vizier to sultan by being a cunning strategist, strong military leader, and unrelenting ruler. During his reign, Balban restored the dignity and authority of the government and his people became tractable and obedient. The Turkish slave, risen to the sultanate, had reduced his people to the state he had once endured: obedient and submissive, or rather, slaves themselves.

Section III: Critical Thinking

The student may not use his text to answer this question.

Raziyya was "a great sovereign." She was "sagacious, just, beneficent . . . and of warlike talent." However, several officers once loyal to Raziyya's father Iltumish did not support her rule, even though she was an excellent leader. Write a paragraph explaining why the vizier of Delhi and his supports would want to put one of Iltumish's useless sons on the throne instead of the capable and strong Raziyya.

There are two reasons former supporters of Iltumish, and others, did not support Raziyya's rule.

First, Raziyya was a woman. It did not matter that she was wise, kind, and a great warrior because she was not a man. For example, on page 326 the Tabakat-i-Nasiri *tells us "she was endowed with all the admirable attributes and qualifications necessary for kings; but, as she did not attain the destiny, in her creation, of being computed among men, of what advantage were all these excellent qualifications to her?" In other words, no matter how great she was, it didn't matter because she was not a man. Raziyya did what she could to make herself appear masculine, like wearing a man's armor and headdress, but in the end that did not change her essential nature.*

Second, it made sense for the Turkish officials in Delhi's government to support one of Raziyya's brothers for the throne because that meant they would have more control and more power. Raziyya was a strong ruler and was in control of her throne. Raziyya's brothers, however, were more easily manipulated. Bahram, who stole the throne from his sister, only lasted two years before his own soldiers assassinated him. Then, the Forty, the most powerful mamluk warriors and courtiers in Delhi, struggled for power while supporting a puppet sultan. At first they were loyal to Raziyya's alcoholic nephew and then her youngest brother, Nasiruddin. Nasiruddin was devoted to fasting and prayer and the study of the Holy Word. He was a model of all gentle virtues: compassion, clemency, humility, and harmlessness. Causing no harm, he received none. He gave himself over to study and charity, and turned the running of the sultanate over to his Turkish officials. In this way he survived as ruler for two decades. The fourteenth-century poet and historian Isami explains that "The Sultan expressed no opinion without their permission. [H]e did not move his hands or feet except at their order. He would neither drink water nor go to sleep except with their knowledge." The Forty now had a direct line into ruling Delhi because they were able to control the sultan. This kind of power would not have been possible if Raziyya were still on the throne.

EXAMPLE ANSWER:

There are two reasons former supporters of Iltumish, and others, did not support Raziyya's rule. First, Raziyya was a woman. It did not matter that she was wise, kind, and a great

warrior because she was not a man. Raziyya did what she could to make herself appear masculine, like wearing a man's armor and headdress, but in the end that did not change her essential nature. Second, it made sense for the Turkish officials in Delhi's government to support one of Raziyya's brothers for the throne because that meant they would have more control and more power. Raziyya was a strong ruler and was in control of her throne. Raziyya's brothers, however, were more easily manipulated. The Forty, the most powerful mamluk warriors and courtiers in Delhi, struggled for power while supporting a puppet sultan. At first they were loyal to Bahram, then Raziyya's alcoholic nephew, and then her youngest brother, Nasiruddin. Nasiruddin was devoted to fasting and prayer and the study of the Holy Word. He was a model of all gentle virtues. He gave himself over to study and charity, and turned the running of the sultanate over to his Turkish officials. In this way he survived as ruler for two decades. The fourteenth-century poet and historian Isami explains that "The Sultan expressed no opinion without their permission. [H]e did not move his hands or feet except at their order. He would neither drink water nor go to sleep except with their knowledge." The Forty now had a direct line into ruling Delhi because they were able to control the sultan. This kind of power would not have been possible if Raziyya were still on the throne.

Section IV: **Map Exercise**

1. Trace the rectangular outline of the frame for Map 47.1 in black.

2. Using your blue pencil, trace the coastline, including the outline of Sri Lanka. Also trace the line of the Indus and of the Ganges, as well as the Narmada and Kaveri. Repeat until the contours are familiar.

3. Using a contrasting color, trace the lines of the Sultanate of Delhi under Balban. Trace the mountains with small peaks. Using your black pencil, trace the Chola and Orissa areas. Repeat until the contours are familiar.

4. Using a new sheet of paper, trace the rectangular outline of the frame in black. Then, using your regular pencil with an eraser, draw the coastline, including Sri Lanka. Draw the Indus and Ganges and Narmada and Kaveri. Show the mountains with small peaks. Then draw the area of the Sultanate of Delhi under Balban. Erase and redraw as necessary. When you are happy with your map, lay it over the original, and erase and redraw any lines more than ½" off of the original.

5. Now study carefully the Makran, Sind, Mewar, Choa, Orissa, Bengal, and Punjab areas. When you are familiar with them, close the book and mark them on your map. Then study the locations of Herat, Ghazni, Lahore, Bathinda, Delhi, Kannauj, Talsandah, and Laknaur. When they are familiar for you, close the book, and mark them on your map. When you are happy with your map, lay it over the original. Erase and re-mark any marks more than ½" off of the original.

6. Mark the arrows indicating the Mongol incursions as shown in the book.

Chapter Forty-Eight

The Seventh Crusade

The student may use her text when answering the questions in sections I and II.

Section I: Who, What, Where

Write a one or two-sentence answer explaining the significance of each item listed below.

As-Salih Ayyub—**Pg. 332, ¶ 7 to Pg. 333, ¶ 1 and Pg. 335, ¶ 7—As-Salih Ayyub, the older of al-Kamil's sons, won control of his father's empire by imprisoning his brother to ensure his hold on the throne, but his control was fractured when his uncle as-Salih Ismail declared himself ruler of the Syrian half of the Ayyubid empire. Ayyub fought against the Seventh Crusade but died by the time the Crusaders arrived at his encampment at Mansurah.**

As-Salih Ismail—**Pg. 333, ¶ 1—As-Salih Ismail, brother of al-Kamil and governor of Damascus under al-Kamil's sultancy, rebelled against as-Salih Ayyub and declared himself ruler of the Syrian half of the Ayyubid empire, making him the overlord of Jerusalem.**

Baibars—**Pg. 337, ¶ 1—Baibars, a commander in the Bahri Regiment, was angry that Turan-shah suggested that the Bahri was dispensable, so he plotted his leader's assassination. Baibars and his confederates, setting themselves up as a military government in Cairo, decided to honor Ayyub's widow as the titular ruler of Cairo, while they ran the government to suit themselves.**

Charles—**Pg. 333, ¶ 7—Charles, younger brother of Louis IX, sailed with his brother the king, the queen of France, and his brother Robert from Aigues-Mortes on August 25, 1248 to help lead the Seventh Crusade.**

Fakhr-ad-Din—**Pg. 335, ¶ 8—Fakhr-ad-Din, general of the Egyptian army, took control of the Egyptian defense after the death of as-Salih Ayyub.**

Margaret of Provence—**Pg. 333, ¶ 7 and Pg. 336, ¶ 6—Margaret of Provence, wife of Louis IX and queen of France, sailed with her husband from Aigues-Mortes on August 25, 1248 at the start the Seventh Crusade. Margaret gave birth to a son while Louis IX was fighting in Mansurah; with no midwife in the city, she had been forced to ask one of the old knights to** help her deliver the baby and just before the surrender, she was bundled out of the city with her new baby and taken back to Acre.

Robert—Pg. 333, ¶ 7 and Pg. 335, ¶ 8 to Pg. 336, ¶ 1—Robert, younger brother of Louis IX, sailed with his brother the king, the queen of France, and his brother Charles from Aigues-Mortes on August 25, 1248 to help lead the Seventh Crusade. On February 7, 1249, Robert led a brilliant surprise attack on the Muslim encampment outside of Mansurah, but then he and his men were slaughtered because he decided to lead his knights into Mansurah itself rather than turning back for reinforcements.

Turan-shah—Pg. 335, ¶ 8 and Pg. 336, ¶ 2 & 7—Turan-shah, son and heir to as-Salih Ayyub, arrived unexpectedly from war in Syria, cut off the Crusaders from behind, and blocked their line of supply from Damietta. Turan-shah agreed to Louis IX's request for surrender, but the deal between the men almost did not happen because Turan-shah was murdered suddenly in an uprising of the Turkish soldiers who made up a good part of his armed force.

Section II: Comprehension

Write a two or three-sentence answer to each of the following questions.

1. What motivated Louis IX to go on crusade?

A1.—Pg. 332, ¶ 2-5—When Louis IX was thirty, he became very sick and everyone in his palace thought he was going to die. But after everyone gave up hope, Louis IX suddenly came out of his coma; when he had recovered enough to sit up and speak, he announced that in thanksgiving, he would go on crusade. However, even before his illness, Louis IX had probably been contemplating crusade because in the fall of 1244 Jerusalem had fallen once more into Muslim hands.

2. Why did Frederick II's treaty with al-Kamil come to an end?

A2.—Pg. 332, ¶ 6—Frederick II's treaty with al-Kamil expired in 1239. Islamic law dictated that a treaty made by Muslims with infidels could not last more than ten years. In most cases, treaties were simply renewed once per decade, but al-Kamil died in 1238 causing his two sons to battle over his empire, leaving the treaty with the Holy Roman Emperor to remain expired. 3. Who did as-Salih Ayyub hire to attack his uncle's Syrian domains? What was their history?

A3.—Pg. 333, ¶ 3—As-Salih Ayyub hired the wandering survivors of the Turkish kingdom of Khwarezm that was destroyed by Genghis Kahn in 1219 to attack his uncle's Syrian domains. When the last Shah of Khwarezm, Jalal ad-Din, had fled into India pursued by Genghis's men, his army and family had been wiped out, but Jalal ad-Din himself had survived and then he had spent the next ten years of his life waging guerrilla warfare against the Mongol conquerors. His followers became known as the *Khwarezmiyya*, nomadic mercenaries, claiming to preserve the last remnants of Khwarezm culture, hiring themselves out to whoever could pay.

4. How was Jerusalem retaken by the Muslims?

A4.—Pg. 333, ¶ 4—In 1244, ten thousand Khwarezmiyya, fighting on behalf of the Sultan of Egypt, swept down on Syria. On August 11, they stormed Jerusalem and slaughtered both Muslims and Christians in the streets, broke into the Church of the Holy Sepulchre, and ripped the bones of the Crusader kings of Jerusalem from their crypts. Then the Ayyub of Egypt claimed the city for his own, folding it back into the Muslim world.

5. What did Louis IX do to prepare for the Seventh Crusade?

A5.—Pg. 333, ¶ 6—Louis IX started his preparation for the Seventh Crusade by collecting a special crusade tax from his subjects to pay for the expedition, and recruiting French barons and their knights to join him. From the city of Genoa, he bought scores of ships; over thirty two- and three-decked sailing ships, transport galleys, and war galleys. He also sent provisions like wine, wheat, and barley to Cyprus, where he intended to rendezvous with other Crusader knights.

6. Describe the beginning of the Seventh Crusade.

A6.—Pg. 335, ¶ 2—The beginning of the Seventh Crusade started with everyone arguing with one another. The Crusader army was led by Louis, his brothers, the Grand Master of the Knights Templar, Jean de Joinville, the English Earl of Salisbury, and the Count of Marche, and they all disagreed over strategy. Louis wanted to attack Egypt, which now controlled Jerusalem; the Grand Master of the Templars thought that the Crusaders should start off by making a play for some of the disputed Syrian lands; and several of the French barons suggested that fall was a bad time to set off by ship, since foul weather was almost a certainty. In the end, the Crusaders delayed on Cyprus until the following May, by which point a good deal of the fervor had faded, and most of the food had been eaten.

7. What happened at Damietta?

A7.—Pg. 335, ¶ 4 & 5—When the Crusader ships reached the coast near Damietta as-Salih Ayyub had fortified the city and established a second line of defense at the town of Mansurah, just east of the Nile and seventy-five miles northeast of Cairo. The Crusader attack began on the morning of June 5 and they fought so fiercely that the Turkish defenders retreated back into Damietta and then evacuated the city that night, allowing the Crusaders to march in triumphantly the next day. Ayyub, furious over the easy victory, executed the generals who were responsible for the surrender.

8. Why did the Crusaders stay so long in Damietta? What did they do while they were there?

A8.—Pg. 335, ¶ 6—The Crusaders stayed for a long time in Damietta because the Nile floods were due to begin, and Louis IX had learned his lesson from tales of the disastrous Fifth Crusade. The Crusaders knew it would be impossible to go to Alexandria, Babylon, or Cairo while the Nile was flooded. Instead, the Crusaders lingered in Damietta, transforming its mosque into a cathedral, digging additional fortifications, and waiting for the Nile to recede.

9. What happened after Turan-shah unexpectedly cut the Crusaders off from behind, outside of Mansurah, blocking their supply from Damietta?

A9.—Pg. 336, ¶ 3 & 4—After Turan-shah cut the Crusaders off from their supply of food, they slowly began to starve, first eating horses, donkeys, and mules, and then dogs and cats. Disease followed when the bodies of the Crusaders that were killed by the Egyptians came to the surface of the water; the flesh on the Crusaders' legs dried up, their skin became blotched with black and blue, and their gums rotted. By Easter, the men realized they had to flee but they didn't get far before Louis IX decided to surrender.

10. Why did Turan-shah murder the sick and wounded Crusaders after accepting Louis IX's surrender? What terms were set for the truce after the killing of the sick and wounded?

A10.—Pg. 336, ¶ 5—Turan-shah most likely ordered all of the sick and wounded slaughtered because his guard told him the plague afflicting the Crusaders would spread. The truce set was that in exchange for 800,000 "Saracen bezants" (nearly 400,000 pounds of gold), half of it to be paid on the spot, and the freedom of all Muslim prisoners, Turan-shah would free his Crusader captives.

11. Why did the Turkish soldiers rise up against Turan-shah?

A11.—Pg. 336, ¶ 8 to Pg. 337, ¶ 1—The most elite fighting force in the Egyptian army was a thousand-strong mamluk regiment known as the Bahri Regiment, originally formed as the personal bodyguard of the sultan Ayyub himself. When Turan-shah had arrived in Egypt, though, he had high-handedly promoted his own favorites into key positions instead of advancing the senior mamluks of the Bahri Regiment and he also announced at a drunken dinner party that he intended to chop down his father's mamluks. Angry over the slight, one of the Bahri Regiment's commanders, a Turk named Baibars, plotted Turan-shah's assassination.

12. How did the Seventh Crusade end?

A12.—Pg. 337, ¶ 2-4—The Seventh Crusade ended with Turan-Shah's dead and butchered body swelling with the decay on the ground outside his camp for three days before anyone bothered to bury it and with the Crusaders still in captivity while the Bahri Regiment decided if they were going to honor the agreement the Crusaders made with Turan-Shah. On May 5, the Bahri Regiment agreed to the deal; Louis handed over his half ransom and was set free, along with his two surviving brothers and most of his barons. Though the king had survived, hundreds of Crusader soldiers remained prisoners in Egypt, Louis IX had spent every penny and owed still more for the balance of his ransom, and the Crusade itself had failed: Jerusalem was still in Muslim hands.

Section III: Critical Thinking

The student may not use her text to answer this question.

The Seventh Crusade should have been a success. Louis IX made sure his soldiers were well-prepared, and yet, the Crusade turned into a fiasco with Jerusalem still in Muslim hands. Explain what you think went wrong. What do you think was the main reason the Crusaders failed?

The student can answer this question in a variety of ways. There were several factors that led to the downfall of the Seventh Crusade:

- *When Louis IX, his thirty-eight ships, and score of flat-bottomed transports arrived in Cyprus, a decision could not be made as to how to move forward.*

- *Instead of moving forward, the Crusaders decided to stay on Cyprus until the following May, which led to a decrease in motivation and more importantly, a decrease in food stores.*

- *The Crusaders were successful in Damietta, but by the time they took the city the Nile was about to flood, which meant they had to again wait to go further into Muslim territory. The hesitancy gave the enemy time to prepare for war.*

- *Another of Louis IX's brothers arrived in Damietta with fresh men and the Crusaders marched on Mansura. Robert led a brilliant attack on the Muslim encampments outside of Mansurah, but then he continued into the city rather than waiting for reinforcements, leading to his death and the slaughter of his men. This decreased Crusader morale and manpower.*

- *The Crusaders didn't have enough men after Robert's defeat to take Mansurah, so they had to camp outside the city and rely on food supplied from Damietta. When Turan-shah arrived and cut off the Crusaders' supply, they were trapped. They starved and suffered from disease.*

- *Realizing the Crusaders had to get out of Mansurah, Louis IX led his men north, but the men were hungry and weak, and couldn't continue fighting off their Muslim attackers. This led to Louis IX's surrender.*

The student can pick any one of these moments as the breaking point in the Seventh Crusade. She just has to back up her answer with a convincing argument as to why the particular point she picked was the moment of no return. The example answer reflects how a convincing argument might sound—the student does NOT have to elaborate on the same point.

EXAMPLE ANSWER:

As described in the chapter, the Seventh Crusade was a "fiasco." So many things went wrong even though Louis IX set his crusade up for success. While a series of unfortunate events plagued the Crusaders, the Seventh Crusade failed because there were "too many cooks in the kitchen." When the Crusaders first arrived in Cyprus, they couldn't decide how to move forward. As a result, they used up a lot of their provisions. They moved forward to Damietta, but once there they were off schedule and had to wait out the floods of the Nile, again losing motivation and supplies. This break also allowed the enemy to get ready for the Crusaders' attack. Though new supplies and soldiers came before attacking Mansurah, the lack of leadership foiled the Crusaders again. Robert led a strong attack against the Muslim encampment outside Mansurah, but then he did what he wanted to do and attacked the city itself, leading to his own death and the slaughter of his men. The Crusaders couldn't recover. They were cut off by Turan-shah, starved and riddled with plague, and then they had to surrender. If there was a strong leader with a clear vision for how to take back Jerusalem from the start, maybe the Seventh Crusade would have gone differently. Instead, the various leaders argued about what to do and the result was another failed holy war.

Section IV: Map Exercise

1. Trace the rectangular outline of the frame for Map 48.1: The Seventh Crusade in black.

2. Trace the coastal outline around the Mediterranean, including the Black Sea and the Red Sea. You do not need to include all the small islands around Greece and Turkey. Repeat until the contours are familiar.

3. Using your black pencil, trace the outlines of France, the Holy Roman Empire, the Papal States, Cyprus, the Kingdom of Jerusalem, and the Ayyubid Empire. Repeat until the contours are familiar.

4. Using a new sheet of paper, trace the rectangular outline of the frame of Map 48.1 in black. Using your regular pencil with an eraser, draw the coastline around the Mediterranean and the Red and Black Seas. Then draw the areas of France, the Holy Roman Empire, the Papal States, Cyprus, the Kingdom of Jerusalem, and the Ayyubid Empire. Erase and redraw as necessary. When you are happy with your map, lay it over the original, and erase and remark any marks that are more than ½″ off of the original.

5. Now study carefully the locations of Aigues-Mortes, Paris, Genoa, Damascus, Acre, Jerusalem, Damietta, Mansurah, and Cairo. When you are familiar with them, close the book. Mark and label each location. Then check your labels against the original, and erase and redraw any marks and labels that are more than ½″ off of the original.

6. Mark the areas of France, the Holy Roman Empire, the Papal States, Golden Horde, Cyprus, the Kingdom of Jerusalem, Egypt, and the Ayyubid Empire.

7. Mark the line showing the progress and direction of the Seventh Crusade.

Chapter Forty-Nine

The Splintering Khanate

The student may use his text when answering the questions in sections I and II.

Section I: **Who, What, Where**

Write a one or two-sentence answer explaining the significance of each item listed below.

Alghu—**Pg. 343, ❡ 8**—Alghu, Chagatai's grandson and supporter of Arik-Boke's khanship, seized the fighting over the khanship to declare his own independent rule over the Chagatai Khanate.

Arik-Boke—**Pg. 343, ❡ 3 & 6**—Arik-Boke, the youngest of Mongke's brothers, managed to summon a rump assembly after Mongke's death in Karakorum and get himself elected Great Khan before either of his elder brothers could make it back home and claim the throne themselves. Arik-Boke had to surrender his throne to Kublai on August 1, 1264, after two years of fighting.

Berke—**Pg. 343, ❡ 8 & 9**—Berke, brother to Batu, controlled the lands of the Golden Horde and rejected Kublai's clan to be his overlord. Berke firmed up the independence of the Golden Horde khanship.

Guyuk—**Pg. 339, ❡ 1 & 2 and Pg. 340, ❡ 3**—Guyuk, oldest son of Ogodei, was made Great Khan in 1246 at the age of forty, but not everyone supported his rule. Guyuk was prematurely aged by the traditional Mongol overindulgence in strong drink and as a result in April of 1248 Guyuk died while he was traveling after only two years as Great Khan.

Hulagu—**Pg. 342, ❡ 5 & 6 and Pg. 343, ❡ 9**—Hulagu, Mongke's youngest brother, was successful in his attacks on the Nizari and the Ayyubid holdings, but he had to return to Karakorum before he reached Cairo because the Great Khan had died. Hulagu refused to support any of the rivals for Great Khan because he didn't want to make the wrong choice, so he withdrew from the fight entirely and grew his own holdings in the Middle East into a kingdom that would be known as the Il-khanate.

Kublai—**Pg. 341, ¶ 3 & 5 and Pg. 343, ¶ 4-6—Kublai, Mongke's younger brother, worked to bring down the Southern Song by first attacking the kingdom of Nanzhao and then using the capital city of Dali as his base to begin attacks on the Song border. Kublai had himself confirmed as Great Khan in opposition to Arik-Boke, then he returned to Karakorum and fought against his brother for two years before he finally beat him and took the title for himself.**

Mongke—**Pg. 339, ¶ 2 and Pg. 341, ¶ 1 & 2—Mongke, the oldest son of Genghis Khan's son Tolui, was the preferred choice for Great Khan after Ogodei's death by a healthy segment of Mongol chiefs, but he was beat out by Guyuk. Mongke became Great Khan after Guyuk's death but was elected only by a partial assembly; he remained in full control of the entire empire for nine years but the partial victory cracked the foundation of the Mongol house forever.**

Rukn al-Din—**Pg. 342, ¶ 4—Rukn al-Din, leader of the Nizari at the time of Hulagu's moves west, wanted to surrender when the Mongols arrived but the other Nizaris held him back. Rukn a-Din managed to sneak past his men and surrender to Hulagu on the condition that he be allowed to travel east and appeal to the Great Khan himself, but even though Hulagu agreed, Rukn al-Din was ordered to be killed by the Great Kahn as soon as he arrived at his camp.**

Toregene—**Pg. 339, ¶ 2 & 4—Toregene, Ogodei's widow, insisted that Guyuk take his father's place as Great Khan. Though Guyuk was unpopular, Toregene used her power as regent to get Guyuk elected.**

Tran Hoang—**Pg. 342, ¶ 2—Tran Hoang, son of Tran Canh, was given the Dai Viet throne by his father in 1257.**

Section II: Comprehension

Write a two or three-sentence answer to each of the following questions.

1. Why was Guyuk so unpopular? How did he manage to replace Ogodei as Great Khan despite his unpopularity?

A1.—Pg. 339, ¶ 2-4—Guyuk was unpopular in part because his father had disliked him and had repeatedly suggested that the succession pass him by. However, all of Genghis Kahn's sons were dead, so a grandson had to be made Great Khan, and Toregene, regent until a new khan was elected, insisted on Guyuk's election. Toregene had the force of Mongol law behind her and she was able to delay the election for four years in order to bribe, persuade, and bully clan chiefs into supporting her son.

2. Describe Guyuk's coronation ceremony.

A2.—Pg. 339, ¶ 5—On August 24, beneath a white velvet tent, surrounded by gold-armed clan chiefs, Guyuk was seated on a gold and ivory throne, studded with pearls, and acclaimed as Great Khan. The ceremony was observed by more than four thousand envoys and ambassadors from Moscow, Cairo, Goryeo, the Song court, Baghdad, Georgia, Cilician Armenia, and Rome. Gifts of silk, samite, velvet, brocade, furs and more than five hundred carts filled with gold and silver and silken garments were presented to the new ruler.

3. What kind of gift did Pope Innocent IV send to the Great Khan? How did Guyuk respond?

A3.—Pg. 340, ¶ 1 & 2—Pope Innocent IV did not send an actual gift to the Great Khan; he sent a letter asking him to stop his attacks on the Christian world and to "acknowledge Jesus Christ the very Son of God, and worship His glorious name by practicing the Christian religion." Guyuk responded by saying the pope should serve the Mongols, reminding the pope that the Mongols made known God's command through their successes in conquering the world, and he asked the pope to prove that it was not God's will for the Mongols to triumph. Guyuk reminded the pope that because he was living outside the Christian world, he was one of the few rulers in the world powerful enough to question the pope's authority with absolute impunity.

4. What advances did Guyuk make toward Mongol world domination?

A4.—Pg. 340, ¶ 4—In his two-year reign, Guyuk had set the Mongols back on the road to world domination by returning to the west and entirely subduing the Sultanate of Rum and the remaining holdout lands in Georgia. Guyuk made Cilician Armenia his vassal. Guyuk was about to send Subotai to head a campaign against the Southern Song when he died.

5. How did Mongke follow Guyuk as Great Khan?

A5.—Pg. 340, ¶ 5 to Pg. 341, ¶ 1—The clans argued for three years over Guyuk's successor. When Batu and the Golden Horde threw their favor behind Mongke, the son of Tolui finally gained his long-delayed title of Great Khan. He was acclaimed on July 1, 1251, in a ceremony that lacked the over-the-top magnificence of Guyuk's; Batu had called the assembly himself, and when Mongke's detractors refused to attend, Batu insisted on the appointment of Mongke by the clan chiefs who were present.

6. Why did Kublai start his attack on the Song by going after the kingdom of Nanzhao? Why didn't he kill all of the captives after he won the battle?

A6.—Pg. 341, ¶ 5 & 6—Kublai started his attack on the Southern Song by going after the kingdom of Nanzhao because the Song did not expect him to approach from that direction. After he successfully drove the Nanzhao defenders back to their capital city of Dali and besieged it, Kublai only executed the king himself, and two of his officials who had murdered a Mongol ambassador, because he had been studying Chinese philosophy, and took as his motto an ancient tenet of the Confucian teacher Mencius: He who takes no pleasure in killing people can unite them behind him. It took another two years for Nanzhao to be entirely united under Mongol control, but once the kingdom had reached stability under a Mongol governor, Kublai used it as a base to begin attacks against the Song border.

7. Explain how Goryeo ended up surrendering to the Mongols?

A7.—Pg. 341, ¶ 7 to Pg. 342, ¶ 1—In Goryeo, the state of half war, half peace observed by the court on the island of Kanghwa and the Mongol occupiers in the north broke down. Repeated Mongol attacks on the independent south had killed an untold number. Finally, King Gojong arranged for the assassination of Choe-U, the military dictator responsible for the ongoing resistance, and as soon as Choe-U was dead sent his own son, the Crown Prince, to Mongke's court to offer Goryeo's surrender, which was made official in 1259.

8. Why did Tran Canh abdicate his throne to his eighteen-year-old son Tran Hoang?

A8.—Pg. 342, ¶ 2—Tran Canh had been trying to get off of his throne since the moment he was made king. In 1257, after the Mongols captured the capital city Thang Long, Tran Canh abdicated and crowned his eighteen-year-old son Tran Hoang in his place. Officially, the change in power was intended to keep quarrels over succession from breaking out in the middle of a new invasion, but Tran Canh, despite dreading the Mongol return, had finally gained the chance he had been waiting for: to abandon the throne in favor of the monastery.

9. Describe Hulagu's conquests as he headed west. What stopped his advance towards Cairo?

A9.—Pg. 342, ¶ 4 & 5—After Rukn al-Din surrendered to Hulagu, the Mongol army reduced the Nizari to rubble, and they advanced steadily forward, against the Ayyubid holdings. In 1259, Hulagu reached Baghdad and swept through it, putting the last Abbasid caliph to death, and in 1260, he drove the last Ayyubid governors out of Damascus and Aleppo. Hulagu had to stop his approach to Cairo because the Great Khan died and he had to turn back towards Karakorum to be present for the election of the next Mongol supreme leader.

10. Why wasn't Ari-Boke's nor Kublai's election to Great Khan legitimate? Why did both men think their assemblies were legitimate?

A10.—Pg. 343, ¶ 4—Neither the assembly convened by Ari-Boke nor the assembly convened by Kublai was entirely regular, not according to Mongol law. Arik-Boke had not given the full quota of clan chiefs time to assemble, and Kublai had called his assembly on non-Mongolian soil, which made it unofficial. While neither election was official, both brothers had simply followed the pattern Mongke had established at his own election: they had taken partial support as enough justification to seize the single title of Great Khan.

Section III: Critical Thinking

The student may not use his text to answer this question.

Mongke followed Guyuk as Great Khan, but he did not have the full support of the Mongols behind him. Write a paragraph describing the lasting consequences of Mongke's actions. Use specific examples from the chapter to back up your claim.

Mongke was elected great Khan by a partial assembly. By allowing this election to stand, Mongke set a dangerous precedent: the Khan did not have to have everyone's support to rule.

Kublai was the next-oldest of the brothers, and he expected to be acclaimed Great Khan after Mongke. But he lingered in his fight against the Song and did not rush back for the election. Hulagu, also wanting to throw his hat into the ring, did return home, but he had a long way to travel from Egypt back to Karakorum. Arik-Boke was left in the capital alone. He wanted to be Great Khan himself, so he marshaled the support of the more insular Mongol chiefs—those who were suspicious of Kublai's interest in Chinese culture, and wary of expanding the empire as far as Egypt—and summoned a rump assembly to get himself elected Great Khan before either of his elder brothers could make it back home.

When Kublai found out what Ari-Boke had done, he convened his own assembly near Song territory, made up of the clan chiefs who were with him, and had himself confirmed as Great Khan in his brother's place. Kublai then returned to Karakorum and fought with his brother for over two years. On August 1, 1264, Arik-Boke finally agreed to surrender. Kublai spared his life (although he put most of Arik-Boke's supporters that he could find to death).

Kublai's election did not mend the cracks in the Mongol empire. Berke, brother of Batu, who was in control of the lands of the Golden Horde, rejected Kublai's clan to be his overlord. In the lands east of the Oxus, Chagatai's grandson Alghu—who had supported Arik-Boke's khanship—seized the opportunity to declare his own independent rule over the Chagatai Khanate. And Hulagu, afraid that whoever he swore allegiance to might end up on the bottom of the heap when the fighting stopped, had withdrawn entirely. The result was that Kublai still ruled in the east, but the Golden Horde khanship and the Chagatai Khanate would continue to claim their independence. Hulagu's own conquests, growing apart from the other Mongol lands, would become the Il-khanate, a separate Mongol kingdom in the Middle East. Because Mongke allowed his election to come from partial support only, the empire that had stretched from the Chinese coast to the Black Sea had fractured into quarters, and then broken entirely apart.

EXAMPLE ANSWER:

Mongke was elected great Khan by a partial assembly. By allowing this election to stand, Mongke set a dangerous precedent: the Khan did not have to have everyone's support to rule. The lasting consequences of this decision were that the Mongols no longer felt they had to support the Great Khan, and that led to the kingdom falling apart. This is how the breakdown happened: Arik-Boke marshaled the support of Mongol chiefs in Karakorum and summoned a rump assembly to get himself elected Great Khan before either of his elder brothers could make it back home from their battle fronts. Then, when Kublai found out what Ari-Boke had done, he convened his own assembly near Song territory, made up of the clan chiefs who were with him, and had himself confirmed as Great Khan in his brother's place. Kublai returned to Karakorum and fought with his brother for over two years. On August 1, 1264, Arik-Boke finally agreed to surrender. However, Kublai's election did not mend the cracks in the Mongol empire. Berke, brother of Batu, who was in control of the lands of the Golden Horde, claimed independence for his khanship. Alghu, Chagatai's grandson, claimed independence for the Chagatai Khanate. And Hulagu's own conquests, growing apart from the other Mongol lands, became the Il-khanate, a separate Mongol kingdom in the Middle East. Because Mongke allowed his election to come from partial support only, the Mongol empire that had stretched from the Chinese coast to the Black Sea had fractured into quarters, and then broken apart entirely.

Chapter Fifty

The Mamluks of Egypt

The student may use her text when answering the questions in sections I and II.

Section I: Who, What, Where

Write a one or two-sentence answer explaining the significance of each item listed below.

Al-Malik al-Ashraf—**Pg. 346, ¶ 5 to Pg. 347, ¶ 1 & 2—Al-Malik al-Ashraf, the grandson of the youngest son of al-Kamil, was proclaimed the rightful Ayyubid sultan by mamluk comrades that did not agree with Aybek's sultanhood and he ruled for some time as co-sultan. He was sent into exile when he was ten years old by his co-sultan.**

Al-Mansur Ali—**Pg. 347, ¶ 5—Al-Mansur Ali, son of Aybek, was appointed to be the next sultan of Egypt after his father's death and Shajar al-Durr's murder. Ali was never meant to rule; he was a makeshift caretaker, meant to reassure the people of Cairo that all was in order, while behind his throne the mamluks fought amongst themselves over the sultanate.**

Aybek—**Pg. 346, ¶ 4 and Pg. 347, ¶ 3—Aybek, a mamluk commander but not one of the Bahri Regiment, married Shajar al-Durr; Shajar al-Durr wanted to protect her power so she married Aybek and handed the title of sultan to him. Shajar al-Durr had hoped that the marriage would allow her to keep some power, but Aybek was determined to shut her out so in April of 1257 she had the sultan strangled to death.**

Bohemund VI—**Pg. 351, ¶ 2—Bohemund VI, prince of Antioch, could not stop Qutuz from taking the kingdom, and he was left only with Tripoli after the Muslim attack.**

Faris al-Din Aqtay—**Pg. 347, ¶ 2—Faris al-Din Aqtay, the Bahri regiment general who had largely been responsible for the defeat of Louis and the French army, was murdered by Aybek and Qutuz in 1254. Faris al-Din Aqtay's death broke the Bahri regiment apart.**

Ked-Buqa—**Pg. 347, ¶ 7 and Pg. 348, ¶ 3—Ked-Buqa, Hulagu's general, carried on the westward Mongol advance while Hulagu was in Karakorum; Ked-Buqa led the occupation of Aleppo, Homs, Hama, and Gaza and by early 1260, he had almost reached the Jordan river.**

Ked-Buqa died in battle against the Egyptians on September 3, 1260 in the valley of Ain Jalut, and his death caused the Mongol army to lose heart and flee.

Qutuz—**Pg. 347, ¶ 2 & 6 and Pg. 348, ¶ 6—Qutuz, Aybek's lieutenant and hitman, was proclaimed sultan by his companions on November 12, 1259, sending Al-Mansur Ali into early and peaceful retirement and also welcoming back the Bahri who had fled under the rule of Aybek. Qutuz was able to beat the Mongols in battle, but he was murdered by Baibars and his men in October of 1260 as revenge for Qutuz's murder of Faris al-Din Aqtay.**

Shajar al-Durr—**Pg. 346, ¶ 2 and Pg. 347, ¶ 3 & 4—Shajar al-Durr, as-Salih Ayyub's widow, was recognized as the new sultan after the Bahri Regiment took over control of Egypt's government, but she always represented herself as "Queen of the Muslims and Mother of Khalil" because only as mother of as-Salih Ayyub's son could she claim any right to hold the throne. Shajar al-Durr tried to keep her power by marrying Aybek and giving him the title of sultan, but she ended up having him killed and then she was murdered when Aybek's first wife allowed the house servants to beat Shajar al-Durr to death with their wooden house clogs.**

Section II: Comprehension

Write a two or three-sentence answer to each of the following questions.

1. How did Aybek deal with those who opposed his position as sultan?

A1.—Pg. 347, ¶ 2—At first Aybek accepted al-Malik al-Ashraf as his co-sultan, but he eventually sent Al-Malik al-Ashraf into exile by taking him north and finding him refuge in the Empire of Nicaea. Aybek got rid of the general Faris al-Din Aqtay by having him murdered; the murder caused the Bahri to break apart. Aqtay's friends fled north to Syria; among them was Baibars himself, the assassin of Turan-shah.

2. What did Qutuz do when Ked-Buqa's messengers arrived in Cairo in late August of 1260? Why did he react this way?

A2.—Pg. 347, ¶ 8 to Pg. 348, ¶ 1—When Ked-Buqa's messengers arrived in Cairo in late August of 1260 and ordered Qutuz to surrender, the new sultan put the Mongol messengers to death and stuck their heads up on his city gate. The defiance was intended to spark an explosion; Qutuz knew that the Mongols had been left behind as a skeleton force, and he was convinced that Allah was behind him in his desire to crush the Christian Mongol enemies of Islam. Qutuz even sent a message to Acre, asking the Crusaders there to join him in an alliance; they decided to pass but did offer to help with resupplying the Egyptian army as it marched against the Mongols.

3. What happened when the Egyptians met the Mongols on September 3, 1260 in the valley of Ain Jalut?

A3.—Pg. 348, ¶ 2 & 3—When the Mongols met the Egyptians in the valley of Ain Jalut, they fell into a trap they had set several times before: Qutuz concealed most of his men in the

STUDY AND TEACHING GUIDE FOR THE HISTORY OF THE RENAISSANCE WORLD

hills around Ain Jalut and sent only a small division, led by Baibars, into the Mongol jaws. Ked-Buqa, scenting victory, called for a charge; Baibars turned tail and fled into the hills; and as the Mongols followed, the rest of the mamluks emerged from hiding and surrounded them. The Mongols nearly fought their way free but several hours into the battle, Ked-Buqa fell and his death took the heart out of the Mongol army and they fled.

4. Describe the events that followed the Egyptian victory over the Mongols.

A4.—Pg. 348, ¶ 4-6—After the Egyptians beat the Mongols, news of the mamluk victory was carried triumphantly to Egypt, accompanied by Ked-Buqa's head on a spear. Qutuz himself rode in triumph to Damascus, drove out the Mongol occupiers, and claimed it again for Egypt; within a month, he had also retaken Aleppo, Homs, and Hama; and Egypt and Syria were finally reunited under the Cairo sultanate. Unfortunately, Qutuz was murdered in October of 1260 by Baibars and the Bahri Regiment in retaliation for Qutuz's role in the murder of Faris al-Din Aqtay six years earlier.

5. How did Baibars become sultan of Egypt?

A5.—Pg. 348, ¶ 6 to Pg. 349, ¶ 1—After Baibars orchestrated the revenge murder of Qutuz, he rode back with his men to camp and to face down Qutuz's top official, who was waiting for him. When the man asked "Which of you killed him?" and Baibars answered, "I did," the man told him to sit on the throne in Qutuz's place, making him the new sultan of Egypt.

6. Why did the Mongol Berke make an alliance with the Egyptian Qutuz?

A6.—Pg. 349, ¶ 3 & 4—Baibars wanted to to guard himself from the revenge of the Il-khanates, so he sent envoys north to the Golden Horde to negotiate alliances with Berke, the khan who now ruled the Rus' lands. Berke had converted to Islam and renounced his allegiance to the Great Khan, so he was anxious to protect his own borders against Hulagu's ambitions. The allegiance between Berke and Qutuz also protected the slave trade routes, where thousands of slaves, taken captive by Mongol detachments, were shipped from the shores of the Black Sea (now under Berke's control) to Egypt every year; the slave regiments remained the strongest instrument of Baibars's power.

7. How did Baibars lasso the role of Commander of the Faithful for Egypt? How did this change Egypt's role in the Muslim world?

A7.—Pg. 349, ¶ 5 and Pg. 351, ¶ 1—In 1261, Baibars lassoed the role of Commander of the Faithful by welcoming an Abbasid refugee, fleeing the Mongol-occupied city of Baghdad, into Cairo, and declaring him the new Abbasid caliph, under Bahri protection. The fourteenth-century Arab historian Ibn Khaldun wrote that the Mongols "abolished the seat of the Caliphate and . . . made unbelief prevail in place of belief," but Baibars "rescued the faith by reviving its dying breath and restoring the unity of the Muslims in the Egyptian realms." The result was that Egypt gained the immediate allegiance of the *sharif* of Mecca, the most powerful tribal chief in the Holy City.

CHAPTER FIFTY: THE MAMLUKS OF EGYPT

8. What did Baibars do after making an alliance with the *sharif* of Mecca? How did he reinforce his place as a Muslim leader?

A8.—Pg. 351, ¶ 1 & 2—After making an alliance with the *sharif* of Mecca, Baibars made the land passed through for the *hajj*, the sacred pilgrimage to Mecca, safe, and adopted a new title to show his benevolence: *khadim al-haramayn al-sharifayn*, "Servant of the Two Holy Places," protector of both Mecca and Medina. In the next years, he paid for the renovation of the mosque in Medina that bore Muhammad's name, and supervised the renewed observation of Islamic laws in the sultanate (including the ban on drinking alcohol). He also renewed the war against the Crusader kingdoms.

9. Describe Qutuz's attack on the city of Antioch.

A9.—Pg. 351, ¶ 2 & 3—Baibars started by laying siege to Antioch itself, and the city fell after just four days. Seventeen thousand of its people were taken captive, over a hundred thousand sold into the slave markets, and Bohemund VI, not present at the time of the attack but filled in on the details by a brutally descriptive letter from Baibars, was left with only Tripoli. Baibars wrote to Bohemund VI that "Your houses [were] stormed by pillagers and ransacked by looters, your women sold four at a time . . . the crosses in your churches smashed, the pages of the false Testaments scattered, the Patriarch's tombs overturned . . . your Muslim enemy trampling on the place where you celebrate the mass, cutting the throats of monks, priests, and deacons upon the altars. . . . The God who gave you Antioch has taken it away again; the Lord who bestowed that fortress on you has snatched it away, uprooting it from the face of the earth."

Section III: **Critical Thinking**

The student may not use her text to answer this question.

The Mongols did not fight against the rest of the world because they wanted to covert them to a particular religion. The Mongols were interested in conquest. In this chapter, however, we see religion play a part in the battle between the Egyptians and the Mongols. Write a paragraph or two explaining how religion influenced Egypt's successes against the Mongols.

The student should focus her answer on the section of the chapter that describes the opposition between Christian Mongols and Muslim Egyptians.

Ked-Buqa, leader of the Mongol troops left in place by Hulagu, carried on Mongol conquests while Hulagu attended to the election of the next Great Khan. Ked-Buqa led the occupation of Aleppo, Homs, Hama, and Gaza. Ked-Buqa got close to the Jordan river in early 1260, about to pounce on Cairo. In late August of 1260, Ked-Buqa sent an envoy to Cairo, ordering Qutuz to surrender. Instead, Qutuz put the Mongol messengers to death and stuck their heads up on his city gate.

Qutuz goaded the Mongols on purpose. He knew that the Mongols had been left behind as a skeleton force, and he was convinced that Allah was behind him in his desire to crush the Mongol enemies of Islam. Qutuz saw Ked-Buqa as a religious enemy: like Hulagu's mother, Ked-Buqa was a convert to Christianity. The Egyptians were able to beat the Mongols in the battle at the valley of Ain Jalut by using a military tactic that lulled the Mongols into a false sense of safety. After the defeat of the Mongols, Qutuz himself rode in triumph to Damascus, drove out the Mongol occupiers, and claimed it again for Egypt. Within a month, he had also retaken Aleppo, Homs, and Hama. Egypt and Syria were finally reunited under the Cairo sultanate. And a lasting line had been drawn between the Arabic empire of Cairo and the domain of the Mongols, deeply influenced by Christianity; first Hulagu's mother and now his wife were Christian converts.

Baibars was also able to make an important alliance because of his Muslim faith. Baibars sent envoys north to the Golden Horde to negotiate alliances with Berke, the khan who now ruled the Rus' lands. Berke had converted to Islam. Berke had renounced his allegiance to the Great Khan and he was anxious to protect his own borders against Hulagu's ambitions. The allegiance between Berke and Qutuz also protected the slave trade routes. Thousands of slaves, taken captive by Mongol detachments, were shipped from the shores of the Black Sea (now under Berke's control) to Egypt every year; the slave regiments, continually replenished, remained the strongest instrument of Baibars's power. Islam united the previous Mongol and Egyptian enemies against a new enemy: Christianity.

EXAMPLE ANSWER:

When the Mongols approached Egypt, Qutuz mustered up fervor to fight against them by employing religion. After taking Aleppo, Homs, Hama, and Gaza, Mongol commander Ked-Buqa sent an envoy to Cairo, ordering Qutuz to surrender. Instead, Qutuz put the Mongol messengers to death and stuck their heads up on his city gate. Qutuz goaded the Mongols on purpose. He knew that the Mongols had been left behind as a skeleton force, and he was convinced that Allah was behind him in his desire to crush the Mongol enemies of Islam. Qutuz saw Ked-Buqa as a religious enemy: like Hulagu's mother, Ked-Buqa was a convert to Christianity. The Egyptians were able to beat the Mongols in the battle at the valley of Ain Jalut and after this triumph, Qutuz himself rode in triumph to Damascus, drove out the Mongol occupiers, and claimed it again for Egypt. Within a month, he had also retaken Aleppo, Homs, and Hama. A lasting line had been drawn between the Arabic empire of Cairo and the domain of the Mongols, which was influenced by Christianity.

Baibars was also able to make an important alliance because of his Muslim faith. Baibars sent envoys north to the Golden Horde to negotiate alliances with Berke, the khan who now ruled the Rus' lands. Berke had converted to Islam. Berke had renounced his allegiance to the Great Khan and he was anxious to protect his own borders against Hulagu's ambitions. The allegiance between Berke and Baibars also protected the slave trade routes. Mongol detachments took thousands of slaves captive and then sent them to Egypt. The slave regiment gave Baibars most of his power. Islam united the previous Mongol and Egyptian enemies against a new enemy: Christianity.

Section IV: Map Exercise

1. Trace the rectangular outline of Map 50.1 in black.

CHAPTER FIFTY: THE MAMLUKS OF EGYPT

2. Using your blue pencil, trace all the coastal lines, from the Mediterranean to the Black Sea, Caspian Sea, Red Sea, and Persian Gulf. You do not need to include all the small islands around Greece and Turkey. Repeat until the contours are familiar.

3. Now using contrasting colors trace the Bahri Sultanate and the Il-khanate regions. Repeat until the contours are familiar.

4. Using a new sheet of paper, trace the outline of the frame in black. Then using a regular pencil with an eraser, draw the coastal lines of the Mediterranean to the Black Sea, Caspian Sea, Red Sea, and Persian Gulf. You do not need to include all the small islands around Greece and Turkey. Erase and redraw as necessary. When you are happy with your map, lay it over the original. Erase and redraw any lines which are more than ½″ off of the original.

5. Now study carefully the locations of Antioch, Aleppo, Baghdad, Gaza, Damietta, Cairo, Medina, and Mecca. When you are familiar with them, close the book. Mark and label each one on your map, and then lay your map over the original. Erase and redraw any marks which are more than ½″ off of the original.

6. Now trace on your paper the enlarged box showing the principality of Antioch and the Kingdom of Jerusalem. Study the locations of Hama, Homs, Tripoli, Acre, Beisan, and the Battle of Ain Jalut. Also study the line of the Jordan. When they are familiar to you, close your book, and mark them on your map. Then check your map, and correct any misplaced or incorrect labels.

Chapter Fifty-One

Louis the Saint

The student may use his text when answering the questions in sections I and II.

Section I: Who, What, Where

Write a one or two-sentence answer explaining the significance of each item listed below.

Master of Hungary—**Pg. 354, ¶ 3 & 4 and Pg. 355, ¶ 1—A Hungarian monk who began to preach, throughout northern France, that the Virgin Mary had appeared to him with a revelation—King Louis would be relieved not by barons and knights but by the humble and the poor. He called himself the "Master of Hungary." After leading the Pastoureaux in riots across France, the Master of Hungary was killed by a militant Parisian butcher that struck him on the head with an ax.**

The Pastoureaux—**Pg. 354, ¶ 4-6—The Pastoureaux, or "the shepherds," was the name for a group of people— farmers, swineherds, cowmen, murderers, thieves, and outcasts—who followed a mad Hungarian monk that called himself the "Master of Hungary" and dressed themselves as shepherds. The Pastoureaux were enemies of the church, calling priests and bishops, "money-hunters," and in 1251 they attacked clergymen, burning and raiding as they went, in Orleans, Tours, and Bourges.**

Thomas Aquinas—**Pg. 356, ¶ 3—Thomas Aquinas, a Dominican scholar, arrived in Paris in 1252 and was lecturing and writing there when Louis IX returned to France. Thomas Aquinas, devoted to the study of the Greek masters and their synthesis with Christian thought, would manage to lay out in full, during Louis IX's lifetime, a massive reconciliation of Aristotelian ideas with Christian revelation.**

Section II: **Comprehension**

Write a two or three-sentence answer to each of the following questions.

1. How did Louis IX decide to stay in Acre instead of returning to France?

A1.—Pg. 353, ¶ 2-4—Louis IX asked the hundred surviving men from the Seventh Crusade to decide whether or not he should "return to France, because my kingdom is in great peril, seeing that I have neither peace nor truce with the King of England" or whether he should stay in Acre because he had been told that if he departed, the land would be lost. Most of the surviving barons wanted the king to go back to France to assure the kingdom's safety, and then relaunch the Crusade after proper preparations, while the soldiers were reluctant to abandon the Crusade and the remaining hostages back in Cairo. Ultimately, Louis IX decided to stay, explaining that Queen Blanche had enough people to defend France. If he departed, the kingdom of Jerusalem would be lost.

2. Why did Queen Blanche approve, at first, of the Master of Hungary and his message?

A2.—Pg. 353, ¶ 4 to Pg. 354, ¶ 1 & 5—When Louis IX decided to stay in Acre rather than returning to France, he asked his to support the crusade by being true to God. It seemed that the Pastoureaux were answering that call. At first, Queen Blanche supported the rising up of peasants and shepherds in the name of God, even inviting them to Paris and listening to the Master's message.

3. What happened in January 1251, after the Master of Hungary started preaching an anti-Church message?

A3.—Pg. 354, ¶ 6 to Pg. 355, ¶ 1—In January of 1251, the Pastoureaux entered Orleans, armed and ready to fight; they swept through the city, attacking and killing clergymen, burning and raiding as they went. Queen Blanche immediately withdrew her support of the group, which started a royal manhunt that put an end to the Pastoureaux with hand-to-hand fighting, arrests, hangings, and drownings. The Master of Hungary himself was killed by a militant Parisian butcher wielding an ax, who "struck him on the head and sent him brainless to hell."

4. What caused Louis IX to finally leave Acre and return to France?

A4.—Pg. 355, ¶ 2—In November of 1252, Queen Blanche—well into her sixties—died after a short illness. Hearing of his mother's death, Louis shut himself in his chambers for two days, speaking to no one, and then he finally made preparations to leave Acre and return to France.

5. How did the collapse of the Seventh Crusade change Louis IX?

A5.—Pg. 355, ¶ 3—The collapse of the Seventh Crusade changed Louis IX by making him more pious; though he had managed to free some of his captured followers and had built new fortifications around the Christian cities in the east, he failed to recover Jerusalem and that stuck with him. When he arrived back in Paris on September 7, 1254, he became very devoted to his faith. He was ascetic in clothing, in food and drink, and in his habits,

dedicating more and more of his income to the poor, praying constantly, and studying the scriptures late into the night.

6. Describe the changes Louis IX made to the policies and practices of France's officials and bishops after he returned to his home country.

A6.—Pg. 356, ¶ 1 & 2—Within two years of Louis IX's return, he had passed multiple restrictions on the conduct of his royal officials: they were not to swear or to frequent taverns; they were to treat native Frenchmen and foreigners the same; bribes and gifts were forbidden, as were random seizures, jailing without cause, and violence; he banned duels as a way of settling legal arguments; and he outlawed prostitution, gambling, and public blasphemy. When the French bishops petitioned him to arrest and "constrain" men they had excommunicated, as a way to bring them more quickly to repentance, he refused: it was possible, he told them, that the judgment of the pope might yet declare such men innocent, and the power of France could not be used to support the decisions of local bishops who might be mistaken. Louis IX believed judgment could be wielded only on behalf of God by way of the pope.

7. Why was Louis IX considered a "just" ruler in the Aristotelian sense?

A7.—Pg. 356, ¶ 4—In *The Politics*, Aristotle argued that a just ruler works for the common good of all his subjects. Aristotle's "common good" encompassed justice and prosperity for all, and by his definition Louis IX was indeed a virtuous monarch: Louis IX made finding out how the people were governed his main concern, and he made sure their rights and interests were protected. Because justice prevailed and things were so much better, goods and property in France sold for double their value.

8. How did Thomas Aquinas understand the relationship between the king and the pope?

A8.—Pg. 356, ¶ 5 to Pg. 357, ¶ 1—Thomas Aquinas said that kings have the task of bringing justice and prosperity to their subjects, but leading them to ultimate salvation is beyond the monarch's reach—that was the job of the pope. There was, in Aquinas's mind, no conflict between king and pope, any more than there was a clash between natural law and heavenly law, or between reason and revelation. They walked hand in hand, the king attending to earthly matters, the pope to heavenly ones.

9. What did Louis IX believe when it came to quarreling with the church?

A9.—Pg. 357, ¶ 2—Louis IX believed one should not quarrel with the church. He told his son to "Love and honour all persons in the service of Holy Church." He also told him that even if he felt wronged by the Church, the king should hold his tongue, for considering "the benefits God had bestowed," it was better to give up royal privilege than to struggle against an authority bestowed by God.

Section III: Critical Thinking

The student may not use his text to answer this question.

We have read over and over again about how the personal desires of men were often the motivation behind going on crusade, rather than fighting for God. Write a paragraph explaining who the Master of Hungary was and how he used the criticism of personal gain over piousness to drum up support for the Pastoureaux movement. In your answer, explain who joined the movement, and why you think they did so.

There was a mad monk that preached in northern France, saying that the Virgin Mary had appeared to him with a revelation: King Louis would be relieved not by barons and knights but by the humble and the poor. This revelation spoke to the masses in France; as written on page 354, " 'the poor people . . . pay for all the wars of their lords,' the Norman churchman William the Clerk had written, not a score of years before, 'and often weep thereat and sigh.' " The monk, who called himself the Master of Hungary, struck a chord of resentment in the poor and laboring classes; they were angry with the privileged and powerful, the nobles and the knights.

The Master of Hungary's message assured those same poor shepherds and peasants that they had been "granted by heaven the power, in their humility and simplicity, to rescue the Holy Land . . . for, as he said, the pride of the French soldier was displeasing to God." The message was very popular because it said that the regular people would save France, rather than the rich or the barons that were able to go off on crusade. The Master of Hungary gained great support—thousands of followers made up of farmers, swineherds, cowmen, and a healthy salting of murderers, thieves, and outcasts. They were called the Pastoureaux, the shepherds, because they dressed themselves up as such.

The movement was peaceful at first, and was supported by the Queen. But the clergy were quickly slotted in to the greedy folk condemned by the Pastoureaux. The Master of Hungary began to preach an anti-Church message that condemned all religious orders except for the one he started. He said the Franciscans were vagrants, the Cistercians greedy, the priests and bishops "only money-hunters." Again, the Master of Hungary criticized the greed of all those who profited while the poor struggled to create fervor for his movement. The people that joined his movement were sick of not having money and wealth, of being controlled by barons and overlords and priests. They wanted to be freed from having to pay taxes and tithes, so they partook in the religious movement that gave them power by proclaiming it was the poor that would save France.

EXAMPLE ANSWER:

The Master of Hungary was a monk that preached in northern France, saying that the Virgin Mary had appeared to him with a revelation: King Louis would be relieved not by barons and knights but by the humble and the poor. The monk struck a chord of resentment in the poor and laboring classes; they were angry with the privileged and powerful, and tired for paying for the wars of the nobles and the knights. The Master of Hungary's message assured the poor shepherds and peasants that they had been "granted by heaven the power, in their humility and simplicity, to rescue the Holy Land . . . for, as he said, the pride of the French soldier was displeasing to God." The message was very popular because it said that the regular people would save France, rather than the rich or the barons that were able to go off on crusade. The people that joined the movement, the Pastoureaux, were farmers,

swineherds, cowmen, murderers, thieves, and outcasts. The Pastoureaux were sick of not having money and wealth, of being controlled by barons and overlords and priests. The movement was peaceful at first, and was supported by the Queen. But the Master of Hungary began to preach an anti-Church message that condemned all religious orders except for the one he started. He said the Franciscans were vagrants, the Cistercians greedy, the priests and bishops "only money-hunters." His followers wanted to be freed from having to pay taxes and tithes, so they partook in the religious movement that gave them power by proclaiming it was the poor that would save France.

Section IV: Map Exercise

1. Trace the rectangular frame of Map 51.1 in black.

2. Using your blue pencil, trace the visible coastal outline of the continent. Also trace the line of the Loire. Repeat until the contours are familiar.

3. Using your black pencil, trace the outline of the kingdom of Louis IX. Trace the line showing Normandy as well. Repeat until the contours are familiar.

4. Now using a new sheet of paper, trace the rectangular outline of the frame in black. Using a regular pencil with an eraser, draw the coastline and the line of the Loire. Draw the outline of the kingdom of Louis IX and the line showing Normandy. Erase and redraw as necessary, using the outline of the frame as a reference point. When you are happy with your map, lay it over the original, and erase and redraw any lines which are more than ½" off of the original.

5. Now study carefully the locations of Soissons, Reims, Paris, Orleans, Tours, and Bourges. Also study the sites of Clairvaux and Cluny. When you are familiar with them, close the book. Mark and label each one on your map. Then check your map against the original, and erase and re-mark any incorrect or misplaced labels.

6. Mark the regions of Brittany and Normandy.

Chapter Fifty-Two

The Lion's Den

The student may use her text when answering the questions in sections I and II.

Section I: Who, What, Where

Write a one or two-sentence answer explaining the significance of each item listed below.

Ad Extirpanda—**Pg. 359, ¶ 2**—***Ad Extirpanda* was a papal bull issued by Pope Innocent IV in 1252 that elaborated a set of procedures governing the Inquisition in Italy: every ruling civil official was ordered to appoint committees that would be responsible for hunting out and arresting heretics. The officials themselves were commanded to "force" the heretics to confess by any measure, short of death or permanent disfigurement; it was the first papal legitimization of torture as a tool of inquisition.**

Alexander IV—**Pg. 360, ¶ 4 and Pg. 362, ¶ 5**—**Alexander IV, Pope Innocent IV's successor, excommunicated Manfred and confirmed Edmund as king of Sicily soon after his appointment. Alexander IV died shortly after issuing the papal bull that absolved Henry III from the Provisions of Oxford and Westminster.**

Alfonso X—**Pg. 360, ¶ 6**—**Alfonso X, king of León-Castile, an experienced statesman who also happened to be the grandson of the German baron Philip of Swabia (by way of his mother), was voted for by half of the electors of Germany to be the new king of their state. He did not become king of Germany because Richard of Cornwall took the title.**

Charles of Anjou—**Pg. 364, ¶ 1 and Pg. 365, ¶ 4**—**Charles of Anjou, Louis IX's younger brother, made a deal with Urban IV that gave him the title "king of Sicily" if he would conquer the country, give up all power over the clergymen in Sicily, claim no other title in Italy, pay off the English debt to Rome, and hand over an enormous yearly tribute to the pope. Charles of Anjou defeated Manfred's army and stopped a rebellion by Conradin to end up ruling over Sicily and southern Italy.**

Citra membri diminutionem, et mortis periculum—**Pg. 359, ¶ 2**—***Citra membri diminutionem, et mortis periculum* was a phrase used by Pope Innocent IV in the *Ad Extirpanda* that said officials were** commanded to "force" heretics to confess by any measure, short of death or permanent disfigurement.

Clement IV—**Pg. 364, ❡ 2—Clement IV, the papal name of the French cardinal Guy Foulques le Gros and Urban IV's successor, supported Charles of Anjou's fight for the Sicilian throne.**

Conradin—**Pg. 360, ❡ 1, 2 & 5 and Pg. 365, ❡ 3—Conradin, Conrad's son, only two when his father died and he became king of Germany, was sent to grow up safely in Bavaria while his uncle Manfred ruled as his regent. Conradin, who lost his claim to Germany after both William of Holland and his father died and the electors of Germany did not vote for him to take the title, was beheaded for treason in 1269 after he was captured by Charles of Anjou during a war he started so that he could take northern Italy for himself.**

Edmund—**Pg. 359, ❡ 3 & 4—Edmund, second son of Henry III of England, was offered to be made king of Sicily by Pope Innocent IV. Henry III accepted the offer for nine-year-old Edmund.**

Edward—**Pg. 362, ❡ 5 & 8 and Pg. 363, ❡ 1—Edward, Henry III's oldest son and heir, leader of the royal army, fought in the Second Barons' War in his father's name. After his father surrendered, Edward also surrendered and was put under courteous guard, in the Tower of London, by Simon de Montfort, but Edward escaped his imprisonment, rallied up royal support, and massacred the baronial opposition on August 4, 1265 at the field of Evesham.**

Manfred—**Pg. 360, ❡ 1 & 4 and Pg. 364, ❡ 5—Manfred, Conrad's younger half-brother, claimed to be Conradin's regent as soon as the two-year-old was made king of Germany. Manfred crowned himself king of Sicily in 1258 despite Pope Innocent denying him the title; Manfred, excommunicated by Pope Alexander IV for taking Sicily, died fighting for Sicily in 1266 when Charles of Anjou's army met Manfred's army at Benevento.**

Provisions of Oxford—**Pg. 361, ❡ 5—Provisions of Oxford was the June 11, 1258 document listing the demands of the Curia Regis in exchange for paying the scutage for Henry III's war on Sicily. According to the Provisions of Oxford, Henry III had to expel most of his French-born officials from England; he was to reaffirm all of the provisions of the Magna Carta; and he was to hand final decisions of policy over to a standing council of fifteen who would have to ratify all his decisions, as well as another committee of twelve, and a council of twenty-four leading barons, twelve chosen by him, twelve by the Curia Regis.**

Richard of Cornwall—**Pg. 360, ❡ 6—Richard of Cornwall, Henry III's younger brother and second son of John Lackland, was a contender for the German throne after Conrad's death, and even managed to get Pope Alexander IV on his side. However, when faced with the necessity of conquering over half the country to actually rule it, he soon gave up and went home again.**

Rudolf, Count of Hapsburg—**Pg. 365, ❡ 4 & 5— Rudolf, Count of Hapsburg, was made the next king of Germany by the German electors after the death of Conradin. Rudolf remained in Germany, content with the title "king of Germany" and making no efforts to regain the Holy Roman Empire.**

Simon de Montfort (younger)—**Pg. 361, ¶ 1, Pg. 362, ¶ 4 & 8 and Pg. 363, ¶ 1—Simon de Montfort (younger), Henry III's brother-in-law, led the barons in war against Henry III after he slipped out of the Provisions of Oxford and Winchester by way of papal decree. Simon de Montfort, at first successful in his war against the king, put Henry III and Edward under arrest in the Tower of London, but he lost his control over the monarchy when Edward escaped his prison and the war started up again; he died in battle against Edward in 1265.**

Urban IV—**Pg. 362, ¶ 5—Urban IV followed Alexander IV as pope and confirmed the papal bull written by Alexander IV freeing the king from all obligation to the demands of the barons.**

Section II: Comprehension

Write a two or three-sentence answer to each of the following questions.

1. Why was it a bad idea for Henry III to accept the role of king of Sicily for his son Edmund? Why did he accept anyway?

A1.—**Pg. 359, ¶ 4—To accept the title king of Sicily was to gain nothing for Edmund, or for England, other than debt. The title was empty, but with it Henry III would have to swear, on peril of excommunication, to hand over a substantial payment to Rome, and also to send an army to take Sicily away from Conrad. Nevertheless, Henry III accepted on his young son's behalf because he was an idle, cowardly, and foolish king.**

2. What happened when Pope Innocent IV decided not to endorse Manfred as king of Sicily?

A2.—**Pg. 360, ¶ 2 & 3—When Pope Innocent IV decided not to endorse Manfred as king of Sicily, Manfred exhorted the Sicilians to rise behind him and resist the papal order handing them over to foreign rule. In December, Manfred crossed over to southern Italy with his troops and led an army against the papal soldiers stationed at Foggia, defeating them easily. When Pope Innocent IV heard the news, the sickness he was suffering from took a turn downward and he died on December 7, 1254.**

3. List all of the bad decisions Henry III made as king of England prior to March 1258.

A3.—**Pg. 361, ¶ 1 & 2—Henry III made a lot of bad decisions. He promoted too many of his wife's French relatives into plum court positions, annoying his local courtiers; he raised taxes in an attempt to collect the pope's fee for the Sicilian crown, annoying his subjects. He was spiky and irascible, resentful of any advisor who seemed too controlling; he feuded with his officials; he fell out with his brother-in-law; when he needed the approval of the Curia Regis he summoned only those men who were certain to agree with him; he led expensive and pointless campaigns into the French lands that had once belonged to England; and he was facing excommunication on June 1 of 1258 unless he raised the funds needed to march into Sicily.**

4. How did Henry III end up earmarking the money he needed for Sicily?

A4.—Pg. 361, ¶ 3 & 4—In early April 1258, Henry III summoned the priests and barons of England together in London and demanded more money, which they would give him as soon as he fulfilled their conditions: he was to expel most of his French-born officials from England; he was to reaffirm all of the provisions of the Magna Carta; and he was to hand final decisions of policy over to a chamber of twenty-four leading barons, twelve chosen by him, twelve by the Curia Regis. They also told the king that he should frequently consult them, and listen to their advice.

5. What happened after Henry III agreed to the Provisions of Oxford that led to a war between the barons of England and the king?

A5.—Pg. 361, ¶ 6 to Pg. 362, ¶ 4—First, the money to pay for the army to fight Sicily and the pope's fee did not materialize because a dry season in England led to a drastic shortage of food, which led to famine and disease. Then, at the same time that Pope Alexander IV extended the deadline for payment, the English barons expanded the Provisions of Oxford into the more elaborate Provisions of Winchester, placing even more limitations on Henry's ability to raise money. This prompted Henry III to open secret negotiations with Alexander IV; on April 13, 1261, the pope issued a papal bull freeing the king from all obligation to both Provisions, which led to Simon de Montfort rallying the barons against the king.

6. Describe the events that led to Henry III and Edward's surrender to Simon de Montfort.

A6.—Pg. 362, ¶ 6-8—The barons and the royal army started to go at each other in March of 1264, and on May 14, the armies met at Lewes, on the southern coast of England. Edward, in charge of one wing of the attack, crushed the barons facing him and chased them well into the countryside, but the rest of the royal army faltered and Henry III himself surrendered after his horse was killed underneath him. Edward too was forced to surrender, making Simon de Montfort the most powerful man in England.

7. How did Edward end up winning the Second Barons' War and becoming the de facto ruler of England?

A7.—Pg. 362, ¶ 9 to Pg. 363, ¶ 2—Early in 1265, Edward managed to talk the guards watching him in the Tower of London into racing him while he was riding for exercise, and when the race started he quickly outrode them and took refuge with royal partisans at the castle of Wigmore. He found plenty of support for the royal cause outside of London, assembled a large army, and restarted the war against the barons, driving Simon de Montfort's army back during each clash. In the third encounter between the two forces, at the field of Evesham on August 4, Edward's army massacred the opposition in a brief confrontation, Simon de Montfort himself died in the fighting, the Second Barons' War against the crown came to an end, and it became clear that though Henry III was still on the throne, Edward was the real ruler of England.

8. Explain how Sicily came to be ruled by Charles of Anjou.

A8.—Pg. 364, ¶ 1-5—Charles of Anjou agreed to take over Sicily for the pope in exchange for the title of king; Charles and his wife were crowned king and queen of Sicily in Rome

and, with title in hand, Charles prepared to attack Manfred. Manfred prepared for war in southern Italy but before Manfred could arrive in the south, Charles marched his own army out of Rome and down into Manfred's southern Italian lands through a gap in the border defense that was rumored to have been opened by traitors in Manfred's kingdom. The two kings met at Benevento and Charles of Anjou's battalion easily outmaneuvered the Sicilian soldiers: three thousand of Manfred's men fell, more were drowned in the river nearby as they fled, and Manfred himself was killed at the center of the fighting.

9. How did Conradin end up beheaded for treason?

A9.—Pg. 364, ¶ 6 to Pg. 365, ¶ 3—After the capture of the Sicilian kingdom by Charles of Anjou, the Italian cities in the north declared independence, and Conradin made a play for what remained of his inheritance by crossing through the Alps and trying to rally the Lombard cities against Charles's power. Charles came north against him and drove back Conradin's supporters at the Battle of Tagliacozzo on August 23, 1268. Conradin himself was captured as he fled from the battlefield, imprisoned for a year and then, in October 1269, was publicly beheaded on the order of Charles of Anjou for treason.

Section III: Critical Thinking

The student may not use her text to answer this question.

It is made very clear to the reader in this chapter that becoming the king of Sicily was a thankless job. Nothing was to be gained other than a title. Henry III agreed to Edmund's appointment by Innocent IV because he was a spineless ruler. But Charles of Anjou, who was not known as a coward or a fool, accepted the title happily. Write a paragraph explaining what Charles of Anjou agreed to do in order to become king of Sicily, and why you think he went through all of that trouble just for a title.

We find out on page 364 the practical reason for Charles of Anjou accepting the title king of Sicily and what he had to promise to do in exchange:

> But Urban IV found a more willing candidate in Louis's younger brother, Charles of Anjou: aged forty, constantly in motion, a veteran of the failed Damietta Crusade, impatient with Louis's scruples and ambitious for himself. He agreed at once—over Louis's objections—to both take the crown and conquer the country. And, like Henry III nearly a decade earlier, he accepted a truly awful set of conditions in exchange for the meaningless title. He agreed to give up all power over the clergymen in Sicily, to claim no other title in Italy, to pay off the English debt to Rome, and to hand over an enormous yearly tribute to the pope. In exchange, he got the name of king—and the pope's promise to give anyone who fought against Manfred the rewards of crusade.

It doesn't seem like there was much in the fight for Charles—if he died, he would get the reward of crusade, but he would be dead and no longer a king. The key to Charles of Anjou's agreement comes from the phrase "ambitious for himself." Charles of Anjou wanted to be a king. The title may have been empty, and he might have had to pay a lot for it, but to be a king was to be in the highest position on earth next to the pope. It was to have power over one's people and to have God's support in that power. There was nothing else like being a king, and in Charles of Anjou's case, he must have felt that it was worth the hefty price tag.

EXAMPLE ANSWER:

Charles of Anjou said he would do a lot of things for Pope Urban IV in exchange for the title "king of Sicily." He would kick Manfred off the throne, he would give up all his power over the clergymen in Sicily, he promised to claim no other title in Italy, he said he would pay off the English debt to Rome, and he agreed to hand over an enormous yearly tribute to the pope. He did get the pope's promise to give anyone who fought against Manfred the rewards of crusade, but little else in the material sense. Though the title "king of Sicily" didn't mean much, and was very expensive, it still made Charles a king. Charles of Anjou was forty and ambitious. He wanted power, and the best way to get power was to be a king. A king was in the highest position on earth next to the pope. It was to have power over one's people and to have God's support in that power. There was nothing else like being a king, and in Charles of Anjou's case, he must have felt it was worth the hefty price tag.

Chapter Fifty-Three

The Recapture of Constantinople

The student may use his text when answering the questions in sections I and II.

Section I: **Who, What, Where**

Write a one or two-sentence answer explaining the significance of each item listed below.

Baldwin II—**Pg. 367, ¶ 2 and Pg. 370, ¶ 3 & 6**—Baldwin II, nephew of the Count of Flanders, inherited rule of the Latin Empire in 1228 at the age of eleven and let the empire shrink during his time on the throne. Constantinople was poor and defenseless when Michael VIII invaded; Baldwin II fled, ending up in Italy, still claiming to be the emperor of the Latins even though the Latin Empire ceased to exist after Michael VIII occupied the city.

Ivan Asen—**Pg. 367, ¶ 2**—Ivan Asen, leader of the Bulgarian empire, mounted constant attacks on the Latin Empire's western border. Baldwin II could not fight against the Bulgarian.

John—**Pg. 369, ¶ 2 & 3 and Pg. 370, ¶ 7**—John, son and heir of Theodore II, was made ruler of the Empire of Nicaea at the age of eight, but his rule was promptly co-opted by Michael Palaeologus. After Michael Palaeologus, as Michael VIII, restored rule of Byzantium, he ordered John blinded and imprisoned in a castle on an island in the Sea of Marmara; the sentence was carried out on Christmas Day, 1261, the boy's eleventh birthday.

Michael Palaeologus/Michael VIII—**Pg. 369, ¶ 3 and Pg. 370, ¶ 7**—Michael Palaeologus, an ambitious and well-regarded soldier and aristocrat who was also the great-grandson of the Byzantine emperor Alexius III, declared himself as regent for John, and then with the support of most Nicaeans, promoted himself to co-emperor of the Empire of Nicaea as Michael VIII in 1259. Michael VIII successfully seized Constantinople and began rule over restored Byzantium unopposed (he had his co-emperor John blinded and imprisoned at the age of eleven).

Philip—**Pg. 368, ¶ 1**—Philip, son of Baldwin II, was sent to Venice as a hostage. He would be released once his father repaid the massive amounts of money he had borrowed from the Venetian merchants.

Theodore II—**Pg. 369, ¶ 1 & 2**—Theodore II, thirty-three when he took over rule of the Empire of Nicaea after his father John Vatatzes's death, did not last long on the throne. Theodore II soon sickened and he died before the end of his fourth year as king.

Treaty of Nymphaion—**Pg. 370, ¶ 2**—Treaty of Nymphaion was a deal made between the Genoese statesman Guglielmo Boccanegra and the emperor Michael VIII during the winter of 1260. The treaty promised the Genoese their own tax-free trading quarters in Constantinople, should they help the ambitious emperor to conquer it.

Section II: Comprehension

Write a two or three-sentence answer to each of the following questions.

1. Describe the shrinking of the Latin Empire under Baldwin II's rule.

A1.—Pg. 367, ¶ 2—The Latin Empire was known as a tiny and penniless realm under the rule of Baldwin II. The Bulgarian empire mounted constant attacks on its western border and the Empire of Nicaea assaulted it from the east. A delegation of Franciscan and Dominican friars who visited the city in 1234 reported that city was "deprived of all protection," the emperor a pauper, all mercenaries departed, with the friars worried that the empire was in danger because it was surrounded by enemies.

2. How did Baldwin II spend most of his reign?

A2.—Pg. 367, ¶ 3 to Pg. 368, ¶ 1—Baldwin spent much of his reign out of Constantinople, traveling from court to court in Europe and begging each Christian king to help him protect the city that had once been Christianity's crown jewel in the east.

3. What did Baldwin II do to raise money to save Constantinople?

A3.—Pg. 367, ¶ 3 to Pg. 368, ¶ 1—Baldwin II was able to get some money from Louis IX of France and Henry III of England for the Latin treasury, but it wasn't enough. He had torn the copper roofs from Constantinople's domes and melted them down into coins and he had already sold most of the city's treasures and sacred relics. He even sent his son as a hostage to Venice because he had borrowed so much money from the Venetian merchants that he had to use Philip as collateral until he repaid his debts.

4. How did the Empire of Nicaea change under the rule of John Vatatzes?

A4.—Pg. 368, ¶ 2—The Empire of Nicaea grew under the rule of John Vatatzes, who still claimed to be the Byzantine emperor in exile and who spent most of his thirty-three-year reign fighting. John Vatatzes swallowed most of Constantinople's land, seizing Thrace from Bulgaria and Thessalonica from the third of the mini-kingdoms that Byzantium had broken into, the Despotate of Epirus. By 1254, the Empire of Nicaea stretched from Asia Minor across to Greece and up north of the Aegean.

5. What did Michael VIII do to prepare for war with Constantinople?

A5.—Pg. 369, ¶ 4 and Pg. 370, ¶ 2—**Michael VIII started to prepare for war with Constantinople, so he could reclaim his his great-grandfather's city, from the moment he took the throne. In the first two years of his reign, he made peace on his other borders by concluding treaties with both Bulgaria and the nearby Il-khanate Mongols. Michael VIII also made an alliance with the Genoese, guaranteeing them their own tax-free trading quarters in Constantinople if they helped him conquer the city.**

6. Why were Christians at war with each other in Acre in 1256? What was the result of the war?

A6.—Pg. 369, ¶ 5 to Pg. 370, ¶ 1—**In 1256, the Genoans had quarreled sharply with the Venetians over the ownership of a waterfront parcel of land in Acre because whoever controlled it could block rival ships from the harbor of Acre, and both of the maritime republics wanted this advantage. The Genoese lost the first major sea battle in the war and then between 1257 and 1258 the conflict ballooned until all of Acre was was war. By the end of 1258, the Genoese were losers, having been forced out of Acre completely; the old Genoese quarter in Acre was entirely pulled apart, and the Venetians and Pisans used the stones to rebuild their own trading posts.**

7. Explain how Michael VIII was able to take Constantinople for Nicaea so easily.

A7.—Pg. 370, ¶ 3—**When the small detachment Michael VIII sent to Constantinople arrived at the city, they found it defenseless; most of the remaining Latin army had been sent to attack a Nicaean-held harbor island near the Bosphorus Strait. Michael VIII's troops then climbed into the city under the cover of dark, quickly overwhelmed the tiny remaining guard, and opened the gates. Baldwin II himself, sleeping at the royal palace, woke up at the sounds of their shouts and managed to flee the city, leaving his crown behind him.**

8. How did Michael VIII find out that his men had taken Constantinople? What did he find once he arrived at the city?

A8.—Pg. 370, ¶ 4 & 5—**Michael VIII, camped to the north of Thyateira at the time that his men opened the gates of Constantinople, was told by his sister, "Rise up, emperor, for Christ has conferred Constantinople upon you!" According to Akropolites, he answered, "How? I did not even send a worthy army against it." When he arrived at Constantinople three weeks later, he found a disastrous mess of destruction and ruin, and he also found that the royal palace was so filthy and smoke-stained that it had to be scrubbed from top to bottom before he could take up residence in it.**

Section III: Critical Thinking

The student may not use his text to answer this question.

The Latin Empire, once great, faded away in the twelfth century, as did the power of Constantinople. Write a paragraph or two explaining how Michael VIII turned the fate of Constantinople, and Byzantium, around.

Michael Palaeologus, great-grandson of the Byzantine emperor Alexius III, had a vision. He wanted to restore his family's kingdom.

Baldwin II had let Constantinople, the heart of the old Byzantine Empire, fall even further from its former glory than any previous emperor. He sold all of the city's treasures and did a poor job of defending its territory. In the end he barely had power over the area just outside of the city's walls. Michael VIII didn't even need a whole army to take back the city; he sent a small detachment of men to send threats, but when they got there, they found the city barely guarded. When they entered the city at night, Baldwin II fled, not even bothering to take his crown with him.

Three weeks after Baldwin II fled, Michael VIII entered a city that was a mess. The palace was so dirty that he had to have it professionally scrubbed down before he would live in it. Despite the filth and destruction, Michael VIII was able to retake Constantinople for his family and revive Byzantium with a new dynasty. He ended the Latin Empire and made sure John would not challenge his rule by blinding and imprisoning the eleven-year-old boy. Most importantly, Michael VIII made a treaty with the Genoese, allowing them a tax-free trading post in the city. The Genoese now had a monopoly on trade in the city and held the premier position for trade in the Mediterranean. Michael VIII restored Constantinople's importance by making it a central place for thirteenth-century commerce and by breathing life back into the Byzantine Empire.

EXAMPLE ANSWER:

Michael Palaeologus, great-grandson of the Byzantine emperor Alexius III, had a vision. He wanted to restore his family's kingdom. Baldwin II, the ruler of Constantinople when Michael became regent for John of Nicaea, and then co-emperor, had let Constantinople, the heart of the old Byzantine Empire, fall even further from its former glory than any previous emperor. He sold all of the city's treasures and did a poor job of defending its territory. In the end he barely had power over the area just outside of the city's walls. Michael VIII didn't even need a whole army to take back the city; he sent a small detachment of men to send threats, but when they got there, they found the city barely guarded. When they entered the city at night, Baldwin II fled, not even bothering to take his crown with him.

Three weeks after Baldwin II fled, Michael VIII entered a city that was a mess, with a palace that was unfit to live in. Despite the filth and destruction, Michael VIII was able to retake Constantinople for his family and revive Byzantium with a new dynasty. He ended the Latin Empire and made sure John would not challenge his rule by blinding and imprisoning the eleven-year-old boy. Most importantly, Michael VIII made a treaty with the Genoese, allowing them a tax-free trading post in the city. The Genoese now had a monopoly on trade in the city and held the premier position for trade in the Mediterranean. Michael VIII restored Constantinople's importance by making it a central place for thirteenth-century commerce and by breathing life back into the Byzantine Empire.

Section IV: **Map Exercise**

1. Trace the rectangular outline of the frame for Map 53.1 in black.

2. Trace the coastline around the Mediterranean and the Black Sea in black. You do not need to include most of the small islands around Greece and Turkey, but do include the two larger islands of Cyprus and Crete. Also trace the line of the Danube. Repeat until the contours are familiar.

3. Using contrasting colors, trace the separate areas of Bulgaria, the Empire of Nicaea, the Despotate of Epirus and the Latin Empire, and the areas of the Empire of Trebizond and Il-khanate. Repeat until the contours are familiar.

4. Now using a new sheet of paper, trace the rectangular outline of the frame for Map 53.1 in black. Then using your regular pencil with an eraser, draw the coastline around the Mediterranean as you did before, including just the islands of Crete and Cyprus. Draw the line of the Danube. Then draw the lines of the separate areas of Bulgaria, the Empire of Nicaea, the Despotate of Epirus and the Latin Empire, and the areas of the Empire of Trebizond and Il-khanate. Erase and redraw as necessary. When you are happy with your map, lay it over the original, and erase and redraw any lines which are more than ½″ off of the original. Label each area.

5. Now study carefully the locations of Thessalonica, Thyateira, Constantinople, the Bosphorus Strait, the Sea of Marmara, and Acre. When you are familiar with them, close the book. Mark and label each one on your map, check it against the original, and erase and re-mark any misplaced labels.

Chapter Fifty-Four

The Last Crusades

The student may use her text when answering the questions in sections I and II.

Section I: Who, What, Where

Write a one or two-sentence answer explaining the significance of each item listed below.

Abaqa—**Pg. 374, ¶ 5 and Pg. 376, ¶ 1—Abaqa, Hulagu's son and successor to the Il-khanate dynasty, made an alliance with Edward of England and helped Bohemund IV keep Tripoli by stopping Baibars from invading. Abaqa also sent a delegation to the Second Council of Lyons to show his willingness to fight with the Crusaders against the Egyptian Muslims.**

Abu 'Abdallah al-Mustansir—**Pg. 373, ¶ 1 and Pg. 374, ¶ 2—Abu 'Abdallah al-Mustansir, relation to the twelfth-century prophet and founder of the Almohad movement Ibn Tumart, ruled in Tunis since 1249 and called himself "Commander of the Faithful." Abu 'Abdallah al-Mustansir made a peace treaty with Charles of Anjou after Louis XI's death, bringing the French king's crusade to an end.**

Al-Ashraf Khalil—**Pg. 376, ¶ 6 to Pg. 377, ¶ 1—Al-Ashraf Khalil, son of Qalawun and his father's successor to the Bahri Sultanate, led the Bahris in a successful final push against the last remaining fragment of the final Crusader kingdom: Acre, the sole remaining outpost of the Kingdom of Jerusalem.**

Bohemund VI—**Pg. 374, ¶ 5—Bohemund VI, ruler of the Principality of Antioch, had lost everything but Tripoli to Baibars of Egypt. Edward of England helped Bohemund VI by stopping Baibars from finishing his conquest and by negotiating a truce with the Egyptian.**

Henry the Fat—**Pg. 374, ¶ 2—Henry the Fat, who earned his nickname because of his corpulent appearance, was the younger brother of Theobald, and his brother's successor to the throne of Navarre. Four years after becoming king, Henry the Fat suffocated on his own adipose tissue, leaving his infant daughter Joan as queen of Navarre.**

Idris II—Pg. 372, ¶ 2—Idris II was the last Almohad caliph. Idris II tried to claim the lands surrounding Marrakesh but lost them in 1269 when the Marinids stormed Marrakesh and took it for themselves.

Philip III—Pg. 374, ¶ 2 & 3—Philip III, Louis IX's son and heir, almost died of dysentery while on crusade with his father, but recovered and then began his rule as the king of France.

Qalawun—Pg. 376, ¶ 5—Qalawun, a powerful colleague of the mamluk leader Baibars, seized the throne of Egypt after Baibars's death, driving Baibars's sons into exile. In the decade and half after his accession in 1277, Qalawun's empire crept steadily outwards, including the taking of Tripoli in April of 1289, bringing an end to the Principality of Antioch.

Tebaldo Visconti/Pope Gregory X—Pg. 374, ¶ 7 and Pg. 376, ¶ 1—Tebaldo Visconti, the Milanese priest who had joined Edward to continue the failed Egyptian Crusade, was elected to be the successor to Pope Clement IV in October of 1271. Pope Gregory X's great accomplishment was reunifying the church at the Second Council of Lyons.

Theobald—Pg. 373, ¶ 4 and Pg. 374, ¶ 2—Theobald, king of Navarre and husband of Louis IX's daughter Isabella, was one of the few people to agree to go on crusade with Louis IX against the Hafsids. Theobald died of dysentery shortly after the failed crusade against the Hafsids ended.

Section II: Comprehension

Write a two or three-sentence answer to each of the following questions.

1. What happened to Almohad power in North Africa after the disintegration of the Almohad hold on the Spanish peninsula?

A1.—Pg. 372, ¶ 2—The disintegration of Almohad power on the Spanish peninsula had been followed by the breaking apart of the Almohad empire in North Africa: in Tunis, a former Almohad governor had declared his independence in 1229, establishing the Hafsid dynasty; the Zayyanids ruled from the city of Tlemcen; the Marinids from Fez; and the last Almohad caliph, Idris II, had been able to claim little more than the lands surrounding Marrakesh itself. Even Idris II's claim had fallen when the Marinids stormed Marrakesh in 1269 and took it for themselves.

2. Describe the Hafsid kingdom under the rule of Abu 'Abdallah al-Mustansir.

A2.—Pg. 373, ¶ 1—Tunis, at the heart of the Hafsid kingdom, lay at the end of the central trade route down into Africa; it was already visited by merchants from across the Muslim world, and in Hafsid hands it grew into a mighty political capital as well, with ambassadors visiting from Egypt, West Africa, and Norway, and with the kings of Kanem and James of Aragon keeping permanent embassies there. Abu 'Abdallah al-Mustansir supported both the great theological school of al-Zaytuna, where students of Islam came to work from all over Spain and North Africa, and the Studium Arabicum, a Dominican school intended to train Christian missionaries in their understanding of Muslim beliefs so that they could more effectively argue against them in Tunis. Under his rule, both Dominicans and Franciscans preached freely to the Hafsid Muslims.

3. Why did Louis IX decide to go on crusade against the Hafsid kingdom?

A3.—Pg. 373, ¶ 2—It is not entirely clear why Louis IX decided to go on crusade against the Hafsid kingdom—they were a mighty Muslim empire, but they held no holy sites. He had originally taken the cross intending to fight against Baibars, who had conquered Antioch and was now threatening Acre, and Charles of Anjou announced that he would join the Crusade, which might explain the targeting of Tunis; Charles, now king of Sicily and southern Italy, wanted to claim the North African coast for himself as well. But Louis IX, who was not sympathetic to his brother's ambitions, may have simply thought that the open-minded al-Mustansir was a likely convert to Christianity.

4. How did the crusade against the Hafsids end before it even started?

A4.—Pg. 373, ¶ 4 to Pg. 374, ¶ 2—Louis IX landed in Carthage with his three older sons and Theobald of Navarre on July 18, 1270; he marched his army the fifteen miles towards Tunis and then began to besiege the city, but the fighting was halted when he and his troops started to suffer from dysentery. Louis IX's second son John died, along with many other common folk, and then Louis IX himself died on August 25 after two weeks of suffering. Charles of Anjou, who arrived in Tunis not long after Louis IX's death, negotiated a peace deal with al-Mustansir, who paid him off in order to get rid of the besieging army, and then the demoralized Crusaders returned home.

5. How did Edward of England stop Baibars from taking Tripoli from Bohemund VI?

A5.—Pg. 374, ¶ 5—Edward stopped Baibars from taking Tripoli from Bohemund VI by gathering up three hundred knights and recruiting more from Cyprus for his fight against the Egyptian. But his real strength lay in an alliance he negotiated as soon as he arrived in Tripoli with the ruler of the Il-khanate dynasty, Abaqa. Facing the joint Crusader and Il-khanate Mongol defensive front, Baibars agreed to a truce that would protect the plain of Acre and the road to Nazareth for ten years, ten months, ten days, and ten hours.

6. What were the circumstances that led to Tebaldo Visconti's election as pope?

A6.—Pg. 374, ¶ 7 to Pg. 375, ¶ 2—Pope Clement IV had died in 1268, and for three years the cardinals had been in conclave in the Italian city of Viterbo, just north of Rome, quarreling over the succession: half of them wanted a French pope who would support Charles of Anjou, the rest an Italian pope who would resist him. The citizens of Viterbo, finally fed up with the delay, had banded together and locked the cardinals into a single palace, removed the roof, and threatened them with nothing but bread and water until they chose a new pontiff. They elected Visconti, a compromise candidate who was Italian but had spent most of his career outside Italy, who had never been involved with papal politics, to be Pope Gregory X.

7. Explain how Pope Gregory X reunified the eastern and western churches.

A7.—375, ¶ 8 to Pg. 376, ¶ 1—Pope Gregory X arranged a church council to be held in the eastern French city of Lyons in 1274 and he invited Michael VIII to send a delegation to this Second Council of Lyons to discuss the possibilities of reunifying the divided eastern and western churches. The delegation arrived at Lyons in midsummer, bearing a letter from Michael VIII that conceded almost every theological distinction of the eastern church in favor of the Roman (western) positions. A celebratory Mass was then carried out, with priests from both east and west taking part, and the council moved on to address other issues, including the renewal of crusading in the east.

8. Why didn't Pope Gregory and Michael VIII's vision for a reunified church come to fruition?

A8.—Pg. 376, ¶ 2 & 3— While those present at the Second Council of Lyons agreed to reunify the church, the citizens of Constantinople were dead set against this politically desirable reunion. Monks and priests in the capital protested; even Michael VIII's sister Eulogia snapped, "Better that my brother's empire should perish, than the purity of the Orthodox faith." Though Michael VIII tried to still the dissent, it was useless; Pope Gregory died on January 10, 1276 and the next three popes elected by the cardinals all died within a year, unable to implement any meaningful policies of their own. With them died the vision for a reunified church.

9. Describe the Bahri take over of Acre.

A9.—Pg. 376, ¶ 6 to Pg. 377, ¶ 1—In April of 1291, al-Ashraf Khalil's army, which was so huge that it "stretched over more than twelve miles," surrounded Acre, filled in the moats, and battered at the walls. For some weeks the inhabitants of Acre, led by the Knights Templar, resisted—stopping up the holes in the walls first with stones, then with wood planks, and finally with sacks stuffed with wool and cotton. In the end, they could hold out no longer, the gates were broken down, and the Egyptians flooded in: more than 60,000 people were slain, the riches of the city were plundered, and the walls and strongholds of the city were broken down and set aflame.

Section III: **Critical Thinking**

The student may not use her text to answer this question.

In the crusading world, God is the ultimate authority. However, God is only able to speak through man, and men often find it hard to separate their desire for power from their desire to serve Him. Write a paragraph or two explaining how both the trouble Louis IX had drumming up support for his crusade and the quarrel between the eastern and western churches reflected man's conflict between power and piety.

Both of these circumstances—Louis IX's trouble finding support for his crusade against the Hafsids and the division between the eastern and western church—revolved around power and authority.

On page 373, we find out why it was hard for Louis IX to find supporters for his fight against Abu 'Abdallah al-Mustansir:

> Whatever the motivation, enthusiasm for the project among the French knights was nonexistent. "If we take not the cross, we shall lose the King's favour," one of them remarked, in the hearing of Jean de Joinville, "and if we take the cross, we shall lose the favour of God, since we take not the cross for Him, but for fear of the King." James of Aragon refused to have anything to do with the war against his allies, and Joinville himself decided not to accompany his king: "They all did mortal sin that counselled his going," he wrote, "because . . . all the realm was at good peace with itself and with all its neighbors . . . after he had gone, the state of the realm [did nothing but] worsen."

The French kings were in a bind: if they followed their king they would do so knowing that it was only because they were afraid of his disapproval, not because they were doing the work of God. To go on crusade was to fight for God's kingdom, and the French knights felt that the only reason they would go on this crusade was to please their king.

On page 376, we read about why the eastern and western churches were quarrelling. The footnote explains:

> The thorniest issue was the western church's insistence that the Holy Spirit "proceeded," or issued, from both the Father and the Son. The east refused to use this formulation, known as the "Filioque clause." Eastern believers thought that to speak of the procession of the Holy Spirit "from the Father and the Son" suggested that God the Father and Jesus Christ were separate beings in a way that violated the unity of the Trinity. However, the real quarrel between east and west was one of authority: whether pope or patriarch ultimately had the last word on which Christian beliefs were or were not orthodox.

While church doctrine was important, the leaders of the separated Christian churches were arguing not over what was God's formation but who had more power: the pope or the patriarch. The desire for authority over the last word got in the way of unified worship for all Christians.

In her answer, the student should explain how power and piety conflict in both scenarios and link the two together by this common theme.

EXAMPLE ANSWER:

In both the case of Louis IX's trouble finding support for his crusade against the Hafsids and the division between the eastern and western church, men were conflicted or arguing over who had more power—God or man. While Louis IX wanted to go on crusade against the Hafsids, there really wasn't a reason for religious war. The French knights had a hard time supporting him because they felt they weren't fighting for God, but that they were fighting because they were afraid of upsetting their king: "If we take not the cross, we shall lose the King's favour, and if we take the cross, we shall lose the favour of God, since we take not the cross for Him, but for fear of the King." To go on crusade was to fight for God's kingdom,

and the French knights felt that the only reason they were going on this crusade was to please their king.

In this chapter we also read about the division between the eastern and western Christian churches. The main issue between the churches was over the Holy Spirit, where it came from, and if God the Father and Jesus Christ were separate beings in a way that violated the unity of the Trinity. This issue was really a way of arguing over authority; did the pope or the patriarch have the last word on which Christian beliefs were or were not orthodox?

While church doctrine was important, the leaders of the separated Christian churches were arguing not over what was God's formation but who had more power. The desire for authority over the last word got in the way of unified worship for all Christians. In both cases, Christians were confused about what to do because the desire for power and authority got in the way of piety; to truly do what would be good for God would be to go against his earthly representatives—men that were often swayed by the desire for power.

Section IV: Map Exercise

1. Trace the rectangular outline of Map 54.1 in black.

2. Using your blue pencil, trace the visible coastline around Europe and Africa. Using contrasting colors, trace the separate areas of the Marinids, Zayanids, and the Hafsid. Repeat until the contours are familiar.

3. Using a new sheet of paper, trace the rectangular outline of the frame in black. Then using your regular pencil with an eraser, draw the coastline and the areas of the Marinid, the Zayanid, and the Hafsid areas. Erase and redraw as necessary. When you are happy with your map, lay it over the original. Erase and redraw any lines which are more than ½" off of the original.

4. Now study carefully the locations of Marrakesh, Rabat, Seville, Fez, Tlemcen, and Granada. When they are familiar for you, close the book. Mark each one on your map. Then check your map against the original, and erase and re-mark any labels more than ¼" off of the original.

5. Trace the rectangular outline of the enlarged box showing Carthage and Tunis. Draw the outline of the coast and mark the locations of Tunis and Carthage.

6. Show the lines of the former Almohad Empire.

Chapter Fifty-Five

Kublai Khan

The student may use his text when answering the questions in sections I and II.

Section I: Who, What, Where

Write a one or two-sentence answer explaining the significance of each item listed below.

Bayan—**Pg. 382, ¶ 5—Bayan, one of Kublai Khan's generals, led his armies on a successful mission along the Yangtze river; city after city fell to them and by the end of 1275, they had reached the southern Song capital of Hangzhou.**

Bing—**Pg. 383, ¶ 1—Bing, the youngest son of Song Duzong, was concealed in a Buddhist temple far to the south after Emperor Gong's regent surrendered to the Mongols. Bing was guarded by his mother (a younger concubine of Duzong), her father, and the mother of the Duanzong and survived until 1279, when he was drowned by his guardians in the sea in order to avoid capture; Bing's death brought a final end to the Southern Song.**

Chungnyeol—**Pg. 382, ¶ 1—Chungnyeol, forced into submission by Kublai Khan, was known as king of Goryeo rather than emperor. Chungnyeol was also tied to Kublai Khan because his wife was a Mongol princess, but this was not a great privilege because Kublai Khan, who had twenty-two sons by his four wives, twenty-five by his concubines (who numbered at least a hundred), and an untold number of daughters, used marriages to his children to tie his vassals close to him.**

Duanzong—**Pg. 382, ¶ 7—Duanzong, middle son of Song Duzong, was ordered by a partisan group to act as emperor in exile. He died not long after his acclamation.**

Emperor Chengzong—**Pg. 386, ¶ 4—Emperor Chengzong was the name given to Kublai Khan's grandson when he inherited his grandfather's rule. He was no longer a Great Khan, but the second emperor of the Yuan dynasty.**

Emperor Gong—**Pg. 382, ¶ 6—Emperor Gong was the imperial name given to Song Duzong's five-year-old son after the death of his father. Gong's mother, his regent, surrendered to the Mongols; in January of 1276 the gates of Hangzhou were opened and Emperor Gong and his** mother were treated kindly, with Gong living out the rest of his life as a Buddhist monk in the north of China.

Hojo Tokimune—**Pg. 382, ¶ 2 and Pg. 383, ¶ 3—Hojo Tokimune, regent for the Kamakura shogun, refused to pay tribute to the Mongols and give in to Kublai Khan's demands for Japanese submission. When Kublai Khan sent another embassy to demand submission two years after his first defeat in Japan, Hojo Tokimune beheaded the ambassadors and prepared for war.**

Indravarman V—**Pg. 385, ¶ 3 & 4—Indravarman V, king of Champa, sent an embassy to Kublai's court to negotiate a treaty, hoping to both avoid war and subjection, but Kublai chose to regard the embassy as a surrender, and at once appointed two Yuan vice-regents to rule Champa on his behalf. Indravarman V refused to recognize their authority and launched a guerilla war against the Mongols that drove out almost all of the invaders by the summer of 1285.**

Jayavarman VIII—**Pg. 385, ¶ 3—Jayavarman VIII, Khmer king, sent Kublai Khan tribute and submitted as a vassal. He wanted to buy peace with the Mongols after they turned their attention to the Khmer following their two defeats by the Japanese.**

Kamikaze—**Pg. 383, ¶ 7—Kamikaze is the Japanese word for "a divine wind sent to protect the island." A Japanese Buddhist monk gave this name to the typhoon that destroyed the invading Mongol fleet.**

Marco Polo—Pg. 381, **¶ 1—Marco Polo was a Venetian traveler who wrote about his time spent with the Mongols in the thirteenth century.**

Song Duzong—**Pg. 379, ¶ 3—Song Duzong, emperor of the Song, could not handle the relentless and frightening Mongol aggression his empire faced so he turned to wine and feasting, his harem of concubines, gambling and games to distract himself from the coming end.**

Toghan—**Pg. 385, ¶ 5 to Pg. 386, ¶ 1—Toghan, one of Kublai Khan's sons, led a Mongol army to Thang Long in 1284, was halted by guerilla warfare, and was forced to return to his father to ask for reinforcements. Toghan's Mongol troops were slaughtered by the Dai Viet upon their return, and Toghan fled the carnage.**

Tran Quoc Toan—**Pg. 385, ¶ 5 to Pg. 386, ¶ 1—Tran Quoc Toan, a fervent nationalist and cousin of the ruling Dai Viet emperor, guided Dai Viet soldiers in a guerilla war against the invading Mongols in 1284 and led his men to defeat the Mongols. Tran Quoc Toan was honored as the hero of the resistance and was later worshipped as divine under his posthumous name, Tran Hung Dao.**

Section II: **Comprehension**

Write a two or three-sentence answer to each of the following questions.

1. Explain how the Mongols were finally able to take the double city of Xiangyang and Fancheng.

A1.—Pg. 379, ⁋ 4 to Pg. 380, ⁋ 1—Though the Song managed to hold out against the Mongol attack on the double city of Xiangyang and Fancheng by resupplying their cities by the Yangtze river, as time went on, the Mongol blockade strengthened and Song resupply ships could make it through only with massive casualties. Then, in March of 1272, a team of siege engineers led by Ala al-Din of Mosul arrived from the west, sent to Kublai Khan by his nephew Abaqa of the Il-khanate Mongols as a gesture of goodwill, and they brought with them a new weapon: trebuchets that used counterweights, instead of brute pulling strength, to hurl unusually massive stones at the walls of Fancheng. By early February of 1273, they were breached, the Mongols stormed in and executed over ten thousand of the city's inhabitants, and when the trebuchets began to systematically break down the walls of Xiangyang, the city's commander surrendered.

2. Describe Kublai Khan's dual capital cities in the north and south of China.

A2.—Pg. 380, ⁋ 4 to Pg. 381, ⁋ 1—Kublai Khan's summer home, the capital in the north of China, Shangdu, or "Supreme Capital," featured a stately palace on sixteen miles of fertile meadows, pleasant springs, and delightful streams, where all sorts of animals roamed and a house of pleasure moved around, too, all within a surrounding wall. In the south, Kublai Khan built his second capital, Dadu, or "Great Capital," right next to the burned remains of Zhongdu. Dadu was perfectly square, surrounded by white battlements, with arrow-straight streets and carefully laid-out allotments of land for each family and clan chief, protected by a wall around the city with twelve gates, three on each side of the square, with every gate guarded by a thousand men.

3. What happened when the Mongols set sail from Goryeo in 1274 to attack Japan?

A3.—Pg. 382, ⁋ 3 & 4—The Mongols set sail from Goryeo in 1274 to fight against Japan with just over twelve thousand men and perhaps three hundred vessels. On November 19 the fleet arrived at Hakata Bay, on the northern end of the island of Kyushu itself, but the Goryeo contingent scented bad weather, and they talked the Mongol commanders into withdrawing after a single day of fighting. Even so, the ships were caught by a storm on their way out of the bay, and perhaps a third of them were lost.

4. How did the Japanese stop a second Mongol invasion two years after the Mongols' first attempt at defeating the Kamakura shogunate?

A4.—Pg. 383, ⁋ 3-6—The Japanese prepared themselves well for the Mongol attack: Hojo Tokimune summoned samurai from across western Japan to defend the coast, he had eight-foot stone walls along the beaches of Hakata Bay and other ports built, and the Japanese assembled a special navy of small, very fast boats. While the samurai fought hard on land, protected in part by the stone walls, the small Japanese ships launched constant quick strikes against the Mongols while keeping them on perpetual alert; packed together, unable

to escape the fast Japanese boasts, the Mongol soldiers on board began to suffer from an epidemic that killed thousands and weakened more. Then, a typhoon blew down on the Mongol fleet and for two full days, it battered the anchored ships, sinking something like 90 percent of the vessels, drowning nearly a hundred thousand men and leaving thirty thousand soldiers stranded on the beach where they were massacred by the Japanese.

5. What did the Dai Viet do in order to win against Prince Toghan after he returned to Thang Long with reinforcements from his father?

A5.—Pg. 385, ¶ 6 & 7—When Prince Toghan came back with a massive army of both men and river craft, Tran Quoc Toan lured him into a battle at the Bach Dang river, the site of the great Dai Viet defeat of the Song in 1076. The Dai Viet army had prepared for the invasion by staking the bottom of the river with bronze spikes. When the tide began to run out, the Mongol river barges were caught, causing a slaughter of Mongols so massive that the water in the river ran red.

Section III: Critical Thinking

The student may use his text to answer this question.

There may be a dispute over the start of the Yuan dynasty (variously considered to have begun in 1263 when Kublai founded his new capital city, 1271, 1279, when the last Song heir died, and 1280) but there is no disputing that Kublai Khan transformed his kingdom from a khanate into an empire. Write a few paragraphs explaining all of Kublai Khan's accomplishments, and how he was able to turn the savage Mongols into the citizens of the Yuan dynasty.

Because there is so much detail in this chapter regarding Kublai Khan's accomplishments, the student may use his text while planning the answer to this question.

The first mention in the chapter of Kublai Khan's transformation from khan to emperor came when we read about how Kublai Khan declared war against the Southern Song. Shortly after the seizure of Xiangyang, Kublai Khan issued a declaration of war to Song Duzong. He said, "Since the time of Genghis Khan, we have communicated diplomatically with the Song . . . [asking for] a cessation of hostilities and respite for the people. . . . This could have provided a plan for all humanity. Yet [you] . . . continued to dispatch troops year after year. The dead and injured now pile up while prisoners and hostages grow. This all suggests that the Song has brought peril to its own people." While the Mongols had been at war with the song for four decades, and Kublai Khan himself had spent fourteen years conquering the south, the formal declaration of war signaled a shift in Kublai Khan's approach to war. He was no longer the Great Khan of a vast rough-hewn nomadic empire, built by invasion; he was one king pointing out the faults of another. He was defending the legitimacy of his attack.

After this description, we read about all the ways Kublai Khan transformed his reign into the beginning of a new Chinese dynasty. He built two new capitals, a summer home in Shangdu and a winter home in Dadu. Shangdu, the "Supreme Capital," was a beautiful and fecund place full of vegetation, wildlife, and the opportunities for pleasure. Dadu, the "Great Capital," was very organized and well-defended, with every gate of the city wall watched by a thousand men. The security of the city reflected Kublai Khan's strengthening grasp on the lands around him, and on his own empire.

Kublai Khan's whole reign was marked by great accomplishments in war and also in prosperity. As written on page 386,

> He kept a personal guard of twelve thousand horsemen; he could seat forty thousand of his subjects at a festival banquet and serve them all from gold and silver vessels; he could mount a hunt for his friends with ten thousand falconers and five thousand hunting dogs. He printed his own money, accepted by traders from Shangdu to Venice; he could send messages through a network of post offices and riders that webbed his entire kingdom. He welcomed to his court, says Marco Polo, "kings, generals, counts, astrologers, physicians, and many other officers and rulers" from all over the world.

While Japan and the southeast were not conquered by Kublai Khan, the Great Khan had managed to transform his kingdom. He died not a leader of nomads but as the first emperor of the Yuan dynasty of China.

EXAMPLE ANSWER:

Kublai Khan may have started out continuing the leadership tradition of the nomadic Mongols before him, but he ended his reign as an emperor. Everything about Kublai Khan's reign, from the capitals he built to the way he declared war, suggested his power as a civilized sovereign. He built two new capitals, a summer home in Shangdu and a winter home in Dadu. Shangdu, the "Supreme Capital," was a beautiful place full of vegetation, wildlife, and opportunities for pleasure. Dadu, the "Great Capital," was very organized and well-defended, with every gate of the city wall watched by a thousand men. The security of the city reflected Kublai Khan's strengthening grasp on the lands around him, and on his own empire.

The way he declared war also changed. For example, instead of just attacking the Song like a mad-man, Kublai Khan issued a declaration of war. He said, "Since the time of Genghis Khan, we have communicated diplomatically with the Song . . . [asking for] a cessation of hostilities and respite for the people. . . . This could have provided a plan for all humanity. Yet [you] . . . continued to dispatch troops year after year. The dead and injured now pile up while prisoners and hostages grow. This all suggests that the Song has brought peril to its own people." By pointing out the faults of the Song, Kublai Khan focused on what he wanted to do to the Song going forward rather than harping on the decades of fighting that had gone on between the kingdoms.

The changes in style of rule marked Kublai Khan's transformation from Great Khan to the first Emperor of the Yuan Dynasty. Kublai Khan's wealth was great, and widely acknowledged. He could seat forty thousand of his subjects at a festival banquet and serve them all from gold and silver vessels, and he could mount a hunt for his friends with ten thousand falconers and five thousand hunting dogs. He printed his own money, and he could send messages through a network of post offices and riders that webbed his entire kingdom. His court, protected by a personal guard of twelve thousand horsemen, welcomed kings, generals, counts, astrologers, physicians and other officers and rulers from all over the world. While Japan and the southeast were not conquered by Kublai Khan, the Great Khan had managed to transform his kingdom. He died not a leader of nomads but a powerful emperor.

Chapter Fifty-Six

The Sicilian Vespers

The student may use her text when answering the questions in sections I and II.

Section I: **Who, What, Where**

Write a one or two-sentence answer explaining the significance of each item listed below.

Alfonso III—**Pg. 392, ¶ 4—Alfonso III, son of Peter III of Aragon, was given the crown of Aragon after his father's death.**

Andronicus II—**Pg. 389, ¶ 5 and Pg. 391, ¶ 7—Andronicus II, son and heir to Michael VIII's Byzantine throne and a staunch Orthodox believer, refused to let his father, who he saw as a traitor to the Byzantine church, be buried in consecrated ground, and he also immediately revoked the Union of Lyon, which had brought the eastern and western churches together. After Charles of Anjou's death, the Venetians began peace talks with Andronicus II, aiming to get back their trading quarters in the east.**

Charles II/Charles the Lame—**Pg. 391, ¶ 2 and Pg. 392, 6-9—Charles II/Charles the Lame (named for his slight limp), Charles of Anjou's oldest son and most trusted officer, was taken prisoner in the fighting that followed the Sicilian Vespers. In order to get out of prison, Charles the Lame agreed to a peace with Sicily and Aragon; he would pay fifty thousand marks of silver for the expenses of the war his father had started and he would acknowledge that Sicily and southern Italy were now two separate kingdoms. But as soon as he returned home he got out of the treaty and that started another war between Naples, Sicily, and Aragon.**

Giacomo Savelli/Pope Honorius IV—**Pg. 391, ¶ 8 and Pg. 392, ¶ 8—Giacomo Savelli was elected to be pope after the death of Martin VI when he was eighty-five. Giacomo Savelli, who was given the papal name Honorius IV, only lived for two years after his election.**

James II—**Pg. 392, ¶ 4 & 6—James II, second son of Peter III of Aragon, was given the crown of Sicily after his father's death. James hoped to be a Christian monarch; keeping Charles the Lame, the rightful king of Naples, who also happened to be the first cousin of the king of**

France, in prison was not the act of a God-fearing king so he brokered a peace deal with his prisoner with the help of Edward of England.

John of Procida—**Pg. 389, ¶ 7 to Pg. 390, ¶ 2—John of Procida, a Sicilian nobleman, was at the head of an alliance of anti-Anjou soldiers and officials supported by the king of Aragon, Peter III.**

Martin IV—**Pg. 389, ¶ 3 & 4—Martin IV, a French Franciscan named Simon de Brion, was elected to be pope through Charles of Anjou's use of intimidation; he was so unpopular in Italy that he did not dare enter Rome and he had to be consecrated at Orvieto, north of Saint Peter's city. Martin IV furthered Charles of Anjou's ambitions by promoting him to the position of Senator of Rome, promoted pro-Anjou French priests into positions of power, and threw his complete agreement behind Charles of Anjou's scheme to conquer Constantinople for himself.**

Nicholas IV—**Pg. 392, ¶ 8—Nicholas IV followed Honorius IV as pope. Nicholas IV absolved Charles the Lame of the obligations of the peace agreement he made with James II of Sicily in exchange for Charles's acknowledgement of the final and supreme authority of the pope in Sicily and any other lands he might rule.**

Ottocar II—**Pg. 388, ¶ 2 & 3—Ottocar II, King of Bohemia, would not acknowledge Rudolf of Hapsburg as his overlord, so he refused to show up to an imperial diet in 1274 and then he openly revolted against the king of Germany. Ottocar II kept fighting against the king for the next four years, but was killed in 1278 in a fight against Rudolf on the banks of the Danube.**

Peter III/Peter of Aragon—**Pg. 390, ¶ 2 and Pg. 391, ¶ 3—Peter III, son of James of Aragon and successor to his throne, married the daughter of Manfred, whose kingdom was taken over by Charles of Anjou; Peter III supported the alliance against Charles of Anjou headed by John of Procida. After successfully attacking Sicily and taking Charles of Anjou's son prisoner, Peter III of Aragon was proclaimed king of Sicily and Aragon at Palermo on August 30, 1282.**

Roger of Lauria—**Pg. 391, ¶ 9—Roger of Lauria, an Aragonese admiral, led a sea attack against Philip III in Roussillon that dispersed the French fleet.**

Sicilian Vespers—**Pg. 390, ¶ 3 to Pg. 391, ¶ 2—Sicilian Vespers was the name given to the massacre of French soldiers and civilians across Sicily during Easter week of 1282. The men conspiring against Charles of Anjou used a riot in Palermo between the French and the Sicilians to spread the war across Sicily, slaying the French across the island.**

Wenceslaus—**Pg. 388, ¶ 3—Wenceslaus, son of Ottocar II, was wed to Rudolf of Hapsburg's daughter in a marriage alliance.**

Section II: **Comprehension**

Write a two or three-sentence answer to each of the following questions.

1. Describe the circumstances of Rudolf of Hapsburg's crowning as king of Germany, and the state of his kingdom once he sat on the throne.

A1.—Pg. 388, ¶ 1 & 2—Rudolf of Hapsburg's crowning ceremony was already underway when someone realized that the royal regalia, the scepter and crown of Frederick II, had disappeared sometime during the anarchy of the previous decade and Rudolf of Hapsburg was forced to improvise, grabbing a nearby crucifix as a symbol of his royalty, and redemption. The state of Germany when Rudolf became king was a wreck: the treasury was empty, the countryside afflicted by roving bandits, and the dukes were engaged in private warfare. For example, Ottocar II of Bohemia was in open revolt against the king.

2. Why was Ottocar II of Bohemia in open revolt against the German king?

A2.—Pg. 388, ¶ 2—Ottocar II of Bohemia was in open revolt against the German king because the Dukes of Bohemia, since early in the century, had been granted the right by the emperor to claim the title of king of Bohemia, a lesser monarch subject to the German throne. When Ottocar II was summoned to an imperial diet in 1274 to do homage to his new overlord, he refused to show up, and instead fortified his boundaries for war.

3. How did Rudolf whip Germany back into shape at the start of his reign?

A3.—Pg. 388, ¶ 3 to Pg. 389, ¶ 1—Rudolf took as his motto the Latin phrase *Melius bene imperare, quam imperium ampliare*: Better to govern the empire well than to enlarge it. Instead of expanding his borders, he destroyed the headquarters of robber bands, reestablished the rule of law in Germany, and killed the rebellious Ottocar II in 1287. Rudolf destroyed sixty castles occupied by bandits and private warlords; he whipped the troublesome kingdom of Moravia into line; he made a marriage alliance between Ottocar II's son Wenceslaus and his own daughter, and made another treaty with the king of Hungary; and he restored Frederick's laws, spending countless months traveling through Germany, visiting each local court.

4. What did Charles of Anjou do to fix the papal election following the death of Nicholas III in 1280?

A4.—Pg. 389, ¶ 3—In 1280, after the sudden death of Nicholas III, Charles of Anjou fixed the election of the next pope by intimidating the cardinals that did the electing. Charles of Anjou favored the election of the Franciscan Simon de Brion, a native of Tours, but the Italian cardinals objected to the election of another Frenchman, so Charles imprisoned two of them. The rest, properly intimidated, elevated Brion to the papal seat as Martin IV.

5. Why was there a secret revolt brewing against Charles of Anjou? How did the revolt come to a head?

A5.—Pg. 389, ¶ 7 to Pg. 390, ¶ 1—The people of Sicily resented Charles of Anjou's French rule, and they hated him for his drastic tax policies, so they started a secret revolt against him led

by John of Procida and supported by Peter of Aragon, husband of the daughter whose father was kicked out of the Kingdom of the Two Sicilies by Charles of Anjou. The revolt came to a head in Palermo during Easter week of 1282 when a Frenchman insulted a Sicilian woman and rioting broke out between the French and the Sicilians. As the Sicilians shouted "Death to the French" and the headquarters of the royal government in Palermo were rapidly overrun, the conspirators seized their opportunity and carried the war against Charles of Anjou across Sicily.

6. How did Pope Martin IV, Philip III of France, and Edward of England react to the war between Peter III of Aragon and Charles of Anjou?

A6.—Pg. 391, ¶ 4—After Peter III of Aragon was proclaimed king of Sicily and Aragon at Palermo, Pope Martin IV obediently excommunicated Peter III of Aragon and preached a crusade against both Aragon and Sicily. Philip III of France, Charles of Anjou's nephew, joined the fight against Peter and the Sicilian rebels, bringing France and Aragon to open war. Edward of England got involved when he thought about refereeing single combat between Charles of Anjou and Peter of Aragon, but he decided against it.

7. Describe the state of Philip III and his army in the days leading up to the Battle of the Col de Panissars. What happened after the battle?

A7.—Pg. 391, ¶ 9 to Pg. 392, ¶ 3—Philip III of France marched through Languedoc into the eastern Aragonese territory known as Roussillon with an enormous army—over a hundred thousand foot soldiers, cavalry, and bowmen, supported by a hundred French ships off shore—but the Aragonese, joined by the people of Roussillon, put up a fierce resistance. The land forces began to suffer from dysentery so Philip III decided to retreat back across the Pyrenees, but before he could lead his army to safety, an Aragonese army came up behind them and attacked; the assault was known as the Battle of the Col de Panissars. After the Battle of the Col de Panissars, which lasted for two days, little more than the royal vanguard itself remained and Philip III himself faded: on October 5, four days after his army had been slaughtered, he died at Perpignan of dysentery.

8. What happened after Charles the Lame was released from prison?

A8.—Pg. 392, ¶ 7-9—After Charles the Lame was released from prison, he was able to convince Nicholas IV to get him out of the peace treaty he made with James II of Sicily in exchange for Charles's acknowledgement of the final and supreme authority of the pope in Sicily and any other lands he might rule. Nicholas IV said he released Charles the Lame from the agreement because no ruler should be forced to abide by conditions that were made in captivity. But his nullification of the treaty began another war between Naples, Sicily, and Aragon that would drag on for a full twenty-four years.

Section III: **Critical Thinking**

The student may not use her text to answer this question.

The revolt against Charles of Anjou in Palermo was given the name "Sicilian Vespers." What are "vespers"? After doing some research, write a paragraph that defines "vespers," and then explains why, literally and metaphorically, the revolt at Palermo was named as such.

According to the United States Conference of Catholic Bishops, vespers is the word used to describe "evening prayer." Vespers is part of the Liturgy of the Hours, which is also known as the Divine Office. The Liturgy of the Hours specifies particular times to pray, and the most important times are called the "hinge hours," which include Morning Prayer (takes place upon rising) and Evening Prayer (takes place as dusk begins to fall).*

When the student looks up "Sicilian Vespers," she will find that the revolt against Charles of Anjou started during the evening prayer at the Church of the Holy Spirit in Palermo. This is how the revolt got its literal name. Metaphorically, the name suggests the ending of Charles of Anjou's rule, and the French occupation, of Sicily. Evening prayer takes place as dusk begins to set—in other words—lights out. We can also think of the curtain being drawn, or the darkening of a screen. The student could also make a play on the idea of prayer, as in the French had to pray for safety, or Charles of Anjou needed divine intervention in order to beat the rebellion. While the student can play around with the different possible innuendos and meanings, she must explain clearly why any particular reading makes sense.

*From "Vespers," United States Conference of Catholic Bishops. Accessed January 2016: http://www.usccb.org/prayer-and-worship/liturgy-of-the-hours/vespers.cfm

EXAMPLE ANSWER:

"Vespers" means "evening prayer." It is the prayer said when dusk begins to fall. The Sicilian Vespers got its name because the Sicilian rebellion against the French started during vespers. The riot that broke out in Palermo between the French and the Sicilians turned into a war that spread across Italy and resulted in the slaughter of thousands of French people. This is why the name "vespers" is metaphorically appropriate for the fighting. The Sicilian Vespers meant the end of the day, like dusk, for the French occupation of Sicily. Like the sun goes down, it was lights out for Charles of Anjou and his rule over the Kingdom of the Two Sicilies.

Section IV: **Map Exercise**

1. Trace the rectangular outline of Map 56.1 in black.

2. Using your blue pencil, trace the visible coastline around the Holy Roman Empire and France through the Mediterranean and around Italy and Greece. As usual, you do not need to include small islands around Greece, but do include Sicily, Sardinia, and Corsica. Repeat until the contours are familiar.

3. Now using your black pencil, trace the separate areas of Aragon, France, the Holy Roman Empire, Hungary, the Papal States, and the Kingdom of the Two Sicilies. Trace the mountains with small peaks. Repeat until the contours are familiar.

4. Now using a new sheet of paper, trace the rectangular outline of the frame in black. Then using your regular pencil with an eraser, draw the coastline around the Holy Roman Empire and France through the Mediterranean and around Italy and Greece, including Sicily, Sardinia, and Corsica. Draw the separate areas of Aragon, France, the Holy Roman Empire, Hungary, the Papal States, and the Kingdom of the Two Sicilies. Show the mountains with small peaks. When you are happy with your map, lay it over the original. Erase and redraw any lines which are more than ½″ off of the original. Label each region.

5. Now study carefully the locations of Tours, Aachen, Venice, Genoa, Perugia, Orvieto, Rome, Benevento, Palermo, and Trapani. When they are familiar for you, close the book. Mark each one on your map. Lay your map over the original, and erase and redraw any marks which are more than ½″ off of the original. Label the Strait of Messina.

6. Now trace the outline of the enlarged box showing the Battle of the Col de Panissars. Mark the site of the Battle and the location of Perpignan.

7. Mark Catalonia and the Pyrenees mountains.

Chapter Fifty-Seven

The Wars of Edward I

The student may use his text when answering the questions in sections I and II.

Section I: Who, What, Where

Write a one or two-sentence answer explaining the significance of each item listed below.

Alexander III—**Pg. 397, ❡ 6 & 7—Alexander III, king of the Scots since 1249, had made an alliance with Henry III by marrying his daughter Margaret, Edward I's younger sister, but after the wedding, he had refused Henry III's demands that he pay homage to the English king as his overlord. After his wife died, Alexander III married a young French woman named Yoleta de Dru in the hopes of producing a male heir that could continue ruling Scotland as an independent kingdom, but he died before any children were born.**

Dafydd—**Pg. 395, ❡ 3-6 and Pg. 397, ❡ 2 & 3—Dafydd, Llywelyn ap Gruffudd's younger brother, joined Edward I in his fight against the Prince of Wales and was given rule over a chunk of the Gwynedd principality that had once belonged to his brother after Llywelyn was defeated. Dafydd started a rebellion against the English just before Easter of 1282; he was turned over to the English in June of 1283 after his brother's death by a handful of his own men and then he was drawn, hung, and quartered by Edward I.**

Edward II—**Pg. 401, ❡ 4—Edward II, Edward I's son and future king of England, was betrothed to Isabella of France when he was fifteen and she was five as part of a peace negotiation made between his father and the French king in 1299.**

Isabella—**Pg. 401, ❡ 4—Isabella, daughter of Philip IV, was betrothed to Edward I's son Edward II as part of a peace negotiation made between her father and the English king in 1299.**

John Balliol—**Pg. 398, ❡ 2 & 4 and Pg. 399, ❡ 4—John Balliol, a great-great-great-grandson of David I, was elected to be king of Scotland by a gathering of 104 Scottish aristocrats and Edward I of England in 1292. After John Balliol agreed to send Scottish troops to the king of England for the fight against Philip IV for Aquitaine, he earned the nickname *Toom Tabard*** or "Empty Suit" because the aristocrats of Scotland took away his power, saying he could not longer act by himself.

Llywelyn ap Gruffudd—**Pg. 394, ❡ 3 to Pg. 395, ❡ 1 & 4 and Pg. 397, ❡ 1**—Llywelyn ap Gruffudd, the second brother of the dead prince of the Kingdom of Gwynedd, was able to drive the English out of Perfeddwlad and then he spent the next twenty years fighting against the English outposts in Wales and against his fellow Welsh princes; in 1267, Henry III had been forced to recognize Llywelyn ap Gruffudd with the title Prince of Wales, the first Welsh ruler to claim anything more than local authority. Llywelyn ap Gruffudd was forced to make a treaty with the English after Edward I decided to reclaim the Perfeddwlad, and later in December of 1282, Llywelyn ap Gruffudd was killed in the fighting against the English started by his brother just before Easter of that year.

Margaret (granddaughter)—**Pg. 397, ❡ 8 to Pg. 398, ❡ 2**—Margaret, the granddaughter of Alexander III, child of his dead daughter Margaret and her husband, the king of Norway, was the sole surviving heir of Alexander III and was made queen of the Scots when she was just three by the nobles of Scotland. Margaret was to be married to Edward I's son, according to the Treaty of Birgham, but this did not happen because Margaret died when she was just seven.

Marguerite—**Pg. 401, ❡ 4**—Marguerite, sister of Philip IV, was married to Edward I as part of a peace negotiation made between her brother and the English king in 1299.

Marion of Lanark—**Pg. 400, ❡ 6**—Marion of Lanark, the beautiful daughter of a Scottish landowner, fell in love with William Wallace and married him in secret because Lanark was the seat of a powerful English sheriff. When William Wallace was caught visiting Marion, he had to fight his way out of Lanark, killing a good number of English soldiers on the way, and then the sheriff put Marion to death in retaliation.

Philip IV—**Pg. 398, ❡ 7, Pg. 399, ❡ 5, and Pg. 401, ❡ 5**—Philip IV, Philip the Bold's successor as king of France, married Queen Joan of Navarre, uniting France and Navarre together under one royal couple. Philip IV agreed to the Treaty of Paris with the Twelve Peers of Scotland in 1295 but in 1299, after realizing the war against the English was too expensive, Philip IV made peace with Edward I and agreed to give no further aid to the Scots.

Reginald de Gray—**Pg. 395, ❡ 5**—Reginald de Gray, the English sheriff appointed to supervise Welsh affairs, was harsh, dragging up decades-old offenses for trial and threatening petitioners with the death penalty, turning relations between the Welsh and their English overlords sour.

Robert Bruce the Fifth—**Pg. 398, ❡ 2 & 3**—Robert Bruce the Fifth, Alexander III's second cousin and a frontrunner for the Scottish throne after the death of Margaret, was eighty when he decided to go for the Scottish crown. He lost his bid to John Balliol.

Robert Bruce the Sixth—**Pg. 398, ❡ 3 and Pg. 399, ❡ 6**—Robert Bruce the Sixth, son of Robert Bruce the Fifth, was well known to Edward I because he had joined Edward on the Ninth Crusade and helped him in the English campaign against Wales. Robert Bruce the Sixth was placed in charge of the northern fortress Carlisle Castle on the Scottish border when Edward I went after John Balliol and the Scottish resistance.

Scottish Wars/Wars of Independence—**Pg. 399, ¶ 5—Scottish Wars/Wars of Independence were the names given to the wars between the Scottish and the English started in 1295 with the signing of the Treaty of Paris between the Scottish and the French. The English called the decades of fighting the "Scottish Wars," while the Scots called them the "Wars of Independence."**

Statute of Rhuddlan—**Pg. 397, ¶ 4—Statute of Rhuddlan formally added Wales to the English Empire in 1284. Llywelyn ap Gruffudd became known as Llywelyn the Last because after the Statute of Rhuddlan, Wales would never again have an independent ruler.**

Stone of Scone—**Pg. 398, ¶ 4 and Pg. 400, ¶ 1—Stone of Scone, a chunk of sandstone said to have been brought to Scotland by the legendary first king of the Scots, Fergus, sixteen hundred years before the coronation of John Balliol, was where Scottish kings sat while they were crowned at Scone Abbey. Edward I took the Stone of Scone to England and set it on the royal coronation seat of England after taking John Balliol prisoner so that future English kings would be crowned kings of Scotland as well.**

Treaty of Birgham—**Pg. 397, ¶ 8 to Pg. 398, ¶ 2—Treaty of Birgham, made by the nobles of Scotland in the hopes of bringing a lasting peace, said that Margaret would marry Edward I's son; this would create a personal union between the two kingdoms of England and Scotland on the condition that Scotland would always keep its independence. The arrangement all fell apart in 1290, when Margaret died in the Orkney Islands, aged seven.**

William Wallace—**Pg. 400, ¶ 3 to Pg. 401, ¶ 1—William Wallace started his fight against the English by launching attacks on English garrisons and plundering English-held castles and then, in 1297, he killed the sheriff that killed his wife, the first act of coordinated Scottish rebellion against the English. Edward I sent a large force to fight Wallace and on September 11, 1297, Wallace's army wiped out the English and killed their general, beginning the First War of Scottish Independence.**

Section II: Comprehension

Write a two or three-sentence answer to each of the following questions.

1. Why was Wales vulnerable to the whims of the English kings?

A1.—**Pg. 394, ¶ 2—Wales had never possessed a High King who could boast the allegiance of the whole country. Instead, it had rival princes who claimed to rule one or more of a handful of small kingdoms: Gwynedd and Powys, Dyfed and Deheubarth, Morgannwg and Ceredigion. This made Wales vulnerable to the English kings, should they choose to push west past Offa's Dyke, the border between Powys and the English county of Mercia as Henry III did in 1247; he taken the northern territory known as the Perfeddwlad away from the**

Kingdom of Gwynedd and had then granted the Perfeddwlad to Edward, the crown prince, as his own particular possession.

2. How did Edward I reclaim the Perfeddwlad for himself?

A2.—Pg. 395, ¶ 2-4—Edward I ordered Llywelyn ap Gruffudd to travel to England and pay him homage, but when Llywelyn refused, Edward prepared to march into Gwynedd. Edward I was able to raise an army by promising the English barons that supported the cause gifts of conquered Welsh land, and Edward I was also supported by the Welsh princes that had been forced into submission by Llywelyn ap Gruffudd. Edward I cut off Llywelyn ap Gruffudd by land and hemmed him in by sea, and by November 1277, Llywelyn was forced to agree to the Treaty of Conway, leaving him only his original small northwest corner of Gwynedd.

3. Why did the Treaty of Conway fall apart?

A3.—Pg. 395, ¶ 5 & 6—Five years after it was made, the Treaty of Conway fell apart because English barons, as overlords to their Welsh tenants, were both dismissive and demanding. The English sheriff appointed to supervise Welsh affairs, Reginald de Gray, was harsh, dragging up decade-old offenses for trial and threatening petitioners with the death penalty, and the Welsh were upset because they were forced to obey English laws in their own lands. Then, just before Easter 1282, Dafydd rallied the Welsh princes behind him and attacked the English-held castle, Hawarden.

4. How did Edward I deal with Dafydd after he was turned over by his own companions to the English?

A4.—Pg. 397, ¶ 3—Dafydd was drawn, hung, and quartered, a barbaric punishment carried out on a still-living rebel. He was dragged through the streets of London behind a horse, as a traitor; hung as a thief; and then cut down when still alive, disemboweled and his intestines burned in front of his eyes, an ancient penalty for homicide. Finally, says the contemporary *Chronicle of Lanercost*, "his limbs were cut into four parts as the penalty of a rebel, and exposed in four of the ceremonial places in England as a spectacle:" his right arm went to York, his left to Bristol, his right leg to Northampton, his left to Hereford, and his head, bound in iron to keep it from falling apart as it decayed, was stuck on a spear shaft at the Tower of London.

5. Why, in 1294, did Philip IV order Edward I to appear at the French royal court?

A5.—Pg. 398, ¶ 8 to Pg. 399, ¶ 2—Philip IV hero-worshipped his dead grandfather Louis, and hoped to model himself after Philip Augustus, his great-grandfather. In order to show how he was like the great men that came before him, Philip IV exerted his authority over the independent-minded dukes who still held much of his kingdom, and the most independent-minded of these was Edward I, who was Duke of Aquitaine as well as king of England. In 1294, Philip IV ordered Edward I to appear at the French royal court in order to answer for the behavior of Norman sailors who had taken part in a brawl with French ships just off the coast, but he really summoned Edward I because he wanted to show his power over the English king.

6. How did Edward I deal with the Scottish resistance after his disobedient vassal kingdom signed the 1295 Treaty of Paris with Philip IV?

A6.—Pg. 399, ¶ 6 to Pg. 400, ¶ 1—Edward I started his assault on the disobedient Scottish vassal kingdom by personally leading an army towards the Scottish city of Berwick while also sending a navy to assault John Balliol by sea; Berwick was taken easily and then one by one the castles of Scotland fell. Balliol then gave up at Montrose, was taken prisoner and locked up in the Tower of London; the Stone of Scone was taken, too, set on the royal coronation seat of England, so that future English kings would be crowned kings of Scotland as well.

Section III: Critical Thinking

The student may not use his text to answer this question.

William Wallace is a well-known Scottish hero. In this chapter we learned about Wallace's life through the work of the poet Blind Harry, who wrote about the rebel 150 years after his life ended. In the 19th century famous Scottish writer Sir Walter Scott explored the life of William Wallace, and in the 20th century, Mel Gibson portrayed William Wallace in the Academy Award-winning 1995 film, *Braveheart*. William Wallace is certainly an epic figure, and with that comes mystery and exaggeration. For example, we learn in the chapter that Marion of Lanark might not have been real. Do some research and find out more about William Wallace's original organized rebellion against the English. You can explore any angle you'd like—did Marion exist? Was William Wallace on the run because of the slaughter of English men? How did the organized rebellion against Sir William Heselrig come about? Just make sure to start with a clear research question. Write your question down, and then explain what you found and how you found it, in a well-organized paragraph. Make sure you to cite your sources!

In this Critical Thinking question the student is challenged to pick one research question and reflect on his research process. The question should be clear. After the student writes down his question, he should take notes on what he finds, marking clearly where his information is coming from. Then, he should write a paragraph that starts with his research question, explains what information he found out about his question, and where that information came from.

Example research question:
    Who was Marion of Lanark?
Research notes:
    Searched the internet via a search engine: "Who was Marion of Lanark?"
    Looked first at Wikipedia article "Action at Lanark"
        repeats chapter info (death of Heselrig)
        Marion's name: Marion Braidfute of Lamington
    Searched for "Marion Braidfute of Lamington"
    Found website "Clan McAlister of America" page "On the topic of William Wallace and Marion Braidfute" by Jared Savory
        Marion's father died—brother killed by Heselrig (brother didn't like him)

Stays in Lanark at her father's (Braidfute) home
Marion supposed to marry Heselrig's son
Marion and William Wallace fall in love, have affair
Soldier finds them, he is killed by Wallace in a crowd
Wallace and his men kill the men in the crowd to save their own lives
Marion tries to protect Wallace, killed by Heselrig
Searched for "Who was Marion Braidfute"
Found same info on Education Scotland website, "William Wallace" page
Found same info from article "William Wallace: The Man Behind the Legend" by DeAnna Stevens (Saber and Scroll, March 2013)

EXAMPLE ANSWER:

Who was Marion of Lanark? In the chapter Susan Wise Bauer writes, "Marion's existence cannot be traced." I found in my research that because her existence cannot be traced, it is hard to find out more about William Wallace's supposed wife. I started my search by looking up "Who was Marion of Lanark?" and I found a Wikipedia article called "Action at Lanark." From this page I found Marion's full name, Marion Braidfute of Lamington, but no other new information. Then I looked up the full name and found a website called "Clan McAlister of America" with a page entitled "On the topic of William Wallace and Marion Braidfute" by Jared Savory. The information on this page matched information on other pages I found in my research, like the Education Scotland "William Wallace" page, and the article called "William Wallace: The Man Behind the Legend" by DeAnna Stevens. Savoy's essay gives a very detailed account of the legendary love between Marion and William Wallace. After Marion's father died, she became the sole heir of his estate, but she decided to stay in her Braidfute home rather than return to Lamington. I also found out that Marion's brother was killed by Sir William Heselrig because he didn't like the English sheriff. Though Marion was supposed to marry Heselrig's son, she fell in love with Wallace and started an affair. They may or may not have gotten married. One of Heselrig's men found out about the affair and confronted Wallace in the street. Wallace and his men killed the officer, and then slaughtered their way through the crowed, killing several English men, in order to save their own lives. Marion tried to protect Wallace so he could get away and hide, and as a result she was killed in her home, on the spot, by Heselrig. I did find out more about Marion from Savoy's writing, but the veracity of the site is questionable; much of what Savoy writes is sourced as "legend has it," and that's not verifiable.

Section IV: Map Exercise

1. Trace the rectangular frame of Map 57.1 in black.

2. Using your blue pencil, trace the outline of the continent and of Wales, England, and Scotland. You do not need to include all the small islands around Scotland, but do include the Orkney Islands. Repeat until the contours are familiar.

3. Now using a new sheet of paper, trace the rectangular outline of the frame for Map 57.1 in black. Using your regular pencil, draw the line of the coast around the continent and the islands of Wales and England and Scotland, including the Orkney Islands. Erase and redraw until you are happy with your map. Then lay it over the original, and erase and redraw any lines which are more than ½″ off of the original.

4. Now study carefully the locations of Scone, Lanark, Berwick, Montrose, Edinburgh, Dunbar, Stirling, Carlisle, Hawarden, Perfeddwlad, Gynedd, Irfon, Ceredigion, Deheubarth, Dyfed, Powys, Morgannwg, and London. When they are familiar for you, close the book. Mark and label each location on your map. Check your map against the original, and erase and re-mark any labels more than ½″ off of the original.

5. Study the locations of the Battle of Stirling Bridge, Hadrian's Wall, and Offa's Dyke. Close the book, mark them on your map, and check your marks against the original.

Chapter Fifty-Eight

The Second Sultanate of Delhi

The student may use her text when answering the questions in sections I and II.

Section I: **Who, What, Where**

Write a one or two-sentence answer explaining the significance of each item listed below.

'Ala'-ud-Din—**Pg. 404, ¶ 7 to Pg. 405, ¶ 3 and Pg. 407, ¶ 6 to Pg. 408, ¶ 1—'Ala'-ud-Din, nephew of Jalalu-d din Firu Khilji, husband of one of his daughters, and also his chief general, stockpiled his wealth, killed his uncle, marched into Delhi and then claimed the throne. After defeating the Mongols in 1296 and 1299, 'Ala'-ud-Din named himself "The Second Alexander" and had this title embossed on his coins, announcing his intentions to go out like Alexander the Great and conquer the known world.**

Bughra Khan—**Pg. 403, ¶ 2 & 5—Bughra Khan, Balban's second son, and governor of the eastern Ganges delta territories known as Bengal, abandoned allegiance to his son Mu'izzu-d din and named himself Sultan of Gaur, an independent ruler.**

Duwa—**Pg. 406, ¶ 1 and Pg. 407, ¶ 5—Duwa, great-grandson of Chagatai and ruler of the Chagatai khanate, was friendly with the Golden Horde khan but hostile to Kublai's rule, and firmly opposed to the Il-khanate, which led to bloody fighting over the right to claim Khurasan. After taking Khurasan, Duwa launched attacks on India intending to take it for himself, but he could not beat 'Ala'-ud-Din and he even lost his own son as the Mongols retreated from war outside of Delhi in 1299.**

Ghazan—**Pg. 405, ¶ 7—Ghazan, great-grandson of the Il-khanate founder Hulagu, took the Il-khanate throne in 1295, and like his grandfather, he was an enemy of the Egyptian sultanate and the Golden Horde khanate north of the Black Sea. He allied himself with Christian interests, made overtures of friendship to Andronicus II of Constantinople, and kept up a friendship with the distant Chinese khanate of Kublai.**

Jalalu-d din Firu Khilji—**Pg. 404, ¶ 2-4—Jalalu-d din Firu Khilji, one of Balban's favored slaves and governor of the city of Samana, was pulled from his post by Mu'izzu-d din to administer the palace's affairs after the death of Nizamu-d din. Soon after he arrived in**

Delhi, he engineered the placement of Mu'izzu-d din's son as sultan, then he made the son disappear and declared himself sultan in 1289, starting a new dynasty: the Khilji.

Malik Kafur—**Pg. 407, ¶ 1—Malik Kafur was a eunuch taken captive after 'Ala'-ud-Din sent a successful invasion force against the Hindu state of Gujarat. 'Ala'-ud-Din saw Malik Kafur and was "captivated" by the slave's beauty; from that time on, Malik Kafur was the sultan's constant companion.**

Mu'izzu-d din—**Pg. 403, ¶ 2 & 4 and Pg. 404, ¶ 3—Mu'izzu-d din, Bughra Khan's son, was made sultan of Delhi after Balban's death when he was seventeen and he spent the four years of his reign having fun with his friends in an enormous palace and garden he built for himself. After bringing the ambitious Jalalu-d din Firu Khilji to administer the government, Mu'izzu-d din contracted a paralyzing illness and was replaced on the throne by his infant son.**

Nizamu-d din—**Pg. 404, ¶ 1—Nizamu-d din, Chief Justice, figured out how to get Mu'izzu-d din to eliminate his rivals; he would present himself before the young sultan when he was drunk, and get from him permission to kill anyone he pleased. Nizamu-d din died by his own game: a court official convinced the intoxicated Sultan to authorize Nizamu-d din's murder, and then put poison in his wine.**

Ulugh—**Pg. 406, ¶ 3 and Pg. 407, ¶ 5—Ulugh, 'Ala'-ud-Din's brother, who was sent at the head of a large army to meet the invading Mongols in the north of India in 1296, won an easy victory against the enemy, helping to strengthen the authority of 'Ala'-ud-Din. Ulugh also helped his brother defeat the invading Mongols outside of Delhi in 1299, securing 'Ala'-ud-Din's greatness as sultan.**

Zafar—**Pg. 406, ¶ 3 and Pg. 407, ¶ 5—Zafar, 'Ala'-ud-Din's close friend, was sent at the head of a large army to meet the invading Mongols in the north of India in 1296 and he won an easy victory, helping to strengthen the authority of 'Ala'-ud-Din. Zafar was killed in the attack on the Mongols outside of Delhi in 1299.**

Section II: Comprehension

Write a two or three-sentence answer to each of the following questions.

1. How did Jalalu-d din Firu Khilji become Sultan of Delhi and the first Sultan of the Khilji dynasty?

A1.—**Pg. 404, ¶ 2-4—Jalalu-d din Firu Khilji, one of Balban's favorite slaves and governor of Samana, was pulled to the royal palace by Mu'izzu-d din to administer the government. Before long, the young sultan was struck by a mysterious paralyzing illness and Jalalu-d din presided over the enthronement of the boy's infant son as the next sultan, took the job of regent, and then with the help of his sons, kidnapped the baby. In 1289 he declared himself sultan in the child's place, bringing an end to the mamluk dynasty of Balban and inaugurating a new dynasty, that of the Khilji.**

STUDY AND TEACHING GUIDE FOR THE HISTORY OF THE RENAISSANCE WORLD

2. Why did Jalalu-d din Firu Khilji rule from Kilu-ghari instead of from Delhi?

A2.—Pg. 404, ¶ 4—Jalalu-d din Firu Khilji was Turkish by descent, but the Khilji had been Indianized over several generations, and the Turks of Delhi at first resisted his rule. He was forced to establish his headquarters at Kilu-ghari, a few miles from Delhi, and for the first two years did not even try to enter the capital city. Instead, he governed from Kilu-ghari, distributed alms, recruited a sizable army, and then finally sent his sons ahead of him to clear opposition out of Delhi before his arrival.

3. How did Jalalu-d din Firu Khilji deal with threats against him?

A3.—Pg. 404, ¶ 5—Jalalu-d din Firu Khilji dealt with threats in different ways, depending on whether or not he deemed the threat real. For example, when a treasonous plot was uncovered in his palace, he burned the traitors alive and had their leader crushed by an elephant. But when he received reports that a group of drunken nobles had spoken about killing him, he did nothing and simply remarked, "Men often drink too much, and then say foolish things. Don't report drunken stories to me."

4. Explain how Jalalu-d din Firu Khilji's reign came to an end.

A4.—Pg. 404, ¶ 7 to Pg. 405, ¶ 2—Jalalu-d din Firu Khilji gave his chief general and nephew, 'Ala'-ud-Din, the governorship of Kara and had allowed him to keep a good part of the booty and treasure from various raids down into the Hindu kingdoms of the Deccan, the dry lands south of the Narmada river, which 'Ala'-ud-din used to raise and equip an army of his own. Though Jalalu-d din Firu Khilji was warned that 'Ala'-ud-Din was planning a coup, Jalalu-d din Firu Khilji refused to listen. As his nephew arrived back from a raid carried out against the rich southern city of Devagiri, 'Ala'-ud-Din knelt down in front of Firu to pay homage which was a signal to 'Ala'-ud-Din's men to attack: the sultan was beheaded and his men were cut down as well.

5. What gave the Chagatai an advantage in their battle for Khurasan? What were they able to do once they took hold of Khurasan?

A5.—Pg. 406, ¶ 1-3—The Chagatai took advantage of the internal struggle for the Il-khanate throne after Hulagu's death right before Ghazan's khanship began. Chagatai soldiers were finally about to drive the Il-khanates out of Khurasan. Once the Chagatai had a hold of the city, Duwa could plan a conquest of Indian lands from the capital city.

6. Why did 'Ala'-ud-Din go against his councillors's advice to prepare for Delhi's siege by the approaching Mongol army in 1299? What was the result of the battle that followed?

A6.—Pg. 407, ¶ 3-5—As the Mongol army approached Delhi, 'Ala'-ud-Din's councillors advised him to prepare for siege, but 'Ala'-ud-Din ignored their advice because Delhi was not prepared for war: the old fortifications had not been kept in repair. 'Ala'-ud-Din led his army outside of Delhi and the battle lines between the two massive armies stretched on for miles. His own troops, equipped with hundreds of elephants, broke the Mongol line and after nearly a full day of fighting, the Mongols began to retreat.

7. How did 'Ala'-ud-Din want to commemorate his triumph over the Mongols?

A7.—Pg. 407, ¶ 6—'Ala'-ud-Din wanted to commemorate his triumph over the Mongols by starting a new religion. He told his courtiers "My sword . . . will bring all men to adopt it. Through this religion, my name and that of my friends will remain among men to the last day, like the names of the Prophet and his friends." He also named himself "The Second Alexander" and had that title embossed on his coins.

Section III: Critical Thinking

The student may not use her text to answer this question.

As soon as Balban died and his court officials chose not his dead son's younger child to be sultan but rather Mu'izzu-d din, Delhi fell apart. There was no confidence in the stability of the kingdom, chiefs and nobles quarreled with each other, men were killed for no reason other than suspicion and doubt—the security of life in Delhi was lost. One man could tear a kingdom apart, and one man could put it back together. Write a paragraph explaining how 'Ala'-ud-Din was the latter kind of man, turning Delhi into one of the most efficient, tightly controlled, and aggressive empires in the world.

'Ala'-ud-Din started his reign by rewarding his friends and hurting his enemies, making sure those in his court were loyal to him. He distributed offices and gold to all his supporters: the gifts, and the honors, earned him security. Those around him quickly forgot that he killed his own uncle, put his head on a spear, and paraded it around Delhi. He also ordered his cousin, Jalalu-d din Firu Khilji's oldest son, blinded to disqualify him from ever laying claim to the throne.

'Ala'-ud-Din then showed the world that Delhi could win at war. In the second year of his reign, 'Ala'-uh-Din defeated the Mongol invasion in the north of India. At Jalandhar, the Delhi army won an easy victory over the Mongols: "Many were slain or taken prisoners and many heads were sent to Delhi." The victory strengthened 'Ala'-ud-Din's authority.

As the Mongols prepared for a bigger attack on India, 'Ala'-ud-Din realized his capital city was not prepared for war. He decided to meet the Mongols in 1299 outside of the city, and his great army, filled with elephants and fierce warriors, defeated the invading force. On his return to Delhi, 'Ala'-ud-Din announced his intention of founding a new religion; he named himself "The Second Alexander," had this title embossed on his coins, and announced his intentions to go out like Alexander the Great and conquer the known world.

'Ala'-ud-Din realized, after the Mongol invasions, that he had to prepare his city for attack. He also realized that if he wanted to conquer the rest of the world, he'd have to have an efficient kingdom behind him in order to do it. As a result, he created a huge standing army with a standing cavalry of 475,000 horsemen. He made sure the army was always ready to fight by paying regular salaries to his soldiers so that they could live comfortably. 'Ala'-ud-Din made sure these wages were adequate by introducing fixed prices into the markets of Delhi, setting state-controlled limits on the costs of grain, fruit, sugar, oil, even shoes and coats. Merchants who were caught price gouging were arrested; if convicted, they were punished with the removal of flesh equal to the weight of the falsely priced goods sold. To funnel money towards defense, 'Ala'-ud-Din also restricted the ability of his noblemen to

live luxuriously. Anyone who wanted to throw a huge party or indulge in a major purchase had to get permission from the Market Controller, a new office introduced into Delhi's government by the sultan.

Once a system to pay for the army was created, 'Ala'-ud-Din secured Delhi by repairing all of the frontier forts, garrisoning them with well-trained regiments, and branding the military's horses to prevent theft or unauthorized sale. He also put into place an espionage system to warn him of Mongol movements and unprepared fortress commanders, of discontented soldiers and possible revolt. By the century's turn, 'Ala'-ud-Din turned the sultanate of Delhi into one of the most efficient, tightly controlled, and aggressive empires in the world. He was ready to beat the Mongols should they strike again, and he was ready to take over the rest of the world.

EXAMPLE ANSWER:

'Ala'-ud-Din was an aggressive ruler with a clear vision for Delhi. He killed his uncle to take the throne, and then rewarded his friends and hurt his enemies in order to make sure those in his court were loyal to him. He protected his kingdom from invasion by the Mongols in 1296, and again in 1299, spurring him to found a new religion and call himself "The Second Alexander," with the intention to conquer the known world. He created a standing army with a standing cavalry of 475,000 horsemen that he paid regular salaries to so they could live in comfort when not fighting. 'Ala'-ud-Din made sure these wages were adequate by introducing fixed prices into the markets of Delhi, setting state-controlled limits on the costs of most goods. Merchants who were caught price gouging were arrested; if convicted, they were punished with the removal of flesh equal to the weight of the falsely priced goods sold. To funnel money towards defense, 'Ala'-ud-Din also restricted the ability of his noblemen to live luxuriously. Anyone who wanted to throw a huge party or indulge in a major purchase had to get permission from the Market Controller, a new office introduced into Delhi's government by the sultan. Once a system to pay for the army was created, 'Ala'-ud-Din secured Delhi by repairing all of the frontier forts, garrisoning them with well-trained regiments, and branding the military's horses to prevent theft or unauthorized sale. He also put into place an espionage system to warn him of Mongol movements and unprepared fortress commanders, of discontented soldiers and possible revolt. By the century's turn, 'Ala'-ud-Din turned the sultanate of Delhi into one of the most efficient, tightly controlled, and aggressive empires in the world. He was ready to beat the Mongols should they strike again, and he was ready to take over the rest of the world.

Chapter Fifty-Nine

The End of the Papal Monarchy

The student may use his text when answering the questions in sections I and II.

Section I: Who, What, Where

Write a one or two-sentence answer explaining the significance of each item listed below.

Albert of Hapsburg—**Pg. 410, ¶ 3 and Pg. 414, ¶ 4—Albert of Hapsburg was Rudolf of Hapsburg's son and his successor as king of Germany. Albert of Hapsburg was assassinated in 1308.**

Babylonian Captivity—**Pg. 413, ¶ 5—Babylonian Captivity was the term given to the time the pope was in residence in Avignon, starting with the term of Clement V on June 5, 1305. For seventy years the papacy remained out of Rome and under French control.**

Benedict XI—**Pg. 413, ¶ 3—Benedict XI was Boniface VIII's successor as pope. He ruled for only a few months before dying.**

Boniface VIII—**Pg. 410, ¶ 1, Pg. 411, ¶ 2 and Pg. 413, ¶ 2—Boniface VIII's mission as pope was to restore the power of the papal monarch, but there was no Holy Roman Emperor to support his cause, so he had to negotiate with all of the complicated and opposing powers that surrounded him. Boniface VIII fought most notably with Philip IV; the stress caused by the French king's excommunication led to Boniface VIII's death at the age of sixty-eight.**

Charles of Valois—**Pg. 411, ¶ 3-5—Charles of Valois, Philip IV's younger brother, was brought into Italy by Boniface VIII to help settle the fight in the Guelph family, between the branch of the Cancellieri called the Bianchi and another branch called the Neri. Charles mismanaged the Florentine purge of the Bianchi, which rapidly became much bloodier than the pope had intended, and as a result of the mess and running out of money, Charles of Valois was forced to return to France.**

Clement V—**Pg. 413, ¶ 4 & 5—Clement V was the papal name of Bertrand, the French archbishop of Bordeaux and Philip IV's first choice for Benedict XI's successor. After being made pope on June 5, 1305, Clement V revoked the French king's excommunication and** promised him a tithe of all the Church's income, making him, for all intents and purposes, Philip IV's lapdog.

Dante Alighieri—**Pg. 411, ¶ 4—Dante Alighieri, the great Florentine poet, was a White loyalist in Italy at the time of Charles of Valois's raids, and as a result he lost his house, his possessions, and was forced to flee from the city. The rest of his life was spent in exile, which accounts for his sour assessment of Charles of Valois in the *Divine Comedy* ("Not land, but sin and infamy, / Shall [he] gain").**

Henry VII—**Pg. 414, ¶ 4 & 5 and Pg. 416, ¶ 1-3—Henry VII was the royal name of Henry of Luxembourg, chosen by the German electors to become king of Germany in 1308; he also wanted to be the Holy Roman Emperor so in 1310 he went to Italy to be crowned by a cardinal sent by Pope Clement V. After fighting against those who did not want another emperor, Henry VII was crowned in the church of St. John Lateran, just outside of Rome, on June 29, 1312 but he wasn't Holy Roman Emperor for long: he died on August 24, 1313 from malarial fever.**

Ghibelline—**Pg. 410, ¶ 5—Ghibelline, an Italian political party that rivalled the Guelphs, had started out in the twelfth century, as the support team for Conrad of Hohenstaufen as candidate for the Holy Roman Emperorship. The Hohenstaufens had successfully snagged the title, meaning that the family's Ghibelline loyalists in Italy were ardent supporters of the empire's power over the perpetually rebellious Lombard lands.**

Guelph—**Pg. 410, ¶ 5 and Pg. 411, ¶ 3—Guelph, an Italian political party that rivalled the Ghibellines, had started out in the twelfth century, as the support team for Henry the Lion as candidate for the Holy Roman Emperorship. By turn of the 14th century the Guelphs were embroiled in an internal fight between the Bianchi (the "White Guelphs") and the Neri (the "Black Guelphs").**

Guillaume de Nogaret—**Pg. 412, ¶ 5 to Pg. 413, ¶ 2—Guillaume de Nogaret, Philip IV's Keeper of the Seal, was sent to Anagni on September 7, 1303 to kidnap the pope just after he excommunicated the French king and just before he issued a bull of deposition that would remove Philip IV from the French throne. Guillaume de Nogaret's actions were for naught because three days after his kidnapping, the pope was rescued by friends and taken to the Vatican, where he died a month later.**

Jacques de Molay—**Pg. 414, ¶ 1 & 2—Jacques de Molay, sixty-year-old Grand Master of the Knights Templar, confessed that when he had joined the Templars he had been required to spit on a cross and deny the divinity of Christ, but only after he was imprisoned, starved, and threatened with torture. Though he recanted the confession, his statement was used to convince other Templars to confess to a whole range of blasphemous and idol-worshipping rituals that led to the burning at the stake of fifty-four Templars, including Jacques de Molay.**

Philip V—**Pg. 417, ¶ 1-3—Philip V, brother of Louis, was made the king's son's regent after his brother's death, but when the baby died Philip V made a play for the French throne himself.**

Philip V stopped Joan of Navarre from inheriting the throne by invoking Salic Law and then he managed to get himself crowned on January 9, 1317.

Princess Joan of Navarre—**Pg. 417, ¶ 2 & 3—Princess Joan of Navarre, Louis X's daughter, was stopped from becoming queen of France by Philip. He argued that Salic Law barred women from inheriting the throne, and because Salic Law was always considered part of French law, Princess Joan could inherit only the crown of Navarre.**

Robert—**Pg. 416, ¶ 5—Robert, son of Charles the Lame and his successor as king of southern Italy, was offered the position of Vicar of Italy by Clement V, which meant he would be vice-regent of the north, theoretically under papal authority. The position was good for Robert because it doubled the size of his kingdom but it also made him obliged to be loyal to Clement V because he owed him for the land.**

Section II: Comprehension

Write a two or three-sentence answer to each of the following questions.

1. How did Pope Innocent IV undermine the power of the pope during his rule?

A1.—Pg. 410, ¶ 2—Though Pope Innocent IV set up the idea of the papal monarchy, he had also unintentionally put an expiration date on the power of Saint Peter's heir. He had excommunicated Frederick II, authorized civil war in the Holy Roman Empire, and helped to split Germany, Sicily, and Italy apart. In doing so, he had deprived the papacy of its strongest potential ally, a Holy Roman Emperor with the power to protect the Church's interest across all three lands.

2. Why were the Ghibelline and Guelph parties still fighting a hundred years after their formation?

A2.—Pg. 410, ¶ 6 to Pg. 411, ¶ 1—Like any political party that survives for more than a century and a half, the Guelphs and the Ghibellines had taken on a culture and life of their own, divorced from their original purpose. A hundred years after their formation, the Ghibelline and Guelph parties had lost most of their pro- and anti-empire leanings but they were still fighting because members of each struggled for control of Italian cities north of the Papal States. By this point, those struggles had lost any identification with the fate of the empire: they were struggles for control over ports, trading privileges, and tax breaks.

3. Why did Charles of Valois agree to help Pope Boniface VIII with the messy political situation in Italy? What was the result of his involvement?

A3.—Pg. 411, ¶ 4 & 5—Charles of Valois got involved in the messy political situation in Italy because he hoped to become Holy Roman Emperor. Charles of Valois negotiated an alliance with the Neri, the Black Guelphs, and in November of 1301, with papal approval, he led his soldiers, along with the Neri, on a feud-ending attack on the White Guelphs and Ghibelline in Florence. Six days of sacking and burning, looting of shops, and the murder of White partisans followed, and though he did the pope's bidding, Charles of Valois was forced to return to France having run out of money.

4. Explain why Philip IV was on bad terms with Pope Boniface VIII, what the pope did about it, and how Philip IV responded.

A4.—Pg. 411, ¶ 6 to Pg. 412, ¶ 1—Philip IV was on bad terms with Pope Boniface VIII because he imposed taxes on the French church in order to help pay for his ongoing wars and he also insisted on his right to try clergymen in royal courts and to control the appointments of French priests to empty cathedral posts. In December of 1301, Pope Boniface VIII sent the king a papal letter reasserting the arguments of his powerful forerunners, telling Philip IV that the pope was his superior, that his predecessors had deposed three kings of France in the past, and that he would do the same should Philip IV continue to be uncooperative. After Philip IV read the letter, he responded by setting it on fire.

5. How did Philip IV guard himself from the public backlash that would follow excommunication by Pope Boniface VIII?

A5.—Pg. 412, ¶ 2—To guard himself from the public backlash that would follow excommunication by Pope Boniface VIII, Philip IV summoned to Paris the two most powerful bodies of men in the country: the dukes who ruled the great counties of France, and the leading French churchmen. To these he added, for the first time, a third group: the "deputies of the good towns," the mayors, prominent citizens, and wealthy merchants of the largest cities. During the month of April, 1302, all three assemblies agreed with Philip IV; Boniface was in the wrong, and Philip's defiance was entirely justified.

6. What happened on July 11, 1302 when a large French army commanded by the distinguished Robert of Artois faced down a force of Flemish foot soldiers?

A6.—Pg. 412, ¶ 3—The French army was horribly defeated by the Flemish foot soldiers that fought on July 11, 1302. The battlefield, crisscrossed with ditches dug by the Flemish, tripped up the French cavalry; the horses became entangled, falling into the water-filled trenches and throwing their riders, and the Flemish infantry systematically advanced through them, finishing off both men and horses. The Flemish commander Guy de Namur ordered that everything with spurs on be killed and within three hours, an entire army of elite French knights, including Robert of Artois, had been slaughtered.

7. Why did Philip IV exile the Jews from France in 1306?

A7.—Pg. 413, ¶ 6— Philip IV exiled all the Jews from France in 1306 so that he could confiscate their property. This was just one way he paid off his war debts.

8. Why was Henry VII crowned Holy Roman Emperor outside of Rome?

A8.—Pg. 415, ¶ 1 to Pg. 416, ¶ 1—As Henry VII crossed into Italy in 1310 on his way to be crowned Holy Roman Emperor, he was welcomed by the Ghibellines who joined him in war against the Guelphs, who turned the Florentines, the Bolognese, the Lucchese, the Sienese, the Pistoians, the people of Volterra, and all the other Guelf cities against the Emperor. Henry VII fought through the summer and by September of 1311, Brescia surrendered, Genoa agreed to a twenty-year oath of loyalty, and Pisa, historically pro-emperor, declared itself on his side, offered him six hundred bowmen, and provided him with transport down the coast to Rome on thirty Pisan ships. When Henry VII arrived in Rome to be crowned, the

gates were shut against him by the Romans so he was forced to go to the church of St. John Lateran, beyond the city's limits, for his coronation.

9. Describe the deaths, birth, and invocation of obscure law that led to Philip V's coronation as king of France.

A9.—Pg. 416, ❡ 7 to Pg. 417, ❡ 3—After Philip IV died from a fall that happened during a boar hunting accident, his son Louis of Navarre became king of France in 1305. He ruled as king of France and Navarre for only eighteen months before dying unexpectedly at the age of twenty-seven and his unborn son was named king, with his younger brother Philip to serve as his regent; unfortunately, the baby only lived for six days. The relatives of Prince Joan of Navarre argued that she should inherit the throne as the direct descendent of the oldest son, but Philip stopped her from becoming queen by invoking Salic Law, which he said barred women from inheriting the crown, and he managed to get himself crowned Philip V on January 9, 1317.

Section III: Critical Thinking

The student may not use his text to answer this question.

The Knights Templar was a highly respected religious order of knights that protected Christianity. Why would Philip IV want to tear them apart? Write a paragraph explaining what happened between the Knights Templar and Philip IV in the early 14th century. Make sure to include what Philip IV got out of ruining the order in your answer.

The breakdown of what happened between the Knights Templar and Philip IV is presented on pages 413 and 414. Philip IV convinced Clement V to remove his protection over the Knights Templar. As soon as he did, Philip IV issued a letter ordering the arrest of the Templars throughout France, on charges that the Templars indulged in all sorts of secret and occultish acts of demon worship. Philip IV wanted them treated as heretics. He wrote to the chief inquisitor of Paris that "You will hold them captive to appear before an ecclesiastical court. . . . [Y]ou will seize their movable and immovable goods and hold the seizures under strict supervision in our name." Their "movable and immovable goods" included a vast amount of treasure, held in the Templar fortress right outside the walls of Paris. The inquisitor duly sent out his agents, and all through France the Templars were suddenly arrested and imprisoned.

Through imprisonment, starvation and the threat of torture, Grand Master Jacques de Molay was forced to confess to heresy. He said that when he had joined the Templars forty-two years earlier, he had been required to spit on a cross and deny the divinity of Christ; which he had done, but "not with his heart." Though he recanted, the interrogators used his confession to convince other Templars to confess to a whole range of blasphemous and idol-worshipping rituals, including black magic and ritual acts of sodomy. In 1310, Philip IV ordered fifty-four Templars burned at the stake outside the walls of Paris. On March 24, 1312, Clement V officially abolished the Templars, and in 1314, the elderly Grand Master was removed from his prison cell and burned to death on a tiny island in the middle of the Seine.

Philip IV wanted the Templars's money and treasures. He had already denied Pope Boniface VIII the taxes demanded by the Church, which led to his excommunication until the appointment of Clement V. Philip IV already kicked the Jews out of France so he could confiscate their goods and property for himself. Philip IV destroyed the Knights Templar so he could have their money.

EXAMPLE ANSWER:

Philip IV was a greedy king, and he accused the Knights Templar of heresy in order to take their wealth for himself. Philip IV convinced Clement V to remove his protection over the Knights Templar. As soon as he did, Philip IV issued a letter ordering the arrest of the Templars throughout France, on charges that the Templars indulged in all sorts of secret and occultish acts of demon worship. He was able to get the Grand Master Jacques de Molay to confess to spiting on the cross and denying the divinity of Christ by imprisoning him, starving him, and threatening him with torture. Philip IV's interrogators were then able to use Molay's confession to get other Templars to confess to a whole range of blasphemous and idol-worshipping rituals, including black magic and ritual acts of sodomy. In 1310, Philip IV ordered fifty-four Templars burned at the stake outside the walls of Paris. On March 24, 1312, Clement V officially abolished the Templars, and in 1314, the elderly Grand Master was removed from his prison cell and burned to death on a tiny island in the middle of the Seine. Once the Templars were destroyed, Philip IV was able to take the vast amount of treasure hidden in the Templar fortress outside of France for himself. After denying Pope Boniface VIII the taxes demanded by the Church, and kicking the Jews out of France so he could confiscate their goods and property for himself, it shouldn't have been surprising that Philip IV would go after the Knights Templar and their booty.

Section IV: Map Exercise

1. Trace the rectangular outline of Map 59.1 in black.

2. Trace the coastal outline above France and Germany and through the Mediterranean. Include Sicily, but you do not need to include other islands. Also trace the line of the Seine. Repeat until the contours are familiar.

3. Using your black pencil, trace the different regions of France, Germany, Lombardy, the Papal States, the Kingdom of Naples, and Sicily. Trace the mountains with small peaks. Repeat until the contours are familiar.

4. Using a new sheet of paper, trace the rectangular outline of the frame for Map 59.1. Using your regular pencil, draw the coastline above France and Germany and through the Mediterranean, including Sicily. Then draw lines showing the regions of France, Germany, Lombardy, the Papal States, the Kingdom of Naples, and Sicily. Show the mountains with small peaks. When you are happy with your map, lay it over the original. Correct any lines which are more than ½″ off of the original.

5. Study closely the locations of Uzeste, Avignon, Bordeaux, Lyons, Paris, Courtrai, Brescia, Genoa, Lucca, Pisa, Volterra, Siena, Florence, Pistoia, Bologna, Venice, Rome, Anagni, and Naples. When you are familiar with them, close the book. Mark each one on your map. Then place your map over the original, and erase and re-mark any locations that more than ½″ off of the original.

6. Now study the regions of Gascony, Flanders, Bavarian, Austria, and the site of Fontainebleau. When you have learned them, close the book, mark each one, check your marks, and make any needed corrections.

Chapter Sixty

The Appearance of the Ottomans

The student may use her text when answering the questions in sections I and II.

Section I: Who, What, Where

Write a one or two-sentence answer explaining the significance of each item listed below.

Andronicus III—**Pg. 422, ¶ 4-8 and Pg. 423, ¶ 4—Andronicus III, son of Michael IX and co-emperor to his grandfather Andronicus II, declared war on his grandfather after he was kicked off the throne for having his mistress's lover (also his half-brother) Manuel killed. Andronicus III launched a successful coup against his grandfather and became emperor himself at thirty-one; he spent his reign fighting against the Turks and died just shy of his forty-fifth birthday in 1341 from a high fever.**

Catalan Company—**Pg. 420, ¶ 4 and Pg. 421, ¶ 4—Catalan Company was a group of mercenary soldiers brought together by Roger de Flor from Aragon proper and from the Aragonese-controlled countship known as Catalonia, on the eastern Spanish coast. The soldiers of the Catalan Company were at first hired by Andronicus II to fight against the Turks and then they were massacred by the Byzantine army after Roger de Flor led them in a raid into Byzantine territory.**

Empress Anne—**Pg. 423, ¶ 6 and Pg. 425, ¶ 3—Empress Anne, mother of John V, with the help of the Patriarch of Constantinople, paid off, promised, and flattered a critical mass of officials to declare her regent for her son in place of Cantacuzenus. Empress Anne had Cantacuzenus declared an enemy of the empire but he won out; after running out of money Anne had to negotiate with Cantacuzenus and he became co-emperor to John V.**

John Cantacuzenus—**Pg. 423, ¶ 1, & 5-7 and Pg. 425, ¶ 3—John Cantacuzenus, Andronicus III's longtime friend and chief official (*megas domestikos*), became the regent for John V after Andronicus III's death but was stripped of his duties and declared an enemy of Constantinople by Empress Anne and the Patriarch of Constantinople, prompting him to declare war on Constantinople to re-claim not just the regency but to take the crown of** co-emperor for himself. After making an alliance with Orhan of the Ottoman Turks, John Cantacuzenus marched into Constantinople and was crowned John VI, co-emperor of John V.

John V—Pg. 423, ¶ 4—John V was son and heir to Andronicus III. After a civil war started over who would rule with John V, John Cantacuzenus came out as John IV, John V's co-emperor.

Manuel—Pg. 422, ¶ 4 & 5—Manuel, Andronicus III's half-brother, was suspected by Andronicus III of sleeping with his mistress. Andronicus III hired hit men to stalk his mistress and to kill the man with whom she was having the affair; it was Manuel, and he died in the dark, on the streets of Constantinople.

Michael IX—Pg. 420, ¶ 2 and Pg. 422, ¶ 2 & 3—Michael IX, son of and co-emperor to Andronicus II, was sent into Asia Minor with a huge army after Osman drove back a Byzantine army at Baphaeum, but found himself so outnumbered that he retreated without giving battle. Michael IX was never able to beat the Catalan Company and after their retreat in 1315 he suffered from some progressive and undefined illness, possibly aggravated by depression, leading to his death in 1320.

Oljeitu—Pg. 421, ¶ 2—Oljeitu, brother of Ghazan and successor to his Il-khanate throne, agreed to a marriage alliance with Andronicus II, marrying one of his daughters in exchange for troops to fight against Osman.

Orhan—Pg. 422, ¶ 7 and Pg. 425, ¶ 2—Orhan, son of Osman, fought a steady and successful campaign towards Byzantium. He was then offered a powerful political position: John Cantacuzenus offered a marriage alliance with one of his own daughters should Orhan help him retake Constantinople; this would make the Ottoman chief son-in-law of the emperor.

Osman—Pg. 419, ¶ 4, Pg. 420, ¶ 1 and Pg. 422, ¶ 7—Osman, Turkish chief of a small tribe from Sogut, embarked on a conquest spree in 1290, ransacking the nearby countryside, conquering Eskenderum, occupying Pergamum and intruding into Phrygia, all with the goal of taking Constantinople for himself. Osman extended his kingdom as far as Ephesus and then held his ground against the Byzantine army until his death in 1327.

Roger de Flor—Pg. 420, ¶ 4 & 5 and Pg. 421, ¶ 1—Roger de Flor, a onetime Knight Templar who been thrown out of the order by Grand Master Jacques de Molay for piracy, had assembled around him a mercenary crew called the Catalan Company. After turning against Byzantium and raiding the lands of his employer, Roger de Flor was murdered in April 1305 by assassins hired by Andronicus II.

Stefan Dushan—Pg. 424, ¶ 2-4—Stefan Dushan, the great-great-great-grandson of Stefan Nemanja, the Serbian Grand Prince who had managed to free his country from Constantinople's control, had been crowned in 1331 and started an attack on Byzantium. Stefan Dushan had himself crowned Emperor of the Romans and Czar of the Serbs by the Doge of Venice, after which he planned to take Constantinople.

Section II: **Comprehension**

Write a two or three-sentence answer to each of the following questions.

1. Who ruled over the Turkish sultanate of Rum? Why wasn't Ghazan bothered by the Turkish agitation in Asia Minor?

A1.—Pg. 419, ¶ 2-4 and Pg. 420, ¶ 1—The Turkish sultanate of Rum was ruled over not by a sultan—he was only a figurehead—but by Il-khanate viziers. There were challengers to the Il-khanate overlords, but Ghazan, the Il-khanate ruler, was not worried about the unrest because the agitation in Asia Minor was nothing new. The Turks of Asia Minor had been running rampant for decades, laying waste the lands between the coast of the Black Sea and the southern island of Rhodes, and the Mongol khans ignored the Turks, as long as they stayed where they were supposed to.

2. What happened that put Andronicus II on edge when the Catalan Company showed up to help the Byzantine army in September of 1302?

A2.—Pg. 420, ¶ 5—When Roger de Flor showed up in September of 1302 to help Andronicus II (on a fleet of Genoese-built ships that he did not pay for), he had already led his eight thousand paid soldiers on a sack of the Venetian island of Ceos (not part of the deal he made with Andronicus II). Though the Catalan Company began to engage Osman's troops and did the Turks significant harm, Roger de Flor also showed himself completely willing to rob any Christian settlements in his way. This made Andronicus II very worried, especially when when Roger de Flor demanded more money and, not getting it, started to raid Byzantine territory.

3. How did Andronicus II plan to stop Roger do Flor and the Catalan Company from their attack on Byzantine territory? Was he successful?

A3.—Pg. 420, ¶ 6 to Pg. 421, ¶ 2—When, in the winter of 1304, the Catalan Company retreated to Gallipoli, Andronicus II hired a second set of mercenary soldiers to waylay Roger de Flor on a planned visit to Prince Michael IX at Adrianople and murder him. The plot, carried out in April 1305, succeeded: the assassins killed Roger de Flor and all the men that were with him, and at the same time Byzantine soldiers laid siege to the remaining Catalan Company at Gallipoli. Andronicus II's plan was partly successful; Roger de Flor was dead, but the Catalan Company fought back, which meant that Andronicus II's army was now spread thin fighting two wars, one against Osman and another against the Catalan Company.

4. How did Andronicus III become emperor of Byzantium? What happened to Andronicus II?

A4.—Pg. 422, ¶ 4, 8, & 9—After being kicked off his co-emperor throne for murdering his half-brother, Andronicus III had been carrying on a constant propaganda campaign from Thrace, promising lower taxes and faster action against the Turks, and the people of Byzantium—overtaxed to pay for all of the ongoing fighting—were inclined to think that the time had come for a change in leadership. On the evening of May 23, 1328, supporters inside Constantinople opened the gates for Andronicus III and his troops. Andronicus III allowed his grandfather to abdicate and enter a monastery in safety; old Andronicus II lived there

another five years, dying peacefully at the age of seventy-four, while Andronicus III ruled as emperor of Byzantium.

5. Why was Orhan's territory called the Ottoman Empire?

A5.—Pg. 423, ¶ 1 & *— Orhan renamed his territory after his father. His subjects were actually known as "Osmanli," the "descendants of Osman," which came over into western languages as "Othmanli" or "Ottoman." Even though the words aren't the same, we say the Ottoman Empire was given its name by Orhan in memory of his father.

6. Describe Orhan's advances on the Byzantine empire and how we know the Byzantine people were in a panic about this encroaching enemy.

A6.—Pg. 423, ¶ 1-3—When Andronicus III first came face-to-face in battle with Orhan, near the Marmara straits, Andronicus III was wounded, and the Byzantine ranks broke and fled. In 1331, Orhan took Nicaea and then he advanced to Nicomedia and laid siege to it; for the next six years, the Byzantine armies fought to drive him out and by 1337 Nicomedia was forced to surrender, no longer able to resupply its defenders. The following year Turkish raids into Thrace took thousands of Greek prisoners; three hundred thousand, according to contemporary chroniclers, a wildly inflated number that revealed the panic the Byzantines felt in the face of this ongoing, apparently unstoppable, assault.

7. Why was Stefan Dushan such a threat to Byzantium?

A7.—Pg. 424, ¶ 3 & 4—Stefan Dushan successfully invaded Byzantine territory and city after city fell in front of him, until he had reached almost as far as Thessalonica. On Easter Sunday, 1346, Stefan Dushan made his intentions perfectly clear. He had already written to the Doge of Venice, whom he hoped to pacify with an alliance, claiming lordship of almost all of the *imperii Romaniae*; now he had himself coronated as Emperor of the Romans and Czar of the Serbs, with the intention of taking the throne of Constantinople, too.

8. How did John Cantacuzenus manage to retake his place of power in Constantinople?

A8.—Pg. 425, ¶ 2 & 3—John Cantacuzenus made an alliance with Orhan of the Ottoman Turks: if he helped John Cantacuzenus become co-emperor of Constantinople, then John Cantacuzenus would marry one of his daughters to the Ottoman chief, making him the son-in-law of the emperor. In 1347, with a thousand of his own men with him and the threat of a much larger Turkish force hovering behind, John Cantacuzenus marched into the city through a gate opened to him by a supporter inside. Empress Anne was broke and defenseless and the people of Constantinople were ready for a competent emperor, so Cantacuzenus had no trouble negotiating a settlement: he would rule with young John V as equal co-emperor, taking the royal name John VI, and all the intrigues, hostilities, and injuries of the previous six years would be covered under a blanket amnesty.

Section III: **Critical Thinking**

The student may not use her text to answer this question.

In this chapter we read about many different people's desire to rule Constantinople. Write a paragraph describing Osman's dream of conquering Constantinople, and explain how through his actions, and the actions of his son, his dream came closer and closer to being a reality.

Osman's dream is described on page 419: "later legends tell of a dream Osman had, of a great tree growing up to shadow the whole world; the Tigris, Euphrates, Nile, and Danube flowed from its roots; beneath its limbs were built scores of cities filled with minarets, where the faithful came to pray; the leaves of the tree were sword blades, and a wind blew against them and pointed them towards Constantinople, which lay in the distance 'like a diamond . . . the precious stone of the ring of a vast dominion which embraced the entire world.' "

The dream suggests that all of Osman's conquests over the Turkish tribes were building towards a conquest of Constantinople. Over the course of his lifetime, Osman took the countryside surrounding Sogut, he conquered the tribe of the Eskenderum to his north, occupied territory near Ephesus and Pergamum, and intruded into Phrygia. Osman drove back a Byzantine army at Baphaeum, near Nicaea, causing Andronicus II to enlist the help of the Il-khanate against the Turks. Oljeitu sent thirty thousand men against the Turks in 1308. Oljeitu claimed victory but Osman seemed unhindered. He then took Ephesus, fought down the coast, and made a pass at Rhodes. He did not advance further but kept a tight grip on the territory he had gained. He left his principality to his son Orhan.

Orhan continued his father's conquests. He expanded the Ottoman Empire to Nicaea and Nicomedia. Then Orhan was offered a great opportunity. If he helped John Cantacuzenus regain his power in Constantinople, Orhan would marry one of John Cantacuzenus's daughters, making him the son-in-law of the emperor. Osman's dream was edging closer to reality. The boundaries of the Ottoman Empire crept towards Constantinople. With the marriage alliance between Orhan and John Cantacuzenus's daughter, the Turks were now in the house of Constantinople, making Osman's dream even more possible.

EXAMPLE ANSWER:

Osman had a dream of a great tree that cast a shadow over the whole world. On the leaves of the trees were sword blades and when the wind grew the blades pointed toward the jewel of Constantinople. The dream suggests that all of Osman's conquests over the Turkish tribes were building towards a conquest of Constantinople. Over the course of his lifetime, Osman took the countryside surrounding Sogut, conquered the tribe of the Eskenderum to his north, occupied territory near Ephesus and Pergamum, and intruded into Phrygia. Osman drove back a Byzantine army at Baphaeum, near Nicaea, causing Andronicus II to enlist the help of the Il-khanate against the Turks. Oljeitu sent thirty thousand men against the Turks in 1308. Oljeitu claimed victory but Osman then took Ephesus, fought down the coast, and made a pass at Rhodes. He did not advance further but kept a tight grip on the territory he had gained. Orhan, Osman's son, continued his father's conquests. He expanded the Ottoman Empire to Nicaea and Nicomedia. Then Orhan was offered a great opportunity. If he helped John Cantacuzenus regain his power in Constantinople, Orhan would marry one of John Cantacuzenus's daughters, making him the son-in-law of the emperor. Osman's

dream was edging closer to reality. The boundaries of the Ottoman Empire crept towards Constantinople. With the marriage alliance between Orhan and John Cantacuzenus's daughter, the Turks were now in the house of Constantinople, making Osman's dream even more possible.

Chapter Sixty-One

The Fall of the Khilji

The student may use his text when answering the questions in sections I and II.

Section I: **Who, What, Where**

Write a one or two-sentence answer explaining the significance of each item listed below.

Ghazi Malik Tughluq/ Sultan Ghiyas-ud-Din—**Pg. 431, ❡ 2 & 3—Ghazi Malik Tughluq, governor of one of the outlying areas in the Punjab, rallied an opposition party against Khusru Khan, which led to the sultan's beheading outside the walls of Delhi. After Khusru Khan's death, Ghazi Malik Tughluq was proclaimed Sultan Ghiyas-ud-Din by the Delhi governors, and in the course of one week he brought the business of Delhi into order.**

Khusru Khan—**Pg. 430, ❡ 1-4 and Pg. 431, ❡ 2—Khusru Khan, a young Hindu prisoner of war who had converted to Islam and with whom Qutb-ud-Din Mubarak Shah was obsessed, led a palace revolt against his lover, had the sultan murdered, and then had himself recognized as the new sultan. Khusru Khan was beheaded during a confrontation between the royal army and a collection of Muslim governors because he had denounced Islam once he became sultan.**

Padmini—**Pg. 428, ❡ 2-4—Padmini, wife of the Mewar shah Rana Ratan Singh, was said by the sixteenth-century poet Jayasi to have rescued her husband from 'Ala'-ud-Din by tricking the sultan into thinking she was going to trade places with her captive husband and instead ambushed his guards and stole Rana Ratan Singh away. Padmini was said to have thrown herself on her husband's funeral pyre after his death so she wouldn't have to submit to 'Ala'-ud-Din.**

Qutb-ud-Din Mubarak Shah—**Pg. 429, ❡ 4 and Pg. 430, ❡ 1-4—Qutb-ud-Din Mubarak Shah, older son of 'Ala'-ud-Din, was meant to act as regent to his younger brother, but instead he had the eyes of the six-year-old king and a third brother cut out and then he had himself proclaimed sultan. Qutb-ud-Din Mubarak Shah was murdered by his eunuch lover Khusru Khan after an incompetent but crowd-pleasing four-year rule.**

Rajput kingdoms—**Pg. 427, ❡ 1—Rajput kingdoms were the Hindu warrior clans, the "sons of kings," in India. Muslim sultan 'Ala'-ud-Din wanted to obliterate the Rajput kingdoms.**

Rana Ratan Singh—**Pg. 428, ❡ 2-4—Rana Ratan Singh, Mewar shah, was said by the sixteenth-century poet Jayasi to have been kidnapped by 'Ala'-ud-Din and then rescued by his wife, who engineered a Trojan horse attack on 'Ala'-ud-Din's men. Rana Ratan Singh died during the eight-month siege 'Ala'-ud-Din laid on Chittor.**

Section II: Comprehension

Write a two or three-sentence answer to each of the following questions.

1. Describe the conquests made in the later part of 'Ala'-ud-Din's reign.

A1.—Pg. 428, ❡ 5 to Pg. 429, ❡ 1—'Ala'-ud-Din was able to conquer more and more Hindu kingdoms in the later part of his reign. The Pandyan realm, divided by civil war between two princes, fell in 1308; the northern part of the Sri Lankan island declared its independence, and Delhi armies occupied the Pandyan capital. Other Hindu kingdoms south of the Deccan survived: the Yadava (ruling from Devagiri), the Kakatiya (centered at Warangal) and the Hoysala (with its capital at Dwarasamudra), but they too suffered from constant attacks, with thousands dying in the raids.

2. Why did 'Ala'-ud-Din build a black pavilion in the middle of Delhi?

A2.—Pg. 429, ❡ 2—'Ala'-ud-Din built a black pavilion in the middle of Delhi so it would be like the Ka'aba in the navel of the earth. The Ka'aba was Islam's most sacred shrine; at Mecca, it housed the Black Stone, a sacred rock (possibly a meteorite) oriented towards the east. 'Ala'-ud-Din's "Ka'aba" was visited by kings and princes of Arabia and Persia to prostrate themselves not just before the duplicate Ka'aba but before the sultan as well.

3. Why was Malik Kafur such a menace to the running of Delhi? How was the menace taken care of?

A3.—Pg. 429, ❡ 3-5—Before 'Ala'-ud-Din died, he made Malik Kafur commander of his army and he also made him vizier even though no one wanted him to be; this new power may have led to a plot for more power that involved blinding all of 'Ala'-ud-Din's sons. However, only the young king and the oldest son were blinded, so it is possible that Malik Kafur ran into too much opposition before he could finish the job. Malik Kafur didn't last much longer than the young king, and thirty-five days later he was assassinated, beheaded in the halls of the palace by courtiers, or possibly by army officials.

4. What did Qutb-ud-Din Mubarak Shah do during his rule as sultan?

A4.—Pg. 430, ❡ 1— While sultan, Qutb-ud-Din Mubarak Shah made every crowd-pleasing decision he could. He removed all of 'Ala'-ud-Din's price controls, he abandoned the tax code, he gave the noblemen freedom to pursue their own power-building schemes, he raised salaries, and he scattered gold lavishly around the court to buy loyalties. He also occupied himself with pleasure, wine, and overspending.

5. How did Khusru Khan become sultan?

A5.—Pg. 430, ¶ 3 & 4—Khusru Khan led an army of rebellious ex-slaves into the royal palace and placed them outside of the sultan's door while he went in to supposedly see his lover. While the rebels killed the guards, Khusru Khan attacked Qutb-ud-Din Mubarak Shah and then his conspirators came in to the room and helped him finish off the job. Qutb-ud-Din's headless, dismembered body was thrown into the courtyard, Khusru Khan and his men carried out a palace purge, murdering all of the sultan's supporters, and then, at midnight, all of the remaining officials assembled in the courtyard by torchlight and recognized Khusru Khan as the new sultan.

6. What did Khusru Khan do to lead to his beheading?

A6.—Pg. 430, ¶ 6 to Pg. 431, ¶ 2—As soon as he was secure on his new throne, Khusru Khan renounced his profession of Islam and returned to Hindu practice. Khusru began to promote Hindu officers and courtiers through the ranks, but the coherence of the Delhi sultanate was largely due to 'Ala'-ud-Din's vision of the empire as an Islamic realm, bringer of truth to the heathens, and Khusru Khan's reconversion quickly wiped out his support. Two months after Khusru's accession, Ghazi Malik Tughluq rallied an opposition party against him and Khusru was beheaded during a pitched battle outside the walls of Delhi.

Section III: Critical Thinking

The student may not use his text to answer this question.

'Ala'-ud-Din's biggest obstacle as he worked to destroy the Rajput kingdoms was Mewar. Gujarat, Malwa, and Ranthambhore fell to 'Ala'-ud-Din, but Mewar, the kingdom of the Guhlia, was harder to crack. Not only was the kingdom fierce, fighting successfully for five hundred years against Muslim invaders, but the fight was also personal: 'Ala'-ud-Din was supposedly enamored with the wife of the Mewar shah. Write a paragraph explaining the story of Rana Ratan Singh's capture, escape, and death. Then write a paragraph explaining why this story might not be true, and how the symbolic role 'Ala'-ud-Din was supposed to play in Jayasi's allegory matched his real-world actions as a conquering ruler.

The story of what happened between 'Ala'-ud-Din, Padmini, and Rana Ratan Singh is found on page 428:

> 'Ala'-ud-Din chose to attack Mewar because he hoped to kidnap Mewar's beautiful queen: Padmini, wife of the Mewar shah Rana Ratan Singh. He began the attack with deception: he visited the capital city of Chittor, ostensibly in peace, but with men hidden outside the gates. When Rana Ratan Singh courteously escorted him to the gates at the end of the visit, 'Ala'-ud-Din's men sprang out of hiding, seized the king of Mewar, and dragged him off to the sultan's camp.
>
> To save her husband, Padmini sent a message to the sultan, offering to exchange herself for her husband, as long as she could bring her beloved

maids and attendants with her. 'Ala'-ud-Din agreed; and the next day, a whole procession of curtained litters, each carried by six slaves, wended its way towards the camp. But the slaves were Rajput warriors, and the litters were so many Trojan horses, crammed with fully armed soldiers. Once inside the camp, the soldiers leapt out, slaughtered the guards around 'Ala'-ud-Din's camp, rescued their king, and fought their way back to Chittor.

We then find out that the details of this heist were most likely invented by the sixteenth-century poet Jayasi. Jayasi was working out a detailed allegory in which 'Ala'-ud-Din represents lust, Rana Ratan Singh love, and Padmini herself wisdom. According to Jayasi, when 'Ala'-ud-Din finally did conquer Chittor, Rana Ratan Singh died fighting, while Padmini sacrificed herself on his funeral pyre rather than submitting to 'Ala'-ud-Din.

There are some facts in Jayasi's allegory. 'Ala'-ud-Din did conquer Chittor after an eight-month siege. He also seems to have taken the resistance of Chittor very personally; the chronicler Amir Khusru, who was there, notes that when Chittor finally fell, the sultan ordered thirty thousand of the Hindu inhabitants massacred, which was not his style.

We don't know enough from the chapter about Padmini and Rana Ratan Singh to explain how their lives might have matched up with their allegorical roles, but we do know enough about 'Ala'-ud-Din to see how Jayasi could paint him as representing "lust." On the surface it is clear that 'Ala'-ud-Din lusted for Padmini. On a deeper level, 'Ala'-ud-Din lusted for power. In this chapter we see his desire to conquer the Rajput kingdoms, and we see 'Ala'-ud-Din succeed in taking one Hindu kingdom after the next. In Chapter Fifty-Eight we read about 'Ala'-ud-Din's desire to be a ruler as great as Alexander, and his notion to start a religion with him at the center after his defeat of the Mongols. All of these actions point towards 'Ala'-ud-Din's great lust, or desire, for power.

EXAMPLE ANSWER:

According to the the sixteenth-century poet Jayasi, Rana Ratan Singh was kidnapped by 'Ala'-ud-Din because the sultan wanted to take the shah's wife for himself. Mewar, a Rajput kingdom 'Ala'-ud-Din hoped to subdue contained a bonus: a beautiful queen named Padmini. 'Ala'-ud-Din made a peaceful visit to the capital city of Chittor but when Rana Ratan Singh courteously escorted him to the gates at the end of the visit, 'Ala'-ud-Din had his men seize the king and drag him off to the sultan's camp. To save her husband, Padmini offered to exchange herself for her him, as long as she could bring her beloved maids and attendants with her. 'Ala'-ud-Din agreed. When Padmini supposedly arrived, she came into 'Ala'-ud-Din's camp in a procession of curtained litters, each carried by six slaves. However, the slaves were Rajput warriors, and the litters were Trojan horses, crammed with fully armed soldiers. Once inside the camp, the soldiers leapt out, slaughtered the guards around 'Ala'-ud-Din's camp, rescued their king, and fought their way back to Chittor. Rana Ratan Singh did die at the hand of 'Ala'-ud-Din after the sultan laid siege to Chittor for eight months. Jayasi says that Padmini threw herself on her husband's funeral pyre instead of submitting to 'Ala'-ud-din. Whatever happened, it is true that the sultan took the city, and massacred thirty thousand Hindu inhabitants, seemingly because of a personal grudge.

The story might not be true in all of its details because Jayasi was working out a detailed allegory in which 'Ala'-ud-Din represents lust, Rana Ratan Singh love, and Padmini herself

wisdom. Whether the details are all real or not, it is clear that 'Ala'-ud-Din did lead India as a man with a lust for power. In this chapter we see his desire to conquer the Rajput kingdoms, and we see 'Ala'-ud-Din's successful takeover of Hindu kingdom after Hindu kingdom. In Chapter Fifty-Eight we read about 'Ala'-ud-Din's desire to be a ruler as great as Alexander, and his notion to start a religion with him at the center after his defeat of the Mongols. All of these actions point towards 'Ala'-ud-Din's great lust, or desire, for power.

Section IV: Map Exercise

1. Trace the rectangular outline of the map in black.

2. Trace the coastal outline around India, including the coastline of Sri Lanka. Also trace the lines of the Indus, the Ganges, and the Narmada. Repeat until the contours are familiar.

3. Using a contrasting color, trace the outline of the sultanate of Delhi. Using your black pencil, trace the mountains with small peaks. Repeat until the contours are familiar.

4. Using a new sheet of paper, trace the rectangular outline of the frame for Map 61.1. Then using your regular pencil, draw the coastline; the Indus, Ganges, and Narmada rivers; the mountain peaks; and the area of the Sultanate of Delhi. Erase and redraw as necessary. When you are happy with your map, lay it over the original. Erase and redraw any lines which are more than ¼″ off of the original.

5. Now study carefully the Pandya, Hoysala, Kakatiya, Yadava, Gujarat, Mewar, Malwa, and Chuahan areas. When you are familiar with them, close the book. Mark each area on your map, and then check it against the original. Erase and re-mark any misplaced labels.

6. Now study carefully the locations of Delhi, Chittor, Devagiri, Warangal, and Dwarasamudra. When you are familiar with them, close the book, and mark and label each location on your map. Use the frame and geographical markers as a reference point. When you are happy with your map, lay it over the original. Erase and re-mark any labels which are more than ¼″ off of the original.

7. Mark the location of Ranthambhore.

Chapter Sixty-Two

The Triumph of the Bruce

The student may use her text when answering the questions in sections I and II.

Section I: Who, What, Where

Write a one or two-sentence answer explaining the significance of each item listed below.

John Menteith—**Pg. 434, ¶ 2—John Menteith, the English-appointed governor of Dumbarton Castle, took William Wallace prisoner, most likely because of a tip given to him by Wallace's own servant, Jack Short.**

Piers Gaveston—**Pg. 435, ¶ 4 & 5 and Pg. 436, ¶ 4—Piers Gaveston, close friend of Edward II, was made Earl of Cornwall by the young king after his father's death, and when Edward II went to France to marry Isabella, daughter of Philip the Fair, Gaveston was left as regent of the kingdom in his place. Piers Gaveston made many enemies in England because he used his friendship with the king to act badly: in early 1213, Gaveston was beheaded, the result of a murder plot put together by the English barons.**

Section II: Comprehension

Write a two or three-sentence answer to each of the following questions.

1. What is the significance of Edward I naming Edward II Prince of Wales?

A1.—**Pg. 433, ¶ 2—William Wallace successfully invaded England after his victory at Stirling Bridge but the following year an English army crushed Wallace's men in the Forth valley near Falkirk, and Wallace was driven into hiding. After four more years of fighting that yielded no real advantage for either side, and no single leader of the Scottish cause coming to the fore, Edward, anticipating a victory yet to be won, awarded the title Prince of Wales to his oldest son. This was significant because Edward I expected to win, and because it was the first time an English heir apparent had claimed the title.**

2. What was the "War-wolf"? How was the "War-wolf" used to put a showy end to Scottish resistance in 1304?

A2.—Pg. 433, ¶ 4 to Pg. 434, ¶ 1—The "War-wolf" was a mammoth trebuchet commissioned by Edward I to demonstrate English strength; the "War-wolf" was still being assembled by five carpenters and fifty master craftsmen outside of Stirling Castle's walls when the Scottish tried to surrender. Edward I wanted to show his power by using the "War-wolf;" only after the "War-wolf" was assembled and deployed, battering the walls of Stirling Castle to bits, did Edward I allow the fighting to end. After the English show of strength, ending with a flourish via the "War-wolf," the Scottish made their submission and the English army returned home, leaving only a Chief Warden to rule as vice-regent in the king's place.

3. How did William Wallace meet his end?

A3.—Pg. 434, ¶ 2—Eleven months after the English "War-wolf"-ed Stirling Castle, William Wallace was taken prisoner by John Menteith most likely because of a tip given to Menteith by Jack Short, Wallace's own servant. Wallace was sent to London, where, after a trial that consisted of a recitation of his crimes without any chance for defense, he was hanged, cut down and disemboweled alive, and then beheaded as his intestines were burned in front of him. Then his body was split into four quarters to hang in four towns: his head at London, his quarters spread throughout Scotland.

4. Why did Robert Bruce the Sixth decide to turn back on his alliance with the English?

A4.—Pg. 434, ¶ 4—Robert Bruce the Sixth had become disenchanted with the English administration of Scotland because he was indignant at the cruel bondage of the kingdom and the ceaseless ill-treatment of the people. What frustrated Robert Bruce the Sixth even more was that he had spent a good deal of his own money on the English campaign but he had not been reimbursed by the crown, nor had Edward I rewarded his loyalty in any way. In March of 1306, he mounted a renewal of the Scottish rebellion, declaring himself King of the Scots and taking Edward completely by surprise.

5. What happened immediately after Robert Bruce the Sixth renewed the rebellion against England?

A5.—Pg. 434, ¶ 5 to Pg. 435, ¶ 1—Right after Robert Bruce the Sixth renewed the Scottish rebellion against England, English armies marched into Scotland and then defeated him twice in succession, the first time in June near Perth, the second time on August 11 at Dalry. Bruce's men were forced into hiding, and Bruce himself became a fugitive. Bruce wasn't captured by the English however, so while Bruce was at large, the Scots still hoped for victory.

6. Why was Piers Gaveston banished to Gascony? How did Piers Gaveston later end up as regent of England?

A6.—Pg. 435, ¶ 4 & 5—Piers Gaveston, a close childhood friend of Edward II, annoyed Edward I: the two young men had become so inseparable that the older Edward believed his son loved Gaveston too much. When the Prince of Wales demanded that Gaveston be given the title Count of Ponthieu (a Norman countship that had belonged to Edward I himself), the king flew into a fury and banished Gaveston to his ancestral lands in Gascony. After Edward

I's death, and against his dead father's wishes, Edward II invited Piers Gaveston back into England, made him the Earl of Cornwall, and when in 1308 Edward II traveled to France to celebrate his marriage to Isabella, he left Gaveston as regent of the kingdom in his absence.

7. For what reason did the English court hate Piers Gaveston? How did Edward II choose to deal with the situation?

A7.—Pg. 436, ¶ 1 & 2—Though there were rumors that Piers Gaveston and Edward II were lovers, the English barons did not hate him because of this possible sexual relationship but because of how Edward II treated him with such obvious favoritism. The barons demanded that Edward II get rid of Gaveston. The king chose to deal with the situation by sending Piers Gaveston to Ireland to act as his lieutenant there, but he also prepared for civil war because he was disturbed the the united hostility of the barons against him.

8. Describe the circumstances that led to Piers Gaveston's death, and explain what happened to his body.

A8.—Pg. 436, ¶ 2, 4 & 5—After Piers Gaveston was sent to Ireland to act as Edward II's lieutenant there, Edward II's preparation for civil war allowed him to round up enough support for Gaveston's return via gifts and promises. However, once restored to England, Gaveston acted worse than ever before, calling his enemies by insulting nicknames and using his power to grant offices and privileges to his own favorites. Fed up, the barons of England, led by the Earl of Lancaster, had Gaveston beheaded; they left him where he fell, but nearby Dominican friars gathered up the body and head, and buried them together.

9. Who were the two enemies facing Edward II just before and after Piers Gaveston's death? How did he react to them?

A9.—Pg. 436, ¶ 3 & 6—The two enemies facing Edward II were the English barons, who were against his friendship with Piers Gaveston, and Robert Bruce the Sixth, who was fighting for Scotland's independence. In the fall of 1310, Edward II marched into Scotland with an army, but Bruce and his freedom fighters evaded him and the campaign dragged on for months with Bruce gaining in strength and the English losing horses, men, and confidence. Edward II dealt with his other enemies, the barons, after Piers Gaveston's death by accepting a mediated peace; the barons protested that they had acted only to preserve the king's power, and with his good in mind.

10. What happened when Edward II decided to attack Robert Bruce the Sixth in Scotland during the summer of 1314?

A10.—Pg. 436, ¶ 7 to Pg. 437, ¶ 1—In the summer of 1314, Edward II marched into Scotland with additional reinforcements, hoping to bring the ongoing and exasperating war to an end, but the invasion failed. The English army met the Scots at Bannockburn, where the Scots— fighting almost entirely on foot—managed to draw the heavier English cavalry forward, across pits that had been dug and covered over lightly. The horses floundered in the pits; the cavalry behind panicked and retreated; Edward himself, at the rear of the army, turned and rode to safety as fast as possible.

11. How did Robert Bruce the Sixth become "King of Scotland" once again? What was Robert Bruce's first act as so-called king?

A11.—Pg. 437, ¶ 2 to Pg. 438, ¶ 1—After the English were defeated at Bannockburn, the whole land of Scotland rejoiced and Robert Bruce the Sixth, no longer a rebel, was commonly called King of Scotland. Bruce's first act as so-called king was to launch a war of conquest, sending ships to Ireland and marching over the border into northern England to raid, burn, and plunder.

Section III: **Critical Thinking**

The student may not use her text to answer this question.

In this chapter we read more about the Scottish fight for independence. William Wallace was captured and killed, but Robert Bruce the Sixth took up the fight and soldiered on. This 14th century desire for independence still burns in the 21st century. Scotland has tried to declare its independence from England as recently as 2014. Write a paragraph explaining the Scottish Independence Referendum and what happened when voters were asked "Should Scotland be an independent country"?

This critical thinking question will require research. The student should not use Wikipedia as an answer source for her question, but she may look over the article to gain general knowledge and she can use the footnotes from the Wikipedia article to find reliable sources. Some places to start would be "Scotland's Referendum," via the Scottish Government (http://www.scotreferendum.com/) and "Scottish independence referendum (Archived)" via the United Kingdom's government website (https://www.gov.uk/government/topical-events/ scottish-independence-referendum/about).

The student's paragraph should explain what the Scottish Independence Referendum is, including when it was created, who created it, and why. She should then explain the election results.

EXAMPLE ANSWER:

The Scottish Independence Referendum asked the question "Should Scotland be an independent country?" and voters had to say yes or no. According to the website "Scottish independence referendum," the "The Scottish independence referendum was a once-in-a-generation opportunity for people in Scotland to have their say about the country's future" and it happened "because the Scottish National Party, who campaign for Scotland to be independent, won a majority at the last Scottish Parliament election." An article from BBC News called "Scottish independence: What's going on in Scotland" by Andrew Black explains that when the Scottish National Party won the Scottish Parliament election by a landslide, First Minister Alex Salmond argued that the union between England and Scotland no longer worked. He said that "an independent Scotland, aided by its oil wealth, would be one of the world's richest countries," while UK Prime Minister David Cameron said "Britain is one of the world's most successful social and political unions." The referendum took place on September 18, 2014. The result was that 55.3% of voters said "no," Scotland should not be independent, while 44.7% said "yes." While there are a lot of people who think Scotland should be independent, more continue to believe that Scotland should remain part of the United Kingdom.

Chapter Sixty-Three

The Great Famine

The student may use his text when answering the questions in sections I and II.

Section I: Who, What, Where

Write a one or two-sentence answer explaining the significance of each item listed below.

Medieval Warm Period/ Medieval Climatic Anomaly—**Pg. 443, ¶ 1 & 2—The Medieval Warm Period, also known as the Medieval Climactic Anomaly, was a warm "blip" that covered the span of about five hundred years. During the Medieval Warm Period food production was abundant and as a result the population of Europe almost tripled.**

Murrains—**Pg. 445, ¶ 3—Murrains was a blanket fourteenth-century term for epidemics of foot-and-mouth disease, streptococcus, and other damp-aggravated illnesses. Murrains was a word used to describe what killed livestock as the Medieval Warm Period came to an end and erratic, wet weather replaced it.**

Section II: Comprehension

Write a two or three-sentence answer to each of the following questions.

1. How did the Medieval Warm Period affect the quality and concentration of life in Europe?

A1.—Pg. 443, ¶ 1—The Medieval Warm Period changed the planting seasons in Europe; in France, planting began in March and then summer began early in June and lasted until the early days of September. In England villages and farms spread far into the north; in the Alps, copper mines that were previously closed by ice during the Roman empire were reopened; and the ice pack in the northern oceans melted back, giving Leif Ericsson passage to the west, deluding his followers into believing that the shores of Greenland were habitable. As a result of the extended growing season, the population mushroomed: in two centuries, the English population tripled, and in France, the 6.2 million men and women that populated the country around 1100 had grown to at least 17 million by the beginning of the fourteenth century.

2. What were the first signs that the the Medieval Warm Period was coming to an end?

A2.—Pg. 443, ¶ 3 to Pg. 445, ¶ 1—The first signs that the Medieval Warm Period was coming to an end came around 1310, when the temperature started to dip lower than ever been experienced within living memory. With these dips came soaring temperature highs, violent storms, deluges, and flooding. Rain poured down in the spring, grain rotted in the field, and famine spread across Europe; cattle died and men were forced to feed on the flesh of horses and other beasts.

3. How was England and the northwest of Europe affected by rain between the years 1314 and 1316?

A3.—Pg. 445, ¶ 2 & 3—In England and the northwest of Europe, the summer of 1314 was one of the wettest in memory, but the summer of 1315 was worse, filled with downpours and flooded low-lying areas, with hay so drowned in water that it could not be mowed nor gathered, nor could it ripen because there was no sun to nourish it. The German town of Salzburg saw such flooding that the Great Flood was referenced. Things didn't get any better in 1316: sheep and goats died of foot-and-mouth, streptococcus, and other damp-aggravated illnesses; in the south of England, the harvest weighed in at half its normal bulk, the lowest yield in fifty years; in Germany, the Neustadt vineyard gave only "a trifling quantity of wine,"; the French city of Ypres lost one person in ten to famine; and in Tournai, an observer wrote that so many "perished every day . . . men and women, rich and poor, young and old . . . that the very air stank."

4. What was the significance of the comet that was visible throughout most of Europe for a good portion of 1315 and 1316?

A4.—Pg. 445, ¶ 3—Geoffrey de Meaux, royal physician to the king of France and amateur astronomer, noted that the comet's brilliance was so great that it was visible day and night. Fourteenth-century scholars were in agreement that such a brilliant comet signified a coming time of bad crops, a time when robbery and mayhem would increase, truth and justice decline, and the sea would rise to swallow many: "The whole world was troubled," wrote a German chronicler, surveying the multiple reports of disaster from the Baltic Sea to the Mediterranean coast.

5. Describe how Europeans first dealt with the Great Famine, and then what hard choices they had to make.

A5.—Pg. 447, ¶ 1—At the beginning of the Great Famine, everyone suffered, but the aristocrats, with their larger reserves, suffered less. The mass of peasants, living week to week, found themselves on the constant edge of starvation, so they survived only by using up everything tucked away for the future: seed grain, future stores, and draft animals. Then hard choices came: old people starved themselves to keep grandchildren alive and young parents were forced to choose between their children or their lives, knowing that their deaths would ultimately mean the starvation of their young ones.

6. How is the German folktale "Hansel and Gretel" related to the Great Famine?

A6.—Pg. 447, ¶ 2—The German folktale "Hansel and Gretel" was collected by the Grimm brothers in the nineteenth century from a story told about the Great Famine. The story begins with the line "There was great famine in the land," and considers what happened to the children at the time. Their parents, unable to face voluntary starvation or infanticide, led their children into the woods to abandon them where at least they would not then see the young ones die; the father thinks "Surely it would be better to share the last bite of food with one's children!" while the stepmother, perhaps clutching babies of her own, still desperately hopes to live.

7. Explain the erratic weather that hit Europe between the summer of 1317 and mid-March of 1321.

A7.—Pg. 447, ¶ 3 & 4—The summer of 1317 brought some relief to Europe because it was a littler dryer, but in August the rains returned, and between October 1317 and Easter 1318, temperatures sank to unheard-of lows: the North Sea froze and Cologne suffered from a snowstorm on June 30. By fall 1318, the weather remained unpredictable, with violent winds and thunder-storms rocking Europe through 1319. In 1321, there was a hard winter, killing nearly all the animals; the snow was everywhere and it didn't go away, with the thickest snow lasting through mid-March, to the middle of Lent.

8. How did the Great Famine affect the population of Europe?

A8.—Pg. 447, ¶ 5—The Great Famine left a tenth of Europe's men and women dead; in some places, as much as a quarter of the population died. The children who survived the famine were, for the rest of their lives, weakened by scurvy. Their teeth were poor, their growth was stunted, and their immune systems were compromised.

Section III: Critical Thinking

The student may not use his text to answer this question.

The Medieval Climatic Anomaly has been used by politicians opposed to legislation to reduce carbon dioxide emissions as proof that climate change happens independent of human action. At the same time, those who say humans do affect the temperature of the earth have downplayed the warming period or deny that it happened at all in order to lay all the blame of climate change on people. Find one example of each side of the argument using the Medieval Climatic Anomaly as proof of their own stance on climate change. Write a paragraph that explains your findings. As always, make sure to cite your sources.

The student may use the internet to research this question. If a student is not using the internet, he could work with a local librarian to search newspapers and magazines for stories related to contemporary mentions of the Medieval Climatic Anomaly.

A search using the words "Medieval Climatic Anomaly as proof climate change not caused by humans" yields pages of results from reputable sources. Similarly, a search for "Medieval Climatic Anomaly not real" also brings up pages of results. The student should use sources that come from verifiable organizations or credited news outlets rather than personal blogs or websites. The example answer uses Chicago-style footnotes for citations.

EXAMPLE ANSWER:

Michael Mann, Distinguished Professor of Meteorology at Penn State, writes in an article for livescience.com that climate change deniers must stop distorting the evidence and admit that climate change is caused by humans.[1] Mann does not deny the Medieval Warm Period, but he does say it cannot justify the earth's temperatures warming independent of humanity. He explains that while during the Medieval Climatic Anomaly there were areas of the world that reached temperatures as warm as those reached in the late twentieth century, the average temperature of the whole earth was much cooler than it is today. Mann uses an article by David Rose for Britain's *Daily Mail* as an example of how the Medieval Climatic Anomaly is misused by climate change deniers. David Rose's article is titled "World's top climate scientists confess: Global warming is just a QUARTER what we thought—and computers got the effects of greenhouse gases wrong."[2] Rose uses the Medieval Climatic Anomaly to question the veracity of the Intergovernmental Panel on Climate Change's assertion that the world is warmer than it ever has been. Rose argues that the world's temperatures fluctuate regardless of the production of greenhouse gases.

Section IV: Map Exercise

1. Trace the rectangular outline of Map 63.1 in black.

2. Using your blue pencil, trace the outline of the coast. Take your time, since there is a significant amount of coast on this map. Trace the coast of Greenland, Iceland, and all around Britain and the continent through the Mediterranean. You do not need to include all the small islands around Scotland and the Baltic Sea. Repeat until the contours are familiar.

3. Now using a new sheet of paper, trace the rectangular outline of the frame in black. Using your regular pencil, draw the coastline as you traced it before: around Greenland and Iceland around the continent and through the Mediterranean. As before, you need not include small islands around the Baltic Sea and Scotland. When you are happy with your map, lay it over the original. Erase and redraw any lines which are more than ½" off of the original.

4. Now study carefully the areas of Greenland, Iceland, Scotland, Germany, and France. Study carefully also the more local areas of the Pennine Moors, Dartmoor, Northumberland, Flanders. Also be sure you know the North Sea, the Baltic Sea, and the Mediterranean Sea. When they are familiar for you, close the book, and mark each. Then compare your map to the original, and make any needed corrections.

---

1. Michael Mann, "Climate-Change Deniers Must Stop Distorting the Evidence (Op-Ed)," *livescience.com*, September 26, 2013, http://www.livescience.com/39957-climate-change-deniers-must-stop-distorting-the-evidence.html
2. David Rose, "World's top climate scientists confess: Global warming is just a QUARTER what we thought—and computers got the effects of greenhouse gases wrong," *dailymail.co.uk*, September 14, 2013, http://www.dailymail.co.uk/news/article-2420783/Worlds-climate-scientists-confess-Global-warming-just-QUARTER-thought--computers-got-effects-greenhouse-gases-wrong.html

5. Now study carefully the locations of York, Ypres, Tournai, Cologne, Neustadt, and Salzburg. When they are familiar for you, close the book. Mark each on your map, using the frame and coastlines as reference. When you are happy with your map, lay it over the original. Erase and re-mark any labels which are more than ½″ off of the original.

6. Mark the areas of famine and flood on your map. If you can replicate the skulls and water drops on the original map, feel free to do so! Otherwise, use a marker of your preference.

Chapter Sixty-Four

The Sultan and the Khan

The student may use her text when answering the questions in sections I and II.

Section I: Who, What, Where

Write a one or two-sentence answer explaining the significance of each item listed below.

Abu Sa'id Bahadur Khan—**Pg. 450, ¶ 5 and Pg. 452, ¶ 3 & 6—Abu Sa'id Bahadur Khan, son and heir of Oljeitu, became khan at the age of ten, with Chupan serving as his regent. Abu Sa'id was able to get rid of Chupan after he became jealous of his power; Abu Sa'id was not the ruler Chupan was, and the Il-khanate spiraled out of control under his leadership.**

Al-Nasir Muhammad ibn Qalawun—**Pg. 449, ¶ 4 & 5, Pg. 450, ¶ 2 and Pg. 451, ¶ 2—Al-Nasir Muhammad ibn Qalawun, Khalil's younger brother, was elevated to the sultanate twice between 1293 and 1310, both times as a figurehead, and by the time he was twenty-four he was ready to take the title and power of sultan for himself. After taking the sultanate al-Nasir turned Egypt from disordered and chaotic to the single strongest power between Morocco and the Persian Gulf.**

Baybars—**Pg. 450, ¶ 2—Baybars proclaimed himself sultan two years before al-Nasir decided to take the sultanate for himself. When al-Nasir approached Cairo, Baybars met him on foot, carrying a grave cloth to show that he was ready to die; al-Nasir, who was already a clever politician, magnanimously forgave Baybars in public, and then had him strangled in private a few hours later.**

Chupan—**Pg. 450, ¶ 5 & 6 and Pg. 452, ¶ 3—Chupan, one of Oljeitu's most distinguished generals and Abu Sa'id Bahadur Khan's regent, started his regency by making peace with the vassal king of Georgia and by making a peace treaty with the mamluks in 1323 that set the Euphrates river as the boundary between the Il-khanate state and the mamluk empire. Because Chupan did an excellent job as regent, Abu Sa'id was threatened by him and as a result Chupan fled to Herat where the governor, his friend but also loyal to the khan, put him to death.**

George V—**Pg. 450, ¶ 6 and Pg. 453, ¶ 1—George V, the vassal king of Georgia, was rewarded by Chupan for showing up at Baghdad to attend the coronation of Abu Sa'id Bahadur Khan by**

347

giving him back full control of a southwestern piece of Georgia that previous khans had ruled directly. George V immediately declared its independence from the Mongols after Abu Sa'id's murder in 1335.

Ghiyath al-Din—**Pg. 452, ¶ 6—Ghiyath al-Din, a good but incompetent man and one of Abu Sa'id's favorites, was hired by the khan to replace Chupan. Ghiyath al-Din filled the government with other incompetent people, and as a result the Il-khanate went into a downward spiral.**

Khatun—**Pg. 452, ¶ 1, 5 & 6—Khatun, Chupan's daughter and a famous beauty, was married to an Il-khanate nobleman but in 1325 Abu Sa'id demanded her for himself. After they were married following Chupan's death, Khatun grew jealous of another of Abu Sa'id's lovers and poisoned the khan.**

Uzbek—**Pg. 451, ¶ 1—Uzbek was khan of the Golden Horde at the time of al-Nasir's rule. He made an alliance with al-Nasir and sent one of his daughters to marry the sultan to seal the deal.**

Section II: Comprehension

Write a two or three-sentence answer to each of the following questions.

1. What happened to Egypt in the years following the assassination of Khalil in 1293?

A1.—Pg. 449, ¶ 3—Egypt fell into chaos after the assassination of Khalil: in the seventeen anarchic years that followed, the sultanate changed hands four times. The mamluks of Egypt had no tradition of father-to-son succession: the strongest man was the one who could lay hold of the sultan's scepter. And although all of the would-be rulers were mamluk, none of them belonged to the Bahri Regiment, and the Bahri who had been very young men at the time of the Regiment's rise to power were in their seventies, meaning the next generation of mamluks was agitating for its share of power.

2. How did al-Nasir Muhammad ibn Qalawun survive the anarchic years following his older brother's death?

A2.—Pg. 449, ¶ 4 & 5—Al-Nasir Muhammad ibn Qalawun, only eight at the time of Khalil's murder, was elevated to the sultanate twice between 1293 and 1310, both times as a figurehead. He spent most of his life under house arrest. Power had always remained in the hands of an ambitious regent, and al-Nasir had survived only by accepting his complete lack of authority and living in retirement.

3. What were the circumstances that gave al-Nasir the confidence to seize the sultanate?

A3.—Pg. 449, ¶ 6 to Pg. 450, ¶ 2—When the Nile suddenly failed to rise in 1310, the people of Egypt, who had grown tired of the constant chaos and purges at the sultan's palace, pitched their discontent to a new high, and al-Nasir seized his chance. He left the castle of Kerak, where he had been living for some time in exile, and set out for Damascus, collecting followers as he

went. By the time he arrived at the city, the governors of the mamluk-held cities of Aleppo and Jerusalem had decided to join his cause, followed by most of the empire as he journeyed from Damascus to Cairo to claim his throne.

4. How did Oljeitu's attack on Egypt turn into a gain for al-Nasir?

A4.—Pg. 450, ¶ 4—Oljeitu, who had allied himself with the Byzantine empire against the mamluks, tried in 1305 to persuade the French and English kings to join him in an attack on Egypt. In 1312, he organized an invasion of Syria, across the Euphrates, which failed completely to conquer any mamluk-held cities. In retaliation, al-Nasir sent an army into Il-khanate territory and seized the eastern cities of Kahta, Gerger, and Malatya for himself, turning Oljeitu's attack into a gain for himself.

5. Why did Abu Sa'id demand Chupan's daughter Khatun for himself?

A5.—Pg. 451, ¶ 5 to Pg. 452, ¶ 2—Abu Sa'id suspected that Chupan was planning to install his own son as his successor, in a shogun type of arrangement that would leave Abu Sa'id entirely out of the circles of power. In 1325, he prodded hard at Chupan's authority by demanding Chupan's daughter, who had two years earlier been married to an Il-khanate nobleman, be turned over to him, for it was a custom of the Mongols for the king to have any woman he pleased. While some chalked this demand up to romantic love, or to two beautiful people being together, it was Abu Sa'id's way of showing Chupan who was in control.

6. Describe the circumstances that led to Chupan's death.

A6.—Pg. 452, ¶ 3—Chupan refused to order his daughter to obey Abu Sa'id's demands, so Abu Sa'id waited until Chupan was out of Baghdad, and then ordered Chupan's oldest son arrested and executed on charges that the young man was sleeping with one of the khan's own concubines. Chupan, hearing the news, realized that a purge was upon him and he fled to the Il-khanate city of Herat, believing that the governor—a personal friend— would protect him. But the governor refused to defy the khan and instead he offered his old acquaintance a choice between beheading and the more honorable death of strangulation; Chupan chose strangulation.

7. What happened to Chupan's family after his death?

A7.—Pg. 452, ¶ 5—After their father died, Chupan's children suffered under the will of Abu Sa'id. Chupan's second son fled to Cairo, but al-Nasir was also unwilling to offend Abu Sa'id; he put the boy in jail and then executed him the following year. Abu Sa'id then forced the beautiful Khatun to divorce her husband, and married her himself.

8. How did Abu Sa'id's death change the Il-khanate kingdom?

A8.—Pg. 453, ¶ 1—As soon as Abu Sa'id was killed in 1335, the Christian kingdom of Georgia declared its independence under George V. Almost at the same time, Muslim dynasties, ruling over mini-kingdoms, sprang up all over the old Il-khanate lands, with governors assuming the running of the district over which they had been placed. Almost overnight, the entire Il-khanate vanished.

Section III: Critical Thinking

The student may use her text to answer this question.

Al-Nasir Muhammad ibn Qalawun had a very successful time as sultan of Egypt. Explain how Egypt flourished under al-Nasir, and what circumstances allowed this flowering to happen.

The student should connect peacetime to al-Nasir's success as sultan. The student may use her text to refer to the details of Egypt's successes under al-Nasir. The most important part of this question is spelling out the relationship between peace and prosperity in Egypt.

Al-Nasir came to the throne after a time of chaotic rule, so most of his enemies had killed each other off, and the people of Egypt were eager for a strong ruler. Rather than worrying about threats to his own power, al-Nasir was immediately able to focus on reorganizing the country's disorderly affairs. He commissioned a survey of the empire's land, its owners, and the taxes paid by each, a formal audit called a rawk, and then he redistributed estates to those who were most loyal to him. He did this four times in total during his reign. He always paid attention to detail, personally supervising the work of the scribes and surveyors.

While al-Nasir was getting his kingdom's affairs in order, his greatest threat, the Il-khanate kingdom ruled by Oljeitu, was falling apart. After Oljeitu's death, al-Nasir was able to make a treaty with Chupan, regent to the young khan Abu Sa'id Bahadur Khan, that set the boundary between the Il-khanate state and the mamluk empire at the Euphrates. He also made a marriage alliance with the leader of the Golden Horde; al-Nasir married one of Uzbek's daughters. With his enemies under control, al-Nasir was able to focus all of his time and money on the building up of his kingdom.

Under al-Nasir, Egypt blossomed; Egypt was now the single strongest power between Morocco and the Persian Gulf. Cairo alone was populated by perhaps 600,000 people. It stood at the intersection of the spice route that ran from the Red Sea to the Nile and then to the west of Africa, and al-Nasir's efficient administration meant that the Egyptian sultanate collected a percentage of the trade passing through.

The Muslim traveler Ibn Battuta came to Cairo in 1325 at the midpoint of al-Nasir's reign. He reported that there were supposedly "twelve thousand water carriers and thirty thousand mocaris [renters of beasts of burden]; thirty-six thousand watercraft on the Nile belonging to the sultan and his subjects that do nothing but come and go . . . laden with merchandise of every kind. . . . There is a continuous series of bazaars from the city of Alexandria to Cairo. . . . Cities and villages succeed one another along its banks without interruption and have no equal in the inhabited world, nor is any river known whose basin is so intensively cultivated as that of the Nile."

Al-Nasir was able to fund this growth by putting the tax money he collected from his citizens back into Cairo and the surrounding cities. He built at least thirty mosques and schools, dug new canals and wells, and ordered bridges and waterwheels constructed on the Nile. Al-Nasir was able to make Egypt flourish because he funneled all of his money into the building up of his kingdom rather than protecting it from outside threats or using it to expand through his own wars of conquest. Peace allowed Egypt to prosper.

EXAMPLE ANSWER:

Al-Nasir's reign over Egypt was peaceful. He guaranteed this peace by making a treaty with the Il-khanate khan and regent that set the boundary between the Il-khanate state and the

mamluk empire at the Euphrates. He also made a marriage alliance with the leader of the Golden Horde; al-Nasir married one of Uzbek's daughters.

With his enemies taken care of, al-Nasir could focus on organizing his kingdom. He commissioned a survey of the empire's land, its owners, and the taxes paid by each, a formal audit called a rawk, and then he redistributed estates to those who were most loyal to him. He did this four times in total during his reign. He always paid attention to detail, personally supervising the work of the scribes and surveyors.

Under al-Nasir, Egypt blossomed; Egypt was now the single strongest power between Morocco and the Persian Gulf. Cairo alone was populated by perhaps 600,000 people. It stood at the intersection of the spice route that ran from the Red Sea to the Nile and then to the west of Africa, and al-Nasir's efficient administration meant that the Egyptian sultanate collected a percentage of the trade passing through. According to the Muslim traveler Ibn Battuta, who came to Cairo in 1325, "there is a continuous series of bazaars from the city of Alexandria to Cairo. . . . Cities and villages succeed one another along its banks without interruption and have no equal in the inhabited world, nor is any river known whose basin is so intensively cultivated as that of the Nile."

Al-Nasir was able to fund this growth by putting the tax money he collected from his citizens back into Cairo and the surrounding cities. He built mosques and schools, dug new canals and wells, and ordered bridges and waterwheels constructed on the Nile. Al-Nasir was able to make Egypt flourish because he funneled all of his money into the building up of his kingdom rather than protecting it from outside threats or using it to expand through his own wars of conquest. Peace allowed Egypt to prosper.

Section IV: Map Exercise

1. Trace the rectangular outline of the frame for Map 64.1: The Collapse of the Il-khanate in black.

2. Using your blue pencil, trace the coastal outline through the Mediterranean, the Black Sea, the Red Sea, and the Persian Gulf. As usual, you need not include the small islands around Greece and Turkey. Include the lines of the Tigris and Euphrates from the Persian Gulf. Using your black pencil, trace the lines of the Spice Routes. Repeat until the contours are familiar.

3. Using contrasting colors, trace the outline of the Sultanate of Egypt and of the former Il-khanate. Repeat until the contours are familiar.

4. Using a new sheet of paper, trace the rectangular frame of the map in black. Then, using your regular pencil with an eraser, draw the coastline through the Mediterranean, the Black Sea, the Red Sea, and the Persian Gulf. As usual, you need not include the small islands around Greece and Turkey. Include the lines of the Tigris and Euphrates from the Persian Gulf. Draw the lines of the Spice Routes. Erase and redraw as necessary. When you are happy with your map, lay it over the original. Erase and redraw any lines which are more than ½″ off of the original.

5. Now study carefully the locations of Cairo, Gaza, Jerusalem, Mecca, Medina, Damascus, Aleppo, Baghdad, Kahta, Gerger, Malatya, and Herat. When they are familiar to you, close the book. Mark each location on the map. Then lay your map back over the original, and erase and re-mark any labels which are more than ¼″ off of the original.

6. Now mark each body of water, the location of Kerak, the Euphrates, and Georgia.

Chapter Sixty-Five

Mansa Musa of Mali

The student may use his text when answering the questions in sections I and II.

Section I: Who, What, Where

Write a one or two-sentence answer explaining the significance of each item listed below.

Abubakari II—**Pg. 455, ¶ 2, 5 & 6**—**Abubakari II, nephew of Sundiata, founder of Mali, wanted to find out what lay on the other side of the Atlantic Ocean, so he sent out 200 ships and told them not to return until they came to the end of their food and drink. When the expedition failed, Abubakari II himself set sail at the head of two thousand ships, hoping to find what lay on the other side of the world; that was the last the people of Mali saw of Abubakari II.**

Cresques Abraham—**Pg. 457, ¶ 3**—**Cresques Abraham, a Jewish cartographer, made the Catalan Atlas, an ambitious world map produced for Peter of Aragon. The Catalan Atlas shows Mansa Musa seated on a golden throne, holding a golden scepter and a golden orb, wearing a crown of gold.**

Fomba—**Pg. 459, ¶ 4**—**Fomba, Mansa Sulayman's son, tried for the Mali throne after his father's death. Civil war erupted between his supporters and the supporters of Mari Diata II and Fomba was killed in the fighting.**

Ibn Amir Hajib—**Pg. 456, ¶ 3**—**Ibn Amir Hajib, governor of Old Cairo, became friends with Mansa Musa while he was staying in Cairo. Mansa Musa told Ibn Amir Hajib about Mali's strength and riches, and after their talks Ibn Amir Hajib came to believe that the gold in Africa grew in the ground, on gold plants, with roots of gold, that simply needed to be pulled up and shaken.**

Maghan—**Pg. 457, ¶ 5**—**Maghan, Mansa Musa's son, served as regent during his father's extended absence from the country while he was on *hajj* and then he inherited his father's crown after Mansa Musa's death. Maghan died after a brief four-year reign.**

Mansa Musa—**Pg. 455, ¶ 7 and Pg. 457, ¶ 3**—**Mansa Musa, Abubakari II's cousin, was made king of Mali after Abubakari II failed to return from his expedition to discover what was on the other**

STUDY AND TEACHING GUIDE FOR THE HISTORY OF THE RENAISSANCE WORLD

side of the Atlantic Ocean. Twelve years into his rule, Mansa Musa made the *hajj* and brought with him so much gold and so much wealth that he put Mali on the European map of the world.

Mansa Sulayman—Pg. 457, ¶ 5 and Pg. 459, ¶ 2—Mansa Sulayman, Maghan's uncle, claimed the Mali throne after his nephew's death. During Mansa Sulayman's twenty-four years on the throne, he made Mali a safe and pious kingdom, and the people of Mali remained devoted to him as a ruler.

Mari Diata II—Pg. 459, ¶ 4—Mari Diata II, son of Maghan, sized the Mali throne after civil war broke out between his supporters and the supporters of Fomba, who was killed in the fighting. Mari Diata II was known as a wicked ruler because of the torture and tyranny he inflicted upon his subjects.

Ndiadiane N'Diaye—Pg. 459, ¶ 5 & 6—Ndiadiane N'Diaye is what tradition tells us was the name of the first elected Emperor of the Wolofs. Ndiadiane N'Diaye was a magician; he was not an Islamic king, but a traditional African ruler, meaning beneath the surface veneer of Muslim loyalty in Mali, the old practices had survived.

Section II: Comprehension

Write a two or three-sentence answer to each of the following questions.

1. Who did Abubakari II first send out to explore the Atlantic Ocean? What happened to them?

A1.—Pg. 455, ¶ 4 & 5—Abubakari II first sent out 200 ships filled with men and 200 ships equipped with gold, water, and provisions enough to last them for years on the strict orders that they were to sail west, and not to return until they had come to the end of their food and drink. Long after, only a single ship returned; its captain reported to the king that the entire fleet had been caught in a strong current, with only his craft left behind. The Mali expedition had been caught in the North Equatorial Current, the Drifts of the Trade Winds, the current that flows westward into the Caribbean Sea.

2. What was the effect on Mansa Musa's treasury because of his distribution of gold in Cairo?

A2.—Pg. 457, ¶ 2—Mansa Musa spent most of his money on his initial passage through Cairo. By the time he returned through the city after his pilgrimage to the Ka'aba, he was broke. He had to borrow from Cairo's moneylenders to fund his trip back across the desert, to Mali, and the moneylenders charged him compound interest; he ended up paying back 233 percent on each dinar borrowed.

3. Why was Mansa Sulayman suspicious of Ibn Battuta?

A3.—Pg. 457, ¶ 6 to Pg. 458, ¶ 1—Mansa Sulayman was not just suspicious of Ibn Battuta, but of all new arrivals to his kingdom, because in Mansa Musa's wake, more and more outsiders had made their way to Mali, looking for the gold plants that lay on the ground, and counting on the gullibility of the Malians to make a quick profit. The governor of Old Cairo, a generation before, had noted that the merchants of Cairo exploited Mansa Musa's caravan by raising the prices for objects an extraordinary amount and counting on the simplicity and trustfulness of the Africans to accept whatever offer was given. Later, Africans formed a very poor opinion of Egyptians because of their outrageous behavior when price-fixing.

4. What was Ibn Battuta's lasting impression of Mali?

A4.—Pg. 458, ¶ 2 to Pg. 459, ¶ 1—After his stay, Ibn Battuta left Mali impressed by the safety provided in the kingdom, and by the piousness of the people. He said that a traveler could proceed alone in Mali without fear, and that it was not uncommon for the men of Mali to have committed the entire Koran to memory.

5. How was Mansa Sulayman treated during his twenty-four years on the Mali throne?

A5.—Pg. 459, ¶ 2—Mansa Sulayman was revered by his people during his twenty-four years on the throne. His subjects prostrated themselves and threw dust upon their heads in his presence. He was treated as an emperor: he had gold arms and armor; ranks of courtiers and Turkish mamluks; warrior slaves bought from Egypt; and everyone in his court was required to keep solemn and attentive in his presence.

6. What happened to the Mali government after Mansa Sulayman's death in 1359?

A6.—Pg. 459, ¶ 3-6—After Mansa Sulayman's death in 1359, the political factions that had been slowly coalescing during his reign—each one centered on a different descendant of Mansa Musa—broke the country apart. After Mari Diata II seized the throne, a chunk of Mali between the Senegal and Gambia rivers revolted. Instead of submitting to the despotic Mari Diata II, three distinct but neighboring clans—Waalo, Baol, and Kajoor, all of them Wolof-speakers—formed a confederation, each independent but all three united under a single king named Ndiadiane N'Diaye.

Section III: Critical Thinking

The student may not use his text to answer this question.

Abubakari II went out to discover the world, but it was Mansa Musa that brought the world to Mali. When Mansa Musa first become king of Mali, he decided he wanted to go to Mecca, to make the *hajj*. Explain how Mansa Musa's pilgrimage to Mecca changed Mali's position in the world, for good and for bad.

When Mansa Musa made the hajj in 1324 he took with him a massive caravan of slaves, soldiers, officials, and five hundred of his wife's maids. He journeyed along the Niger valley and then northeast towards Cairo, crossing over the trade routes and passing through Taghaza on his way. Mansa Musa also brought with him thousands and thousands of gold ingots: eighty loads weighing 120 kilograms (260 pounds) each, a total of over ten tons.

Mansa Musa had to stop in Cairo because Mecca was under the protection of the Bahri sultan. When he was in Cairo, Mansa Musa told Ibn Amir Hajib that his country was very extensive and contiguous with the Ocean. He told he him that with his sword and his armies he had conquered 24 cities, each with its surrounding district with villages and estates. Then Mansa Musa explained that from all of these conquered cities, he demanded tribute in gold. Ibn Amir Hajib came away from the conversation convinced that the gold in Africa grew in the ground, on gold plants, with roots of gold, that simply needed to be pulled up and shaken. Mansa Musa's tales were reinforced by his lavish distribution of gold; he distributed so much that the worth of gold in Cairo fell as much as 25 percent.

After Mansa Musa's trip east, Mali appeared more and more often on European maps of the world. The Catalan Atlas, an ambitious world map produced for Peter of Aragon by the Jewish cartographer Cresques Abraham, shows Mansa Musa himself seated on a golden throne, holding a golden scepter and a golden orb, wearing a crown of gold. In the remaining years of Mansa Musa's rule, European traders and embassies from European governments traversed the Sahara again and again, seeking gold and forging alliances. After Mansa Musa's death in 1337, Mali remained strong. But outside the country, the exaggerated legends of Mali's wealth, of the riches that needed only to be plucked from the ground, continued to grow. After Mansa Musa's death, more and more outsiders came to Mali, looking for the gold plants that lay in the ground. Mansa Musa put Mali on the map, and now it was subject to the greed of outsiders.

EXAMPLE ANSWER:

When Mansa Musa made the hajj in 1324 he took with him a massive caravan of slaves, soldiers, officials, and five hundred of his wife's maids. By showing Mali's wealth to those in the towns and cities he passed through, he proved Mali's greatness. But he also made Mali vulnerable to those who wanted to take those riches for themselves.

When Mansa Musa was in Cairo, he told Ibn Amir Hajib that his country was very extensive, that with his sword and his armies he had conquered 24 cities, and that from all of these conquered cities, he demanded tribute in gold. After talking with Mansa Musa, Ibn Amir Hajib came to believe that gold grew in the African ground, on gold plants that just had to be pulled up and shaken in order for one to get the gold. Mansa Musa's tales were reinforced by his lavish distribution of gold; he distributed so much that the worth of gold in Cairo fell as much as 25 percent.

After Mansa Musa's trip east, Mali appeared more and more often on European maps of the world. In the remaining years of Mansa Musa's rule, European traders and embassies from European governments traversed the Sahara again and again, seeking gold and forging alliances. After Mansa Musa's death in 1337, Mali remained strong. But outside the country, the exaggerated legends of Mali's wealth continued to grow. More and more outsiders came to Mali, looking for the gold plants that lay in the ground, and the leaders had to be suspicious of outsiders. Mansa Musa put Mali on the map, but his successors had to deal with the greed of those hoping to come to Mali and take its wealth for themselves.

Chapter Sixty-Six

After the Famine

The student may use her text when answering the questions in sections I and II.

Section I: **Who, What, Where**

Write a one or two-sentence answer explaining the significance of each item listed below.

Charles IV—**Pg. 463, ¶ 4, Pg. 464, ¶ 4 and Pg. 465, ¶ 1—Charles IV, brother of Philip V and his successor to the French throne, was also brother to Isabella, queen of England. Charles IV backed his sister in her fight against Edward II by providing her with enough money to buy an army to attack England.**

Edward III—**Pg. 465, ¶ 3 and Pg. 467, ¶ 4 to Pg. 468, ¶ 1—Edward III, son of Edward II and Isabella, was made king of England in 1327 after his father was deposed by his mother and her army. When he was eighteen, Edward III dissolved the regency by having his mother put under house arrest for the rest of her life and by having Roger Mortimer drawn and quartered as punishment for the death of his father.**

Hugh Despenser the Younger—**Pg. 463, ¶ 4 to Pg. 464, ¶ 2 and Pg. 465, ¶ 4 & 5—Hugh Despenser the Younger, son of the Earl of Winchester and favorite of Edward II (after the death of Piers Gaveston), was coddled with gifts and favors by the king. Hugh Despenser meddled in the marriage between Isabella and Edward II, which caused the queen to turn against the king, raise an army, and have him deposed; Hugh Despenser was taken prisoner by this same army and was then drawn and quartered.**

Philip of Valois—**Pg. 467, ¶ 2—Philip of Valois, the Count of Anjou, followed Charles IV as king of France, bringing an end to the direct line of Hugh Capet, which had been in power for 340 years. Philip of Valois was crowned in 1328 and was the first king of the Valois line.**

Pope John XXII—**Pg. 461, ¶ 4 and Pg. 462, ¶ 5—Pope John XXII, a French lawyer named Jacques d'Euse, was made pope in 1316 and he lived in Avignon, dependent on the French king, an exile from Rome, powerless over the politics of Germany and Italy. Pope John XXII implored the people of France to fight against the Pastoureaux after the roaming shepherds started to kill off the Jews living in France.**

Robert III ("the Lion of Flanders")—**Pg. 462, ¶ 1—Robert III ("the Lion of Flanders"), the young and independent-minded count of Flanders, worked for Flanders's freedom against Philip V and the unwilling submission given by the previous count in 1305.**

Roger Mortimer—**Pg. 464, ¶ 5 and Pg. 466, ¶ 1 & 2 and Pg. 468, ¶ 1—Roger Mortimer was an exiled English Baron who had been imprisoned by Edward II in 1321, after leading an armed attempt to drive Hugh Despenser out of London, and who had escaped from the Tower of London, fled to France, and there became queen Isabella's lover. Roger Mortimer, who acted as co-regent for Edward III and tried to get the boy on the French throne, was drawn and quartered at the demand of Edward III once the king was eighteen, as punishment for the death of Edward II.**

Treaty of Edinburgh-Northampton—**Pg. 466, ¶ 1—Treaty of Edinburgh-Northampton was made by Edward III under the guidance of Isabella and Roger Mortimer. The treaty brought an end to the First War for Scottish Independence by recognizing Robert the Bruce as king of Scotland.**

Section II: Comprehension

Write a two or three-sentence answer to each of the following questions.

1. When did Philip V of France try to start up a new crusade? How did the pope's living situation affect Philip V's power to rally excitement for a new crusade?

A1.—Pg. 461, ¶ 3-5—Philip V of France hoped to go on crusade in 1318; then in 1319, he called a council in Paris to discuss the possibilities but the crusade was not undertaken, nor did it happen in 1320. Philip V could not rally support for a crusade because the pope did not wield enough power to gather men around him; Pope John XXII lived in Avignon, was dependent on the French king, and lived in exile from Rome, powerless over the politics of Germany and Italy. If a crusade were to happen, one of the monarchs of Europe would have to spearhead it, and Philip V of France was too preoccupied with troubles in France to start up the crusade.

2. What obstacles did Philip V face as he tried to plan his next crusade?

A2.—Pg. 461, ¶ 5 to Pg. 462, ¶ 1—Philip V's coronation had coincided with the last severe year of famine and cold; the worst had now passed, but the world that greeted the survivors of famine was still jagged and unreliable, troubled with windstorms and torrential tides, dry months and sharp unbearable cold snaps. Prices of grain and salt were seesawing wildly, England was perpetually hostile, and Flanders, forced into unwilling submission in 1305, was agitating again under its new count, Robert III ("the Lion of Flanders"). Also, the rebellious religious shepherds known as the Pastoureaux had reemerged and were causing trouble in the countryside.

3. How did the Pastoureaux come to murder over 150 Jewish people in Toulouse in a single day in 1320?

A3.—Pg. 462, ⁋ 3 & 4—The reemergence of the Pastoureaux started with begging for alms in order to accompany the proposed royal crusade in June 1320, but like the first bands of Pastoureaux, they were soon joined by bandits and outlaws and begging turned to plundering wealthy priests and well-to-to monasteries. Next the Pastoureaux turned against France's Jewish population, and in Bordeaux, Albi, Toulouse, and in a dozen smaller villages, the Jewish population was herded together by the Pastoureaux and given the choice between forcible baptism and death. After 337 Jews died at Montclus and 152 Jews were murdered in Castelsarrasin, officials arrested twenty-four wagons full of marauders and hauled them Toulouse for trial, but in the last wagons some of the Pastoureaux asked for help, were freed, and then all the Pastoureaux were out of the wagons calling "Death, death, let's kill all the Jews!'" which led to the death of over 150 Jews in Toulouse in a single day.

4. What did Pope John XXII do to end the Pastoureaux uprising?

A4.—Pg. 462, ⁋ 5 to Pg. 463, ⁋ 2—When Pope John XXII heard of the troubles the Pastoureaux were causing, he at once sent letters to every major town in France, condemning the Pastoureaux and ordering all Christian people to join together in protecting the Jews. By the second week of July in 1320, the letters had spread across the country, and the civil authorities had begun to act. Thousands of Pastoureaux, marching across Aigues-Mortes, were surrounded by the men of Carcassonne and slaughtered; as a result, the leaderless movement collapsed almost immediately.

5. Who did the English blame for their misfortune post-famine? Use part of the excerpt presented on page 463 from the protest poem "The Simonie" in your answer.

A5.—Pg. 463, ⁋ 5 & 6—English farmers and peasants blamed greedy merchants and corrupt judges for their troubles. In "The Simonie" it is written, "Every bailiff and beadle seeks how he may most oppress poor men/ Once there were merchants who honorably bought and sold,/ And now is that custom abrogated, and has not been observed for a long time." The chain of culpability continued on: the merchants and judges blamed the English barons for their hardship, and the barons blamed the king.

6. Describe the favors and gifts lavished on Hugh Despenser by Edward II, and what finally caused Isabella to leave England and seek refuge with her brother Charles IV, king of France.

A6.—Pg. 464, ⁋ 1-3—In 1318, Edward II made Hugh his chamberlain and afterwards, the royal accounts record a startling amount of money paid out on behalf of Hugh Despenser: supplies bought for his chambers, armor and weapons for himself and his castles, and out-and-out grants of money for personal use. New private chambers were built for Hugh Despenser within the royal castle at Winchester and a great new warship built for the king's fleet was named *La Despenser*. Isabelle, Edward II's wife, had enough of the friendship when Despenser convinced Edward II to stop seeing his wife; fed up with playing a distant third, she left London and went to Paris, taking refuge with her brother, the newly crowned Charles IV of France.

7. How was Isabella able to raise an army against Edward II without her husband really noticing?

A7.—Pg. 464, ¶ 4-6—After Isabelle took refuge in France with her brother Charles IV, her brother ordered French armies to invade the English-held Duchy of Guienne and then Isabella returned to England on the pretense of helping her husband make peace with Charles IV. In 1325, she visited Paris for a second time; while there she gathered around her a powerful ring of English exiles. Isabella was also able to secure the support of the English barons in the fight against her husband as long as she showed up in England with reinforcements for the cause, and she did all of this with her husband only getting a twinge of what was going on.

8. What happened to King Edward II and Hugh Despenser after Isabella arrived in England with an army behind her?

A8.—Pg. 465, ¶ 3-6—When Isabella arrived in England, her conquest was almost instant; the lords and common people rose up against the king, Edward II was taken prisoner in Berkeley Castle and stripped of his crown, and Hugh Despenser was drawn, hung and quartered. Everyone thought that Edward II died in jail, suddenly, and of natural causes. For centuries, most chroniclers assumed that Roger Mortimer had ordered the king suffocated but, in 1878, a letter written by the fourteenth-century bishop Manuele de Fieschi was uncovered in Church archives at Montpellier, France that said Fieschi had met Edward II himself and that the king had escaped from Berkeley Castle by murdering a guard, ultimately ending up in Italy.

9. Describe the political decisions made by Edward III under the guidance of his mother and Roger Mortimer during the first four years of his reign.

A9.—Pg. 466, ¶ 1 to Pg. 467, ¶ 2—In the first four years of his reign, Edward III made peace with Charles IV of France by paying over fifty thousand sterling marks to buy back his own Duchy of Guienne and he also made peace with Robert the Bruce. Under his regents' guidance, he also made a go at the French throne. Mortimer suggested that Edward III was the logical choice to fill Charles IV's seat because Salic Law only prevented women from inheriting the throne; it did not prevent inheritance through the female line, as long as the heir himself was male and as Isabella's son, Edward III was the closest living male relative of the French royal house.

10. What happened to Isabella and Roger Mortimer's power in England after Edward III came of age?

A10.—Pg. 467, ¶ 4 to Pg. 468, ¶ 1—When Edward III turned eighteen in 1330, he immediately dissolved the regency of his mother and her lover. He sent two of his younger friends with a party of soldiers to arrest Roger Mortimer and his mother in the middle of the night. Mortimer had a quick trial and then was drawn and quartered for having been involved with the death of Edward II and Isabella was placed under polite house arrest with comfortable rooms, an income, and ladies in waiting, but she was ordered never to go out or show herself in public again.

Section III: **Critical Thinking**

The student may not use her text to answer this question.

Section Three of *The History of the Renaissance World* is called "Catastrophes" and the first catastrophe we encountered was the Great Famine. In this chapter, we continue to see the effects of the Great Famine on Europe in the 14th century. Write a paragraph explaining how the treachery associated with the famine in France turned into a fear of lepers, and then a fear of lepers, Jews, and Muslims. Then explain why you think this fear exploded across France in 1321.

The Great Famine caused the people of Europe to lose faith in the sustainability of their livelihoods. The student should remember from her reading in Chapter Sixty-Three that the food shortage was caused by extremely erratic weather, and that wild weather continued to plague France. The people of France could not get ahead of the Famine because they could not count on the success of their agricultural pursuits, or in the perseverance of their livestock.

The student should be able to connect the fear of dying because of lack of resources to the fear of things that are foreign and unknown. Leprosy is a chronic disease that can cause permanent damage to the skin, nerves, limbs, and eyes. Lepers are often looked at as dangerous and are outcast from society. The same can be said for Jews and Muslims in Christian countries in the 14th century. Their religions were foreign and as a result practitioners were looked at as untrustworthy.

On page 463, the student read about a rumor:

> In the spring of 1321, an untraceable rumor sprang up: lepers were poisoning wells throughout France in order to spread their disease to everyone. Soon, the rumor morphed into a conspiracy theory. Lepers, Jews, and Muslims had joined together in a grand plan to throw "poisonous potions" into "waters, fountains, wells, and other places" in "all kingdoms subject to Christ's faith." Terrified villagers seized local lepers and burned them alive. Philip V, thoroughly convinced of the danger, ordered lepers quarantined and Jews evicted; again, a wave of Jewish exiles left France. The panic spread across into Aragon, where the Aragonese king James II ordered all lepers arrested and questioned under torture.

The student's answer should connect the rumor about leprosy being spread in fountains, to Jews, Muslims, and lepers banding together to spread poisonous potions, to the general fear the French had about life in the 14th century. There was no one to blame for the unpredictable weather and the lack of food, so the anger and fear the French had about their own existence turned against those that either looked different or believed in something different. It was easy for everyone, from the peasants to the kings, to scapegoat those that were different in their efforts to release the pressure of fear built up around everyday life.

EXAMPLE ANSWER:

The Great Famine caused the people of Europe to lose faith in the sustainability of their livelihoods. The food shortage was caused by extremely erratic weather, and that wild weather continued to plague France. The people of France could not get ahead of the Famine because

they could not count on the success of their agricultural pursuits, or in the perseverance of their livestock. There was no one to blame for the weather, or the lack of food, so the people of the France turned their anger and fear on those that were different. During the period of unease, a rumor started in 1321 that lepers were poisoning the water wells. That rumor then turned into a conspiracy theory against lepers, Jews, and Muslims. The rumor was that they were all working together to poison those who believed in Christ. This rumor led to Philip V ordering the quarantine of lepers and the eviction of Jews, and the rumor spread to Aragon, where king James II ordered all lepers arrested and questioned under torture. The fear of lepers, Jews, and Muslims was an outlet for the scared and starving French people. They were not able to blame God or Mother Nature for their misfortune and receive a positive or tangible result, so they blamed those that either looked different or believed in something different.

Section IV: Map Exercise

1. Trace the rectangular outline of the frame for Map 66.1 in black.

2. Trace the outline of the coast around Ireland, Scotland, England, the continent, and the visible portion of the Mediterranean. Also trace the lines of the Thames, the Seine, and the Loire. Repeat until the contours are familiar.

3. Now using contrasting colors, trace the outlines of the English Empire and France. Repeat until the contours are familiar. Show the mountains with small peaks. When you are happy with your map, lay it over the original. Erase and redraw any marks which are more than ½" off of the original.

4. Label the areas of Ireland, Scotland, Wales, England, Germany, France, Aragon, and Guienne. Then study carefully the areas of Flanders, Normandy, Brittany, and Anjou. Close the book, label each, and then check your work and make any needed corrections.

5. Study carefully the locations of Hereford, Berkeley, Winchester, London, Paris, Boudeaux, Castelsarrassin, Albi, Toulouse, Montclus, Avignon, and Aigues-Mortes. When you are familiar with them, close the book. Mark and label each one on your map. Lay your map over the original, and erase and redraw any lines that are more than ½" off of the original.

Chapter Sixty-Seven

The Southern and Northern Courts

The student may use his text when answering the questions in sections I and II.

Section I: Who, What, Where

Write a one or two-sentence answer explaining the significance of each item listed below.

Ashikaga Takauji—**Pg. 473, ¶ 2, Pg. 474, ¶ 2 & 6, and Pg. 475, ¶ 2—Ashikaga Takauji, a notorious samurai descended from the Minamoto clan that participated in the war between Go-Daigo and the *shikken*, rotated his loyalties during the war until he came out on top. After imprisoning Emperor Kogon, driving Hojo Takatoki to suicide, and making Go-Daigo flee into the mountains, Ashikaga Takauji established himself as shogun of Japan in 1338, the first shogun of the Ashikaga Shogunate.**

Go-Daigo—**Pg. 471, ¶ 3 & 6 and Pg. 474, ¶ 6—Go-Daigo, part of the junior branch, followed Hanazono as emperor, though most of the junior branch wanted his nephew Kuniyoshi to be emperor; once he was on the throne he began to plot a rebellion against the *shikken* so that he could keep his power. After getting rid of the power of the *shikken*, Go-Daigo was forced to flee south into the mountains by Ashikaga Takauji, who wanted military power for himself; once there, Go-Daigo established a new imperial capital at Yoshino.**

Go-Uda—**Pg. 471, ¶ 7 to Pg. 472, ¶ 1—Go-Uda, father of Go-Daigo, was the oldest Cloistered Emperor at the time Go-Daigo decided to rebel against the Kamakura shogunate, and Go-Daigo took advantage of his father's inclination towards piety and his dislike of administration to garner more power for himself. During the fourth year of his rule, Go-Daigo talked Go-Uda into giving up the traditional lawmaking powers held by the Cloistered Emperor and returning them to the throne.**

Hanazono—**Pg. 471, ¶ 3—Hanazono, from the senior line, abdicated as emperor of Japan in 1318. Go-Daigo, Hanazono's cousin and member of the junior branch, took his place as emperor.**

Hojo Takatoki—**Pg. 472, ¶ 3 and Pg. 474, ¶ 2—Hojo Takatoki, appointed *shikken* in 1311 at the age of eight, did not have to handle the succession crisis that led to the compromise between** the senior and junior branches because he was too young—his chief minister and competent grandmother had handled the matter—but after Takatoki had taken power in his own right, he turned out to be easily distracted from matters of state by his passion for dog fighting (and was even willing to accept dogs in lieu of taxes owed). Hojo Takatoki was at first successful in the war against the rebellious Go-Daigo, but when the emperor came out of exile and restarted the war, Hojo Takatoki was attacked by his own men and committed suicide rather than facing defeat.

Kogon—Pg. 473, ¶ 3 & 4 and Pg. 474, ¶ 2—Kogon was crowned emperor by the *shikken* shortly after Go-Daigo called for open rebellion against the shogunate, but he was widely regarded as Takatoki's puppet; he had not even been properly coronated, since Go-Daigo had refused to hand over the imperial scepter and regalia. After Go-Daigo came out of exile and restarted the war against the *shikken*, Kogon was captured and imprisoned in Kyoto by the rebel army led by Ashikaga Takauji.

Kuniyoshi—Pg. 471, ¶ 4 and Pg. 472, ¶ 2—Kuniyoshi, part of the junior branch, was the nephew of emperor Go-Daigo; though most of the junior branch wanted Kuniyoshi to be emperor, the principle of alternating succession meant that, after Go-Daigo, the crown would have to pass to the other clan, cutting Kuniyoshi out completely. In 1326, Kuniyoshi fell suddenly ill and died within two weeks, disrupting the order of succession designated by the *shikken*.

Muromachi *bakafu*—Pg. 475, *—Muromachi *bakafu* was another name given to the Ashikaga Shogunate. The name came from the district where the Ashikaga Shogunate's headquarters were located.

Nitta Yoshisada—Pg. 473, ¶ 5 to Pg. 474, ¶ 2, 5 & 6—Nitta Yoshisada, a descendent of the Minamoto clan and a commander in the *shikken*'s army, followed Ashikaga Takauji in his turn against the *shikken* to his loyalty to Go-Daigo, and led successful battles against Emperor Kogon and Hojo Takatoki that put Go-Daigo back on the throne. When Go-Daigo declared Ashikaga Takauji an enemy of the throne, Nitta Yoshisada led a successful battle against the emperor in 1336 at the banks of the Minato river that divided the emperor's army and resulted in the death of thousands of imperial soldiers and Go-Daigo fleeing south into the mountains.

Yutahito—Pg. 475, ¶ 1—Yutahito, Kogon's brother, was declared emperor by Ashikaga Takauji after Go-Daigo was driven out of Kyoto.

Section II: Comprehension

Write a two or three-sentence answer to each of the following questions.

1. Explain how the succession of the Chrysanthemum Throne divided at the peak of the Mongol threat. Why were the two lines hostile to each other?

A1.—Pg. 470, ¶ 3 & 4—At the peak of the Mongol threat, the succession to the Chrysanthemum Throne divided because of a complicated argument between two brothers—one the oldest son of the emperor, the other his favorite—and eventually resolved itself into an arrangement

where the sons and grandsons of the older brother (the senior line) and the descendants of the younger (the junior line) alternated on the throne. The two royal families grew increasingly hostile to each other. The junior line followed Confucianism, the senior Buddhism; the junior line patronized Chinese-style scholarship, the senior preferred Japanese literature written in traditional Japanese script; and within the clans, individual families quarreled over the right to put the next emperor on the Chrysanthemum throne.

2. Describe the way *shikken* Hojo Tokimune and his successors ran the military government headquartered at Kamakura, and how the people of Japan reacted.

A2.—Pg. 470, ¶ 5 to Pg. 471, ¶ 2—Hojo Tokimune and his successors acted tyrannically and autocratically: they granted government positions to friends and allies, distributed land to loyalists, and elected more and more Hojo clan members to be the military governors (the *shugo*) who ran the provinces farther away from Kyoto and Kamakura, and they reacted to the lawlessness of the Japanese people by enacting more stringent punishments and enforcing more regulations. For example, to deal with pirates, the Hojo clan members made all ships register and show the name of the owner and the port of registration at all times. The disorder only grew; piracy moved west, and hordes of the *akuto* ("evil bands") increased year by year, until the bands were often a hundred strong, armed with swords and bamboo spears, robbing villages and blocking roadways.

3. What compromise was made by the *shikken* in Kamakura to accommodate the junior line's desire to put Kuniyoshi on the throne?

A3.—Pg. 471, ¶ 5—The *shikken* in Kamakura ordered a compromise to accommodate the junior line's desire to put Kuniyoshi on the throne. Go-Daigo would be coronated, but none of his sons would be eligible for the title of crown prince; Kuniyoshi would follow him, but after that, the crown would revert to the senior line. And, to give more candidates a shot at the throne, all emperors would have to abdicate after ten years of rule.

4. How did Go-Daigo use his father to gain more power as emperor? How did he take advantage of Kuniyoshi's death to remain on the throne, and what did he do in an attempt to safeguard his power?

A4.—Pg. 472, ¶ 1 & 2—Go-Daigo's father, eldest Cloistered Emperor Go-Uda, was convinced by his son to retire and to turn over the traditional law-making powers held by the Cloistered Emperor over to the sitting emperor. In 1326, when Kuniyoshi died, Go-Daigo suggested that, since the original arrangement had clearly designated another member of the junior line as his successor, one of his own sons should now become Crown Prince, but the senior branch argued for the immediate reversion of the title to the senior line. Without a clear successor, Go-Daigo remained on the throne past his ten-year expiration date and at the same time he was developing a strong alliance with the notorious warrior monks on Mount Hiei in an effort to safeguard his power; he sent two of his sons to study there, one becoming a priest, the other an abbot.

5. What was Hojo Takatoki doing while he should have been handling the succession quarrels in Kyoto caused by Go-Daigo?

A5.—Pg. 472, ¶ 3—Instead of dealing with Go-Daigo and his designs on keeping the imperial throne, Hojo Takatoki was enjoying dog fighting, and was even willing to accept dogs in lieu of

STUDY AND TEACHING GUIDE FOR THE HISTORY OF THE RENAISSANCE WORLD

taxes owed. Dog fights were staged twelve days out of every month, and the best dogs were "fed on fish and fowl, kept in kennels having gold and silver ornaments, and carried in palanquins to take the air." When the dogs were brought into public, people had to kneel in obeisance, and the city of Kamakura turned into a spectacle, with "well-fed dogs, clothed in tinsel and brocades and totaling from four to five thousand."

6. What happened to Go-Daigo soon after he called for open rebellion against the corrupt and weakened *shikken*?

A6.—Pg. 473, ¶ 3—In first six months of fighting, the shogunate overpowered the forces loyal to Go-Daigo; the Kamakura army drove Go-Daigo and his samurai into the mountains near Kyoto and trapped them there, and Go-Daigo was forced to surrender with embarrassing speed. He was taken back to Kyoto and housed in a shack behind the palace, where he was forced to listen to the joyous coronation of a prince from the senior line as the new emperor. He was then escorted under guard to Yasuki Harbor, west of the capital, and was taken by ship to desolate Oki Island where he lived for two years in makeshift housing while the new Emperor Kogon ruled in Kyoto and Hojo Takatoki went back to his dog fights in Kamakura.

7. How did Go-Daigo raise an army against Takatoki from exile? What role did Ashikaga Takauji play in Go-Daigo's comeback?

A7.—Pg. 473, ¶ 4 & 5—While in exile, Go-Daigo was able to quietly assemble a network of supporters who wanted to be rid of Hojo Takatoki's rule, and in the winter of 1333, a small band of pirates and fishermen helped Go-Daigo escape from his island. He landed on the shores of Hoki Province and found an army there already assembled, waiting for his leadership. Though Ashikaga Takauji was a commander in Hojo Takatoki's army, he had been carrying on a secret correspondence with Go-Daigo for the last year because he felt that the *shikken* had been slow in rewarding his loyalty; once Ashikaga Takauji, who was supposedly leading forces for the *shikken*, was out of Kamakura, he swapped sides, and fought for Go-Daigo.

8. Describe how Ashikaga Takauji and Nitta Yoshisada took down Emperor Kogon and Hojo Takatoki.

A8.—Pg. 473, ¶ 5 to Pg. 474, ¶ 2—After switching allegiance to Go-Daigo, Ashikaga Takauji and Nitta Yoshisada led a two-pronged attack against Hojo power; Ashikaga Takauji took part of the force into Kyoto and drove out the Hojo officials there, while Nitta Yoshisada led the rest directly against Kamakura. Emperor Kogon and the military governor of Kyoto fled together to the east but were quickly overtaken; the governor was killed on the spot, Kogon was brought back to Kyoto and imprisoned, and Nitta Yoshisada and his men continued to fight in a five-day battle at Kamakura where the Hojo generals and officials began to commit suicide, one after another, in the face of certain defeat. On July 5, 1333, Hojo Takatoki retreated with three hundred supporters to the Kamakura temple where his ancestors were buried; he swigged down a bowl of wine, passed it to his closest companion, plunged a dagger into his side, and his men followed his example—nearly eight hundred men killed themselves in a single day.

9. How did Go-Daigo and Ashikaga Takauji go from allies to enemies?

A9.—Pg. 474, ❡ 3 & 4—During the period known as the Kemmu Restoration, Go-Daigo returned to Kyoto, claiming that he had never actually abdicated and attempted to take back direct rule of the country, but Ashikaga Takauji was simultaneously angling for the vacant position of *shikken* and had already set himself up in the emptied shogunate offices of Kyoto, and from there he appointed military governors just as the Hojo *shikken* had done. In 1335, he moved himself to Kamakura and began to give out grants of land. Go-Daigo had intended to free himself from the dictates of the shogunate, not simply replace one voice of authority with another, so the emperor declared his onetime ally an "enemy of the throne."

10. Explain how, by 1338, Japan had two imperial capitals, two emperors, two courts, one shogun, and no *shikken*.

A10.—Pg. 474, ❡ 5 to Pg. 475, ❡ 2—After Go-Daigo declared Ashikaga Takauji an enemy of the throne, he was driven out of Kyoto by Nitta Yoshisada and established a new imperial capital in the mountains at Yoshino. Ashikaga Takauji claimed Kyoto for himself, building military headquarters in the section of the city called Muromachi, and he declared Kogon's younger brother Yutahito to be the new emperor. In 1338, finally in complete control of Kyoto, Ashikaga Takauji named himself shogun of Japan, resulting in a Japan that had two imperial capitals, two emperors, two courts, one shogun, and no *shikken*.

11. When did the Ashikaga Shogunate begin? What was the Nambokucho era, and how did it coincide with the Ashikaga Shogunate?

A11.—Pg. 475, ❡ 2 & 3—The Ashikaga Shogunate began in 1338 when Ashikaga Takauji declared himself shogun of Japan. The Nambokucho era was the time when there were two courts, "the age of the Southern and Northern Courts." The establishment of the shogunate at Kyoto coincided with the Nambokucho era, with the shogun protecting the senior line in Kyoto and Go-Daigo and his descendants carrying on the junior line from Yoshino.

Section III: Critical Thinking

The student may not use his text to answer this question.

Japan's two-court arrangement may have involved a convoluted plan for the succession to the Chrysanthemum Throne, but it kept the imperial core of Japan stable. As political theorist Kitabatake Chikafusa wrote from his place at the Southern Court:

> From the time of the heavenly founder, there has been no disruption in dynastic succession in Japan. Our country has been ruled without interruption by the sovereigns of a single dynastic line. . . . In our country alone, the imperial succession has followed in an unbroken line from the time when heaven and earth were divided until the present age. . . . This is entirely the result of the immutable mandate of Amaterasu, and is the reason why Japan differs from all other countries. The way of the gods is not readily revealed. Yet if the

divine basis of things is not understood, such ignorance will surely give rise to disorder.

Explain how Ashikaga Takauji tried to comply with dynastic succession and to follow "the divine basis of things" but ultimately failed, throwing Japan into chaos.

When Ashikaga Takauji drove Go-Daigo into the mountains and claimed Kyoto for himself, he knew he could not call himself emperor. He knew that the connection of the imperial right to rule with the bloodline of the royal family was impossible to break. Instead, he declared former Emperor Kogon's younger brother Yutahito to be the new emperor. Then, in 1338, after he was in complete control of Kyoto, Ashikaga Takauji named himself shogun of Japan, ending the Kamakura Shogunate and starting the Ashikaga Shogunate, which would survive for more than two hundred years.

Though the Ashikaga Shogunate would last for a significant amount of time, its existence threw Japan into chaos. There were now two imperial capitals, two emperors, two courts, no shikken, *and a shogun. Go-Daigo's descendants continued to rule from the south at Yoshino, starting the Nambokucho era, the age of the "Southern and Northern Courts," a clear royal schism. The convoluted succession to the Chrysanthemum Throne that was arranged between the junior and senior lines turned into an open breach; the junior line ruled in the south, the senior in the north. As written on page 475, "The divided sovereignty turned Japan into a series of military zones. Unlike the Kamakura shogunate, the Ashikaga shogunate never claimed the loyalty of most of the warrior class; it had a much smaller base of samurai support. And while the Kamakura shogunate had attempted to keep peace between the junior and senior royal branches, the Ashikaga had thrown its fortunes in with the senior line and turned against the junior. Before long, the Ashikaga could claim to be in power only over Kyoto and the lands nearby. Governors of the more distant provinces took control for themselves. Nowhere was there peace; nowhere, order."*

The Ashikaga Shogunate could not get support from the Japanese people because its founder strong-armed his way into power rather than working with the dynastic succession the Japanese people believed was mandated by the heavens. The student may see a connection to the chaos in Japan that occurred during Hojo Tokimune's time as shikken. *Hojo Tokimune acted more and more autocratically, and tyrannically, and each time he tightened his grip on the Japanese people, more crime and chaos broke out. Though Ashikaga Takauji put an emperor on the throne, he did so by disrupting the dynastic succession. Go-Daigo may have started the war between the* shikken *and the emperor, but there was no heavenly mandate for a military ruler in Japan. The imperial line won out, and now it was divided. The only result possible was chaos, fueled by self-serving rulers and divided loyalties.*

EXAMPLE ANSWER:

The Chrysanthemum Throne was filled by a man designated to rule from the heavens. Though a man could gain power outside of the throne, disorder would arise if the divine basis of things was not understood. We saw a little of this during Hojo Tokimune's rule as *shikken*. Hojo Tokimune acted more and more autocratically, and tyrannically, and each time he tightened his grip on the Japanese people, more crime and chaos broke out. Ruling the people was not up to him, it was up to the emperor. Ashikaga Takauji seemed to understand the basis of this idea: when Ashikaga Takauji drove Go-Daigo into the mountains and claimed Kyoto for himself, he knew he could not call himself emperor. He knew that the connection of the imperial right to rule with the bloodline of the royal family was impossible to break. So, he declared former

Emperor Kogon's younger brother Yutahito to be the new emperor. Only after a new emperor was established did Ashikaga Takauji name himself shogun.

Though the Ashikaga Shogunate would last for a significant amount of time, its existence threw Japan into chaos. There were now two imperial capitals, two emperors, two courts, no shikken, and a shogun. The rise of the Ashikaga Shogunate was paralleled by the Nambokucho era, the age of the "Southern and Northern Courts." The convoluted succession to the Chrysanthemum Throne that was arranged between the junior and senior lines turned into an open breach; the junior line ruled in the south, the senior in the north. Imperial succession was not honored, and Japan turned into a series of military zones. The Ashikaga Shogunate supported only the senior line and as a result lost a lot of support which shrunk their sphere of power to Kyoto and the lands nearby. Loyalties divided, governors of distant provinces took power for themselves, and disorder reigned.

Section IV: Map Exercise

1. Using your black pencil, trace the rectangular outline of the frame for Map 67.1: The Southern and Northern Courts.

2. Using your blue pencil, trace all the visible coastline (you do not need to include small islands). Repeat until the contours are familiar.

3. Using a new sheet of paper, trace the rectangular outline of the frame of the map in black. Then using your regular pencil, draw the coastline, using the frame of the map as a reference. Erase and redraw as necessary. When you are happy with your map, lay it over the original, and erase and re-draw any lines which are more than ¼" off of the original.

4. Now study carefully the locations of Oki Island, Yasuki Harbor, Hoki, Kyoto, Mt. Hiei, Yoshino, and Kamakura. Also make sure you know the location of the Battle of the Minato River. When they are all familiar for you, close the book. Mark each location on your map, and then lay it over the original again. Erase and re-draw any labels which are more than ¼" off of the original.

Chapter Sixty-Eight

Rebellions

The student may use her text when answering the questions in sections I and II.

Section I: Who, What, Where

Write a one or two-sentence answer explaining the significance of each item listed below.

Ahsan Shah—**Pg. 480, ¶ 5**—Ahsan Shah, an Indian governor, broke away from Muhammad bin Tughluq in 1335 and announced himself the ruler of the Sultanate of Madura, an independent Muslim realm.

Firoz Shah—**Pg. 482, ¶ 2-6**—Firoz Shah, nephew of Muhammad bin Tughluq, was forced to become sultan after his uncle's death. Firoz Shah was able to get those that had been fighting in the north back to Delhi, and once he was on the throne he began to make reparations for all of the evil done by his uncle, slowing the disintegration of the sultanate.

Harahara and Bukka—**Pg. 480, ¶ 5**—Harahara and Bukka, Kakatiya survivors, brothers who had fled from the sack of Warangal, declared their own freedom from Delhi dominance at Vijayanagara and established themselves around the Tungabhadra river in 1336. Filled with fury and disgust at the violent destruction, joined by other Hindu warriors driven south by Delhi's expansion, they set themselves to reestablish the Hindu kingdom in the south.

Hasan Gangu—**Pg. 481, ¶ 1**—Hasan Gangu, a Muslim officer, declared himself sultan Ala-ud-Din Bahman of the Deccan in 1347. His sultanate, the Bahmani, would rule there for over a century.

Kapaya Nayaka—**Pg. 480, ¶ 6**—Kapaya Nayaka, a Hindu warrior, drove the Delhi occupiers out of Warangal and took it for himself, calling himself Sultan of the Andhra Country.

Malik Haji Ilyas—**Pg. 480, ¶ 7 to Pg. 481, ¶ 1**—Malik Haji Ilyas, a Delhi officer, seized the Bengali city of Lakhnawati, captured Gaur, and made himself Sultan Shams-ud-Din, founder of the Ilyas Shahi dynasty of Bengal. He called himself the Second Alexander on his coins, "the right hand of the caliphate, the defender of the Commander of the Faithful."

Pratapa Rudra—**Pg. 478, ❡ 2 & 4 and Pg. 479, ❡ 1**—Pratapa Rudra, king of the south Indian kingdom of the Kakatiya, took the start of the Tughluq dynasty as an opportunity to fight back against Delhi by not sending tribute to the sultan. Pratapa Rudra was taken prisoner after Ulugh Khan laid waste to Warangal, and died in chains on this way to Delhi; two later inscriptions tell us that the last Kakatiya king took his own life by jumping into the banks of the Narmada because his kingdom and city were gone.

Ulugh Khan (Muhammad bin Tughluq)—**Pg. 478, ❡ 4, Pg. 479, ❡ 2 & 4, Pg. 481, ❡ 2 to Pg. 482, ❡ 1**—Ulugh Khan, son of Ghiyas-ud-Din, put down Pratapa Rudra's rebellion in Warangal and gave himself the royal name Muhammad bin Tughluq when he became sultan following his father's sudden death in Afghanapur. Muhammad bin Tughluq did what he wanted as ruler and as a result faced numerous rebellions which he tried to put down with the sword; Muhammad bin Tughluq died of dysentery on March 20, 1351 while fighting against rebels in the north.

Section II: Comprehension

Write a two or three-sentence answer to each of the following questions.

1. Why did general Malik Kafur give Pratapa Rudra a robe and a parasol? What did Pratapa Rudra do to subvert his acceptance of Malik Kafur's gifts?

A1.—Pg. 478, ❡ 3—Malik Kafur gave Pratapa Rudra a robe and a parasol to symbolize that Pratapa Rudra now ruled "under the shadow" of the Delhi sultan 'Ala'-ud-Din. Pratapa Rudra accepted both after agreeing to send a hefty annual tribute to the sultan, but he continued to act with independence, and was often slow to send the proper tribute to Delhi. He also subverted the sultan's power by reinforcing the stone walls that surrounded Warangal with bastions, suggesting his kingdom was separate from that of 'Ala'-ud-Din.

2. Why did it take two sieges for Ulugh Khan to take Warangal? What happened to Warangal once the son of the sultan breached the city's walls?

A2.—Pg. 478, ❡ 5 to Pg. 479, ❡ 1—The first siege by Ulugh Khan on Warangal in 1231 failed; the city was successfully blockaded, but before the city could surrender, false news of Ghiyas-ud-Din's death arrived from Delhi, and his son retreated. After finding out Ghiyas-ud-Din was alive and well, Ulugh Khan laid siege to the city for a second time and because it was already weakened, surrender came within a few days. Ulugh Khan allowed his men to sack Warangal, to destroy the great temple that housed the Hindu deities to whom Pratapa Rudra paid homage, he ordered the city renamed Sultanpur, and he began to build a huge mosque next to the wrecked Hindu temple.

3. Describe Ghiyas-ud-Din's reconquest of Bengal, and the tragedy that immediately followed.

A3.—Pg. 479, ❡ 2 & 3—Ghiyas-ud-Din himself marched east against the Sultanate of Bengal, ruled by Bughra Khan's grandson. Though he attempted to resist, the reconquest of Bengal happened with remarkable ease; Bughra Khan's grandson was sent to Delhi with a rope

around his neck, and the sultan of Delhi turned to start home. Then tragedy stuck: on his way back to Delhi, Ghiyas-ud-Din halted six miles southeast at Afghanapur to show himself to the residents and as he was watching an elephant parade from a knocked-together royal pavilion, it collapsed on top of him and he died.

4. How did Muhammad bin Tughluq deal with the numerous rebellions against his rule?

A4.—Pg. 481, ¶ 2—The sheer scope of the rebellions overwhelmed Muhammad bin Tughluq. His troops were spread thin; when he did win a victory, he attempted to frighten the remaining rebels into submission with increasingly severe punishments of the captured. However, the more violent his reprisals, the worse the revolts became.

5. What happened to the regiments that were fighting with Muhammad bin Tughluq in the north after he died? How did they manage to get home?

A5.—Pg. 482, ¶ 2-4—The regiments that were with Muhammad bin Tughluq fled the north towards Delhi but they were robbed by bandits; without food and supplies, the women and children who had accompanied the expedition began to die. The remaining officers gathered together and made Muhammad bin Tughluq's nephew Firoz Shah sultan, even though he didn't want to do it and was planning to make the *hajj* when he got back to Delhi. Firoz Shah organized the stragglers into new regiments, turned them to attack the bandits, and under his guidance the regiments were victorious, the robbers fled, and they made it back to Delhi.

6. How did Firoz Shah try to fix the damage done by Muhammad bin Tughluq? Did his actions bring India back together?

A6.—Pg. 482, ¶ 5 & 6—Firoz Shah tried to fix the damage done by his uncle by paying reparations to the heirs of anyone put to death unjustly by Muhammad bin Tughluq: "those who themselves had been deprived of a limb, nose, eye, hand, or foot . . . [were] appeased with gifts," the new sultan himself records. He also repealed a whole raft of taxes, ordered new hospitals and shelters built for the poor, restored confiscated land, and pensioned off or discharged government officials who had taken part in Tughluq's repressive regime. While the disintegration of the sultanate slowed and the borders began to stabilize, Firoz Shah could not bring India back together, and he was just one ruler in a cluttered landscape of many.

Section III: Critical Thinking

The student may use her text to answer this question.

When Ulugh Khan became sultan Muhammad bin Tughluq, he inherited rule at the height of India's expansion. Like the great rulers that came before him, he was energetic and ambitious. But he himself did not turn out to be a great ruler. Explain how Muhammad bin Tughluq's energy and ambition, rather than raising India up, ran India into the ground.

The student may reference her textbook when answering this question because there is a lot of detail to recall. The most important thing the student should note is that though Muhammad bin Tughluq was energetic and ambitious, he did not channel that energy and ambition into positive action. He was short-tempered, inclined to cruelty, and apt to act without forethought. He made decisions on his own and created projects that pleased his own heart but that required all of India to cooperate, whether they wanted to or not.

First, Muhammad bin Tughluq imposed a tax increase that infuriated the rich and ruined the poor. Next, he decided to move the capital city seven hundred miles south, to the city of Devagiri, in an effort to be closer to the new southern expanses of the empire; below the Krishna river, only the Hoysala had continued to resist the sultanate. His courtiers and officers were less than thrilled, and a good number of them refused to move there. The sultan then chose a cross section of the Indian elite and forced them to transplant their families to his new capital, which he renamed Daulatabad. Daulatabad was not prepared to receive the number of new residents who were now settled there, and water ran short. Famine and thirst began to kill the new citizens so in 1330, Muhammad gave up and moved back to Delhi. But the long and grueling journey across the Deccan and the Vindhya mountain range killed thousands more. Because so few of the transplants made it home, Delhi became something like a ghost town.

After returning to Delhi, Muhammad bin Tughluq made an attempt to change the currency of the entire empire over to copper coins. Private mints sprang up throughout India, churning out money that soon sank into complete worthlessness. Then, a seven-year drought and accompanying famine—over three times as long as the Great Famine of Europe—settled over the subcontinent. Thousands died, but Muhammad bin Tughluq put no aid programs into effect; there was no lowering of taxes, no handouts of stored food. Finally, Muhammad bin Tughluq continued to campaign into Khorasan. The ventures of conquest were expensive and unproductive. They made Muhammad bin Tughluq not only poorer, but more and more unpopular. People began to revolt.

Muhammad bin Tughluq thought he was full of good ideas. He had energy and ambition and put all of his ideas into action, but because he did not run these ideas by anyone, or listen to the counsel of his advisors, he pulled India apart rather than bringing it together. His energy and ambition could have made India great, but instead, Muhammad bin Tughluq destroyed his kingdom.

EXAMPLE ANSWER:

Muhammad bin Tughluq was energetic and ambitious, but he did not channel that energy and ambition into positive action. He did not consult anyone about his plans and did what he pleased. Everyone had to cooperate and abide by Muhammad bin Tughluq's ideas, and the result was that India suffered greatly.

First, Muhammad bin Tughluq imposed a tax increase that infuriated the rich and ruined the poor. Next, he decided to move the capital city seven hundred miles south, to the city of Devagiri. He forced a cross section of the Indian elite to move there, and renamed the city Daulatabad. However, Daulatabad was not prepared to receive the number of new residents who were now settled there, and water ran short. Famine and thirst began to kill the new citizens so in 1330, Muhammad gave up and moved back to Delhi. The long and grueling journey across the Deccan and the Vindhya mountain range killed thousands more and few made it home. Delhi became something like a ghost town.

After returning to Delhi, Muhammad bin Tughluq tried to change the currency of the entire empire over to copper coins. Private mints sprang up throughout India, churning out money that soon sank into complete worthlessness. Then, a seven-year drought and famine settled over the subcontinent. Thousands died, but Muhammad bin Tughluq put no aid programs

into effect. Finally, Muhammad bin Tughluq continued to campaign into Khorasan. The ventures of conquest were expensive and unproductive. They made Muhammad bin Tughluq not only poorer, but more and more unpopular. People began to revolt.

Muhammad bin Tughluq thought he was full of good ideas, and he had the energy and ambition to put all of his ideas into action. His ideas were not good, however, and because he did not run these ideas by anyone, or listen to the counsel of his advisors, he pulled India apart rather than bringing it together. His energy and ambition could have made India great, but instead, Muhammad bin Tughluq destroyed his kingdom.

Chapter Sixty-Nine

Naming the Renaissance

The student may use his text when answering the questions in sections I and II.

Section I: Who, What, Where

Write a one or two-sentence answer explaining the significance of each item listed below.

Benedict XII—**Pg. 488, ¶ 4—Benedict XII was elected to be pope very quickly after the death of John XXII thanks to the intervention of Philip VI of France. Benedict XII did not work out a compromise with Louis of Bavaria; Louis remained an excommunicate Holy Roman Emperor and the pope remained in Avignon, a servant of the French king.**

Count of Märstetten—**Pg. 484, ¶ 5—Count of Märstetten was appointed an imperial vicar in 1323 by Louis of Bavaria in an attempt to woo they loyalty of the Lombard cities of Milan and Ferrara towards the German king.**

Defensor Pacis—**Pg. 485, ¶ 4 to Pg. 486, ¶ 2—*Defensor Pacis* was a 1324 treatise written by Marsilius of Padua that both condemned the actions of John XXII and built on the work of Dante to argue that the "true church" is not centered at Rome, made up of those whom the pope recognizes as Christians, but that the true church is made up of all who worship Christ, all over the world, in any place or community. This community— the *ecclesia*, the "invisible church"—is spiritual, not earthly, it is not bound by time or place, and so it cannot have an earthly, time-bound ruler.**

Marsilius of Padua—**Pg. 485, ¶ 5 to Pg. 486, ¶ 1—Marsilius of Padua, an Italian scholar and Louis of Bavaria's personal physician, wrote the *Defensor Pacis* in 1324. Marsilius built on Dante's condemnation of man's claimed power over God's word, asserting that the true church is made up of all who worship Christ with no earthly ruler at its head.**

Nicholas V—**Pg. 486, ¶ 5 and Pg. 487, ¶ 1—Nicholas V, the papal name of the Franciscan priest Pietro Rainalducci, was installed by Louis of Bavaria in his role as Holy Roman Emperor in St. Peter's Basilica in 1328. After Louis of Bavaria left Rome, Nicholas V fled the city, made his way to Avignon, and asked John XXII for absolution; it was granted and Nicholas V faded gratefully into obscurity.**

Siegfried Schweppermann—**Pg. 484, ¶ 2—Siegfried Schweppermann, the knight who fought hardest in the battle between Louis of Bavaria and Frederick of Hapsburg in 1322, was awarded two eggs in honor of his service by Louis (everyone else only got one). Siegfried Schweppermann later put an egg on his family crest to mark the honor.**

Section II: Comprehension

Write a two or three-sentence answer to each of the following questions.

1. How did the conflict over the German crown between Louis of Bavaria and Frederick of Hapsburg end?

A1.—Pg. 484, ¶ 2 & 3—The mostly cold war between Louis of Bavaria and Frederick of Hapsburg ended in 1322 when Louis's men met Frederick and his supporters in person at Mühldorf, in Bavaria. Louis came out on top, Frederick was taken prisoner, and then he was confined in the relative comfort at the Castle of Trausnitz. Louis rewarded his poverty-stricken army with eggs for dinner; it was the most lavish celebration he could afford.

2. Why did John XXII excommunicate Louis of Bavaria?

A2.—Pg. 484, ¶ 4 & 5—Louis of Bavaria wanted to be Holy Roman Emperor, and to do that he had to get control of the north Italians, so in 1323, Louis appointed an "imperial vicar," the Count of Märstetten, and sent him into Italy to woo the Lombard cities of Milan and Ferrara. From his papal palace at Avignon, John XXII objected, insisting that in the absence of a crowned emperor the pope was the protector of the empire and alone had the right to appoint a "vicar" over Italy. Louis refused to retreat from Italy so on July 17, 1324, John XXII had him excommunicated.

3. What was Louis of Bavaria's plan to garner more support from the German dukes after his excommunication from the pope-in-exile?

A3.—Pg. 485, ¶ 2 & 3—In an effort to shore up his support within Germany without yielding to the demands of John XXII, Louis went to see Frederick of Hapsburg, still jailed at Trausnitz, and offered to recognize him as joint king. His proposal was carefully detailed: on odd days, his name would appear on state documents, on even days, Frederick's; they would both receive homage of vassals to the German crown; if one set out for Italy, the other would remain in Germany; Frederick's name would appear on Louis's seal, Louis's become part of Frederick's. Preferring not to stay in prison, Frederick of Hapsburg agreed to the plan.

4. How did the German electors and Pope John XXII react to Louis of Bavaria's plan to split the German throne with Frederick of Hapsburg?

A4.—Pg. 485, ¶ 3 & 4—The German electors opposed Louis of Bavaria's plan. They had the right to choose the king of Germany, none of them had voted for both men, and the compromise would savagely undercut their authority. John XXII also refused to recognize any claim of Frederick's to the throne, condemning him for his willingness to cooperate with the excommunicated Louis.

5. Why were John XXII's actions as pope questioned?

A5.—Pg. 485, ¶ 4—John XXII's actions as pope were questioned because it was increasingly obvious that his decrees were aimed at the eventual declaration of his patron, the king of France, as Holy Roman Emperor. The Avignon papacy had become no more than the tool of the French crown. John XXII's decrees drove the last nail into the coffin of the papal monarchy, that theory placing all popes above any law.

6. What was Dante Alighieri's view on the pope's right to confer the title of Holy Roman Emperor?

A6.—Pg. 485, ¶ 5 to Pg. 486, ¶ 1—Dante Alighieri insisted that the Church had never been given authority over any earthly kingdom, and so could not bestow on any man a power that it did not own. He wrote, "Before Pilate, Christ disclaimed any ruling power of a temporal kind, saying, 'My kingdom is not of this world. . . .' This must not be understood to imply that Christ, who is God, is not Lord of the temporal kingdom . . . but rather to mean that, as exemplar of the Church, He had not charge of this kingdom."

7. How did Marsilius of Padua build on Dante's ideas about man's power in the church? Who else shared views similar to those of Marsilius and Dante?

A7.—Pg. 486, ¶ 1-3—Marsilius agreed with Dante and took his argument even further; he wrote that Christ "did not come into the world to reign with temporal government or dominion," and the bishops of Rome had claimed this power through a "perverted inclination" for power. He said the pope was not the head of the empire, nor the head of the Church itself; that the "true church" is not centered at Rome, made up of those whom the pope recognizes as Christians, but of all who worship Christ, all over the world, in any place or community; and that this community— the *ecclesia*, the "invisible church"—is spiritual, not earthly, nor does it have an earthly, time-bound ruler. Both Dante and Marsilius had given written shape and an intellectual foundation to the impulse that had pushed the Waldensians and Cathars and Pastoureaux to reject both priests and pope.

8. Explain how Louis of Bavaria finally became Holy Roman Emperor and how John XXII ended up deposed.

A8.—Pg. 486, ¶ 4 & 5—Armed with Marsilius's arguments, depending on the goodwill of the Italians who had benefited from the visit of his imperial vicar, Louis of Bavaria marched into Italy to be crowned emperor. On Whitsunday of 1327, he had himself crowned king of Italy at Milan, with the Iron Crown of the Lombards; and on January 17, 1328, he was crowned Holy Roman Emperor by two bishops, aided by the Italian nobleman Sciarra Colonna. John XXII had declared a crusade against Louis of Bavaria, and even though he voided it after Louis's coronation, Louis of Bavaria, now Holy Roman Emperor, still took a stab at the pope and declared him deposed.

9. Why did Louis, now Holy Roman Emperor, leave Rome?

A9.—Pg. 486, ¶ 6—The people of Rome disliked Louis because his underpaid German army was looting and stealing in order to support itself. As a result, he forced Milan and the surrounding cities to hand over a total of 200,000 florins to help pay for his proposed reunification of the empire; and he unwisely threatened priests who remained loyal to John

XXII with execution. After these unpopular actions, Louis decided that it would be wiser to leave Rome.

10. Describe John XXII's November 1, 1331 new interpretation of the Beatific Vision, and how this interpretation did harm to the pope.

A10—Pg. 487, ¶ 2 to Pg. 488, ¶ 3—John XXII's new interpretation of the Beatific Vision was that the righteous dead, who were traditionally thought of as being in the presence of God, were actually in an intermediate state; they were protected by Christ, free from human woes, but still not in the direct presence of God and they would not be until the Last Judgment. For fourteenth-century Christians, whose dead were numerous and close, who lived in the constant knowledge that they too faced the possibility of death from every accidental splinter, every sore throat, every minor burn, it was a fraught and painful message that led to John XXII defending himself from heresy by his cardinals in 1331. John XXII, by now nearly eighty-five, crumbled; on December 3, 1334, he retracted his teaching about the Beatific Vision, acknowledging that he had made a mistake and on the next day, December 4, he died in Avignon.

Section III: Critical Thinking

The student may not use his text to answer this question.

The Italian poet Petrarch revived the honor of the Poet Laureate. He was crowned on Easter Sunday, April 18, 1341, by the Roman Senate. Write a paragraph explaining why Petrarch chose Easter Sunday for his coronation.

The student read about Petrarch when he first started his work with The History of the Renaissance World. Petrarch is credited for giving a name to the renaissance.

Renaissance means "rebirth." Easter is the time when Christians celebrate the rising of Christ from the dead. After Christ was crucified and he died, he was buried. Three days after his burial, Christians believe Christ rose from the dead, and later ascended into heaven. Christ's death and rebirth symbolize the power of God, of faith, and the ultimate salvation of man. The student may look up the holiday and its significance to the Christian faith in order to help him answer this question.

Petrarch picked Easter Sunday to accept the prize of Poet Laureate because he believed the revival of the Poet Laureate position would help to bring about a new age in Rome. On the day of the election, he told the Roman Senate that "I am moved also by the hope that, if God wills, I may renew in the now aged Republic a beauteous custom of its flourishing youth. . . . I am venturing to offer myself as guide for this toilsome and dangerous path; and I trust that there may be many followers." As written on page 489, the path was the path of learning. It was the rediscovery of the truths of the past, the history and literature of Rome's glory days. Like Jesus would save man, poets and scholars, Petrarch explained, would save Italy; poets and scholars would lead the Italian cities back into peace and prosperity.

As Christ was resurrected from his burial ground, Petrarch wanted to resurrect Rome. He wanted a return to the days when the Roman Empire had been whole and powerful, not split between squabbling rulers and priests. And though Petrarch was using Christian ideas to fuel his resurrection, he wanted to bring Italy back to a time before

Christianity, when Rome was in the golden age of Cicero and Virgil, Rome between the coronation of Romulus and the rule of the emperor Titus. He wanted to return to the classical age of light and learning. The revival of the Poet Laureate, conferred on Easter Sunday, marked an official recognition of the glory of the Roman past and Petrarch's desire to return it to the present: the renaissance.

EXAMPLE ANSWER:

Petrarch chose Easter Sunday to be crowned Poet Laureate because he wanted to tie his coronation with the idea of rebirth. Easter is the time when Christians celebrate the rising of Christ from the dead. Christ's death and rebirth symbolize the power of God, of faith, and the ultimate salvation of man. Petrarch picked Easter Sunday to accept the prize of Poet Laureate because he believed the revival of the Poet Laureate position would help to bring about a new age in Rome. Like Jesus would save man, poets and scholars, Petrarch explained during his ceremony, would save Italy; poets and scholars would lead the Italian cities back into peace and prosperity. As Christ was resurrected from his burial ground, Petrarch wanted to resurrect Rome. He wanted a return to the days when the Roman Empire had been whole and powerful, not split between squabbling rulers and priests. He wanted to return to the classical age of light and learning. The revival of the Poet Laureate, conferred on Easter Sunday, marked an official recognition of the glory of the Roman past and Petrarch's desire to return it to the present: the renaissance.

Section IV: Map Exercise

1. Using your black pencil, trace the outline of the frame for Map 69.1: Lands Claimed by Louis of Bavaria.

2. Using your blue pencil, trace the outline of the coast through the Mediterranean. Include the islands of Sardinia, Corsica, and Sicily, but you need not include other islands. Also trace the line of the Rhine. Repeat until the contours are familiar.

3. Using a pencil in a contrasting color, trace the outline of the Holy Roman Empire claimed by Louis. Using your black pencil, show the mountains with small peaks. Repeat until the contours are familiar.

4. Using a new sheet of paper, trace the outline of the frame in black. Then using your regular pencil with an eraser, draw the outline of the coast through the Mediterranean. Include the islands of Sardinia, Corsica, and Sicily, but you need not include other islands. Also draw the line of the Rhine. Draw the mountains with small peaks. Erase and redraw as necessary, using the frame as a reference. When you are happy with your map, place it over the original. Erase and redraw any lines which are more than ½" off of the original.

5. Study the areas of Sardinia, Sicily, Apulia, the Papal States, Hapsburg, Bavaria, Lorraine, Märstetten, Carinthia, and Germany. When you are familiar with them, close the book and mark each area on your map. Then check your map against the book. Erase and re-mark any misplaced labels.

6. Now study closely the locations of Martirano, Rome, Viterbo, Florence, Mantua, Cremona, Milan, Avignon, Lyons, Ravenna, Ferrara, Padua, Verona, Mühldorf, Worms, Mainz, and Koblenz. When they are familiar for you, close the book. Mark each one on your map. Lay your map over the original, and erase and re-mark any locations which are more than ½″ off of the original.

7. Mark the site of Trausnitz.

Chapter Seventy

The Cities in the Lake

The student may use her text when answering the questions in sections I and II.

Section I: **Who, What, Where**

Write a one or two-sentence answer explaining the significance of each item listed below.

Acamapichtli—**Pg. 494, ¶ 4 to Pg. 495, ¶ 2—Acamapichtli, the son of an Aztec father and a Colhuacan mother, was crowned in 1375 as the first ruler of Tenochtitlán. Acamapichtli paid tribute to Tezozomoc; though he made his city a vassal to his neighbor, the peace allowed him to rule in harmony, building up the city and allowing it to grow in strength and wealth.**

Achitometl—**Pg. 492, ¶ 1-3—Achitometl, king of Colhuacan, drove the Mexica out of Tizapan after they killed his daughter in a show of defiance. Achitometl's warriors drew back once they had driven the Mexica into the waters of Lake Texcoco for fear of sparking a fight with the equally powerful city-states of Azcapotzalco and Texcoco.**

Cuacuauhpitzahuac—**Pg. 495, ¶ 3—Cuacuauhpitzahuac, younger son of Tezozomoc of Azcapotzalco, was sent to be king of Tlatelolco. Cuacuauhpitzahuac's rule over Tlatelolco made the city a vassal of Azcapotzalco.**

Huitzilopochtli—**Pg. 491, ¶ 3 and Pg. 493, ¶ 2—Huitzilopochtli was the god worshipped by the Mexica. The Mexica said that Huitzilopochtli had told them that they would know they had reached their true home when they saw an eagle sitting on a cactus with a snake in its beak, the sign they said they saw when they reached Lake Texcoco.**

Lake Texcoco—**Pg. 492, ¶ 4 to Pg. 493, ¶ 1—Lake Texcoco, the eventual home of the Mexica people, was a runoff lake, filled with melted snow that had trickled down from the mountains ringing the Basin of Mexico. The closed lake, filled with salt and minerals from the evaporated water, was shallow and briny, filled with saltwater reeds and dotted with islands of liquid mud, and was completely hostile to settlement.**

Mexica—**Pg. 491, ❡ 3 and Pg. 494, ❡ 1—Mexica was the name of one of the wandering tribes on the Central American land bridge that settled in the Valley of Mexico. After settling on Tenochtitlán in Lake Texcoco, the Mexica transformed into the Aztecs.**

Tenochtitlán—**Pg. 494, ❡ 1—Tenochtitlán, one of the larger islands in Lake Texcoco, was the settling place of the Mexica. On Tenochtitlán, the Mexica trapped, hunted and traded the meat with the surrounding cities for bricks and timber and the other necessities of life, and slowly, the tribe of the Mexica became a nation: the Aztecs.**

Tlatelolco—**Pg. 494, ❡ 2—Tlatelolco was built by four chieftains that left Tenochtitlán because they felt they were not given the right amount of property when the city was divided into barrios. Tlatelolco did not exist peacefully with Tenochtitlán.**

Tezozomoc—**Pg. 494, ❡ 4 to Pg. 495, ❡ 3—Tezozomoc, king of the city-state Azcapotzalco, was alarmed by the rapid growth of Tenochtitlán and demanded tribute from Acamapichtli, which he received. Tezozomoc sent his son to rule over Tlatelolco, making Tenochtitlán's twin city another vassal, but a vassal in higher standing.**

Tizapan—**Pg. 491, ❡ 5—Tizapan was the name of a barren plain south of Chapultepec where the king of Colhuacan settled the Mexica. Tizapan was inhospitable, filled with rocks and poisonous snakes, but the Mexica were tough and they survived in new land, building their strength while serving the Colhuacan.**

Section II: Comprehension

Write a two or three-sentence answer to each of the following questions.

1. Describe the general journey story of the people moving south on the Central American land bridge.

A1.—**Pg. 491, ❡ 2—In general, the refugees from the dusty northwest that were wandering farther and farther south into the more fertile valleys, searching for water and tillable ground, had similar stories: each group of refugees had left its homeland because the gods told them to go. Journeying south, they came first to the ruins of the half-mythical city of Tollan, burned in the middle of the eleventh century and deserted by its people. Tollan had been a blessed city, loved by the gods; but it too had fallen, so the exiles passed through it and traveled on to the lands where they now settled.**

2. How did the Mexica end up at Chapultepec? What happened once they arrived at Chapultepec?

A2.—**Pg. 491, ❡ 3 & 4—The Mexica were led faraway from their home, a place called Aztlan, by their god Huitzilopochtli, and after nearly a century of wandering, they had come to a valley where they built their first homes on the crest of a hill called Chapultepec. The locals were not pleased at the intrusion, and after several years of destructive fighting the Mexica were beaten into submission and turned into slaves and servants. The surrounding tribes divided** the defeated newcomers up; the largest group of Mexica was claimed by the king of Colhuacan, and their new master intended to use them as front-line troops in future wars.

3. What did the Mexica do to show their defiance against the king of Colhuacan?

A3.—Pg. 492, ❡ 1 & 2—Around 1325, the Mexica told their royal master, the king Achitometl, that they wished to elevate his daughter, the princess of Colhuacan, to goddesshood, and asked that she be sent to them so that they could carry out the rituals. The king agreed and the princess was taken with great ceremony out to the highest point of Tizapan, but instead of honoring the princess, the Mexica killed her, flayed her, and dressed a priest in her skin. Then they summoned King Achitometl to come and greet the goddess; when he realized what the Mexica had done to his daughter, he called for their annihilation.

4. How did the Mexica end up in Lake Texcoco? Why didn't the Colhuacan warriors follow the Mexica into Lake Texcoco?

A4.—Pg. 492, ❡ 3—The Mexica were driven out of Tizapan into the waters of Lake Texcoco by the Colhuacan warriors following their murder of the princess of Colhuacan, and once they were splashing in the shallows, the Colhuacan soldiers drew back. While the Colhuacan warriors may have thought the Mexica had perished in the water, it was more likely they drew back because the lake sat in a demilitarized zone, neutral ground that separated Colhuacan from the equally powerful city-states of Azcapotzalco and Texcoco. King Achitometl did not mind wiping out the helpless Mexica, but he did not wish to start a fight with his neighbors so he let the Mexica flounder in the lake.

5. What story did the Mexica tell about their journey to and settlement in Lake Texcoco? How did it help the Mexica deal with their situation?

A5.—Pg. 493, ❡ 1 & 2—The Mexica said their god Huitzilopochtli had told them long that they would know they had reached the end of their wanderings when they saw a sign, an eagle sitting on a cactus with a snake held in its beak: "It is there that we shall fix ourselves, it is there that we shall rule, that we shall wait, that we shall meet the various nations and that with our arrow and our shield we shall overthrow them." When they arrived at Lake Texcoco, the story went on, they sloshed their way into the middle of it and suddenly saw the eagle of prophecy, "poised on a cactus, eating with delight. . . . And they wept, crying, 'At last we have been worthy of our god; we have deserved the reward; with astonishment we have seen the sign: our city shall be here.' " The Mexica were stuck in the lake, surrounded by three major powers, so the story was very useful and allowed them to celebrate the inevitable settlement.

6. How did the Aztecs come to be split between Tenochtitlán and Tlatelolco?

A6.—Pg. 494, ❡ 2—Sometime between 1337 and 1357, a splinter group of Aztecs moved out of Tenochtitlán because of a perceived inequality. Tenochtitlán had grown large enough to be divided into four sections, or *barrios*, with each section parceled out to the men of the city, and some elders felt they deserved more property than they had received. Four chieftains sought out a different place to settle, found a dry piece of land, and built a second city called Tlatelolco.

7. What tribute did Tezozomoc demand from Acamapichtli? Why did Acamapichtli decide to pay the tribute?

A7.—Pg. 494, ¶ 4 to Pg. 495, ¶ 2—Tezozomoc demanded tribute in the form of fish, frogs, willow and cypress trees, maize, chiles, beans, squash, and large loaves of bread made out of the ground redworms called *ezcahuitli*. Though paying the tribute would acknowledge that the Aztecs were vassals and servants to Azcapotzalco, Acamapichtli ordered the people of the city to pay the tribute and keep the peace. Paying the tribute allowed the Aztecs to live in peace, and during the years that they pretended to be content and obedient, they grew stronger, more organized, and more prosperous.

8. Why did the chieftains of Tlatelolco ask Tezozomoc to send them a royal son to be their ruler?

A8.—Pg. 495, ¶ 3—The chieftains of Tlatelolco ignored the election of Acamapichtli, which necessitated that they find their own ruler. Tlateloloc asked Tezozomoc of Azcapotzalco to send them one of his own royal sons as their ruler. Tezozomoc agreed and sent his younger son, Cuacuauhpitzahuac, making Tlatelolco a vassal of the greater city, but a vassal in higher standing than Tenochtitlán.

Section III: Critical Thinking

The student may not use her text to answer this question.

Before the Aztecs were known by that name, they were called the Mexica. The Mexica were driven out of Tizapan to their home of Tenochtitlán by Achitometl because the Mexica murdered his daughter, the princess of Colhuacan. Write a paragraph that connects the princess's murder to the later custom of human sacrifice practiced by the Aztecs. You will have to do some research to answer this question. As always, make sure to cite your sources.

In this answer, the student will use the death of the princess of Colhuacan to explore the later ritual sacrifices of the Aztecs.

The Aztec people practiced human sacrifice regularly. It was an important part of their religion. They believed that Huitzilopochtli was hungry and needed to be fed regularly; their god was nourished by human blood. Human blood was believed to be the force behind life. It kept the people going and it gave the sun the power to rise and set. Captives and criminals were often sacrificed, but people volunteered as well, seeing the sacrifice of their lives as the ultimate sign of grace and nobility.

The Mexica sacrificed the princess of Colhuacan in order to show their defiance of Achitometl. They were forced out of Tizapan after her death, and that led them to Tenochtitlán. While their move to Lake Texcoco was forced, it was later understood to be part of Huitzilopochtli's divine plan. The princess of Colhuacan's death was the first recorded sacrifice of the Aztecs; it was a sacrifice that led the Mexica to their homeland and that started a great civilization. The great civilization of the Aztecs was kept alive, in the spiritual minds of the people, through continued human sacrifice.

For the following example answer, two outside texts are used to substantiate the connection between the death of the princess and the later sacrifices of the Aztecs. To begin the research process, the student should do a keyword search on the internet, using terms such as "human sacrifice," "Mexica human sacrifice," and "Aztec human sacrifice." The most important connection for the student to make is that the Mexica later turned into the Aztecs once they were settled at Tenochtitlán. The move wouldn't have happened without the murder of the princess, so her death is tied directly to the rise of the Aztecs (a civilization that appeased their gods with sacrifice).

EXAMPLE ANSWER:

According to the third edition of *Contemporary Mexican Politics* by Emily Edmonds-Poli and David A. Shirk, the princess of Colhuacan was killed not just in a show of defiance against Achitometl, but as part of a "religious ritual" (12). The *Ancient History Encyclopedia* reports that human sacrifices were a ritual that honored the gods and were "regarded as a necessity to ensure mankind's continued prosperity." Captive warriors, volunteers, and specially-selected individuals chosen to impersonate gods were sacrificed. The sacrifices were "viewed as a repayment for the sacrifices the gods had themselves made in creating the world and the sun." The sacrifice of the princess of Colhuacan did show the Mexica's defiance of Achitometl. It was the catalyst that caused them to be forced out of Tizapan, and that led them to Tenochtitlán. While their move to Lake Texcoco was forced, it was later understood to be part of Huitzilopochtli's divine plan. The princess of Colhuacan's death was the first recorded sacrifice of the Aztecs; it was a sacrifice that led the Mexica to their homeland and that started a great civilization. The great civilization of the Aztecs was kept alive, in the spiritual minds of the people, through continued human sacrifice.

Section IV: Map Exercise

1. Trace the rectangular outline of the frame for Map 70.1 in black.

2. Trace the outline of Lake Texcoco , including the small islands. Repeat until the contours are familiar.

3. Using a new sheet of paper, trace the rectangular outline of the map in black. Then draw the outline of Lake Texcoco, including the small islands. When you are happy with your map, lay it over the original, and erase and re-draw any lines which are more than ¼″ off of the original.

4. Study the locations of Colhuacan, Chapultepec, Tenochtitlan, Tlatelolco, Azcapotzalco, and Texcoco. When they are familiar for you, close the book. Mark and label each one on the map, and then lay your map over the original. Erase and re-mark any labels which are more than ¼″ off of the original.

Chapter Seventy-One

A Hundred Years of War

The student may use his text when answering the questions in sections I and II.

Section I: Who, What, Where

Write a one or two-sentence answer explaining the significance of each item listed below.

Charles of Bohemia—**Pg. 503, ¶ 1 & 2—Charles of Bohemia was elected king of Germany in 1346 to replace Louis IV. Louis IV refused to recognize the election but just as civil war seemed inevitable, he had a stroke during a bear hunt and fell dead from his horse.**

David Bruce—**Pg. 497, ¶ 1 & 2 and Pg. 498, ¶ 5—David Bruce, Robert Bruce's son, was married to the seven-year-old sister of Edward III at the signing of the Treaty of Edinburgh-Northampton in 1328, and was made king of Scotland at five after his father's death in 1329. After Edward Balliol took the Scottish throne for the second time in July of 1333, David Bruce and his child wife Joan were sent to France, where Philip IV agreed to help him regain Scotland in return for David's homage to the French throne.**

Edward Balliol—**Pg. 497, ¶ 3 to Pg. 498, ¶ 2 & 4—Edward Balliol, son of John Balliol, fought his way onto the Scottish throne in October of 1332, but because he had no supporters in Scotland was forced to flee three months later by a reassembled Scottish army loyal to David Bruce. Edward Balliol took the Scottish throne for a second time, this time backed by Edward III's troops, in July of 1333.**

Edward of Woodstock—**Pg. 501, ¶ 4 and Pg. 502, ¶ 4—Edward of Woodstock, Edward III's oldest son, was knighted on July 18, 1346 on the shores of Normandy. Edward of Woodstock fought fiercely against the French at Crécy-en-Ponthieu and was rewarded with a black cuirass from which his nickname, the Black Prince, may have been derived.**

Thomas Randolph—**Pg. 497, ¶ 2 and Pg. 498, ¶ 1—Thomas Randolph was the Earl of Moray and regent and guardian to young King David Bruce. Thomas Randolph died after he was taken suddenly and violently ill on his way to defend King David from Edward Balliol.**

Section II: **Comprehension**

Write a two or three-sentence answer to each of the following questions.

1. What did Robert Bruce and the Early of Moray do to set David up for success as king of Scotland?

A1.—Pg. 497, ¶ 2 & 3— Robert Bruce had done his best to guard his son's claim to the throne by having him betrothed to the seven-year-old sister of Edward III (the marriage was celebrated the same year, and the little girl had come to live in the Scottish royal palace) at the signing of the Treaty of Edinburgh-Northampton in 1328. Robert Bruce also made Thomas Randolph David's regent and guardian; Randolph, the Earl of Moray, was an experienced soldier who had commanded a regiment at Bannockburn and fought by Bruce's side during the War for Scottish Independence. At David's coronation Randolph had it publicly proclaimed that David claimed right to the kingdom of Scotland by no hereditary succession, but in like manner as his father, by conquest alone because he knew that the Scots had a tradition of following the strongest man, not the next in line by blood.

2. Who supported Edward Balliol's first attempt to take the Scottish throne? What happened when the invaders met the Scottish army?

A2.—Pg. 497, ¶ 3 to Pg. 498, ¶ 2—Edward Balliol and his small mercenary army were supported by a handful of English barons who had lost their Scottish territories and wanted them back. The Scottish army was badly defeated by Edward Balliol's army and all of the Scottish leaders died in battle: the Earl of Mar (who had replaced the dead Earl of Moray as regent), Robert, David's illegitimate half brother, and the young son of the dead Earl of Moray. Edward Balliol marched triumphantly to Scone and had himself crowned king of Scotland on October 4, but he had no supporters in Scotland so three months after his coronation, he was forced to flee Scotland by a reassembled Scottish army loyal to David.

3. Why did Edward III choose to support Edward Balliol instead of David Bruce? What was the result of Edward III's support?

A3.—Pg. 498, ¶ 3 & 4—Though David Bruce was married to Edward III's sister, Edward Balliol was English, and supporting him meant a chance at getting Scotland back for England. An English army joined Balliol and his men, and in early July of 1333, the combined armies of Balliol and Edward III successfully attacked the border town of Berwick and then marched to Scone. After taking the throne again, Balliol repaid Edward III for his aid by handing over half of Scotland to the direct control of the English crown.

4. How did the Holy Roman Empire end up entirely independent of the papacy?

A4.—Pg. 499, ¶ 6 to Pg. 500, ¶ 2—Edward III arranged for Louis IV of Germany to declare him the Vicar-General of the Holy Roman Empire "so that all those of the Empire should be at his service," meaning the English king would have the right to recruit soldiers from anywhere in the empire to fight against Philip VI. In order to make the declaration, Louis IV held three meetings over the spring and summer of 1338 where the electors of Germany agreed, almost unanimously, to an imperial policy that said the Holy Roman Emperor derived his authority

not from the pope (more clearly than ever an ally of the French throne) but from the electors, the representatives of the empire and its people, now known formally as the Electoral League. This is how the Holy Roman Empire ended up entirely independent of the papacy, how Louis IV became Holy Roman Emperor by right of his electors alone, and how he was able to give Edward III the support of the Empire in his fight against France.

5. What events led to the signing of the Treaty of Malestroit on January 19, 1343?

A5.—Pg. 501, ¶ 1 & 2—After declaring war on France, Edward III destroyed the French fleet at Sluys, which halted Philip VI's intended invasion of England, but Edward III followed this up with a siege of Tournai that failed and cost far too much money. David of Scotland, accompanied by French troops, returned home in 1341 and began to attack English positions along the Scottish border; the English were made vulnerable because Louis IV's promised soldiers never arrived to help the English, despite repeated appeals from Edward III. By late 1342, neither side had gained a clear advantage and both kings were deep in debt, so they agreed to a three-year peace: the Treaty of Malestroit.

6. Explain how Edward III ended up knighting his sixteen-year-old son, Edward of Woodstock, on Norman soil on July 18, 1346.

A6.—Pg. 501, ¶ 3 & 4—After Edward III declared the Treaty of Malestroit void in April of 1345, insisting that Philip had violated its provisions, a French army laid siege to Aiguillon, in the English-held territory of Gascony. Edward III then supposedly planned for a large army to attack France at Gascony in order to relieve the Castle of Aiguillon, but instead he landed on the shores of Normandy at the head of fifteen thousand men in July of 1346. Once there, Edward III knighted his son, sixteen-year-old Edward of Woodstock, on Norman soil.

7. How did Edward III direct his soldiers to behave once they reached Normandy? What actually happened?

A7.—Pg. 501, ¶ 5 to Pg. 502, ¶ 1—Edward III had given his men orders not to burn the houses of the poor, sack churches, or injure women, children, or the elderly, but this well-intentioned decree was not well enforced. The English romped through Normandy, sacking and pillaging. At the town of Caen, sacked on July 26, Edward's army slaughtered civilians and knights without distinction, and it is claimed that at least some of the English soldiers raped women in the street and indulged in arson and robbery.

8. Describe what happened when the French army, which outnumbered the English three to one, met its enemy at Crécy-en-Ponthieu.

A8.—Pg. 502, ¶ 3 & 4—When the French met the English at Crécy-en-Ponthieu at four o'clock on the afternoon of Saturday, August 25, 1346, the English had their backs to the sun and it shone straight into the eyes of the French. The English then placed their bowmen at the front and overwhelmed the French's front lines with a blizzard of arrows and the French line broke. By nightfall, Philip VI was forced to begin a retreat and took refuge at Amiens; thousands of French foot soldiers and most of Philip VI's knights—by one reliable count, 1,291—lay dead on the field.

9. How did David Bruce end up a prisoner of the English?

A9.—Pg. 502, ❡ 6—After his victory at Crécy-en-Ponthieu, Edward III marched to the strategic port of Calais and laid siege to it, though the defenders did hold out for eleven months. Philip, hoping to lift the attack by distracting his enemy, sent word to David of Scotland asking him to invade England from the north but as David Bruce led the Scottish army towards Durham he encountered, unexpectedly, an English force hastily assembled by the Archbishop of York. Once again, the English archers broke the Scottish line, nearly the whole of the army of Scotland was either captured or slain, and David himself was taken prisoner back to London, where he would remain for the next eleven years.

10. What happened after Philip VI lost Calais?

A10.—Pg. 503, ❡ 3—Philip VI surrendered in August of 1347 after he lost Calais. Edward III immediately established an English colony there, ordering thirty-six well-established English families to settle in the city, along with three hundred "men of lesser standing." He also encouraged the French exodus: "I wish to repopulate Calais with pure-blooded English," he announced.

Section III: Critical Thinking

The student may use his text to answer this question.

As we know from our reading, both in this chapter and previous ones, "War between England and France was nothing new." The reasoning behind the Hundred Years' War, however, is complicated, and is based on the crisscrossing of family lines and rightful claims to the throne. Write a paragraph explaining why English king Edward III claimed the right to the French throne and how he declared war on France. You may want to look back at chapters Fifty-Nine and Sixty-Six when working on your response.

The English claim to the French throne is confusing. This exercise is intended to help the student sort through the mess.

In Chapter Sixty-Six, we read about how Edward II neglected his wife Isabella. When she had enough of being treated poorly by her husband, she fled England for France. Isabella was the sister of the French king Philip V and Charles IV, successor to the French throne. Isabella and Edward II had a son: Edward III. Edward III became king of England, but his bloodline tied him to French royalty. After Charles IV's death, Philip of Valois became king of France, ending the Capetian line. However, the blood of Hugh Capet ran in Edward III's veins. As described on page 499, " 'The King of England,' says Jean Froissart, 'had long wished for an opportunity to assert his right to the crown of France.' When Philip V had resurrected the old Salic Law to take the throne of France away from his niece, he had inadvertently provided a way for the English king to take the French throne. Philip V's end run around his niece's [Joan of Navarre's] right to rule France had led to the barring of his own daughter, his sole child, from the throne, and the appointment of the new House of Valois in the place of Hugh Capet's descendants—leaving Edward III, son of Philip's sister Isabelle, as the sole remaining monarch of direct Capetian descent." This is why Edward III believed he should be king of France: not only did he have a tie to the crown, but he would be restoring the Capetian bloodline to the throne.

The student can review Philip V's barring of Joan of Navarre from the throne by looking over chapter Fifty-Nine.

Edward III's claim to the throne then explains why he started his October 19, 1337 letter to Philip VI by claiming "We are heir to the realm and crown of France by a much closer degree of kingship than yourself, who have entered into possession of our heritage and are holding and desiring to hold it by force. . . . Wherefore we give you notice that we shall claim and conquer our heritage of France. . . . since we consider you as our enemy and adversary."

Edward III felt that he had a more secure hold on the French throne as a descendent of Hugh Capet than Philip VI did as a descendent of the House of Valois. Edward III's assertion led to the Hundred Years' War.

EXAMPLE ANSWER:

Philip V became king of France after he barred Princess Joan of Navarre from taking the French throne by invoking Salic Law. After Philip V died, his brother Charles IV took the throne. After Charles IV's death, Philip of Valois took the throne. Though Isabella, sister of Philip V and Charles IV lived, she was barred from the French throne because of the same law that blocked Joan of Navarre. When Philip of Valois became king, the House of Valois came into power and the Capetian bloodline ended. However, Isabella, married to Edward II of England, had a child: Edward III. Edward III was the the sole remaining monarch of direct Capetian descent. Edward III believed he had a greater right to the French throne than Philip VI, of Valois. This is why Edward III's October 19, 1337 letter to Philip VI starts by claiming "We are heir to the realm and crown of France by a much closer degree of kingship than yourself, who have entered into possession of our heritage and are holding and desiring to hold it by force. . . . Wherefore we give you notice that we shall claim and conquer our heritage of France. . . . since we consider you as our enemy and adversary." Edward III felt that he had a more secure hold on the French throne as a descendent of Hugh Capet than Philip IV did as a descendent of the House of Valois. Edward III's assertion led to the Hundred Years' War.

Section IV: Map Exercise

1. Trace the rectangular outline of the frame for Map 71.1 in black.

2. Using your blue pencil, trace the outline of the coast around Ireland, Scotland, England, and the European continent. You do not need to include small islands. Also trace the line of the Seine and of the Loire. Repeat until the contours are familiar.

3. Using a new sheet of paper, trace the outline of the frame for Map 71.1 in black. Using your regular pencil with an eraser, draw the coastline around Ireland, Scotland, England, and the European continent. You do not need to include small islands. Also draw the line of the Seine and of the Loire. Remember to use the frame of the map as a reference. When you are happy with your map, lay it over the original. Erase and redraw any lines which are more than ½" off of the original.

4. Mark Ireland, Scotland, England, Normandy, Brittany, Poitou, Languedoc, and Gascony. Then study carefully the locations of Scone, Kinghorn, Berwick, Durham, York, London, Calais, Tournai, Crecy, Rouen, Paris, and Caen. When they are familiar for you, close the book. Mark and label each

one on your map. Lay your map over the original, and erase and re-mark any labels that are more than ½" off of the original.

5. Study closely the locations of the Battle of Dupplin' Moor, the Battle of Sluys, and the castle of Aiguillon. When they are familiar, close the book. Mark and label each one on your map. Lay your map over the original, and erase and re-mark any labels that are more than ½" off of the original.

Chapter Seventy-Two

The End of the World

The student may use her text when answering the questions in sections I and II.

Section I: Who, What, Where

Write a one or two-sentence answer explaining the significance of each item listed below.

Toghon Temur—**Pg. 505, ¶ 2 & 3—Toghon Temur, the tenth Yuan emperor and Kublai Khan's great-great-great-grandson, was crowned at the age of thirteen in 1333 and for eleven years he had been the passive ruler of a top-heavy, bureaucrat-stuffed, unevenly taxed empire, run for him by his chancellors. Five years into his rule, the plague struck a little village below Lake Issyk-Kul.**

Section II: Comprehension

Write a two or three-sentence answer to each of the following questions.

1. Where did the plague start, and how do we know it started there? What caused the plague?

A1.—Pg. 505, ¶ 3 & *—The plague started in an obscure little village below Lake Issyk-Kul. We know this only from the hundreds of headstones dated from around 1338 and 1339 found in the village graveyard; an inscription on one of these headstones reads "This is the grave of Kutluk. He died of the plague with his wife." The exact origin of the "Black Death" continues to be debated, as does the identity of the plague. Our text takes the majority view that the fourteenth-century pandemic was bubonic plague caused by the bacterium *Yersinia pestis*, but a solid minority of scientists and historians continue to argue for other causes, such as anthrax, hemorrhagic fever, typhus, or some combination of infectious diseases.

2. What tragedies did contemporary chroniclers record in the years after the deaths near Lake Issyk-Kul? Where and when did the plague make a reappearance?

A2.—Pg. 505, ¶ 2 to Pg. 506, ¶ 1—No contemporary accounts trace the spread of the illness in the six years following the deaths near Lake Issyk-Kul, but plenty of chroniclers record

other disasters: drought and famine in the Huai river valley, torrential flooding rains in the provinces at Canton and Houkouang, locusts in Honan, and an earthquake that carved a new lake into the Ki-Ming-Chan mountain range. Meanwhile, sickness seems to have moved silently west, along the trade routes between the Yuan cities and the markets of India. In 1344, an army from Delhi, marching south to put down a rebellion in Ma'bar, was wiped out by a "pestilence"; the Arab traveler Ibn Battuta, visiting the southeastern city of Madurai, discovered a lethal infection sweeping through it, writing that "Whoever caught it died on the morrow, or the day after."

3. Describe the particular mark of the plague that moved across the world in the 14th century.

A3.—Pg. 506, ¶ 4—The particular mark of the plague that moved across the world in the 14th century was swellings in armpit and groin. The swellings, or buboes, were caused by infected lymph nodes, which filled with pus: a symptom of the presence of *Yersinia pestis*, a bacterial infection carried by fleas. This is known as the bubonic plague.

4. How did the Golden Horde hope to break down Caffa, a Genoese-controlled trading port? How did this strategy spread the plague even further?

A4.—Pg. 506, ¶ 6 to Pg. 507, ¶ 1—Golden Horde warriors hurled the corpses of their dead companions over the city walls of Caffa with catapults, hoping to kill the defenders either with the illness itself, or with the stench of the decaying bodies; a handful of the inhabitants escaped by ship from the terror and made their way to Messina and they died, as did everyone else who had any contact with them. Most likely, the plague spread into and out of Caffa not via the dead members of the Mongols, but on the backs of black rats that lived in the holds of ships, ran in and out of cities, and shed fleas wherever they went. And in a perfect storm of disrupted weather cycles, overcrowded cities, weakened population, far-flung merchant navies, and far-roving armies, the plague burned across Europe as it had burned across Asia and India and Syria.

5. Explain some of the ways that the plague took its victims.

A5.—Pg. 507, ¶ 2 & 3—Millions died writhing in pain from the swollen buboes, their skin blackened with internal bleeding, lips and noses turning gangrenous, vomiting blood. Millions more died when the infection settled in the lungs and caused pneumonia, killing so quickly—often within forty-eight hours—that the buboes never had a chance to form. John Cantacuzenus watched his thirteen-year-old son die and described how "Great abscesses were formed on the legs or the arms, from which, when cut, a large quantity of foul-smelling pus flowed. . . . There was no help from anywhere . . . there was no hope left."

6. What did the poet Giovanni Boccaccio see in Florence that amazed him? What happened to the towns whose inhabitants were wiped out by the plague? How did Pope Clement VI react to the fast-spreading disease?

A6.—Pg. 507, ¶ 4 & 5— In Florence, the poet Giovanni Boccaccio watched in amazement as two pigs on the street nosed the cast-off rags of a plague victim, and then collapsed, struggling and dying as if poisoned. Houses stood empty everywhere, entire families wiped out within hours of each other; in some villages, everyone died and crops were left untended, doors open,

churches deserted and the cows and sheep wandered free. In Avignon, Pope Clement VI bought a field just outside the city and consecrated the entire thing so that sixty-two thousand bodies could be buried there.

7. How did the plague affect England, Ireland, and Egypt?

A7.—Pg. 507, ¶ 6 to Pg. 508, ¶ 2—The plague crossed over to England and Ireland in 1348, spreading from the southwest up and across the islands; nearly half of England died and many villages and hamlets were deserted because everyone who had lived there was dead, and according to the Irish monk John Clynn, there was scarcely anyone left in the villages, cities, castles and towns of Ireland, too. John Clynn himself wrote "I, waiting among the dead for death to come, have committed to writing what I have truly heard. . . . I leave parchment for continuing the work, in case anyone should still be alive in the future" and beneath these last words is added, in the handwriting of another, "Here, it seems, the author died." In Egypt, between October of 1348 and February of 1349, a hundred thousand died in Cairo alone.

8. What was the effect of the plague on Europe's economy after the spread of the disease began to slow?

A8.—Pg. 509, ¶ 4 to Pg. 510, ¶ 2—The survivors of the plague found themselves facing newly emptied countrysides, deserted villages, and wasted fields. Because there were no workers left, there was a massive shortage of crops, and in England, prices of essentials had tripled or quadrupled. Farmhands, now a rare commodity, began to charge exorbitant fees for their labor, sometimes up to three times what they would have been paid before the plague.

9. How did survivors of the plague explain its existence?

A9.—Pg. 510, ¶ 3—The faculty of the medical school in Paris published a report blaming the plague on the conjunction of "three planets in Aquarius," which had caused the "deadly corruption of the air." King Edward III of England, mourning the loss of his fifteen-year-old daughter, blamed the spiritual wickedness of his people and in France and Germany, Jews were accused of poisoning the wells; hundreds were seized and murdered by angry mobs. From Avignon, Pope Clement VI condemned this violence and composed a Mass for the turning away of plague.

Section III: Critical Thinking

The student may not use her text to answer this question.

The plague started its deadly creep across the world in 1338. It wasn't until 1346 that the Western world started to record the horrible death occurring the the East. One of the first accounts of the illness from an observer comes from the Arab scholar Abu Hafs 'Umar Ibn al-Wardi. He writes, "It began in the land of darkness [and] it has been current for fifteen years. . . . Plague sat like a king on a throne and swayed with power, killing daily one thousand or more and decimating the population. It destroyed mankind with its pustules. . . . How amazingly does it pursue the people of each house! One of them spits blood, and everyone in the household is certain of death." Write a paragraph or two that recounts another first-hand account of the plague. In your answer, attempt to pry some greater meaning from the account. What can you tell about the conditions at the time from the writer's description? A useful place to start your research would be with the list of books recommended in the footnote on page 505, but you do not have to use one of those texts as the source for your answer.

The student will need to find a primary source on the plague in order to answer this question. A primary source is an original document or object. For example, the United States Constitution is a primary document. A guide to understanding the Constitution is a secondary source. Secondary sources act as interpretations, or guides, to primary sources.

Susan Wise Bauer recommends several texts on the plague in the footnote on page 505. She points to Rosemary Horrox's The Black Death *(Manchester University Press, 1994) as a useful collection of primary sources, though the student does not have to use this text in her research. Whatever text the student uses, she must cite her sources clearly.*

In the example that follows, one of the accounts from Rosemary Horrox's book is presented in a mix of direct quotation and paraphrase. There is also some analysis of the firsthand account. The author, Ralph Hidgen, notes that few lords and great men died during the plague. This suggests that money allowed some men to separate themselves from the masses. Wealth could not stop the disease from killing the men once it was contracted, but money did allow the men to isolate themselves in an attempt to not be in contact with the plague in the first place.

EXAMPLE ANSWER:

In the book *The Black Death,* **Rosemary Horrox presents many firsthand accounts of the plague and its spread across the world. In this example, Horrox presents the reader with Ralph Hidgen's understanding of how the plague moved across the world (pages 62-3). Hidgen was a Benedictine monk that lived in the monastery of St. Werburgh's in Chester. The account comes from a continuation of his book** *Polychronicon,* **which was a history of the world from its creation to 1340. He writes, "In 1348 there was an inordinately heavy rain between Midsummer and Christmas, and scarcely a day went by without rain at some point in the day or night. During that time a great mortality of men spread across the world and was especially violent in and around Roman Curia at Avignon, and around the coastal towns of England and Ireland." He then continues to explain how the plague made its way across England: "This year around the feast of St. John [24 June] the aforesaid pestilence attacked the Bristol area and then travelled to all the other parts of England in turn, and it lasted in England for more than a year." Hidgen's says "scarcely a tenth of mankind was left alive." Dead animals followed, land went to waste because there was no one to keep it up, and Hidgen feared that the world would not "regain its previous condition" because "so much misery ensued." He does note that few lords or great men died during the plague, suggesting that wealth allowed them to separate themselves from the masses and hide from the disease.**

Chapter Seventy-Three

The Will to War

The student may use his text when answering the questions in sections I and II.

Section I: Who, What, Where

Write a one or two-sentence answer explaining the significance of each item listed below.

Charles V—**Pg. 517, ¶ 2 and Pg. 521, ¶ 5—Charles, son and heir to John II, was the first prince to be known as the Dauphin. In a plot concocted by Charles of Navarre, the Dauphin Charles tried to overthrow his own father but failed; the Dauphin was crowned King Charles V of France after his father died while renegotiating the terms of his ransom with the English.**

Charles of Navarre—**Pg. 516, ¶ 3, Pg. 517, ¶ 5, and Pg. 519, ¶ 5—Charles of Navarre, Joan's son and heir, and husband of King John II of France's daughter, long thought of himself as a Frenchman, and launched a bid for the French throne. After failing to overthrow John II with the Dauphin Charles's help, Charles of Navarre was placed in prison, but escaped and made another failed bid for the throne while John II was held in captivity by the English.**

Enrique of Trastámara—**Pg. 522, ¶ 3 and Pg. 523, ¶ 1—Enrique of Trastámara, Pedro of Castile's illegitimate half brother, challenged Pedro's rule soon after Charles V's coronation. With the help of Charles V, Enrique of Trastámara was able to defeat (and kill) his half brother and take the Castilian throne.**

Estates-General—**Pg. 516, ¶ 5—Estates-General was the name for the first representative gathering of the French people; the Estates-General, which had no power to pass laws, nor was it able to force the king to do anything. It could only offer counsel and advice. The three groups that made up the Estates-General—the French nobility, clergy, and leading townsmen—was first called by Philip the Fair in 1302, and had been called several more times by Philip's successors, mostly to approve new taxes.**

Etienne Marcel—**Pg. 519, ¶ 5 and Pg. 520, ¶ 4—Etienne Marcel, a powerful Parisian merchant and supporter of parliamentary rule, led the Estates-General at the time of John II's captivity. Etienne Marcel was assassinated in Paris a few weeks after the ending of the Jacquerie.**

Louis of Anjou—Pg. 520, ❡ 5 and Pg. 521, ❡ 3—Louis of Anjou, John II's second son, was sent to Calais to be a hostage of the English until the full amount of his father's debt to the English was paid as part of the compromise signed at Bretigny on May 8, 1360. Louis of Anjou escaped from Calais and returned home; his father went to England to renegotiate the terms of the treaty and when he departed he left nothing for Louis of Anjou to rule as his own.

Jacques Bonhomme—Pg. 520, ❡ 2 & 4—Jacques Bonhomme, meaning "Silly Jack," was the name given by the French elite to the country's peasants. The Jacques Bonhomme came together to revolt against the French upper class in May 1358 in an uprising called the Jacquerie.

John II—Pg. 515, ❡ 6 to Pg. 516, ❡ 1, Pg. 518, ❡ 3, and Pg. 521, ❡ 1—John II, Philip VI's successor, inherited a country that was in disarray: the English occupied much of France (including Calais), the treasury was exhausted, famine and draught had weakened the country and war and bubonic plague weakened it further. John II was taken prisoner by the English in 1356 and was not able to return to France until May of 1360, after signing away half of his country to the English.

John of Gaunt—Pg. 517, ❡ 5—John of Gaunt, English prince and third son of Edward III, helped Philip of Navarre attack John II's Norman holdings in revenge for Charles of Navarre's imprisonment; Edward III himself furnished twenty-seven ships for the attack.

Pedro of Castile—Pg. 515, ❡ 5 and Pg. 522, ❡ 4 & 6—Pedro, ruler of Castile following the death of his father Alfonso XI, began a war for territory with the king of neighboring Aragon, Pedro IV. Pedro of Castile was forced to flee his country by his half brother Enrique of Trastámara; he was eventually killed by Enrique at the Battle of Campo de Montiel.

Philip the Bold—Pg. 518, ❡ 3 and Pg. 521, ❡ 3—Philip, King John's favorite son, was taken prisoner, along with his father, by the Black Prince after the English defeated the French at Poitiers in September of 1356. When John II returned to England in 1364 to renegotiate the terms of the compromise signed in Bretigny on May 8 1360, Philip the Bold was given control of Burgundy as well as the title Duke of Burgundy.

Philip of Navarre—Pg. 517, ❡ 5—Philip of Navarre, Charles of Navarre's brother, recruited John of Gaunt to help him attack King John of France's holdings in Normandy as revenge for his brother's imprisonment.

Section II: Comprehension

Write a two or three-sentence answer to each of the following questions.

1. Describe the deaths of Joan, queen of Navarre, Philip VI of France, and King Alfonso XI of León-Castile.

A1.—pg. 515, ❡ 2-4—Joan of Navarre, Philip VI, and Alfonso XI all died of the plague. The first victim was Joan, who died in 1349, followed by King Alfonso XI of León-Castile who succumbed to the disease on March 27, 1350 in a campaign tent near Gibraltar while fighting against the Muslim kingdom of Granada. On August 22, 1350 Philip VI of France died; he was fifty-two years old and newly married to Joan's nineteen-year-old daughter.

2. Why did Charles of Navarre think he had a shot at the French throne?

A2.—Pg. 516, ¶ 3 & 4—Charles of Navarre, Joan's son and heir, had long thought of himself as a Frenchman because he had inherited from his father, the Count of Évreux, substantial family lands in the north of France. Also, he had married King John II's daughter, had lived in France for much of his life, and even after his coronation, he used Navarre mostly as a source for income and soldiers. Most importantly, Charles of Navarre was the grandson of Louis X, the strongest heir to the Capetian throne.

3. How did Charles of Navarre make himself an attractive candidate to replace the French king?

A3.—Pg. 516, ¶ 6—Charles of Navarre played on the narrative of reform that was attractive after the disorder that followed the plague in France. He made complicated and careful alliances, presenting himself as a possible "reform king," willing (should he gain the throne) to give more authority to the Estates-General. He was thought shrewd and charming by both the common people and the men of substance and power.

4. What were the terms of the truce made between Edward of England and John of France in April 1354? What happened to the truce?

A4.—Pg. 516, ¶ 7 to Pg. 517, ¶ 2—In April 1354, John of France agreed to hand over to Edward of England all of the western French lands south of Normandy (except for Brittany), and to yield Calais. In exchange, Edward III would give up his claim to the French crown. A year later, however, Edward repudiated the treaty; by then, John II had already gained a reputation for weakness, Charles of Navarre's campaign gained strength, and it seemed the French throne was up for grabs again.

5. How did John II's son and heir come to be called the "Dauphin Charles"?

A5.—Pg. 517, *—The Dauphin took his title from the province of Dauphiné, which was his particular possession. Charles was the first heir to the French throne to hold this designation; after his accession, he decreed that all future heirs to the crown would receive it.

6. What happened to Charles of Navarre's plot with the Dauphin Charles to overthrow King John of France?

A6.—Pg. 517, ¶ 3-5—The Dauphin Charles and Charles of Navarre were not able to overthrow the king of France because John II found out about their plot before it was executed. In April of 1356, the two men were throwing a banquet for some thirty potential allies at Rouen Castle in Normandy when John II unexpectedly arrived, fully armed, at the head of a band of soldiers. John arrested four of the Norman leaders and ordered them executed. John II spared his son-in-law, but the king of Navarre was taken off in chains and moved from secure prison to secure prison until he ended up in the Fort of Arles, surrounded by a swamp.

7. How did King John of France and his son Philip end up as prisoners of the Black Prince?

A7.—Pg. 517, ❡ 6 to Pg. 518, ❡ 3—Edward the Black Prince had been leading raids into Languedoc from his father's territory of Gascony; in August 1356, Edward marched out of Gascony, towards the Loire river, with eight thousand men. John II turned to meet Edward, and the two armies came face-to-face at Poitiers, where the French, despite being better rested and better organized, were driven back by the English. The defeat led to the capture of King John of France and his fourteen-year-old son Philip.

8. How did the governing power in France shift while John II was held captive in England? How did this shift open up room for Charles of Navarre to, once again, make a bid for the French throne?

A8.—Pg. 519, ❡ 4 & 5—While John II was being held prisoner, the Estates-General came to the conclusion that the king's sons were too young and incompetent to run the country, so each of the Estates agreed to nominate twelve "of the wisest from among themselves, to consider and determine what would be most advisable." This council of thirty-six took control of the country, with the young Dauphin Charles "styled Regent" but not granted much in the way of actual power. The French did not transition easily into parliamentary rule, so Charles of Navarre, after escaping from his swampland fortress in November of 1357, made his way to Paris, where a complicated power struggle began between his supporters, the Estates-General, and the Dauphin.

9. What caused the Jacques Bonhomme to come together in Saint-Leu-d'Esserent in armed revolt, the Jacquerie, against the French nobility in May 1358? What put an end to the revolt?

A9.—Pg. 520, ❡ 2-4—The Jacques Bonhomme were sick of struggling to raise their crops and tend their livestock in a countryside constantly trampled by the armed forces of English, French, and Navarrese; they were sick of paying sudden arbitrary taxes imposed by the Crown and collected by force; and they had had enough when the Dauphin decided to give his army captains permission to pillage the countryside in order to supplement their skimpy wages. In May 1358, the Jacques Bonhomme rose up in armed revolt and for two weeks rampaged through the north of France, armed with pikes and plow pieces, burning castles, murdering knights, and massacring noble households and families. The uprising, nicknamed the Jacquerie, barely lasted three weeks before the Dauphin and Charles of Navarre, fighting separately, brought it to an end by wiping out the major roving bands of Jacques Bonhomme insurgents.

10. Describe Charles of Navarre's final attempt to take the French throne after John II's death.

A10.—Pg. 521, ❡ 5—After John II died in England, Charles of Navarre sent a Navarrese army, under joint Navarrese and English command, into Normandy; at the same time, three thousand men were dispatched intending to intercept the Dauphin Charles on the way to his coronation and prevent it. But the French royal army, pressing rapidly forward, met the invaders near the village of Cocherel, north of Paris. Charles of Navarre's army was defeated and three days later the Dauphin was crowned King Charles V of France.

11. How did Enrique of Trastámara become king of Castile?

A11.—Pg. 522, ❦ 3-6—Enrique of Trastámara challenged the rule of his half brother Pedro of Castile and was backed by the French in his contest; a Castilian king who owed his throne to the French could be very useful in the continuing attacks from Navarre. At first Enrique of Trastámara was defeated and had to flee to France, but after Charles V sent more reinforcements, Enrique of Trastámara was able to beat his half brother at the Battle of Campo de Montiel and take Pedro Captive. Enrique of Trastámara killed his half brother and was then crowned king of Castile.

Section III: Critical Thinking

The student may not use his text to answer this question.

The idiom "a king's ransom" means a very large amount of money. In this chapter we read about literal cases of kings being held captive until a ransom was paid. For example, David of Scotland was able to free himself from his eleven-year imprisonment in England by finally agreeing to paying 100,000 marks. For this critical thinking question, explain why the Black Prince took King John of France prisoner. Then, explain what ransom was paid, and if that ransom did the job of not only releasing King John but guaranteeing peace between England and France.

In the 1500s, ransom was a way to raise revenue; taking a wealthy opponent captive and holding him until a sizable payment was made offered a quick way to refill an empty treasury. At the time of King John's capture, Edward III of England had spent much of his kingdom's money on war. After the plague, the tax revenue dwindled because there were few people left to pay taxes. Taking John II prisoner meant that the English could demand payment from the French, payment that would refill the king's treasury.

Edward III suggested the French pay three million crowns to free their king, which would equal something around what we would understand to be 500 million dollars. The French king negotiated a slightly different settlement. On May 8, 1360, a compromise was signed at Bretigny that allowed John II to return home. The conditions were that John II could buy his freedom by handing over Aquitaine, Normandy, Poitou, Touraine— almost half of his country. He would also have to raise the three million crowns of his ransom, although Edward III graciously allowed him six years to pay the debt off. His second son, Louis of Anjou, was sent to Calais to be a hostage of the English until the full amount was paid. In return, Edward III gave up his claim to Normandy and also agreed (for the second time) to surrender any claim to the French throne, a concession that also extended to his son the Black Prince.

After John II returned home, he realized he would not be able to to talk the Estates-General into raising taxes for the payment of the ransom. Louis of Anjou, seeing no end to his captivity, escaped from Calais and made his way home. In January of 1364, John himself announced that he would journey back to England to renegotiate the terms. His country was a mess and he had no other choice. John II arrived in England was put up in style, but the negotiations were stalled and John II died before new terms were agreed upon.

After Pedro of Castile was forced to flee his country by Enrique of Trastámara, he asked Edward the Black Prince to help him regain his power. As justification, Pedro pointed out that he and the Black Prince were blood kin. The Black Prince's great-grandmother, wife of Edward I, was Eleanor of Castile, Pedro's great-great-great-aunt,

CHAPTER SEVENTY-THREE: THE WILL TO WAR

which made the two men cousins, three times removed. The Black Prince agreed because the alliance would bring him face-to-face with the French again, and without breaching the Treaty of Bretigny.

Pedro was eventually killed by Enrique of Trastámara, and Enrique was crowned king of Castile. The French, emboldened by the triumph and secure in their alliance with Castile, were ready again for war with England. Charles V declared that the English had not fulfilled all of the terms of the Treaty of Bretigny, so peace between the two countries was no longer possible. In the summer of 1369, Charles V prepared for all-out war.

While the ransom for John II provided a temporary peace, it did not end war between France and England. In fact, the next French king used the terms of the ransom as a way to justify another invasion of England.

EXAMPLE ANSWER:

The Black Prince took John II of France prisoner in order to raise money for England. At the time of King John's capture, Edward III of England had spent much of his kingdom's money on war. After the plague, the tax revenue dwindled because there were few people left to pay taxes. Taking John II prisoner meant that the English could demand payment from the French, payment that would refill the king's treasury.

On May 8, 1360, the kings of France and England agreed to the Treaty of Bretigny. The treaty stated that John II could buy his freedom by handing over Aquitaine, Normandy, Poitou, Touraine— almost half of his country. He would also have to raise the three million crowns of his ransom, to be paid over the course of six years, guaranteed by keeping Louis of Anjou, John II's second son, hostage. In return, Edward III gave up his claim to Normandy and also agreed (for the second time) to surrender any claim to the French throne, a concession that also extended to his son the Black Prince.

After John II returned home, he realized he would not be able to to talk the Estates-General into raising taxes for the payment of the ransom. John II was forced to return to England to renegotiate the terms of the treaty not only because he didn't have the money but also because Louis of Anjou escaped and returned to France. After returning to England, John II died in the middle of negotiations.

Soon after Charles V replaced his dead father as king of France, Pedro of Castile was forced off his throne by his half brother Enrique of Trastámara. The French backed Enrique and the English backed Pedro; backing Pedro gave the Black Prince a way to attack the French without technically violating the Treaty of Bretigny. Enrique kept the throne after killing Pedro, and the French grew bold. Charles V declared that the English had not fulfilled all of the terms of the Treaty of Bretigny, so peace between the two countries was no longer possible. In the summer of 1369, Charles V prepared for all-out war. While the ransom for John II provided a temporary peace, it did not end war between France and England. In fact, Charles V used the terms of the ransom as a way to justify another invasion of England.

Section IV: Map Exercise

1. Trace the rectangular outline of the frame for Map 73.1 in black.

2. Using your blue pencil, trace the coastline around England and the continent, up through and around the Mediterranean. Also trace the lines of the Oise, the Seine, the Loire. Repeat until the contours are familiar.

3. Using a pencil in a contrasting color, trace the English-held lands. Repeat until the contours are familiar. Use small peaks to trace the mountains.

4. Using a new sheet of paper, trace the rectangular outline of the map frame in black. Then using your regular pencil with an eraser, draw the coastline around England and the continent, up through and around the Mediterranean. Also draw the lines of the Oise, the Seine, the Loire. Remember to use the frame as a reference, erasing and re-drawing as necessary. When you are happy with your map, lay it over the original, and erase and re-draw any lines which are more than ½" off of the original.

5. Now label the areas of England, Normandy, Brittany, Touraine, Burgundy, Poitou, Aquitaine, Gascony, Languedoc, Navarre, Aragon, Portugal, and Granada.

6. Next, study carefully the locations of Calais, Rouen, Saint-Leu-d'Esserent, Paris, Evreux, Bretigny, Toulouse, Marseille, Granada, and Gibraltar. When you are familiar with them, close the book, and mark each one on your map. When you are done, lay your map over the original. Erase and re-mark any marks more than ½" off of the original.

7. Finally, study the locations of the Battle of Cocherel, the Battle of Poitiers, Arles, the Battle of Navarette, and the Battle of Campo de Montiel. When you are familiar with them, close the book, and mark each one on your map. When you are done, lay your map over the original. Erase and re-mark any marks more than ½" off of the original.

Chapter Seventy-Four

White Lotus, Red Turban

The student may use her text when answering the questions in sections I and II.

Section I: Who, What, Where

Write a one or two-sentence answer explaining the significance of each item listed below.

Amitabha—**Pg. 525, ¶ 3—Amitabha, or Pure Land Buddhism, is an old form of Buddhism that promises rebirth into an undefiled and perfect world, the Western Paradise, for all who believe in the Buddha.**

Ayushiridara—**Pg. 527, ¶ 2—Ayushiridara, son of Toghon Temur, was Crown Prince and heir to the Yuan throne. Toghto forgot to organize a ceremony for Ayushiridara's recognition and was fired as a result.**

Chen Youliang—**Pg. 527, ¶ 3 & 6—Chen Youliang, a former Yuan provincial official and leader of the Red Turban rebellion in the southwest, proclaimed himself emperor of China in Jiangzhou, adopting the name *Dahan*, meaning "Great Han." Chen Youliang's rebellion died after Zhu Yuanzhang's forces defeated Chen Youliang's navy and Chen Youliang was shot in the eye with an arrow that killed him instantly.**

Corvée labor—**Pg. 526, ¶ 4—Corvée labor, workers drawn from the peasant and farmer classes that were required to work without being paid for a certain number of months per year, was the method Toghto used to rebuilt the Yellow river. Corvée labor, imposed on almost two hundred thousand Chinese residents of the central Yuan empire, was horrendously unpopular; while the workers were digging up silt, their fields at home were going untended, and they would return to a reduced harvest and the same tax burdens as before.**

Embroidered Uniform Guards—**Pg. 529, ¶ 3—Embroidered Uniform Guards, the Hongwu Emperor's secret police, acted as spies and hit men. They had the authority to arrest and confine, in secret prisons, anyone who might threaten the security and tranquility of the realm.**

403

STUDY AND TEACHING GUIDE FOR THE HISTORY OF THE RENAISSANCE WORLD

Fang Guozhen—**Pg. 526, ¶ 3 and Pg. 527, ¶ 3—Fang Guozhen, a pirate, took advantage of Dadu's helplessness at the time of the Yellow river's shifting, and assembled a fleet of outlaws that pranced along the coast, robbing coastal cities and intercepting grain ships sailing to Dadu at will. After the failed siege of Gaoyou, Fang Guozhen seized the southern coast south of Hangzhou for his own.**

Han Lin'er—**Pg. 526, ¶ 7—Han Lin'er, son of Han Shantong, declared by his father to be crown prince and heir apparent to the Chinese throne, went into hiding after his father was executed and his rebellion was put down.**

Han Shantong—**Pg. 526, ¶ 6—Han Shantong, a White Lotus follower press-ganged into the Yellow river project, announced that he had uncovered, in the silt of the Yellow river, a one-eyed statue prophesying the arrival of the Prince of Light. Other White Lotus believers flocked to him, donning the red turbans as their mark, and with their support Han Shantong proclaimed himself the rightful ruler of China, descendant of the last Northern Song emperor, sent to oust the oppressive and foreign Yuan powers.**

Hu Wei-yung—**Pg. 529, ¶ 3—Hu Wei-yung, longtime friend and chief minister to the Hongwu Emperor, was tried for treason in 1380 because the emperor felt he was growing too powerful. Hu Wei-young was executed by his old friend.**

Mao Ziyuan—**Pg. 525, ¶ 3—Mao Ziyuan, a twelfth-century charismatic Pure Land monk, preached that the Western Paradise could be experienced on earth, mystically: in the mind of the believer who was willing to meditate unceasingly on the name of the Buddha, concentrating all thought and will on the Pure Land. His followers took the name White Lotus Society.**

Toghto—**Pg. 526, ¶ 1-6 and Pg. 527, ¶ 2 & 3—Toghto, soldier-historian and chancellor to Emperor Huizong, imposed corvée labor on the Yuan Chinese in order to rebuild the Yellow river, which drove the Chinese to rebel against the government. Toghto was fired after he forgot to plan a celebration marking Ayushiridara's status as Crown Prince in 1354, an he died a year later in exile.**

White Lotus Society—**Pg. 525, ¶ 3—White Lotus Society, the name of the group that followed Mao Ziyuan, flowered and divided, and by the fourteenth century spread into energetic subsects all over Yuan China. These White Lotus worshippers, who believed a Prince of Light, a manifestation of the Buddha, would appear in the present and bring the Pure Land on earth, looked forward to immediate deliverance and often adopted red turbans as a sign of their unity.**

Zhu Yuanzhang (the Hongwu Emperor)—**Pg. 527, ¶ 3 and Pg. 528, ¶ 3—Zhu Yuanzhang, a Buddhist monk and originally a follower of Han Lin'er, was the leader of a Red Turban movement in the northeast of Yuan China, and after he captured Nanjing declared himself founder of the new Wu dynasty. After defeating Chen Youliang and Toghon Temur, Zhu Yuanzhang had himself crowned emperor at his capital city of Nanjing where he announced the start of another new dynasty, the Ming, beginning with the New Year of 1368; for himself, he took the imperial name Taizu, and named the era of his reign *Hongwu*, "Most Warlike" (he is generally known by his era name: the Hongwu Emperor).**

Section II: **Comprehension**

Write a two or three-sentence answer to each of the following questions.

1. What are some causes for the drop in the Chinese population—forty million people—between the beginning and the end of the fourteenth century?

A1.—Pg. 525, ¶ 1 & 2—One obvious cause for the drop in the population was the bubonic plague, though it went almost unrecorded in China. In addition, the Mongol invasions and the establishment of the Yuan at the beginning of the century cost millions of lives. Also, like the rest of the world, China had seen severe weather patterns—heat and drought, rain and mold, floods and windstorms—that all played a part in famine, failed crops, and ultimately deaths from starvation.

2. Why did Toghto have to direct a massive repair project in the center of the empire in 1351?

A2.—Pg. 526, ¶ 2 & 3—The Yellow river's outlet to the sea frequently shifted—the land near the coast was flat, and silt buildup constantly pushed the river's course back and forth—but the flooding of the last years had now moved it far to the north, above the Shangdong Peninsula. The flooding had also blocked the Grand Canal and it had become impossible to transport grain from the rich farmland around the Yangtze to the southern capital, Dadu, except by sea. Moving the Yellow river back to its old bed would make it possible to clean out and unblock the Grand Canal, meaning the grain shipments from south to north could resume, protected by the shore from the pirate Fang Guozhen and his bandits.

3. How did Han Shantong's rebellion end? What were the lasting effects of his uprising?

A3.—Pg. 526, ¶ 7 to Pg. 527, ¶ 1—Han Shantong's little rebellion was immediately squashed into the mud by Toghto, who dispatched Yuan soldiers to arrest him. Han Shantong was promptly executed; his followers scattered, and his son Han Lin'er, whom he had declared his crown prince and heir apparent, disappeared into hiding. However, Red Turban rebellions began to pop up all over the Yuan realm, and after Han Shantong, at least five men proclaimed themselves the new emperor of China, and six or seven war leaders without imperial titles added themselves to the mix.

4. Why did Toghto lose his job as chancellor in 1354? How did he react to being fired?

A4.—Pg. 527, ¶ 2—Toghto lost his job as chancellor because the emperor was annoyed that Toghto had not found the time to organize the elaborate ceremonial recognition of his son, Ayushiridara, as Crown Prince and heir. Toghto, loyal to the end, stepped down at once. He was in the middle of conducting a siege of the rebel-held city of Gaoyou; it was on the verge of surrender, but when Toghto left, the Red Turbans who held it took heart.

5. What happened to Yuan China after the failed siege of Gaoyou?

A5.—Pg. 527, ¶ 3—After the failed siege of Gaoyou, Toghto took himself into exile and died a year later (possibly poisoned by one of the Crown Prince's allies). The Yuan army was divided by squabbling generals, each hoping for ultimate command; spread too thin, fighting too many rebels, the imperial force was unable to wipe any of them out and by the end of the

decade, the emperor Toghon Temur controlled only the land directly around Dadu. The Red Turban rebels divided into two major movements, one in the northeast led by Zhu Yuanzhang and one in the southwest led by Chen Youliang, and at the same time the pirate Fang Guozhen seized the southern coast south of Hangzhou for his own.

6. How did Zhu Yuanzhang defeat Chen Youliang and the southern Red Turban movement?

A6.—Pg. 527, ❡ 4-6—On August 30, 1363, Chen Youliang and Zhu Yuanzhang fought for for two days on Lake Poyang without victory. On the third day, Zhu Yuanzhang ordered dummy ships, manned by straw-stuffed uniforms and loaded with gunpowder, to be launched towards the enemy; set fire with long fuses, the fireships blew into Chen Youliang's line and exploded. This battle was followed a month later by a second short naval encounter during which Chen Youliang was struck in the eye by an arrow, dying instantly, which brought an end to the southern Red Turban movement.

7. What happened to Toghon Temur's holdings after Zhu Yuanzhang's success against Chen Youliang?

A7.—Pg. 528, ❡ 1 & 2—In November of 1367, after the Yuan court held out at Dadu for four years, Zhu Yuanzhang mounted a final attack on Dadu and overran it with ease. Toghon Temur fled with his court into the old Mongolian homeland to the north and though he only controlled Shangdu, he was still boldly proclaiming himself emperor of China. However, he had become merely another northern warlord, clinging to a tiny local kingdom, and a year later, he lost Shangdu was forced even farther into the steppe.

8. How did the Hongwu Emperor manage the aristocratic clans that lived on in Ming China?

A8.—Pg. 529, ❡ 3—The Hongwu emperor broke up the power of aristocratic clans that might unite against him by ruthlessly moving them off their land, resettling them far apart, and then taking their fields. In payment, he gave them monthly allowances of rice and cloth, making them completely dependent on his goodwill alone.

Section III: Critical Thinking

The student may not use her text to answer this question.

At the end of the chapter we read that "the new Ming empire would be peaceful, and no price was too high to pay for peace." The Hongwu Emperor refused to eat meat, wore patched shirts, and ordered the crown prince to plant his own vegetable garden to save money. He acted with iron self-control and determination to keep his kingdom tranquil. But is tranquility the same as peace? Describe China under the first leader of the Ming dynasty, and then explain whether or not you think the kingdom was peaceful, or if its people were forced into submission by their ruler.

When Zhu Yuanzhang became emperor of the Ming dynasty, he took the name Taizu and named the era of his reign Hongwu, or "Most Warlike." He became known as the Hongwu Emperor, or the most warlike emperor. Though the Hongwu Emperor won his kingdom in battle, he wanted his people to live in a peaceful way.

First, he installed his twenty-three sons across the new empire as prince-regents. They were place in strategic locations, and acted as symbols of the emperor's power. Then, as written on page 529, "he appointed a committee of scholars to revise, expand, and reissue the old Tang law code, replacing the knotty tangle of old customs and nomadic practices that the Yuan had followed. He poured money into the Confucian schools and reinstituted the old Confucian civil service tests, as a way of bringing competent officials to his notice: 'The empire is of vast extent,' one of his very first decrees read; 'because it most certainly cannot be governed by my solitary self, it is essential that all the worthy men of the realm now join in bringing order into it.'

Next the Hongwu Emperor had his friend and chief minister Hu Wei-yung, who he thought was growing too powerful, tried for treason and executed. Then he created the Embroidered Uniform Guards who acted as spies and hit men, and held people in secret prison if he felt they threatened his authority and/or the realm. And he broke up aristocratic families by taking away their land and giving them monthly allowances in return (making them dependent upon him for survival) so that they would not grow too strong and take over his power.

The Hongwu Emperor wrote to a letter to the Byzantine emperor introducing the Ming dynasty, and explaining that, under the Yuan, his homeland had suffered nearly two decades of misery. He wanted the Byzantine emperor to know that his new kingdom would be peaceful. The letter explained "We, as a simple peasant of Huai-yu, conceived the patriotic idea to save the people . . . [and we have now] established peace in the Empire, and restored the old boundaries. . . . Although We are not equal in wisdom to our ancient rulers whose virtue was recognized all over the universe, We cannot but let the world know Our intention to maintain peace within the four seas."

The student can argue for or against the supposed peacefulness of the first years of the Ming dynasty. Although the Hongwu Emperor cleaned up the kingdom and led an ascetic life himself, he created strict rules and had a secret police force to instill fear and order into his subjects. The example answer below includes both arguments.

EXAMPLE ANSWER:

Part 1 (Same for both answers):

When Zhu Yuanzhang became emperor of the Ming dynasty, he took the name Taizu and named the era of his reign Hongwu, or "Most Warlike." He became known as the Hongwu Emperor, or the most warlike emperor. Though the Hongwu Emperor won his kingdom in battle, he wanted his subjects to live in a peaceful way. First, he installed his twenty-three sons across the new empire as prince-regents. They were placed in strategic locations, and acted as symbols of the emperor's power. Next the Hongwu Emperor revised the old Tang law code and revamped the Confucian school and civil service tests. He wanted to make sure that his officials were capable. Then he got rid of any threats to his power: he had Hu Wei-yung executed, he used the Embroidered Uniform Guards as spies and hit men, and he broke up the power of the aristocratic families.

Part 2 (Yes, peaceful):

The Hongwu Emperor lived through a time of misery while the Yuan were in control of China. Though he used war to get the throne, his main interest was to create a peaceful kingdom. He even wrote to the Byzantine emperor, telling him that "We cannot but let the world know Our intention to maintain peace within the four seas." He used strict rules and the threat of punishment to keep his people controlled, and the result was his desired tranquil kingdom.

Part 2 (No, not peaceful):

Though the Hongwu Emperor said his top priority was to have a peaceful kingdom, what he really meant was that he wanted to have a controlled kingdom. The name he used means "Warlike," not "Tranquil." He used intimidation and fear of secret prisons to keep his subjects under control. He murdered those that threatened him, like his good friend Hu Wei-yung, and he made sure no groups could come together to rebel against him, like the old aristocratic families. A kingdom is not peaceful if everyone is too afraid to make waves.

Section IV: Map Exercise

1. Trace the rectangular outline of the map in black.

2. Using your blue pencil, trace all the visible coastline. Include the line of the Yellow River, the Yangtze, and Lake Poyang. Repeat until the contours are familiar.

3. Using contrasting colors, trace the areas of Ming China and the Yuan Dynasty. Using contrasting colors, trace the alternate course of the Yellow River and the line of the Grand Canal. Repeat until the contours are familiar.

4. Using a new sheet of paper, trace the rectangular outline of the map in black. Using your regular pencil with an eraser, draw the coastline, the Yellow and Yangtze Rivers, Lake Poyang, and the separate areas of Ming China and the Yuan Dynasty. Use the frame as a reference, erasing and redrawing as necessary. Draw the lines of the Grand Canal and the alternate course of the Yellow River. When you are happy with your map, lay it over the original, and erase and redraw any lines which are more than ½" off of the original.

5. Study carefully the locations of Shangdu Dadu, Gaoyou, Nanjing, Hangzhou, Nancheng, and Jiangzhou. When they are familiar for you, close the book. Mark each one on your map, and then lay your map over the original. Erase and re-mark any labels which are more than ½" off of the original.

6. Mark the Shandong Peninsula.

Chapter Seventy-Five

After the Mongols

The student may use his text when answering the questions in sections I and II.

Section I: Who, What, Where

Write a one or two-sentence answer explaining the significance of each item listed below.

Borommaracha—**Pg. 532, ¶ 4-6—Borommaracha of Suphanburi, Ramesuan's mother's brother, challenged his nephew's claim to to the Ayutthaya throne and won. Borommaracha spent almost the entire eighteen years of his rule mounting attacks against the Sukhothai borders and by the time of his death, in 1388, he had managed to force the king of Sukhothai into swearing allegiance to him.**

Che Bong Nga of Champa (the Red King)—**Pg. 533, ¶ 4 to pg. 534, ¶ 3, 5, & 7—Che Bong Nga of Champa, known to the Dai Viet as the Red King, roused the Cham into their first major assault on the Dai Viet in 1361 and after more attacks Che Bong Nga managed to gain the imprimatur of the Chinese emperor on his kingship in 1369, a recognition that gave yet more energy to his attempts to conquer the Dai Viet. Che Bong Nga led the Champa in successful attacks against the Dai Viet but was killed by a gunshot wound, leading his troops to retreat and bringing Champa power to an end.**

Jayavarmaparamesvara—**Pg. 531, ¶ 2—Jayavarmaparamesvara was the last Khmer king that was given a distinct name and description. After Jayavarmaparamesvara, the kings became faceless.**

Le Quy Ly—**Pg. 534, ¶ 4 & 8 and Pg. 535, ¶ 3—Le Quy Ly, a soldier of Chinese blood who had risen through the ranks of the Dai Viet army to become its supreme commander, was able to stop the Red King from taking hold of Thang Long. After defeating the Cham with the use of Chinese firearms, Le Quy Ly usurped the throne of the Dai Viet, taking the royal Chinese name Ho in 1399 and renaming his country Ta Yu, after the Second Sage Emperor Yu.**

Prince An—**Pg. 535, ¶ 2 & 3—Prince An took the the Dai Viet throne at the age of three, after his father abdicated the throne. When Prince An was seven, in 1399, he relinquished his crown to his grandfather, Le Quy Ly.**

Ramathibodi (U Thong)—**Pg. 532, ¶ 2 & 3—Ramathibodi, originally named U Thong, built up the Thai kingdom at Lopburi and then moved his kingdom to Ayutthaya because an epidemic of smallpox drove him out of his home city of Lopburi. Ramathibodi was an aggressive ruler and in 1352 he led his new kingdom of Ayutthaya into its first conflict with the Khmer; over ten years of slow and excruciating war followed, with victories balanced by defeats.**

Ramesuan—**Pg. 532, ¶ 4-8—Ramesuan, son of Ramathibodi, followed his father as king, but his rule was challenged by his mother's brother Borommaracha of Suphanburi and Ramesuan left the throne and retreated to Lopburi as a result. After Borommaracha's death, Ramesuan reclaimed the throne, and worked to enfold the people of Khmer into the Thai culture.**

Syam—**Pg. 531, ¶ 3—Syam, a vassal people of the Khmer, slipped out of Khmer control and founded a kingdom centered at the city of Sukhothai in the 12th century. The kingdom was the first independent state governed by the people of the valley, known to us as the Thai.**

Thong Lan—**Pg. 532, ¶ 7—Thong Lan, Borommaracha's son and heir, was executed by his cousin Ramesuan after Borommaracha's death. He was executed in the traditional manner: he was placed in a velvet sack and then beaten to death.**

Tran Due-tong—**Pg. 534, ¶ 3—Tran Due-tong became king of the Dai Viet after his brother abdicated because he could not stop the Cham invaders from sacking his cities and kidnapping his subjects. Tran Due-tong gained a reputation as a cowardly and greedy king; after one invasion, he fled from the capital city on a raft and waited at a distance until the Cham had retreated and then took all of his treasure up into the mountains and buried it so that neither the Cham nor his subjects would be able to get their hands on it.**

Tran Thuan Tong—**Pg. 535, ¶ 2—Tran Thuan Tong, sitting emperor and son-in-law of Le Quy Ly, was convinced by his father-in-law to abdicate his throne to the emperor's son (the general's grandson) Prince An. After he abdicated, Lu Quy Ly had Tran Thuan Tong executed.**

Section II: Comprehension

Write a two or three-sentence answer to each of the following questions.

1. What happened to the Khmer after they became a vassal of the Mongols to buy peace?

A1.—Pg. 531, ¶ 2—After the Khmer became a vassal of the Mongols to buy peace, the power of Angkor Wat went into decline. The last inscription recording the rule of a Khmer king at Angkor Wat, the obscure Jayavarmaparamesvara, comes from 1327; the kings after him are faceless. Also, after becoming a vassal of the Mongols, Khmer building had almost ceased and their rice fields had grown over with weeds.

2. Describe the rise of U Thong's power at Lopburi.

A2.—Pg. 531, ¶ 4 to Pg. 532, ¶ 1—In 1351, the ambitious leader U Thong, known to some as the son of a Chinese merchant who had settled at Lopburi, one of a number of Chinese expatriates to carry on a lucrative trade with the Thai valley as their home, and others as a native of

Lopburi, became king of his clan. He then built a kingdom to rival the Syam by marrying into a rich merchant clan at another Thai city-state, Suphanburi, and claiming leadership of it as well. U Thong then changed his name to the royal Ramathibodi and the two cities together became the twin nuclei of his new domain.

3. How did Borommaracha of Suphanburi take Ramesuan's throne?

A3.—Pg. 532, ¶ 4 & 5—The Thai kingdoms, like most brand-new states, had no tradition of father-to-son succession, so while Ramesuan managed to get himself crowned as his father's successor, his mother's brother, Borommaracha of Suphanburi, soon arrived at Ayutthaya and demanded the throne. Borommaracha, a short-tempered but experienced soldier in his sixties, had almost the entire city behind him because he was the uncle who rescued the Ramesuan from Khmer captivity, and had followed this up with an impressive victory outside the walls of Angkor Wat itself. Ramesuan had no victories of his own to boast of, so seeing his uncle's popularity, he left the throne and retreated to Lopburi.

4. Explain how the Khmer culture was already part of the Thai culture, and how Ramesuan continued that intermingling.

A4.—Pg. 532, ¶ 8 to Pg. 533, ¶ 1—The Thai and Khmer cultures had already entwined around each other during the years when the Khmer had dominated the valley; the Thai already used the Khmer writing system and had already borrowed Khmer ways of irrigating their crops. Ramesuan went to war against the Khmer after he retook the throne in order to enfold the Khmer people into the Thai. Captive Khmer—particularly if they were artists, writers, musicians, or high-ranking civil officials—were deported to Ayutthaya, where they were encouraged to continue their work, intermingling the two cultures and turning them into something new.

5. How did Che Bong Nga influence the abdication of the Dai Viet king?

A5.—Pg. 534, ¶ 2 & 3—In 1371, Che Bong Nga organized a massive sea invasion, landing his soldiers along the Dai Viet coast. They rampaged inland all the way to the capital city of Thang Long, which the Cham soldiers sacked and burned, and girls and young men alike were kidnapped and hauled back to Champa as slaves. Unable to halt the raids, the Dai Viet king abdicated and handed his throne over to his brother, Tran Due-tong.

6. Describe Le Quy Ly's final defeat of the Cham.

A6.—Pg. 534, ¶ 6 & 7—Le Quy Ly had been arming his soldiers with weapons imported from his Chinese homeland: *huochong*, a brand-new military technology, handguns sold by the Ming. In 1390, a defector from Cham's ranks had told them which of the river vessels carried the Red King, and the Dai Viet trained a hail of gunfire on it, which killed Che Bong Nga and caused the Dai Viet army to panic and retreat. In a more traditional gesture, Le Quy Ly ordered Che Bong Nga's head cut off and taken to the capital city, signaling the end of Champa's brief stint as a major power.

7. How did Le Quy Ly manage to usurp the Dai Viet throne? What royal heritage did he claim, and how was that reflected in his new name for the Dai Viet?

A7.—Pg. 535, ¶ 2 & 3—Le Quy Ly married one of his daughters into the Dai Viet royal family, and in 1395 he convinced the sitting emperor Tran Thuan Tong, his son in-law, to relinquish the throne to Prince An, aged three: the emperor's son, grandson of the general. Le Quy Ly then executed the abdicated emperor and declared himself regent for his grandson after which the child obediently abdicated in 1399, at the age of seven, and relinquished the crown to his grandfather. Le Quy Ly changed his name to the Chinese Ho and began to claim descent from the legendary Second Sage Emperor Yu of antiquity, renaming the country itself to Ta Yu, after the great emperor.

Section III: Critical Thinking

The student may not use his text to answer this question.

The Champa were strong under the leadership of Che Bong Nga. They drove the Dai Viet back again and again. In 1389, Dai Viet general Le Quy Ly suffered the greatest defeat of his career. Fighting on the Luong river, his soldiers were massacred and he was forced to scramble away through the rough countryside with one of his surviving captains moaning "The enemy is stronger than we are, and resistance is impossible!" But as we found out, the traditional strength of the Champa was no match for the new technology used by Le Quy Ly. A single shot from a *huochong*, for all intents and purposes, ended the Champa's aggressive campaign against the Dai Viet. We learned just a little bit about *huochong* in this chapter. Do some research on your own and write a paragraph describing the evolution of the *huochong* from the fire lance. Make sure to cite your sources!

In the chapter we learn that Le Quy Ly had been arming his soldiers with weapons imported from his Chinese homeland. The Dai Viet carried huochong: *"a brand-new military technology, handguns sold by the Ming."*

There is some dispute about the form Chinese firearms first took, and often huochong *is a term used for both guns and cannons. The idea that* huochong *is like a cannon most likely comes from the technology called a fire lance. The fire lance was created in 10th century China, and is often referred to as the first fire arm. Charles Le Blanc writes in* Chinese Ideas About Nature and Society: Studies in Honour of Derk Bodde *that "the fire-lance or fire-pike constituted a five-minute flame-thrower, in the guise of a rocket attached to a pole, with its open end directed towards the adversary; if sufficient supplies were available, one can have little difficulty imagining that the weapon would have discouraged enemy troops from climbing up and invading one's city wall" (295). The fire lance was effective only at short distances. The next step was to have the fire lance shoot out its flame in greater distances, thus the evolution of the gun. The fire lance was usually made out of bamboo. Once the fire lance evolved to having a metal shaft, more power was able to be harnessed and exploded inside of the tube, meaning the projection of the fire (and a bullet lodged inside the tube) could go much farther and faster. We can see the change in the weapon in its terminology. At first it was just called* huo ch'iang, *fire-spear; next came* huo t'ung *(fire tube); and eventually we have* ch'ung *(the later specific name for a gun of any kind) (297).*

Your student's answer will vary depending on the sources he uses. The example answer below is just one possible response.

EXAMPLE ANSWER:

Chinese firearms developed in the 10th century. At first soldiers used fire lances, which were nothing more than flame-throwers. Charles Le Blanc writes in *Chinese Ideas About Nature and Society: Studies in Honour of Derk Bodde* that the fire lance was only effective at short distances. The fire lance was good for protecting walls or barriers, but didn't do much good to stop a faraway advance. The bamboo shaft of a fire lance prevented it from encasing extreme heat or blasts, so the explosion of fire and gunpowder in the shaft was limited. Once the tube of the fire lance was made out of a metal, the explosion inside the tube could be much greater, meaning the fire could travel much further. Now we can see the development of the *huochong*. Once a powerful explosion could be harnessed inside the metal tube, a bullet could be launched and travel long distances with great speed. Thus we have the first guns used in battle, as described in the death of Che Bong Nga.

Chapter Seventy-Six

The Turks and the Desperate Emperor

The student may use her text when answering the questions in sections I and II.

Section I: Who, What, Where

Write a one or two-sentence answer explaining the significance of each item listed below.

Innocent VI—**Pg. 539, ¶ 7 and Pg. 540, ¶ 6—Innocent VI, a Frenchman and lawyer by training, followed Clement VI as pope. He died in September of 1362.**

Manuel—**Pg. 541, ¶ 7—Manuel, oldest son of John V and governor of Thessalonica, managed to bail his father out of debt in Venice by confiscating treasure from the churches and monasteries in Thessalonica.**

Matthew—**Pg. 537, ¶ 2, Pg. 538, ¶ 2, and Pg. 539, ¶ 2—Matthew, oldest son of John VI, was given rule of Andrianople by his father and was made co-emperor by John VI after he deposed John V. After John V escaped from the island where he was imprisoned, both Matthew and his father John VI lost their hold on the Byzantine throne and John V became sole emperor.**

Murad—**Pg. 539, ¶ 8 to Pg. 540, ¶ 3—Murad, second son of Orhan, replaced his brother Suleyman Pasha as governor of Gallipoli and leader of the Turkish invasion into Byzantium. Murad, said to be the most powerful of the line of the Ottomans, turned the occupation of Byzantine territory into an out-and-out invasion, one that only gained strength after Orhan died and Murad took his place as sultan.**

Suleyman Pasha—**Pg. 537, ¶ 4, Pg. 538, ¶ 2, and Pg. 539, ¶ 8—Suleyman Pasha, son of Orhan of the Ottomans, led a detachment of Turkish soldiers into Byzantium after John VI asked Orhan to help his son Matthew fight off a 1352 attack from John V; after the defeat of John V, Suleyman Pasha seized a fortress called Tzympe in Thrace and refused to leave. Suleyman Pasha was killed in a riding accident in 1357.**

Urban V—**Pg. 540, ¶ 6 to Pg. 541, ¶ 3—Urban V, the papal name of the Benedictine monk named William Grimoard, followed Innocent VI as pope; he did not, however, follow in Innocent VI's luxurious lifestyle. He also did not believe the papacy could serve both God and the king of**

414

CHAPTER SEVENTY-SIX: THE TURKS AND THE DESPERATE EMPEROR

France, so he moved the papacy back to Italy soon after he became the leader of the Catholic church.

Section II: **Comprehension**

Write a two or three-sentence answer to each of the following questions.

1. Why was John V frustrated by his co-rule with John VI?

A1.—Pg. 537, ¶ 1 & 2— John V's rule was already stunted because he had to share governance of a plague-battered city, a half-empty countryside, and a sadly shrunken empire: all that was left of glorious Byzantium was the old Roman province of Thrace, a handful of northern Aegean islands, and the city of Thessalonica. In addition, John VI had already handed parts of the empire over for his two surviving sons to govern: the remote southernmost tip of the Greek peninsula to the younger and the strategically valuable city of Adrianople to his oldest, Matthew. John V was frustrated by his own lack of power.

2. How did John V end up as a prisoner of John VI?

A2.—Pg. 537, ¶ 3 to Pg. 538, ¶ 1—In the summer of 1352, John V marched into John VI's son Matthew's territory and laid siege to Adrianople. Matthew retaliated by asking his father for help, which arrived in the form of a detachment of Turkish soldiers led by Suleyman Pasha, and in response John V was able to gather four thousand troops from Stefan Dushan. The Ottomans crushed the Serbs, John V's allies retreated, and John himself was taken prisoner; John VI ordered him deported to Tenedos, a fifteen-mile-long island just off the coast of Asia Minor.

3. Why did John VI grow unpopular after he made his own son Matthew co-emperor?

A3.—Pg. 538, ¶ 2-4—John VI grew unpopular after he made Matthew co-emperor because the public was frustrated that he had raided the churches and monasteries of Constantinople for enough gold and silver to pay the Turks he invited to help his son fight John V. After the battle, the Turks rampaged their way through the villages near Adrianople, taking what they pleased and John VI was widely thought to have given them permission. Even worse, Orhan's son Suleyman Pasha had seized a fortress in Thrace—Tzympe, on the coast—and now refused to leave.

4. How did the Turks use the March 2, 1354 earthquake to their advantage?

A4.—Pg. 538, ¶ 4 & 5—The earthquake that hit the entire coastline of the Aegean Sea on March 2, 1354 caused the walls of Constantinople to shift and crack; throughout Thrace houses and fortresses crumbled; some villages entirely disappeared; the city of Gallipoli, the key point for controlling passage over the Hellespont, was flattened; thousands died and the survivors were lashed by fierce storms of alternating rain and snow. Suleyman Pasha, hearing of Gallipoli's destruction, rounded up a massive crowd of Turkish soldiers and civilians and descended on the deserted ruins where they occupied the wrecked empty houses, repaired the walls, and claimed the city as their own. More Turks dispersed through the countryside, doing the same whenever they found a shattered village, quietly and effectively occupying Byzantine territory.

5. What did John VI do to deal with the Turkish squatters, and what was the outcome of this approach?

A5.—Pg. 538, ¶ 6 to Pg. 539, ¶ 2—John VI hoped to get the Turks out of Byzantine territory through diplomacy, but when he appealed to Orhan, the Ottoman leader stalled. John V took advantage of the situation; in November he escaped from his island and returned to Constantinople where the citizens welcomed him, shouting his name in the streets and demanding his return to power. On December 10, John VI abdicated as co-emperor of the Byzantine realm and handed all power over to the younger man and then entered the Monastery of St. George in Constantinople where he remained for the rest of his life.

6. What saved John V from the Serbians after he was given the throne by John VI?

A6.—Pg. 539, 3—Soon after John V returned to the throne, the Serbians started to gear up for battle. However, in December 1355, forty-seven-year-old Stefan Dushan suffered from a stroke. He had named no heir and his empire immediately split apart under battling successors.

7. How did John V attempt to deal with the Turks after he reclaimed the Byzantine throne?

A7.—Pg. 539, ¶ 6-8—John V was willing to attack the Turks, but he needed help: he sent a letter to the pope saying that in exchange for Christian soldiers and ships, John V would convert to Catholicism and return the entire empire to the Catholic fold. Innocent VI politely sent a papal legate to instruct the emperor in the faith, but he ignored the request for soldiers. After the pope, John V tried to get aid from the Serbs (too embroiled in their own civil wars), Genoa and Venice (unable to supply the necessary numbers), and the king of Hungary (too busy with his own war against Bulgaria), but no one would help him.

8. Describe the return of the papacy to Italy.

A8.—Pg. 541, ¶ 1-3—When Urban V became pope, he immediately began a return of the papacy to Rome. The cardinals, most of whom preferred France, objected; but the Roman Senate sent messages of encouragement, and the poet Petrarch sent a long and flowery appeal. In April of 1367, Urban V set sail from Marseille and took the papacy, along with the unwilling cardinals; when they arrived in Italy they found the papal palace was in ruin, so they took up temporary residence near Viterbo.

9. What did Urban V do in exchange for John V's conversion to the Catholic faith?

A9.—Pg. 541, ¶ 6—In return for John V's conversion to the Catholic faith, Urban V supplied him with three hundred soldiers, which was hardly enough to mount an attack on the Ottomans. However, he also issued an official bull ordering all Christian monarchs in the west to do everything possible to assist the emperor, as he was now a full brother in the faith.

10. How did John V manage to get home after he realized the Doge of Venice was not going to forgive the 30,000-ducat loan taken out by his mother Anne, back in the days of the civil war with John Cantacuzenus?

A10.—Pg. 541, ¶ 6 & 7—After the Doge of Venice politely refused to forgive John V's mother's debt, John V had no money left for travel, meaning the emperor of Byzantium was stranded in Venice. Eventually John V's oldest son Manuel managed to raise the cash by confiscating treasure from the churches and monasteries in Thessalonica, where he was governor. After being bailed out by his son, John V arrived at his capital city, humiliated, converted, and penniless, in October 1371.

Section III: Critical Thinking

The student may not use her text to answer this question.

Many of us have heard a derivation of the verse from 2 Samuel 1:25, "How the mighty have fallen!" Write two or three paragraphs describing the decline of John V. In your answer, explain how John V started as the Orthodox co-emperor of Byzantium and ended up as a Catholic Turkish vassal.

John V's reign was contested from the start, and he was forced to rule as co-emperor with John VI. Frustrated by John VI's power grabbing and his distribution of lands to his sons, John V invaded Matthew's land in retaliation. This started a fight between John V and John IV. John V had to ask the Serbs and Stefan Dushan for help, while John IV had to ask Orhan of the Ottomans. The Turkish-reinforced troops ended up beating John V. This could have been the end of the emperor. However, John VI became unpopular after the Turkish mercenaries took up residence in Byzantium and increased their occupation after an earthquake hit in 1354. John VI couldn't get the Turks out of Byzantine land, and John V saw his chance to get his power back. He escaped from the island where he was imprisoned by John VI and returned to Constantinople with the citizens shouting his name. John VI abdicated and John V became sole emperor. In another stroke of luck, Stefan Dushan died suddenly at the age of forty-seven with no named heir. The Serbian empire split apart and was no longer a threat to John V.

The Turkish threat, however, grew. In an effort to get more troops, John V appealed to the pope and said he, and the rest of the Orthodox church, would convert to Catholicism in exchange for reinforcements against the Turks. Innocent VI was happy to convert John V, but he sent no troops. John V found no help from the Serbs, Genoa and Venice, nor Hungary. He tried the papacy again after Innocent VI's death. Urban V had just returned to Italy and seemed more sympathetic to the roiled emperor's plight. This time, though, John V promised only his conversion, hoping the Orthodox back in Constantinople would follow. Urban V performed the ceremony, gave John V three hundred troops, and issued an official papal bull ordering all Christian monarchs help John V. The bull did not work. When John V arrived in Venice, the Doge refused to help and in fact demanded payment on a loan made to John V's mother. John V was only able to leave Venice after his son Manuel confiscated treasures from the churches and monasteries in Thessalonica to pay his father's debts. When John V arrived back in Constantinople, he was penniless and humiliated. On top of that, he found out that Murad had just led the Ottoman army in a shattering defeat of the Serbians, killing two of the princes who had claimed parts of the Serbian empire after Stefan Dushan's death. The Turks were now deep into Serbian territory, flanking Byzantium, cutting the remnants of the empire off from the rest of Europe; only by water could John return home.

This is when the emperor gave up. Though there are no records of the treaty, by 1373, John V had sworn a vassal's oath to Murad and was carrying out his duties by fighting with Murad against rival Turkish tribes in Anatolia. This was the end to John V's fall. He had once been an Orthodox Byzantine emperor and he ended up a Catholic Turkish vassal. On his journey, he had lost everything but Constantinople itself.

EXAMPLE ANSWER:

John V never liked sharing the throne with John VI, and he had enough when John VI made Matthew governor of Adrianople. John V invaded Matthew's land and this started a fight between John V and John IV. John V had to ask the Serbs and Stefan Dushan for help, while John IV had to ask Orhan of the Ottomans. The Turkish-reinforced troops ended up beating John V. John V was imprisoned by John VI, but he escaped after John VI became unpopular because the Turkish mercenaries took up residence in Byzantium and increased their occupation after an earthquake hit in 1354. The people of Constantinople wanted John V on the throne; John VI abdicated and John V became sole emperor. In another stroke of luck, Stefan Dushan died suddenly at the age of forty-seven with no named heir. The Serbian empire split apart and was no longer a threat to John V.

The Turkish threat, however, grew. John V couldn't get any help. Pope Innocent VI did not send troops, and John V found no help from the Serbs, Genoa and Venice, nor Hungary. He tried the papacy again after Innocent VI's death. Urban V had just returned to Italy and seemed more sympathetic to the roiled emperor's plight. John V promised his conversion, hoping the Orthodox back in Constantinople would follow. Urban V performed the ceremony, gave John V three hundred troops, and issued an official papal bull ordering all Christian monarchs help John V. The bull did not work. When John V arrived in Venice, the Doge refused to help and in fact demanded payment on a loan made to John V's mother. John V was only able to leave Venice after his son Manuel confiscated treasures from the churches and monasteries in Thessalonica to pay his father's debts. When John V arrived back in Constantinople, he was penniless and humiliated. On top of that, he found out that Murad had just led the Ottoman army in a shattering defeat of the Serbians, killing two of the princes who had claimed parts of the Serbian empire after Stefan Dushan's death. The Turks were now deep into Serbian territory, flanking Byzantium, cutting the remnants of the empire off from the rest of Europe. The situation was so bad that John V could only return home by water.

This is when the emperor gave up. By 1373, John V had sworn a vassal's oath to Murad and was carrying out his duties by fighting with Murad against rival Turkish tribes in Anatolia. This was the end to John V's fall. He had once been an Orthodox Byzantine emperor and he ended up a Catholic Turkish vassal. On his journey, he had lost everything but Constantinople itself.

Section IV: **Map Exercise**

1. Using your black pencil, trace the rectangular outline of the frame for Map 76.1: The Ottoman Empire.

2. Using your blue pencil, trace the outline of the coast around the Mediterranean Sea and the Black Sea. As usual, you need not include the very small islands around Greece. Also trace the line of the Danube. Repeat until the contours are familiar.

3. Now using contrasting colors, trace the outlines of the Byzantine Empire and the Ottoman Turks. Repeat until the contours are familiar.

4. Now using a new sheet of paper, trace the outline of the frame for Map 76.1 in black. Then using your regular pencil with an eraser, draw the coastline around the Mediterranean and the Black Sea. Draw the line of the Danube. Erase and redraw as necessary, using the frame of the map as a reference. Draw the separate areas of the Byzantine Empire and Ottoman Turks. When you are happy with your map, lay it over the original. Erase and re-draw any lines which are more than ½" off of the original.

5. Study closely the areas of Greece, Thessalonica, Serbia, Bulgaria, Thrace, and Asia Minor. When you are familiar with them, close the book. Mark and label each one on your map. Then check your map against the original, and erase and re-mark any misplaced labels.

6. Now study closely the locations of Thessalonica, Didymoteichon, Edirne, and Constantinople. When they are familiar for you, close the book. Mark and label each one on your map. Then lay your map over the original, and erase and re-draw any locations which are more than ½" off of the original.

7. Mark the location of the Battle of Marica River.

Chapter Seventy-Seven

The Disintegration of Delhi

The student may use his text when answering the questions in sections I and II.

Section I: Who, What, Where

Write a one or two-sentence answer explaining the significance of each item listed below.

'Ali Hujwiri—**Pg. 545, ¶ 1 & 2**—'Ali Hujwiri, an eleventh-century Sufi scholar, was born in Ghazni, and then traveled throughout the old Persian lands where Sufism flourished. He settled in the north Indian city of Lahore, and had found ready ears among both the Muslim poor and the Hindu underclass.

Awliyâ'—**Pg. 545, ¶ 1**—Awliyâ' was the Sufi name for saint. Sufi believers held strongly that those who had preach inward purity—the awliyâ'—were the true rulers of men.

Bahman Shah—**Pg. 546, ¶ 2**—Bahman Shah, known as Zafar Khan during his time as an officer in Delhi, moved his capital city to Gulbarga, also known as Karnataka, and built himself a massive citadel there; it still survives today. By the time of his death, in 1358, he had expanded the Bahmani kingdom until it stretched from Bhongir in the east to Daulatabad in the west; and from the Wainganga river in the north to Krishna in the south.

Bukka Raya—**Pg. 546, ¶ 1**—Bukka Raya was the brother and successor of Harihara Raya.

Harihara Raya—**Pg. 545, ¶ 6 to Pg. 546, ¶ 1**—Harihara Raya, the first Vijayanagara ruler, conquered himself a territory that reached from Kaveri to Krishna by the time of his death in 1356.

Harihara Raya II—**Pg. 547 ¶ 2, and Pg. 548, ¶ 3**—Harihara Raya II, son and successor of Bukka Raya, faced solid opposition from Muhammad Shah I from the north, so he made a tentative prod into Sri Lanka, sending a few soldiers over the Palk Strait. Harihara Raya II's troops did not make it far into Sri Lanka; the island troops were strong and the kings at Jaffna and Kotte were able to buy the Vijayanagara ruler off with an insignificant tribute.

Muhammad Shah I—**Pg. 546, ⁋ 3 to Pg. 547, ⁋ 1—Muhammad Shah I, Bahman Shah's son and successor, began a war with Vijayanagara over possession of the fertile land between Krishna and Tungabhadra. Muhammad Shah I was a fierce warrior; he was the first to use gunpowder in his wars in the Deccan and during the years of his fighting against Vijayanagara, half a million people died.**

Shaikh 'Ala al-Haq—**Pg. 545, ⁋ 3—Shaikh 'Ala al-Haq was a Bengali Sufi teacher that had achieved sainthood within the Sufi hierarchy. Sultan Shams-ud-Din was a patron and follower of Shaikh 'Ala al-Haq, announcing on a mosque inscription that "He is the guide to the religion of the Glorious . . . may his piety last long."**

Sikandar—**Pg. 545, ⁋ 4—Sikandar, son of Shams-ud-Din, followed his father as sultan of Bengal. Firoz Shah did not have the strength to compel the Bengali sultan, and he was forced to retreat after Sikandar offered him nothing more than a token tribute payment.**

Sufism—**Pg. 544, ⁋ 5 to Pg. 545, ⁋ 1—Sufism, a mystical strain of Islam, taught that the present, not the hereafter, was what mattered. Practitioners sought inner purification, working hard to rise to higher and higher levels of piety; they fasted, meditated, prayed, gave alms; internally, they practiced gratitude to God, tried to exist in a constant awareness of the divine bond between God and the believer, and strove for a heart-felt affirmation of the oneness of the divine.**

Section II: **Comprehension**

Write a two or three-sentence answer to each of the following questions.

1. How did Firoz Shah Tughluq cultivate loyalty from his subjects in Delhi?

A1.—Pg. 544, ⁋ 1 & 2—Firoz Shah Tughluq cultivated loyalty from his subjects by making massive government loans to the people of Delhi "for the purpose of restoring the land, villages, and the quarters which had fallen into ruin during the days of famine," and then forgiving the loans. Firoz Shah's good domestic policy ensured that everyone had plenty of gold and silver, that wealth and comfort abounded, and that all were supportive of their leader.

2. Describe the interpretation of Sufism given by the eleventh-century scholar 'Ali Hujwiri. Why was this version of Islam so appealing to the Muslim poor and the Hindu underclass?

A2.—Pg. 545, ⁋ 1 & 2—'Ali Hujwiri explained that Sufi saints—the awliyâ'—were the true rulers of men, chosen by God to be the governors of His kingdom, purged of natural corruptions and delivered from their subjection to their lower soul and passion, so that all their thoughts were of Him. The Sufi saints were entirely devoted to God, and because of their purity and devotion were the governors of the universe. 'Ali Hujwiri's message found ready ears among both the Muslim poor and the Hindu underclass because that meant there was a chance to rise through spiritual discipline from the mud of their daily lives to a dazzling high place in the world where the authority of a saint trumped the power of a king.

3. Why did Shams-ud-Din embrace Sufism?

A3.—Pg. 545, ⁋ 3—Shams-ud-Din embraced Sufism as part of his break away from Delhi. He became a patron and follower of the Sufi teacher Shaikh 'Ala al-Haq, a native Bengali who had achieved sainthood within the Sufi hierarchy. Sufism gave Shams-ud-Din a useful way to distinguish his rule from that of his former master.

4. Explain what happened to the rule of Sri Lanka after the decay of Pandyan power.

A4.—Pg. 547, ⁋ 3 to Pg. 548, ⁋ 3—Since the decay of Pandyan power, the north of Sri Lanka had been independent under a king who ruled from Jaffna; the first Jaffna king may well have been a Pandyan general who remained in the island when his native country fell to Delhi. The kingdom of Jaffna had flourished for a time but over several obscure decades, the center of power had migrated from Dambadeniya to the capital city of Gampola, a little farther to the south, and from there to the fortress city of Kotte.

5. Why was Firoz Shah a successful ruler even though is expeditions against neighboring kingdoms failed?

A5.—Pg. 548, ⁋ 5-7—Even though Firoz Shah's expeditions almost universally failed, he was considered to be a successful ruler at home because of the attention he devoted to administration, and as a result, his country grew more and more prosperous. Firoz Shah himself believed that justice and compassion were the greatest qualities of his reign, shunning the method former kings had employed to keep their power, such as pouring molten lead into the throat, crushing the bones of the hands and feet with mallets, and driving iron nails into the hands, feet, and bosom in the hopes that dread and obedience would come into the hearts of his subjects. Despite his unwarlike rule, Delhi had mostly held together (only Khandesh was lost) because Firoz Shah had proved to be an excellent administrator, an enthusiastic mosque builder and garden planner, and a competent manager of the empire's finances; under Firoz Shah grain remained cheap in the capital, soldiers and officials were well paid, and taxes were reasonable.

6. What happened to the sultanate of Delhi after Firoz Shah's death?

A6.—Pg. 549, ⁋ 1—The sultanate of Delhi immediately fell apart after Firoz Shah's death. The governors of Jaunpur, Malwa, and Gujarat joined Bengal and Khandesh in independence, while in Delhi, a handful of claimants battled over the weakened throne. It was only Firoz Shah that was keeping Delhi together; as soon as he departed, the people were dispersed.

Section III: Critical Thinking

The student may not use his text to answer this question.

Muhammad Shah I was known as a no-holds-barred warrior. He was the first to use gunpowder in his wars in the Deccan. As we learned in the chapter, "His gunpowder projectiles were inaccurate and unpredictable, valuable for noise and confusion more than for actual defense; they came from China, and the Indians called them hawai, 'rockets.'" Yet their use began to change the landscape. Write a paragraph that explains just how the hawai changed the landscape, and how military-mindedness has affected other landscapes. In order to complete this critical thinking question you must do some research. After you are done researching, pick one architectural or landscape change that came about as a result of military-mindedness.

The student learned that the hawai affected the Indian landscape because new forts were being built that were given slit holes through which projectiles could be fired. This straightforward answer is found on page 546 of the text.

The student may conduct his research on the internet. Make sure all sources are cited. He can write about any kind of change as long as he explains how the change in landscape or architecture was related to the military.

EXAMPLE ANSWER:

Muhammad Shah I used gunpowder projectiles in his wars against Vijayanagara. The use of hawai, or rockets, wasn't very effective. The projectiles were not accurate; mostly they made a lot of noise and caused confusion. They did have a large effect on the landscape, though, because forts began to be built with slit holes through which projectiles could be fired.

Another way that military growth changed a landscape was the building of roads in Ancient Rome. According to the History.com article, "10 Innovations That Built Ancient Rome," the Romans "built over 50,000 miles of road by 200 A.D., primarily in the service of military conquest. Highways allowed the Roman legion to travel as far as 25 miles per day, and a complex network of post houses meant that messages and other intelligence could be relayed with astonishing speed." Roman roads were made of dirt, gravel, and bricks. The engineers made arrow-straight roads that were sloped to allow for water drainage. The network of roads in Rome not only allowed for speedy communication between conquering troops, but also ensured efficient administration of the "sprawling domain."

Section IV: **Map Exercise**

1. Trace the rectangular outline of the frame for Map 77.1: Bahmani Expansion in black.

2. Using your blue pencil, trace the coastal outline, including Sri Lanka. Also trace the lines of the Kaveri, Tungabhadra, Wainganga, Narmada, and Indus. Repeat until the contours are familiar.

3. Now using contrasting colors, trace the outline of the Delhi, Bahmani, Vijayanagara, and Jaffna areas. Show the mountains with small peaks. Repeat until the contours are familiar.

4. Now using a new sheet of paper, trace the outline of the map in black. Then using your regular pencil with an eraser, draw the coastal outline, including Sri Lanka. Also draw the lines of the Kaveri, Tungabhadra, Wainganga, Narmada, and Indus, using the frame of the map as a reference. When you are happy with your map, lay it over the original. Erase and re-draw any lines that are more than ½" off of the original. Mark each of the rivers.

5. Now study carefully the Punjab, Himalaya, Jaunpur, Bengal, Malwa, Jaunpur, Gujarat, Deccan, and Sri Lanka areas. Mark each on your map, check it against the original, and make any necessary corrections.

6. Next study carefully the locations of Ghazni, Lahore, Delhi, Chittor, Gaur, Daulatabad, Gulbarga, Vijayanagara, Jaffna, Dambadeniya, Gampola, and Kotte. When they are familiar for you, lay your map over the original. Erase and re-draw any locations that are more than ½″ off of the original.

7. Label Palk Strait.

Chapter Seventy-Eight

The Union of Krewo

The student may use her text when answering the questions in sections I and II.

Section I: Who, What, Where

Write a one or two-sentence answer explaining the significance of each item listed below.

Aldona—**Pg. 554, ¶ 7—Aldona was Lithuanian wife of Casimir the Great. She converted to Christianity at the time of her marriage, though the Lithuanians did not follow her and remained pagan.**

Casimir the Great—**Pg. 551, ¶ 3 and Pg. 552, ¶ 3 & 4—Casimir the Great, king of Poland, gathered together world leaders at a meeting known as the Congress of Krakow in the hopes of starting a crusade against the Ottoman Turks. Casimir the Great created a unified, powerful Poland but he was not able to produce a male heir, dying on November 5, 1370 after a hunting accident with only daughters to carry on his legacy.**

Charles II—**Pg. 553, ¶ 5—Charles II, king of Naples, arrived in Hungary in 1386 in order to take Mary's place on the throne. He was assassinated a month later, by agents of Mary's mother Elizabeth, who had hoped to rule as regent for her young daughter.**

Congress of Krakow—**Pg. 551, ¶ 3 to Pg. 552, ¶ 1—The Congress of Krakow was called by Casimir the Great as a way to whip the assembled kings and aristocrats up into an enthusiasm for a new crusade against the eastern threat of the Ottoman Turks. While the Congress was unsuccessful in its efforts to start a new religious war (and turned into a jousting tournament instead), it did demonstrate to the world that Poland had joined the first rank of nations.**

Hedwig—**Pg. 553, ¶ 4, Pg. 554, ¶ 3 and Pg. 555, ¶ 3—Hedwig, Mary's younger sister, was supported by a strong party of dukes to be the Polish queen; her place on the throne would break the union of Poland and Hungary and preserve Poland's separate existence. Hedwig was crowned king of Poland on October 16, 1384, she married the Grand Duke of Lithuania in 1385, and she died in 1399 within a week of giving birth to a daughter that also died shortly after she was born.**

Jogaila—**Pg. 554, ¶ 7 to Pg. 555, ¶ 3—Jogaila, the Grand Duke of Lithuania, was married to Hedwig of Poland on the condition that he convert to orthodox Christianity. Jogaila was a sincere and honest man with a good head for politics; he agreed to the arrangement by signing the Union of Krewo and all power passed into his hands.**

Mary—**Pg. 553, ¶ 3 and Pg. 554, ¶ 2—Mary, Louis of Anjou's oldest surviving daughter, was married to the Roman Emperor Charles IV's second son, Sigismund, and she was placed on the Polish and Hungarian thrones after her father's death. In the contest over her succession, Mary was forced to watch her mother be strangled to death and to give up her power to her husband.**

Privilege of Košice—**Pg. 553, ¶ 2—Privilege of Košice was a deal Louis of Anjou made with the Polish dukes after he became king that reduced their obligations to the crown to three duties: payment of a small land tax, military service within Poland only, and the upkeep of castles and fortifications.**

Sigismund—**Pg. 553, ¶ 3 and Pg. 554, ¶ 2—Sigismund, the second son of Roman Emperor Charles IV, was arranged to marry ten-year-old Mary, daughter of Louis of Anjou and queen of Hungary and Poland. After Mary's death, with no heir to the throne, Sigismund was able to take over sole rule as king of Hungary.**

Union of Krewo—**Pg. 555, ¶ 2—Union of Krewo was the formal agreement made between Jogaila, the Grand Duke of Lithuania, and Hedwig's regents that said if he converted to orthodox Christianity and married Hedwig, he would become king of Poland and Lithuania. The agreement was signed on August 14, 1385; Hedwig remained queen, but all power passed into Jogaila's hands.**

Wladyslaw the Elbow-High—**Pg. 552, ¶ 2—Wladyslaw the Elbow-High, Casimir the Great's father, a Duke of Piast before he became king of Poland, had made a good try at rounding up all of the dukes to create a unified Poland, but the Polans in the north and east had remained outside of his control.**

Section II: Comprehension

Write a two or three-sentence answer to each of the following questions.

1. How did Casimir create a unified Poland?

A1.—Pg. 552, ¶ 3—As soon as Casimir was crowned he worked to create peace around his country: he made a treaty with the Teutonic Order that settled an ongoing quarrel over his northern border; he paid off the king of Hungary and in return was given control over the duchy of Mazovia; and he fought other duchies into submission. He then started work on the infrastructure of his country: he built at least fifty new castles across Poland to help hold the newly expanded country together; he founded schools and convinced the pope to approve the charter of a new university in Krakow; and he sponsored the massive revision and republication of a law code for all Polans. Finally, he threw himself into the renovation of his

capital city: "He found Poland dressed in timber," says an old Polish proverb, "and left her dressed in brick."

2. Describe Casimir the Great's funeral.

A2.—Pg. 553, ¶ 1—Casimir the Great's funeral was massive and elaborate, with a mile-long ceremonial procession of knights and courtiers and the distribution of silver coins to the people. At the end of the funeral mass, his royal standard was broken into pieces. When the standard was broken, the Polish subjects in attendance cried out both in sorrow and in fear that the peace to which they had grown accustomed would meet the same end as their beloved king.

3. Explain how Louis of Anjou managed to become the Polish king. What arrangement did he make with the dukes of Poland in order to keep his place on the throne?

A3.—Pg. 553, ¶ 2—Louis of Anjou's mother was Casimir's sister, so he was the closest male relative of the dead king and thus had a claim to the Polish throne; in addition, Casimir himself had promised him the crown. Louis came to an agreement with the Polish dukes that said they would recognize him as king of Poland and in return he would leave them alone. He further sweetened the deal with a proclamation issued in 1374, the Privilege of Košice, that reduced their obligations to the crown to three duties, he redistributed hundreds of acres of royal land among them, and he rarely came into Poland.

4. What happened to Mary's place on the Polish throne after her father's funeral?

A4.—Pg. 553, ¶ 4—After Louis of Anjou's funeral, the aristocrats of both Poland and Hungary objected to Mary's rule. In Poland, a strong party of dukes argued for the election of Mary's younger sister Hedwig instead; this would break the union of the two crowns and preserve Poland's separate existence. In Hungary, a dissenting party of Hungarian nobles who disliked the idea of female rule invited the king of Naples to come in and take the crown.

5. How did Mary end up as a prisoner in Croatia, and how did she get out?

A5.—Pg. 553, ¶ 5 to Pg. 554, ¶ 1—One month after Charles II, king of Naples, arrived in Hungary in 1386 to take the throne away from Mary, he was assassinated by agents of Mary's mother. In retaliation, the supporters of the dead king kidnapped Mary and her mother and dragged them off to Croatia, where, in a mountain fortress, Mary's mother was strangled in front of her daughter's eyes. Mary's husband Sigismund, with his father's assistance, put together a force of German soldiers and Venetian sailors and arrived in Hungary a few months later; he managed to negotiate Mary's release on the promise that Mary would have no more power than a queen consort.

6. What happened between Sigismund and Mary after she returned to Hungary?

A6.—Pg. 554, ¶ 2—Mary suspected that her new husband had been complicit in her mother's death, so she refused to live with him. Mary and Sigismund lived in two separate households until her accidental death in a riding accident in 1395. Mary was pregnant with their first child; her death prevented the crown from passing out of Sigismund's hands, and after that he reigned alone as king of Hungary.

7. In what ways did the Teutonic Knights, invited into the Polish duchies to help conquer the Lithuanians, actually strengthen the Lithuanians and their relationship with Poland?

A7.—Pg. 554, ¶ 5 & 6—The Teutonic conquest of the Lithuanian-speaking region of Prussia had had the side effect of uniting the Lithuanians to the east into a stronger and stronger block of resistance, governed and directed by a Grand Duke who ruled from the capital city of Vilnius. Teutonic aggression had also convinced Casimir's father that an alliance with the Lithuanians would provide good protection against both the German-Prussian state and the possible expansion of the Golden Horde. In 1325, he had arranged for Casimir to marry the daughter of the Grand Duke, creating a union between the two countries.

Section III: Critical Thinking

The student may not use her text to answer this question.

When Hedwig was made the ruling monarch of Poland on October 16, 1384, she was called "king" and not "queen." We only learn a little bit about Hedwig's life in this chapter. For this critical thinking question, explain why Hedwig was king, and not queen. In your answer, define the term "queen regnant." Then, after finding out at least three more facts about Hedwig's rule via your own research, write a paragraph that tells the reader more about the Polish "king." As always, make sure to cite your sources.

On page 554 we learn that Hedwig was crowned king on October 16, 1384. Polish queens had always simply been the wives of the king, so they had no name for a queen that ruled. Thus, she was called king. A "queen regnant" is a queen that rules in her own right, rather than a queen who is just the companion of a king. The Polans did not have a term for a queen regnant because they were used only to a queen consort.

Hedwig, also known as Jadwiga, was canonized by Pope John Paul II on June 8, 1997. Hedwig was known for her missionary work in Lithuania, which naturally followed the conversion of her husband, Jogaila, to orthodox Christianity. The student might pursue research on Hedwig's personal life, her role as queen consort, or her work as a proponent of the Catholic faith. The student's answer should include at least *three facts about Hedwig that were not included in the chapter.*

The Chicago Manual of Style is used to for the footnotes in this example answer. You may designate the style guide to be used by the student.

EXAMPLE ANSWER:

When Hedwig was crowned as the Polish monarch, she was called "king." The Polans only knew a queen to be a consort, or companion, to a king. They did not have a term for a queen that ruled in her own right, or a queen regnant. So, she was called "King Hedwig." Hedwig was a pre-teen when she married the Grand Duke of Lithuania, Jogaila. Though Hedwig ended up marrying Jogaila as a way to unite Lithuania and Poland, and to appease those that did not want to have a woman ruling their country, Hedwig was actually in love with an Austrian Prince named William. Their marriage was arranged, but when they met, the two teens fell in love. The rising problems with the Teutonic knights gave the Polish aristocracy many worries,

and they believed Jogaila was a better match, so Hedwig's engagement to William was called off.[3]

Hedwig died shortly after having a child (that also died) in 1399. In her short time as monarch, she made a strong mark on the world. Hedwig was a strong believer in education. She breathed new life into the university in Krakow and she created a college in Prague for Lithuanians.[4] She was also invested in religious development in the nations that she had united. Her work spreading Catholicism in Lithuania later earned her the title of "saint;" she was canonized by Pope John Paul II on June 8, 1997.[5]

---

3. Thomas J. Craughwell, "A patron saint for queens," *Catholicherald.com,* last modified February 24, 2015, http://catholicherald.com/stories/A-patron-saint-for-queens,28361.

4. *Ibid.*

5. "Jadwiga," *Encylopædia Britannica,* accessed May, 5, 2016, http://www.britannica.com/biography/Jadwiga.

Chapter Seventy-Nine

The Rebirth of the Mongol Horde

The student may use his text when answering the questions in sections I and II.

Section I: Who, What, Where

Write a one or two-sentence answer explaining the significance of each item listed below.

Amir Husayn—**Pg. 557, ¶ 2 & 3 and Pg. 558, ¶ 4—Amir Husayn, governor of the Mongol city of Balkh, was a powerful amir that was known as a kingmaker; he had personally engineered the coronation of his Chagatai khan, Kabil Shah. Amir Husayn was murdered by one of Timur-Leng's officers (a man that had a blood feud against the amir) after Timur-Leng laid siege on his former master.**

Kabil Shah—**Pg. 557, ¶ 3—Kabil Shah was made Chagatai Khan by the power of Amir Husayn, one of the most prominent kingmakers among all the local Mongol chiefs.**

Nasiruddin Mahmud—**Pg. 561, ¶ 5 and Pg. 563, ¶ 1—Nasiruddin Mahmud of the Tughluq dynasty was ruling over Delhi at the time of Timur-Leng's 1398 invasion. After Timur-Leng sent Nasiruddin's war elephants back through his own army when they followed by the Mongol forces when the two sides met outside Delhi, the sultan fled to Gujarat.**

Pir Muhammad—**Pg. 561, ¶ 4 & 5—Pir Muhammad, Timur-Leng's grandson, led an exploratory force into India, after which he was joined by his grandfather in April of 1398. Pir Muhammad was at his grandfather's side in India, and together they raided through the Punjab.**

Timur-Leng (Timurlane)—**Pg. 557, ¶ 1 & 2, Pg. 558, ¶ 4 & 5, Pg. 561, ¶ 2 and Pg. 563, ¶ 2—Timur-Leng (Latinized to Timurlane), meaning the Iron Cripple, a name earned after Timur-Leng fought through to the end of a battle despite having been wounded in both arms and legs, was a Mongol soldier from the Chagatai Khanate that set out to recover the glorious Mongol empire in 1367. After defeating his brother-in-law Amir Husayn, and then taking Khwarezm, Isfahan, Tabriz, and the lands south of the Caspian Sea for himself, Timur-Leng successfully conquered the Golden Horde and Delhi.**

Toktamish—**Pg. 560, ₵ 3 and Pg. 561, ₵ 1—Toktamish, the leader of the Golden Horde, was a man from the Chagatai lands and descendent of Genghis Khan's son Juchi that had previously sworn a vassal's oath to Timur-Leng himself. Toktamish was attacked by Timur-Leng twice; after the second attack in 1395, Toktamish fought for three days before having to flee, after which he spent his life as a fugitive, wandering through Siberia trying to stay alive.**

Section II: Comprehension

Write a two or three-sentence answer to each of the following questions.

1. What kind of a fighter was Timur-Leng? Why were those that fought with him so loyal?

A1.—Pg. 558, ₵ 2 & 3—Timur-Leng was a fierce and charismatic fighter; it was said by those who had seen him in battle that when he seized his sword, he "made such sparks fly from it that / The sun in comparison seemed dark / He charged down like a roaring lion." His battle frenzies had won him a loyal following among Amir Husayn's soldiers, and their loyalty was only increased by his habit of giving away much of the battle spoil to his troops. He gave them clothing, jewels, horses, weapons, and belts, and thanked them for their bravery by sending them, "in cups of gold, the most delicious wines by the hands of the most beautiful women in the world."

2. Describe Timur-Leng's treatment of his enemies and conquered subjects.

A2.—Pg. 558, ₵ 8 to Pg. 560, ₵ 1—Timur-Leng had no interest in diplomacy, often scolding his officers for displaying too much restraint. After a battle against the city of Isfizar, seventy miles south of Herat, he ordered the defenders of the city piled up and cemented into towers while still alive; when Isfahan fell, he had seventy thousand opponents executed; he left pillars of skulls across the former Il-khanate lands to mark his progress; and in Sistan, he ordered his troops to wreck all of the irrigation works they could find, destroying the countryside's ability to grow crops and simultaneously its will to resist. Timur-Leng put his enemies to death and spared his allies because he was a practical man whose only ethic was victory.

3. Why did Timur-Leng think he would be able to conquer the Golden Horde?

A3.—Pg. 560, ₵ 3—The Golden Horde seemed poised for plucking because plague had weakened both the Rus' cities and the Mongol government that oversaw them and in 1359, a fight between two brothers of the khanship had spread into a khanate-wide struggle. In the years before Timur-Leng's arrival, pretenders all over the Horde—at one time, seven simultaneously—claimed to be the rightful khan. The man who eventually came out on top was a man that came from Chagatai lands called Toktamish and some years before, he had sworn a vassal's loyalty to Timur-Leng himself.

4. How did Toktamish assert his place as the Khan of the Golden Horde against Rus' resistance?

A4.—Pg. 560, ₵ 4—Toktamish asserted his place as the Khan of the Golden Horde by descending on those who resisted his rule with full Mongol ferocity. He plundered his dissenters' treasuries, burned their houses, and slaughtered their women and children. By

the time Timur-Leng arrived at his borders, Toktamish had terrorized the Rus' back into submission.

5. What happened the first time Timur-Leng attacked Toktamish? What did Timur-Leng do after the armies met in 1391 near the Volga river?

A5.—Pg. 560, ¶ 6-8—When Timur-Leng first attacked Toktamish, he met not only Toktamish but the Rus' princes Toktamish had previously attacked; they chose to fight with their oppressor because Timur-Leng had a reputation for being a terrible torturer and destroyer. Timur-Leng defeated Toktamish's forces when they met near the Volga river in 1391, giving Timur-Leng control of the eastern part of the Horde Territory. During the next year, Timur-Leng fought his way through the Rus' cities as far as Elets, he put down rebellions south of the Caspian Sea, and he had his eye on Baghdad, which he entered with little difficulty in August of 1393.

6. What happened the second time Timur-Leng attacked Toktamish? What happened to the Golden Horde after the attack?

A6.—Pg. 560, ¶ 8 to Pg. 561, ¶ 2—Timur-Leng launched a second invasion against Toktamish in 1394 and once again Toktamish and his Rus' princes were defeated. On the Terek river, in 1395, Toktamish fought against Timur-Leng for three entire days before he was forced to flee, running for the rest of his life through Siberia as a fugitive, just trying to stay alive. After Toktamish fled, Timur-Leng sacked the Golden Horde capital city of Sarai, on the Volga, and then spent eight months in the land of the Rus', destroying fortresses and reducing towns to rubble.

7. How did Timur-Leng prepare for his invasion of Delhi?

A7.—Pg. 561, ¶ 6 & 7—Timur-Leng prepared for his invasion of Delhi by ordering all the Indian prisoners still held in his camp massacred, for fear that they might break out during the battle and join in Delhi's defense. Every soldier was ordered to kill his fair share of the prisoners; contemporary accounts suggest that as many as 100,000 were slaughtered, their bodies piled into a bloody mountain outside the camp. Timur-Leng also prepared for the opposition's use of war elephants whose tusks had been poisoned by ordering his men to pile hay on the backs of camels, set the hay on fire, and drive the camels towards the elephants, which caused the elephants to stampede back through the sultan's army.

8. Describe what happened to Delhi and its population after Timur-Leng defeated Nasiruddin Mahmud.

A8.—Pg. 563, ¶ 2 & 3—After Nasiruddin Mahmud fled Delhi, Timur-Leng entered the city and allowed his forces to plunder and kill: the official court account recorded ten thousand beheaded in a single hour, wives and children taken as slaves, grain stores burned, and jewels torn from the ears and fingers of Delhi's women. When Timur-Leng withdrew to Samarkand he took with him thousands of captives: artists, writers, competent officials, stonemasons, bricklayers, and weavers, intending to put them to work as slaves in his own realm. When Nasiruddin Mahmud finally crept back to his wrecked city, he found it stripped and burned, corpses stacked in the street, and its entire culture transported over the mountains, to captivity in distant Samarkand.

Section III: Critical Thinking

The student may not use his text to answer this question.

Power does not always come from the person designated by a government to wield power. We can see this clearly when looking at Timur-Leng's pursuit of Mongol power. Write a paragraph that explains how power was distributed between the governors and the khan in the Chagatai realm. Then explain who Timur-Leng wanted to get rid of, and why.

On page 557 we read about the distribution of power in the Chagatai Khanate. The Chagatai were theoretically ruled over by a Mongol Khan that claimed to be a direct descendant of Genghis Khan. However, the Chagatai Khanate had never gained the stability that the other three parts of the Mongol empire (the Golden Horde, the Il-khanate, and the Yuan) at some point, even if briefly, enjoyed. The Chagatai khans ruled from the eastern side of the Khanate, an area that had gained the nickname Mughulistan, "Land of the Mongols." The Chagatai khans had never been able to wield very much power in the western reaches of the kingdom, Transoxania (the lands just east of the Oxus river). There, local Mongol chiefs—called amirs—wielded the real power. Without them, the Chagatai khans had no hope of retaining their thrones.

Amir Husayn, brother-in-law to Timur-Leng, was the Mongol governor of the city of Balkh. He was also one of the most powerful of the amirs. He was known as a prominent kingmaker, and he had personally engineered the coronation of his Chagatai khan, Kabil Shah. While Kabil Shah may have been called "khan," it was Amir Husayn that had the real power.

We learn in the chapter that Timur-Leng wanted his own power, and he saw the path to that power through rebellion against the khan. However, Timur-Leng was not a descendent of the royal clan of Genghis Khan, so he could not pursue the khanate itself. Rebelling against the khan wasn't the plan anyway, because the khan was a mere puppet. Timur-Leng wanted power, not a title. He did not want to appear to rule, he wanted to dominate. As such, he had to go after his brother-in-law, the kingmaker. Amir Husayn had the real power, and Timur-Leng wanted it for himself.

EXAMPLE ANSWER:

The Chagatai were ruled over by a Mongol khan that had to be the direct descendant of Genghis Khan. But the khan didn't have that much power. The real power came from the amirs, or the local Mongol chiefs, in Transoxania. The Chagatai khans ruled from Mughulistan, "Land of the Mongols," on the eastern side of the Khanate; their power did not extend to the western reaches of the kingdom where the amirs were in control. Only with the support of the amirs could a khan keep his throne. Amir Husayn, brother-in-law to Timur-Leng, was the Mongol governor of the city of Balkh. He was also one of the most powerful of the amirs. He was known as a prominent kingmaker, and he had personally engineered the coronation of his Chagatai khan, Kabil Shah. While Kabil Shah may have been called "khan," it was Amir Husayn that had the real power.

Timur-Leng wanted his own power, and he saw the path to that power through rebellion against the khan. However, Timur-Leng was not a descendent of the royal clan of Genghis Khan, so he could not pursue the khanate itself. Usurping the khan's place wasn't the plan anyway because the khan was a mere puppet. As such, he had to go after his brother-in-law, the kingmaker. Amir Husayn had the real power, and Timur-Leng wanted it for himself.

Section IV: Map Exercise

1. Trace the rectangular outline of Map 79.1 in black.

2. Trace the coastal outline in blue, including the Persian Gulf and Caspian Sea. Trace the lines of the Oxus and Indus. Repeat until the contours are familiar.

3. Using contrasting colors, trace the areas of the Golden Horde and Chagatai Khanate. Show the mountains with small peaks. Repeat until the contours are familiar.

4. Using a new sheet of paper, trace the outline of the frame in black. Using your regular pencil with an eraser, draw the coastal outline, including the Persian Gulf and Caspian Sea. Draw the lines of the Oxus and Indus. Then draw the lines of the areas of the Golden Horde and the Chagatai Khanate. Draw the mountains with small peaks. When you are with happy your map, lay it over the original. Erase and re-draw any lines which are more than ½″ off of the original.

5. Now study the areas of Sistan, Khwarezm, Transoxania, Mughulistan, Punjab, and Gujarat. When you are familiar with them, close the book. Mark each one on your map, and then check your map against the original. Make any needed corrections.

6. Now study the locations of Tabriz, Baghdad, Isfahan, Isfizar, Herat, Balkh, Samarkand, and Delhi. When you are familiar with them, close the book. Mark each one on your map, and then lay your map over the original. Erase and re-mark any locations more than ½″ off of the original.

7. Mark the directions of Timur's campaigns.

Chapter Eighty

Compromises and Settlements

The student may use her text when answering the questions in sections I and II.

Section I: **Who, What, Where**

Write a one or two-sentence answer explaining the significance of each item listed below.

Ashikaga Yoshimitsu—**Pg. 566, ¶ 5, Pg. 568, ¶ 5 and Pg. 569, ¶ 4—Ashikaga Yoshimitsu, appointed shogun in 1368 when he was just ten years old, held every title that his father and grandfather had claimed by the age of twenty-one and by 1380, aged twenty-three, he had become the Minister of the Left, the second-highest position at court; he even called himself "King of Japan" in his dealings with the Ming emperor. Yoshimitsu made a compromise with Go-Kameyama that legitimized the Kyoto emperor's rule, thus bringing an end to the Nambokucho era.**

Cheonsang yeolcha bunya jido—**Pg. 568, ¶ 4 & *—Cheonsang yeolcha bunya jido is the name of the star map Taejo commissioned in 1395. The map, based on a rubbing of a first-century star map, was a representation of the sky with 1,467 stars, the Milky Way, and almost three hundred constellations, and it also showed representations of the relative brightness of each star, with dim stars carved smaller, and brighter ones larger.**

Go-Kameyama—**Pg. 569, ¶ 2 & 3—Go-Kameyama, the southern Japanese emperor, was in possession of the sacred regalia of the Japanese emperors, but he could boast little other power. Go-Kameyama made a compromise with Yoshimitsu: Go-Kameyama would travel to Kyoto with the sacred regalia and hand it over to the northern emperor (an act that would ritually legitimize the Kyoto emperor's rule), and then the shogun would see that Go-Kameyama was awarded the title of Cloistered Emperor.**

Gongmin—**Pg. 565, ¶ 3 and Pg. 566, ¶ 6—Gongmin, king of Goryeo, worked to cleanse his kingdom of Mongol influence by sending messages of respect to the new Hongwu Emperor and by having Shin Ton purge the Mongols in Goryeo's government. Gongmin's anti-Yuan, pro-Ming policies led to his assassination in 1374 by those who saw Ming power looming too close.**

Hosokawa Yoriyuki—Pg. 566, ¶ 5—Hosokawa Yoriyuki, highly capable and conscientious, was made regent of the young shogun Ashikaga Yoshimitsu. Unfortunately, Hosokawa Yoriyuki was forced out of Kyoto by his political rivals and was unable to continue advising the young shogun.

Shin Ton—Pg. 565, ¶ 3 and Pg. 566, ¶ 1 & 6—Shin Ton was a Buddhist monk appointed by King Gongmin to help carry out a purge of the Mongols in Goryeo's government after the decline of Yuan power and the coronation of the Hongwu emperor. With the king's approval, Shin Ton created a new agency, the "Directorate for Reclassification of Farmland and Farming Population," whose sole task was to investigate pro-Yuan landholders with the intent of taking their land and slaves away, redistributing the land and freeing the slaves (an endeavor that cost him his life in 1371).

Wu—Pg. 567, ¶ 1 & 4—Wu, King Gongmin's son (though widely rumored to be not Gongmin's son at all, but the illegitimate son of the dead monk Shin Ton), was eleven when he was made king of Goryeo, though Yi In-im took over control of the government. King Wu was deposed by Yi Seong-gye in 1388 after he refused to listen to the general's opinion that war against the Ming was ill-advised.

Yi In-im—Pg. 567, ¶ 1 & 2—Yi In-im, King Gongmin's chief general, was the architect of the king's assassination because Yi In-im was pro-Yuan, and anti-Ming, and believed that Goryeo would find independence only in resisting all Ming demands. Yi In-im took control of the government after putting Wu on the throne but later fell in the ongoing conflict between pro-Ming and Ming-phobic factions.

Yi Seong-gye (Taejo)—Pg. 566, ¶ 3 and Pg. 567, ¶ 4 & 5—Yi Seong-gye, one of Gongmin's generals and famous for his skills as an archer, was made personally responsible by Gongmin for picking off the most notorious of the Japanese pirates, the much-feared Akibatsu, with his own arrow. Yi Seong-gye led a peaceful coup against King Wu because Wu wanted to fight the Ming; Yi Seong-gye crowned himself ruler of Goryeo in 1392, renamed himself Taejo, and renamed Goryeo as Joseon.

Section II: Comprehension

Write a two or three-sentence answer to each of the following questions.

1. Explain Goryeo's relationship with the Yuan dynasty, and how King Gongmin started to reclaim his power after the coronation of the Hongwu emperor.

A1.—Pg. 565, ¶ 2 & 3— Goryeo was deeply connected to the Yuan: Kublai Khan had forced them to replace their traditional title of emperor with the lower rank of vassal king, and had further tied the royal family to his own through marriage; one of his (many) daughters had been sent to Goryeo as a royal bride, and since then, Goryeo kings had continued to marry Mongol wives. However, when Yuan might started to decline during the Red Turban rebellions, King Gongmin of Goryeo began to reclaim his power. The Hongwu Emperor's coronation, in 1368, was a green light; King Gongmin immediately sent messages of friendship and respect to the

new Ming emperor, and at the same time appointed the Buddhist monk Shin Ton to help carry out a purge of the Mongols in his own government.

2. How do we know that the Mongol thread woven through Goryeo's life was a constant humiliation to Gongmin?

A2.—Pg. 565, ¶ 4 & 5—For nearly a century, Goryeo's kings had not only married Mongol wives but had gone to Yuan China for their education; Gongmin himself had spent years studying politics and Confucian thought at the Mongol capital Dadu. But a contemporary chronicle gives us a glimpse into the resentment that must have simmered around him, after his return, through a story that tells us Gongmin's father scolded him for wearing Mongolian clothing. The Mongol influence was a constant reminder of Goryeo's subjugation, and thus a constant humiliation to King Gongmin.

3. Why didn't all of Gongmin's subjects want to remove the Yuan influence from Goryeo culture?

A3.—Pg. 566, ¶ 2— Not everyone in Gongmin's court wanted to do away with the Yuan presence in Goryeo because many of Gongmin's people believed the ways of the Yuan had simply become their ways. Yuan supporters felt that the foreigners to be feared were the Ming, the aggressive new empire that no one yet knew or understood.

4. Who was terrorizing Goryeo's shores and how did the people of Goryeo react?

A4.—Pg. 566, ¶ 3 & 4—Japanese pirates, called _wokou_, ranged lawlessly through the sea and raided Goryeo's coast; these raids grew so severe that Gongmin ordered warehouses on the coast, used for storing official taxes paid in rice, moved inland. Peasants who had always farmed the fertile lands along the water gave up and fled from the sea. Gongmin gave the defense against pirates over to his general Yi Seong-gye, who he made personally responsible for picking off the most notorious of the pirates, the much-feared Akibatsu, with his own arrow.

5. Why didn't the Japanese government do anything to stop the _wokou_?

A5.—Pg. 566, ¶ 4—The Ashikaga shogunate had been powerless to restrain the _wokou_ because it was powerless to restrain most bandit activity that took place far away from Kyoto. The Japanese monarchy itself was divided, with an emperor from the senior imperial line ruling in Kyoto, and a rival emperor from the junior line holding court in the southern mountains. The Ashikaga shogun had tied his fortunes to the emperor in Kyoto; and that emperor's reach was short and weak, unable to stop not only raids off the coast in Goryeo but also the Ming coast.

6. What did King Wu demand that led to his deposition as king?

A6.—Pg. 567, ¶ 3-5—In the summer of 1388, the Ming Hongwu Emperor made a demand for the return of the northern lands once held by the Yuan, and under the influence of his anti-Ming advisors, King Wu ordered General Yi Seong-gye to lead an attack on the nearest Ming territory. Yi Seong-gye protested saying it was a very bad idea, but King Wu refused to listen and as a result, Yi Seong-gye arrested both the young king and his anti-Ming advisor and then made sure Wu was firmly deposed.

7. How did Yi Seong-gye become Taejo and Goryeo become Joseon?

A7.—Pg. 567, ¶ 5 to Pg. 568, ¶ 1—After King Wu was deposed, Yi Seong-gye and his allies chose a new king to serve as their puppet; but in April of 1392, Yi Seong-gye crowned himself ruler of Goryeo. He renamed himself Taejo and declared the following year, 1393, to be the first year of a new era, with a new king and a newly renamed country: from now on Goryeo would be Joseon, the name he also gave to his new dynasty.

8. What did Taejo do during his transition into power to minimize bloodshed and show his own strength and purpose?

A8.—Pg. 568, ¶ 1—In effort to keep bloodshed to a minimum, the new emperor Taejo ordered that all government officials be removed from their posts, deprived of their titles, and put under house arrest; then he appointed a new administration. To show his strength and purpose, he announced the construction of a new capital city: the city of Hanyang, which was renamed Hanseong, and known widely simply as the *seoul*, a common noun meaning "capital." A massive building project, recruiting almost twenty thousand laborers, began, and a massive new royal wall was built around the city during the cold season, when the laborers were not needed on their own farms, resulting in a city that had had four gates: Great East, Great South, Great West, and Sukjeongmun the north gate, barred so that it could not be used except for ritual purposes.

9. How did the Nambokucho era, the age of the "Southern and Northern Court," come to an end?

A9.—Pg. 569, ¶ 2-4—In 1392, Ashikaga Yoshimitsu negotiated a compromise with Go-Kameyama: if Go-Kameyama would travel to Kyoto with the sacred regalia of the Japanese emperors and hand it over to the northern emperor (an act that would ritually legitimize the Kyoto emperor's rule), the shogun would see that Go-Kameyama was awarded the title of Cloistered Emperor, that the next ruling emperor would come from the junior line, and that rule would alternate between the senior and the junior branches of the family. Even though it was exactly the same compromise that had failed sixty years before, Go-Kameyama chose to be an optimist and journeyed to Kyoto and surrendered the regalia. In recognition, Yoshimitsu sponsored a three-day sacred festival in Kyoto where nightly dances dedicated to the gods (*kagura*) celebrated the spiritual triumph of reunification, the joy of the end of the Nambokucho era, the conclusion of the age of the "Southern and Northern Court."

Section III: Critical Thinking

The student may not use her text to answer this question.

Diplomacy is the art and practice of conducting negotiations between nations. It is also the word we use when we talk about handling affairs with sensitivity, or without arousing hostility. To be duped is to be deceived or cheated. Write a paragraph explaining whether or not you think Taejo was acting diplomatically or he was being duped in his relations with the Ming. Then write a paragraph describing your thoughts on the end of the Nambokucho era: was Yoshimitsu being diplomatic, or was he duped? For both answers, make sure to explain your assertion fully with examples from the chapter.

For this answer the student can argue either diplomacy or duped for both situations. Each paragraph below explains the situation for Taejo and Yoshimitsu. The example answers show how the student could argue both ways for each leader.

Taejo believed, from his time as a general under King Gongmin and King Wu, that Goryeo should serve the Ming. In his letter to King Wu against the attack on the Ming after their demands for the return of northern lands once held by the Yuan, Taejo wrote

> *First, it is not profitable for a small kingdom to attack a bigger kingdom.*
> *Second, it is not appropriate to mobilize large troops in summer.*
>
> *Third, there is the possibility of Japanese pirates invading the southern*
> *parts if large troops are concentrated in the northern parts.*
>
> *Fourth, bows cannot be used due to the melting of the bowstrings in summer when it is*
> *rainy and sweltering much, and soldiers suffer from many diseases.*

The first line of his letter is very telling: "it is not profitable for a small kingdom to attack a bigger kingdom." If this were true, our History of the Renaissance World would be a very different text. We continue to see Taejo's desire to please the Ming after he took control of Goryeo (Joseon). We learn on page 568 that "Joseon, [Taejo] believed, was 'a small nation serving a greater nation,' and there was both honor and virtue in acting with proper submission. Despite his years of army service, King Taejo was a diplomat through and through. When the Ming emperor sent a demand for tribute to be paid every three years, Taejo sent a counterproposal: he would send it three times per year instead. Somewhat startled, the Hongwu Emperor agreed. He was not excessively concerned with his own dignity, merely with the survival of his country and the stability of his own throne." He was successful in achieving prosperity. His people were happy and the king had a long reign. The star map "Cheonsang yeolcha bunya jido" is evidence of the peace in Taejo's kingdom. He was able to concentrate his efforts on observing the night sky, not fighting off outside enemies.

The Ashikaga shogun Yoshimitsu was interested in gaining more and more power. By age twenty-three he was Minister of the Left, the second-highest position at court, and he had taken to calling himself "King of Japan" in his dealings with the Ming emperor. Reuniting the Japanese thrones would be a great win for Yoshimitsu. In 1392, Ashikaga Yoshimitsu managed to negotiate a compromise: if Go-Kameyama would travel to Kyoto with the sacred regalia of the Japanese emperors and hand it over to the northern emperor (an act that would ritually legitimize the Kyoto emperor's rule), the shogun would see that Go-Kameyama was awarded the title of Cloistered Emperor. He also promised that the next ruling emperor would come from the junior line, and that rule would alternate between the senior and the junior branches of the family. This was exactly the same compromise that had failed sixty years before, but Go-Kameyama went through with it anyway. After the regalia was handed over, Yoshimitsu sponsored a three-day sacred festival in Kyoto with nightly dances dedicated to the gods that celebrated the spiritual triumph of reunification, the joy of the end of the Nambokucho era, the conclusion of the age of the "Southern and Northern Court." However, as written on page 569, "the compromise, which theoretically brought the struggle between north and south to an end, had done nothing to bring the fractured military zones back under central rule. It had done nothing to corral the independent-minded warlords out in the provinces. The victory dances were empty: ritual with no reality behind them."

EXAMPLE ANSWER (TAEJO DIPLOMACY):

Taejo believed, from his time as a general under King Gongmin and King Wu, that Goryeo should serve the Ming. He believed that it was not profitable for a small kingdom to attack a bigger kingdom. Taejo believed that Joseon was a small nation serving a bigger nation. He wanted to keep the peace so that his small nation could prosper. He believed there was both honor and virtue in acting with proper submission. When the Ming emperor sent a demand for tribute to be paid every three years, Taejo sent a counterproposal: he would send it three times per year instead. Of course the Hongwu emperor did not turn this offer down. Taejo's excessive tribute guaranteed peace for Joseon, and his kingdom was able to thrive. His people were happy and the king had a long reign. The star map "Cheonsang yeolcha bunya jido" is evidence of the peace in Taejo's kingdom. He was able to concentrate his efforts on observing the night sky, not fighting off outside enemies.

EXAMPLE ANSWER (TAEJO DUPED):

While Taejo may have always believed that a small nation should serve a big nation, his submission to the Ming made him less of a diplomat and more of a vassal. Taejo feared conflict with the Ming, so he overcompensated when the Ming demanded tribute. The Ming emperor said he wanted a payment every three years, and Taejo responded by saying he would send tribute three times a year. Who would not agree to this excessive generosity? Taejo's belief that it was not profitable for a small kingdom to attack a bigger kingdom filtered its way into his relationship with the Ming and he overpaid to keep his country safe.

EXAMPLE ANSWER (YOSHIMITSU DIPLOMACY):

The Ashikaga shogun Yoshimitsu was interested in gaining more and more power. The best way to do this would be to reunite his broken country. Yoshimitsu was able to make a compromise with the southern emperor Go-Kameyama; if Go-Kameyama brought the sacred regalia of the Japanese emperors north, thereby legitimizing the northern emperor's rule, the shogun would see that Go-Kameyama was awarded the title of Cloistered Emperor. He also promised that the next ruling emperor would come from the junior line, and that rule would alternate between the senior and the junior branches of the family. Go-Kameyama agreed and the Nambokucho era came to an end. Reuniting his nation was the ultimate act of diplomacy for Yoshimitsu.

EXAMPLE ANSWER (YOSHIMITSU DUPED):

The Ashikaga shogun Yoshimitsu was interested in gaining more and more power. The best way to do this would be to reunite his broken country. Yoshimitsu was able to make a compromise with the southern emperor Go-Kameyama; if Go-Kameyama brought the sacred regalia of the Japanese emperors north, thereby legitimizing the northern emperor's rule, the shogun would see that Go-Kameyama was awarded the title of Cloistered Emperor. He also promised that the next ruling emperor would come from the junior line, and that rule would alternate between the senior and the junior branches of the family. Go-Kameyama agreed and the Nambokucho era came to an end. However, this was the same failed compromise that divided the country in the first place. Yoshimitsu's reunification of Japan was a sham: the military zones were not under central rule and the war-lords out in the provinces were not unified. The deal existed on paper, but Japan was still broken.

Chapter Eighty-One

The House of Visconti and the Papal States

The student may use his text when answering the questions in sections I and II.

Section I: Who, What, Where

Write a one or two-sentence answer explaining the significance of each item listed below.

Bernabò Visconti—**Pg. 571, ¶ 5 to Pg. 572, ¶ 2 and Pg. 575, ¶ 1—Bernabò Visconti, who ruled from the city of Bologna, which he had seized from the Papal States, was a fearsome opponent that showed no fear or respect to the pope. Bernabò Visconti was overthrown by his nephew and taken prisoner; he died seven months later, still under guard, after eating a big meal sent to him by his nephew.**

Gian Galeazzo Visconti—**Pg. 575, ¶ 1 & 2—Gian Galeazzo Visconti, Bernabò Visconti's nephew, overthrew his uncle and then gathered the support of the Milanese by offering them drastic tax cuts. Gian Galeazzo Visconti captured Verona in 1387 and Padua in 1388 and then Bologna, Assisi, Perugia, Siena, Pisa, and Lucca.**

Giovanni Visconti—**Pg. 571, ¶ 5 to Pg. 572, ¶ 1—Giovanni Visconti divided the rule of Milanese territory with his brother Bernabò in 1356; Giovanni ruled from Milan.**

Gregory XI—**Pg. 572, ¶ 8 to Pg. 573, ¶ 2 and Pg. 574, ¶ 2—Gregory XI, nephew of Urban V's predecessor Clement VI and Urban V's successor, knew that the papacy was in danger of losing the Papal States unless it returned to Rome, but he was also aware that he was no more capable of dealing with the Viscontis than Urban had been, so, from Avignon, he worked to unify a league of Lombard cities against the Visconti, a plan that plunged Italy into war. By 1377, both Gregory XI and the antipapal league were sickened by the war, and on August 21, they agreed to a cease-fire; Gregory XI was still in the middle of negotiations when he died, in March of 1378.**

John Hawkwood—**Pg. 573, ¶ 3 to Pg. 574, ¶ 1—John Hawkwood, an English mercenary who fought in turn for Florence, Milan, and Gregory XI during the war between the pope and the**

Viscontis, was in the pope's service when he led his men in a sack of the Italian city of Faenza that ended in massacre of the civilians, rape of every woman under the age of sixty, and wholesale looting. A Sienese chronicle says that Hawkwood himself killed at least one young woman, and that a priest with the expedition stood at the gates of Faenza, calling out to the rape victims to submit because "this is good for the army."

Matteo Visconti—Pg. 571, ¶ 4—Matteo Visconti was maneuvered by his uncle Ottone Visconti, the archbishop of Rome, into Milan's secular government as Captain of the People, leader and spokesman for the merchants and craftsmen. Thirty years later, the Holy Roman Emperor Louis IV appointed Matteo's grandson Perpetual Lord of Milan, and after that appointment, the House of Visconti dominated Milan's politics.

Ottone Visconti—Pg. 571, ¶ 4—Ottone Visconti, the archbishop of Rome, started the rise of Visconti power by maneuvering his nephew Matteo into Milan's secular government as Captain of the People, leader and spokesman for the merchants and craftsmen.

Robert of Geneva—Pg. 574, ¶ 1 and Pg. 574, ¶ 4—Robert of Geneva, the pope's legate, led an attack at Cesena during the war in Italy in which at least four thousand unarmed citizens were killed: "women, old and young, and sick, and children, and pregnant women, were cut to pieces at the point of a dagger" and Robert himself was heard to shout out, during the attack, "I will have more blood! kill all!—blood, blood!" Robert of Geneva was elected antipope Clement VII by the French cardinals after Urban VI was elected in Italy.

Urban VI—Pg. 574, ¶ 3-5—Urban VI, the papal name for the Italian-born Bartolomeo Prignano, was declared deposed by the French cardinals, though he continued a paranoid rule in Italy. Urban VI deposed all of the cardinals who had taken part in the election of Clement VII (the "antipope," according to the Romans) and then quarreled with their replacements, accusing them of conspiracy, and ordering them tortured and executed.

Section II: Comprehension

Write a two or three-sentence answer to each of the following questions.

1. Describe the state of governance in Italy following Pope Urban V's return to Rome.

A1.—Pg. 571, ¶ 2—When Pope Urban V returned to Rome, he found that Italy was seething. South of the Papal States, the Kingdom of Naples was friendly to the pope, but torn by palace intrigues and an ongoing feud with Sicily and the Papal States themselves had been without a head for sixty-five years, ever since the papacy had removed itself to Avignon; the cities within the Papal States were ruling themselves. Control of Rome itself had seesawed violently between Senate and various competing aristocratic families and in the north, the Lombard cities had reverted to their old independent ways, with little interference from the Holy Roman Emperor Charles IV, who was far more interested in Germany than in the old *regnum Italicum* of the empire (when he had gone to Rome for his own coronation, he had arrived in the morning, been crowned, and then left without even spending the night in the city).

2. What kind of a person was Bernabò Visconti? How did he react when he was excommunicated by Pope Urban V?

A2.—Pg. 572, ❡ 2—Bernabò was a fearsome opponent: a notorious libertine, father of seventeen legitimate and some twenty illegitimate children; an enthusiastic hunter who kept five thousand hunting dogs; a cruel and capricious ruler who had once ordered a deer poacher thrown into his dog kennel to be eaten, and who had executed a young man for confessing that he had "dreamed" of killing one of his master's game boars. After Urban V had excommunicated Bernabò for his trespass into the Papal States, he sent two papal legates with a bull of excommunication to Bologna to confront Bernabò in person. Bernabò had listened, and then had forced the legates to eat the bull—parchment, silk ribbons, lead seals and all and when Urban V protested Bernabò retorted, "I would have you know that I am pope, emperor and king in my own domains. God Himself cannot do here what is contrary to my will."

3. What happened when Charles IV entered Italy in May of 1368 at the request of Urban V?

A3.—Pg. 572, ❡ 3 & 4—Charles IV entered Italy in May of 1368 and started marching on Milan. Although he was not popular in Italy, he could easily have mustered the other northern Italian cities against the Viscontis; Florence, Padua, and Mantua were all worried about the growing Visconti power. Instead, the emperor allowed the Visconti brothers to buy him off with a good-sized tribute and then he then tried to base himself in Lucca, but the people of Lucca, indignant over his pacification of the Visconti tyrants, refused to welcome him, so he gave up and went home.

4. How did the Franciscan nun Birgitta of Vadstena react when she found out that Urban V wanted to return to Avignon? Was she right in her prophecy?

A4.—Pg. 572, ❡ 6 & 7—When the Franciscan nun Birgitta of Vadstena found out about Urban V's wish to return to Avignon, she visited the papal court and told the pope that she had received a direct word from the Mother of God. "I led Pope Urban by my prayer and the work of the Holy Spirit from Avignon to Rome. . . ," she declared, speaking in Mary's voice. "What did he do to me? He turns his back on me. . . . An evil spirit has brought him to this by deceiving him. He is weary of his divine work and wants his own physical comfort." If Urban V returned to Avignon, Birgitta prophesied, he would die within the year; she was right—Urban V returned to Avignon in September, and died in November after a brief and sudden illness.

5. Explain how Gregory XI's plan to unify a league of Lombard cities against the Visconti went wrong.

A5.—Pg. 573, ❡ 2 & 3—In his plan, Gregory XI had hoped that Florence would join the anti-Visconti league, but the papal legate he sent to finalize the alliance swapped sides and took up with the Viscontis. The Florentines, already suspicious of the pope's motivations, rallied Siena, Lucca, and Pisa against the Papal States. Almost immediately, the conflict mutated into Italians against French, the defense of the homeland against a foreign pope; in ten days, eighty cities and towns joined this antipapal alliance and soon a nasty, complicated, and bloody war followed.

6. What did Pope Urban V's death in Italy mean for the Roman cardinals? How did the French cardinals react?

A6.—Pg. 574, ¶ 3—The Roman cardinals had the chance to elect an Italian pope because Pope Urban V drew his last breath in Italy. They then elevated the Italian-born Bartolomeo Prignano as Pope Urban VI, but the French cardinals, indignant over the new pope's first months in office (he refused to even visit Avignon, and he was appalled by the luxury in which the cardinals lived; one of his first acts was to decree that they could have only one course at dinner), soon revolted. They left Rome en masse, reassembled at Fonti, declared Urban VI deposed, and elected an antipope: Robert of Geneva, leader of the massacre at Cesena.

7. How did the papacy end up divided, with one pope in Rome and another pope in Avignon?

A7.—Pg. 574, ¶ 3 & 4—After the French cardinals declared Urban VI deposed and elected Robert of Geneva as Pope Clement VII, a dual papacy developed, one at Rome and one at Avignon. King Charles of France, the King of Spain, the Earl of Savoy, the Duke of Milan, the Queen of Naples, and the whole of Scotland acknowledged Clement VII to be the true pope. But Germany and Lord Lewis of Flanders declared themselves for Urban VI, thus dividing the Christian world.

8. What was going on in Italy while Urban VI was occupied with his cardinals after the split of the church?

A8.—Pg. 575, ¶ 1 & 2—While the pope was occupied with his own troubles, Genoa and Venice, always rivals, restarted their own series of battles; and in 1380, the Venetians destroyed most of the Genoese fleet in a sea battle at Chioggia, a blow from which Genoa never fully recovered. In Milan, Bernabò Visconti's nephew, Gian Galeazzo Visconti, plotted the overthrow of his uncle; in 1385, he launched an armed raid that took both Bernabò and his two sons prisoner, and declared himself Lord of Milan. Gian Galeazzo Visconti then went on a kingdom-building spree, capturing Verona in 1387 and Padua in 1388, and then Bologna, Assisi, Perugia, Siena, Pisa, and Lucca.

Section III: Critical Thinking

The student may not use his text to answer this question.

To this day, the symbol of Milan is a biscione, or giant snake. In the modern version, the snake is eating a child, though when the symbol was first introduced, during the days of the House of Visconti, the snake was eating something else. Find out what the snake was eating when the symbol was introduced, and then write a paragraph based on what you have learned about the House of Visconti in this chapter that explains why you think the Viscontis chose this particular symbol.

The student can find an image of the symbol for Milan, and the House of Visconti, through a simple internet search. The symbol for the House of Visconti is a biscione eating a human, often noted as a Saracen or Moor. One legend says that Ottone Visconti attacked Jerusalem during the Second Crusade and there he challenged the

Saracen Voluce to a duel. Ottone won, and took the Saracen's coat of arms as his own. The student might suggest that the "otherness" of the Saracen or Moor figure represents the insularity of the family, and the desire to keep up Italian dominance. There is another myth that says the biscione is giving birth to a child, rather than eating one. The birth of the child also reinforces the power of the family by showing the continuation of the family's power through birth.

The student should recognize that the ruthless power of the Visconti family is represented in their family symbol. The student should also see that the growing power of the Visconti family from their base in Milan was so influential that the house symbol continues to this day as the symbol of the city.

EXAMPLE ANSWER:

The original symbol for the House of Visconti was a a biscione eating a human, often noted as a Saracen or Moor. One legend says that Ottone Visconti attacked Jerusalem during the Second Crusade and there he challenged the Saracen Voluce to a duel. Ottone won, and took the Saracen's coat of arms as his own. In the version with the grown man, the otherness represented by what could be called a Saracen or Moor represents the insularity of the family, and the desire to keep up Italian dominance. There is another myth that says the biscione is giving birth to a child, rather than eating one. In the version of the symbol where a child is being birthed by the snake, we can see the power of the family by the representation of the family's legacy through birth.

The Visconti family, with its seat in Milan, was very powerful. For example, when Pope Urban V excommunicated Bernabò Visconti for his trespass into the Papal States, Bernabò responded by saying "I would have you know that I am pope, emperor and king in my own domains. God Himself cannot do here what is contrary to my will." The Viscontis took more and more of Italy under their grasp, and they did it ruthlessly. The Visconti family didn't rule forever, but their influence in Milan was so great that the house symbol lives on as the symbol of the city.

Section IV: **Map Exercise**

1. Trace the outline of the rectangular frame of Map 81.1: War in Italy in black.

2. Using your blue pencil, trace the coastal outline around France and through the Mediterranean around France, the Holy Roman Empire, and the visible coastline of Africa. Include the line of the Seine. Trace the mountains with small peaks. Repeat until the contours are familiar.

3. Using contrasting colors, trace the outlines of the Holy Roman Empire, France, the Papal States, the Kingdom of Naples, and Sicily. Repeat until the contour are familiar.

4. Using a new sheet of paper, trace the rectangular outline of the frame for Map 81.1. Using your regular pencil with an eraser, draw the coastal outline around France and through the Mediterranean around France, the Holy Roman Empire, and the visible coastline of Africa. Include the line of the Seine. Draw the mountains with small peaks. Then draw the outlines of the Holy Roman Empire, France, the Papal States, the Kingdom of Naples, and Sicily. When you are happy

with your map, place it over the original. Erase and re-mark any lines which are more than ¼″ off of the original.

5. Now study carefully the areas of Gascony, Flanders, France, Germany, and the regions you drew: the Holy Roman Empire, the Papal States, the Kingdom of Naples, and Sicily. When they are familiar, mark them on the map, and then make any needed corrections.

6. Now study the locations of Bourdeaux, Uzeste, Avignon, Paris, Geneva, Fonti, Milan, Pavia, Genoa, Lucca, Pisa, Siena, Rome, Anagni, Naples, Verona, Mantua, Bologna, Florence, Perugia, Assisi, Faenza, Cesena, Padua, and Venice. When they are familiar for you, close the book. Mark each one on your map, using the frame of the map as a reference. Erase and re-mark as necessary. When you are happy with your map, lay it over the original. Erase and re-mark any labels which are more than ¼″ off of the original.

7. Mark the site of the Battle of Chioggia.

Chapter Eighty-Two

Bad Beginnings

The student may use her text when answering the questions in sections I and II.

Section I: Who, What, Where

Write a one or two-sentence answer explaining the significance of each item listed below.

Bertrand du Guesclin—**Pg. 578, ¶ 1 & 3—Bertrand du Guesclin, a professional soldier, was appointed to be the new chief commander of the French offensive, with the title Constable of France (a position generally awarded to a nobleman rather than to a common-born soldier) by Charles V. Constable Guesclin recovered almost all of the land between the Loire and the region of Gironde for France after the English fleet was defeated at La Rochelle in 1372.**

Charles VI—**Pg. 579, ¶ 2 and Pg. 581, ¶ 2 & 3—Charles VI, son and successor to Charles V, led a successful attack against a rebellious Flemish army and used this win to boost his power at home. When he arrived back in Paris, he put down the rebellion of his citizens and put heavy fines on anyone who protested publicly.**

John Ball—**Pg. 582, ¶ 4 and Pg. 584, ¶ 6—John Ball, known as the "mad priest," traveled through the English countryside calling for a radical reorganization of English society, demanding communal holding of all property and the extinction of class difference. John Ball tried to flee into the countryside when Richard II sent his English army after the rebels, but he was arrested and brought back to London, where he was drawn and quartered.**

John Wycliffe—**Pg. 582, ¶ 3—John Wycliffe, a doctor of theology at Oxford University, argued that the church of Rome was not the head of all the churches, that the pope at Rome did not have greater power than any other ordained priest, and that the Gospel was a sufficient guide in this life for any Christian. These beliefs were not new, but Wycliffe's ideas, expressed both in scholarly writings and in the pulpit, gained him a considerable following.**

Louis, the Duke of Anjou—**Pg. 579, ¶ 5—Louis, the Duke of Anjou, used his appointment as regent to Charles VI to raid the treasury and raise an army for his own pursuit of Naples's throne. Louis managed to get himself crowned king by Clement VII in Avignon, but when he marched into Italy a harsh winter and the reluctance of the Italians to provide him with fodder** killed most of the horses; food ran short, Urban VI declared Louis to be a heretic, and then he died on campaign in September of 1384 as plague spread throughout the remnants of his army.

Richard II—Pg. 578, ¶ 5 and Pg. 584, ¶ 2 & 6—Richard II, son of the Black Prince, made heir to the English throne after his father's death, made a deal with Wat Tyler, leader of the civilian rebellion against the king, saying he would grant all of the requests of the rebels. Richard II's promises were empty; he was buying time in order to prepare his English army to punish the rebels in full force.

Wat Tyler—Pg. 583, ¶ 6 to Pg. 584, ¶ 3—Wat Tyler, the chief spokesman for the people's cause in the civil war against poll taxes, met with Richard II on June 14 and 15, 1381, after the peasant army ransacked London, and demanded that laws passed during Edward III's reign in order to give landowners more power over the peasants who worked the land were to be repealed, the legal category "outlaw" be abolished, all of the wealth of the English church was to be redistributed among the people, all bishops would be stripped of their rank and only John Ball would hold that title, all of the ranks and titles of English aristocracy would be done away with, and finally, he demanded that there be no more villains in England. After Richard II agreed to all of Tyler's requests, Tyler asked for a mug of beer to toast the arrangement; within ten minutes, due to either Tyler's aggression or the taunting of Richard II's party, Wat Tyler was mortally wounded.

Section II: Comprehension

Write a two or three-sentence answer to each of the following questions.

1. How did the Black Prince react to the voluntary surrender of Limoges to the French? What is the most likely reason he reacted this way?

A1.—Pg. 577, ¶ 4-6 & *—When the Black Prince found out that the citizens of Limoges surrendered at the request of the French, without a fight, he became vexed and insisted on laying siege to retake it. English sappers, tunneling under the walls, brought a large chunk of the defenses down without too much trouble, but the Black Prince had worked himself up into a towering fury at the town's inhabitants, who had been so quick to open the gates to the French, that he ordered killed whoever he could once inside the city. The Black Prince most likely acted this way because he had porphyria, a genetic disorder that produces an imbalance of certain chemicals in the body, often produces vomiting, diarrhea, and stomach cramps, along with seizures and mental symptoms such as paranoia and hallucinations.

2. What led to the truce between Charles V of France and Edward III of England?

A2.—Pg. 578, ¶ 3—The Black Prince, growing progressively sicker, returned to England after the massacre at Limoges and Edward III announced that he would personally arrive in France to lead the English army; however, he was now into his sixties and showing some signs of early senility and he never left England. In 1372, the English fleet was defeated at La Rochelle; by the following year, the constable Guesclin had recovered almost all of the land between the Loire and the region of Gironde for France and only Bordeaux, Bayonne, and Calais remained in English hands. The English now possessed the same French lands they had claimed in 1337, before the war had begun, and Edward II realized it was time to call a truce.

3. How was the death of Edward III good for Charles V? Why didn't Charles V take full advantage of his political good fortune?

A3.—Pg. 579, ¶ 2—Richard II was placed on the English throne after his grandfather Edward III's death; England was being governed by a child, so Charles V finally launched his fleet across the Channel. Between 1377 and 1380, French ships raided all along the southern coast: Rye, Sussex, the Isle of Wight, Dartmouth, Plymouth, Southampton, and Dover all suffered from French invasion, but Charles V was unable to seize victory. Charles V didn't take full advantage of his political good fortune because he too was suffering from a chronic illness and he saw his death coming; he summoned his brothers and solemnly charged them to look after young Charles VI and on September 16, 1380, Charles V died.

4. What kind of bad advice did Charles VI get from his uncles after he lost the council of his regent Louis, the Duke of Anjou?

A4.—Pg. 579, ¶ 6—After Louis, the Duke of Anjou died, the group of uncles recommended a tax increase in Paris; the incensed citizens rioted, and Paris grew so dangerous that Charles VI and his uncles fled to Meaux. At the same time the Duke of Berry was diverting royal funds to buy himself rare manuscripts and beautiful works of art, which he added to his extraordinary collection. Then the Duke of Burgundy, motivated by his own political aspirations, suggested that Charles VI go off and fight in Flanders to put down a growing rebellion against the Count of Flanders—who happened to be the Duke of Burgundy's own father-in-law.

5. Describe Charles VI journey to Flanders and the battle that ensued near the village of Rosebecque.

A5.—Pg. 579, ¶ 7 to Pg. 581, ¶ 1—As Charles VI and the royal army marched towards Flanders they increased the royal treasury by looting for cloth, linen, knives, money in gold and silver, silver dishes, and plates. Once they met the rebellious Flemish army outside of Rosebecque, the long-speared French infantrymen spitted the close-packed Flemish foot soldiers until the ranks broke and fled. The Flemish captain was found dead in a ditch without a wound on him; he had been trampled and suffocated by the masses of men climbing across him.

6. Explain the three poll taxes imposed in England by Richard II based on the guidance of his governing council.

A6.—Pg. 581, ¶ 6, 7, & *—To raise money for the ongoing war with France, the king's council orchestrated a series of new taxes: "poll taxes," flat payments imposed on everyone in the country. The first of these, collected in 1377, required each person in England to pay one groat—a coin roughly equivalent to the price of a goat (the tax was slightly higher for clergymen); the second, passed in 1379, required a groat from the poor, but much more from knights and landowners; the third, proposed in December of 1380, required three groats from every man and woman in England over the age of fifteen. And while there was a provision requiring the rich to make up shortfalls if the poor were simply unable to pay—the overall intention was to impose a flat tax across all of England.

7. What happened as tax collection began in England in the spring of 1381?

A7.—Pg. 582, ¶ 1 & 2—As tax collection began in England in the spring of 1381, tax collectors noticed that five hundred thousand or so laborers, shepherds, and farmers seemed to have simply disappeared from England since 1377. Devon was particularly afflicted by this strange vanishing-peasant phenomenon; apparently its population had dropped by half in three years. The size of the quiet tax revolt suggests massive underground organization, and an almost universal agreement that enough was enough; the laborers of England were fed up.

8. How did the royal council at first deal with the tax revolt in England? What was the result of this plan?

A8.—Pg. 583, ¶ 2-5—The royal council had decided to deal with the tax revolt by appointing special inquiry agents with powers of arrest and punishment to go out and find the peasants that seemed to have disappeared when it came to paying poll taxes. In June of 1381, the inhabitants of the village of Brentwood greeted the arrival of one of these inquiry agents fully armed and when the agent ordered them arrested, they drove him out of Brentwood by force. Immediately, organized revolt engineered by thousands of English commoners that had fought in France spread across the south of England; it was a civil war.

9. What made Richard II agree to a parley with Wat Tyler?

A9.—Pg. 583, ¶ 7 & 8—When the revolt against the king and his taxes made it to London, restraint broke. The elaborate London mansion owned by John of Gaunt, the Savoy Palace, was set on fire; Temple Bar, where London's lawyers practiced, was destroyed; the peasant army opened the gates of Fleet Prison and set the prisoners free; fires burned all over London; and the Archbishop of Canterbury, the Treasurer of England, a chief poll-tax collector, and two other men were dragged out of the Tower of London and executed. After Richard II retreated to a royal storehouse called the Wardrobe, where he was trapped with his advisors, he found himself forced to agree to a parley with Wat Tyler.

10. Richard II agreed to a parley with Wat Tyler but what was his real purpose for meeting with the rebellious leader? What was his purpose in telling the rebellious English that he would be their captain and leader, and grant their requests?

A10.—Pg. 584, ¶ 4 & 5—Richard II met with Wat Tyler, listened to his demands, and agreed to all of them, as a way to buy time for the London militia; as the men were negotiating, the militia had been quietly assembling behind the scenes, and immediately after the death of Wat Tyler they surrounded the peasant army. Massive bloodshed seemed inevitable, but when Richard II called out "I will be your king, your captain and your leader, and grant your requests," the peasant soldiers began to lay down their arms and retreat. Richard II had no intention of keeping his word; he was just buying time to allow the English army to assemble in full force and begin punishment of the rebels.

Section III: **Critical Thinking**

The student may not use her text to answer this question.

When Charles VI became king of France, he was twelve. Richard II, who was already on the English throne, was thirteen at the time of Charles VI's coronation. Both young kings had to face considerable obstacles at the start of their reigns, most notably bad advisors and unruly citizens. Explain how both sovereigns used similar approaches to assert their power as young kings.

The student should recall that both Charles VI and Richard II faced uprisings by their own people that challenged their authority. Charles VI managed his rebellion by scaring his citizens into complacency. Richard II put down any challenge to his authority by tightening even further the restrictions that caused his people to revolt in the first place.

On page 581 we read about how Charles VI asserted himself against his rebellious citizens:

> High on triumph [against the rebellious Flemish army], Charles returned to Paris. The residents came out to greet him in arms, determined to show their new young king just how much power they had; in response, Charles ordered his captains to remove the gates from the city and clear the streets, so that he could stampede the entire army into the city to put down any further rebellion. This proved adequately terrifying: the Parisians slunk back into their homes, "so fearful of being punished," Froissart says, "that, as the King entered the city, none dared to venture out of doors, or even to open a window." In retaliation, Charles VI and his advisors levied heavy fines on those who had protested publicly: "as a punishment for their past behavior, and as an example to other towns in the kingdom of France."

Richard II of England was devious in his subduing of rebellion. He met with the leader of the peasant rebellion, Wat Tyler, and agreed to all of Wat Tyler's requests. He had no intention of fulfilling those requests, he was just buying time while the London militia prepared to attack the peasant army. When massive bloodshed seemed inevitable between the militia and the peasants, Richard II told the rebels "I will be your king, your captain and your leader, and grant your requests." Again, Richard II did not mean what he said, though the rebels didn't know that. After a few tense moments, the peasant soldiers began to lay down their arms. The militia allowed them to disperse; over the next few days, more and more of them trickled back to their homes. The diffusion of the peasant soldiers gave the king time to assemble the English army. When the peasants realized their king would not make good on his promise, rioting began, but the army was prepared. Rebels were dragged behind horses, put to the sword, hanged in the gallows, or dismembered. Richard gave the Mayor of London absolute military authority to keep order in the city. Richard II had no tolerance for the revolts, and he showed the people of England his strength by giving them nothing in return for their rebellious behavior. This was exemplified in Richard II's response to a delegation of laborers that requested an audience with him in Essex on June 22: They asked for the fulfillment of his promises: for the abolishment of serfdom, for equality with their lords. Richard, "completely amazed at such boldness," retorted, "Peasants you were, and peasants you are. You will remain in bondage, not as before, but in an incomparably worse state. For as long as we are alive to achieve this and by the grace of God rule this kingdom, we shall work our minds, powers and possessions to keep you in such subjection . . . that now and in the future men like you shall always have before their eyes, as if in a mirror, your miseries, as a reason for cursing you and fearing to commit similar crimes themselves" (585).

EXAMPLE ANSWER:

Both Charles VI and Richard II had to prove they could stand up to rebellious citizens in order to show their worthiness as kings. When Charles VI came back from Flanders, victorious, he was greeted by an armed rebellion of citizens in Paris. Instead of backing away, he ordered his captains to clear the streets so he could bring the entire army into the city to put down any further agitation. The Parisians were scared and slunk back in their homes for fear of being punished. Those that did publicly protest were fined heavily as punishment for their behavior and as an example for other towns of what would happen if the king of France was crossed.

Richard II was a little more extreme in the assertion of his power. Richard II's advisors told him to levy flat taxes across the English people. This wasn't the best idea, but Richard II followed along. When the inevitable rebellion came, Richard II did not chastise his advisors but rather punished his citizens. He met with the leader of the peasant rebellion, Wat Tyler, and agreed to all of Wat Tyler's requests. He had no intention of fulfilling those requests, he was just buying time while the London militia prepared to attack the peasant army. When massive bloodshed seemed inevitable between the militia and the peasants, Richard II told the rebels "I will be your king, your captain and your leader, and grant your requests." Again, Richard II did not mean what he said, though the rebels didn't know that. After a few tense moments, the peasant soldiers began to lay down their arms. The militia allowed them to disperse; and over the next few days, more and more of them went home. The diffusion of the peasant soldiers gave the king time to assemble the English army. When the peasants realized their king would not make good on his promise, rioting began, but the army was prepared. Rebels were dragged behind horses, put to the sword, hanged in the gallows, or dismembered. Richard gave the Mayor of London absolute military authority to keep order in the city. When another group of laborers asked for Richard II's audience in Essex, he agreed to listen to their demands for the abolishment of serfdom and for equality with their lords. His response showcased his severity. He told the laborers that they would remain in bondage, in conditions worse than the ones they were already in, and he said he would work to keep them subjugated, by the grace of God, for as long as he was able. Richard II had no tolerance for the revolts, or the demands of the laborers, and he showed the people of England his strength and iron-will by giving them nothing in return for their rebellious behavior.

Section IV: Map Exercise

1. Trace the rectangular outline of Map 82.1 with your black pencil.

2. With your blue pencil, trace the coastline around Ireland, England, and the continent, through the visible Mediterranean. Also trace the line of the Loire. Repeat until the contours are familiar.

3. Using contrasting colors, trace the separate territories of the Empire of Richard II and the Kingdom of Charles VI. Repeat until the contours are familiar.

4. Using a new sheet of paper, trace the outline of the frame for Map 82.1 in black. Using a regular pencil, draw the lines of the coast around Ireland, England, and the continent, through the visible Mediterranean. Also draw the line of the Loire. Then draw the separate territories of the Empire of Richard II and the Kingdom of Charles VI. Erase and re-draw as necessary, using the map's frame as a reference. When you are happy with your map, lay it over the original. Erase and re-draw any lines which are more than ¼" off of the original.

5. Label the areas of Ireland, England, and France. Study carefully the areas of Wales, Devon, Essex, Sussex, Kent, Flanders, Anjou, Burgundy, Berry, Gironde, and Languedoc. When they are familiar for you, close the book. Mark and label each one on your map. Check your map against the original, and make any needed corrections.

6. Now study carefully the locations of Plymouth, Dartmouth, Southampton, London, Brentwood, Rye, Dover, Calais, Meaux, Paris, Limoges, Bordeaux, and Bayonne. When they are familiar for you, close the book. Mark and label each one on your map. Then lay your map over the original, and erase and re-mark any labels which are more than ¼" off of the original.

7. Mark the sites of the Isle of Wight, the Battle of Rosebecque, and the Battle of La Rochelle.

Chapter Eighty-Three

Dislocation

The student may use his text when answering the questions in sections I and II.

Section I: Who, What, Where

Write a one or two-sentence answer explaining the significance of each item listed below.

Bayajidda—**Pg. 588, ¶ 5—Bayajidda, son of the "king of Baghdad," is known as the founder of the seven kingdoms. After marrying a Bornu princess and then falling out with her father, Bayajidda traveled to Daura, where he supposedly killed a snake that was terrorizing the town, married Daura's queen, and had seven children that founded the seven kingdoms.**

Bornu—**Pg. 588, ¶ 2—Bornu, the land west of Lake Chad where 'Umar ibn Idris chose to settle, had probably been an independent kingdom at some time long past. The memory of that separate existence was almost gone, but survived in the ongoing tendency of the Kanem kings to claim the title "King of Kanem and Lord of Bornu."**

Bulala—**Pg. 587, ¶ 3—Bulala was the name of a people, farmers and shepherds who had drifted westward, possibly from the highlands of the Nile, ahead of Arab settlement, that started to raid Kanem's borders at the beginning of the fourteenth century. The Bulala still held to their traditional religious practices, and their dislike of Kanem may have been motivated by Kanem's slave trading practice; since Islamic law forbade one Muslim to sell or own another, the unconverted tribes nearby were Kanem's only source of slaves.**

'Umar ibn Idris—**Pg. 588, ¶ 2—'Umar ibn Idris, a Kanem king fighting the Bulala, made the decision in 1380 to abandon the lands east of Lake Chad and to move away from the capital city Njimi, choosing to settle himself west of the lake, placing it between his people and the Bulala threat.**

Section II: **Comprehension**

Write a two or three-sentence answer to each of the following questions.

1. Why was it so hard for Kanem to defend its borders?

A1.—Pg. 1 & 2—Kanem was huge, starting on the Egyptian side at a town called Zella and ending on the other side at a town called Kaka; it took three months to travel the twelve hundred miles between one town and the other. The king of Kanem did not rule over everyone that lived between Zella and Kaka; he did not need the northern Saharan tribes to pay homage, he merely wanted to keep the trade routes within his borders safe. As such, Kanem's borders were a commercial reality, not a political one, and this made them difficult to define and even more difficult to defend.

2. On what did Kanem's prosperity depend?

A2.—Pg. 587, ¶ 2—Kanem's prosperity depended on trade through the Sahara, along the eastern trade route that led to Tripoli, and along a less-traveled and rougher road that led, more directly, to Egypt. Salt, ivory, ostrich feathers, and grain went north from Kanem's mines, fields, and forests; war horses, wool, copper, and iron weapons came south. The monarchs of Kanem were charged with the responsibility of keeping the roads safe so that they could continue trade with the Mediterranean markets.

3. Why did 'Umar ibn Idris move away from Njimi to Bornu?

A3.—Pg. 588, ¶ 2—'Umar ibn Idris made the decision in 1380 to abandon the lands east of Lake Chad and to move away from the capital city Njimi, choosing to settle himself in Bornu, because of the Bulala threat. The attacks from the neighboring tribe were constant, and tradition says that the last six rulers on Kanem's throne died in battle fighting the Bulala.

4. Describe the Hausa kingdoms.

A4.—Pg. 588, ¶ 4—The Hausa kingdoms, which had existed in the wide fork of the Niger as small settlements, some of them for centuries, were each centered around a mud-walled city where soldiers were based and where trade was carried out. They traded up towards Tripoli: gold, ivory, leather, and ostrich feathers traveling north to the Mediterranean, paper and parchment, weapons and armor making their way back down south. There were seven Hausa kingdoms: Kano, whose oral tradition puts the first Kano ruler around AD 1000 and the completion of the city's walls sometime around 1150, and Rano, both known for trading indigo; warlike Gobir; Zaria, whose wealth was built on slaves; Biram, Daura, and Katsina.

5. Explain the legend of Bayajidda and the foundation of the seven kingdoms.

A5.—Pg. 588, ¶ 5—According to a legend about the origin of the Hausa kingdoms, Bayajidda, son of the "king of Baghdad," quarreled with his father, left home, and then went to Bornu, where he married a Bornu princess. Then he quarreled in turn with his father-in-law and left this kingdom too, continuing west to Daura where he found the people afflicted with a problem: an enormous snake in the village well, which allowed the people to draw water only

on Fridays. **Legend says he killed the snake, married Daura's queen, and had seven sons, who scattered out to found the seven kingdoms.**

6. What can we learn about the legend of Bayajidda and the ancestral development of the Hausa kingdoms?

A6.—Pg. 588, ¶ 6 to Pg. 589, ¶ 1—The legend of Bayajidda tells us that all the Hausa kingdoms were linked by some ancient tribal relationship; they are linked by a common ancestral bond. We can also see that the legend of Bayajidda tries to tie the origins of the kingdoms to Islam, though in the fourteenth century the Hausa kingdoms were not yet Muslim. Finally, the story gives us a royal origin for the seven kingdoms.

Section III: Critical Thinking

The student may not use his text to answer this question.

While oral traditions can sometimes be unreliable, looking at the details of legends can help us to learn about the development of a culture. Write a paragraph that explains what we can learn about Bornu's changing religion based on the legend of Bayajidda.

The student learns about the legend of Bayajidda on page 588:

> A later legend about the origin of the Hausa preserves a journey from the east. Bayajidda, son of the "king of Baghdad," quarreled with his father and left home. He came to Bornu, where he married a Bornu princess; and then he quarreled in turn with his father-in-law and left this kingdom too. Continuing west, he came to Daura and there found the people afflicted with a problem: an enormous snake in the village well, which allowed the people to draw water only on Fridays. He killed the snake, married Daura's queen, and had seven sons, who scattered out to found the seven kingdoms.

We know that the Hausa were not yet Muslim in the fourteenth century, so we can see a created lineage for the Muslim faith in this legend. Even more tellingly, we can see a co-mingling of traditional religion and Islam in the interpretation of the story of the snake. The student read on page 589 that "The villagers in Daura had tried to pacify the monster by sacrificing black chickens, black he-goats, and black dogs. But only Fridays (the Muslim holy day) and the sword of the Muslim prince could block it from its prey." This suggests a battle between traditional African religion, where sacrifice was practiced to appease the gods, and the Muslim faith, which is the faith that saved the day.

It is possible that the story reflects the conflict between traditional religion and the religion the Kanem king introduced to the west; when he moved to Bornu, he brought with him the entire array of Islamic government: soldiers and settlers, scholars and imams. The full Muslim court existed, for the first time, just above the Hausa kingdoms. The common frontier between Bornu and the Hausa allowed for the exchange of information and culture, and the comingling of religions, as evidenced by the killing of the Daura serpent.

EXAMPLE ANSWER:

The legend of Bayajidda, son of the "king of Baghdad," tells of how a Muslim man saved Daura from a treacherous serpent. The Hausa kingdoms, of which Daura was a part, were not always Muslim, so we know that the story is intended to give the kingdom a Muslim origin after-the-fact. More interestingly, in the story, the villagers tried to appease the snake in the well by sacrificing black chickens, black he-goats, and black dogs. These sacrifices did not work. It was only Fridays, the Muslim holy day, when the citizens were allowed to draw water from the well, and it was only the sword of a Muslim royal that could kill the serpent. The story reflects the conflict between traditional religion, the sacrificing of animals, and Islam, the religion that beat the snake. When the Kanem king moved to Bornu, he brought with him the entire array of Islamic government: soldiers and settlers, scholars and imams. The full Muslim court existed, for the first time, just above the Hausa kingdoms. The common frontier between Bornu and the Hausa allowed for the exchange of information and culture, and the comingling of religions, as evidenced by the killing of the Daura serpent.

Section IV: Map Exercise

1. Trace the rectangular outline of Map 83.1 in black.

2. Using your blue pencil, trace the coastal outline around the Mediterranean and Africa. Include the each body of water visible on the map. Trace the line of the Nile. Repeat until the contours are familiar.

3. Using contrasting colors, trace the regions of the Empire of Kanem and the Kanem Influence. Repeat until the contours are familiar.

4. Using a new sheet of paper, trace the outline of the map in black. Using your regular pencil with an eraser, draw the coastal outline around the Mediterranean and Africa. Include the each body of water visible on the map. Draw the line of the Nile. When you are happy with your map, lay it over the origina. Erase and re-draw any lines which are more than ¼″ off of the original.

5. Now study carefully the locations of Tunis, Tripoli, Zella, Bilma, Njimi, and Kaka. When you are familiar with the locations, close the book. Mark and label each one on your map. Lay your map over the original, and erase and re-mark any labels which are more than ¼″ off of the original.

6. Mark the Sahara Desert, the Nile, the area of Bulala, and the location of Lake Chad.

Chapter Eighty-Four

Madness and Usurpation

The student may use her text when answering the questions in sections I and II.

Section I: Who, What, Where

Write a one or two-sentence answer explaining the significance of each item listed below.

Blanche of Lancaster—**Pg. 591, ¶ 2—Blanche of Lancaster, John of Gaunt's first wife, brought him the title Duke of Lancaster. She died at the age of twenty-three after she had borne John seven children, three of whom survived.**

Constance of Castile—**Pg. 591, ¶ 2—Constance of Castile, daughter of the deposed and murdered king of Castile, Pedro the Cruel, was married to John of Gaunt at the age of seventeen. John of Gaunt thought the he could claim the throne of Castile in the name of his wife.**

Henry Bolingbroke—**Pg. 595, ¶ 5 to Pg. 596, ¶ 2—Henry Bolingbroke, oldest son of John of Gaunt, was kicked out of England by Richard II for challenging the Duke of Norfolk to a duel, and while he was out of the country, Richard II confiscated the dead John of Gaunt's vast Lancaster estate, which now belonged to Henry, for the crown. Henry returned to England to gather support to overthrow the king and soon after he had six thousand soldiers on his side; Richard II didn't fight back and on September 29 he formally abdicated the throne to Henry Bolingbroke.**

Isabella—**Pg. 594, ¶ 7 to Pg. 595, ¶ 2—Isabella, Charles VI's daughter, was married to King Richard II of England at six years old; the marriage was part of the peace treaty made between England and France in 1396. After the marriage, Isabella was given her own household in the southern English castle of Portchester.**

John of Aviz—**Pg. 592, ¶ 1 & 2—John of Aviz, who claimed the right to rule in Portugal, led a combined English-Portuguese army with John of Gaunt in a war against Castile in 1383; the war with Castile turned into an assertion of Portuguese independence against Castilian might and of John of Aviz's right to rule as sole sovereign. In August of 1385, John of Aviz defeated the French-Castilian forces at the Battle of Aljubarrota, bringing a crashing end to Castilian** attempts to reclaim Portuguese land, a victory that made John of Aviz a hero in the eyes of his people and strengthened his claim on the throne.

John (of Castile)—Pg. 591, ¶ 5 to Pg. 592, ¶ 1—John, son of Enrique of Trastámara, was on the throne of Castile when war began with Portugal in 1382.

Louis—Pg. 594, ¶ 2 & 3—Louis, brother of Charles VI and Duke of Orleans, was attacked by his brother during a punitive expedition against the Duke of Brittany when his brother suffered from an attack of madness.

Section II: Comprehension

Write a two or three-sentence answer to each of the following questions.

1. Why did John of Gaunt, Duke of Lancaster, make an urgent request from the king of England for money and ships?

A1.—Pg. 591, ¶ 2—John of Gaunt, duke of Lancaster, claimed that he needed funds and ships to defend the English coast from the French enemy for a whole year. The money and ships were granted, but everyone knew that the fleet was not merely for defense of the coast from the French, but also so that John of Gaunt could attack Castile and hope to claim it for himself on behalf of his wife.

2. How did John of Gaunt plan to get into Castile? Why did the king of Portugal agree to the plan?

A2.—Pg. 591, ¶ 4—John of Gaunt intended to seize the throne of Castile by entering through Portugal. He negotiated an alliance with the king of Portugal. The king of Portugal was amenable to the plan because the Portuguese were consistently suspicious that Castile would try to absorb them again, and a war against Castile would help assure them of independence.

3. What did John of Gaunt do after his first war with Castile proved fruitless? What did the king of Castile do in response?

A3.—Pg. 592, ¶ 3 to Pg. 593, ¶ 1—After the first war with Castile proved fruitless, John of Gaunt took up the king of Portugal's offer to keep on fighting against Castile. Parliament reluctantly agreed to fund another invasion force: twelve hundred knights, two thousand archers, a thousand foot soldiers, and enough money to pay them all for at least six months. In answer, the king of Castile appealed to the court of France for help; Charles VI said the French would help, but by attacking England in order to draw away the foreign troops from Castile.

4. How did the French prepare for the invasion of England? What happened to their planned attack?

A4.—Pg. 593, ¶ 2 & 3—In order to prepare for the English invasion, planned for August of 1386, a new tax was declared in France that would fund the building of more warships; Charles VI ordered vessels commandeered from every port in France. Months were spent baking ship's biscuit, salting meat, and drying egg yolks so that they could be powdered and stored on board. The French fleet did not catch a fair wind until the end of October and then, twenty miles out of port, a contrary wind began blowing in their faces causing them to be driven home and driven into each other, so that some ships were wrecked in the very entrance to the port they had just left.

6. When did negotiations for a peace treaty between England and France start? When did they end, and what were the terms of the treaty?

A6.—Pg. 593, ¶ 6 & 7 and Pg. 594, ¶ 7 to Pg. 595, ¶ 1—In 1391, the French chamberlain opened tentative discussion of a possible peace treaty. Officials from both countries had endless lists of bullet points to be ticked off before any peace treaty could be sworn out, and discussions dragged out, slowed down ever further by Charles VI's spells of insanity; finally, in March 1396, the final stamp was put on a twenty-eight-year truce between the two countries. It froze hostilities between the two countries, prohibited the building of any new castles along the existing frontiers, and created a marriage alliance between King Richard II of England and Charles VI of France's six-year-old daughter Isabella (though Isabella's children were to have no claim to France).

7. What did Richard II do to upset the period of peace that was supposed to follow the 1396 treaty with France and his marriage to Isabella?

A7.—Pg. 595, ¶ 3—Things seemed to be going very well in England, but then, without warning, Richard II arrested and imprisoned three men he distrusted because he thought they were plotting against him; the earls of Warwick and Arundel, and his own uncle, the Black Prince's youngest brother Thomas. No one was completely convinced of the charges, but Richard II was determined to get rid of possible rivals. The Earl of Warwick was imprisoned for life, Arundel was beheaded, and the royal Thomas died unexpectedly in prison, though it was Richard II that arranged the death by dispatching a hired assassin to smother him without leaving marks.

8. Explain the circumstances of Richard II's abdication, and of his death.

A8.—Pg. 596, ¶ 2-5—Richard II, who knew he was unpopular and could not win against his rival, abdicated the throne to Henry Bolingbroke, Duke of Lancaster, without a fight on September 29. After Henry accepted the crown, Richard II made a single remark: "After all this, I hope that my kinsman is willing to be a good lord and friend for me." By February 1401 the king was dead: he was confined to Pontefract Castle by Henry IV where most believe he sank into deep despair and starved himself to death, though some believe that the knight Piers of Exton heard Henry sigh, "Have I no faithful friend who will deliver me from him?" and then he set out to assassinate the disgraced king.

9. Why was Henry IV's acceptance speech at his coronation significant, and how did his coronation mark a shift in the ruling house of England?

A9.—Pg. 596, ¶ 3, 6, & *—When Henry IV accepted the crown, he gave his acceptance speech in English—the first time, since the Norman Conquest, that an English king had used his native language for the coronation address. Though Richard II and Henry IV were cousins, Henry's father John of Gaunt had been a younger son of the king, and Henry IV was considered a member of a different family, the House of Lancaster, a "cadet branch" of the Plantagenets, a branch made up of the descendants of the younger sons of a monarch or patriarch. So, Henry

IV's reign marked the beginning of the House of Lancaster's possession of the English throne, and it marked the end of the Plantagenet line.

Section III: Critical Thinking

The student may not use her text to answer this question.

Just two chapters ago you wrote an explanation of how both Charles VI of France and Richard II of England asserted themselves by standing up to their own people. In this chapter, we see both kings, once again, having parallel experiences. In this critical thinking question, explain what similar experience the kings had, and how these separate but linked experiences cost each king his own power.

Young Charles VI and Richard II had such potential, but both kings' reigns had rough starts, and things didn't get any easier for either of them as time went on.

In this chapter we learn that Charles VI was a flighty and uninterested ruler, his uncles constantly jostled each other for more power at court, and intrigues, private agreements, and feuds prevented any unified war strategy against England from taking place. In London, Richard II was no more effective. He made unwise favorites, quarreled with the two uncles still in England, and plotted to get rid of unwanted council members. Clashes and spats took place along the French and the English coasts, but neither king was capable of planning, let alone carrying out, a grand strategy.

Things got even worse for the kings when they both, in parallel experiences, went mad.

Charles VI lost it first. In 1392, Charles VI began to suffer from a chronic fever. His family and doctors noticed that his intellect wasn't intact, but nothing was done because Charles VI wouldn't listen to their advice. Then, in the first week of August 1392, Charles VI insisted on leading a troop of soldiers on a punitive expedition against the Duke of Brittany, who had insulted the Chief Constable of France. It was a hot day, but he was fully dressed in a black velvet jacket and crimson hood, and the young pages who rode behind him were elaborately dressed in silks and armor, with polished steel caps; one of them carried the king's lance. As they were riding, the children grew negligent and the one holding the lance fell asleep. The lance then fell on the helmet of the page riding in front of him and the sound of steel on steel startled Charles VI. He screamed "Advance, advance!," turned on his own pages, who scattered in terror, and then Charles VI pointed his horse directly toward his brother Louis with his sword in his hand.

Panicked, Louis spurred his horse away and then rode back around in a circle so that the squires and knights could surround the king. Charles VI seemed to recognize no one; they backed away and circled, letting him chase them, until he was sweat soaked and exhausted. Finally, his chamberlain came up behind him and caught him by the arms so that others could take his sword away. The king didn't recognize anyone, his eyes rolled around in his head, and he didn't speak. The king was brought to Le Mans, where he laid in a coma for three days. When he recovered consciousness he had no memory of the event; he was weak, but completely rational. Charles VI was never again the same. He suffered from sudden severe attacks of pain and he had fits in which he recognized no one, turned on his friends and family, and ran through the palace for hours until he collapsed. The madness, unpredictable and never lasting, made it impossible for a regent to legally claim power, but it also meant that Charles VI was unfit to rule. Charles VI's uncles returned to court and the country fell into their hands.

Richard II's madness was not as severe as Charles VI's, but it still cost him the throne.

After marrying Isabella and signing a peace treaty with France, Richard II snapped. He arrested and imprisoned three men he distrusted; the earls of Warwick and Arundel, and his own uncle, the Black Prince's youngest brother Thomas. He accused the three of plotting against him. No one was completely convinced of the charges, but Richard was determined to get rid of possible rivals. The Earl of Warwick was imprisoned for life, Arundel was beheaded, and Thomas was murdered in prison.

The king was most likely suffering from paranoia. His behavior after the purge was not exactly rational. He became preoccupied with the possibility that Arundel's head might have been miraculously rejoined to his body, and ordered a couple of earls to go dig up the coffin at four o'clock in the morning to check. (It was still detached.) He also grew increasingly autocratic; he borrowed money in vast amounts from his subjects and made no effort to repay it; he expected any man who caught his eye to fall on his knees; he forced some of his courtiers to sign and seal blank sheets of paper so that he could write accusations later, should he need an excuse to rid himself of them. The final straw was when Richard II made Henry Bolingbroke leave England because he challenged the Duke of Norfolk to a duel and then seized Henry's dead father's estate—which now belonged to Henry—for the crown. Henry Bolingbroke recognized that the king was unjust and gathered up an army to challenge him. In something like a moment of clarity, Richard II knew he couldn't win so he abdicated peacefully and named Henry Bolingbroke to the throne. Richard II's paranoia and autocratic actions led to his deposition and to his death (he died in prison after Henry Bolingbroke had him locked up).

EXAMPLE ANSWER:

Young Charles VI and Richard II had such potential, but both kings' reigns had rough starts, and things didn't get any easier for either of them as time went on. When they were younger, both kings had to assert their power by showing their citizens who was boss. Then, later, both of them lost their power because of madness.

In the summer of 1392 Charles VI started to suffer from chronic fever. Even though he didn't feel good, he led an expedition to Brittany. It was hot when Charles VI left, but he was wearing a black velvet jacket and a crimson hood anyway. He also had his pages dressed up in silks and armor, with steel caps, and one of them carried his lance. As the journey continued on, the page carrying the lance fell asleep. The lance hit the steel cap of the other page, and Charles VI panicked. He thought he was being attacked. The pages scattered and then Charles VI pulled his sword out and charged his brother Louis. Charles VI didn't recognize his brother, or any of his party. The rest of the knights and squires circled around and let Charles VI chase them and then finally his chamberlain was able to catch him from behind and hold his arms down. Charles VI was taken to Le Mans where he laid in a coma for three days. When he woke up, he didn't know what happened. Charles VI was never again the same. He suffered from sudden severe attacks of pain and he had fits in which he recognized no one, turned on his friends and family, and ran through the palace for hours until he collapsed. His madness, unpredictable and never lasting, made it impossible for a regent to legally claim power, but it also meant that

Charles VI was unfit to rule. Charles VI's uncles returned to court and the country fell into their hands.

Richard II's madness was not as severe as Charles VI's, but it still cost him the throne, and his life. After marrying Isabella and signing a peace treaty with France, Richard II snapped. He arrested and imprisoned the earls of Warwick and Arundel, and his own uncle, the Black Prince's youngest brother Thomas. He accused the three of plotting against him. No one was completely convinced of the charges, but Richard was determined to get rid of possible rivals. The Earl of Warwick was imprisoned for life, Arundel was beheaded, and Thomas was murdered in prison. The king was most likely suffering from paranoia. His behavior after the purge continued to be motivated by suspicion and fear. He thought that Arundel's head was somehow back on his body and so he ordered a couple of earls to dig up the coffin at four o'clock in the morning to check. They found that the head was still detached. He also turned into an autocratic ruler. He borrowed money from his subjects with no intention of repaying it; he thought any man who saw him should fall on his knees in reverence; and he forced some of his courtiers to sign blank sheets of paper so that later, if Richard II wanted to, he could write accusations with their signature on them as an excuse to have them killed. The final straw was when Richard II made Henry Bolingbroke leave England and then he seized Henry's dead father's estate—which now belonged to Henry—for the crown. Henry Bolingbroke recognized that the king was unjust and gathered up an army to challenge him. Richard II knew he couldn't win so he abdicated peacefully and named Henry Bolingbroke to the throne. Richard II's paranoia and autocratic actions led to his deposition, imprisonment, and death.

Chapter Eighty-Five

The Battle of Nicopolis

The student may use his text when answering the questions in sections I and II.

Section I: Who, What, Where

Write a one or two-sentence answer explaining the significance of each item listed below.

Bayezid—**Pg. 598, ¶ 4 to Pg. 599, ¶ 1 and Pg. 602, ¶ 3**—Bayezid, who was called Yildirim, meaning "the thunderbolt," was an aggressive ruler that called himself the Sultan of Rum and that planned, in addition to his other conquests, to be the sultan of the second Rome, Constantinople itself. Bayezid continued to conquer the kingdoms outside of Byzantium until the only holdout was Constantinople itself.

Hannsen Greif—**Pg. 601, ¶ 8 to Pg. 602, ¶ 1**—Hannsen Greif was a noble of Bavaria who was taken prisoner by Bayezid after the attack at Nicopolis. Hannsen Greif consoled the other prisoners waiting to die by telling them that "when our blood this day is spilled for the Christian Faith we by God's help shall become the children of heaven."

Helena—**Pg. 599, ¶ 6**—Helena, a Serbian princess, was married to Manuel in 1392 in a lavish ceremony that pretended Manuel's empire was still great.

Lazar—**Pg. 598, ¶ 3**—Lazar, a Serbian nobleman who had established himself as a local ruler on the Morava river, had rallied the competing Serbian leaders behind him for a last defense against the Ottomans, but they were badly outnumbered, and divided on strategy; when the Turkish troops met them at Kosovo on June 15, thousands of Serbian soldiers were slaughtered. Lazar himself was taken captive and immediately beheaded, though his son was spared when he agreed to swear loyalty, pay tribute, and fight for the Turks.

Yakub—**Pg. 598, ¶ 4**—Yakub, Bayezid's favorite brother and loyal commander, was ordered to be strangled by Bayezid with a bowstring after Bayezid took Murad's place as leader of the Turks. Bayezid had Yakub killed because Yakub had fought bravely at Kosovo, and Bayezid was worried Yakub might one day challenge his might.

Section II: **Comprehension**

Write a two or three-sentence answer to each of the following questions.

1. Describe the Ottomans' campaign of conquest through Murad's taking of Serbia and Bulgaria.

A1.—Pg. 598, ¶ 1-3—Murad made John V of Constantinople his vassal, then he moved past Byzantium, into Serbia and Bulgaria. The Turks moved into Serbia, taking So in 1385, Nis the following year, Thessalonica in 1387, and Kosovo in the early summer of 1389; after Kosovo fell, Serbia belonged to the Turks. Bulgaria, mounting a last-ditch rebellion against Murad's dominance, was overrun with Turkish troops; the Bulgarian king was trapped and compelled to swear loyalty.

2. Give an overview of Bayezid's new policy regarding his place at the head of the Ottoman empire and his dealing with vassal rulers.

A2.—Pg. 599, ¶ 1—Bayezid had a new policy regarding his place at the head of the Ottoman empire: he adopted a new title—the Sultan of Rum— because he intended to be the sultan of the second Rome, Constantinople itself. He also had a new policy regarding vassal rulers: rather than allowing the vassal rulers under his control to continue on, he planned to aggressively drive them out. New campaigns began in Bulgaria and in the other vassal territories of the Ottoman empire, with Bayezid determined to replace vassal kings with slave governors who were entirely devoted to him.

3. How did John V react to Bayezid's aggression? How was John V's death related to his reaction to Bayezid's aggression?

A3.—Pg. 599, ¶ 3 & 4—Alarmed by Bayezid's aggression, John V of Constantinople ordered the gates of the city reinforced, stripping marble from the dilapidated churches around the city to do so. This did not please Bayezid, who then demanded that the reinforcements be pulled down, and that the Golden Gate of the city be demolished and thrown open. John V agreed to Bayezid's commands only after he threatened to blind Manuel; John V then lost his pride and retreated to his own apartments, lying motionless and without food, until he died in February of 1391 at the age of fifty-eight.

4. What happened between Manuel and Bayezid after John V's death?

A4.—Pg. 599, ¶ 5 & *—After John V's death, Manuel escaped from the sultan's territory and made his way back to Constantinople, where he claimed the throne. Bayezid was later heard to say that he wished he had murdered his hostage while he had the chance, but apparently the sultan reconsidered this threat; three months after Manuel's enthronement, he summoned Manuel to his court, and the new emperor arrived in safety. Manuel had decided to stave off Bayezid's inevitable attack on Constantinople itself by demonstrating his loyalty, and he spent seven months assisting Bayezid's next military campaign before returning to his position as emperor in January 1392.

5. How was Manuel's wedding to the Serbian princess Helena an example of his denial regarding the true state of Constantinople?

A5.—Pg. 599, ❡ 6 to Pg. 600, ❡ 2—When Manuel married Helena, he held a ceremony that trumpeted the empire's greatness, with Constantinople dressed in silks, parades and feasts held leading up to an all-night celebration of the Eucharist, after which the newlyweds greeted the gathered court from their golden thrones, crowned and jeweled. However, the real crown jewels were actually still in Venice, held as surety for the unpaid debt. Also, Constantinople was no longer the center of a great empire; all that was left now lay within the walls of Constantinople because the outside belonged to the Turks.

6. How did Constantinople survive the first siege laid upon it by Bayezid in 1394?

A6.—Pg. 600, ❡ 3—Constantinople survived the first siege laid upon it by Bayezid in 1394 because the Turks were not yet able to blockade the city by sea; their fleet was rudimentary, their skills on the water poor, and Constantinople was for a time able to resupply itself by ship. Also, because the fields and woods outside the city were inaccessible, the people inside the city managed to sustain themselves by growing vegetables in their tiny city plots and pulling down outbuildings and cottages so that there was enough firewood to bake bread.

7. Why did Sigismund of Hungary agree to help Manuel? What happened when he tried to get a crusade going against the Turks?

A7.—Pg. 600, ❡ 4 to Pg. 601, ❡ 3—With Bulgaria succumbing to Turkish attack and Serbia already gone, Sigismund of Hungary could see his own doom on the horizon, so he agreed to help Manuel and begged the kings of the Christian West for one more crusade, this time against the Turks. The response was lackluster: the Avignon pope promised indulgences; only a few English soldiers arrived, none of them under the command of royalty; Charles VI of France was in no shape to go on crusade so his uncle the Duke of Burgundy promised to attend in his place, but backed out at the last minute and sent his son instead; Venice, hoping to preserve its right to trade with the east through the Black Sea, sent troops; and the military order of the Knights Hospitaller provided a few more. By the end of September 1396, the crusading force that had gathered in Hungary was at its strongest, a formidable force only because Sigismund himself had reinforced their ranks with sixty thousand Hungarians.

8. How did Bayezid defeat the crusading force sent to attack him at Nicopolis in 1396?

A8.—Pg. 601, ❡ 5—In order to defeat the crusading force sent to attack him at Nicopolis, Bayezid drew the French knights, who were anxious to claim credit for the first attack, out with a small advance force, hiding the bulk of his army behind a nearby hill. The French contingent galloped impressively out against the small visible band of Turks; they were at once surrounded and wiped out and then the Turkish army charged down against the remaining Crusaders who were taken by surprise and slaughtered in droves. The Crusader camp outside Nicopolis was surrounded, all of the goods and tents falling into Turkish hands.

9. Explain what Bayezid did with the prisoners taken at Nicopolis.

A9.—Pg. 601, ❡ 6-8—The day after the battle at Nicopolis, Bayezid ordered his men to bring out all of their prisoners. According to Islamic custom, the prisoners belonged to their captors,

although Bayezid could claim one-fifth of the battle spoils for himself, but Bayezid told one of the French captives, a Burgundian who had once fought for the Ottomans as a mercenary and spoke some Turkish, to identify twenty of the richest prisoners to be held for ransom and then he ordered the rest of the prisoners decapitated. However, no one under the age of twenty was killed.

Section III: **Critical Thinking**

The student may not use his text to answer this question.

Our chapter ends with Bayezid's triumph at Nicopolis. Bayezid did not treat his prisoners in a traditional manner, however. Write a paragraph that explains what Bayezid did with the prisoners that remained after his win at Nicopolis, making sure to include what Bayezid did that was off-script. Then write a paragraph that explains why you think the author of our text, Susan Wise Bauer, chose to include the story of Hannsen Greif's end alongside the story of Bayezid's treatment of his prisoners.

The student read about what Bayezid did to his prisoners on page 601 of the text:

> The day after the battle, Bayezid ordered his men to bring out all of their prisoners.
>
> According to Islamic custom, the prisoners belonged to their captors, although Bayezid could claim one-fifth of the battle spoils for himself. But the sultan had a different ending in mind. He told one of the French captives, a Burgundian who had once fought for the Ottomans as a mercenary and spoke some Turkish, to identify twenty of the richest prisoners to be held for ransom. The man did so; the young heir to Burgundy was among them. Then Bayezid ordered the rest decapitated.

What is important about Bayezid's treatment of his prisoners is that he did not follow religious tradition. His actions were against both Christian and Islamic practice, but Bayezid was not concerned with holy war, he was concerned with conquest.

Hannsen Greif's final words are presented at the end of the chapter to contrast Bayezid's ruthlessness. Hannsen Grief believed he was fighting in a holy war. Johann Schiltberger, a young German foot soldier, recounts Hannsen Grief's last moments:

> Then I saw lord Hannsen Greif, who was a noble of Bavaria, and four others bound with the same cord. When they saw the great revenge which was taking place, he cried with a loud voice and consoled the cavalry and infantry who were standing there to die. Stand firm, he said, when our blood this day is spilled for the Christian Faith we by God's help shall become the children of heaven. When he said this he knelt and was beheaded together with his companions.

Hannsen Grief's words provide a foil to Bayezid's indiscriminate slaughter. Hannsen Grief's last moments were spent in prayer. He believed he was going directly into the presence of God because he was fighting in a holy war.

Bayezid, however, in his ignoring of custom and his excessive violence, showed the he had only one master to serve—himself.

EXAMPLE ANSWER:

After his big win at Nicopolis, Bayezid ordered his men to bring out all of their prisoners. Islamic tradition states that the prisoners belonged to the men that captured them, although Bayezid could claim one-fifth of the battle spoils for himself. Bayezid didn't follow the tradition however, and demanded that the twenty richest men be held for ransom, and the others decapitated. Bayezid didn't follow with Islamic tradition because he was interested not in the rules of religion but in the path of conquest. One of the men to be killed was Hannsen Grief, a Bavarian nobleman. Hannsen Grief believed he was fighting in a holy war. He told the men he was grouped with, right before they were killed, that they should stand firm because "when our blood this day is spilled for the Christian Faith we by God's help shall become the children of heaven." Susan Wise Bauer most likely ended the chapter with the juxtaposition of Bayezid's and Hannsen Grief's actions to show the different motivation in fighting at Nicopolis. Hannsen Grief's last moments were spent in prayer. He believed he was going directly into the presence of God because he was fighting in a holy war. Bayezid, however, in his ignoring of religious custom and his excessive violence, showed that he had only one master to serve—himself.

Chapter Eighty-Six

The Union and Disunion of Kalmar

The student may use her text when answering the questions in sections I and II.

Section I: Who, What, Where

Write a one or two-sentence answer explaining the significance of each item listed below.

Albert—**Pg. 605, ¶ 1 & 8 and Pg. 607, ¶ 1—Albert, cousin of Magnus Ericsson, was invited by the Swedish nobles to take the throne in 1364, though he never gained the full allegiance of the noblemen in the west of his country, and when he tried to commandeer noble-held lands and castles for his own use, their opposition against his rule crystallized. Albert was taken prisoner by Margaret's troops after a secret treaty was made that put her in power.**

Christian of Oldenburg—**Pg. 609, ¶ 4—Christian of Oldenburg was elected king of Denmark after Christopher of Bavaria's death.**

Christopher of Bavaria—**Pg. 609, ¶ 3 & 4—Christopher of Bavaria, Eric's sister's son, was elected king of Denmark after Eric fled to Gottland, though he was a young and inexperienced ruler, and his acclamation meant that control of the country actually fell into the hands of the Danish nobles. Eventually Sweden agreed to recognize his kingship as well and soon Norway followed, though Christopher never even visited the country after his coronation.**

Eric—**Pg. 605, ¶ 6, Pg. 607, ¶ 3, Pg. 608, ¶ 6 and Pg. 609, ¶ 1 & 2—Eric, the grandson of Margaret's dead older sister, was adopted when he was five by Margaret so that she could claim an heir to the Norwegian throne, and he became king of a united Scandinavia under Margaret's watch. Eric married Philippa of England and the alliance should have completed the transformation of Eric into the position of one of the premier monarchs of Europe, but instead, he overtaxed and undergoverned the Union, and in 1438, after four years of open revolt, he took the royal treasury and fled to the island fortress of Gottland.**

Haakon—**Pg. 605, ¶ 1 & 2—Haakon, son of Magnus Ericsson, became king of Norway in 1355 after his father was kicked off of the throne. Haakon married the Danish princess Margaret, laying the ground work for another confederation of Scandinavian kingdoms.**

STUDY AND TEACHING GUIDE FOR THE HISTORY OF THE RENAISSANCE WORLD

Karl Knutsson—**Pg. 609, ¶ 4—Karl Knutsson, a Swedish aristocrat who had led the fighting against Eric when open revolt first broke out, was elected king of Sweden after Christopher of Bavaria's death.**

Magnus Ericsson—**Pg. 604, ¶ 5 to Pg. 605, ¶ 2—Magnus Ericsson, elected king of Sweden, also inherited the rule of Norway from his grandfather in 1319, but neither the Swedes nor the Norse were content under the combined crowns; after multiple uprisings and revolts, Magnus Ericsson was forced to pass the throne of Norway to his son Haakon in 1355 and then, in 1364, he lost the throne of Sweden as well, when the Swedish nobles invited his cousin Albert to become king instead. After losing both thrones, Magnus Ericsson took refuge with his son in Norway, drowning in a shipwreck some ten years later.**

Margaret—**Pg. 605, ¶ 2 & 3, Pg. 606, ¶ 1 and Pg. 607, ¶ 1 & 2—Margaret, daughter of Valdemar IV of Denmark, married Haakon of Norway and bore him one son named Olaf; Margaret acted as Olaf's regent and when he died early in 1387, Margaret became the de facto ruler of both Norway and Denmark. Margaret unified Sweden, Denmark and Norway after defeating Albert and taking Stockholm for herself, earning the name "All-Powerful Lady and Rightful Mistress of Sweden."**

Olaf—**Pg. 605, ¶ 2—Olaf, son of Haakon and Margaret, became king of Denmark in 1375 after being elected by the Danehof in the wake of his grandfather's death. He then became king of Norway in 1380, by right of inheritance, after his father Haakon died prematurely.**

Philippa—**Pg. 608, ¶ 6—Philippa, daughter of Henry IV of England, was married to Eric on December 8, 1405 in Westminster Abbey; Philippa was eleven and her groom, aged twenty-four, was not even present at the wedding. The marriage was celebrated for a second time in Sweden's Lund Cathedral on October 26, 1406 with two hundred and four of Philippa's attendants, who were brought by her from England as part of her household.**

Valdemar IV of Denmark—**Pg. 605, ¶ 2—Valdemar IV of Denmark, father of Margaret, had only one son, and he died. When Valdemar IV died in 1375, Margaret's son Olaf was elected king of Denmark by the Danehof, the Danish electors.**

Section II: Comprehension

Write a two or three-sentence answer to each of the following questions.

1. Describe the dispersal of the Scandinavians through the formation of the kingdoms of the Suetidi, the Dani, and the Hordar, and then describe the relationship of these three Scandinavian kingdoms.

A1.—Pg. 604, ¶ 2 & 3—The Scandinavians had lived in the cold northern lands since far before the eighth century, but after they grew too big for their land, some of them went to Lombardy, northern Italy, others crossed the Baltic Sea and built trading posts, founding Rus' villages along the rivers and streams, and still others had set sail as marauding pirates into the Frankish and British lands, where they became known as Vikings. Those that remained

in their native lands formed three kingdoms called the Suetidi, the Dani, and the Hordar: the Swedes, the Danes, and the Norse. The Norse had been united under Harald Tangle-Hair around 900 AD and afterwards had sent ships westward to colonize Iceland and Greenland, while the Danes had claimed England for a time, and the Swedes formed alliances with the Danish and English kingdoms.

2. In general, how did kings come to the throne in Scandinavia?

A2.—Pg. 604, ¶ 4—In general, kings in Denmark and Sweden were elected to the throne, as per the old warrior-clan tradition, however the kings were usually elected from the royal families. In Norway, kings came to the throne through succession; a son followed his father as king.

3. How did Margaret come to be known as "All-Powerful Lady and Mistress"?

A3.—Pg. 605, ¶ 5—Margaret held power in Norway and Denmark after she became the de facto ruler following Olaf's death, for whom she was serving as regent. The Danehof were inclined to keep her on the throne because she was the only surviving child of Valdemar IV and they preferred to keep the crown within the royal family. The Danehof had no title for a woman holding such a position, so Margaret was known by the appellation "All-Powerful Lady and Mistress."

4. What did Margaret do in order to become the ruler of Norway?

A4.—Pg. 605, ¶ 6—Margaret knew she needed to have an heir in order to rule Norway because of its tradition of blood succession. To boost her claims there, Margaret adopted a son and heir: her dead older sister's grandson Eric, a child of five. It worked: the year after her recognition by the Danehof, Margaret was acclaimed as ruler of Norway as well.

5. How did Margaret come to be known as "All-Powerful Lady and Rightful Mistress of Sweden"?

A5.—Pg. 605, ¶ 8 to Pg. 606, ¶ 1—Albert of Sweden was not a popular leader; he had never gained the full allegiance of the noblemen in the west of his country (these men had preferred Magnus Ericsson and they had felt an affection for his son Haakon and grandson Olaf, and now were ready to offer their loyalty to Margaret) so when Albert incautiously tried to commandeer noble-held lands and castles for his own use, their opposition to his rule crystallized. A secret treaty, sworn out in January of 1388, promised Margaret the use of a series of castles and fortresses across Sweden, as well as recognition of the queen of Norway and regent of Denmark as "All-Powerful Lady and Rightful Mistress of Sweden." In exchange, Margaret pledged to protect "the rights, freedoms, and privileges" that the Swedish aristocrats had enjoyed "before King Albert came to Sweden"; even more important, she promised to restore to Sweden all lands that had been filched by Denmark and Norway over the past decades, returning the country to its old boundaries.

6. What happened to Albert after he added "Queen Breechless" to Margaret's list of monikers?

A6.—Pg. 606, ¶ 2 to Pg. 607, ¶ 1—After Albert nicknamed Margaret "Queen Breechless" and showed that he had nothing but scorn for his opponent, civil war broke out in Sweden. The violent but brief war came to head in February of 1389, on a plain east of Falköping, when

Margaret's army defeated Albert's men in straight battle and Albert was taken prisoner. Margaret, who had not appreciated her new nickname, ordered him crowned with a fool's cap and taken back to the Danish castle of Lindholm where he would remain imprisoned for the next six years.

7. What did Margaret do to ensure the unity of Sweden, Denmark, and Norway?

A7.—Pg. 607, ¶ 2 & 3—After Stockholm surrendered, Margaret ordered a constitution drafted that would formalize the union of Sweden, Denmark, and Norway. All three kingdoms would be "eternally united" under a single king; each would keep its own laws and customs; each was obligated to fight to defend the other two; and foreign alliances made by one would bind all three. On June 17, 1397, this constitution was signed by aristocrats from all three countries in a ceremony at Kalmar and young Eric was crowned king of a united Scandinavia, but Margaret was the real sovereign.

8. Who challenged Margaret's rule of Scandinavia fifteen years after the death of Olaf? How did Margaret deal with the pretender?

A8.—Pg. 608, ¶ 1-4—Fifteen years after the death of the Olaf, a penniless stranger arrived in the Teutonic state of Prussia, where he was discovered by some merchants who claimed, because he looked so much like the dead King Olaf, that surely he was the king, and they called him the King of Denmark and Norway. The merchants, most likely native schemers attempting to upset Margaret's power, set up a court for him, gave him everything he wanted, and even made a seal for him. When he came into Margaret's presence, it was clear he was pretending because he wasn't born in the kingdom and didn't even speak the language; he confessed that he was actually a native of northern Hungary and that he had accepted his new identity only because the people of Danzig had heaped him with honors, a confession that earned him death by burning at the stake.

9. What happened to rule of Norway after Christopher of Bavaria's death?

A8.—Pg. 609, ¶ 4 & 5—After Christopher of Bavaria died, the Norwegians split into three support camps—some wanted to elect a native ruler from the extended family of Haakon, others favored the Swedish king, and still others the Danish ruler. Ultimately, the Danish party won out, and Norway and Denmark submitted to a single crown.

Section III: Critical Thinking

The student may not use her text to answer this question.

Over the course of our textbook we have read about the governing bodies of various countries not knowing how to address female sovereigns. Margaret of Denmark faced this dilemma herself, and eventually was given the appellation "All-Powerful Lady and Rightful Mistress of Sweden." Her enemy, Albert, gave her a different title, however. Write a paragraph that explains what name Albert gave Margaret, and why he gave her that name. If you do any research to answer this question, make sure to include citations in your paragraph.

Albert called Margaret "Queen Breechless," meaning a queen without pants. According to Merriam-Webster, breeches are "short pants covering the hips and thighs and fitting snugly at the lower edges at or just below the knee." Breeches are also "pants," or "the hind of the body." Breeches were a typical garment worn by men.

Margaret became "All-Powerful Lady and Mistress" when she took hold of the Danish crown. The next year, Margaret was recognized by Norway as their leader. The Swedish took a little bit longer to come around because Albert was still in power. However, a secret treaty was made in January of 1388 that recognized Margaret's power in Sweden through the appellation "All-Powerful Lady and Rightful Mistress of Sweden." Albert did not give up his throne when he heard of this designation. Instead, he gave Margaret the name "Queen Breechless." Sweden broke out into civil war when the Danish and Norse troops marched into the country. A contemporary chronicle laments:

> *One brother slew another*
> *And sons moved against father*
> *No one asked after law or right*
> *For some they held to the king*
> *And some the queen would follow*

Apparently some Swedes felt the same as Albert and did not want to have a queen ruling their country. Albert's nickname for Margaret played on her ability to rule as a woman. She may have been a sovereign, the "queen," but she didn't wear the right clothes to be a true leader because she was not a man, thus she was "breechless." Albert's nickname played on Margaret's femaleness as the reason that she should not be ruler, though he is the one that ended up in prison and Margaret is the one that ended up uniting Scandinavia.

EXAMPLE ANSWER:

Albert called Margaret "Queen Breechless," meaning a queen without pants. According to Merriam-Webster, breeches are "short pants covering the hips and thighs and fitting snugly at the lower edges at or just below the knee." Breeches are also "pants," or "the hind of the body." Breeches were a typical garment worn by men. Albert was most likely jealous of Margaret's power. She had become "All-Powerful Lady and Mistress" when she took hold of the Danish crown. The next year, Margaret was recognized by Norway as their leader. Then, a secret treaty was made in January of 1388 that recognized Margaret's power in Sweden through the appellation "All-Powerful Lady and Rightful Mistress of Sweden." Albert did not give up his throne when he heard of this designation. Instead, he gave Margaret her nickname and prepared to fight for his throne. Albert's nickname for Margaret played on her ability to rule as a woman. She may have been a sovereign, the "queen," but she didn't wear the right clothes to be a true leader because she was not a man, thus she was "breechless." Albert's nickname played on Margaret's femaleness as the reason that she should not be ruler, though he is the one that ended up in prison and Margaret is the one that ended up uniting Scandinavia.

Section IV: Map Exercise

1. Trace the rectangular outline of map 86.1 in black.

2. Using your blue pencil, trace the outline of the coast around Scandinavia and Europe. Try to include the islands and inlets as best you can. Repeat until the contours are familiar.

3. Using contrasting colors, trace the outlines of Norway, Sweden, Denmark, and Prussia. Repeat until the contours are familiar.

4. Using a new sheet of paper, trace the outline of the rectangular frame of the map in black. Then using your regular pencil with an eraser, draw the outlines of the coast around Scandinavia and Europe. Then draw the outlines of Norway, Sweden, Denmark, and Prussia. Erase and redraw as necessary. When you are happy with your map, lay it over the original. Erase and re-draw any lines which are more than ½″ off of the original.

5. Label Norway, Sweden, Denmark, and Prussia. Then study the locations of Stockholm, Gottland, Kalmar, Lindholm, Scania, Danzig and Graudenz. When they are familiar for you, close the book. Mark each one on your map. Lay your map over the original, and erase and re-draw any labels which are more than ½″ off of the original.

6. Mark the site of the Battle of Falköping.

Chapter Eighty-Seven

The Hussite Uprising

The student may use his text when answering the questions in sections I and II.

Section I: Who, What, Where

Write a one or two-sentence answer explaining the significance of each item listed below.

Alexander V—**Pg. 615, ¶ 2 & 6—Alexander V, elected by the College of Cardinals as a compromise candidate, a third pope after the Avignon and Roman popes were deposed, condemned Wycliffism in a 1409 papal bull. Alexander V died suddenly and unexpectedly after only ten months on the third papal throne.**

Benedict XIII—**Pg. 612, ¶ 4 and Pg. 617, ¶ 6 & 8—Benedict XIII, supported by the king of France, succeeded Clement VII as the Avignon Pope and refused to be deposed during the international church council at Constance. Benedict XIII was deposed after the king of Aragon voiced his support for the deposition.**

Boniface IX—**Pg. 612, ¶ 4 & 6—Boniface IX, supported by the German throne, succeeded Urban VI as the Roman Pope. When Wenceslaus IV and Charles VI agreed to ask both popes to resign in order to elect a third pope that would bring the papacy back together, Boniface IV fought back by offering to give the German electors the authority to depose their king in exchange for their support of his papacy.**

First Defenestration of Prague—**Pg. 618, ¶ 3 & 4—First Defenestration of Prague was the name given to the riot caused by the Hussites in Prague in July of 1419. The Hussites broke into the town hall and demanded that the officials release the imprisoned guests, after which the Hussites threw thirteen Prague administrators out of the windows (seven died in the street below).**

Gregory XII—**Pg. 617, ¶ 5—Gregory XII, Boniface IX's successor as pope, offered to abdicate at the international church council in Constance as long as Benedict XIII also be deposed.**

Hussites—**Pg. 618, ¶ 2 & 3—Hussites were followers of John Hus that could not forget his death; his followers in Bohemia began to gather weapons and organized themselves into groups. The**

Hussites formed an increasingly bold movement that was rapidly transforming into a popular army; their first act of violence was the First Defenestration of Prague.

Jan Hus—Pg. 613, ¶ 4 & 5, Pg. 615, ¶ 1 and Pg. 617, ¶ 3, 4. & 6—Jan Hus, a Bohemian priest, rector of the University of Prague, and follower of John Wycliffe, was dismissed from his position at the University of Prague in 1403 when he continued to defend Wycliffe after the university banned his teachings. John Hus agreed to speak at the Council of Constance on the condition that he be given safe passage; he was treated as a heretic instead, imprisoned, tried for heresy, and then burned at the stake at a site known as the Devils' Place.

John XXIII—Pg. 615, ¶ 7 and Pg. 617, ¶ 4—John XXIII, Alexander V's successor in Pisa, confirmed Hus's excommunication and criticized Bohemia for being "full of heresy." John XXIII was deposed in 1415 at the Council of Constance.

Lollards—Pg. 614, ¶ 2—Lollards was the name given to the people, both poor and among the knightly class, that followed the teachings of John Wycliffe. Lollards were silenced by Henry IV in 1401 when he approved a parliamentary statute that forbade English subjects to own Wycliffe's Bible and that said anyone preaching without a license granted by the Church could be arrested and tried; the statute never mentioned the Lollards, but it instantly prohibited them from ever speaking their beliefs out loud, on pain of death.

Martin V—Pg. 617, ¶ 8 to Pg. 618, ¶ 1 & 3—Martin V, a Roman priest, was elected to be pope in 1417—a single pope—after the deposition of the Roman, Avignon, and Pisa popes at the Council of Constance. Martin V excommunicated all of Hus's followers in early 1418, which forced King Wenceslaus to act against them or be accused of defying the one true Church.

Wenceslaus IV—Pg. 611, ¶ 2, Pg. 612, ¶ 2, and Pg. 613, ¶ 2—Wenceslaus IV, given the imperial throne because his father Charles IV bought his crown, spent the first ten years of his reign fighting the Swabian League and then spent the next ten years putting down rebellious German dukes that disliked his methods of raising money, his treatment of the clergy, his excessive drinking, and the paperwork he generated in the governing of the empire. Wenceslaus IV continued to rule from Bohemia after he refused to recognize his deposition by the German electors, but his power ended at the Bohemian border.

Rupert of Germany—Pg. 613, ¶ 1-3—Rupert of Germany was made king of Germany by the electors after they deposed Wenceslaus IV. Rupert of Germany faced the same problems as Wenceslaus IV: he marched into Italy in 1401 to reduce the power of Gian Galeazzo Visconti, now the Duke of Milan, but Visconti's troops halted the imperial army at Brescia, and when he returned home the following year he found himself embroiled in the same rebellions, complaints, and intrigues as his predecessor.

Section II: Comprehension

Write a two or three-sentence answer to each of the following questions.

1. What were "imperial cities" *(Reichsstädte)*, and what did it mean to "mortgage" an imperial city?

A1.—Pg. 611, ¶ 3 & 4—"Imperial cities" were cities founded on royal-owned land, or cities that had grown up around imperial castles. They were directly under the authority of the Holy Roman Emperor; imperial cities paid their taxes straight into the royal treasury, answered only to the emperor's appointed governor (and not to any duke or elector, even if they stood within his duchy), and swore allegiance to the emperor alone. To "mortgage" an imperial city was to hand it over to the control of another in return for payment.

2. How did Charles IV guarantee that his son Wenceslaus IV would be given his throne?

A2.—Pg. 611, ¶ 2 & 4—Just before his death in 1378, Charles IV had guaranteed his son's election to the imperial throne by distributing cash presents to the electors. To raise the money, Charles had mortgaged a cluster of imperial cities in Swabia. He had sold the right to appoint magistrates and other civil officials to a local Swabian aristocrat, the Count of Württemberg, which effectively put the cities under the Count's power.

3. How did the Swabian city of Ulm challenge Wenceslaus IV's rule? What brought an end to the German king's war with the Swabian League?

A3.—Pg. 611, ¶ 5 to Pg. 612, ¶ 1—The Swabian city of Ulm led thirteen others in revolt against Charles IV; they declared themselves a League, a political alliance of German cities pledged to resist any outside princes who might try to dictate their affairs, and to reject the election of young Wenceslaus as their new emperor. Charles IV had barely begun to fight back against the rebellious Swabian League before his death in 1378; Wenceslaus spent the next decade struggling to force the cities into submission to his rule. The war came to an end in 1389 when Wenceslaus agreed to give the Swabian cities a carefully enumerated set of self-governing privileges (including the settlement of quarrels between "the lords and the cities who are in this peace" by an independent commission) in exchange for their recognition of him as their king—and the dissolution of the league.

4. Why did the German dukes continue to rebel against Wenceslaus IV?

A4.—Pg. 612, ¶ 2—The German dukes resented Wenceslaus IV's methods of raising money, like recognizing Gian Galeazzo Visconti, the Lord of Milan, as a full duke, in exchange for an enormous payment. The German dukes also objected to Wenceslaus IV's dealings with the clergy; for example, he had reacted to an ongoing conflict with the Archbishop of Prague by tossing the archbishop's subordinates into jail. The dukes criticized the king's heavy drinking and they complained about the amount of paperwork Wenceslaus IV generated in the governing of the empire.

5. How did Palatine Rupert come to be nominated by the German electors as Wenceslaus IV's replacement?

A5.—Pg. 612, ⁋ 5 to Pg. 613, ⁋ 1—In 1398, Wenceslaus IV of Germany and Charles VI of France met at Reims and agreed that they would ask both the Roman and Avignon popes to resign, and a third would be elected to bring the papacy back together. Boniface IX fought back by offering to give the German electors the authority to depose their king in exchange for their support of his papacy. They accepted the offer and on August 20, 1400 the Archbishop of Mainz declared Wenceslaus IV to be "useless, idle, and incapable," no longer worthy of the crown, and that the Elector Palatine Rupert should be the next king of Germany.

6. Why did John Wycliffe want to translate the Bible from Latin into English? Who opposed this project?

A6.—Pg. 613, ⁋ 6 & 7—John Wycliffe wanted to translate the Bible from Latin into English because he believed that "no simple man of wit should be afraid to study in the text of holy Writ." He argued that the pride and greed of England's priests caused them to be blind to the true understanding of the word of God and that the New Testament was "open to the understanding of simple men." After the publication of Wycliffe's Bible, the English abbot Henry Knighton showed his opposition to the project when he said "By him, Scripture is become common and more open to the lay folk and to *women* than it used to be to clerics of a fair amount of learning. . . . Thus, the Gospel pearl is cast forth and trodden under foot of swine. . . . and the jewel of the clergy is turned into the sport of the laity."

7. What other anticlerical beliefs did John Wycliffe hold, in addition to his belief that everyone should be able to study the bible without the help of the clergy?

A7.—Pg. 613, ⁋ 8 to Pg. 614, ⁋ 1—John Wycliffe also held the anticlerical belief that the Church doctrine of transubstantiation (the transformation of the bread and wine of the Eucharist into the actual body and blood of Christ) was unscriptural and idolatrous. He said "We worship a false god in the chalice . . . [for] a sacrament is no more but a sign . . . of a thing passed, or a thing to come," which was in opposition to the clergy because they claimed that they alone had the divine right to handle the sacred body and blood. Wycliffe also condemned indulgences as a "manifold blasphemy," since promising sinners that their punishment would be revoked gave Christ's saving power to the pope.

8. Why did Wenceslaus IV reprimand the Archbishop of Prague? How was this action contradictory to his earlier support of Alexander V?

A8.—Pg. 615, ⁋ 4-6—Wenceslaus IV reprimanded the Archbishop of Prague because, against the pleas of Jan Hus and several other Bohemian supporters of Wycliffe's ideas, he took their copies of Wycliffe's writings and burned them in a bonfire, supposedly saving the gold bindings and knobs from the most valuable books for himself. Groups of rioters burst into churches and chased the priests away from the altars; Hus preached a sermon that strongly suggested that the archbishop might be the Antichrist, and Wenceslaus IV ordered the archbishop to pay back the cost of the burned books. This action was contradictory to Wenceslaus IV's earlier support of Alexander V because Alexander V issued a papal bull in

1409 condemning Wycliffism; by making the archbishop responsible for payment to Hus, Wenceslaus IV was doing the opposite of condemning Wycliffism.

9. What did Sigismund hope to achieve at the Council of Constance? What was the setting like during the meeting?

A9.—Pg. 616, ¶ 5 & 6—Sigismund hoped to recover Bohemia, corral Italy, and solve the embarrassment of the triple papacy at the Council of Constance. The scene in Constance was lively: nearly four hundred high-ranking clergy members—archbishops, abbots, priors, and priests—were present, but they were outnumbered by university leaders, scholars, and ambassadors from the courts of Europe. There were also hundreds of merchants, clowns, jugglers, conjurers, musicians, barbers, and prostitutes carousing in the streets during the meeting; one local resident estimated that seventy thousand outsiders descended on the city during the Council's deliberations.

10. How did the Hussites react to Wenceslaus IV's order that priests in Prague who had allowed laypeople to serve the Eucharist be arrested?

A10.—Pg. 618, ¶ 3—When Wenceslaus IV ordered that priests in Prague who had allowed laypeople to serve the Eucharist be arrested, the Hussites rioted because this rule was a condemnation of the Hussite acceptance of the radical ideas first proposed by Wycliffe. In July of 1419, Hussites stormed through the streets of Prague, breaking into the town hall and demanding that the officials there release the imprisoned priests. In the scuffle that followed, Hussites threw thirteen Prague administrators out of the windows, seven of which were killed in the street below.

Section III: Critical Thinking

The student may not use his text to answer this question.

Niccolò Machiavelli was a famous sixteenth-century political philosopher; his treatise *The Prince* is, arguably, his most well-known work. We met Machiavelli in this chapter; he described the condition of the German dukes and their relationship to Wenceslaus IV: "The cities of Germany enjoy a very extensive liberty. . . . [They] obey the emperor when they please, under no apprehension of being attacked either by him or by others, for the towns are defended by strong walls and deep ditches, and are provided with artillery and provisions for a year, so that the siege of these cities would be both long and painful." For this critical thinking question, write a short biography for Machiavelli. Then, give a brief description of his most famous work, *The Prince*. As always, make sure to cite your sources.

The student will have to do research to answer this question. The citation style may be chosen at your discretion; just make sure your student is consistent. There is a plethora of information available about Niccolò Machiavelli, both online and in print. The student should give a brief biographical summary of Machiavelli's life, and then give a brief summary of The Prince's *main point. The student should note that Machiavelli is often called the father of modern political theory, and that* The Prince *suggests a leader rule based on fear rather than adoration.*

The example answer provides the minimum amount of information to be given by the student. Chicago Style footnotes are used in the example answer.

EXAMPLE ANSWER:

Niccolò Machiavelli was born on May 3, 1469. Machiavelli was a historian and philosopher, and is often called the father of modern political theory. During his early career, he worked as an Italian diplomat, but he was fired when the Medici family came back into power in 1512 because he supposedly was trying to organize a militia to fight their return.[6] Machiavelli had time to reflect on his own political theories after his dismissal, and he began to write. His most famous work, *The Prince,* **was published in 1513 as a pamphlet, but it wasn't released as a book until after his death in 1532. In** *The Prince,* **Machiavelli says that new princes should rule the world according to what it is, rather than what they want it to be. This is why he is called the founder of modern political science, because he said the one should govern based on the actual state of the world rather than be guided by utopic ideals.[7] In** *The Prince,* **Machiavelli claims that fear through "the dread of punishment" will make subjects obey a new prince. He also writes that a leader should not count on the support of his subjects but rather "one's own arms," meaning a prince should not rely on others and he should raise his own army to carry out his orders.[8]**

---

6. "Niccolò Machiavelli," *Biography.com*, accessed May 27, 2016, http://www.biography.com/people/niccolò-machiavelli-9392446
7. Harvey Mansfield, "Niccolò Machiavelli," *Encyclopædia Britannica*, last updated May 22, 2015, date accessed May 27, 2016, http://www.britannica.com/biography/Niccolo-Machiavelli
8. *Ibid.*

Chapter Eighty-Eight

The Taking of France

The student may use her text when answering the questions in sections I and II.

Section I: **Who, What, Where**

Write a one or two-sentence answer explaining the significance of each item listed below.

Catherine (of France)—**Pg. 625, ¶ 6 & 7—Catherine, Charles VI's daughter, was married to Henry V as part of the terms of the Treaty of Troyes.**

Catherine (of Wales)—**Pg. 621, ¶ 2 & 3—Catherine, daughter of Owain Glyndwr, was married to Edmund Mortimer as part of a bargain the two men made where Edmund Mortimer would help Wales gain independence from the English and in exchange Owain Glyndwr would help put Edmund Mortimer on the throne. Catherine and the four children she had with Edmund Mortimer died of illness after being taken to the Tower of London following the surrender of Harlech Castle in 1409.**

Charles—**Pg. 622, ¶ 6 to Pg. 623, ¶ 1 and Pg. 625, ¶ 1—Charles, successor to the dukedom of Orleans after the murder of his father, married the daughter of the Count of Armagnac in 1410. The Duke of Orleans was taken captive by the English after their success at the Battle of Agincourt.**

Dauphin Louis—**Pg. 621, ¶ 7 and Pg. 625, ¶ 6—Dauphin Louis, Charles VI's son and heir, was married to the daughter of the Duke of Burgundy when he was just eleven. Louis lost his place as heir to the throne in the Treaty of Troyes; Henry V would be the French king's heir.**

Edmund Mortimer—**Pg. 620, ¶ 2 and Pg. 621, ¶ 2 & 3—Edmund Mortimer, the Earl of March, was the son of Philippa, the only daughter of Edward III's second son Lionel of Antwerp, but he had died before his father; Philippa, who was still senior to Henry IV, had been Richard II's heiress, and after her death in 1382, her claim on the throne passed to Edmund Mortimer. Edmund Mortimer fought with Henry Percy and Owain Glyndwr in civil war against Henry IV, a war that caused his death in January of 1409.**

Henry V—**Pg. 623, ❡ 3, Pg. 625, ❡ 3, 6 & 7**—Henry V, crowned at Westminster on April 9, 1413, triumphed over the French at Agincourt and when he returned home to London he was hailed as "King of England and of France." Henry V married Catherine after agreeing to the Treaty of Troyes in May 1420, which stated that he would be France's regent, he would be heir to Charles VI, and he would marry Charles VI's daughter so that Charles VI's grandchildren would still rule France.

Henry Percy—**Pg. 621, ❡ 1-3**—Henry Percy, Edmund Mortimer's brother-in-law, had been leading the resistance to the Scots when Mortimer was taken prisoner in battle with Owain Glyndwr; Henry Percy offered to ransom him out of his captor's hands, but Henry IV refused to allow it. Henry Percy joined Edmund Mortimer and Owain Glyndwr in war against Henry IV; nicknamed "Hotspur" because of his tendency to act first and think later, Henry Percy was killed almost immediately in the middle of battle in July 1403 when he lifted his faceplate and was struck by a random arrow.

Isabeau—**Pg. 621, ❡ 7**—Isabeau was the wife of Charles VI. By 1404, she had borne Charles VI eight children.

Jehan Petit—**Pg. 622, ❡ 5**—Jehan Petit, a noted theologian, helped the Duke of Burgundy mount a public defense for himself regarding the death of the Duke of Orleans. Petit argued that the killing was not murder but tyrannicide.

John—**Pg. 621, ❡ 7 to Pg. 622, ❡ 1 & 4, and Pg. 625, ❡ 4**—John, made the Duke of Burgundy after his father's death in 1404, gained popularity in France when he said a heavy tax that Charles VI hoped to impose on the people should not be levied; his popularity was so strong that he remained in the favor of the French people after he had the Duke of Orleans murdered. The Duke of Burgundy was assassinated by Armagnac thugs after he opened secret negotiations with Henry V, willing to entertain the idea of accepting the English king in place of Charles VI.

Owain Glyndwr—**Pg. 620, ❡ 3 and Pg. 621, ❡ 2**—Owain Glyndwr, a wealthy Welsh farmer, began to lead attacks on the English living in the north of Wales in early 1401; these attacks marked the beginning of Owain Glyndwr's challenge to Henry IV's rule over Wales. Owain Glyndwr made an alliance with Edmund Mortimer and Henry Percy that started civil war in England.

Philip the Good—**Pg. 625, ❡ 6 & 7**—Philip the Good, who followed John as Duke of Burgundy, was the mastermind behind the compromise, the Treaty of Troyes, between Charles VI and Henry V. The Treaty of Troyes stated that Charles VI would remain on the throne of France but Henry would become France's regent, that Henry would become the king's heir, and that Henry V would marry Catherine, guaranteeing that Charles VI's grandchildren would still rule France.

Section II: Comprehension

Write a two or three-sentence answer to each of the following questions.

1. How did Henry IV's putting down of the Welsh revolt turn into a civil war?

A1.—Pg. 620, ¶ 5 to Pg. 621, ¶ 2—After Edmund Mortimer, who had been loyally fighting for the English cause against the Welsh, was taken prisoner in a battle with Owain Glyndwr, his brother-in-law Henry Percy offered to ransom him out of Owain Glyndwr's hands, but Henry IV refused to allow it. Both Mortimer and Henry Percy, who until this point had been supporters of Henry IV, were indignant, and Owain Glyndwr seized on the indignation: he set Mortimer free, gave him his own daughter Catherine as wife, and made an alliance with both Mortimer and Percy. The alliance was that the Englishmen would help Wales gain independence from England, and Owain Glyndwr would in turn help put Mortimer on the English throne, thus starting a civil war.

2. Why did the Duke of Burgundy flee Paris after the Feast of Saint Clement in 1407?

A2.—Pg. 622, ¶ 3 & 4—In 1407, on the Feast of Saint Clement, the Duke of Orleans was ambushed in the streets of Paris, late at night, by a gang of armed men. He was knocked off his horse and beaten to death in the street so savagely that, the next morning, his servants went back to scrape up the brain matter that had been scattered across the stones so that it could be buried with him; they also found his right hand, which had been severed in the attack. The ambushers had been hired by the Duke of Burgundy; fearing arrest, the Duke of Burgundy fled from Paris and made his way back to his own domains.

3. How did the Duke of Burgundy get away with murdering his cousin the Duke of Orleans?

A3.—Pg. 622, ¶ 4-6—After finding out that the people of Paris were happy that the Duke of Orleans was dead, the Duke of Burgundy returned to Paris and mounted a public defense with help of theologian Jehan Petit, arguing that the murder was tyrannicide, and so it was ethical and justified. Petit offered a syllogism to defend the murder: "The major: It is permissible and meritorious to kill a tyrant. The minor: The duke of Orleans was a tyrant. The conclusion: Therefore the duke of Burgundy did well to kill him." Then, Charles VI, anxious to keep the peace in Paris, granted his cousin a free pardon the very next day.

4. What brought France to the brink of civil war in the early fifteenth century?

A4.—Pg. 622, ¶ 7 to Pg. 623, ¶ 1—After Charles VI pardoned the Duke of Burgundy, the indignant supporters of the Duke of Orleans, led by his wife, formed an anti-Burgundy faction, uniting behind fourteen-year-old Charles, the new Duke of Orleans. After Charles married the daughter of the Count of Armagnac and the Count became the leader of the anti-Burgundy party, more people joined the cause: they were called the Armagnacs and were from the west and south and included the Dukes of Berry and Bourbon, and the Constable of France. The opposition, the Burgundy party, was from the north and the east, and the two parties set France on the brink of civil war.

5. How did Henry V of England get involved in the French struggle between the Armagnac party and the Duke of Burgundy supporters? What was his reaction to the French internal conflict?

A5.—Pg. 623, ¶ 4-6—Two sets of envoys arrived at the English court soon after Henry V was crowned, one from the Armagnac party (which now counted Charles VI himself among its adherents) and one from the Duke of Burgundy, both asking to be "strengthened" in their struggle against the other party. Henry V offered to drive a bargain with the Armagnac party; he would defeat the Duke of Burgundy, in exchange for the crown of France, marriage with the king's daughter Catherine, and a dowry of two million crowns. This was not so much an offer as an incitement to war: the French internal conflict had opened the door to English invasion.

6. Describe the English siege of Harfleur.

A6.—Pg. 623, ¶ 7 to Pg. 624, ¶ 1—Henry V landed in Normandy on August 15, 1415, with nearly fifteen hundred ships behind him, and with six thousand foot soldiers and twenty-three thousand archers on the ground; the force of archers probably numbered closer to ten thousand but the English longbows seemed like their number was greater because they were so deadly. Harfleur held out for a month, with the English bombarding the walls with cannon by day and mining beneath them by night. Meanwhile, dysentery had swept through the English tents; thousands died, many more were forced to return to England, and by the time he had accepted Harfleur's surrender, Henry V had lost a good part of his army, with only eight thousand archers and foot soldiers remaining.

7. What happened when the English army met the French army on October 25, 1415 near the wood of Agincourt?

A7.—Pg. 624, ¶ 3 to Pg. 625, ¶ 2—When the exhausted and weak English army met the refreshed French army on October 25 near the wood of Agincourt, the French offered to carry out further negotiations, but Henry V ordered his men to begin the charge. The first volley from the English archers, coordinated into a single devastating hail, brought down the entire French front line; the horses behind, many of them wounded, wheeled and charged back into the massed ranks while others slipped in the mud—the field where they fought was newly planted with grain—and trapped their knights. The English foot soldiers drove forward with swords and hatchets, slaughtering thousands: perhaps eight thousand French soldiers died and the English declared victory.

Section III: Critical Thinking

The student may not use her text to answer this question.

When French envoys arrived at the English court shortly after Henry V's coronation, Henry V gave the Armagnacs an offer they could refuse: he would defeat the Duke of Burgundy in exchange for the crown of France, marriage with the king's daughter Catherine, and a dowry of two million crowns. This was not so much an offer of support as an incitement to war. Explain how the inability of the Armagnacs and the Burgundy party to work together caused their crown, for all intents and purposes, to be turned over to the English king. In your answer, make sure to compare

Henry V's original demands given to the Armagnac and Burgundian envoys to the terms of the Treaty of Troyes.

When the Armagnacs and the Burgundians found themselves equally balanced in power in France, they hoped that the new English king would break the stalemate.

Soon after Henry V was crowned, two sets of envoys showed up from France, one from the Burgundy party and one from the Armagnacs. Henry V decided to drive a bargain with the Armagnac party. He said he would defeat the Duke of Burgundy in exchange for the crown of France, marriage with the king's daughter Catherine, and a dowry of two million crowns. This was a ridiculous offer. First, the two house parties didn't want Henry V to take over rule of their country, they just wanted him to back up one of their houses. Second, the payment Henry V asked for was ludicrous; two million crowns was the equivalent of over thirteen thousand years of middle-class income. Henry V's demands were not feasible, so the French saw that he was inadvertently declaring war, seizing on the king's weakness and the destabilization of the country because of the feuding houses.

Henry V started his invasion in the summer of 1415. He did well against the French at Harfleur. The French response was slow, made worse by the unwillingness of the Burgundian and Armagnac parties to fight side by side. Most of the French fighters were Armagnac. The Duke of Burgundy had promised to fight, but did not keep his word. Then, Henry V defeated the French at Agincourt. Soon after, the leaders of the two houses were killed. The Count of Armagnac, who became Constable of France, was murdered in a riot along with many other Armagnac supporters. Then, the Duke of Burgundy, who was carrying on secret negotiations with Henry V, was assassinated by Armagnac thugs.

In 1417, Henry V returned to France, a fresh army with him, and started to fight his way through Normandy. Rouen fell on January 19, 1419; it had been in French hands for two centuries and its loss cut the heart out of the French resistance. By the end of 1419, the French were ready to make a deal. Philip the Good brokered the Treaty of Troyes, which was finalized in 1420. The treaty stated that Charles VI would remain on the throne of France, but Henry V would act as his regent. This gave Henry V power over France's decision making. Next, the treaty stated that Henry V would become Charles VI's heir, meaning that when Charles VI died, Henry V would take the French throne. Finally, Henry V would marry Charles VI's daughter Catherine, guaranteeing that Charles VI's grandchildren would still rule France.

Henry V's original demands were that he become king of France, he marry Catherine, and that he receive a huge dowry. The Treaty of Troyes tells us he would be France's regent and then France's king once Charles VI died, and that he would marry Catherine. Perhaps if the French enjoys had agreed to Henry V's original demands, thousands of lives would have been spared. Nevertheless, Henry V got almost everything he wanted.

EXAMPLE ANSWER:

The Treaty of Troyes, finalized in May of 1420, was very similar to the original demands made by Henry V of England when he was visited by Burgundian and Armagnac envoys shortly after his coronation. Henry V decided to back the Armagnacs and made this offer: he would defeat the Duke of Burgundy in exchange for the crown of France, marriage with the king's daughter Catherine, and a dowry of two million crowns. The Armagnacs did not oblige the English king. First, they didn't want Henry V to take over rule of their country, they just wanted him to back up their house against their rivals. Second, the payment Henry V asked for was ludicrous; two million crowns was the equivalent of over thirteen thousand years of middle-class income. Henry V's demands were not feasible, so the French saw that he was inadvertently declaring war, seizing on the king's weakness and the destabilization of the country because of the feuding houses.

When Henry V started his invasion of France in the summer of 1415, the Armagnacs and the Burgundians could have worked together to stop him, but they didn't. The Duke of Burgundy said he would help out but he never showed up, and the army that came out to meet advancing English troops were mostly Armagnac. After Henry V defeated the French at Harfleur and Agincourt, and after the leaders of the Armagnac and Burgundy parties were killed, a compromise was finally brokered by Philip the Good: the Treaty of Troyes. The treaty stated that Charles VI would remain on the throne of France, but Henry V would act as his regent. This gave Henry V power over France's decision making. Next, the treaty stated that Henry V would become Charles VI's heir, meaning that when Charles VI died, Henry V would take the French throne. Finally, Henry V would marry Charles VI's daughter Catherine, guaranteeing that Charles VI's grandchildren would still rule France. Henry V's original demands were that he become king of France, he marry Catherine, and that he receive a huge dowry. Perhaps if the French enjoys had agreed to Henry V's original demands, thousands of lives would have been spared. Nevertheless, Henry V got almost everything he wanted.

Section IV: Map Exercise

1. Trace the rectangular outline of the frame for Map 88.1 in black.

2. Using your blue pencil, trace the outline of all the visible coastline. Include the lines of the Thames in England and the Seine in France. Repeat until the contours are familiar.

3. Now using contrasting colors, trace the outlines of England and France. Repeat until the contours are familiar.

4. Using a new sheet of paper, trace the rectangular outline of the frame for Map 88.1: Agincourt in black. Then using your regular pencil with the eraser, draw the lines of the visible coast, including the Thames and Seine rivers. Then draw the outlines of France and England. Erase and re-draw as necessary, using the frame as a reference. When you are happy with your map, lay it over the original. Erase and re-draw any lines which are more than ¼" off of the original.

5. Now study carefully the locations of London, Dover, Calais, Harfleur, Paris, Meaux, and Troyes. When you are familiar with them, close the book. Mark each location on your map. Then lay your map over the original, and erase and re-mark any locations over ¼" off of the original.

6. Mark the locations of the Battle of Shrewsbury, the Battle of Agincourt, and the castle of Rouen.

7. Label Normandy and Wales.

Chapter Eighty-Nine

After Timurlane

The student may use his text when answering the questions in sections I and II.

Section I: Who, What, Where

Write a one or two-sentence answer explaining the significance of each item listed below.

Al-Zahir Barquq—**Pg. 628, ¶ 4—Al-Zahir Barquq was the Circassian mamluk who first ruled after the Bahri, the founder of the Burji dynasty. He took as his palace the great Citadel of Cairo and his dynasty took its nickname from the Arabic word for the citadel's spires, *burj*.**

Faraj—**Pg. 628, ¶ 5 & 6—Faraj followed his father al-Zahir Barquq as sultan of the Burji dynasty though Faraj had no power of his own; his emirs made decisions for him. Faraj found his kingdom attacked by Timur when his emirs refused to surrender the sultanate's Syrian lands.**

Firoz—**Pg. 627, ¶ 2 and Pg. 628, ¶ 1 & 2—Firoz, sultan of the Bahmani kingdom, sent diplomats loaded with gifts to Samarkand and begged Timur to accept Firoz as his vassal; Timur agreed and sent the message that Firoz could, by his grace, rule over Malwa and Gujarat. Though Firoz wasn't actually the ruler of Malwa and Gujarat, submitting to Timur meant that the Mongol warrior would leave the Bahmani alone.**

George VI—**Pg. 630, ¶ 5—George VI, son and heir of George the Brilliant, was given a small amount of authority by Timur in Georgia in exchange for tribute money. But Timur returned and took that authority away, sweeping across the countryside, flattening seven hundred villages and destroying all the churches in Tbilisi.**

Ibn Khaldun—**Pg. 629, ¶ 1 & 2—Ibn Khaldun, a well-known traveler and historian, was trapped inside Aleppo during Timur's siege of the city, but when Timur heard he was inside he asked to speak to the famous man. After Ibn Khaldun was lowered over the walls in a basket (so that the gates of the city would not be opened to the enemy), he ate and drank with Timur, complimented him for being "sultan of the universe and the ruler of the world," and was allowed to leave in peace, later going back to Cairo.**

John VII—Pg. 629, ¶ 5-7—**John VII, who acted as regent of the Byzantine empire in the place of his uncle Manuel, begged European courts for money in the fight against Bayezid, but he had no luck; the great kings were preoccupied, broke, invested elsewhere, or insane. John VIII found help in his fight against the Ottomans from an unlikely source: Timur.**

Mehmed—Pg. 632, ¶ 6 to Pg. 633, ¶ 2—**Mehmed, the sixth son of Bayezid, declared himself both the undisputed sultan of the Ottoman realm and the loyal friend of Constantinople; the emperor Manuel had provided Mehmed with Byzantine warships and troops to help him fight and kill his brother Musa. After his victory against Musa, Mehmed signed a peace treaty with Manuel and then annexed the Hungarian principality of Wallachia.**

Mircea the Elder—Pg. 633, ¶ 2—**Mircea the Elder was the independent prince that ruled over the Hungarian principality of Wallachia. His kingdom was annexed by Mehmed and he became the Ottoman sultan's vassal.**

Musa—Pg. 630, ¶ 4 and Pg. 632, ¶ 6—**Musa, one of Bayezid's sons, escaped from Timur's hands and fought fiercely with two of his brothers over the Ottoman heartland. Musa was defeated and then strangled to death by his brother, Mehmed.**

Qara Yusu—Pg. 632, ¶ 5—**Qara Yusu was the chief of the Black Sheep. He worked out a truce with the mamluks of Egypt that would guarantee the existence of the Black Sheep as an independent kingdom, making them the most powerful Turkish kingdom in the east for a short time.**

Shah Rukh—Pg. 632, ¶ 4—**Shah Rukh, Timur's youngest son, was serving Pir Muhammad as governor in the eastern part of the empire when Pir Muhammad was murdered. Then Shah Rukh took the east for himself.**

Suleyman—Pg. 630, ¶ 4—**Suleyman, Bayezid's third son, managed to seize the western Ottoman territories. Suleyman held on to the western territories by freeing Manuel from his vassal status and allowing him to reclaim Thessalonica for Byzantium.**

Threshold of Paradise—Pg. 627, ¶ 2—**Threshold of Paradise was the nickname given to Samarkand. Samarkand, once razed by Genghis Khan, was brought back to splendid life by Timur; he spared architects, artists, and craftsmen from execution and brought them back to his capital to work towards creating a wondrous city.**

Vlad—Pg. 633, ¶ 2—**Vlad, son of Mircea the Elder, took his father's place as Wallachia's prince and Mehmed's vassal. He would become known as Vlad Dracul, Vlad the Dragon; builder of Castle Dracul, father of the violent and bloodthirsty Wallachian prince Vlad the Impaler.**

Section II: **Comprehension**

Write a two or three-sentence answer to each of the following questions.

1. Describe Samarkand as it existed in Timur's lifetime.

A1.—Pg. 627, ⁋ 3—Under Timur, Samarkand was filled with mosques and minarets, green parks and marble houses, paved courtyards and cobbled streets, with a wide commercial street traversing the heart of the city with rows of shops on both sides, each shop uniformly built and fronted with a stone bench for shoppers, the street itself domed over and lined with water fountains: the first indoor shopping mall. The merchants visiting the city were so numerous that they camped outside the walls, in a tent city of fifty thousand, and they came into the city to sell their goods along the commercial street: there one could find leather and linen from the Rus', silks and embroidery from China, rubies and diamonds and pearls from India; nutmegs, cloves, and ginger; game, fowl, bread, and fruit; hemp and flax, silver and copper, glass and porcelain, rhubarb and musk. The royal palace of Samarkand stood inside the city walls, doubly protected by a river that curved through the city and around its walls, with a splendid public garden so huge that one ambassador's horse, escaping into the leafy retreat, stayed missing for six whole weeks before it could be located.

2. How did Firoz of Bahmani benefit from becoming the supposed ruler of Malwa and Gujarat even though he did not actually rule over either kingdom?

A2.—Pg. 628, ⁋ 1 & 2—Even though Firoz of Bahmani did not actually rule over either Malwa or Gujarat (in fact, his rival, the sultan of Vijayanagara, was busy establishing diplomatic relationships with both), getting Timur to accept him as vassal meant that Timur was in no hurry to plow back down and wreck the Bahmani. Though the ceremonial dance between the two was meaningless as far as rule over Malwa and Gujarat was concerned, it was meaningful to Firoz, who secured the projection of the Bahmani people.

3. How did the Burji dynasty come into existence, and where did they get their name from?

A3.—Pg. 628, ⁋ 4—The Bahri sultanate, drawn from the old regiment that had once protected the Ayyubid ruler of Egypt, had decayed; in 1390 a new mamluk dynasty, the Burji, had claimed the rule of Egypt. The Burji dynasty drew its sultans from a different military regiment, originally made up of slave warriors bought from the Caucasus mountain ranges that were known as the Circassian mamluks. The Circassian mamluk who first ruled after the Bahri, al-Zahir Barquq, took as his palace the great Citadel of Cairo, built by Saladin himself, and his dynasty took its nickname from the Arabic word for the citadel's spires, *burj*: they were the mamluks of the Tower.

4. What did Timur do after Faraj's emirs declined to surrender Egypt's Syrian lands (and cut Timur's messenger in half at the waist)?

A4.—Pg. 628, ⁋ 6 to Pg. 629, ⁋ 3—After Faraj's emirs refused to give over Egypt's Syrian lands to Timur (and after his messenger was cut in half at the waist), Timur marched on Aleppo. Soldiers from a dozen Egyptian-held Syrian cities hurried to reinforce Aleppo's defense, but Timur crushed the Burji army, broke through the city's gates, and allowed his men to

slaughter the population. He then laid siege to Damascus, and after the city surrendered, Timur robbed the city of all of its wealth and goods and then set it on fire.

5. How did John VII get rid of the Ottomans without the help of the European kings?

A5.—Pg. 629, ¶ 7 to Pg. 630, ¶ 2—Timur helped John VII get rid of the Ottoman threat; on his side were numerous Turkish chiefs who had been displaced by the spread of the Ottoman empire and that wanted revenge. Timur blocked the Ottomans from nearby water sources, so that they went into battle thirsty, and he planned to repeat the fire attack that had worked so well in Delhi; this time, soldiers launched "Greek fire" (unquenchable streams of burning liquid, probably sulfur-based) into the enemy ranks from the backs of thirty-two specially trained elephants. Fighting began early on the morning of July 28 and continued for the entire day, but by the end of it the Ottoman troops had been driven back; Bayezid himself and two of his sons were taken captive and John of Constantinople, following the directions of Timur, guarded the Strait of Bosphorus with Byzantine galleys so that the defeated Ottoman troops could not flee across it and escape.

6. Why did Timur help John VII protect Constantinople? What did the Mongol warrior really want?

A6.—Pg. 629, ¶ 7 and Pg. 630, ¶ 3—Timur helped John VII protect Constantinople because his greatest desire was to recreate the old Mongol empire; Constantinople lay beyond the Mongol border past which Timur was not inclined to pass. After getting rid of the Ottoman threat in Constantinople, the Timurids raided deep into the Ottoman lands. Within a matter of weeks, the Ottoman empire had shrunk back to its core domains, with Timur claiming dominion over the rest.

7. How far did Timur get in achieving his goal of recreating the Mongol empire? What brought an end to his years of conquest?

A7.—Pg. 630, ¶ 6 to Pg. 632, ¶ 3—Timur had sacked the lands of the Golden Horde and claimed the lands of the Il-khanate, and he already controlled the Chagatai Khanate, so his final push was to reclaim the old land of the Yuan, the last quarter of the former Mongol empire. By January of 1405, he had made it as far as Utrar, 250 miles east of Samarkand, but was forced to halt by extreme cold and deep snows; he warmed himself with a three-day feast during which he ate little, but drank a lot. He slipped into a coma, emerging only long enough to declare that his grandson Pir Muhammad should inherit the throne of Samarkand before dying on February 18, 1405.

8. Who took over the western reaches of Timur's empire after his death?

A8.—Pg. 632, ¶ 4 & 5—The western reaches of Timur's empire were claimed by the Turks between the Caspian and the Black Seas; the tribes there were linked together into two separate confederations, the Black Sheep ("Qara Qoyunlu") and White Sheep ("Aq Qoyunlu") Turkomans. They occupied adjacent and overlapping territories, the White Sheep just south of the Black Sea where they took Mardin and the surrounding lands, the Black Sheep on the southwestern Caspian shore, where they captured Tabriz in 1406 and Baghdad in 1410. Soon the Black Sheep halted the White Sheep expansion and overran the remnants of the kingdom of Georgia, and then their chief, Qara Yusu, worked out a truce with the mamluks of Egypt that would guarantee the existence of the Black Sheep as an independent kingdom—temporarily, the most powerful Turkish kingdom in the east.

9. How did the Ottoman leader Mehmed come to make peace with Manuel?

A9.—Pg. 632, ¶ 6 to Pg. 633, ¶ 1—When Mehmed decided to challenge his brother Musa, he asked Manuel for help; Manuel obliged him and gave him warships and troops to win the fight against his brother. When Mehmed came out on top, he was grateful to Manuel. Then Mehmed signed a treaty of peace with Manuel and went to work rebuilding his army, firming up his control over his Serbian lands, and battling to keep the Black Sheep back.

10. Why did Manuel rebuild the Hexamilion Wall?

A10.—Pg. 633, ¶ 3 & 4—Manuel rebuilt the Hexamilion Wall because rebuilding it guaranteed that the Turks would be able to conquer this final outpost of Byzantium only by sea. Manuel did have a peace treaty with Mehmed, but he did not put all of his faith in the sultan's goodwill. Just in case the Turks decided to attack, Manuel built the wall and counted on the Byzantine navy to keep the peninsula safe.

Section III: Critical Thinking

The student may not use his text to answer this question.

Vlad the Impaler, son of Vlad Dracul, is well known as the inspiration for Bram Stoker's 1897 *Dracula*. Yet the violent and bloodthirsty Wallachian prince has, in reality, very little in common with Stoker's demonic vampire. Do some research and find out why Vlad the Impaler is often cited as the real Dracula, even if he really was nothing like the famous vampire. Write a paragraph explaining your findings, and make sure to give credit to your sources.

There is a wealth of information about Vlad the Impaler and his relation to Bram Stoker's Dracula *available on the internet. The student's answer should clearly address the relation between Vlad and Dracula. The student may include how the two men were different, but he does not have to include that in his answer. The student may use the citation style of his choosing. Chicago Style footnotes are used in the example answer.*

EXAMPLE ANSWER:

According to the article "The Real Dracula: Vlad the Impaler" by Marc Lallanilla, Bram Stoker named Dracula after Vlad the Impaler. Vlad's father was inducted into the knightly order "The Order of the Dragon" in 1431, giving him a new surname: Dracul. Lallanilla writes that "Dracul came from the old Romanian world for dragon, 'drac.'" Vlad Dracul's son then became known as "the son of Dracul." In old Romanian, the word for "the son of Dracul" was "Draculea," or as we know it, "Dracula." Lallanilla also explains that in modern Romanian, "drac" refers to the devil.[9] Vlad the Impaler was a ruthless ruler; in fact, *Business Insider*

---

9. Marc Lallanilla, "The Real Dracula: Vlad the Impaler," *Livescience.com,* last updated October 24, 2014, date accessed June 1, 2016, http://www.businessinsider.co.id/most-ruthless-leaders-2016-4/9/#.V06-iWNGPH0

names him as one of the "25 most ruthless leaders of all time." Elena Holodny explains that the principality of Wallachia was in disarray when Vlad became the ruler, so "Vlad invited his rivals all to a banquet, where he stabbed and impaled them all. (Impaling was his favorite method of torture.)" She continues, "Though it's difficult to determine whether this story was embellished, it characterizes Vlad's rule: He tried to bring stability and order to Wallachia through extremely ruthless methods."[10] It is clear that Bram Stoker used Vlad the Impaler's family name, Dracul, the name's relation to something evil, the devil, and his brutal ruling style as the inspiration for the name of his famous vampire.

Section IV: Map Exercise

1. Trace the rectangular frame of Map 89.1 in black.

2. Using your blue pencil, trace the outline of the coast through the Mediterranean and around the Middle East and Far East, including the Black Sea, Persian Gulf, and Caspian Sea. As usual, you need not include all the small islands around Greece. Trace the lines of the Indus and Sutlej. Repeat until the contours are familiar.

3. Using contrasting colors, trace the outlines of the regions of Byzantium, the Ottoman Turks, the Burji Dynasty, Georgia, and Timur's Empire. Trace the mountains with small peaks. Repeat until the contours are familiar.

4. Using a new sheet of paper, trace the outline of the map's frame in black. Then using your regular pencil with an eraser, draw the outline of the coast through the Mediterranean and around the Middle East and Far East, including the Black Sea, Persian Gulf, and Caspian Sea. Draw the lines of the Indus and Sutlej. Draw the outlines of the regions of Byzantium, the Ottoman Turks, the Burji Dynasty, Georgia, and Timur's Empire. Draw the mountains with small peaks. When you are happy with your map, lay it over the original. Erase and re-draw any lines more than ½″ off of the original.

5. Label each of the regions which you traced and drew. Then study carefully the areas of Hungary, Wallachia, Thessalonica, Caucasus, White Sheep, Black Sheep, the Sayyids, Kirman, Malwa, Gujarat, Deccan, Bahmani, and Vijayanagara. When they are familiar, close the book. Label each one on your map, and check your work against the original. Make any necessary corrections.

6. Study carefully the locations of Constantinople, Mardin, Edessa, Aleppo, Damascus, Cairo, Baghdad, Tabriz, Tbilisi, Isfahan, Yazd, Shiraz, Balkh, Utrar, Samarkand, Multan, Lahore, and Delhi. When they are familiar, close the book. Mark and label each one on your map. Lay your map over the original, and check your work. Correct any marks more than ¼″ off of the original.

7. Mark the Battle of Ankara, Khyber Pass, and Fort Bhatner.

---

10. Elena Holodny, "The 25 most ruthless leaders of all time," *Business Insider,* last updated April 26, 2016, date accessed June 1, 2016, http://www.businessinsider.co.id/most-ruthless-leaders-2016-4/9/#.V06-iWNGPH0

Chapter Ninety

The Withdrawal of the Ming

The student may use her text when answering the questions in sections I and II.

Section I: Who, What, Where

Write a one or two-sentence answer explaining the significance of each item listed below.

Cheng Ho—**Pg. 638, ¶ 4—Cheng Ho, Grand Eunuch, the superintendent of all royal eunuchs, was the commander in chief of the six massive naval expeditions launched by the Yongle Emperor from the coast of China between 1405 and 1422.**

Esen Tayisi—**Pg. 642, ¶ 7 and Pg. 643, ¶ 3 & 7—Esen Tayisi inherited the leadership of the Oirat and was very good at welding more and more of the surrounding Mongol tribes and petty states into his following. After leading a successful defense against Ming soldiers in 1449, Esen Tayisi was murdered by his own men in 1455 during a sharp struggle between the tribes over control of the coalition.**

Fang Xia—**Pg. 638, ¶ 2—Fang Xia, Jianwen's chief counselor, refused to recognize the new Yongle Emperor as legitimate. He was sentenced to death by public dismemberment by Zhu Di: *zhe*, a version of drawing and quartering that could take as long as three days.**

Forbidden City—**Pg. 640, ¶ 4—Forbidden City was the name of the Yongle Emperor's gargantuan new royal residence, a city within the city, for use by the emperor and the royal family alone. The Forbidden City was built in Beijing, the new name for Dadu, the Yongle Emperor's personal capital.**

Hongxi—**Pg. 642, ¶ 2—Hongxi followed his father the Yongle Emperor as leader of the Ming. Hongxi ruled for only two years.**

Jianwen—**Pg. 638, ¶ 1—Jianwen, oldest son of the dead crown prince of the Hongwu emperor, succeeded the Hongwu emperor on the throne. After three years of civil war, Zhu Di and his army marched into Nanjing in 1402 and burned down young Jianwen's imperial palace, where Jianwen was said to have died (but rumors of his reappearance would spread constantly through the rest of his uncle's reign).**

Le Loi/Binh Dinh Vuong—**Pg. 640, ❡ 6 & 7, Pg. 641, ❡ 2 and Pg. 642, ❡ 5**—Le Loi, a northern Dai Viet aristocrat, organized a resistance to the Chinese occupation; at first, he chose to throw his weight behind the restoration of the old and vanished Tran dynasty, picking an inoffensive Tran figurehead and proclaiming that he would help return the Tran to the throne, but then he simply led the rebellion himself, under the royal name Binh Dinh Vuong: Pacifying King of the Dai Viet. For ten years Le Loi and Nguyen Trai fought a guerilla war against the Ming, and in 1428, after the Ming soldiers withdrew, he started the Le dynasty, which would rule Dai Viet until the eighteenth century.

Nguyen Trai—**Pg. 640, ❡ 7 to Pg. 641, ❡ 2**—Nguyen Trai, Binh Dinh Vuong's right-hand man and chief general, helped to rally the Dai Viet countryside behind Binh Dinh Vuong's cause and for ten years he carried on a guerrilla war that sucked away at the Ming army.

Oirat—**Pg. 637, ❡ 2**—Oirat was the name given to a coalition of four western Mongol tribes that formed after the Yuan dynasty fell apart.

Ma-Huan—**Pg. 638, ❡ 4 & 5**—Ma-Huan, geographer, accompanied Cheng Ho on five of the six massive naval expeditions launched from China under the Yongle Emperor. Ma-Huan made note of the customs, the landscapes, and the food and drink of a dozen different countries.

Wang Zhen—**Pg. 642, ❡ 8 and Pg. 643, ❡ 3**—Wang Zhen, Zhengtong's chief eunuch, advised the Ming emperor to personally lead an army against the Oirat in 1449. Wang Zhen was killed in the fighting against the Oirat; he was probably murdered by his own angry and terrified men.

Xuande—**Pg. 642, ❡ 2, 3 & 7**—Xuande, son and successor of Hongxi, decided to halt Ming sea expeditions and withdraw from the war in Dai Viet. Xuande died after just ten years on the throne.

Zhengtong—**Pg. 642, ❡ 7 & 8 and Pg. 643, 3-5**—Zhengtong, who followed his father Xuande as Ming emperor, personally led his men against the Oirat in 1449; the attack was a disaster and Zhengtong was taken prisoner. His brother took control of the Ming and Zhengtong was named Grand Senior Emperor, but when he returned to Beijing to take back his throne, he found little support, so he lived out the rest of his life within the walls of the Forbidden City.

Zhu Di—**Pg. 638, ❡ 1-4, and Pg. 640, ❡ 3 & 4**—Zhu Di, the Hongwu Emperor's fourth son and military governor of the old Mongol city of Dadu, drove Jianwen off the throne and then named himself the Yongle Emperor. The Yongle Emperor ordered six massive naval expeditions of conquest between 1405 and 1422, he took the Dai Viet as vassals and renamed their kingdom Jiaozhi, he pushed the Ming border all the way out to the Amur river, and he renamed Dadu Beijing and there built the Forbidden City.

Section II: **Comprehension**

Write a two or three-sentence answer to each of the following questions.

1. What happened to the Yuan dynasty after the Hongwu emperor came into power?

A1.—Pg. 637, ¶ 1 & 2—After the Hongwu emperor took control of China, the inner workings of the country had been entirely revamped, opposition mowed down, and the remnants of the Yuan dynasty were thoroughly beaten. The ruined Yuan court, retreating to the north, hunkered down at the old Mongol city of Karakorum, but the Ming army pushed into it, sacked and burned it, and took seventy thousand men prisoner. The title of Yuan emperor survived, claimed by more and more distant relations of the long-dead Kublai Khan, but with the center of the Mongol homeland violated, the Yuan name lost the last of its cohesive power, digging into its last remaining territory in the northeast.

2. Why did the Hongwu emperor build a string of fortresses out into the steppe country?

A2.—Pg. 637, ¶ 3—The Hongwu emperor knew that there was a distinction between Chinese and barbarian, though he wasn't exactly sure where the physical line was drawn between the civilized Chinese and the barbarian Yuan Mongols. The Hongwu emperor was cautious by nature and did not want to launch unnecessary campaigns, so he aimed to chase the Mongols out of China and then build a border to keep them out. By the end of his reign, in 1398, he had built a string of fortresses out into the steppe country, bases from which to raid deep into Northern Yuan and Oirat lands.

3. How did Zhu Di try and establish legitimacy at the start of his rule?

A3.—Pg. 638, ¶ 2—Zhu Di established legitimacy at the start of his rule by naming himself the Yongle Emperor and ordering that the brief rule of his nephew be wiped from the official Ming record books. Then, he crushed all possible opposition with an immediate purge: tens of thousands of Jianwen's supporters (or suspected supporters) were murdered. He even ordered the boy's chief counselor, Fang Xia, sentenced to death by public dismemberment after Fang Xia refused to recognize him as legitimate.

4. Where were the naval expeditions ordered by Zhu Di heading, and what was the intention behind them?

A4.— Pg. 638, ¶ 4 & 5—The six massive naval expeditions ordered by Zhu Di were heading out to China's western ports: first to India and then to the shores of south Asia, to Sri Lanka, to the islands of the Maldives, to Mecca, and finally to the eastern edge of the African continent. The intention behind the expeditions was conquest, not diplomacy, with the orders that "Upon arriving at foreign cities, capture those barbarian kings who resist civilization and are disrespectful [and] exterminate those bandit soldiers that indulge in violence and plunder." Zhu Di's intentions were clear because he sent out hundreds and hundreds of nine-masted ships, thousands of deck-mounted bronze cannons, and tens of thousands of Ming marines packed aboard to carry out his will.

5. How did the Dai Vet kingdom become known, once again, as the Jiaozhi?

A5.—Pg. 640, ¶ 1 & 2—The Yongle Emperor sent an army of five hundred thousand south, supposedly to restore the Tran dynasty to the throne of the Dai Viet, and to remove the usurping Ho ruler. However, once the Ming soldiers had destroyed Ho power—the capital city was overrun in 1406, the usurping king Ho and his son taken prisoner in 1407—the Emperor Yongle found himself unwilling to let it out of his hands. Instead, he sent an administrator to run the country, formally annexing it as a province of Ming China, and he renamed it Jiaozhi, its name in ancient times, when it had been claimed by the Tang dynasty.

6. What did Nguyen Trai do to make the uneducated villagers in Dai Viet believe that Le Loi was picked by the heavens to rule?

A6.—Pg. 641, ¶ 1—Nguyen Trai is said to have gone into the forest and written "Le Loi is the king and Nguyen Trai his servant" with animal fat on hundreds of leaves. When the ants ate away the fat, the message showed up as perforated letters, making the uneducated villagers in the Dai Viet countryside believe the rebel leader was chosen by the heavens to rule. They saw the leaves as a supernatural prophecy.

7. How did Emperor Xuande start his reign? How did his advisors react?

A7.—Pg. 642, ¶ 3-5—Emperor Xuande, faced with a shrinking treasury and an unending war in the south, chose to halt the sea expeditions and withdraw from the troublesome Dai Viet war at the start of his reign. His advisors were divided, half of them protesting that withdrawal would be a dangerous sign of weakness, the other half pointing out that the Dai Viet kingdom was always a problem, and that no Chinese dynasty had ever managed to hold on to it without headaches. The decision was made when, after a series of concerted attacks on the Chinese front, at least ninety thousand Ming soldiers had fallen in the Dai Viet jungles; Ming soldiers were withdrawn after Xuande called a halt and then the final sea expedition of the Ming returned in 1433.

8. Describe the Oirat advance into Ming territory after the death of Xuande.

A8.—Pg. 642, ¶ 7—As Emperor Zhengtong's advisors argued over strategy, the Oirat advance pushed the Ming front steadily backwards. Frantic fortification of the Great Wall and a series of new barriers inside it—the "inner Great Wall," *nei-ch'ang-ch'eng*— did little to hold the Oirat off. By the time Zhengtong turned twenty-one, Esen Tayisi had advanced to within two hundred miles of Beijing itself.

9. What happened to the Ming army after they decided to turn around from the Oirat front and head home?

A9.—Pg. 643, ¶ 2 & 3—As the Ming army neared the Oirat front they passed heaps of unburied Ming corpses, victims of a recent Oirat attack on the nearby fortress of Datong, two weeks earlier. After seeing the eerily empty landscape, and more and more piles of bodies, Emperor Zhengtong decided to turn around and go back to Beijing, but it was too late: Esen Tayisi had silently surrounded them, cutting off their escape route. With the Ming army camped at Tumu, the Oirat suddenly emerged, cutting down thousands with a hail of arrows and then charging over the bodies to scatter the rest; the eunuch Wang Zhen died in the fighting, and Emperor

Zhengtong himself, recognizing defeat, sat down on the ground and waited silently to be taken prisoner.

10. Why did Esen Tayisi let Zhengtong go free? How was Zhengtong treated when he returned to Beijing?

A10.—Pg. 643, ¶ 4 & 5—After Esen Tayisi captured Zhengtong, he sent a demand for a massive ransom payment to Beijing; had expected the Ming to hand over cash to retrieve their emperor without quarrel but instead, the royal court at Beijing simply declared the captive Zhengtong to be Grand Senior Emperor and crowned his younger brother Junior Emperor in his place. Disgusted, Esen Tayisi set his young prisoner free; he probably hoped that the merciful act would eventually give him a foothold in Beijing. However, when Zhengtong returned home, he found his brother less than pleased to see him and his people uninclined to restore him to full reign, so he spent the rest of his life in the Forbidden City, walled away from his people, remote and withdrawn.

Section III: **Critical Thinking**

The student may not use her text to answer this question.

Emperor Yongle was a big spender. When an ambassador from Baghdad visited the capital city Beijing in 1421, he was asked to attend a royal feast where a thousand different dishes were served: "geese, fowls, roasted meat, fresh and dry fruits . . . filberts, jujubes, walnuts, peeled chestnuts, lemons, garlics and onions pickled in vinegar . . . and various kinds of intoxicants." The diplomats present were required to perform eight prostrations in front of the emperor and in return they were loaded with lavish presents of silver, weapons, hawks, and horses. This is just one example of Yongle's lavish ruling style. While things looked good from the outside, the emperor's massive spending had severe consequences on Ming power. For this critical thinking question, write a paragraph that connects Emperor Yongle's expansiveness to later Ming isolationist policy.

In the answer to this question, the student should connect Emperor Yongle's overreaching ruling style to later Ming problems that were a result of Ming overextension. Emperor Yongle was ambitious: at the start of his reign he launched six naval expeditions of conquest. These expeditions cost a lot of money—he employed tens of thousands of Ming soldiers and equipped them with hundreds and hundreds of nine-masted ships and thousands of deck-mounted bronze cannons. At the same time, Emperor Yongle led five different ground campaigns against the Oirats and the Norther Yuan. He also sent five hundred thousand men south to Dai Viet; he formally annexed the kingdom as a province of Ming China and sent an administrator to run the country. And during all of this fighting, he rebuilt Dadu as his own capital city of Beijing, complete with a gargantuan new royal residence called the Forbidden City.

All of this would have been well and good if no one was fighting back. However, the war with the Dai Viet was expensive, as was the upkeep of the northern border. Instead of funneling all of his funds towards war, Yongle continued to spend lavishly on his lifestyle. This was an impossible course of action. When Xuande came to power, the royal treasury was not able to keep up all that Yongle had started. For ten years the Dai Viet had been chipping away at the Ming army, luring soldiers into the jungle; they never came out. This was very expensive for

Ming China. While some advisors told Xuande that he had to keep fighting in the south, other said that no Chinese emperor was ever able to hold on to the Dai Viet. Perhaps if Xuande had more money, money that Yongle had spent on his Forbidden City or on great feasts, he would have been able to fund a larger offensive in the south. But Xuande didn't have the money or the manpower, so he retreated and Le Loi started the Le dynasty. At the same time, Xuande put an end to the sea expeditions. He didn't have any more money to fund China's sea expansion, so he had to call off that plan, too.

The final break in Ming power came in 1449 when Emperor Zhengtong led an army against the Oirat. Esen Tayisi had pushed the Ming border steadily backwards. When Zhengtong met the Oirat, he was outsmarted and his men were slaughtered. After Zhengtong's defeat, the days of ambitious military campaigns, wide-ranging sea voyages, and international diplomacy trickled to an end. No new offenses were planned, no campaigns to foreign lands, no diplomatic missions demanding tribute. The manpower and tax revenue remaining to the Ming all went to the support of a passive internal policy: the fortification of boundary walls, a retreat to the safe land within them.

Yongle's extreme spending caused the Ming empire to fold in on itself. After his death there was little money left in the treasury to continue his lavish and warring ways. By the time Zhengtong was tucked away in the Forbidden City, Ming policy became about sustaining what was already there and protecting what was left within its own borders.

EXAMPLE ANSWER:

Emperor Yongle was ambitious: at the start of his reign he launched six naval expeditions of conquest. These expeditions cost a lot of money—he employed tens of thousands of Ming soldiers and equipped them with hundreds and hundreds of nine-masted ships and thousands of deck-mounted bronze cannons. At the same time, Emperor Yongle led five different ground campaigns against the Oirats and the Norther Yuan. He also sent five hundred thousand men south to Dai Viet; he formally annexed the kingdom as a province of Ming China and sent an administrator to run the country. And during all of this fighting, he rebuilt Dadu as his own capital city of Beijing, complete with a gargantuan new royal residence called the Forbidden City.

All of this would have been well and good if no one was fighting back. However, the war with the Dai Viet was expensive, as was the upkeep of the northern border. Instead of funneling all of his funds towards war, Yongle continued to spend lavishly on his lifestyle. This was an impossible course of action. When Xuande came to power, the royal treasury was not able to keep up all that Yongle had started. For ten years the Dai Viet had been chipping away at the Ming army, luring soldiers into the jungle; they never came out. This was very expensive for Ming China. Perhaps if Xuande had more money, money that Yongle had spent on his Forbidden City or on great feasts, he would have been able to fund a larger offensive in the south. But Xuande didn't have the money or the manpower, so he retreated and Le Loi started the Le dynasty. At the same time, Xuande put an end to the sea expeditions. He didn't have any more money to fund China's sea expansion, so he had to call off that plan, too.

The final break in Ming power came in 1449 when Emperor Zhengtong led an army against the Oirat. With little money left in the treasury and the awareness of Esen Tayisi's strength,

the royal counselors were divided over strategy. Zhengtong proceeded nonetheless; he was outsmarted and his men were slaughtered. After Zhengtong's defeat, the days of ambitious military campaigns, wide-ranging sea voyages, and international diplomacy came to an end. The manpower and tax revenue remaining to the Ming all went to the support the fortification of boundary walls. Yongle's extreme spending caused the Ming empire to fold in on itself. After his death there was little money left in the treasury to continue his lavish and warring ways. By the time Zhengtong was tucked away in the Forbidden City, Ming policy became about sustaining what was already there and protecting what was left within its own borders.

Chapter Ninety-One

Failure

The student may use his text when answering the questions in sections I and II.

Section I: Who, What, Where

Write a one or two-sentence answer explaining the significance of each item listed below.

Albert—**Pg. 650, ¶ 1—Albert, the Duke of Austria and Sigismund's son-in-law, claimed the right to all of Sigismund's titles. He had no difficulty ascending the Hungarian throne, and in March of 1438 the German electors agreed to recognize his claim to Germany, but Bohemia rejected him.**

Beatrice Lascaris—**Pg. 645, ¶ 5 and Pg. 646, ¶ 1 & 2—Beatrice Lascaris, wife of Facino Cane, married Filippo Maria Visconti after her husband died of fever. The match was never happy; the two coexisted in mutual hostility until 1418, when Filippo Maria Visconti accused Beatrice Lascaris of adultery and ordered her beheaded.**

Compacts of Basel—**Pg. 649, ¶ 5—Compacts of Basel, the *Compactata*, was a compromise made between the hard-line Hussites and the moderate Hussite-Catholic alliance, sworn out in 1436, that recognized the Hussites as part of the Catholic Church although different in practice and belief. The pact was the first time that western Christianity had recognized the existence of a distinct sect as inside Christianity, yet outside pure Catholic doctrine.**

Eugene IV—**Pg. 648, ¶ 2 & 5, Pg. 649, ¶ 1, and Pg. 651, ¶ 5—Eugene IV, a Venetian who replaced Martin V as pope after his death, kept falling out with the attendees at the Council of Basel, which held up Sigismund's coronation as Holy Roman Emperor. Later, at the Council of Florence, Eugene IV promised John VIII three hundred warships and twelve thousand florins for the fight against the Turks.**

Facino Cane—**Pg. 645, ¶ 5 & 6—Facino Cane, a soldier of fortune, ruled Milan with his wife Beatrice Lascaris through the puppet duke Gian Maria. Facino Cane died of fever in 1412.**

Felix V—**Pg. 650, ¶ 3 & 4—Felix V, a northern Italian aristocrat, was elected by the members of the Council of Basel that refused to go to Florence as the "antipope." While most of**

Christendom recognized that the Council of Basel had become the Council of Florence, for the next ten years, Felix V continued to claim the title of pope.

Filippo Maria Visconti—**Pg. 645, ¶ 6 to Pg. 646, ¶ 2-5**—Filippo Maria Visconti, younger brother of Gian Maria, became Duke of Milan after Gian Maria's murder, and in order to increase his power, he married Beatrice Lascaris, the widow of Facino Cane. After hiring Francesco Carmagnola and regaining his lost territories in Milan and claiming Genoa, Filippo Maria Visconti was at the top of the Italian pyramid, ruling northern Italy with something close to an emperor's power.

Francesco Carmagnola—**Pg. 646, ¶ 4**—Francesco Carmagnola was a mercenary hired by Filippo Maria Visconti to head the Milanese army. By 1421 Francesco Carmagnola had reconquered for Milan almost all of the territories that had fractured away from the Duke's control and as a bonus, he added Genoa, which changed its alliance from the mad king of France to Filippo Maria instead.

Gian Maria—**Pg. 645, ¶ 5 & 6**—Gian Maria, the older son of Gian Galeazzo Visconti, fell under the control of the soldier of fortune Facino Cane and his wife Beatrice Lascaris; for a decade, this formidable couple ruled Milan through the puppet duke, while the cities and lands that had once been under Milanese control were claimed, one by one, by other Milanese captains and merchants. Gian Maria was murdered in 1412 by a band of Facino Cane's enemies.

John VIII—**Pg. 650, ¶ 7 and Pg. 651, ¶ 4-7**—John VIII, son and successor of Manuel II, went to the Council of Florence to ask the Christian west to unify against the Ottoman east for the sake of Constantinople's survival. John VIII arrived home in February 1440 after the Council of Florence, however he did not publish the Decrees of Union in Constantinople because he realized that the regular churchmen of Constantinople were not behind the compromise.

John Zizka—**Pg. 646, ¶ 7 and Pg. 647, ¶ 2**—John Zizka, veteran of wars against the Teutonic Order of Prussia, an ex-captain of the dead Wenceslaus IV, rose up as the leader of the Hussite rebellion. John Zizka fought against Sigismund until his death from the plague.

Murad II—**Pg. 650, ¶ 6 & 7**—Murad II, son of Mehmed, followed his father as leader of the Ottoman empire. Soon after taking the throne, Murad II laid siege to Constantinople but eased up in 1424 after Manuel II paid him off.

Prokop the Shaven—**Pg. 647, ¶ 2 and Pg. 649, ¶ 5**—Prokop the Shaven was a scholar-soldier that became the leader of the Hussite rebellion after the death of John Zizka. Prokop the Shaven led the hard-line Hussites in a siege on the the Catholic city of Plzen after the Council of Basel only partially conceded to Hussite demands.

Section II: **Comprehension**

Write a two or three-sentence answer to each of the following questions.

1. Why did Filippo Maria Visconti marry Beatrice Lascaris? Why was the relationship between them so unhappy?

A1.—Pg. 646, ¶ 1 & 2—Filippo Maria Visconti, twenty at the time of his accession, married the forty-year-old Beatrice Lascaris because he was able to claim control of her alliances and also of her rather extensive family lands. However, Filippo Maria Visconti had an odd and unattractive personality; he was intelligent, and a shrewd user of men, but pathologically frightened of thunder, obese, and so self-conscious about his hooked nose and vast girth that he lived in secret rooms, changing them frequently, scuttling away from his subjects in the street and refusing to allow his portrait painted. Beatrice, in turn, was a powerful and wealthy woman twenty years his senior, which resulted in a tense relationship that ended in 1418 when Filippo Maria accused his wife of adultery and ordered her beheaded.

2. How did Filippo Maria Visconti's status change after he hired Francesco Carmagnola?

A2.—Pg. 646, ¶ 4 & 5—Filippo Maria Visconti's reach of power grew after he hired Francesco Carmagnola: Carmagnola had reconquered for Milan almost all of the territories that had fractured away from the Duke's control by 1421, plus Genoa. Though the conquests were vicious and unsparing—one account says that, at the city of Piacenza, so many citizens were slaughtered by the Milanese that only three people remained alive within its walls—they set Filippo Maria at the top of the Italian pyramid. In name, he was a subject duke of the Holy Roman Empire; but in practice, he ruled the north of Italy with something close to an emperor's power.

3. What demands were made by the Hussites in the Four Articles of Prague?

A3.—Pg. 647, ¶ 1—The Articles of Prague asked the king of Germany, first, to allow open preaching of the Gospel without restriction; second, to permit the Eucharist served *sub utraque specie*, "in both kinds" (in the Bohemian churches, a practice had evolved since the twelfth century of serving the bread to the Christians in the pews, but reserving the wine for ordained priests alone); third, to require all clergy to take a vow of poverty, giving up the Church's right to accumulate wealth; and finally, to punish actions "against divine law" (*legi divinae contrariae*) openly and promptly. Specifics were also mentioned in the Articles: drunkenness and theft; adultery and wantonness; unjustified tax and interest rate hikes; and the sudden raising of feudal rents were all to be banned. The Hussites fought against all entitlement and privilege.

4. Why did the Hussites include serving the Eucharist "in both kinds" in the Four Articles of Prague?

A4.—Pg. 647, *—The practice of serving the bread to the Christians in the pews, but reserving the wine for ordained priests alone, which was defended by both Peter Lombard and Thomas Aquinas, seems to have grown out the doctrine of transubstantiation; if the bread and wine are literally transformed into Christ's body and blood, taking part of either means that the

worshipper has shared in the consumption of Christ, so both are not necessary. Because the wine was more easily spilled and abused (and, possibly, more expensive), many priests throughout France, Italy, and Germany refused to serve wine to the laity. The practice was resented by the Hussites for drawing a sharp line of privilege between ordained and nonordained believers, so they included it in the Four Articles of Privilege, which was a list of grievances against the privilege and entitlement of the clergy.

5. How did the Hussites respond to Sigismund after he refused to grant the Four Articles of Prague?

A5.—Pg. 647, ¶ 2 & 3—After Sigismund refused to grant the Articles of Prague, he lost more and more ground to the Hussites. In 1421, while Sigismund was stalled outside Prague, the Bohemian Diet, the gathered princes of the kingdom, declared him deposed. By 1427, the Hussites were venturing out of Bohemia into Germany, raiding and burning in revenge for German attacks on their homes.

6. Why did Sigismund have to negotiate with Filippo Maria Visconti in order to become Holy Roman Emperor? What were the terms of their negotiation?

A6.—Pg. 648, ¶ 2 & 3—Sigismund had to negotiate with Filippo Maria Visconti because, even if he convinced Eugene IV to give him the imperial crown, he could not march through the Lombard lands towards Rome unless he treatied with or defeated Milan. As an incentive, he offered imperial soldiers to aid Milan in its battles with Florence and Venice, and imperial friendship with Milan against those two rival cities. In return, Filippo Maria Visconti agreed to allow Sigismund to enter Milan and be crowned with the Iron Crown of the Lombards.

7. How did Sigismund display his power after being crowned Holy Roman Emperor in 1433?

A7.—Pg. 649, ¶ 2—After Sigismund was crowned Holy Roman Emperor, he showed his power by adopting a new seal: a double-headed eagle, representing his dual identity as king of Germany and Holy Roman Emperor. Later in that same year, he returned to the Council of Basel to weigh in on its discussions and negotiations and speaking to the assembled priests in Latin, he used the feminine gender for a neuter noun; when a nearby canon tactfully corrected him, Sigismund retorted, "I am the Emperor of the Romans, and above grammar" (*Ego Imperator Romanus sum, et super grammaticam*). Sigismund's refusal to follow the rules of grammar was another way that he showed his power.

8. What terms did the Council of Basel agree upon regarding the Hussites? How did the Hussites react to the Council's recommendations?

A8.—Pg. 649, ¶ 3 & 4—On November 26, 1433 the Council of Basel agreed to withdraw condemnation of the Hussites as heretics, to allow Bohemian laypeople to receive the cup of wine at the Eucharist, and to permit preaching by anyone who was "commissioned" by a "superior." The Hussite leaders in Prague, receiving this news from Basel, were inclined to accept the partial concession because Bohemia was a small country; for over a decade, the regular business of trading, farming, and living had been completely disrupted by war, with over a hundred thousand men dead from the fighting, and waves of plague sweeping across the country again and again. However, the Hussite party had subdivided, and the most radical of the Hussites refused to agree to any compromise.

9. Describe Sigismund's death.

A9.—Pg. 649, ¶ 7—Sigismund died on December 9, 1437 after serving as Holy Roman Emperor for four years. He was a few months away from his seventieth birthday, probably suffering from diabetes; the toes on his left foot had been amputated not long before. Feeling the end approach, he ordered himself dressed in the imperial robes and managed to get himself onto the imperial throne, where he sat and waited for death to come.

10. How did the Council of Basel end up dividing and producing an antipope?

A10.—Pg. 650, ¶ 2 & 3—While the Council of Basel had semisettled the Hussite question, a plethora of other matters, including various church reforms and the possibility of attempting to draw the Greek Orthodox church of Constantinople back into the Roman fold, were unsettled. Factions had developed within the Council. Pope Eugene IV and his supporters insisted on moving the deliberations to Florence, where the wealthy merchant-politician Cosimo de'Medici had assured them of a welcome, while a stubborn rump Council remained behind, insisting that the pope had acted without proper consideration of the Council's authority, and elected a replacement: a northern Italian aristocrat who became the "antipope" Felix V.

11. What was the "Decrees of Union," and why didn't John VIII publish the document in Constantinople?

A11.—Pg. 651, ¶ 4-7—The Decrees of Union was the document that listed the compromise statements made at the Council of Florence that supposedly brought together the Roman Catholic church and the Greek Orthodox church. When John VIII and his party arrived back in Constantinople after the Council, the priests who had accompanied the emperor retorted, "We have sold our faith overseas, we have exchanged piety for impiety!" because only the very top levels of the Greek church and court were behind the compromise; the priests who labored in Constantinople's churches and the laity in the pew saw it as a sellout. John VIII delayed in publishing the Decrees of Union because he saw that the people would not be behind the document.

Section III: Critical Thinking

The student may not use his text to answer this question.

The Hussite rebellion was driven by the group's frustration with the entitlement and privilege of the Catholic clergy. Write a paragraph that explains how the behavior of the clergy at the Council of Florence, in particular during the time of John VIII's request for the Christian west to unify against the Ottomans, reinforced the complaints of the Hussites.

The Hussites were bothered by the extreme privilege of the clergy. This is clear in the complaints lodged against the church in the Four Articles of Prague. The Hussites were fed up of being told they were not holy enough to preach the Gospel, that they were not permitted to eat the body of Christ and drink of his blood, of the outrageous spending of the clergy, of the clergy's drinking, and their unjustified taxes and interest hikes and sudden raising of feudal rents. All of the actions represented, to the Hussites, the clergy's belief that they were better than everyone else. The Hussites believed this attitude needed to be tempered.

The clergy confirmed all the complaints of the Hussites in their actions at the Council of Florence. John VIII went to the Council of Florence to ask the Christian west to unify against the Ottoman east for the sake of Constantinople's survival. On page 651 we learn that "even before the arrival of the emperor's party (which included seven hundred priests, court officials, theologians and scholars), the patriarch of Constantinople was infuriated by a message reminding him that he was supposed to kiss the foot of the pope when he was presented."

The Patriarch and the Pope were jousting over rank, each one wanting to be more important and privileged than the other. Then, "Once at the Council, the Byzantines and Europeans argued over the best seats, priority during meals, whether or not the Patriarch got to decorate his dais with curtains like the Pope, where Easter services should be held, and (eventually) church doctrines." The Council of Florence argued for over a year—from June 4, 1438 to July 5, 1439—"over the theological points that divided them: the exact way in which the Holy Spirit related to the other two persons of the Trinity, the use of leavened versus unleavened bread for the Eucharist, the precise degree of authority that the Pope held over the Greek church, and a host of related minutia." One wonders whether or not the two sides were arguing for what they believed in, or just to be right, and to have more power.

EXAMPLE ANSWER:

The Hussites were bothered by the extreme privilege of the clergy. This is clear in the complaints lodged against the church in the Four Articles of Prague. The Hussites were fed up of being told they were not holy enough to preach the Gospel, that they were too common to eat the body of Christ *and* drink of his blood, of the outrageous spending of the clergy, of the clergy's drinking, and their unjustified taxes and interest hikes and sudden raising of feudal rents. All of the actions represented, to the Hussites, the clergy's belief that they were better than everyone else.

The clergy confirmed all the complaints of the Hussites in their actions at the Council of Florence. Even before John VIII arrived, hoping to unify the Christian west against the Ottoman threat, the patriarch of Constantinople was complaining about having to kiss the pope's feet. He wanted to be more important than the pope, so he didn't want to defer to him upon his arrival. During the Council, the men argued over who had the best seats, who got to eat first, whether or not the Patriarch got to decorate his dais with curtains like the Pope, and where Easter services should be held. All of these petty arguments centered around being more important than the other side—they were all arguments about who was more privileged or entitled. The Council of Florence did eventually address church doctrine, though they argued about that, too. They feuded over the way the Holy Spirit related to the Trinity, what kind of bread to use for the Eucharist, and what authority the Pope held over the Greek church. One wonders whether or not the two sides were arguing for what they believed in, or just to be right, and to have more power. Ultimately, we can see that the Hussites were justified in their complaints about the clergy; they seemed to care most about their own comfort and power.

Section IV: **Map Exercises**

1. Trace the rectangular frame of the map in black.

2. Using your blue pencil, trace the outline of the coast around Italy and the surrounding coasts. Include all major islands and the small visible coast of Africa. Repeat until the contours are familiar.

3. Using contrasting colors, trace the areas of Naples and the Empire of Sigismund. Using your black pencil, trace the area of Bohemia within the Empire of Sigismund. Show the mountains with small peaks. Repeat until the contours are familiar.

4. Using a new sheet of paper, trace the rectangular outline of the frame in black. Using your regular pencil, draw all the coastline from Africa all around Italy, including the major islands. Use the frame of the map as a reference, erasing and re-drawing as necessary. Show the mountains with small peaks. When you are happy with your map, lay it over the original. Erase and re-draw any lines which are more than ¼″ off of the original.

5. Now label the areas of Germany, Bohemia, Austria, Hungary, Naples, and Sicily. Study carefully the locations of Plzen, Prague, Lipany, Basel, Milan, Pavia, Piacenza, Venice, Genoa, Florence, and Rome. When they are familiar for you, close the book. Mark and label each one on your map. Then lay your map over the original, and erase and re-mark any locations which are more than ¼″ off of the original.

Chapter Ninety-Two

Perpetual Slavery

The student may use her text when answering the questions in sections I and II.

Section I: **Who, What, Where**

Write a one or two-sentence answer explaining the significance of each item listed below.

Afonso V—**Pg. 657, ¶ 4 and Pg. 659, ¶ 3 to Pg. 660, ¶ 2—Afonso V, son of Edward, became king of Portugal at the age of six; his mother Eleanor and his uncle Peter of Coimbra served as his co-regents. After Afonso V came of age, he convinced pope Nicholas V to approve the enslavement of African captives, and he was able to get the church to protect the Portugese slave enterprise exclusively.**

Black Moors—**Pg. 658, ¶ 1—Black Moors was the name given to the inhabitants of the West African coast that were captured and sold into slavery by the Portuguese.**

Edward—**Pg. 655, ¶ 3, Pg. 656, ¶ 2 & 4 and Pg. 657, ¶ 4—Edward, the oldest son and heir of John of Portugal, was at his father's side when he attacked the port of Ceuta. Edward, crowned king of Portugal in 1433 after his father's death, led a failed attack on Tangiers and died eleven months later, either of the plague or from the deep despair and guilt he felt over his brother Ferdinand's imprisonment in Fez.**

Ferdinand—**Pg. 656, ¶ 4, Pg. 657, ¶ 2 & 3 and Pg. 658, ¶ 1—Ferdinand, the youngest of John I's sons, was taken prisoner after a failed Portuguese attack on Tangiers; he was supposed to be freed once the Portuguese gave up Ceuta, but the Cortes refused to honor Henry's promise to give up the city so Ferdinand remained in miserable captivity in Fez, chained in a cell at night and forced to do back-breaking work with other prisoners during the day. Ferdinand died in captivity in 1443.**

Gil Eannes—**Pg. 656, ¶ 2 & 3 and Pg. 658, ¶ 3—Gil Eannes was the first Portuguese explorer to sail past the Cape of Bojador where he found not the dreaded territory of rumor but calm seas and a long fertile coastline. Gil Eannes piloted one of the six raiding ships sent past Cape Blanc in 1444, ships that held men that would later charge into the West African forest to capture at least 250 slaves and kill many more.**

Guanches—**Pg. 654, ❡ 4 & 6**—Guanches was name of the African tribal people that lived on the Canary Islands. After Jean de Béthencourt became king of the Canary Islands, the Guanches were almost extinguished because they were taken to Europe as slaves.

Henry—**Pg. 655, ❡ 4 and Pg. 658, ❡ 1 & 2**—Henry, one of John of Portugal's sons, was appointed to be Ceuta's permanent governor after the Portuguese took control of the port. Henry was able to significantly increase the slave trade in Portugal by having sailors move past Cape Bojador and raid the West African coast for villagers and goods; he offered yearly rewards to expeditions that pushed into unknown territory and he protected his business by having his brother Peter Coimbra give him the exclusive right to control all trade that went south of the cape.

Jean de Béthencourt—**Pg. 654, ❡ 4 & 5**—Jean de Béthencourt, a French adventurer, landed in the Canary Islands in 1402 with the hope of conquering the islands and bringing Christianity to the people. After returning to the port of Cadiz with African tribal people to sell as slaves, Jean de Béthencourt asked to rule over the Canary Islands as a vassal of Castile; the king of Castile agreed and Jean de Béthencourt was made king of the Canary Islands.

Peter of Coimbra—**Pg. 657, ❡ 4, Pg. 658, ❡ 2 and Pg. 659, ❡ 3**—Peter of Coimbra, one of John of Portugal's sons, served as co-regent for Afonso, and in his capacity as regent, granted Henry the exclusive right to control all trade that went out south of Cape Bojador. Peter of Coimbra tried to fight and keep his position of power when Afonso V came of age but Afonso's troops defeated him in a pitched battle at the river Alfarrobeira, during which Peter was struck through the heart with an arrow.

Nicholas V—**Pg. 660, ❡ 2 & 3**—Nicholas V, Eugene IV's papal successor, agreed to view Portugal as conducting a crusade in Africa. In the papal bull *Dum Diversas,* and later in the charter confirming the bull, *Romanus Pontiflex,* the pope gave his seal of approval on the enslavement of African captives.

The Cortes—**Pg. 656, ❡ 4**—The Cortes was the name of Portugal's lawmaking assembly.

Section II: **Comprehension**

Write a two or three-sentence answer to each of the following questions.

1. How did Castile take control of the Canary Islands? What happened to the Canary Islands after they became part of Castilian territory?

A1.—Pg. 654, ❡ 4-6—In 1402, the French adventurer Jean de Béthencourt landed in the Canary Islands and immediately captured some of the inhabitants, an African tribal people known as the Guanches, and brought them back to the port of Cadiz to sell as slaves. Béthencourt then went to the court of Castile and asked the king to recognize him as king of the Canary Islands, vassal to the throne of Castile, and the king agreed. Before long the Guanches were almost extinguished, taken to Europe as slaves; the Canary Islands were repopulated by Castilian peasants brought over to farm and fish.

2. Why did John I of Portugal think he would be successful in taking over the port city of Ceuta?

A2.—Pg. 655, ¶ 1—John I of Portugal believed he would be successful in taking over the port city of Ceuta because he could convince his people that the battle for the port was part of the Reconquista, the Christian reconquest of Muslim-taken territories. He could do this because the port was in the hands of the North African sultan of the Marinids. John I also thought he would be successful because he had five legitimate sons and they had a lot of young ambitious male energy that could be funneled towards the conquest.

3. Describe the Portuguese assault on Ceuta. What did John I have to do in order to keep control of the port?

A3.—Pg. 655, ¶ 3 & 4—The Marinids abandoned the fight against the Portuguese at Ceuta after just one day. After the defenders fled, the mosque of Ceuta was thoroughly scrubbed out, refitted with Christian altars and crucifixes, cleansed with consecrated water, and all three Portugese princes were knighted by their father there. However, the Marinids launched constant attacks on Ceuta; John I spent a tremendous amount of money defending it, and in 1418 he was forced to send an army under his son Henry to help lift a Marinid siege of the city.

4. Why was Ceuta a disappointment to the Portuguese and how did Henry end up using the port? Why was this alternative use for the port also a disappointment at first?

A4.—Pg. 655, ¶ 5 to Pg. 656, ¶ 1—Ceuta was a disappointment to the Portuguese because Marinid resistance made it impossible to use the city as a base for expansion into the north of Africa. Henry held Ceuta secure and then made it a base to send out ships into the Mediterranean, through the Strait of Gibraltar, and then south towards Cape Bojador. This second use for the port was also a disappointment at first because men were afraid to sail past Cape Bojador because of an ancient rumor that any ship that passed the Cape would never be able to return.

5. What happened when Edward of Portugal and his brother Ferdinand attacked Tangiers?

A5.—Pg. 656, ¶ 5 to Pg. 657, ¶ 3—When Edward of Portugal and his brother Ferdinand arrived in Tangiers they were met by the the same Marinid official who had been governing Ceuta at the time of its conquest by the Portuguese. The official opened the gates of Tangier to draw the Portuguese army in, then sent a detachment around behind to trap them in front of the city, and when yet more Marinid reinforcements arrived, Henry was forced to give up. He managed to negotiate the freedom of most of his men by promising to give up Ceuta, but he was obliged to leave Ferdinand and twelve other Portuguese knights as hostages to assure the city's surrender.

6. How did Henry eventually get many captains to sail south of Cape Bojador?

A6.—Pg. 658, ¶ 1 & 2—During the time of Ferdinand's captivity, Henry's expeditions south of Cape Bojador continued. Sailors would take black Moors prisoner and the sell them at slave markets in Lisbon for a startling good price. When people saw how much money there was to be made in the slave trade, Henry founding himself with no shortage of captains willing to sail south past Cape Bojador.

7. Explain the purpose of the expeditions past Cape Bojador. What would happen if explorers did not find villagers?

A7.—Pg. 658, ¶ 2—The purpose of the expeditions past Cape Bojador was to search for new inlets, new rivers, and more slaves. Kidnapping and exploration went hand in hand; Portuguese ships would anchor off a new stretch of coast, the men would go ashore, and if they found villagers, they would capture them and bring their prisoners back on board. If not, they would sail farther south, making a note of what they saw.

8. What were some techniques used by the Portuguese to capture African slaves?

A8.—Pg. 658, ¶ 2 & 3—One technique used by the Portuguese to capture African slaves was to take a mother's child on a Portuguese boat and hope that maternal love would make the mother follow the child onto the boat, thus capturing both mother and child. Another technique was to send several ships at once to the African coast, as Henry did in 1444 ahead of his planned mass arrival of slaves into Lagos. The men on the expedition captured at least 250 slaves and killed many more as they charged into the West African forests with the battle cry "Santiago, São Jorge, and Portugal!"

9. How did the chronicler Zurara comfort himself in the face of the suffering slaves at the Lisbon market?

A9.—Pg. 659, ¶ 1—Zurara, who was moved by the suffering of the slaves at the Lisbon market, comforted himself by reflecting that they were still better off than before, when they had lived in "damnation of souls . . . like animals." Now, he believed, they were to be dressed and fed, and to be "loved and turned with good will to the path of the Faith." Their captivity had brought them into a Christian land where they would hear the Gospel; this, believed Zurara, was all to the good.

10. What documents written by the pope gave approval for the enslavement of African captives?

A10.—Pg. 660, ¶ 2 & 3—On June 18, 1452, Nicholas issued the papal bull *Dum Diversas*, giving Afonso V "full and free power, through the Apostolic authority . . . to invade, search out, capture, vanquish, and subdue all Saracens and pagans whatsoever, and other enemies of Christ wheresoever placed, and . . . to reduce their persons to perpetual slavery." *In perpetuam servitutem*: the bull had placed the papal seal of approval on the enslavement of the African captives. Three years later, when Nicholas V confirmed the bull once more in the charter *Romanus Pontifex*, he took the further step of outlining the geographical areas in which Afonso V could seize and enslave.

Section III: Critical Thinking

The student may not use her text to answer this question.

For this critical thinking question, read Susan Wise Bauer's article "Spoiling for a Fight, Fighting for God" and then use Bauer's main point to explain the Portuguese justification for the slave trade.

"Spoiling for a Fight, Fighting for God" was first published on the website *Psychology Today* on June 2, 2016. You might remember some of the information covered if you also studied Susan Wise Bauer's *The History of the Medieval World: From the Conversion of Constantine to the First Crusade.*

Susan Wise Bauer, Ph.D.

"Spoiling for a Fight, Fighting for God"

Religious language doesn't create warriors—it just gives them permission.

In 1095, Pope Urban II asked the Christians of Europe to march to Jerusalem and take the Holy City away from its Muslim rulers.

And his appeal succeeded beyond his wildest hopes. Thousands upon thousands of warriors turned east, launching the First Crusade.

Urban's call certainly featured some good rhetoric. He hit on three themes that would pop up frequently, over the next millennium, in religious speech employed for political ends: a recounting of the dreadful deeds of those who hold other (or no) faiths ("the Turks and Arabs . . . have occupied more and more of the lands of those Christians . . . have killed and captured many, and have destroyed the churches and devastated the empire!"); an appeal to fear, warning that worse will inevitably follow ("If you permit them to continue thus . . . the faithful of God will be much more widely attacked by them!"); and, last but certainly not least, the certain claim to be speaking for God ("Moreover, Christ commands it!").

But the rhetoric itself doesn't necessarily account for Urban's success.

To find out why his call resonated so deeply with his listeners, you actually have to go back a century—to the death of the French king Louis the Sluggard, in 987. Louis had ruled for only a single year, and (as his name suggests) wasn't much of a king. He was important only because he was the last king of the Carolingian dynasty, the final royal descendent of Charlemagne.

The powerful Frankish noblemen Louis had attempted to rule rejected the idea of finding a distant Carolingian relation to elevate. Instead, they crowned a king from a new family: Hugh Capet, son of the count of Paris, one of their own. Without much royal authority to wield, Hugh Capet found himself trying to control a disorderly mass of competing dukes who were accustomed to carrying on vicious private feuds without interference. Private warfare between French dukes, private oppression of farmers by aristocrats, armed spats between men of different loyalties and languages: France was a sea of chaos from border to border.

In 989, Christian priests gathered at the Benedictine abbey of Charroux to look for a solution. If France were to survive, someone had to quench the flames of private war that had followed the disintegration of strong royal power. The priests had no army, no money, and no political power, but they had the authority to declare the gates of heaven shut. And so they began to wield it.

They announced that noncombatants—peasants and clergy, families and farmers—should be immune from ravages of battle. Any soldier who robbed a church would be excommunicated. Any soldier who stole livestock from the poor would be excommunicated. Anyone who attacked a priest would be excommunicated (as long as the priest wasn't carrying a sword or wearing armor).

This meeting at Charroux was the first step in a gathering Christian movement known as the Peace and Truce of God. Over the next fifty years, two church councils extended the conditions of the Peace and Truce. Merchants and their goods joined peasants, clergymen, and farmers as official noncombatants, immune from attack. Certain days were now completely off limits for fighting: under threat of excommunication, no one could wage war on Fridays, Sundays, church holidays, or any of the forty days of Lent.

In 1041, Henry III of Germany (which had its own troubles with feuding aristocrats) decreed that the Peace and Truce would be observed in Germany from Wednesday evening through Monday morning of every week of the year. Then, in 1063, priests in the northern German city of Terouanne put together another set of regulations for the Peace and Truce of God. "These are the conditions which you must observe during the time of the peace which is commonly called the truce of God," the document began. "During those four days and five nights no man or woman shall assault, wound, or slay another, or attack, seize, or destroy a castle, burg, or villa, by craft or by violence." Furthermore, the Peace would be observed during every day of Advent and Lent, as well as between the church feasts of Ascension and Pentecost—a schedule that made nearly three-quarters of the year off-limits for fighting.

The result? Scores and scores of German and French noblemen who were absolutely spoiling for a fight—and couldn't find one without risking excommunication. So when, in November of 1095, at the French town of Clermont, Urban II announced that it was time to recapture Jerusalem, he gave all those aristocrats who had been chafing under the restrictions of the Peace and Truce of God something useful to do with their energy.

"Let those who have been accustomed unjustly to wage private warfare against the faithful now go against the infidels," Urban II told his audience. "Let those who for a long time have been robbers, now become knights. Let those who have been fighting against their brothers and relatives now fight in a proper way against the barbarians. . . . Let those who go not put off the journey. . . . As soon as winter is over and spring comes, let them eagerly set out on the way with God as their guide." And those who eagerly set out would receive the greatest possible reward: "All who die by the way, whether by land or by sea, or in battle against the pagans, shall have immediate remission of sins," Urban promised.

And so they went. Then, just as today, religious rhetoric brought about political ends most efficiently—when it gave justification to something that the hearers already wanted, for entirely secular reasons, to do.

The article's main point is "Then, just as today, religious rhetoric brought about political ends most efficiently— when it gave justification to something that the hearers already wanted, for entirely secular reasons, to do."

The student should then connect the use of religious rhetoric for political ends to the use of religious rhetoric for increased wealth and power. Afonso V "appealed to Rome to recognize the throne of Portugal as conducting, in Africa, a crusade: a holy war against the enemies of the Church, an assault on the powers of darkness." Nicholas V approved of this holy war, stating that Afonso V had the "full and free power, through the Apostolic authority . . . to invade, search out, capture, vanquish, and subdue all Saracens and pagans whatsoever, and other enemies of Christ wheresoever placed, and . . . to reduce their persons to perpetual slavery." The slave trade wasn't just about enemies of Christ, however. By 1452, two years before the papal bull Dum Diversas, *at least 3,500 slaves were sold a year, as well as tusks of elephant ivory, gold, fine cotton cloth, and much other merchandise. In fact, we read in the chapter that "the king of Portugal decided to protect his country's interests in Africa by appealing to the pope." Spreading Christianity to the African coast was a far lower priority than making an extreme fortune. However, once the slave trade was transferred into the realm of the holy, once their enslavement was viewed as their salvation, once their sale was baptized as a righteous duty, there was no moral argument to be made against the practice. Nicholas V explained in the charter confirming* Dum Diversas, Romanus Pontifex, *that because the kings of Portugal had spent so much "labor, danger and expense" in sending "swift ships" to Africa, because this had "caused to be preached to them the unknown but most sacred name of Christ," and because this had "gained for Christ" the souls of so many, the entire Portuguese enterprise was now protected by the Church. Only the Portuguese could sail to West Africa, preach the gospel, and bring Africans back to Europe. The pope gave the Portugese a monopoly on the slave trade but couched it in terms saving the Africans' souls. Just as the first crusade justified the eleventh-century everyman's desire for violence and revenge as battling for Christ, the African slave trade used evangelization as impenetrable justification for the capturing, selling, and owning of human beings.*

EXAMPLE ANSWER:

In the article "Spoiling for a Fight, Fighting for God," Susan Wise Bauer connects rhetoric to the start of the first crusade. She explains that the Peace and Truce of God left men itching to fight, and that Urban II played on that itch by channeling common frustration into holy war. The article's epigraph, "Religious language doesn't create warriors—it just gives them permission" helps us to understand how religion can be used to excuse bad behavior. This is fully explained at the end of the article, where Bauer clearly spells out her main point: "Then, just as today, religious rhetoric brought about political ends most efficiently—when it gave justification to something that the hearers already wanted, for entirely secular reasons, to do." Giving someone a religious reason to do something secular that they already wanted to do makes the person infallible, for they can say they are doing the action in the name of God. This is exactly how Afonso V and Nicholas V justified the enslavement of African captives.

Afonso V "appealed to Rome to recognize the throne of Portugal as conducting, in Africa, a crusade: a holy war against the enemies of the Church, an assault on the powers of darkness." Nicholas V approved of this holy war, stating that Afonso V had the "full and free power, through the Apostolic authority . . . to invade, search out, capture, vanquish, and subdue all Saracens and pagans whatsoever, and other enemies of Christ wheresoever placed, and . . . to reduce their persons to perpetual slavery." The slave trade wasn't just about enemies of Christ, however. By 1452, two years before the papal bull *Dum Diversas*, at least 3,500 slaves were sold a year, as well as tusks of elephant ivory, gold, fine cotton cloth, and much other merchandise. In fact, we read in the chapter that "the king of Portugal decided to protect his country's interests in Africa by appealing to the pope." Spreading Christianity to the African coast was a far lower priority than making an extreme fortune. However, once the slave trade was viewed as a crusade rather than as a way to make a great fortune (that just happened to be a fortuitous side effect) there was no moral argument to be made against the practice. Just as the first crusade justified the eleventh-century everyman's desire for violence and revenge as battling for Christ, the African slave trade used evangelization as impenetrable justification for the capturing, selling, and owning of human beings.

Chapter Ninety-Three

The Loss of France

The student may use his text when answering the questions in sections I and II.

Section I: **Who, What, Where**

Write a one or two-sentence answer explaining the significance of each item listed below.

Duke of Bedford—**Pg. 663, ¶ 2 & 3 and Pg. 669, ¶ 1—Duke of Bedford, Henry VI's regent, married the Duke of Burgundy's sister, strengthening the French-English alliance. When the Duke of Bedford's wife died in 1432, the Duke quickly remarried, causing a rift between the English and the French.**

Charles VII—**Pg. 663, ¶ 1 & 2, Pg. 665, ¶ 4 and Pg. 669, ¶ 5—Charles VII, acting for Charles VI since the age of fourteen as Dauphin, was hailed as king by the Armagnacs in 1422 but civil war followed; after Jeanne d'Arc reinvigorated the royalist army, Charles VII mounted an elaborate coronation ceremony in the ancient cathedral at Reims, following the tradition established by the Frankish king Clovis centuries before. On November 12, 1437, after the Treaty of Arras was signed and the French royal army broke through the gates of Paris, Charles VII reclaimed the city; it was the first Sunday in Advent, the beginning of the season of the Messiah's arrival, a day when kings marched into their own cities in triumph.**

Écorcheurs—**Pg. 669, ¶ 6 and Pg. 670, ¶ 2—Écorcheurs, "skinners," or "flayers," were robber bands formed by Charles VII's previous royalist soldiers that continued to storm the countryside after Charles VII reclaimed Paris. Dukes that were angry at Charles VII for reorganizing the army and putting an end to private armies also joined the écorcheurs.**

Henry VI—**Pg. 662, ¶ 3, Pg. 663, ¶ 1 and Pg. 670, ¶ 3—Henry VI was proclaimed "king of England and France," ruler of England and heir to the throne in Paris at the age of nine months; when Charles VI died, the Burgundians and the English claimed Henry VI to be king of France. In 1444, after years of war and the loss of almost all of England's French territories, Henry VI agreed to a temporary cease-fire and he married Charles VII's niece in 1445.**

Jeanne d'Arc—**Pg. 664, ¶ 2 & 3 and Pg. 668, ¶ 4—Jeanne d'Arc, a seventeen-year-old girl who dressed like a man, who was full of courage, and heard voices and saw visions, arrived in**

Chinon in March of 1429 to explain her mission to Charles VII: she was going to rescue France from the English and see the Dauphin crowned as the one rightful king of the French people. After helping the French regain much of their country, Jeanne d'Arc was captured by the English, tried for heresy, and burned at the stake.

John Talbot—**Pg. 670, ¶ 5—John Talbot, son of the Earl of Shrewsbury, was at the head of an English army of five thousand that landed at Bordeaux in October of 1452. The French army arrived to fight back with cannon; over a thousand English died, including Talbot, the rest fled back to England, and the Hundred Years' war breathed a dying gasp.**

Pierre Cauchon—**Pg. 668, ¶ 2—Pierre Cauchon, a Paris-trained canon lawyer who was also the Bishop of Beauvais, prosecuted Jeanne d'Arc. Pierre Cauchon led the assembled court—131 lawyers, priests, and scholars—through seventy different accusations, twelve of which were proven and carried the sentence of lifelong imprisonment.**

Treaty of Arras—**Pg. 669, ¶ 3—Treaty of Arras, signed on September 21, 1435 by the Duke of Burgundy after the Duke of Bedford died, concluded that any French obligation to the English was at an end. The treaty did not finish off the war, but it reunified the Burgundian party to the crown, bringing an end to the split that had allowed the English to make a play for France in the first place.**

Section II: Comprehension

Write a two or three-sentence answer to each of the following questions.

1. Explain Henry V's position as king of France through his sudden death from dysentery on August 30, 1422.

A1.—Pg. 662, ¶ 1—Henry V had taken France; he had the support of the Duke of Burgundy, but the anti-Burgundian party, the Armagnacs, had allied themselves behind the young disinherited Dauphin. Charles VII had handed over the Dauphin's right to inherit; but the old king was still alive, and Henry V spent the years after the Battle of Agincourt fighting against the Dauphin's supporters. By 1422, a large part of his army went back to England, weakened from fighting and lack of food, planning never to return to France again.

2. What important question did Charles VI's death raise? How was the question answered?

A2.—663, ¶ 1 & 2—The important question raised by Charles VI's death was who would succeed him as king of France: the infant Henry VI of England, whose claim was supported by the Burgundians and the English, or the Dauphin Charles, whose claim was supported by the Armagnac party? Both of the candidates were hailed king simultaneously: the baby Henry in Paris with the English Duke of Bedford serving as his regent and Charles VII in the chapel of Mehun, near Bourges. The double claim led to intensified civil war, with the English Duke of Bedford and the French Duke of Burgundy fighting together to expand their power from Paris and the Loire valley south, and Charles VII and the Armagnacs based at Bourges and fortified by soldiers from rebellious Scotland and French-loyal Castile.

3. Describe the civil war in France through the appearance of Jeanne d'Arc.

A3.—Pg. 663, ¶ 3 to Pg. 664, ¶ 2—The first six years of the civil war saw victory after victory for the English. After the Duke of Bedford married the Duke of Burgundy's sister, and the French-English alliance grew that much stronger, Charles VII's army was badly damaged by a horrible loss in July 1423, with three thousand Scottish troops lost and an equal number of French killed or captured. The towns of Coucy, Meulan, Rambouillet, Meung, and Compiègne fell as the English alliance pushed north and south; fortress after fortress surrendered, the Dauphin hid out at a court he set up in Poitiers, and when, in October of 1428 the Duke of Bedford laid siege to Orleans, Charles VII found himself in great distress because he might have to leave his country.

4. What happened when Jeanne d'Arc met Charles VII at Chinon in March of 1429?

A4.—Pg. 664, ¶ 4—When Jeanne d'Arc arrived at Chinon, she immediately went to the Dauphin, who was wearing no identifying royal robes and standing with a group of his counselors, indistinguishable from them. She then told him "Gentle dauphin, I am Joan the Maid, and the King of Heaven commands that through me you be anointed and crowned in the city of Reims as a lieutenant of the King of Heaven, who is king of France," and after further questions asked by the king, Joan said to him anew: "I say to you, on behalf of the Lord, that you are the true heir of France, and a king's son, and He has sent me to you to lead you to Reims, so that you can receive your coronation and consecration if you wish it." Then, the king said to his courtiers that Joan had told him a certain secret that no one knew or could know except God and that is why he had great confidence in her.

5. How did Charles VII's fortune change after Jeanne d'Arc started leading his army against the Burgundian-English forces?

A5.—Pg. 665, ¶ 4 & 5—At the end of April of 1429, Jeanne d'Arc led Charles VII's army in three quick assaults on the Burgundian-English camps at Orleans; the royalist army forced the besiegers to break camp and retreat by the end of the first week of May. It was the initial victory in a string of triumphs and the Dauphin's army followed the "Maid of Orleans" into battle after battle—and fought brilliantly. The English-held Tournelles surrendered on May 8; Jargeau in June; Troyes and Reims in July; and St. Denis in August.

6. What happened when Jeanne d'Arc and the royalist army attacked Paris?

A6.—Pg. 665, ¶ 5—When Jeanne d'Arc and the royalist army arrived at Paris, Jeanne d'Arc had thought that the people would come over to the side of the rightfully crowned king of France, but there were too many Burgundians and English in the city. After a few initial assaults in late August, she led a major attack against Paris's walls on September 8, 1429, but, sensing division in their leadership, the French army faltered. Jeanne d'Arc herself was badly injured, taking a serious arrow wound to the thigh; the royalist army finally retreated and something had shifted—Jeanne's injury had turned the angel of the Lord into a vulnerable woman.

7. How did Jeanne d'Arc plan to recapture the momentum of the royalist army? What happened instead?

A7.—Pg. 667, ❡ 2 & 3—Jeanne d'Arc hoped to recapture the old momentum of the royalist army by going, with two thousand loyal soldiers, to the city of Compiègne, where she hoped to use the city as a base for a surprise attack on English troops nearby. Instead, she marched out from its gates and was almost at once driven backwards by the Duke of Burgundy's men, and then she was shut outside of the city when someone raised the drawbridge, blocking her out. Jeanne d'Arc was forced to surrender and was taken captive to the Duke of Burgundy's camp at Marigny where she was treated not as a prisoner of war but as a heretic, accused of "many crimes, sorceries, idolatry, intercourse with demons, and other matters relative to faith and against faith."

8. How were women accused of heresy supposed to be treated by the court? Why was there a confusion of procedure at Jeanne d'Arc's trial?

A8.—Pg. 667, ❡ 5 to Pg. 668, ❡ 1—Women accused of heresy were supposed to be given a lawyer and allowed the company of other women; instead Jeanne d'Arc was kept in a military prison, given no lawyer for her defense, and denied the company of other women, which were all blatant violations of Church laws protecting women accused of heresy. It was a confusion of procedure caused in large part by Jeanne's own insistence that God was speaking to her directly, independent of any Church voice or setting, and that He did not approve of the Treaty of Troyes (which had given Henry V the right to claim the crown of France). "Asked whether God hates the English," the Latin transcript of her trial tells us, "she said she knows nothing about the love or hate that God has for the English, nor what he will do with their souls; but she knows for certain they will be driven from France, except those who stay and die, and that God will grant the French victory over the English."

9. Why was Jeanne d'Arc burned at the stake when she was originally supposed to be imprisoned for life?

A9.—Pg. 668, ❡ 2-4—During her trial, Jeanne d'Arc, who was exhausted, abandoned, and poorly fed, sank into an illness that reduced her almost to coma so she was in no clear state of mind when, on Thursday, May 24, she allowed her hand to be guided into marking a cross at the bottom of the accusations levied against her. This acknowledgment of guilt sentenced her to lifelong imprisonment, but then a spark of resistance flared back up in the battered recesses of her soul and she renounced her confession. At once, she was condemned as an unrepentant heretic and sentenced to death by burning; on May 30, 1431, she was led out to the square of Rouen and burned at the stake.

10. What caused the relationship between the English-French alliance to fracture after Jeanne d'Arc's death?

A10.—Pg. 669, ❡ 1 & 2—After Jeanne d'Arc's death, the Duke of Burgundy had been contemplating how he could be reconciled to his king because of the resurgence of the king's power, and he was pushed even further from his alliance with the English when the Duke of Bedford's wife, his sister, died and the Duke of Bedford quickly remarried. Then, in the late

summer of 1435, Henry VI's London council agreed to send ambassadors to Arras to meet with two cardinals sent from Rome to help establish a peace between the warring kings; the Duke of Burgundy was also in attendance, as were representatives from a number of French countries, and diplomats sent by Charles VII, but the Duke of Bedford remained away. The English ambassadors faced secret meeting between the French parties and the demand that King Henry give up the claim to be king of France in exchange for sovereignty over certain French territories; by early September they were fed up, so they abandoned the talks and returned to England.

11. How did Charles VII upset the dukes in France after reclaiming power in Paris?

A11.—Pg. 670, ¶ 1 & 2—Charles VII upset the dukes in France by reorganizing the army. With the cooperation of the Estates-General at Orleans, he decreed that from now on, a permanent, government-controlled army would defend France, that all officers were under the direction of the king, and that no French duke could have soldiers of his own without the permission of the king. After making a strike against one of the most treasured privileges of the French aristocracy, private armies, some of the dukes resisted and joined forces with the *écorcheurs*; they tried to mount an armed rebellion but the government army, under the direction of the Constable of France, squelched the resistance before it even really got started.

12. Why did Charles VII go on the offensive against the English in June of 1449? What was the result of this turn?

A12. Pg. 670, ¶ 4—In June of 1449, Charles VII abruptly accused the English of failing to abide by the terms of the cease-fire, and of attempting to incite the French Duke of Brittany, Charles's nephew, to rebel against the crown. In a series of campaigns between July 31, 1449, and August 22, 1451, the French army reconquered almost every fortress, town, and strategic position in both Normandy and Gascony, the latter English-held for the last three hundred years. Reinforcements never came from Henry VI, and finally the only English territory remaining in France was a tiny strip encompassing Calais and Guînes.

13. Describe the illnesses faced by Charles VII and Henry VI.

A13.—Pg. 670, ¶ 6 to Pg. 671, ¶ 2—Starting in late 1453, Charles VII was sick with an illness, perhaps syphilis, or a chronic genetic disorder, that eventually made his hands too shaky to sign official papers. He was forced to wear dressings on one leg to absorb a constant discharge of pus; he ordered special stockings for his bad foot, and his meals were carefully ground up because of a badly ulcerated mouth. In August of the same year, Henry VI suddenly lost his wits (just like his grandfather Charles VI); he did not regain awareness for over a year, and even when he again recognized his wife and children, he continued to hear voices, fall into catatonia, see visions, and retreat into an imaginary world.

Section III: Critical Thinking

The student may not use his text to answer this question.

Jeanne d'Arc reignited the French army in the fight against the English, and she saved Charles VII from losing his throne. Yet, when she was captured by the English and tried for heresy, Charles VII did nothing to help her. Explain how, though devastating, Charles VII's refusal to help Jeanne d'Arc actually benefitted the French cause.

For this critical thinking question, the student should see that Jeanne d'Arc's martyrdom sparked fury in the French, and pushed the royalist cause forward.

Jeanne d'Arc's mission in life was to rescue France from the English, to see the Dauphin crowned as the one rightful king of the French people. She had seen visions and heard voices that verified this life path. In March of 1429, she arrived at Chinon to explain her mission to Charles VII, and he had great confidence in her after she told him a secret that no one knew of and could not know, except God.

Jeanne d'Arc led successful campaigns against the Duke of Bedford at Orleans, followed by successes against the English-held Tournelles, which surrendered on May 8; Jargeau, which fell in June; Troyes and Reims, taken back in July; and St. Denis recovered in August. With Reims finally back in his hands, the Dauphin mounted an elaborate coronation ceremony in the ancient cathedral, following the tradition established by the Frankish king Clovis centuries before.

This is where the momentum slowed. Now that Charles VII was crowned and anointed, he believed in himself, and was less desperate for Jeanne d'Arc's help. His dispassion was not helped by Paris's resistance to the royalist army. After a few initial assaults in late August, Jeanne d'Arc led a major attack against Paris's walls on September 8, 1429 that failed.

Hoping to recapture the old momentum, Jeanne d'Arc left Charles VII in the spring of 1430 and went, with two thousand loyal soldiers, to the city of Compiègne. Compiègne had remained loyal to Charles VII, defying the English. However, Jeanne d'Arc was sold out, and when she arrived at the city the drawbridge was raised. She was forced to surrender and then she taken captive by the Duke of Burgundy. Charles VII made no effort to ransom her. There is no reasoning behind his abandonment. Jeanne d'Arc reinvigorated his army, reclaimed much of France for him, and allowed him to be anointed and crowned, but Charles VII did nothing to help her.

Jeanne d'Arc was put on trial for heresy at Rouen, in Normandy, on February 21, 1431. She was accused of seventy different crimes and the assembled court—131 lawyers, priests, and scholars—decided that twelve of them could be proven. Jeanne, weak with illness, first acknowledged her crimes, but then, with a spark of resistance, renounced her confession a week later. At once, she was condemned as an unrepentant heretic and sentenced to death by burning. On May 30, 1431, was brought to the stake in the square at Rouen, continuing to praise God and the saints while lamenting devoutly; the last word she cried in a high voice as she died was: "Jesus!"

It would seem that Jeanne d'Arc's execution would be a blow to the French. She was, after all, the reason that the army came back to life. However, the sight of Jeanne d'Arc dying with the name of Christ on her lips had not gone over well with the population of English-held Rouen, and she was more and more widely spoken of as a martyr. The executioner himself later went to a priest, begging for absolution; he was damned, he said, because he had burned a holy woman. Rumors began to circulate that her heart had survived the flames, a miracle in the ashes. When the Duke of Bedford brought Henry VI to Paris to be crowned at Notre Dame after Jeanne d'Arc's execution, the people of Paris were so hostile to the king that he fled to Normandy. Jeanne d'Arc's martyrdom had actually fueled the French cause by sparking hatred for the English—they burned one of God's warriors to death, an act that could not be forgiven.

EXAMPLE ANSWER:

Jeanne d'Arc's mission in life was to rescue France from the English, to see the Dauphin crowned as the one rightful king of the French people. After gaining Charles VII's confidence, she led successful campaigns against the Duke of Bedford at Orleans, followed by victories at Tournelles, Jargeau, Troyes, Reims, and St. Denis. At Reims, the Dauphin had himself crowned and anointed in the tradition of the Frankish king Clovis.

This is where the momentum slowed. Now that Charles VII was crowned and anointed, he believed in himself, and was less desperate for Jeanne d'Arc's help. His dispassion was not helped by Paris's resistance to the royalist army. After a few initial assaults in late August, Jeanne d'Arc led a major attack against Paris's walls on September 8, 1429 that failed. Hoping to recapture the old momentum, Jeanne d'Arc left Charles VII in the spring of 1430 and went to the city of Compiègne which had remained loyal to the French king. However, Jeanne d'Arc was sold out, and when she arrived at the city the drawbridge was raised. She was forced to surrender, and then she taken captive by the Duke of Burgundy. Charles VII made no effort to ransom her. There is no reasoning behind his abandonment. Jeanne d'Arc reinvigorated his army, reclaimed much of France for him, and allowed him to be anointed and crowned, but Charles VII did nothing to help her.

Jeanne d'Arc was put on trial for heresy at Rouen, in Normandy, on February 21, 1431. She was ultimately beaten into a confession that would have imprisoned her for life. She felt one last spark of resistance and renounced her confession, which led to her death by burning at the stake. On May 30, 1431, was brought to the square at Rouen and burned to death, continuing to praise God and the saints.

It would seem that Jeanne d'Arc's execution would be a blow to the French. She was, after all, the reason that the army came back to life. However, the sight of Jeanne d'Arc dying while calling out to Christ had not gone over well with the population of English-held Rouen, and she was more and more widely spoken of as a martyr. The executioner himself believed he was damned because he had burned a holy woman. Rumors of a miracle began to circulate, that her heart had survived the flames. When the Duke of Bedford brought Henry VI to Paris to be crowned at Notre Dame after Jeanne d'Arc's execution, the people of Paris were so hostile to the king that he fled to Normandy. Even though Charles VII abandoned his woman warrior, Jeanne d'Arc's martyrdom actually fueled the French cause by sparking hatred for the English—they burned one of God's messengers to death, an act that could not be forgiven.

Section IV: Map Exercise

1. Trace the rectangular outline of frame of Map 93.1: The Dauphin against the English in black.

2. Using your blue pencil, trace the coastal outline around Ireland, England, and Europe, including the small visible portion of the Mediterranean. Also trace the line of the Loire. Repeat until the contours are familiar.

3. Using contrasting colors, trace the outlines of the areas loyal to England and loyal to France. Repeat until the contours are familiar.

4. Using a new sheet of paper, trace the rectangular outline of the map in black. Then using your regular pencil with an eraser, draw the coastal outline around Ireland, England, and Europe, including the small visible portion of the Mediterranean. Also draw the line of the Loire.Then draw the outlines of the areas loyal to England and loyal to France. When you are happy with your map, lay it over the original. Erase and re-draw any lines which are more than ½" off of the original.

5. Label the areas of Ireland, England, Normandy, Brittany, and Gascony. Then study carefully the locations of Plymouth, Dartmouth, Southampton, London, Brentwood, Dover, Rye, the Isle of Wight, Calais, Guines, Arras, Tournelles, Compiegne, Coucy, Reims, Rouen, Meulan, St.-Denis, Paris, Rambouillet, Domremy, Troyes, Orleans, Meung, Mehun, Chinon, Poitiers, Bordeaux, and Bayonne. Then lay your map over the original. Erase and re-mark any locations which are more than ½: off of the original.

7. Mark the location of Mehun.

Chapter Ninety-Four

The Fall

The student may use her text when answering the questions in sections I and II.

Section I: Who, What, Where

Write a one or two-sentence answer explaining the significance of each item listed below.

Aleddin—**Pg. 676, ¶ 1—Aleddin was Murad II's oldest and best-loved son. After he died of a swift and unexpected illness, Murad II grew weary and decided to abdicate his throne to his next son, Mehmet.**

Casimir—**Pg. 674, ¶ 3 and Pg. 677, ¶ 4—Casimir, the younger brother of Wladyslaw III, was made king of Poland three years after the death of his brother at the Battle of Varna.**

Constantine XI Palaeologus—**Pg. 677, ¶ 7 and Pg. 680, ¶ 1—Constantine XI Palaeologus, younger brother of John VIII and his replacement as leader of Byzantium, faced Mehmet II's bombardment of Constantinople. Constantine died defending his city during the final attack on May 28; his body was never found.**

Frederick of Hapsburg—**Pg. 675, ¶ 1 and Pg. 677, ¶ 5—Frederick of Hapsburg, Albert II's first cousin, was made king of Germany after Albert II's death. Eight years after the Battle of Varna, Frederick would be crowned Holy Roman Emperor by Pope Nicholas V; the last Holy Roman Emperor to ever be crowned in Rome.**

Halil Pasha—**Pg. 676, ¶ 1, Pg. 678, ¶ 1, and Pg. 680, ¶ 3—Halil Pasha, vizier for Mehmet, remained on the sultan's staff after he came into power, though he had fully expected to be done away with. Halil Pasha was executed after Mehmet II took Constantinople because he was no longer necessary in the sultan's eyes.**

John Huniades—**Pg. 675, ¶ 4 & 5 and Pg. 676, ¶ 6 to Pg. 677, ¶ 1—John Huniades, the military governor for Szörény and supposed illegitimate son of Sigismund, offered his allegiance to Wladyslaw III, defeated Murad II's troops at the Iron Gate in 1442, and in 1443 marched directly across the Balkan mountains in an audacious and aggressive move known as the Long Campaign, which led to a string of Turkish losses and Murad II's acceptance of a ten-year truce** with Wladyslaw and Huniades in February of 1444. John Huniades accompanied Wladyslaw III in the Battle at Varna; Huniades fled with Vlad Dracul into Wallachia, where they had a private falling-out that ended with Huniades in a Wallachian prison.

Ladislaus—**Pg. 675, ¶ 2 and Pg. 677, ¶ 4**—**Ladislaus, Albert II's posthumous son, was unanimously elected to replace the dead Wladyslaw II as king of Hungary.**

Mehmet—**Pg. 676, ¶ 1, Pg. 677, ¶ 4 & 8, and Pg. 680, ¶ 2**—**Mehmet, son of Murad II, was made sultan of the Ottomans at age twelve, then he was demoted after Murad II came out of retirement after the Battle at Varna, then he was reinstated after his father died in 1451. Mehmet II successfully took Constantinople for the Turks; the first thing he did after taking the city was to go through the St. Romanus gate into the Hagia Sophia to say the first Muslim prayers inside it.**

The Battle at Varna—**Pg. 676, ¶ 5 to Pg. 677, ¶ 2**—**The Battle at Varna, fought in November of 1444, was the last Christian attempt to organize a crusade against the Turks. Murad II came out of retirement and led his one hundred thousand men in devastating defeat over the Hungarian and Wallachian forces.**

Urban—**Pg. 678, ¶ 4 and Pg. 679, ¶ 1**—**Urban, a Hungarian cannon maker, came to Constantinople and offered his services to Constantine; he was too expensive for Constantine, so with regret the emperor turned him away and then Urban went to Cutter of the Strait instead, where Mehmet promptly hired him. Urban created a bombard that shot out stones weighing eighteen hundred pounds and were more than seven feet around; it had taken sixty oxen pulling thirty wagons to haul it from its forging place in Edirne to the city's walls, and road workers had spent two months fortifying bridges and roadways ahead of it.**

Wladyslaw III—**Pg. 674, ¶ 3, Pg. 675, ¶ 1 and Pg. 676, ¶ 6**—**Wladyslaw III, king of Poland, made an alliance with Murad II that was voided after Wladyslaw III accepted the Hungarian crown, uniting Poland and Hungary. Wladyslaw III was killed in the Crusade against Murad II; his body was never found, although rumors circulated for years that he had survived and was wandering through the east as a pilgrim, always searching for Jerusalem.**

Section II: Comprehension

Write a two or three-sentence answer to each of the following questions.

1. Describe Murad II's actions as Ottoman sultan through the destruction of the Hexamillion Wall.

A1.—Pg. 673, ¶ 1—Murad II grew into a fierce and mature ruler, laying siege to Constantinople twice, both times withdrawing only after the payment of tribute and the surrender of yet more Byzantine lands. He had ruthlessly wiped out budding revolts in Wallachia and Serbia, both now under his control; after capturing the massive Hungarian fortress of Golubac, on the Danube river, he had forced the Hungarians to give it over to him permanently; in 1430 he seized Thessalonica; and he had begun to invade the Venetian-held lands on the Adriatic Sea.

In 1431, his troops had knocked down the Hexamillion Wall, built by Manuel to block just such an extension of Turkish power.

2. What things did Albert II fail to do before his death on October 27, 1439?

A2.—Pg. 674, ¶ 2—Albert II failed to get the Bohemians to recognize his kingship. In 1439, Albert II decided to turn southward against the Turkish front in Serbia, but he failed to do anything in particular during that campaign. He also failed to actually be crowned as king of Germany before he died on October 27, 1439; he died as king-elect.

3. How did Murad II plan to stop Hungary and Poland from unifying against him? Why did the plan fail?

A3.—Pg. 674, ¶ 3 to Pg. 675, ¶ 2—In order to prevent Hungary and Poland from unifying against him, Murad II sent an ambassador to the king of Poland, Wladyslaw III, with an offer: the Turks would help the king's younger brother, Casimir, take control of Bohemia, removing it completely from the control of either Germany or Hungary, and instead making it a subject kingdom of Poland—as long as Poland promised not to help the Hungarians attack the Turkish front. Wladyslaw III accepted the treaty, but the Turkish ambassadors had not yet even left Krakow when news of Albert II's death arrived, along with an offer from the Hungarian nobles to recognize Wladyslaw as king of Hungary in his place. Wladyslaw III accepted the Hungarian crown, which annoyed Murad II; when his messengers returned to his capital city of Edirne and told him that Poland and Hungary were now under a single ruler, he declared the treaty with Hungary void and began to gather his forces for an attack.

4. Why did Murad II attack Belgrade? What happened when he attacked?

A4.—Pg. 675, ¶ 2 & 3—Albert II's widow gave birth to a posthumous son, four months after Albert's death, and a minority of the Hungarian nobles lobbied for retracting the offer of kingship to Wladyslaw III in favor of the infant. Fighting broke out, and Murad II must have believed that the divisions in Hungary would make the country vulnerable so in 1440, he advanced forward to Belgrade, the gateway into Hungary, and laid siege to it. To Murad II's shock, the siege failed.

5. Explain how Belgrade and its defenders were able to hold off the Turks.

A5.—Pg. 675, ¶ 3—Belgrade, built between two rivers, was further protected by a double wall and five forts, and its harbor was shut off with a chain that ran between two strong towers. The Turkish army was equipped with stone throwers and cannon, but after several months of bashing at the walls without effect, Murad II ordered a secret tunnel built under the walls, beginning the construction a good distance away and behind a high hill to conceal it. Belgrade's defenders discovered the tunnel, booby-trapped it with gunpowder, and waited until it was filled with advancing Turkish foot soldiers; then they set off the explosion, killing every last man in the tunnel, which caused Murad II to retreat.

6. How did a papal legate convince Wladyslaw III and John Huniades to go on a Crusade against Murad II? What happened to the forces that were supposed to gather to fight the Ottoman sultan?

A6.—Pg. 676, ¶ 3 & 4—A papal legate promised both Wladyslaw III and John Huniades that they were not bound by the terms of the truce they had signed with Murad II since he was an infidel, and he sweetened his persuasions of going on Crusade by promising Huniades that the pope would recognize him as king of Bulgaria if he could manage to drive the Turks out of the old Bulgarian lands. Even before the Crusade could gather momentum, other Crusaders backed out: John VIII refused to take the risk of annoying the Turks into another attack on Constantinople; the Serbian leader, whose daughter was married to Murad, decided that he would be better off working his family connections than trying to kill his daughter's new family; and the Venetians never came up with the expected ships. By the time the Crusaders had planned to march along the Danube, into the Turkish front, the force had shrunk to the Hungarians under King Wladyslaw and John Huniades and a small Wallachian force commanded by Vlad Dracul.

8. What was the purpose of Boğazkesen, "Cutter of the Strait?" How did it claim its first victim?

A8.—Pg. 678, ¶ 2 & 3—Boğazkesen, "Cutter of the Strait," a fortress built on Byzantine land by Mehmet II, on the western shore of the Bosphorus Strait that stood directly across from a fortress built by his grandfather Bayezid on the Turkish shore, had only one purpose—to serve as a base for the conquest of Constantinople. As soon as the fortress was completed, Mehmet announced that all ships passing through the strait would pay a toll. In November 1452, a Venetian merchant ship refused to stop and shell out the tax; Turkish cannon blasted the ship to bits, killing most of the crew, and the captain was hauled out of the water and impaled on the shore where other ships could see him.

9. Describe the preparations Mehmet II made for his attack on Constantinople.

A9.—Pg. 678, ¶ 5 to Pg. 679, ¶ 1—After building Cutter of the Strait, Mehmet II established his own headquarters right across from the gate known as St. Romanus and established other camps all along the walls. He had somewhere between 160,000 and 400,000 men; among them were at least 60,000 archers and 40,000 horsemen; some of the foot soldiers armed only with scimitars, but others with iron helmets and French chain mail. Mehmet II also had bombards, wide-mouthed cannon that hurled granite balls, culverins, smaller cannon that could be fired by hand, and a massive bombard built by Urban that shot out stones that were seven feet around and weighed eighteen hundred pounds.

10. How did Mehmet II get around the massive chain that blocked the Golden Horn?

A10.—Pg. 679, ¶ 3—Mehmet II knew that the Golden Horn was blocked with a massive chain, and that the chain was guarded by towers. To deal with this obstacle, his engineers had outfitted about seventy of his ships with wheels. In the night of April 22, 1453, his men hauled the ships by land over the hills north of the Golden Horn and then slipped them into the water, behind the protective chain, so that when dawn came on the twenty-third, the Golden Horn was filled with enemy ships.

11. What finally caused the fall of Constantinople?

A11.—Pg. 679, ¶ 6 to Pg. 680, ¶ 2—On May 28, after attacking the city non-stop for almost two months, the bombardment suddenly ceased; but then, just after midnight, a final attack came. Every man, every cannon, every horse, every archer Mehmet commanded—was flung against and over the city walls; Constantine himself came out, sword in hand, to join the fighting and he was killed with the thousands of others that died in the battle. By the morning of May 29, Constantinople belonged to the Turks and Mehmet himself came in through the St. Romanus gate, went directly to the Hagia Sophia, the great cathedral of the Greek church, to say the first Muslim prayers inside it.

Section III: Critical Thinking

The student may not use her text to answer this question.

The Turkish bombardment of Constantinople began on April 4, 1453. The weak forces inside of the city could barely defend themselves, and after the Golden Horn filled with enemy ships, and two more attempted invasions through the breaches in the walls took place on May 7 and May 18, Constantine asked Mehmet for terms on which the sultan would withdraw. Mehmet responded "Either I shall take this city, or the city will take me, dead or alive. . . . The city is all I want, even if it is empty." It was very important for Mehmet II to take Constantinople. Write a paragraph that connects his treatment by his father to his desire for conquest. How did his appointment to sultan, and then his demotion, relate to his burning desire to take the Christian Jewel on the Black Sea?

There are many reasons Mehmet II may have wanted to take Constantinople for the Ottomans, however one becomes quite clear in the narrative presented in our chapter.

Mehmet II was made sultan after Murad II lost his favorite son Aleddin. Murad II was so sad that he no longer wanted to rule, so he abdicated and made Mehmet sultan. However, when the Hungarian forces marched towards the Turkish-held city of Varna, the Turkish vizier begged Murad II to come out of retirement and lead the attack, much to the dismay of Mehmet. The Ottomans were successful and Murad decided to come back to the head of the Ottoman empire, demoting his son to the heir apparent once again. Mehmet II retreated into the shadows, waiting for his father to die. Mehmet II was never close to his father; Murad II had two other, older sons that he preferred to Mehmet II, but both had died young. When Murad II died, Mehmet used his place as leader of the Ottomans to prove his worth; the worth his father did not see. He kept Halil Pasha on staff, even though he was Murad II's right-hand man, because he was experienced, well-liked, and well-connected. This would help Mehmet II in his plan for conquest. At the same time, however, he had his infant half-brother killed—the days of sibling rivalry were over for Mehmet II.

What is striking about Mehmet's attitude is his singularity in purpose. As soon as he was made sultan again after his father's death, he arranged truces with Hungary, Venice, Wallachia, and the Greek cities on the southern peninsula so that he could put all of his energy into building Cutter of the Strait, the fortress built for the sole purpose of taking down Constantinople. He would stop at nothing to take the city. He armed himself with hundreds of thousands of soldiers, bombards, culverins, and cannon that could fire boulders seven feet around.

Unlike his grandfather Bayezid and his father Murad II, who were unable to take the city, Mehmet II would prove his strength and worthiness to rule by bringing down the Christian jewel on the Black Sea.

EXAMPLE ANSWER:

Mehmet II thought he was going to be sultan of the Ottomans when he was twelve. Murad II lost his favorite son Aleddin and was so sad that he no longer wanted to rule, so he abdicated and made Mehmet sultan. However, when the Hungarian forces marched towards the Turkish-held city of Varna, the Turkish vizier begged Murad II to come out of retirement and lead the attack, much to the dismay of Mehmet. The Ottomans were successful and Murad decided to come back to the head of the Ottoman empire, demoting his son to the heir apparent once again.

After this demotion, Mehmet waited quietly for his father to die. They did not have a good relationship. Murad II had two other, older sons that he preferred to Mehmet II, but both had died young. When Murad II died, Mehmet used his place as leader of the Ottomans to prove his worth; the worth his father did not see. He kept Halil Pasha on staff, even though he was Murad II's right-hand man, because he was experienced, well-liked, and well-connected. This would help Mehmet II in his plan for conquest. At the same time, however, he had his infant half-brother killed—the days of sibling rivalry were over for Mehmet II.

Mehmet II got to work on his plan to show everyone his power. He arranged truces with Hungary, Venice, Wallachia, and the Greek cities on the southern peninsula so that he could put all of his energy into building Cutter of the Strait, the fortress built for the sole purpose of taking down Constantinople. Then, he armed himself with hundreds of thousands of soldiers, bombards, culverins, and cannon that could fire boulders seven feet around. Mehmet II would not fail, like his grandfather Bayezid and his father Murad II. He was going to prove his strength and worthiness to rule by bringing down the Christian jewel on the Black Sea.

Student Study Guide

FOR

THE HISTORY OF THE RENAISSANCE WORLD

How To Use This Study Guide

On Research and Citations

Many of the critical thinking questions in *The History of the Renaissance World: Study & Teaching Guide* require research. The student may be prompted to use a specific citation style in the question, or he may be given a choice. The most common citation styles for writing in the humanities are MLA (Modern Language Association), The Chicago Manual of Style, and APA (American Psychosocial Association). The most up-to-date versions of these style guides can be purchased through each association's website:

MLA (Modern Language Association) https://www.mla.org/Publications/Bookstore/Nonseries/MLA-Handbook-Eighth-Edition

The Chicago Manual of Style, and APA (American Psychosocial Association)

http://www.chicagomanualofstyle.org/home.html

APA (American Psychosocial Association)

http://www.apastyle.org/manual/

The most recent version of each style guide should be used, as citation guidelines and rules are constantly changing, especially when it comes to online and digital sources.

You may also consider purchasing a style and citation reference book, like Diana Hacker's *A Writer's Reference* (Bedford/St. Martin's), which includes guidelines for all three style guides listed above. Again, make sure to acquire the most recent edition. Also, Purdue University's Online Writing Lab (OWL) is an excellent, free, web-based resource: https://owl.english.purdue.edu/owl/

Students should be aware that all sources are not made equal. Here is a quick checklist that can be used to test the reliability of a source.

Credibility check:

- Is the source credible?
- Who is the author/publisher/source/sponsor?
- Can you find the author or publisher's credentials?
- What does the web address end in? Sites that end in .edu and .gov are generally credible, but beware of student and employee blog posts.
- Have you heard of the author/website/publishing house before? If not, can you find information about it easily?
- Is the information in the text supported by evidence? If you answered "no," the source you are working with is most likely not reliable.
- Has the information been reviewed? If you are looking at a blog post, is it part of a reviewed publication (like a national newspaper or cable network)? If you answered "no," the source you are working with is most likely not reliable.
- Are there any spelling or grammar mistakes? Are there typos in the writing? If you answered "yes," the source you are working with is most likely not reliable.

Application check:

- Is this source appropriate for the topic you are writing about? Is it relevant to your topic?
- Is the text written for the appropriate audience (not too basic or too advanced for your work)?
- Is the text written to persuade or convince someone of a point? If so, is the text too biased to use as a source in your research? Can you pull objective information from it? If you answered "no," the source you are working with is most likely not reliable.
- Is the source a stated piece of opinion or propaganda? If you answered "yes," the source you are working with is most likely not reliable.
- Are personal biases made clear? Do these biases affect the objective transmission of information? If you answered "yes," the source you are working with is most likely not reliable.
- Is the source trying to sell you something? If you answered "yes," the source you are working with is most likely not reliable.
- Is this the only source you've found? Is limiting your research detrimental to your final writing product?

Timeliness check:

- When was the information posted or published?
- Has the information been updated or revised recently?
- Is the information outdated? Has the information been proven wrong or inaccurate? If you answered "yes," the source you are working with is most likely not reliable.

***Please note that the checklist above is a guideline for considering the reliability of a source, not a hard and fast list of rules. If you are working on a piece of writing about public relations, for example, and are using an advertisement (trying to sell the reader something) in your work, the article *would* be a good source because it is necessary for your essay, even if it does not pass the test above.

Preface

You may use your text when answering the questions in sections I and II.

Section I: Who, What, Where

Write a one or two-sentence answer explaining the significance of each item listed below.

Age of Enslavement

Gerard of Cremona

Petrarch

Pope Nicholas V

Romanus Pontifex

Tursun Bey

Section II: Comprehension

Write a two or three-sentence answer to each of the following questions.

1. Why did Gerard of Cremona go to the Spanish peninsula in order to find a copy of the Almagest?

2. What did Gerard of Cremona do once he found so many treasured texts in Toldeo? How did he pick what texts to translate?

3. What was Petrarch's personal interest in "a Renaissance"?

4. What is the "Twelfth-Century Renaissance"?

5. When will the history covered in your text end? Why does Susan Wise Bauer choose to end where she does?

6. What commonly written about historical periods followed the Renaissance? How did these periods start?

Section III: Critical Thinking

You may not use your text to answer this question.

The History of the Renaissance World begins with a "Preface." Why? Write a paragraph that first defines what a preface is and second explains why Susan Wise Bauer starts her story of the Renaissance with a preface.

Chapter One

Logic and Compromise

You may use your text when answering the questions in sections I and II.

Section I: Who, What, Where

Write a one or two-sentence answer explaining the significance of each item listed below.

Anselm of Canterbury

Boethius

Calixtus II

Domesday Book

Feudalism

Henry I

Henry V

Lanfranc

Matilda

Paschal II

Robert

Trans-substantio

Walter Tyrrell

William II

Section II: **Comprehension**

Write a two or three-sentence answer to each of the following questions.

1. What did the first article of Henry I's Charter of Liberties declare? What did the remaining thirteen articles of the Charter of Liberties deal with, and what in particular did the Charter assure English barons?

2. How were the *thegns,* or "thanes," of England treated under William the Conqueror?

3. What was an English baron's relationship to his land? What was the *servitium debitum*?

4. Though the Charter of Liberties seemed to benefit English barons, how did it really reinforce Henry I's power?

5. What is investiture? Why was having power over investiture so important in the renaissance world?

6. Why was Aristotelian logic frowned upon by most churchmen?

7. How did ninth-century Irish theologian Johannes Scotus Erigena and eleventh-century teacher Berengar of Tours use Aristotelian logic in relation to theology? Why were they men excoriated for their use of Aristotle?

8. What is the pallium? When Anselm was nominated to be Archbishop of Canterbury, why did he refuse to take the pallium from William II's hand?

9. What could Henry I lose if he continued to fall out with Paschal II over the right of investiture?

10. Explain the terms of the Concordat of London, the agreement made in 1107 that signaled a truce between Henry I and Paschal II.

11. How did Henry V convince Paschal II to come to a compromise about investiture? What were the terms of their agreement?

12. What happened when the bishops of Rome heard the details of Paschal II's compromise with Henry V on the morning of Henry V's coronation ceremony? How did Paschal II end up in Henry V's "protective custody"?

13. How did Paschal II get out of Henry V's "protective custody"? What were the effects of the agreement made with Paschal II on Henry V's rule?

14. Explain the terms of the Concordat of Worms, the agreement made in 1112 between Henry V and Calixtus II.

Section III: Critical Thinking

You may not use your text to answer this question.

In this first chapter of *The History of the Renaissance World* we see immediately how the reintroduction of classical thinking affects the players in our story. While Aristotelian logic was seen by some as threatening to the church, it was used by others to prove God is real. Write a paragraphing explaining how Anselm of Canterbury used Aristotelian logic to affirm God's existence. In your answer, make sure to explain how the dialectic and use of ontological argument helped Anselm of Canterbury in his assertion.

Section IV: Map Exercise

1. Using a black pencil, trace the rectangular outline of the frame for Map 1.1.

2. Using a blue pencil, trace the Mediterranean coastline around Italy, Francia, and Africa. Also trace the coastline around Britain/Ireland and up around Germany. You do not need to include small islands. Repeat until the contours are familiar.

3. Using your black pencil, trace the outlines of the Holy Roman Empire. Repeat this also until the contours are familiar.

4. Trace the rectangular outline of the frame in black. Remove your tracing paper from the original. Using a regular pencil with an eraser, draw the coastline around England, Germany, Western Francia, and Italy. Remember to use the distance from the map frame as a guide.

5. When you are pleased with your map, lay it over the original. Erase and redraw any lines which are more than ¼" off of the original.

6. Study carefully the major regions of England, Normandy, Western Francia, Germany and the Holy Roman Empire, Italy, and the Papal States. Then close the book and mark them on your map. After you checked and corrected any misplaced labels, study the locations of London, Canterbury, Tinchebray, Bec Abbey, Worms, and Rome. When you are familiar with them, close the book. Mark each location with your regular pencil. Check your map against the original, and erase and re-draw any misplaced labels.

Chapter Two

The Crusader Enemy

You may use your text when answering the questions in sections I and II.

Section I: Who, What, Where

Write a one or two-sentence answer explaining the significance of each item listed below.

Alexius Comnenus

Bohemund

Bohemund II

John Comnenus (II)

Leo I

Section II: Comprehension

Write a two or three-sentence answer to each of the following questions.

1. Why did Bohemund fake his own death? How did he get people to believe he was dead?

2. How was Bohemund able to recruit an army of Italians for his fight against Constantinople?

3. Explain how Crusader power in the east continued to grow after Bohemund's defeat in 1108.

4. Explain Jerusalem's relationship to Tripoli after the city was conquered in 1109. Over what other powerful "lordships" did the king of Jerusalem have authority?

5. Describe the division of power in twelfth-century Italy.

6. What was the relationship between the maritime republics and the Crusader kingdoms?

7. What deal did Alexius Comnenus make with the Venetians before the First Crusade? What happened after John Comnenus cancelled the deal?

8. Why did John Comnenus back down and reinstate Venice's privileges in Constantinople?

9. Why did John Comnenus attack Cilicia? How did he come to be allied with Bohemund II of Antioch?

Section III: Critical Thinking

The student may not use her text to answer this question.

The Crusades, military campaigns sanctioned by the pope, were meant to restore Christian power in the Holy Land. The land conquered during these Holy Wars was supposed to be handed over to the Christian emperor. However, we know that didn't happen. Write a paragraph explaining why Alexius Comnenus had the Crusaders that came through Constantinople swear an oath before going off to war. In your answer, explain what was even more motivating to some Crusaders than fighting for God.

Section IV: Map Exercise

1. Using a black pencil, trace the rectangular outline of the frame for Map 2.1.

2. Using a blue pencil, trace the coastal outline of the Mediterranean and the Black Sea. It is not necessary to trace any of the multiple small islands around Turkey and Greece, but be sure to include the passageway from the Aegean through to the Black Sea (the Hellespont (opening passage), Propontis (small sea in the middle), and Bosphorus; the Bosphorus Strait is noted on the map).

3. Using contrasting colors, trace the outlines of the Dukedom of Apulia and Calabria, the Papal States, the Holy Roman Empire, the Republic of Venice, Byzantium, Asia Minor, Cilician Armenia, the County of Edessa, the Principality of Antioch, the Kingdom of Jerusalem, and the Fatimid Caliphate in Egypt. Mark the Sultanate of Rum. Repeat until familiar.

4. When you feel confident, trace the rectangular outline of the map onto a new sheet of paper, using your black pencil. Using your blue pencil, draw the outlines of the Mediterannean and the Black Sea (and passage into it). Remove your paper from the original, and draw the lines of the Dukedom of Apulia and Calabria, the Papal States, the Holy Roman Empire, the Republic of Venice, Byzantium, Asia Minor, Cilician Armenia, the County of Edessa, the Principality of Antioch, the Kingdom of Jerusalem, and the Fatimid Caliphate in Egypt. Mark the Sultanate of Rum.

5. When you are happy with your map, lay it over the original. Erase and redraw any lines which are more than ¾" off of the original.

6. Carefully study the locations of the Countship of Sicily, Rome, Pisa, Genoa, Venice, Dyrrachium, the Bosphorus Strait, Constantinople, Antioch, Aleppo, Tyre, and Jerusalem. When you are familiar with them, close the book. Using your regular pencil, label all 12 on your map. Compare with the original, and erase and re-mark your labels as necessary.

Chapter Three

Anarchy

You may use your text when answering the questions in sections I and II.

Section I: Who, What, Where

Write a one or two-sentence answer explaining the significance of each item listed below.

The Anarchy

Baldwin II

Fulk V

Geoffrey the Handsome

Lothair III

Louis VI

Melisande

Stephen

Section II: Comprehension

Write a two or three-sentence answer to each of the following questions.

1. What were the circumstances of Matilda's younger brother William's death?

2. How did Matilda become first in line for the English throne? How did Henry V's status change because of his marriage to Matilda and the death of her brother?

3. Why did Matilda return to England?

4. Describe the make up of Western Francia/France at the time of Matilda's betrothal to Geoffrey the Handsome.

5. Who was Fulk the Black? What did he do to become famous, and feared?

6. How was it that Matilda had children with Geoffrey the Handsome after she walked out on their marriage?

7. How did Henry I of England die?

8. Describe the first four years of Stephen's rule of England.

9. What happened to England after Matilda invaded with troops from Anjou and Normandy in 1139?

Section III: Critical Thinking

You may not use your text to answer this question.

When the noblemen of England heard that Henry I was dead, they panicked. He had no son to succeed him on the throne . . . but he did have a daughter. The noblemen were scared of both the French influence that would come with Matilda's husband were she to take the throne, but perhaps they were even more resistant to her rule because she was a woman. Strong and influential women have often caused waves of fear to ripple through society. Write a paragraph or two about another powerful woman of your choosing that influenced English history.

Chapter Four

The Lost Homeland

You may use your text when answering the questions in sections I and II.

Section I: Who, What, Where

Write a one or two-sentence answer explaining the significance of each item listed below.

Akuta

Annam

Dai Viet

Do Anh Vu

Gaozong

Jaya Indravarman III

Jayavarman II

Li Qingzhao

Ly Than Tong

Ly Thuong Kiet

Qinzong

Shaoxing Treaty

Suryavarman II

The Imperial Commissioner's Office for the Control and Organization of the Coastal Areas

Yueh

Section II: **Comprehension**

Write a two or three-sentence answer to each of the following questions.

1. Describe the Jurchen invasion of the Song empire between 1127 and 1130.

2. What factors slowed the invading Jurchen down? How did the Song save themselves from complete destruction by the Jurchen?

3. Why did Song Gaozong agree to a peace treaty with the Jurchen in 1141?

4. Though a firm border north of the Dai Viet capital Thang Long was drawn after the defeat of the Song by Ly Thuong Kiet in 1076, how did Chinese culture still manage to infiltrate Dai Viet?

5. Why did Suryavarman II believe it was his duty to subjugate the earth? In your answer, define *Devaraja* and *Chakravartin*.

6. For what reason did Suryavarman II invade Dai Viet?

7. Describe the city of Angkor and its water supply during the time of Suryavarman II's rule.

8. Describe the place Suryavarman II had built for himself in which he would live forever.

9. What happened to Khmer's hold on Champa when Suryavarman II was no longer in power?

Section III: **Critical Thinking**

The student may not use her text to answer this question.

It is clear that Jaya Indravarman III was not a great ruler. Sources remember him as "mild and resourceless," and during his reign the north of Champa was conquered by Suryavarman II. But though Suryavarman II was an ambitious leader, that does not mean he did much better than Jaya Indravarman III for the kingdom of Khmer. Write a paragraph describing how Suryavarman II's determination did just as much harm as it did good for Khmer.

Section IV: **Map Exercise**

1. Using a black pencil, trace the rectangular outline of the frame for Map 4.1: The Kingdoms of China and Southeast Asia.

2. Using a blue pencil, trace the coastline down from the top of the map around the regions of Jin, Southern Song, Dai Viet, Champa, and Khmer to the bottom of the map, around the Bay of Bengal. You do not need to trace the islands to the right of the mainland, though do take note of them. **Do** trace the outline of the island to the right of the Gulf of Tonkin. With your blue pencil, trace the lines of the Yellow, Huai and Yangtze Rivers and also the Bach Dang. Repeat until the contours are familiar.

3. Using pencils in contrasting colors, trace the outlines of the Jin region, the Southern Song region, the Dai Viet region, the Champa region, and the Khmer regions. Repeat until the contours are familiar.

4. Using a new sheet of paper, trace the rectangular frame of the map with your black pencil. Remove your tracing paper from the original. Using your regular pencil with an eraser, draw the coastline down from the top of the map around the regions of Jin, Southern Song, Dai Viet, Champa, and Khmer to the bottom of the map, around the Bay of Bengal. Draw the lines of the Yellow, Huai, and Yangtze Rivers and the Bach Dang. Also draw the outlines of the Jin region, the Southern Song region, the Dai Viet region, the Champa region, and the Khmer regions.

5. When you are pleased with your map, lay it over the original. Erase and redraw any lines which are more than ½" off of the original. Looking at the map, draw the cluster of islands to the right of the mainland.

6. Now carefully study the locations of Zhongdu, Kaifeng, Yangzhou, Nanjing, Lin'an, Ningbo, Quanzhou, Thang Long, My Son, Vijaya, and Ankora. When you are familiar with them, close the book. Using your regular pencil, mark each location on the map. Check your map against the original, and correct any locations that were misplaced or mislabeled.

Chapter Five

Crusade Resurrected

You may use your text when answering the questions in sections I and II.

Section I: Who, What, Where

Write a one or two-sentence answer explaining the significance of each item listed below.

Bernard of Clairvaux

Conrad III

Eleanor

Great Seljuk

Jihad

Louis VII

Manuel

Nur ad-Din

Pope Eugenius III

Quantum praedecessores

Raymond

Zengi

Section II: **Comprehension**

Write a two or three-sentence answer to each of the following questions.

1. Describe the state of the Turkish empire after the death of its establishment by the great conqueror Malik Shah.

2. How did the earthquake that occurred in October of 1138 physically affect the Turkish empire?

3. Why do earthquakes hold such a sacred place in the Muslim culture? How are they viewed by the Muslim people?

4. Why didn't any Christian armies come to Edessa's aid when Zengi and his Muslim soldiers attacked in 1144?

5. Why were Christian soldiers so eager to fight in the Second Crusade?

6. What happened at the beginning of Louis VII's reign that made him want to join the Second Crusade?

7. How might have Louis VII's religious background affected his ability to produce an heir with his wife, Eleanor?

8. What happened to the German, and then the French and German, armies as they attempted to attack Edessa in 1147 and 1148?

9. What advice did Raymond of Poitiers give to Louis VII regarding his next military move after defeat near Laodicea in the Second Crusade? What did Louis VII want to do instead?

10. How did the Second Crusade end?

Section III: **Critical Thinking**

You may not use your text to answer this question.

The actual causes of war, while perhaps clear in historical accounts, are often murky. In this chapter we see two very different cases that show us indirect causes (or excuses) for war. Explain the first and second catalysts for Zengi's attack on Edessa and Louis VII's engagement in the Second Crusade. In your writing, explain how important the secondary cause was in giving legitimacy to each man's first impetus for war.

Section IV: Map Exercise

1. Using a black pencil, trace the rectangular outline of the frame for Map 5.3.

2. Using a blue pencil, trace the coastal outlines of the Mediterranean and the Black Seas including the passage into the Black Sea. Also trace the visible portions of the Caspian Sea (toward the top of the map), the Persian Gulf (into which the Tigris and Euphrates Rivers flow), and the Red Sea. Trace the lines of the Tigris, Euphrates, and Nile. Repeat until the contours are familiar.

3. Now select three contrasting colors to show the territories of Byzantium, the conquests of Zengi, and the conquests of Nur ad-Din. Trace the outlines of each section with the color you choose, as shown by the key on the map. Repeat until the contours are familiar.

4. When you feel confident about the outlines, remove your paper from the original, and close the book. Draw the coastal outlines of the Mediterranean and the Black Seas, including the passage into the Black Sea. Also draw the visible portions of the Caspian Sea, the Persian Gulf, and the Red Sea and the lines of the Tigris, Euphrates, and Nile. Then draw the territories of Byzantium, the conquests of Zengi, and the conquests of Nur ad-Din.

5. When you are pleased with your map, lay it over the original. Erase and redraw any lines which are more than ½″ off of the original.

6. Now carefully study the locations of Constantinople, Nicaea, Dorylaeum, Laodicea, Mount Cadmus, Aleppo, Baghdad, Damascus, Acre, Jerusalem, Damietta, Alexandria, Tanis, Cairo, and Fustat. When you are familiar with them, close the book. Using your regular pencil, mark their locations. Check and correct any locations that were misplaced or mislabeled.

7. Looking at the book, mark the various Sultans: the Sultanate of Rum, the Sultan of Baghdad, and the Sultan of Syria. Mark the region of Jerusalem (as opposed to the city), the Principality of Antioch, Fatimid Egypt, Edessa, Cilician Armenia, and the Danishmends.

Chapter Six

Reconquista and Rediscovery

You may use your text when answering the questions in sections I and II.

Section I: Who, What, Where

Write a one or two-sentence answer explaining the significance of each item listed below.

Afonso Henriques

Alfonso VII

Alfonso the Battler

Ali ibn Yusuf

Almohads

Al-Mu'min

Garcia Ramirez

Ibn Tumart

Ramiro II

Reconquista

Urraca

Section II: Comprehension

Write a two or three-sentence answer to each of the following questions.

1. Who are the Almoravids, and how did they start a crusade in Spain that lasted for centuries?

2. Why didn't the Almoravids take advantage of the break up of Spain after Alfonso the Battler's death?

3. Describe the challenges Alfonso VII faced as he attempted to take Almoravid Oreja. What was the outcome of Alfonso VII's siege on Oreja?

4. Name the Western thinkers described in this chapter that travelled to Toledo before Gerard of Cremona and list their discoveries.

5. What did Gerard of Cremona discover in Toledo? How was he able to translate the texts he found?

Section III: Critical Thinking

You may not use your text to answer this question.

We may not know what happened at the Battle of Ourique, but we do know that Afonso Henriques was victorious, and that his victory prompted him to declare himself the independent King of Portugal. Write a paragraph explaining how the lost details of the Battle of Ourique turned into an epic Portuguese myth by the sixteenth century. In your paragraph, offer an explanation as to how national pride helped turn the Battle of Ourique into such a grandiose story.

Section IV: Map Exercise

1. Using a black pencil, trace the rectangular outline of the frame for Map 6.1.

2. Using a blue pencil, trace the coastline of the Mediterranean around France and Africa through the Straits of Gibraltar and then the Atlantic up around the coastlines of Portugal, Spain, and France. Then trace the line of the Loire River. Repeat until the contours are familiar.

3. Using pencils with contrasting colors, trace the outlines of Western Francia, Navarre, Aragon, Leon-Castile, and Portugal. Use small peaks to show the mountains around Aragon and Navarre. Repeat until the contours are familiar.

4. Using a new sheet of paper, trace the rectangular outline of the map with your black pencil. Remove your tracing paper from the original. Using a regular pencil with an eraser, draw the coastal outlines around the Mediterranean and Atlantic and the Loire River. Then trace the outlines of Western Francia, Navarre, Aragon, Leon-Castile, and Portugal. Use small peaks to show the mountains around Aragon and Navarre.

5. When you are pleased with your map, lay it over the original. Erase and redraw any lines that are more than ¼″ off of the original.

6. Now study the locations of Toulouse, Barcelona, Valencia, the Castle of Oreja, Toledo, Cordoba, Seville, the Battle of Ourique, and the Straits of Gibraltar. Also study the mark showing the Almohad Advance. When they are familiar for you, close the book. Using your regular pencil, mark each location. Check your map against the original, and correct any locations that were misplaced or mislabeled.

Chapter Seven

Questions of Authority

You may use your text when answering the questions in sections I and II.

Section I: Who, What, Where

Write a one or two-sentence answer explaining the significance of each item listed below.

Bernard of Chartres

Collationes

Concordance of Discordant Canons

Fulbert

Gratian

Heloise

Peter Abelard

Peter Lombard

Sentences

Sic et Non

Theologia Scholarium

Section II: Comprehension

Write a two or three-sentence answer to each of the following questions.

1. How did Peter Abelard end up teaching at the cathedral school of Notre Dame, the most prestigious cathedral school in Western Francia?

2. Why couldn't Peter Abelard publicly marry Heloise?

3. What agreement was made between Peter Abelard and Fulbert regarding Heloise and the couple's love child? What did Fulbert do that went against the agreement?

4. Why did Peter Abelard send Heloise to live in a convent, and what were the consequences of his decision?

5. How did Peter Abelard apply some of Plato's philosophies to the doctrines of the church?

6. Why was Bernard of Clairvaux so against the work of Peter Abelard?

7. Why didn't Peter Abelard have to fulfill his sentence of silence? What happened to him after his death?

Section III: Critical Thinking

You may not use your text to answer this question.

When Peter Abelard started working on the *Theologia Scholarium*, one traditional-minded churchman told him, "we recognize only the words of authority." Though couched in terms of religious propriety, the desire for blind faith had more to do with power than it had to do with God. Write a paragraph explaining why traditional churchmen wanted to do away with reason and support only orthodox, accepted understandings of Christianity. In your answer, explain why Peter Abelard's appeal to the Bishop of Sens and to the pope in response to Bernard of Clairvaux's investigation hurt his case rather than helped it.

Chapter Eight

The New Song

You may use your text when answering the questions in sections I and II.

Section I: Who, What, Where

Write a one or two-sentence answer explaining the significance of each item listed below.

Agricultural Treatise

Hangzhou

Prince Hailing

Shizong

Xiaozong

Zhu Xi

Zhongdu

Section II: Comprehension

Write a two or three-sentence answer to each of the following questions.

1. Why did the Jin keep Song Qinzong alive?

2. What did Song Gaozong's court want him to do regarding the Jin? What did Song Gaozong actually do to help the Song during his reign?

3. Where did the French word "satin" come from?

4. Described the tenets of traditional Confucianism.

5. How did Zhu Xi transform Confucianism? In your answer, make sure to define *li* and *qi*.

STUDY AND TEACHING GUIDE FOR THE HISTORY OF THE RENAISSANCE WORLD

6. In what way is Neo-Confucianism like dialectical inquiry? In what way is the origin of Neo-Confucianism unlike the origin of dialectical inquiry?

7. How did Prince Hailing show his love of Song culture?

8. How did Prince Hailing prepare for his invasion into Song territory? What did the Song forces do to beat the Jin troops back?

9. How did the Song and Jin come to sign the Longxing Peace Accord?

Section III: Critical Thinking

You may not use your text to answer this question.

No matter what a ruler might do to silence his critics, voices of dissent always manage to be heard. Write a paragraph explaining how Song Gaozong planned to cut off criticism over the way his dynasty handled the Jin invasion and how that criticism was expressed regardless of the emperor's desires. Use some of the poetry found on page 56 of your text as a way to illustrate your explanation; make sure to explain what you think Lu Yu's words mean.

Chapter Nine

The Heiji Disturbance

You may use your text when answering the questions in sections I and II.

Section I: **Who, What, Where**

Write a one or two-sentence answer explaining the significance of each item listed below.

Go-Sanjo

Go-Shirakawa

Horikawa

Kiyomori

Konoe

Masakiyo

Minamoto

Nijo

Nobuyori

Samurai

Shirakawa

Shoshi

Sohei

Sutoku

Taira

Tametomo

Tameyoshi

Toba

Tokuko

Yoshitomo

Section II: Comprehension

Write a two or three-sentence answer to each of the following questions.

1. How does the thirteenth-century Japanese history, the *Gukansho*, describe the general feeling towards Fujiwara power during the reign of Go-Sanjo?

2. What reforms did Go-Sanjo make in Japanese government in an attempt to tamp down Fujiwara power?

3. Explain the Japanese tradition of Cloistered Emperors.

4. What were the benefits of the Cloistered Emperor tradition?

5. What was the cause for civil war in Japan in 1156? What happened at the Hogen Incident on July 29, 1156?

6. Describe the events of the Heiji Disturbance.

7. What happened to power in the capital after the Heiji Disturbance?

Section III: Critical Thinking

You may not use your text to answer this question.

Eleventh-century Japan was stifled by the power of the Fujiwara clan. As written on the first page of Chapter Nine, "Generation after generation, imperial princes had married Fujiwara brides. Fujiwara ministers of state, usually close male relations of the reigning empress, dominated weak or young rulers. Emperor after emperor was crowned and then retreated behind the scenes to pursue poetry and luxurious living, political ceremony and religious ritual." Emperors were rendered powerless by the Fujiwara and Emperor Go-Sanjo was sick of it. Write a paragraph explaining how Go-Sanjo got out from under the grasp of the Fujiwara and then explain whether or not you think Japan was better off with Go-Sanjo's new system.

Section IV: Map Exercise

1. Using a black pencil, trace the rectangular outline of the frame for Map 9.1: Japan under the Cloistered Emperors.

2. Trace the coastline around Japan. You need not include the very small unmarked islands around the coastline. Repeat until the contours are familiar.

3. Using a new sheet of paper, trace the rectangular outline of the map in black. Then using a regular pencil with an eraser, draw the Japanese coastline. Erase and redraw as necessary.

4. When you are pleased with your map, lay your paper over the original, and erase and redraw any lines which are more than ½" off of the original.

5. Mark Honshu. Then study carefully the locations of Minamoto, Mt. Hiei, Kamo, Nara, Kumano, and Taira. When you are familiar with them, close the book. Using your regular pencil with an eraser, label each location. Check your map against the original, and correct any misplaced or mismarked labels.

Chapter Ten

Death of an Army

You may use your text when answering the questions in sections I and II.

Section I: **Who, What, Where**

Write a one or two-sentence answer explaining the significance of each item listed below.

Chung-heon

Chung-su

Chungbang

Han Roe

Heaven-Sent Force of Loyalty and Righteousness

Injong

Jeong Jung-bu

Kim Bo-dang

Kim Ton-jung

Kyong

Myeongjong

Sinjong

Uijong

Yi Ko

Yi Uibang

Section II: **Comprehension**

Write a two or three-sentence answer to each of the following questions.

1. What are the two major systems for rendering Korean names into the Roman alphabet? What system is used in present day South Korea, and in your textbook? What system is used in present day North Korea?

2. What internal divisions did Goryeo face during the Injong's reign?

3. Explain the relationship between Uijong and Kyong, and how Kyong ended up in exile in 1156.

4. How did Jeong Jung-bu, Yi Ko and Yi Uibang come together in resentment against Uijong? What was the last straw before they decided to go forward with their rebellion?

5. Why did Jeong Jung-bu institute a second purge of civilians after he had already gotten Uijong off the throne? What was the result of the second purge?

6. Why didn't Chung-heon want to rule over the Goryeo army? Why didn't he want to put his own sons on the Goryeo throne after he took power?

7. How did Chung-heon take the rule of Goryeo into his private control?

8. What was left of the Goryeo government after Chung-heon privatized most the running of the country?

Section III: **Critical Thinking**

You may not use your text to answer this question.

Plato's Phaedrus said, "Things are not always what they seem." Write a paragraph explaining one of the following accounts of deceptive appearances that occurred in this chapter. You can write about the appearance of peace Uijong cultivated and why some continued to support him after he was overthrown, or you can write about the true meaning of the king being entertained by Jeong Jung-bu's burning beard. In your answer, explain what the world saw and then explain the truth found beneath.

Section IV: **Map Exercise**

1. Using a black pencil, trace the rectangular outline of the frame for Map 10. 1: Goryeo.

2. Using a blue pencil, trace the visible coastline around China and Japan. Include Koje Island and the other few distinct islands between the coastlines. Repeat until the contours are familiar.

3. Using a black pencil, trace the Goryeo region, and repeat until the contours are familiar.

4. Using a new sheet of paper, trace the rectangular outline of the frame in black. Using your regular pencil, draw the coastlines of China and Japan, the islands, and then also the specific region of Goryeo.

5. When you are pleased with your map, lay it over the original, and erase and redraw any lines which are more than ¼"off.

6. Now study carefully the locations of P'yongyang, Kaesong, and Koje Island. When they are familiar, close the book, and label each location. Then check them against book, and make any needed corrections.

Chapter Eleven

The First Plantagenet

You may use your text when answering the questions in sections I and II.

Section I: **Who, What, Where**

Write a one or two-sentence answer explaining the significance of each item listed below.

Eustace

Henry

William of Conches

Section II: **Comprehension**

Write a two or three-sentence answer to each of the following questions.

1. What areas of England did Stephen control during the civil war? What areas did Matilda control? What did the land look like in between?

2. Describe Henry's first war adventure in England.

3. What happened when Capetian king Louis VII asked the pope for an annulment from Eleanor of Aquitaine?

4. What happened the second time Capetian king Louis VII asked the pope for an annulment from Eleanor of Aquitaine?

5. Why did Louis VII attack Henry after his marriage to Eleanor? What were the terms of the truce made between the two men?

6. Why did Henry agree to a truce with Louis VII that included being submissive to the French throne?

7. How did Stephen and Henry come to sign the Treaty of Wallingford? What were the conditions of the treaty?

8. What did Henry order on Christmas Day of 1154? Why did he make such an order?

Section III: **Critical Thinking**

You may not use your text to answer this question.

At the age of fourteen Matilda's son Henry sailed to England with a small band of soldiers. After losing several small fights, Henry's men deserted him and he was left stranded in England. His mother's treasury was empty, so the King of England himself had to supply the funds to send Henry back to Western Francia and his teenage studies. This was not an auspicious start for young Henry. However, at twenty-one, Henry was Count of Anjou, Duke of Normandy, Ruler of Aquitaine and King of England. Write a paragraph explaining what made Henry a strong ruler. In your answer, explain both political and military decisions Henry made that helped to secure his power.

Section IV: **Map Exercise**

1. Using a black pencil, trace the rectangular outline of the frame for Map 11.1, Anjou, Normandy, and England.

2. Using a blue pencil, trace the coastline around England and around the continent. Also trace the line of the Thames. Repeat until the contours are familiar.

3. Now using a black pencil, trace the outlines of the Domains of the King of France. Repeat until the contours are familiar.

4. Using a new sheet of paper, trace the outline of the map's frame in black. Then remove your paper from the original. Using your regular pencil with an eraser, draw the outline of the coast around England and the continent, the line of the Thames, and the Domains of King of France. When you are done with this, check your map against the original, and erase and redraw any lines which are more than ½" off of the original.

5. Mark England, the Domains of the King of France, and Western Francia. Now carefully study the areas of Kent, Normandy, Anjou, and Aquitaine. When you are familiar with them, mark and label their locations. Then study the locations of London, Malmsbury, Paris, and Poitiers. When you are familiar with them, mark them on your map. Check your map against the original, and erase and redraw any marks more than ½" off of the original.

Chapter Twelve

Frederick Barbarossa

You may use your text when answering the questions in sections I and II.

Section I: Who, What, Where

Write a one or two-sentence answer explaining the significance of each item listed below.

Adrian IV

Alexander III

Callixtus III

Frederick Barbarossa (Frederick of Swabia)

Henry the Lion

Lombard League

Paschal III

Roman commune

Victor IV

Wends

Section II: Comprehension

Write a two or three-sentence answer to each of the following questions.

1. Who did the German crusaders want to be the objects of their holy war? How did they convince Bernard of Clairvaux and Pope Eugenius III to approve the target of their crusade?

2. Why did the Wendish Crusade fail as a holy war?

3. If Henry the Lion was the son of the Duke of Bavaria and Saxony, why didn't he inherit command of Bavaria and Saxony after his father died?

4. What deal did Frederick Barbarossa make with Pope Eugenius III that resulted in the German king being crowned Holy Roman Emperor?

5. How did the people of Rome react to Frederick Barbarossa's coronation as Holy Roman Emperor?

6. Using Genoese and Milan as examples, describe Frederick Barbarossa's reception as Holy Roman Emperor by the papal states.

7. Why did Henry the Lion found the city of Munich on the Isar river and build the port at Lübeck?

8. How was Frederick Barbarossa finally able to conquer Milan? What did he do after he took the city?

9. Why didn't Frederick Barbarossa's men attack the Lombard League as soon as it formed? What did the Lombard League do while Frederick Barbarossa's men were tied up?

10. What were the terms of the peace made between the Lombard League and Frederick Barbarossa in 1177?

11. How did Frederick Barbarossa gain such a strong grasp over Germany after his failure in Rome?

Section III: Critical Thinking

You may not use your text to answer this question.

Frederick Barbarossa knew his power as Holy Roman Emperor was tenuous. He more-or-less forced Pope Eugenius III into giving him the title, and the people of Rome and the papal states were less than pleased with his coronation. Though Frederick Barbarossa ultimately lost power over Rome and the papal states, how did he attempt to use divine right as a way to legitimize his title?

Chapter Thirteen

The Almohads in Spain

You may use your text when answering the questions in sections I and II.

Section I: **Who, What, Where**

Write a one or two-sentence answer explaining the significance of each item listed below.

Alfonso VIII

Extremadura

Fernando (Ferdinand II)

Gerald the Fearless

Ibn Mardanish

Maimonides

Rabbi Maimon ben Joseph

Saladin

Sancho

Yusuf I

Section II: **Comprehension**

Write a two or three-sentence answer to each of the following questions.

1. What happened to remnants of the Almoravid empire in Spain after the fall of Almoravid rule?

2. Why did Rabbi Maimon ben Joseph move his family to Egypt?

3. How did Gerald the Fearless get kicked out of Spain?

4. Even though Gerald the Fearless was aligned with Yusuf I, how did he come to be killed by the caliphate?

5. Why did Yusuf I's siege on Huete fail?

6. What did the battle at Huete between the Almohads and the Christian leaders do for the Christian kingdoms in Spain?

Section III: **Critical Thinking**

You may not use your text to answer this question.

In the last chapter we read about Frederick Barbarossa's struggles to quell the many cities in the papal states that were loyal to their own. Cultural and religious allegiances can often outweigh the benefits of gold and glory. Using allegiance as the key, write a paragraph explaining how Rabbi Maimon ben Joseph/Maimonides, Yusuf I's failure to take Huete, and the Christian kingdoms coming together in 1177 are all related.

Section IV: **Map Exercise**

1. Trace the rectangular outline of the frame for Map 13.1 in black.

2. Using your blue pencil, trace the coastal outline around Western Francia down around the Strait of Gibraltar and the African coastline. Also trace the lines of the Loire and Ebro. Repeat until the contours are familiar.

3. Using your black pencil, trace the lines of the regions of Western Francia, Navarre, Aragon, Castile, Leon, Portugal, Morocco, the Kingdom of Ibn Mardanish, and the Almohads. Repeat until the contours are familiar.

4. Using a new sheet of paper, trace the outline of the frame using your black pencil. Using your regular pencil with the eraser, draw the coastline from Western Francia down around Africa. Then draw the lines of When you are pleased with your map, lay it over the original. Erase and redraw any lines which are more than ½" off of the original.

5. Now study carefully the locations of the regions you traced before: Western Francia, Navarre, Leon, Castile, Aragon, and Portugal, Morocco, the Kingdom of Ibn Mardanish, and the Almohads. When you know them well, close your book. Mark each one on your map with your regular pencil. Then check it against the book, and correct any incorrect labels.

6. Next study carefully the locations of Pamplona, Zaragoza, Barcelona, Toledo, Santiago de Compostela, the Castle of Oreja, Valencia, Badajoz, Lisbon, Evora, Cordoba, Baeza, Seville, Granada, Almeria, and Murcia. Lay your paper over the original, and erase and redraw any marks that are more than ½" off of the original.

Chapter Fourteen

"Many Nations"

The student may use her text when answering the questions in sections I and II.

Section I: Who, What, Where

Write a one or two-sentence answer explaining the significance of each item listed below.

Abu Abdulluh al-Bakri

Ali ibn al-Hassan

Dawud b. Sulayman

Diara Kante

Dunama

Dunama II

Ærediauwa I

Eweka

Girgam

Hajje

Humai

Ife

Ile-Ibinu

Kumbi-Saleh

Oba

Obatala

Ogiso

Ogiso Owodo

Ólodùmarè

Oranmiyan

Salmama I

Soninke People

Sosso

Sumanguru Kante

Zaghawa

Section II: **Comprehension**

Write a two or three-sentence answer to each of the following questions.

1. What does "people" refer to in Susan Wise Bauer's narrative of African history? What does "tribe" refer to?

2. What were some typical goods from the west and center of Africa that traveled the North African trade routes? What was life like in Taghaza and Bilma, the desert mining towns that provided salt for the trade routes?

3. Describe early African slave trade. How did Africans find a way around the rule that forbade Muslims from enslaving fellow Muslims?

4. Where were the three major North African trade routes located?

5. How was Dunama I able to do a brisk trade in slaves in Kanem if Muslims were not allowed to enslave other Muslims?

6. What proof do we have of flourishing Kilwa trade during the Renaissance era?

7. Recount the Yoruba creation story.

Section III: **Critical Thinking**

The student may not use her text to answer this question.

African history existed in oral tradition for centuries. It was only when Islam came to Africa that written chronicles also appeared. Write a paragraph or two explaining how we can see the influence of Islam in the recorded history of Africa that occurred long before the Islamic religion and culture appeared.

Section IV: Map Exercise

1. Trace the rectangular outline of Map 14.1 in black.

2. Using your blue pencil, trace the coastline around the continent of Africa, including the coastline of the Mediterranean and the Red Sea. Trace the lines of the Senegal, the Volta, and the Niger as well. Repeat until the contours are familiar.

3. Using a new sheet of paper, trace the rectangular outline of the map. Remove your tracing paper from the original. Using a regular pencil with an eraser, draw the coastline around Africa, including the Mediterranean and Red Seas. Trace the lines of the Senegal, the Volta, and the Niger as well. When you are happy with your map, lay it over the original. If any of your lines are more than ½″ off of the original, erase and redraw them.

4. Now carefully study the locations of Tunis, Tripoli, Cairo, Mecca, Dar'a, Bilma, Njimi, Sijilmasa, Taghaza, Kumbi Saleh, Ife, and Benin. When you are familiar with them, close the book. Mark and label each one with your regular pencil. Lay your paper over the original, and erase and redraw any locations which are more than ½″ off of the original.

Chapter Fifteen

The Last Fatimid Caliph

You may use your text when answering the questions in sections I and II.

Section I: Who, What, Where

Write a one or two-sentence answer explaining the significance of each item listed below.

Al-Adid

Amalric I

Baldwin III

Manuel I Comnenus

Shawar

Shirkuh

Section II: Comprehension

Write a two or three-sentence answer to each of the following questions.

1. Why did Nur ad-Din bathe himself in the Mediterranean if he was not in control of all of Syria?

2. What stopped Nur ad-Din from taking Jerusalem while Baldwin III was alive?

3. How did Amalric I justify his first attack on Egypt? What did he do to prepare for the assault?

4. Though Amalric I was driven out of Egypt by Shawar, how did his troops end up back in Egypt? How was Amalric I able to secure tribute from the Fatimids?

5. What happened when Shirkuh returned to Egypt with his nephew Saladin in late 1166?

6. How did Amalric I come to fight in Egypt for a third time? What was the result of this siege?

7. Why were so many people against Shawar? Why was Shawar's own son upset with him?

8. How did the Fatimid caliphate come to an end?

Section III: Critical Thinking

You may use your text to answer this question.

In this chapter we read about Amalric I's inability to conquer Egypt. At first he tried to take Egypt on his own, and then he worked with Byzantine emperor Manuel I but they still couldn't shake the Fatimid or Turkish forces. Using your text, write a paragraph in your own words that summarizes the final disastrous attempt of the Crusader-Byzantine armies to take Egypt. After your description, explain why you think the Crusader-Byzantine armies failed (both practically and philosophically).

Chapter Sixteen

Monks and Brahmas

The student may use her text when answering the questions in sections I and II.

Section I: Who, What, Where

Write a one or two-sentence answer explaining the significance of each item listed below.

Baladeva

Basava

Bijjala II

Buddha's Tooth

Giant's Tank

Lingam

Lingayats

Mahakassapa

Parakrama Bahu

Sankama

Sea of Parakrama

Someshvara

Somesvara IV

Vijaya Bahu

Virasaivas

Section II: **Comprehension**

Write a two or three-sentence answer to each of the following questions.

1. How did Parakrama Bahu unify Sri Lanka?

2. What practical renovations did Parakrama Bahu bring to Sri Lanka during his reign?

3. How did Parakrama Bahu balance out the expenses of the restoration and building of dams, reservoirs and canals?

4. In what way were Sri Lankan monks a threat to the unity created by Parakrama Bahu?

5. Describe the character of a Sri Lankan forest monastery during the time of Parakrama Bahu.

6. What was the relationship of the Chalukya with the great twelfth century Chola empire? What happened to that relationship around the time of Vijaya Bahu's rebellion?

7. How did the Hindu temples of central India sustain themselves? How did Brahman priests keep their wealth and power?

8. Why was the philosophy of Basava and the other lingayats a threat to the Brahman priesthood?

9. What did Basava's reckless spending of Bijjala II's treasury have to do with both men's deaths?

10. How did Somesvara IV die? What happened to the Western Chalukya kingdom ruled by Somesvara IV after his death?

Section III: **Critical Thinking**

The student may not use her text to answer this question.

When the Chola were at the height of their power, their king decorated the expanse of Chola land with lingams honoring the power of Shiva. For the Chola king, religious belief tied in with the success of his empire. Religion took on a different role in the kingdom run by Parakrama Bahu. Explain how the Sri Lankan king turned Buddhism not just into Sri Lanka's official religion but also a tool of the state. Begin your answer by explain the reforms Parakrama Bahu made, and then explain the significance of those reforms in terms of Parakrama Bahu's own power and influence.

Section IV: **Map Exercise**

1. Using a rectangular pencil, trace the rectangular outline of the frame for Map 16.1: The Island of Sri Lanka.

2. Using a blue pencil, trace the coastal outline around Sri Lanka and the visible outline of India. Include the small island with Mannar, but you need only draw small circles to show the other

islands. Using your black pencil, trace the dotted line across the center. Repeat until the contours are familiar.

3. Using a new sheet of paper, trace the rectangular outline of the map in black. Then using your regular pencil with the eraser, draw the coastline of Sri Lanka and India, including the island with Mannar. When you are happy with your map, lay it over the original, and erase and redraw any lines which are more than ½″ off of the original.

4. Study carefully the locations of the areas of Mannar, the "Rice Bowl," the "Giant's Tank," Polonnaruwa, the city of Polonnaruwa, the previous Chola-held Land, the Southern Country, Ruhuna, and the Sea of Parakrama. When you are confident that you know them, close the book. Mark and label each location with your regular pencil. Then check it against the original. Erase and redraw any labels which are more than ¼″ off of the original.

Chapter Seventeen

Conquest of the Willing

You may use your text when answering the questions in sections I and II.

Section I: **Who, What, Where**

Write a one or two-sentence answer explaining the significance of each item listed below.

Ahmed Sanjar

Al Biruni

'Ala' al-Din Husain

Atman

Bahram Shah

Ballal Sen (Ballalsena)

Classical Buddhism

Dharma

Firdausi

Ghiyas ad-Din Ghuri

Gopala

Jivatman

Karma

Khusrau Malik

Lakshman Sen (Lakshmanasena)

Mahayana Buddhism

Madanapala

Muhammad

Prithvi Raj

Ramapala

Theravada Buddhism

Vijay Sen (Vijayasena)

Section II: Comprehension

Write a two or three-sentence answer to each of the following questions.

1. Explain the thousand year cycle of rebellion and conquest in the subcontinent of northeastern India.

2. Describe the Buddhism of the Palas under Gopala.

3. What was the religious climate like in the Pala realm under the kings that followed Gopala?

4. How did Vijay Sen symbolically represent the ritual of the Great Gift? What meaning did the ritual hold for Vijay Sen?

5. How did Bahram Shah attempt to deal with the Ghurid threat to his kingdom? What was the result of his plan?

6. Who were the Rajputs, or "sons of kings"? Where did the Rajputs come from?

7. What are some possible reasons for the great Rajput army's defeat by the smaller Ghurid forces?

Section III: Critical Thinking

You may not use your text to answer this question.

Vijay Sen and his son Ballal Sen attempted to use social and religious reform to strengthen the Hindu ruler's hold over the Sena kingdom. However, these reforms actually ended up pulling the kingdom apart. Describe the caste system in India as it existed before and after Vijay Sen's rule, and explain the religious reforms imposed by Vijay Sen. Then explain how Vijay Sen's policies ended up being the death of the Sena empire.

Section IV: Map Exercise

1. Using a black pencil, trace the rectangular outline of the frame for Map 17.1.

2. Using a blue pencil, trace the coastline of India and the lines of the Indus and the Ganges. Repeat until the contours are familiar.

3. Using a black pencil, trace the area of the Ghurid advance. Show the mountains with small peaks. Repeat until the lines are familiar.

4. Using a new sheet of paper, trace the rectangular outline of the frame. Remove your tracing paper from the original. Using a regular pencil with an eraser, draw the coastline. Then draw the lines of the Ghurid advance and the peaks of the mountains.

5. When you are happy with your map, lay it over the original. Erase and redraw any lines which are more than ½″ off of the original.

6. Now study the locations of Khorasan, Ghaznavid, Solankis, Parihars, Chauhans, Ponwars, Nepal, Bihar, Sena, Pala, and Bengal. When you are familiar with them, close the book. Label each location. Check your marks against the original map, and erase and redraw any locations which are more than ¼″ off of the original.

7. Now study the locations of Lahore, Delhi, Vikrampur, Gaur, the Second Battle of Taurain, and the Odantapuri Monastery. When you are happy with your map, lay it over the original. Erase and redraw any misplaced or mismarked labels.

Chapter Eighteen

Death of a Priest

The student may use her text when answering the questions in sections I and II.

Section I: **Who, What, Where**

Write a one or two-sentence answer explaining the significance of each item listed below.

Ranulf de Broc

Theobald of Bec

Thomas Becket

Section II: **Comprehension**

Write a two or three-sentence answer to each of the following questions.

1. How were English church courts like English secular courts? How were they different?

2. What does "the rule of souls" mean, and how did policing the "rule of souls" affect English law enforcement?

3. Why was there a sharp increase in clergymen in England after the Anarchy? How could someone "prove" he was in the clergy?

4. What was the catalyst for Henry II's church court reforms?

5. What changes to the church court did the Constitutions of Clarendon propose?

6. What was the Assize of Clarendon? How did the Assize of Clarendon change the nature of crime in England?

7. Describe what each man, Henry II and Thomas Becket, had to lose when the two met in 1170 outside of Freteval to make peace. What was the outcome of their meeting?

8. What did Thomas Becket do almost immediately after returning to England from his safe-haven in France? Why was this such an aggressive act?

9. How did Thomas Becket die?

10. Describe Henry II's reaction to Thomas Becket's death. If the king wanted the archbishop out of the way, why was he so upset?

Section III: **Critical Thinking**

The student may not use her text to answer this question.

Henry II was an energetic king. He had strong ideas about his ruling of England and did everything he could to realize those ideas. He was, in every way, a leader. Thomas Becket, however, was not. While he rose up from a political career to be the Archbishop of Canterbury, he didn't necessarily get there by blazing new paths. Explain how Thomas Becket rode the power of adaptation and conformity to the most powerful position in the English church. Then explain why it isn't surprising that Henry II had a falling out with Thomas Becket after his appointment as archbishop.

Section IV: **Map Exercise**

1. Trace the rectangular outline of the frame for Map 18.1 in black.

2. Trace the coastal outline around England and the continent in blue. Repeat until the contours are familiar.

3. Use contrasting colors to trace lands claimed by Henry II and lands claimed by Louis VII. Repeat until the contours are familiar.

4. Using a new sheet of paper, trace the outline of the frame in black. Remove your paper from the original. Using a regular pencil with an eraser, draw the coastal outlines around Britain and by Louis VII. When you are happy with your map, lay it over the original. Erase and redraw any lines which are more than ¼″ off.

5. Now study the locations of York, London, Canterbury, Clarendon, Normandy, Paris, Freteval, and Poitiers. When they are familiar, close the book. Mark each location on your map. Then check them against the original, and erase and redraw any marks which are more than ¼″ off of the original.

Chapter Nineteen

Foreign Relations

You may use your text when answering the questions in sections I and II.

Section I: **Who, What, Where**

Write a one or two-sentence answer explaining the significance of each item listed below.

Aimery of Limoges

Andronicus

Béla

Constance

Géza II

John Ducas

Mary of Antioch

King Colomon of Hungary

Raynald of Chatillon

Stefan Nemanja

Stephen III

Thoros II

Section II: **Comprehension**

Write a two or three-sentence answer to each of the following questions.

1. Review: When and how was the Abbasid caliphate established? Who did the Abbasids have to wipe out in order to come to power, and what tensions related to the caliphate continued on?

2. Describe the deterioration of the Turkish realm during the reign of Ahmed Sanjar.

3. What happened, generally, to the Turkish lands after Ahmed Sanjar's death?

4. Where were the borders of Byzantium at the coronation of Manuel I compared to reaches of the empire under Justinian six hundred years earlier?

5. How did Byzantium grow during the fifteen years of Manuel I's reign?

6. Why did Constance of Antioch remarry after Raymond's death? Who did she end up marrying?

7. How did Thoros II end up as the exiled prince of Cilician Armenia? Where was he in his struggle for power at the time Raynald of Chatillon suggested an alliance?

8. Describe the Antiochene-Armenian attack on Cyprus.

9. What happened to Raynald of Chatillon, and the leadership of Antioch, after his attack on Cyprus?

10. How did the kingdom of Croatia change after King Colomon of Hungary declared himself to be Croatia's sovereign? How did it stay the same?

11. Outside of Croatia, how was the rest of the old Roman province of Illyricum divided in the first half of the twelfth century?

12. How was Manuel I involved in the fighting over Hungary's throne after Géza II's death?

Section III: **Critical Thinking**

You may not use your text to answer this question.

Manuel I told Andronicus not to attack the Hungarian forces at Semlin because the astrological signs were unfavorable. Andronicus attacked anyway, and the Byzantine army came out on top. Did he make the right choice? Write a paragraph arguing whether or not Andronicus's decision was the right one, using the aftermath of the attack at Semlin as evidence.

Chapter Twenty

The Venetian Problem

The student may use her text when answering the questions in sections I and II.

Section I: Who, What, Where

Write a one or two-sentence answer explaining the significance of each item listed below.

Alexius

Alexius II

Andronicus Comnenus

Isaac Angelus

Vitale Michiel

William the Good

Section II: Comprehension

Write a two or three-sentence answer to each of the following questions.

1. Describe the relationship between Venice and Byzantium before the Venetians made a treaty with Hungary.

2. Why did the Venetians want to make a treaty with Hungary, their previous enemy? What were the terms of the treaty?

3. How did Manuel I retaliate against the Venetians after they made an alliance with Hungary? What was the response of the Venetians living in Constantinople to Manuel I's countermeasure?

4. How did all the Venetians living in Byzantium come to be arrested on March 12, 1171?

5. What happened between the Venetians and the Byzantines after Doge Vitale Michiel declared war on Manuel I?

6. How did Vitale Michiel's failure in Chios affect Serbia? How did it affect the Venetian prisoners that were being held in Constantinople?

7. Describe Andronicus Comnenus's approach to getting and keeping hold of Byzantine power.

8. How did Andronicus Comnenus die?

Section III: Critical Thinking

The student may not use her text to answer this question.

Manuel I died in 1180. He increased the Byzantine empire's power, but ruined its alliances and friendships. It seems from our reading in this chapter that the people of Constantinople were unperturbed by the foreign hostility Manuel I created. For this critical thinking question, write a paragraph that explains the difference between patriotism and nationalism, and also suggests which sentiment motivated the actions of the mob that revolted against the government run by Alexius II, his regent Mary of Antioch and her chief advisor Alexius. You may look up the definitions of both patriotism and nationalism before composing your answer.

Section IV: Map Exercise

1. Trace the rectangular outline of Map 20.1 in black.

2. Using your blue pencil, trace the coastline of the Mediterranean and the Black Sea. Trace the line of the Danube as well. You do not need to trace all the small islands around Greece and Turkey, but include Chios as it is marked and the entirety of the Kingdom of Sicily. Repeat until the contours are familiar.

3. Using contrasting colors, trace the areas belonging separately to Byzantium and the Holy Roman empire. Using a third contrasting color, trace the outline of the Kingdom of Sicily. Repeat until the contours are familiar.

4. Using a new sheet of paper, trace the rectangular outline of the frame in black. Then remove your paper from the original, and, using your regular pencil, draw the coastline and the outlines of the territories of Byzantium and the Holy Roman Empire. Mark the Kingdom of Sicily as well. When you are happy with your map, lay it over the original, and erase and redraw any lines which are more than ½″ off of the original.

5. Now study the locations of Genoa, Pisa, Rome, Venice, Dyrrachium, Chalcis, Euboea, Chios, the Bosphorus Strait, Constantinople, and Bursa. When you are familiar with them, close the book. Mark and label each location on your map. When you are happy with your map, check it against the original. Erase and redraw any marks which are more than ¼″ off of the original.

6. Mark the areas of the Republic of Venice, the Papal States, Croatia, Bosnia, Serbia, Byzantium, Asia Minor, Paphlagonia, and Cilician Armenia.

Chapter Twenty-One

Resentments

You may use your text when answering the questions in sections I and II.

Section I: **Who, What, Where**

Write a one or two-sentence answer explaining the significance of each item listed below.

Adele of Champagne

Aoife—Pg. 149, ⁋ 1

Diarmait Mac Murchada

Geoffrey

Henry the Younger

Isabelle

John

Margaret

Philip II Augustus

Richard

Richard de Clare

Rory O'Connor

Rosamund Clifford

Treaty of Windsor

Section II: **Comprehension**

Write a two or three-sentence answer to each of the following questions.

1. Why was the High King of Ireland called "co fresabra"? How did being "co fresabra" influence Rory O'Connor's decision to support the king of Meath in his fight with Diarmait Mac Murchada?

2. How did Henry II get control of the port cities in Ireland?

3. Why did most of the Irish kings pledge loyalty to the king of England after Richard de Clare pledged his loyalty?

4. Why couldn't Henry II claim the north of Ireland as his vassal?

5. What happened when Louis VII made an act of war with Henry the Younger against Henry II? Why did some of the English barons side with Louis VII? Why might Eleanor of Aquitaine have encouraged her sons to rebel against their father, Henry II?

6. What happened to Eleanor of Aquitaine as she tried to escape to the court of Louis VII?

7. Summarize the end of Henry the Younger and Louis VII's rebellion against Henry II.

8. How did the French dukes challenge Philip II Augustus at the beginning of his reign? What did he do to show that he would not be taken advantage of by the dukes?

9. Why did Philip II Augustus expel the Jews from France in 1182?

Section III: **Critical Thinking**

You may not use your text to answer this question.

We have read about myriad reasons for a country going to war with its neighbor. One of those reasons pops up more often than not: family feuds. Write two or three paragraphs explaining how the family affairs of Henry II caused the conflicts he faced in this chapter with Louis VII and Philip II Augustus.

Chapter Twenty-Two

Saladin

The student may use her text when answering the questions in sections I and II.

Section I: Who, What, Where

Write a one or two-sentence answer explaining the significance of each item listed below.

Al-Salih Ismail

Guy

Raymond of Tripoli

Sibylla

Section II: Comprehension

Write a two or three-sentence answer to each of the following questions.

1. Why didn't Saladin complete his attack on the castle of Montreal in October of 1171 and force the Christian enemy to surrender?

2. What excuse did Saladin give Nur ad-Din for leaving Montreal in the hands of the Christians? How did Nur ad-Din react?

3. Describe how Saladin turned on al-Salih Ismail.

4. How did Saladin increase both his own power and the power of the Egypt in his first years as sultan?

5. Why did Saladin want Raynald of Chatillon dead?

6. Where did the Crusaders gather in an effort to fight off Saladin? What did Saladin do in response, and for what reason?

7. What happened at the Battle of Hattin? How did Saladin treat King Guy of Jerusalem and Raynald of Chatillon after their capture?

8. Why did the citizens of Christian Acre let Saladin into their city without protest?

9. How Saladin bring together the king of France, the king of England, the Holy Roman Emperor?

Section III: Critical Thinking

The student may not use her text to answer this question.

At the beginning of the chapter, we read a passage including the words of ibn Shaddad about Saladin's ruling style. Official court biographers sometimes stretch the truth about the traits of their masters. Write a paragraph that analyzes ibn Shaddad's portrayal of Saladin. Do Saladin's actions match Ibn Shaddad's description? Use examples from the chapter to support your answer.

Section IV: Map Exercise

1. Using your black pencil, trace the rectangular outline of map 22.1.

2. Using your blue pencil, trace the coastline of the Mediterranean and the visible portion of the Red Sea. Also trace the lines of the Nile and of the Tigris and Euphrates. Repeat until the contours are familiar.

3. Using contrasting colors, trace the territory belonging to Byzantium and the conquests of Saladin. Repeat until the contours are familiar.

4. Using a new sheet of paper, trace the rectangular outline of the map. Using a regular pencil with an eraser, draw the coastline of the Mediterranean, the Red Sea, the Nile, and the Tigris and Euphrates. Then draw the lines of the separate territories of Byzantium and the Conquests of Saladin. When you are happy with your map, lay it over the original. Erase and redraw any lines which are more than ½″ off of the original.

5. Now study carefully the locations of Antioch, Aleppo, Edessa, Mosul, Irbil, Tripoli, Baghdad, Damascus, Tyre, Sephoria, the site of the Battle of Hattin, Acre, Tiberias, Jerusalem, Ascalon, Tanis, Danietta, and Fustat. When you are familiar with them, close the book. Mark each location: Antioch, Aleppo, Edessa, Mosul, Irbil, Tripoli, Baghdad, Damascus, Tyre, Sephoria, the site of the Battle of Hattin, Acre, Tiberias, Jerusalem, Ascalon, Tanis, Danietta, and Fustat. Check them over the original map, and erase and redraw any lines which are more than ½″ off of the original.

6. Mark the castle of Montreal.

Chapter Twenty-Three

The Gempei War

You may use your text when answering the questions in sections I and II.

Section I: **Who, What, Where**

Write a one or two-sentence answer explaining the significance of each item listed below.

Antoku

Gempei War

Go-Toba

Minamoto Yoritomo

Munemori

Shigemori

Shogun

Takakura

Tokuko

Utaisho

Yorimori

Yoshinaka

Section II: **Comprehension**

Write a two or three-sentence answer to each of the following questions.

1. How did the Taira clan come to have so much power after the Heiji Disturbance?

2. How did Go-Shirakawa plan to check Taira power? What happened instead?

3. Why did Munemori attack Yoshinaka before attacking Minamoto Yoritomo? What was the result of Munemori's military strategy?

4. Describe the culminating battle of the Gempei War that took place on April 25, 1185. What happened to Antoku, Kiyomori's widow, and Munemori during the battle?

Section III: Critical Thinking

You may use your text to answer this question.

In this chapter we learn briefly about the war that ended the Taira clan and resulted in the shogunate rule of Japan: the Gempei War. We moved quickly through Japan's 12th century civil war because *The History of the Renaissance World* is such a sweeping volume. In this critical thinking question, take some time to look up a topic from this chapter that interests you. Then, write a paragraph that starts with an explanation of why are you are interested in the topic, how you went about finding more information about the topic, and finally give us some of the details you found out about your topic. Make sure to cite your source(s)!

Section IV: Map Exercise

1. Trace the rectangular outline of Map 23.1 in black.

2. Using your black pencil, trace the coastal outline of Japan and the visible outline of the mainland. Repeat until the contours are familiar.

3. Using a new sheet of paper, trace the rectangular outline of the frame in black. Remove your paper from the original, and, using your regular pencil with an eraser, draw the outline of Japan and the mainland.

4. Now study the locations of Shinano, Kamakura, Kyoto, the Battle of Kurikara, the Dan-no-Ura Strait, and Mt. Hiei. When they are familiar to you, close the book. Mark each one on your map with your regular pencil. When you are happy with your map, check it against the original, and erase and redraw any marks which are more than ¼" off of the original.

Chapter Twenty-Four

Kings' Crusade

The student may use her text when answering the questions in sections I and II.

Section I: Who, What, Where

Write a one or two-sentence answer explaining the significance of each item listed below.

Alys

Ban Kulin

Bohemund III

Henry VI

Section II: Comprehension

Write a two or three-sentence answer to each of the following questions.

1. Describe the dynamic between Henry II and his son Richard around 1188. In what way did the relationship between father and son influence Richard's friendship with the French king, Philip II?

2. Why were both Richard and Philip II threated by Richard's younger brother John? How did they relate their feelings of frustration over John to Henry II?

3. Explain what happened between Henry II, Richard and Philip II after Richard and Philip II made their demands to the English king.

4. Why did Henry II agree to a peace treaty with his son and the French king Philip II? What were Richard and Philip II's final demands, and what great deceit did Henry II discover via the negotiations?

5. Why was Richard given the nickname "Lionheart"? What were his first actions as the English king?

6. What obstacles did Frederick Barbarossa face as he tried to get his Crusader army through Constantinople?

7. What stopped the Crusaders from taking Acre for their own before the arrival of Richard?

8. Explain the terms of the truce made at Acre after Richard's arrival. Why did the truce break down so quickly?

9. What happened when Saladin met Richard north of Arsuf of September 7, 1191?

10. Why did Saladin and Richard agree to make peace? List the terms of the treaty made between Saladin and Richard on September 3, 1192.

11. How did Richard find himself in trouble and imprisoned after he made peace with Saladin? How did Richard get the money to be released from his captivity?

12. What were the circumstances of Richard's death?

13. How did John come to pledge allegiance to Philip II? What happened to John after Richard's death?

Section III: Critical Thinking

The student may not use her text to answer this question.

On page 173, we read that "The Third Crusade, beginning with yet another burst of religious fervor, had ended with political compromise between the Crusaders and their enemies, and with bloodshed between men of the same faith. Crusade had become simply another name for war; and its participants were more likely than not to die at the hands of their fellow believers." Write a few paragraphs explaining how the relationship between Richard and Philip II clearly exemplifies the breaking down of the values of Crusade. In your answer, explain how personal desires outweighed fighting in the name of God.

Section IV: Map Exercise

1. Using your black pencil, trace the rectangular outline of map 24.1.

2. Using your blue pencil, trace the coastal outline all around the map: the Atlantic around England and the continent, the Mediterranean Sea, and the Black Sea. Also trace the lines of the Vistula and the Danube. Repeat until the contours are familiar.

3. Using contrasting colors, trace the territories of Byzantium, the Holy Roman Empire, the Lands Claimed by France, and the Lands Claimed by England. Repeat until the contours are familiar.

4. Using a new sheet of paper, trace the outline of the rectangular frame of the map in black. Using your regular pencil with an eraser, draw the coastal outline around the Atlantic, the Mediterranean, and the Black Sea. Also draw the lines of the Vistula and the Danube. Then draw the lines of the

territories of Byzantium, the Holy Roman Empire, the Lands Claimed by France, and the Lands Claimed by England. Erase and redraw as necessary.

5. When you are happy with your map, lay it over the original. Erase and redraw any lines that are more than ½" off of the original.

6. Mark the locations of Aquitaine, Normandy, Germany, Poland, Hungary, Rus, the Republic of Venice, the Papal States, the Dukedom of Apulia and Calabria, Croatia, Bosnia, Serbia,Dalmatia, Duklja Raska, the Sultan of Rum, Armenia, Cyprus, Edessa, and Jerusalem.

7. Now study the locations of Bonsmoulins, Chinon Castle, Limoges Castle, Poitiers, Rouen, Marseille, Genoa, Vienna, Pisa, Rome, Palermo, Venice, Constantinople, Nicea, Antioch, Aleppo, Damascus, and Jerusalem.

8. When they are familiar to you, close the book. Mark each one on your map: Bonsmoulins, Chinon Castle, Limoges Castle, Poitiers, Rouen, Marseille, Genoa, Vienna, Pisa, Rome, Palermo, Venice, Constantinople, Nicea, Antioch, Aleppo, Damascus, and Jerusalem. Check your marks against the original, and erase and redraw any that are more than ½" off of the original.

9. Now study the locations of the Baltic Prussians, the Sea of Marmara, and Saleph. Mark each and check it against the original.

Chapter Twenty-Five

The Sack of Constantinople

You may use your text when answering the questions in sections I and II.

Section I: Who, What, Where

Write a one or two-sentence answer explaining the significance of each item listed below.

Alexius (Older)

Alexius (Younger)

Alexius V Ducas

Baldwin I

Emeric

Enrico Dandolo

Foulques

Irene

Otto

Philip

Pope Innocent III

Section II: Comprehension

Write a two or three-sentence answer to each of the following questions.

1. How did Pope Innocent III hope to persuade the heads of state in Europe to join in a renewed fight for the Holy Land?

2. Who were the participants in the Fourth Crusade? What problems did they face even before the Crusade started?

3. How did Zadar come to be returned to the Doge of Venice?

4. Why was Philip eager to help Alexius, his wife Irene's brother, take back the Byzantine throne? How did Philip and Alexius plan to remove the usurper from Constantinople?

5. What did Alexius and Philip expect to happen when they arrived with their Crusader army at Constantinople? What actually happened?

6. Why did the people of Constantinople turn on young Alexius?

7. How did the mission of the Fourth Crusade turn into the rescue of Constantinople?

Section III: Critical Thinking

You may not use your text to answer this question.

Throughout Chapter Twenty-five we read about how the boredom of the men in the Fourth Crusade turned into anger. With nothing else to do, the Crusaders got into brawls, harassed the citizens of the cities in which they were settled and set fire to things for fun. The bloody end of the Fourth Crusade, then, should not have been a surprise. Write a description of the end of the Fourth Crusade and explain how it was the appropriate conclusion to this particular holy war.

Chapter Twenty-Six

Westward

The student may use her text when answering the questions in sections I and II.

Section I: Who, What, Where

Write a one or two-sentence answer explaining the significance of each item listed below.

Aconcagua

Chimu

Chan Chan

Cuzco

Hunac Ceel

Manco Capac

Moche

Nazca

Tacaynamo

Section II: Comprehension

Write a two or three-sentence answer to each of the following questions.

1. Describe the way of life in the northern part of the Yucatán peninsula under the descendants of Hunac Ceel.

2. What is a rain shadow? Give an example from the chapter of an area that is in a rain shadow.

3. How did the Nazca people survive in the Atacama Desert?

4a. What did the center of Moche civilization look like before it disappeared?

4b. What did the areas surrounding the center of the Moche civilization look like before they too disappeared?

5. What brought an end to the Nazca and Moche civilizations?

6. What did the Moche do in an effort to stop the natural disasters that were ruining their civilization? What evidence do we have of these precautionary actions?

7. According to Inca legend, where did Manco Capac come from? What does the legend about Manco Capac tell us about his ruling style and the general character of the Inca?

Section III: Critical Thinking

The student may not use her text to answer this question.

The early history of the South American peoples is, as we read in this chapter, "a puzzle." We have to read the clues left behind and figure out what they mean. However, sometimes that is not possible. Write a paragraph that describes the line drawings at Nazca and explains what some historians have suggested the line drawings might mean. Then write a paragraph explaining what you think the art historian George Kubler meant when he said of the line drawings that "the lines 'inscribe human meaning upon the hostile wastes of nature.'"

Section IV: Map Exercise

1. Trace the rectangular outline of the frame for map 26.2 in black.

2. Trace the coastline in black. Trace the mountain peaks. Repeat until the contours are familiar.

3. Using a new sheet of paper, trace the rectangular outline of the frame in black. Then using your regular pencil with the eraser, draw the coastline. Show the mountains with small peaks. Check it against the original, and erase and redraw any lines more than ¼" off of the original.

4. Study the areas of the Andes, the Atacama Desert, and the Equator. Close the book, mark and label them, check them against the original, and correct any mistakes.

5. Then study the locations of the Moche and the Nazca, the Chimu, and of Chan Chan, Cuzco, and the Place of the Sun and Place of the Moon. Close the book, and mark them on your map. Check them against the original, and erase and redraw any that are more than ¼" off of the original.

Chapter Twenty-Seven

The Mongol School of Warfare

You may use your text when answering the questions in sections I and II.

Section I: Who, What, Where

Write a one or two-sentence answer explaining the significance of each item listed below.

Borjigid

Borte

Genghis Khan

Ilah Ahai

Jamuqa

Li Anchaun

Li Renxiao

Merkit

Taichi'ut

Temujin

Toghrul

Weiming Chunyou

Weishaowang

Western Xia

Section II: **Comprehension**

Write a two or three-sentence answer to each of the following questions.

1. Who were the Mongols? Where did they come from and how was their society structured?

2. Describe the circumstances of Temujin's childhood that led to his preparation as a great fighter and survivor.

3. How did Jamuqa meet his end? What was his final request?

4. How did Genghis Khan change the role of the Mongol khan?

5. Why did the Mongols choose to attack the Western Xia?

6. What tactic did the Mongols use to break past the Western Xia at the mountain pass north of the Chung-hsing?

7. How did Genghis Khan expect his dam to help him in the fight against the Western Xia? How did it actually help him?

8. What happened when Genghis Khan and the Mongols attacked the Jin capital of Zhongdu in 1214?

9. How did the Mongols conduct themselves after the Zhongdu governor took poison and the city's defenses collapsed?

Section III: **Critical Thinking**

You may not use your text to answer this question.

In this chapter we read about the rapid growth of the Mongol state. Temujin turned into Genghis Khan and he created a huge mobile government that traveled with him wherever he went. Yet, the increasing sophistication of the Mongols did not outweigh their nomadic and warring background. In fact, these roots often helped the Mongols in their conquests. Write a paragraph or two explaining how the rough background of the Mongols aided in their quest to build an empire.

Section IV: **Map Exercise**

1. Trace the outline of the rectangular frame of Map 27.1 in black.

2. Trace the coastline in blue (just a little). Also trace the line of the Yellow River. Repeat until the contours are familiar.

3. Trace the areas of the Western Xia, the Jin, and the Southern Song in contrasting colors. Trace mountains with small peaks. Repeat until the contours are familiar.

4. Using a new sheet of paper, trace the rectangular outline of the frame in black. Using your regular pencil with an eraser, draw the coastline. Then draw the line of the Yellow River. Then draw the areas of the Western Xia, the Jin, and the Southern Song. Show the mountains with small peaks. When you are happy with your map, lay it over the original. Erase and redraw any lines that are more than ¼" off of the original.

5. Now study the Altai, Khentil, and Goryeo areas. Then study the locations of Zhongdu, Chunghsing, Kaifeng, and Yangzhou. When they are familiar for you, close the book, and mark and label them on your map. Check them against the original, and erase and remark any that are more than ¼" off of the original.

6. Finally, study the movements of Ghangis Khan: the Negotiations 1209, Dominance 1209, Initial invasion 1210, and Initial Invasion 1211. Also study the location of Lake Baikal and Burkhan Khaldun, the birthplace of Genghis Khan. When they are familiar for you, close the book, and mark and label them on your map. Check them against the original, and erase and remark any that are more than ¼" off of the original.

Chapter Twenty-Eight

John Softsword

The student may use her text when answering the questions in sections I and II.

Section I: Who, What, Where

Write a one or two-sentence answer explaining the significance of each item listed below.

Arthur

Constance

Isabella of Angoulême

Simon de Montfort

Stephen Langton

Section II: Comprehension

Write a two or three-sentence answer to each of the following questions.

1. What happened between John and Philip after Richard the Lionheart's death? How did Philip once again disrupt English family affairs?

2. Why did John want to marry Isabella of Angoulême? What enemy did John make after arranging his marriage to the young French girl?

3. How did John start to refill the treasury after his coronation and during his war in Western Francia?

4. What strategy did John use to refill his treasury after the war in Western Francia ended?

5. How did John justify seizing the Archbishop of Canterbury's estates and their revenue for himself?

6. What happened after Pope Innocent III put England under interdict?

7. Describe the decision John made about the Jews living in England in 1210. Why did he make this decision? How did John treat other religious clergy?

8. How did John respond to the rapidly growing resentment against him?

Section III: **Critical Thinking**

The student may not use her text to answer this question.

Nicknames can be endearing and they can also be cruel. Often nicknames show us something of our true nature. Explain how the military actions of King John of England earned him the nickname "Johannem Mollegladium," or John Softsword. In your answer, explain what you think the nickname means.

Chapter Twenty-Nine

Sundiata of the Mali

You may use your text when answering the questions in sections I and II.

Section I: Who, What, Where

Write a one or two-sentence answer explaining the significance of each item listed below.

Epic of Sundiata

Griots

Keita

Nare Fa Maghan

Sundiata

Section II: Comprehension

Write a two or three-sentence answer to each of the following questions.

1. Why was control over Ghana so desired by African leaders?

2. What brought the Muslim faith to the Keita?

3. How did Nare Fa Maghan's successor handle the conflict between the Keita and the Sosso? What did this mean for the reach of Sumanguru's power?

4. How did the Keita use the marriage treaty made with the Sosso to undo their rival clan?

5. In what way does the *Epic of Sundiata* reflect religious tensions between the Keita and the Sosso? Explain what real world circumstances caused the Keita to view Sumanguru as a religious enemy.

6. Describe the destruction of Sumanguru's kingdom.

7. In what way was Sundiata's success dependent on the African slave trade?

Section III: Critical Thinking

You may not use your text to answer this question.

What is a *jinn*? In the excerpt of the *Epic of Sundiata,* Sumanguru's father is called a *jinn.* After looking up the word *jinn,* use what you know from the chapter about how the Keita viewed Sumanguru and write a paragraph explaining why this detail was included in the epic. Also explain how Sumanguru's ruthlessness, as portrayed in the excerpt from the chapter given on page 207, is tied to the word *jinn.*

Section IV: Map Exercise

1. Using your black pencil, trace the rectangular outline of the frame for map 29.1 in black.

2. Using your blue pencil, trace the coastline. Also trace the line of the Niger and the Senegal. Using contrasting colors, trace the outlines of the separate territories of the Sosso, the Mali, and the Old Ghanan Empire. Repeat until the contours are familiar.

3. Using a new sheet of paper, trace the rectangular outline of the frame in black. Using your regular pencil with an eraser, draw the coastline. Also draw the line of the Niger and the Senegal and the outlines of the separate territories of the Sosso, the Mali, and the Old Ghanan Empire.

4. When you are happy with your map, lay it over the original. Erase and redraw any lines that are more than ¼″ off of the original.

5. Now study carefully the locations of Niani, Gao, Kumbi Saleh, and Mani. Study also the Central Trade Route to Tunis. When they are familiar, close the book, and mark and label them on your map. Check them against the original, and erase and remark any that are more than ¼″ off of the original.

Chapter Thirty

The Jokyu War

The student may use her text when answering the questions in sections I and II.

Section I: **Who, What, Where**

Write a one or two-sentence answer explaining the significance of each item listed below.

Bakufu

Go-Horikawa

Go-Takakura

Goseibai shikimoku (regulation)

Goseibai Shikimoku (book)

Hojo Masako

Hojo Tokimasa

Juntoku

Minamoto Yoriie

Sanetomo

Shikken

Yasutoki

Yoshitoki

Section II: **Comprehension**

Write a two or three-sentence answer to each of the following questions.

1. Why couldn't the Kamakura *bakufu* replace the ancient authority of the Japanese emperor in Kyoto?

2. How did Minamoto Yoritomo work around the Kamakura bakufu's inability to take all power completely from the emperor?

3. After the establishment of the shogunate, what were the official ruling positions in the Japanese imperial government and the Kamakura *bakufu*? Why did the court priest Jien write in the *Gukansho* that it was "strange" for Go-Toba to be in power by himself?

4. Why did Go-Toba retire to the role of Cloistered Emperor in 1198?

5. How did the Japanese emperor's seat acquire the nickname the "Chrysanthemum Throne"?

6. Why did Go-Toba want to go to war against Yoshitoki and Masako?

7. What happened when Go-Toba's plans to attack the shogunate were found out?

Section III: **Critical Thinking**

The student may not use her text to answer this question.

Minamoto Yoritomo took a great risk when he established shogunate rule of Japan. Explain the gamble Minamoto Yoritomo took and why taking this risk was necessary for the establishment of the shogunate. In your answer, use the Jokyu War as an example of how the skills of the samurai helped them to gain power.

Chapter Thirty-One

The Unwanted Throne

You may use your text when answering the questions in sections I and II.

Section I: **Who, What, Where**

Write a one or two-sentence answer explaining the significance of each item listed below.

Alexius Comnenus

Boril

Despot and Despotate

Henry

John III Vatatzes

Kaloyan

Michael

Partitio Romaniae

Philip

Robert of Courtenay

Theodore Comnenus Ducas

Theodore Lascaris

Yolanda

Section II: **Comprehension**

Write a two or three-sentence answer to each of the following questions.

1. What were the terms of the *Partitio Romaniae*?

2. Why was the French Crusader Boniface, Marquis of Monferrat, given his own realm after the sack of Constantinople?

3. How did the king killer and traitor Mourtzouphlus (Alexius V Ducas) finally meet his end?

4. Why was it hard for Baldwin to maintain unified control over Byzantium?

5. What circumstances brought Emperor Baldwin and the Doge of Venice to work together to save Byzantium?

6. What happened to Bulgaria after the death of Andronicus?

7. How did the Latin moment of dominance over Byzantium start to unravel?

8. How did Greek culture thrive under Theodore Lascaris?

Section III: **Critical Thinking**

You may not use your text to answer this question.

Constantine united his men in battle behind Christ in the 4th century, leading to a unified empire under one God. We are reading now of the failed Crusades and their aftermath. Inspired by Constantine's devotion to God but lacking the true faith the great emperor held, these Crusades created empires that quickly fell apart. Using religious devotion as the common point between the two empires, compare the Latin Empire to the Empire of Nicaea. In your answer, explain why you think one failed and the other succeeded.

Chapter Thirty-Two

The First Delhi Sultanate

The student may use her text when answering the questions in sections I and II.

Section I: **Who, What, Where**

Write a one or two-sentence answer explaining the significance of each item listed below.

Ali Mardan

Aram Shah

Dhimmi

Fidaiyan (fidawi)

Firoz

Ghulams

Hasan Sabbah

Iltumish

Jaitra Singh

Mahmud

Mamluks

Mulahidah (Nizari)

Qutb-ud-din

Raziyya

Section II: **Comprehension**

Write a two or three-sentence answer to each of the following questions.

1. How did Islamic rulers cultivate loyalty in the Turkish slaves they owned?

2. What happened to the mamluks after they converted to Islam and were set free?

3. What is the different between a Shi'ite Muslim and a Sunni Muslim?

4. What happened to the Ghurid empire after Muhammad Ghuri's murder?

5. How did Qutb-ud-din create a particularly Indian Muslim land?

6. How did Iltumish spend the first twenty-five years of his sultanate?

Section III: **Critical Thinking**

The student may not use her text to answer this question.

Political conspiracies are often at the heart of murder-mystery novels and television shows. The secretive world of backroom politics is undeniably intriguing. In this chapter we learn about one of these secret societies, the Mulahidah/Nizari. Write a paragraph explaining how this sect emerged. Then write a paragraph that explains how the English word for political killings has its origins in the history of this group.

Section IV: **Map Exercise**

1. Trace the outline of the frame for Map 32.2 in black.

2. Trace the coastline in blue, including Sri Lanka. Also trace the lines of the Indus, the Ganges, the Narmada, and the Kaveri. Trace until the contours are familiar.

3. Using a black pencil, trace the area for the Sultanate of Delhi under Iltumish. Trace the mountains with small peaks. Repeat until the contours are familiar.

4. Using a new sheet of paper, trace the rectangular outline of the frame in black. Using your regular pencil with an eraser, draw the lines of the coastline and the Indus, Ganges, Narmada, and Kaveri rivers. Show the Himalaya mountains and the Salt Range with small peaks. Draw the line of the territory of the Sultanate of Delhi under Iltumish. When you are happy with your map, lay it over the original. Erase and redraw any lines which are more than ¼" off of the original.

5. Study the locations of Herat, Ghazni, Lahore, Delhi, Ranthambore, Gwalior, and Aghata. When they are familiar for you, mark and label them on the map. Check them against the original, and erase and redraw any lines which are more than ¼″ off of the original.

6. Now study the Makran, Sind, Mewar, Vindhya, Chola, Orissa, Himalaya, Punjab, and Salt Range areas. Label them on the map, check them against the original, and correct any incorrect labels.

7. Label the Arabian Sea and Sri Lanka.

Chapter Thirty-Three

Heresy

You may use your text when answering the questions in sections I and II.

Section I: **Who, What, Where**

Write a one or two-sentence answer explaining the significance of each item listed below.

Albigensian Crusade

Arnold, the Abbot of Cisteaux

Bogomilism

Cathars/Catharism

Dominic de Guzman

Donatists

Peter Waldo

Pierre de Castelnau

Raymond VI

Waldensians

Section II: **Comprehension**

Write a two or three-sentence answer to each of the following questions.

1. How did the Nicene Creed give power to claims of heresy?

2. How does Augustine rationalize the right for Christian kings to punish wrong actions as well as wrong beliefs?

3. What happened to religious heretics, generally, in the medieval world?

4. While most eleventh- and early twelfth century heretics were threatened with imprisonment or financial loss, what gruesome fate did other heretics of the time suffer?

5. What was the common point among the twelfth-century charismatic heretics in the south of Francia? Use examples to back up your answer.

6. Why didn't the people of southern Francia rally against the heretics preaching in their lands?

7. Where was the twelfth-century stronghold of Catharism in southern Francia? Why did Catharism take root in this place?

8. What did Dominic de Guzman find when he traveled barefoot through Languedoc, trying to bring the Cathars back into the orthodox fold?

9. Describe the terms of the crusade declared by Innocent III against the Cathars and Raymond VI.

10. What happened when the bishop of Béziers told the Catholic citizens of the city to "quit the city and leave the heretics behind"? What was the Abbot of Cisteaux's response?

11. How did Simon de Montfort become the leader of the Albigensian Crusade? How did Simon de Montfort treat those that resisted the armies of God?

Section III: Critical Thinking

You may not use your text to answer this question.

What is heresy? Heresy is defined on page 233 as "a departure from orthodoxy that was not merely dangerous, but placed the thinker outside the gates of the kingdom of God. Heresy was more than error. Error was wrong belief; error became heresy when the believer, confronted by the Church's condemnation, refused to give it up." In order for heresy to exist, there had to be a set of rules in place regarding religion and worship. The first boundaries were drawn when the Nicene Creed was approved by Constantine. But how did Raymond VI, an orthodox Christian, come to be the focus of an attack on heresy? Write a paragraph explaining how Raymond VI came to be the focus of a new crusade and then explain how Pope Innocent III changed the meaning of both crusade and heresy.

Section IV: Map Exercise

1. Trace the rectangular outline of the frame for Map 33.1 in black.

2. Trace the outline of the coast in blue around England and around the continent, including the visible portion of the Mediterranean Sea. Also trace the line of the Herault from the Mediterranean. Using your black pencil, trace the outline of the kingdom of Philip II. Trace the mountains with simple peaks. Repeat until the contours are familiar.

3. Using a new sheet of paper, trace the outline of the rectangular frame in black. Using your regular pencil with an eraser, draw the coastline around England and the continent, including the Mediterranean and also the line of the Herault. Then draw the line of the territory of the Kingdom of King Philip II. When you are happy with your map, lay it over the original. Erase and redraw any lines more than ½" off of the original.

4. Now study the locations of Brittany, Normandy, the Pyrenees, and Languedoc. Mark each on your map, check the book, and correct any mis-markings.

5. Now study the locations of Tours, Chartres, Melun, Paris, Soissons, Reims, Sens, Cluny, Lyons, Beziers, Termes, Lastours, Minerve, Carcassonne, Toulouse, Bram, and Alaric. When you are familiar with them, close the book. Mark and label each one on your map. Check your map with the original, and erase and remark any incorrect labels.

6. Finally, carefully study the locations of Argenteuil, St. Denis, Paraclete, Clairvaux, and Cluny. When you are familiar with them, close the book. Mark and label each one on your map. Check your map with the original, and erase and re-mark any incorrect labels.

Chapter Thirty-Four

Reconquest and Failure

The student may use her text when answering the questions in sections I and II.

Section I: **Who, What, Where**

Write a one or two-sentence answer explaining the significance of each item listed below.

Alfonso IX

Amicia

James

Muhammad al-Nasir

Pedro II

Sancho I

Sancho the Strong

Yusuf II

Section II: **Comprehension**

Write a two or three-sentence answer to each of the following questions.

1. Why was the Albigensian Crusade difficult for Pedro the Catholic to navigate?

2. How did Pedro the Catholic broker a truce in 1210 between Simon de Montfort and his brother-in-law?

3. What happened to Pedro the Catholic's fight against Muhammad al-Nasir after Almohad troops had begun to cross the Strait of Gibraltar in May 1211?

4. Describe the July 16, 1212 battle at Las Navas.

5. Why did Pedro the Catholic and Raymond of Toulouse decide to mount an attack on Simon de Montfort?

6. What happened when the army of knights from Aragon and Toulouse attacked Simon de Montfort's central fortification, the castle at Muret?

Section III: Critical Thinking

The student may not use her text to answer this question.

In the last chapter we read about Raymond of Toulouse's resistance against the Albigensian Crusade. In this chapter we read about Raymond of Toulouse's dragging feet regarding his penance. We also read about the formation of another crusade, this time declared in January 1212 by Pope Innocent III against the Almohads in Spanish territory. Simon de Montfort continued to lead the fight, but the local nobility in Southern France were growing tired of him. Write a paragraph that explains the similarity between Raymond of Toulouse and Simon de Montfort; though Simon de Montfort despised Raymond of Toulouse, explain how both men wanted the same thing.

Chapter Thirty-Five

From Bouvines to Magna Carta

You may use your text when answering the questions in sections I and II.

Section I: Who, What, Where

Write a one or two-sentence answer explaining the significance of each item listed below.

Articles of the Barons

Barons' War

Curia Regis

Frederick II

Henry III

Hugues de Boves

Louis

Magna Carta

Unknown Charter

William Longsword

William Marshal

Section II: Comprehension

Write a two or three-sentence answer to each of the following questions.

1. How did Pope Innocent III plan to resolve the quarrel with John, king of England, over Stephen Langton's appointment as Archbishop of Canterbury?

2. What happened after Innocent III made his intentions to start a war against John clear?

3. How did Philip II redirect his energies after the pope told him he could not attack John?

4. How did Otto IV become the Holy Roman Emperor? Why did the Count of Flanders turn to Otto IV when Philip II decided to march on Flanders?

5. Why did king John of England say "Since I became reconciled to God, woe is me; nothing has gone prosperously with me!" after the battle at Bouvines?

6. For what main reason did the earls and barons of England want John to confirm the Charter of Liberties first penned by Henry I?

7. What was the main desire of the English earls and barons when they attempted to append the Charter of Liberties with a list of "evil customs" to be righted by the king?

8. How did the English noblemen react to John putting off ratifying the Unknown Charter and the Articles of the Barons?

9. What did John do before signing the Magna Carta to ensure he would be able to get out of its bounds?

10. How did Louis, son of Philip the French king, become king of England?

11. How did Louis lose the kingship of England?

Section III: Critical Thinking

You may not use your text to answer this question.

Magna Carta is a very important document. It has influenced modern government in myriad ways; the American Bar Association even has a monument to honor the document, inscribed "To commemorate Magna Carta, symbol of Freedom Under Law." For this critical thinking question, take some time to explore the Magna Carta. Use the sources listed in the chapter in the footnote on page 253, the sources listed below, and/or sources of your own finding and then write a list of eight things you did not know about the Magna Carta, or things that you found very interesting about the document and its history. Make sure to keep track of the bibliographic information that corresponds to each fact/idea. Then, write three questions about the Magna Carta that you could use for a research project at a later date. Remember: a good research question is open-ended, considers "How?" "What?" or "Why?," and stems from thorough preliminary research (your list of facts).

Internet sources:

- Magna Carta Exhibition from the British Library: http://www.bl.uk/magna-carta
- Magna Carta at National Archives & Records Administration: http://www.archives.gov/exhibits/featured_documents/magna_carta/

- Magna Carta from the History Channel:
    http://www.history.com/topics/british-history/magna-carta
- "The Mad King and Magna Carta" by Dan Jones from *Smithsonian Magazine*
    http://www.smithsonianmag.com/history/
  mad-king-magna-carta-180955745/?no-ist

Section IV: **Map Exercise**

1. Using your black pencil, trace the rectangular outline for map 35.1.

2. Using your blue pencil, trace the coastline around England, Ireland, the continent, and the visible portion of the Mediterranean. Include the lines of the Thames, the Seine, and the Loire. Using two pencils in contrasting colors, trace the outlines of the English empire and the regions belonging to France.

3. Using a new sheet of paper, trace the rectangular outline of the frame in black. Using a regular pencil with an eraser, draw the coastline around England and the continent, including the visible portion of the Mediterranean. Then draw the lines of the regions belonging to the English Empire and to France. When you are happy with your map, lay it over the original. Erase and redraw any lines which are more than ½" off of the original.

4. Now mark the areas of Ireland, Wales, and England on your map. Then study carefully the locations of Connacht, Meath, Ulster, Leinster, Flanders, Normandy, Brittany, Poitou, Aquitaine, and Languedoc. When you are familiar with them, close the book. Mark each one and label it on your map. Check it against the original, and erase and remark any mistakes.

5. Now study closely the locations of Waterford, Dublin, St. Edmonds, Rouen, Paris, Tours, Poitiers, and Le Blanc. When you are familiar with them, lay your paper over the original, and erase and remark any marks that are more than ½" off of the original.

6. Now, with your paper still over the original, trace the rectangular outlines of the small boxes that show the enlargement of the areas in England and in Flanders. Remove your paper from the original. Study closely the locations of Windsor, Runnymede, Staines, London, Canterbury, Dover, Tournai, Lille, Valenciennes, and the Battle of Bouvines. When you are familiar with them, close the book, and show the location of each in the enlarged boxes (you can use dots and lines, as the book does). When you are happy with your marks, check them against the original, and erase and remark any misplaced or mislabeled marks.

7. Finally, study the locations of Chatillon and Chinon. Mark them on your map, check your marks against the original, and make any necessary corrections.

Chapter Thirty-Six

The Birth of the Inquisition

The student may use her text when answering the questions in sections I and II.

Section I: **Who, What, Where**

Write a one or two-sentence answer explaining the significance of each item listed below.

Amaury

Dominicans

Fourth Lateran Council

Francis of Assisi

Franciscans

Honorius III

Lateran Council

Louis IX

Raymond VII

Section II: **Comprehension**

Write a two or three-sentence answer to each of the following questions.

1. Why did Pope Innocent III call for the Fourth Lateran Council? What business had to be settled before the pope could follow his original agenda?

2. How did the Fourth Lateran Council proceed after the business with Raymond of Toulouse was taken care of?

3. Describe Raymond of Toulouse's homecoming.

4. What happened to Innocent III's body after he died?

5. How did Simon de Montfort's siege on Toulouse finally come to an end?

6. How did the attack at Marmande strengthen the resistance against Amaury de Montfort and Prince Louis?

7. In what way did Philip II Augustus's reign change Western Francia?

8. Explain the terms of the deal, the Treaty of Paris, made between Raymond VII and Blanche of Castile.

Section III: Critical Thinking

The student may not use her text to answer this question.

At the end of this chapter we learned about a new way to deal with heretics: inquisition. In your own words, describe the method established at the church council in Toulouse in 1229 that would eliminate heretics from southern France. Then explain how this new method could be used for evil rather than for good.

Chapter Thirty-Seven

Moving Westward

You may use your text when answering the questions in sections I and II.

Section I: Who, What, Where

Write a one or two-sentence answer explaining the significance of each item listed below.

Ala ad-Din Muhammad ibn Tekish

Chagatai

David the Builder

George IV

Jalal ad-Din

Jebe and Subotai

Jochi

Mstislav III

Muhammad al-Nasawi

Ogodei

Tamar

Tolui

Section II: **Comprehension**

Write a two or three-sentence answer to each of the following questions.

1. How did Shan Ala ad-Din Muhammad ibn Tekish plan to defend himself against the Mongol front? What actually happened?

2. Describe Genghis Khan's movement east across Khwarezm.

3. What happened to Jalal ad-Din and his family during the effort to attack the Mongols?

4. What had the Rus' been doing since their Christian conversion in the tenth century?

5. How did Genghis Khan die?

Section III: **Critical Thinking**

You may not use your text to answer this question.

As we know from our history reading, and from hearing contemporary news reports, diplomacy is a tricky thing. Describe, in your own words, the attempt at diplomacy carried out by Genghis Khan towards Shah Ala ad-Din Muhammad ibn Tekish. Then write a paragraph explaining why you think the Shah reacted the way he did. What was the key component missing in the negotiation between Genghis Khan and the Shah?

Section IV: **Map Exercise**

1. Trace the rectangular outline of the frame around Map 37.1 in black.

2. Using a blue pencil, trace all visible coastline, including the Caspian Sea, the Aral Sea, and Lake Baikal. Also trace the lines of the Oxus and the Indus. Repeat until the contours are familiar.

3. Using contrasting colors, trace the Western Xia, Jin, and Southern Song areas. Also trace the areas of the Kingdom of Georgia and of Goryeo. Repeat until the contours are familiar. Trace the mountains with small peaks. Finally, using your black pencil, trace the outline of the conquests of Ghengis Khan in black. Repeat all until the contours are familiar.

4. Using a new sheet of paper, trace the rectangular outline of the frame in black. Then using your regular pencil with an eraser, draw the visible coastline and the lines of the Caspian Sea, the Aral Sea, Lake Baikal, and the Oxus and the Indus. Draw the lines of the Western Xia, Jin, and Southern Song areas. Draw the lines of the Kingdom of Georgia and of Goryeo. Show the mountains with small peaks. Then draw the outline of the conquests of Ghengis Khan. Erase and redraw as necessary.

5. When you are happy with your map, lay it over the original. Erase and redraw any lines which are more than ½" off of the original.

6. Now study the locations of Tbilisi, Nishapur, Merv, Bukhara, Balkh, Tirmidh, Samarkand, Khojend, Otrar, Otukan, Ordu-Baliq, Zhongdu, Kaifeng, Yangzhou, and Burkhan Khaldun. When they are familiar for you, close the book. Mark and label each on your map. Then lay your map over the original, and erase and remark any which are more than ½″ off of the original.

7. Mark the areas of the Hindu Kush and Li'pan.

Chapter Thirty-Eight

South of India

The student may use her text when answering the questions in sections I and II.

Section I: Who, What, Where

Write a one or two-sentence answer explaining the significance of each item listed below.

Chandrabhanu

Jatavarman Sundara

Magha

Parakrama Bahu II

Sangha

Sirisamghabodhi

Vijaya Bahu III

Section II: Comprehension

Write a two or three-sentence answer to each of the following questions.

1. Why wasn't Magha able to establish his own power in Orissa or Chola? Why was Sri Lanka a good target for his ambitions?

2. What did Magha do once he arrived in Sri Lanka?

3. How did Sri Lanka come to be divided between Dambadeniya and Polonnaruwa?

4. What did Vijaya Bahu III and Parakrama Bahu II do to revive Buddhism in Sri Lanka and ensure its longevity?

5. What happened to Polonnaruwa after Magha's death in 1255?

6. Where did the Chola go after the rule of Jatavarman Sundara?

Section III: Critical Thinking

The student may not use her text to answer this question.

In the last chapter we read about the failed diplomatic actions of Genghis Khan and Ala ad-Din Muhammad ibn Tekish. In this chapter we again see an attempt at diplomacy, this time for a small kingdom looking to expand without war. Write a paragraph explaining how Dambadeniya used trade rather than battle as a way to grow their influence in the world.

Section IV: Map Exercise

1. Trace the rectangular outline of the frame for Map 38.1 in black.

2. Using your blue pencil, trace the coastline, including around the island. Also trace the line of the Kaveri. Repeat until the contours are familiar.

3. Using a contrasting color, trace the line of the territory of the Pandya. Then using a different color trace the Orissa area. Repeat until the contours are familiar.

4. Using a new sheet of paper, trace the rectangular frame of the map in black. Then using a regular pencil with an eraser, draw the coastline, including the island. Draw the line of the Kaveri. Then draw the line of the Pandyan territory, erasing and redrawing as necessary. When you are happy with your map, lay it over the original. Erase and redraw any lines which are more than ¼" off of the original.

5. Now study carefully the locations of Nellore, Thanjavur, Polannaruwa,and Dambadeniya. When they are familiar to you, close the book. Mark and label each on your map. Then lay your map back over the original, and erase and remark any marks which are more than ¼" off of the original.

6. Finally mark Palk Strait and the Giant's Tank. Also mark the Arabian Sea.

Chapter Thirty-Nine

The Fifth Crusade

You may use your text when answering the questions in sections I and II.

Section I: Who, What, Where

Write a one or two-sentence answer explaining the significance of each item listed below.

Al-Adil

Al-Kamil

Al-Mu'azzam

Andrew II

King John of Jerusalem

Pelagius

Yolande

Section II: Comprehension

Write a two or three-sentence answer to each of the following questions.

1. Why didn't Frederick II of Germany join in the Fifth Crusade?

2. How did the Egyptians protect Damietta from invasion?

3. What happened to Damietta's defenses after al-Adil's death?

4. Why did Francis of Assisi go to Damietta?

5. How did al-Kamil react to Francis of Assisi's visit to Cairo?

6. What happened when the Crusaders finally stormed into Damietta on November 4, 1218?

7. Describe what happened to the Fifth Crusade after the conquest of Damietta.

8. How did the Fifth Crusade end?

9. What hope did the Crusaders have for a future defeat of the Muslim army?

Section III: Critical Thinking

You may not use your text to answer this question.

In this chapter we read that the Fifth Crusade, according to Roger of Wendover, "assembled in great force at Acre, under the three kings of Jerusalem,* Hungary, and Cyprus." The asterisk next to Jerusalem leads us to a footnote that reads "By 'Jerusalem,' Roger of Wendover means the remnants of the Kingdom of Jerusalem centered at Acre; increasingly it was known as the kingdom of Acre." The fight over the boundaries and ownership of Jerusalem (now known as a city in the nation of Israel) is one that continues to this day. Using your research skills, answer the following questions:

- What is the Arab-Israeli conflict?
- How does the "Holy Land" play into the Arab-Israeli conflict?
- What is the current state of the Israeli-Palestinian conflict?
- *What is the Arab-Israeli conflict?*
- *How does the "Holy Land" play into the Arab-Israeli conflict?*
- *What is the current state of the Israeli-Palestinian conflict (as of date of publication)?*

Chapter Forty

From the Golden Bull to the Baltic Crusade

The student may use her text when answering the questions in sections I and II.

Section I: Who, What, Where

Write a one or two-sentence answer explaining the significance of each item listed below.

Béla

Boleslaw

Cumans

Gertrude

Golden Bull

Konrad

Lithuanians

Novae Institutiones

Piast

Polans

Teutonic Knights

Section II: Comprehension

Write a two or three-sentence answer to each of the following questions.

1. What natural occurrence helped King Andrew of Hungary secure his throne? What did Andrew do on his own to safeguard his power?

2. What were the terms of the *novae institutiones*?

3. How did Andrew's marriage to Gertrude affect the social and governmental structure of Hungary?

4. Why did the Teutonic Knights settle in Hungary in 1211? What was expected of the knights?

5. What did Andrew propose to do with the *novae institutions* when he returned from the Fifth Crusade in 1219? What was the reaction of the Hungarian people?

6. How did Andrew and the Teutonic Knights come to fight against one another?

7. Why was a crusade started against the Lithuanians?

8. In what way did the Baltic Crusade change as fighting dragged on?

Section III: Critical Thinking

The student may not use her text to answer this question.

The theme of displacement continues from the last chapter in this Critical Thinking question. Write a paragraph or two explaining how both religious beliefs and the desire for a homeland motivated the Teutonic Knights in their crusade against the Lithuanians.

Section IV: Map Exercise

1. Using your black pencil, trace the rectangular outline of the frame for Map 40.1: The Baltic Crusade.

2. Using your blue pencil, trace the visible coastline of the Baltic Sea and the Black Sea. You do not need to include all the small islands in the Baltic. Also trace the lines of the Danube and the Vistula. Repeat until the contours are familiar.

3. Using contrasting colors, trace the outline of the territories of Rus, Hungary, and the Holy Roman Empire. Show the mountains with small peaks. Repeat until the contours are familiar.

4. Using a new sheet of paper, trace the outline of the frame of Map 40.1 in black. Remove the sheet of paper, and draw the lines of the coast of the Baltic and the Black Seas. Then draw the lines of the territories of Rus, Hungary, and the Holy Roman Empire. Show the mountains with small peaks.

Erase and redraw as necessary. When you are happy with your map, lay it over the original. Erase and redraw any lines which are more than ½″ off of the original.

5. Now study carefully the locations of Bavaria, Austria, Silesia, Polans, Little Poland, Kujawy, Mazovia, Greater Poland, Prussians, Lithuanians, Letts, Transylvania, and Cumans. When they are familiar to you, close the book. Using your regular pencil with the eraser, mark and label each one. Then check it against the original, and correct any misplaced or mislabeled marks.

Chapter Forty-One

Lakeshores, Highlands, and Hilltops

You may use your text when answering the questions in sections I and II.

Section I: Who, What, Where

Write a one or two-sentence answer explaining the significance of each item listed below.

Bulala

Dunama Dibalemi

Ezana

Gebra Maskal Lalibela

Marara

Yekuno Amiak

Section II: Comprehension

Write a two or three-sentence answer to each of the following questions.

1. What happened to Axum after Ezana's death and then the fall of the capital city?

2. How did Gebra Maskal Lalibela use the coronation ceremony to show that the Zagwe king was a descendent of Moses and his Ethiopian wife?

3. Explain the connection Yekuno Amiak claimed to have to King Solomon. How did the connection help Yekuno Amiak?

4. What was the *mune* and why was it so powerful? What did Dunama Dibalemi do to the *mune*?

5. Why didn't Dunama Dibalemi need the *mune*?

6. How do we know that Dunama Dibalemi was a faithful follower of Islam? If he was so devout, why didn't he convert those pagans he captured on his raids of Lake Chad?

7. Why did the Mapungubwe settle near the Limpopo river?

8. Explain how we know that wealth was unevenly distributed among the Mapungubwe.

Section III: Critical Thinking

You may not use your text to answer this question.

Explain how water plays an important role in the histories we read in this chapter. How did water influence/affect the lives of the Zagwe, the Kanem, and the Mapungubwe?

Section IV: Map Exercise

1. Using your black pencil, trace the rectangular frame of Map 41.1: Zagwe, Kanem, and Mapungubwe.

2. Using your blue pencil, trace the outline of the continent, including the Mediterranean and the Red Seas. Also trace the line of the Senegal, the Niger, the Nile, and the Limpopo. Repeat until the contours are familiar.

3. Now using contrasting colors, trace the outline of the Zagwe, Empire of Ghana, Benin, and Empire of Kanem areas. Repeat until the contours are familiar.

4. Using a new sheet of paper, trace the rectangular outline of Map 41.1 in black. Using your regular pencil with an eraser, draw the coastline around the continent and the Mediterranean. Then draw the Zagwe, Empire of Ghana, Benin, and Empire of Kanem areas, erasing and redrawing as necessary. When you are happy with your map, lay it over the original, and erase and redraw any lines which are more than ½" off of the original.

5. Now study carefully the locations of Malinke, Susu, Owan, Ife, Edo, Igbo, Nri, Kumbi Saleh, Taghaza, Sijilmasa, Tunis, Tripoli, Bilma, Nijimi, Aafa, Shewa, Kilwa, and Mapungubwe. Also study Sakalava. When they are familiar for you, close the book. Then mark and label each one on your map. Check your map against the original, and erase and remark any labels which are more than ½" off of the original.

Chapter Forty-Two

The Sixth Crusade

The student may use her text when answering the questions in sections I and II.

Section I: Who, What, Where

Write a one or two-sentence answer explaining the significance of each item listed below.

Balian of Sidon

Conrad

Garnier l'Aleman

Gregory IX

Section II: Comprehension

Write a two or three-sentence answer to each of the following questions.

1. How did Holy Roman Emperor Frederick II also become "King of Jerusalem"?

2. What stopped Frederick II from going on crusade in August 1227? Did he give a good reason to return home?

3. How did Frederick II react to his excommunication from the church by Pope Gregory IX?

4. Why was Frederick II excommunicated for a second time?

5. What was Frederick II's plan to take back Jerusalem with only a tiny army to fight against the Muslim occupants? What wrench was thrown into his plan?

6. How did al-Kamil and Frederick II treat each other after their original agreement fell apart?

7. What were the terms of the treaty made between al-Kamil and Frederick II?

8. What were the reactions of both the Muslims and the Christians to Frederick II's retaking of Jerusalem?

9. Why was Frederick II treated with such disgust as he left Acre, even thought he had just restored the Holy City for Christendom, Jerusalem, to the Christians?

Section III: Critical Thinking

The student may not use her text to answer this question.

Once again we see the motivation for crusade mix with desire for personal gain. In this chapter we saw Holy Roman Emperor Frederick II finally go on crusade. What took him so long? Write a paragraph explaining why Frederick finally decided to fulfill his obligation to fight for God, and how that decision had more to do with his own material desires than his piety.

Chapter Forty-Three

The Tran Dynasty

You may use your text when answering the questions in sections I and II.

Section I: Who, What, Where

Write a one or two-sentence answer explaining the significance of each item listed below.

Bang Klang T'ao

Bo Dala

Cao Tong

Chieu Hoang

Hue Tong

Indravarman II

Jaya Paramesvaravarman II

Pha Muong

Syam

Tran Canh (Thai Tong)

Tran Thu Do

Section II: Comprehension

Write a two or three-sentence answer to each of the following questions.

1. How did Tran Thu Do try and eliminate any possibility of Ly revolt against the Tran family?

2. What happened to the Dai Viet government and system of law under the direction of Tran Thu Do and Tran Canh?

3. Why didn't Pha Muong try to claim rule over the first independent kingdom of the Syam?

4. Describe Champa's prosperity under Jaya Paramesvaravarman II.

5. What were the circumstances of Jaya Paramesvaravarman II's death?

Section III: Critical Thinking

You may not use your text to answer this question.

We don't find out much about Indravarman II in this chapter. Susan Wise Bauer writes that he was "an obscure king almost unknown to the chronicles." What else is out there about Indravarman II? Do some research and find out at least three more things about the little-known Khmer ruler. Make sure to cite your sources in your answers.

Section IV: Map Exercise

1. Trace the rectangular outline of the frame for Map 43.1 in black.

2. Using your blue pencil, trace the coastal outline. You do not need to include the small islands off the coast. Repeat until the contours are familiar.

3. Using contrasting colors, trace the outlines of the Dai Viet, Nam Dinh Province, Syam, Sukhothai, Khmer, and Champa areas. Repeat until the contours are familiar.

4. Using a new sheet of paper, trace the outline of the frame in black. Then using your regular pencil with an eraser, draw all the visible coastline. Then draw the separate areas of the Dai Viet, the Nam Dinh Province, Syam, Sukhothai, Khmer, and Champa areas. Erase and redraw as necessary. When you are happy with your map, lay it over the original. Erase and redraw any lines which are more than ½" off of the original.

5. Study the location of Chao Phraya on your map, and mark it. Check your work, and correct it necessary.

Chapter Forty-Four

Young Kings

The student may use her text when answering the questions in sections I and II.

Section I: **Who, What, Where**

Write a one or two-sentence answer explaining the significance of each item listed below.

Alhambra

Blanche of Castile

Cortes

Crusade indulgence

Ferdinand III

Hugh de Lusignan

Ibn al-Ahmar

Ibn Hud

Isabella of Angoulême

The Peace of Alcalá

Section II: **Comprehension**

Write a two or three-sentence answer to each of the following questions.

1. Why were the French barons against Louis IX, even though France was more prosperous than ever?

2. Describe the plan hatched by the French barons to take power away from the king.

STUDY AND TEACHING GUIDE FOR THE HISTORY OF THE RENAISSANCE WORLD

3. How did Blanche of Castile thwart Henry III's plans to take back the French lands King John had lost?

4. How did Henry III manage to find a friendly shore to land on after his first attempt against France failed?

5. What happened to Henry III's campaign from Brittany against Louis IX?

6. How did Hugh de Lusignan and Isabella of Angoulême come to be taken prisoner by Louis IX?

Section III: Critical Thinking

The student may not use her text to answer this question.

James of Aragon and Ferdinand III of León-Castile fought against the Muslims that occupied Spain and reclaimed the land for Christianity. This was a crusade in everything but name. Write a paragraph, using the information from the chapter, that explains what the Spaniards did differently from the previous crusaders we read about, and how these differences led to success against the Muslim opposition.

Section IV: Map Exercise

1. Trace the rectangular outline of the frame for Map 44.1 in black.

2. Using your blue pencil, trace the coastline all around England and the continent. Also trace the line of the Charente river. Repeat until the contours are familiar.

3. Using contrasting colors, trace the lines of the areas of France and of England (be sure to note the difference between contemporary borders and those depicted in this map). Repeat until the contours are familiar. Then using your black pencil, trace the outline of the area of Normandy. Repeat until the contours are familiar.

4. Using a new sheet of paper, trace the rectangular outline of the frame in black. Then using your regular pencil with an eraser, draw the coastline around England and the continent, including the Charente river. Erase and redraw as necessary. Then draw the separate territories of England and of France. When you are happy with your map, place it over the original, and erase and redraw any lines which are more than ½" off of the original.

5. Now study carefully the locations of Portsmouth, Paris, Montlhery, Corbeil, Saint-Malo, Nantes, Taillebourg, and Bourdeax. Also study the broader regions of Normandy, Brittany, Marche, and Aquitaine.

6. When they are familiar for you, close your book. Mark each location on your map. Check your map against the original, and erase and redraw any location which is more than ½" off of the original.

7. Mark the Charente. Mark the directions of the invasions of Henry III, as the map shows.

Chapter Forty-Five

The Mongol Horde

You may use your text when answering the questions in sections I and II.

Section I: **Who, What, Where**

Write a one or two-sentence answer explaining the significance of each item listed below.

Aizong

Batu

Béla IV

Choe-U

Chormaghan

Gojong

Henry the Pious

Kadan

Orda

Pak So

Sartaq

Yu-ke-hsia

Section II: **Comprehension**

Write a two or three-sentence answer to each of the following questions.

1. How were the lands of the Universal Khan divided after his death?

2. Where did the Jin go after the north of the empire fell, and what had they been up to since the fall?

3. What happened the first time the Mongols found themselves at the Yalu river in 1218?

4. How did Choe-U get the Mongols to retreat from their 1231 attack on Goryeo? Where did he go after the Mongol retreat?

5. Who helped the Mongols get to the Jin? What route did Subotai use to get to the Jin capital of Kaifeng?

6. What happened when the Mongols reached the Jin capital of Kaifeng?

7. Describe Subotai and Batu's tear across Rus territory.

8. Why were the Hungarians doomed in their fight against the Mongols, even though they were heavily armored and seemingly ready to fight?

9. How did the Mongols come to be known as the Antichrist?

Section III: Critical Thinking

You may not use your text to answer this question.

The Mongols were a great and powerful force. But even these fierce fighters were flawed. Write a paragraph explaining the Mongols' weaknesses. In your answer, consider how nature thwarted the Mongols.

Section IV: Map Exercise

1. Trace the outline of the rectangular frame for Map 45.2 in black.

2. Using your blue pencil, trace the coastal outline around northern Europe, the Mediterranean, the Black Sea, the Caspian Sea, and the Aral Sea. Also trace the lines of the Danube, the Vulga, the Amu Darya, and the Syr Darya. Repeat until the contours are familiar.

3. Now using your black pencil, trace the outlines of the Mongol Conquests. Using contrasting colors, show the areas of Hungary and Georgia. Repeat until the contours are familiar.

4. Now using a new sheet of paper, trace the rectangular outline of the map in black. Then using your regular pencil with an eraser, draw the coastline all around the Mediterranean and northern Europe, including the Black Sea and the Caspian Sea. Erase and redraw as necessary. When you are happy with your map, lay it over the original. Erase and redraw any lines which are more than ½" off of the original.

5. Now study carefully the areas of the Holy Roman Empire, Austria, Polans, Greater Poland, the Prussians, the Lithuanians, Hungary, Croatia, Serbia, and Georgia. When they are familiar to you,

close the book. Mark each one on the map. Then check your work against the map, and correct any mismarked or misplaced labels.

6. Now study carefully the locations of Vienna, Liegnitz, Budapest, and Tbilisi. Study the locations of Kiev, Moscow, and Riazan as well. When they are familiar for you, close the book and mark each one on your map. When you are happy with it, then place your map over the original. Erase and re-mark any marks that are more than ½″ off of the original.

7. Study and mark the location of the Battle of the Sajo River. Mark the Volga and the Danube as well.

Chapter Forty-Six

The Debt of Hatred

The student may use her text when answering the questions in sections I and II.

Section I: Who, What, Where

Write a one or two-sentence answer explaining the significance of each item listed below.

Animadversio debita

Excommunicamus

Henry

Henry Raspe

Imperial diet

John of Brienne

Pope Innocent IV

William of Holland

Section II: Comprehension

Write a two or three-sentence answer to each of the following questions.

1. Describe the state of the The Holy Roman Empire as Frederick II returned home from Jerusalem.

2. How did Pope Gregory IX promote the destruction of the Holy Roman Empire? Was his strategy effective?

3. What happened when Frederick II sent for Henry to attend the 1231 imperial diet at Ravenna?

4. How had Frederick treated heresy since the beginning of his reign?

5. Explain how heresy brought Frederick II and Gregory IX to work together.

6. What happened after Henry declared war on his father in December of 1234?

7. How did Gregory IX come to excommunicate and depose Frederick II after working together to fight heresy?

8. Why did Frederick II retreat from his planned attack on Rome in August of 1241? Did this retreat make a difference for Frederick II's ongoing quarrel with the Church?

9. What was happening in Italy while Conrad fought William of Holland's forces in Germany?

10. Where did Frederick II die, and where was he buried?

Section III: Critical Thinking

The student may not use her text to answer this question.

When Pope Innocent IV came to power, he declared that he had an "absolute papal monarchy." Write a paragraph explaining what "absolute papal monarchy" meant to Pope Innocent IV, and what it means to have "absolute" power. Then explain why this kind of power can be very dangerous.

Chapter Forty-Seven

The Shadow of God

You may use your text when answering the questions in sections I and II.

Section I: Who, What, Where

Write a one or two-sentence answer explaining the significance of each item listed below.

Bahram

Balban

Malik Altuniah

Malik Hakut

Naramasimha Deva

Nasiruddin

Section II: Comprehension

Write a two or three-sentence answer to each of the following questions.

1. How did Raziyya handle the rumors that she appointed Malik Hakut to be Master of the Stables because he was her lover?

2. Explain Balban's rise from slave to vizier.

3. What outside threats did Delhi face at the start of Nasiruddin's reign?

4. How did Balban deal with the Hindu and Mongol threats?

5. Why did Balban arrange his daughter to marry Nasiruddin?

6. Why did Balban lead troops into war against the hill country of Mewar in 1260? What was the result of the fighting?

7. How did Balban justify his place as sultan of Delhi?

8. What did Balban do, and what did he have others do, to prove that he was *Zil-i-llahi*?

9. What practical things did Balban do to secure his place as *Zil-i-llahi*?

10. How did Balban go from being a slave to turning his people, for all intents and purposes, into slaves themselves?

Section III: Critical Thinking

You may not use your text to answer this question.

Raziyya was "a great sovereign." She was "sagacious, just, beneficent . . . and of warlike talent." However, several officers once loyal to Raziyya's father Iltumish did not support her rule, even though she was an excellent leader. Write a paragraph explaining why the vizier of Delhi and his supports would want to put one of Iltumish's useless sons on the throne instead of the capable and strong Raziyya.

Section IV: Map Exercise

1. Trace the rectangular outline of the frame for Map 47.1 in black.

2. Using your blue pencil, trace the coastline, including the outline of Sri Lanka. Also trace the line of the Indus and of the Ganges, as well as the Narmada and Kaveri. Repeat until the contours are familiar.

3. Using a contrasting color, trace the lines of the Sultanate of Delhi under Balban. Trace the mountains with small peaks. Using your black pencil, trace the Chola and Orissa areas. Repeat until the contours are familiar.

4. Using a new sheet of paper, trace the rectangular outline of the frame in black. Then, using your regular pencil with an eraser, draw the coastline, including Sri Lanka. Draw the Indus and Ganges and Narmada and Kaveri. Show the mountains with small peaks. Then draw the area of the Sultanate of Delhi under Balban. Erase and redraw as necessary. When you are happy with your map, lay it over the original, and erase and redraw any lines more than ½" off of the original.

5. Now study carefully the Makran, Sind, Mewar, Choa, Orissa, Bengal, and Punjab areas. When you are familiar with them, close the book and mark them on your map. Then study the locations of Herat, Ghazni, Lahore, Bathinda, Delhi, Kannauj, Talsandah, and Laknaur. When they are familiar for you, close the book, and mark them on your map. When you are happy with your map, lay it over the original. Erase and re-mark any marks more than ½" off of the original.

6. Mark the arrows indicating the Mongol incursions as shown in the book.

Chapter Forty-Eight

The Seventh Crusade

The student may use her text when answering the questions in sections I and II.

Section I: Who, What, Where

Write a one or two-sentence answer explaining the significance of each item listed below.

As-Salih Ayyub

As-Salih Ismail

Baibars

Charles

Fakhr-ad-Din

Margaret of Provence

Robert

Turan-shah

Section II: Comprehension

Write a two or three-sentence answer to each of the following questions.

1. What motivated Louis IX to go on crusade?

2. Why did Frederick II's treaty with al-Kamil come to an end?

3. Who did as-Salih Ayyub hire to attack his uncle's Syrian domains? What was their history?

4. How was Jerusalem retaken by the Muslims?

5. What did Louis IX do to prepare for the Seventh Crusade?

6. Describe the beginning of the Seventh Crusade.

7. What happened at Damietta?

8. Why did the Crusaders stay so long in Damietta? What did they do while they were there?

9. What happened after Turan-shah unexpectedly cut the Crusaders off from behind outside of Mansurah, blocking their supply from Damietta?

10. Why did Turan-shah murder the sick and wounded Crusaders after accepting Louis IX's surrender? What terms were set for the truce after the killing of the sick and wounded?

11. Why did the Turkish soldiers rise up against Turan-shah?

12. How did the Seventh Crusade end?

Section III: Critical Thinking

The student may not use her text to answer this question.

The Seventh Crusade should have been a success. Louis IX made sure his soldiers were well-prepared, and yet, the Crusade turned into a fiasco with Jerusalem still in Muslim hands. Explain what you think went wrong. What do you think was the main reason the Crusaders failed?

Section IV: Map Exercise

1. Trace the rectangular outline of the frame for Map 48.1: The Seventh Crusade in black.

2. Trace the coastal outline around the Mediterranean, including the Black Sea and the Red Sea. You do not need to include all the small islands around Greece and Turkey. Repeat until the contours are familiar.

3. Using your black pencil, trace the outlines of France, the Holy Roman Empire, the Papal States, Cyprus, the Kingdom of Jerusalem, and the Ayyubid Empire. Repeat until the contours are familiar.

4. Using a new sheet of paper, trace the rectangular outline of the frame of Map 48.1 in black. Using your regular pencil with an eraser, draw the coastline around the Mediterranean and the Red and Black Seas. Then draw the areas of France, the Holy Roman Empire, the Papal States, Cyprus, the Kingdom of Jerusalem, and the Ayyubid Empire. Erase and redraw as necessary. When you are happy with your map, lay it over the original, and erase and remark any marks that are more than ½" off of the original.

5. Now study carefully the locations of Aigues-Mortes, Paris, Genoa, Damascus, Acre, Jerusalem, Damietta, Mansurah, and Cairo. When you are familiar with them, close the book. Mark and label each location. Then check your labels against the original, and erase and redraw any marks and labels that are more than ½" off of the original.

6. Mark the areas of France, the Holy Roman Empire, the Papal States, Golden Horde, Cyprus, the Kingdom of Jerusalem, Egypt, and the Ayyubid Empire.

7. Mark the line showing the progress and direction of the Seventh Crusade.

Chapter Forty-Nine

The Splintering Khanate

You may use your text when answering the questions in sections I and II.

Section I: Who, What, Where

Write a one or two-sentence answer explaining the significance of each item listed below.

Alghu

Arik-Boke

Berke

Guyuk

Hulagu

Kublai

Mongke

Rukn al-Din

Toregene

Tran Hoang

Section II: Comprehension

Write a two or three-sentence answer to each of the following questions.

1. Why was Guyuk so unpopular? How did he manage to replace Ogodei as Great Khan despite his unpopularity?

2. Describe Guyuk's coronation ceremony.

3. What kind of gift did Pope Innocent IV send to the Great Khan? How did Guyuk respond?

4. What advances did Guyuk make toward Mongol world domination?

5. How did Mongke follow Guyuk as Great Khan?

6. Why did Kublai start his attack on the Song by going after the kingdom of Nanzhao? Why didn't he kill all of the captives after he won the battle?

7. Explain how Goryeo ended up surrendering to the Mongols?

8. Why did Tran Canh abdicate his throne to his eighteen-year-old son Tran Hoang?

9. Describe Hulagu's conquests as he headed west. What stopped his advance towards Cairo?

10. Why wasn't Ari-Boke's nor Kublai's election to Great Khan legitimate? Why did both men think their assemblies were legitimate?

Section III: Critical Thinking

You may not use your text to answer this question.

Mongke followed Guyuk as Great Khan, but he did not have the full support of the Mongols behind him. Write a paragraph describing the lasting consequences of Mongke's actions. Use specific examples from the chapter to back up your claim.

Chapter Fifty

The Mamluks of Egypt

The student may use her text when answering the questions in sections I and II.

Section I: Who, What, Where

Write a one or two-sentence answer explaining the significance of each item listed below.

Al-Malik al-Ashraf

Al-Mansur Ali

Aybek

Bohemund VI

Faris al-Din Aqtay

Ked-Buqa

Qutuz

Shajar al-Durr

Section II: Comprehension

Write a two or three-sentence answer to each of the following questions.

1. How did Aybek deal with those who opposed his position as sultan?

2. What did Qutuz do when Ked-Buqa's messengers arrived in Cairo in late August of 1260? Why did he react this way?

3. What happened when the Egyptians met the Mongols on September 3, 1260 in the valley of Ain Jalut?

4. Describe the events that followed the Egyptian victory over the Mongols.

5. How did Baibars become sultan of Egypt?

STUDY AND TEACHING GUIDE FOR THE HISTORY OF THE RENAISSANCE WORLD

6. Why did the Mongol Berke make an alliance with the Egyptian Qutuz?

7. How did Baibars lasso the role of Commander of the Faithful for Egypt? How did this change Egypt's role in the Muslim world?

8. What did Baibars do after making an alliance with the *sharif* of Mecca? How did he reinforce his place as a Muslim leader?

9. Describe Qutuz's attack on the city of Antioch.

Section III: Critical Thinking

The student may not use her text to answer this question.

The Mongols did not fight against the rest of the world because they wanted to covert them to a particular religion. The Mongols were interested in conquest. In this chapter, however, we see religion play a part in the battle between the Egyptians and the Mongols. Write a paragraph or two explaining how religion influenced Egypt's successes against the Mongols.

Section IV: Map Exercise

1. Trace the rectangular outline of Map 50.1 in black.

2. Using your blue pencil, trace all the coastal lines, from the Mediterranean to the Black Sea, Caspian Sea, Red Sea, and Persian Gulf. You do not need to include all the small islands around Greece and Turkey. Repeat until the contours are familiar.

3. Now using contrasting colors trace the Bahri Sultanate and the Il-khanate regions. Repeat until the contours are familiar.

4. Using a new sheet of paper, trace the outline of the frame in black. Then using a regular pencil with an eraser, draw the coastal lines of the Mediterranean to the Black Sea, Caspian Sea, Red Sea, and Persian Gulf. You do not need to include all the small islands around Greece and Turkey. Erase and redraw as necessary. When you are happy with your map, lay it over the original. Erase and redraw any lines which are more than ½" off of the original.

5. Now study carefully the locations of Antioch, Aleppo, Baghdad, Gaza, Damietta, Cairo, Medina, and Mecca. When you are familiar with them, close the book. Mark and label each one on your map, and then lay your map over the original. Erase and redraw any marks which are more than ½" off of the original.

6. Now trace on your paper the enlarged box showing the principality of Antioch and the Kingdom of Jerusalem. Study the locations of Hama, Homs, Tripoli, Acre, Beisan, and the Battle of Ain Jalut. Also study the line of the Jordan. When they are familiar to you, close your book, and mark them on your map. Then check your map, and correct any misplaced or incorrect labels.

Chapter Fifty-One

Louis the Saint

You may use your text when answering the questions in sections I and II.

Section I: Who, What, Where

Write a one or two-sentence answer explaining the significance of each item listed below.

Master of Hungary

The Pastoureaux

Thomas Aquinas

Section II: Comprehension

Write a two or three-sentence answer to each of the following questions.

1. How did Louis IX decide to stay in Acre instead of returning to France?

2. Why did Queen Blanche approve, at first, of the Master of Hungary and his message?

3. What happened in January 1251, after the Master of Hungary started preaching an anti-Church message?

4. What caused Louis IX to finally leave Acre and return to France?

5. How did the collapse of the Seventh Crusade change Louis IX?

6. Describe the changes Louis IX made to the policies and practices of France's officials and bishops after he returned to his home country.

7. Why was Louis IX considered a "just" ruler in the Aristotelian sense?

8. How did Thomas Aquinas understand the relationship between the king and the pope?

9. What did Louis IX believe when it came to quarreling with the church?

Section III: **Critical Thinking**

You may not use your text to answer this question.

We have read over and over again about how the personal desires of men were often the motivation behind going on crusade, rather than fighting for God. Write a paragraph explaining who the Master of Hungary was and how he used the criticism of personal gain over piousness to drum up support for the Pastoureaux movement. In your answer, explain who joined the movement, and why you think they did so.

Section IV: **Map Exercise**

1. Trace the rectangular frame of Map 51.1 in black.

2. Using your blue pencil, trace the visible coastal outline of the continent. Also trace the line of the Loire. Repeat until the contours are familiar.

3. Using your black pencil, trace the outline of the kingdom of Louis IX. Trace the line showing Normandy as well. Repeat until the contours are familiar.

4. Now using a new sheet of paper, trace the rectangular outline of the frame in black. Using a regular pencil with an eraser, draw the coastline and the line of the Loire. Draw the outline of the kingdom of Louis IX and the line showing Normandy. Erase and redraw as necessary, using the outline of the frame as a reference point. When you are happy with your map, lay it over the original, and erase and redraw any lines which are more than ½" off of the original.

5. Now study carefully the locations of Soissons, Reims, Paris, Orleans, Tours, and Bourges. Also study the sites of Clairvaux and Cluny. When you are familiar with them, close the book. Mark and label each one on your map. Then check your map against the original, and erase and re-mark any incorrect or misplaced labels.

6. Mark the regions of Brittany and Normandy.

Chapter Fifty-Two

The Lion's Den

The student may use her text when answering the questions in sections I and II.

Section I: Who, What, Where

Write a one or two-sentence answer explaining the significance of each item listed below.

Ad Extirpanda

Alexander IV

Alfonso X

Charles of Anjou

Citra membri diminutionem, et mortis periculum

Clement IV

Conradin

Edmund

Edward

Manfred

Provisions of Oxford

Richard of Cornwall

Rudolf, Count of Hapsburg

Simon de Montfort (younger)

Urban IV

Section II: Comprehension

Write a two or three-sentence answer to each of the following questions.

1. Why was it a bad idea for Henry III to accept the role of king of Sicily for his son Edmund? Why did he accept anyway?

2. What happened when Pope Innocent IV decided not to endorse Manfred as king of Sicily?

3. List all of the bad decisions Henry III made as king of England prior to March 1258.

4. How did Henry III end up earmarking the money he needed for Sicily?

5. What happened after Henry III agreed to the Provisions of Oxford that led to a war between the barons of England and the king?

6. Describe the events that led to Henry III and Edward's surrender to Simon de Montfort.

7. How did Edward end up winning the Second Barons' War and becoming the de facto ruler of England?

8. Explain how Sicily came to be ruled by Charles of Anjou.

9. How did Conradin end up beheaded for treason?

Section III: Critical Thinking

The student may not use her text to answer this question.

It is made very clear to the reader in this chapter that becoming the king of Sicily was a thankless job. Nothing was to be gained other than a title. Henry III agreed to Edmund's appointment by Innocent IV because he was a spineless ruler. But Charles of Anjou, who was not known as a coward or a fool, accepted the title happily. Write a paragraph explaining what Charles of Anjou agreed to do in order to become king of Sicily, and why you think he went through all of that trouble just for a title.

Chapter Fifty-Three

The Recapture of Constantinople

You may use your text when answering the questions in sections I and II.

Section I: **Who, What, Where**

Write a one or two-sentence answer explaining the significance of each item listed below.

Baldwin II

Ivan Asen

John

Michael Palaeologus/Michael VIII

Philip

Theodore II

Treaty of Nymphaion

Section II: **Comprehension**

Write a two or three-sentence answer to each of the following questions.

1. Describe the shrinking of the Latin Empire under Baldwin II's rule.

2. How did Baldwin II spend most of his reign?

3. What did Baldwin II do to raise money to save Constantinople?

4. How did the Empire of Nicaea change under the rule of John Vatatzes?

5. What did Michael VIII do to prepare for war with Constantinople?

6. Why were Christians at war with each other in Acre in 1256? What was the result of the war?

7. Explain how Michael VIII was able to take Constantinople for Nicaea so easily.

8. How did Michael VIII find out that his men had taken Constantinople? What did he find once he arrived at the city?

Section III: Critical Thinking

You may not use your text to answer this question.

The Latin Empire, once great, faded away in the twelfth century, as did the power of Constantinople. Write a paragraph or two explaining how Michael VIII turned the fate of Constantinople, and Byzantium, around.

Section IV: Map Exercise

1. Trace the rectangular outline of the frame for Map 53.1 in black.

2. Trace the coastline around the Mediterranean and the Black Sea in black. You do not need to include most of the small islands around Greece and Turkey, but do include the two larger islands of Cyprus and Crete. Also trace the line of the Danube. Repeat until the contours are familiar.

3. Using contrasting colors, trace the separate areas of Bulgaria, the Empire of Nicaea, the Despotate of Epirus and the Latin Empire, and the areas of the Empire of Trebizond and Il-khanate. Repeat until the contours are familiar.

4. Now using a new sheet of paper, trace the rectangular outline of the frame for Map 53.1 in black. Then using your regular pencil with an eraser, draw the coastline around the Mediterranean as you did before, including just the islands of Crete and Cyprus. Draw the line of the Danube. Then draw the lines of the separate areas of Bulgaria, the Empire of Nicaea, the Despotate of Epirus and the Latin Empire, and the areas of the Empire of Trebizond and Il-khanate. Erase and redraw as necessary. When you are happy with your map, lay it over the original, and erase and redraw any lines which are more than ½" off of the original. Label each area.

5. Now study carefully the locations of Thessalonica, Thyateira, Constantinople, the Bosphorus Strait, the Sea of Marmara, and Acre. When you are familiar with them, close the book. Mark and label each one on your map, check it against the original, and erase and re-mark any misplaced labels.

Chapter Fifty-Four

The Last Crusades

The student may use her text when answering the questions in sections I and II.

Section I: Who, What, Where

Write a one or two-sentence answer explaining the significance of each item listed below.

Abaqa

Abu 'Abdallah al-Mustansir

Al-Ashraf Khalil

Bohemund VI

Henry the Fat

Idris II

Philip III

Qalawun

Tebaldo Visconti/Pope Gregory X

Theobald

Section II: Comprehension

Write a two or three-sentence answer to each of the following questions.

1. What happened to Almohad power in North Africa after the disintegration of the Almohad hold on the Spanish peninsula?

2. Describe the Hafsid kingdom under the rule of Abu 'Abdallah al-Mustansir.

3. Why did Louis IX decide to go on crusade against the Hafsid kingdom?

4. How did the crusade against the Hafsids end before it even started?

5. How did Edward of England stop Baibars from taking Tripoli from Bohemund VI?

6. What were the circumstances that led to Tebaldo Visconti's election as pope?

7. Explain how Pope Gregory X reunified the eastern and western churches.

8. Why didn't Pope Gregory and Michael VIII's vision for a reunified church come to fruition?

9. Describe the Bahri take over of Acre.

Section III: Critical Thinking

The student may not use her text to answer this question.

In the crusading world, God is the ultimate authority. However, God is only able to speak through man, and men often find it hard to separate their desire for power from their desire to serve Him. Write a paragraph or two explaining how both the trouble Louis IX had drumming up support for his crusade and the quarrel between the eastern and western churches reflected man's conflict between power and piety.

Section IV: Map Exercise

1. Trace the rectangular outline of Map 54.1 in black.

2. Using your blue pencil, trace the visible coastline around Europe and Africa. Using contrasting colors, trace the separate areas of the Marinids, Zayanids, and the Hafsid. Repeat until the contours are familiar.

3. Using a new sheet of paper, trace the rectangular outline of the frame in black. Then using your regular pencil with an eraser, draw the coastline and the areas of the Marinid, the Zayanid, and the Hafsid areas. Erase and redraw as necessary. When you are happy with your map, lay it over the original. Erase and redraw any lines which are more than ½″ off of the original.

4. Now study carefully the locations of Marrakesh, Rabat, Seville, Fez, Tlemcen, and Granada. When they are familiar for you, close the book. Mark each one on your map. Then check your map against the original, and erase and re-mark any labels more than ¼″ off of the original.

5. Trace the rectangular outline of the enlarged box showing Carthage and Tunis. Draw the outline of the coast and mark the locations of Tunis and Carthage.

6. Show the lines of the former Almohad Empire.

Chapter Fifty-Five

Kublai Khan

You may use your text when answering the questions in sections I and II.

Section I: **Who, What, Where**

Write a one or two-sentence answer explaining the significance of each item listed below.

Bayan

Bing

Chungnyeol

Duanzong

Emperor Chengzong

Emperor Gong

Hojo Tokimune

Indravarman V

Jayavarman VIII

Kamikaze

Marco Polo

Song Duzong

Toghan

Tran Quoc Toan

Section II: **Comprehension**

Write a two or three-sentence answer to each of the following questions.

1. Explain how the Mongols were finally able to take the double city of Xiangyang and Fancheng.

2. Describe Kublai Khan's dual capital cities in the north and south of China.

3. What happened when the Mongols set sail from Goryeo in 1274 to attack Japan?

4. How did the Japanese stop a second Mongol invasion two years after the Mongol's first attempt at defeating the Kamakura shogunate?

5. What did the Dai Viet do in order to win against Prince Toghan after he returned to Thang Long with reinforcements from his father?

Section III: **Critical Thinking**

You may use your text to answer this question.

There may be a dispute over the start of the Yuan dynasty (variously considered to have begun in 1263 when Kublai founded his new capital city, 1271, 1279, when the last Song heir died, and 1280) but there is no disputing that Kublai Khan transformed his kingdom from a khanate into an empire. Write a few paragraphs explaining all of Kublai Khan's accomplishments, and how he was able to turn the savage Mongols into the citizens of the Yuan dynasty.

Chapter Fifty-Six

The Sicilian Vespers

The student may use her text when answering the questions in sections I and II.

Section I: Who, What, Where

Write a one or two-sentence answer explaining the significance of each item listed below.

Alfonso III

Andronicus II

Charles II/Charles the Lame

Giacomo Savelli/Pope Honorius IV

James II

John of Procida

Martin IV

Nicholas IV

Ottocar II

Peter III/Peter of Aragon

Roger of Lauria

Sicilian Vespers

Wenceslaus

Section II: **Comprehension**

Write a two or three-sentence answer to each of the following questions.

1. Describe the circumstances of Rudolf of Hapsburg's crowning as king of Germany, and the state of his kingdom once he sat on the throne.

2. Why was Ottocar II of Bohemia in open revolt against the German king?

3. How did Rudolf whip Germany back into shape at the start of his reign?

4. What did Charles of Anjou do to fix the papal election following the death of Nicholas III in 1280?

5. Why was there a secret revolt brewing against Charles of Anjou? How did the revolt come to a head?

6. How did Pope Martin IV, Philip III of France, and Edward of England react to the war between Peter III of Aragon and Charles of Anjou?

7. Describe the state of Philip III and his army in the days leading up to the Battle of the Col de Panissars. What happened after the battle?

8. What happened after Charles the Lame was released from prison?

Section III: **Critical Thinking**

The student may not use her text to answer this question.

The revolt against Charles of Anjou in Palermo was given the name "Sicilian Vespers." What are "vespers"? After doing some research, write a paragraph that defines "vespers," and then explains why, literally and metaphorically, the revolt at Palermo was named as such.

Section IV: **Map Exercise**

1. Trace the rectangular outline of Map 56.1 in black.

2. Using your blue pencil, trace the visible coastline around the Holy Roman Empire and France through the Mediterranean and around Italy and Greece. As usual, you do not need to include small islands around Greece, but do include Sicily, Sardinia, and Corsica. Repeat until the contours are familiar.

3. Now using your black pencil, trace the separate areas of Aragon, France, the Holy Roman Empire, Hungary, the Papal States, and the Kingdom of the Two Sicilies. Trace the mountains with small peaks. Repeat until the contours are familiar.

CHAPTER FIFTY-SIX: THE SICILIAN VESPERS

4. Now using a new sheet of paper, trace the rectangular outline of the frame in black. Then using your regular pencil with an eraser, draw the coastline around the Holy Roman Empire and France through the Mediterranean and around Italy and Greece, including Sicily, Sardinia, and Corsica. Draw the separate areas of Aragon, France, the Holy Roman Empire, Hungary, the Papal States, and the Kingdom of the Two Sicilies. Show the mountains with small peaks. When you are happy with your map, lay it over the original. Erase and redraw any lines which are more than ½" off of the original. Label each region.

5. Now study carefully the locations of Tours, Aachen, Venice, Genoa, Perugia, Orvieto, Rome, Benevento, Palermo, and Trapani. When they are familiar for you, close the book. Mark each one on your map. Lay your map over the original, and erase and redraw any marks which are more than ½" off of the original. Label the Strait of Messina.

6. Now trace the outline of the enlarged box showing the Battle of the Col de Panissars. Mark the site of the Battle and the location of Perpignan.

7. Mark Catalonia and the Pyrenees mountains.

683

Chapter Fifty-Seven

The Wars of Edward I

You may use your text when answering the questions in sections I and II.

Section I: **Who, What, Where**

Write a one or two-sentence answer explaining the significance of each item listed below.

Alexander III

Dafydd

Edward II

Isabella

John Balliol

Llywelyn ap Gruffudd

Margaret (granddaughter)

Marguerite

Marion of Lanark

Philip IV

Reginald de Gray

Robert Bruce the Fifth

Robert Bruce the Sixth

Scottish Wars/Wars of Independence

Sir William Heselrig

Statute of Rhuddlan

Stone of Scone

Treaty of Birgham

William Wallace

Section II: **Comprehension**

Write a two or three-sentence answer to each of the following questions.

1. Why was Wales vulnerable to the whims of the English kings?

2. How did Edward I reclaim the Perfeddwlad for himself?

3. Why did the Treaty of Conway fall apart?

4. How did Edward I deal with Dafydd after he was turned over by his own companions to the English?

5. Why, in 1294, did Philip IV order Edward I to appear at the French royal court?

6. How did Edward I deal with the Scottish resistance after his disobedient vassal kingdom signed the 1295 Treaty of Paris with Philip IV?

Section III: **Critical Thinking**

You may not use your text to answer this question.

William Wallace is a well-known Scottish hero. In this chapter we learned about Wallace's life through the work of the poet Blind Harry, who wrote about the rebel 150 after his life ended. In the 19th century famous Scottish writer Sir Walter Scott explored the life of William Wallace, and in the 20th century, Mel Gibson portrayed William Wallace in the Academy Award-winning 1995 film, *Braveheart*. William Wallace is certainly an epic figure, and with that comes mystery and exaggeration. For example, we learn in the chapter that Marion of Lanark might not have been real. Do some research and find out more about William Wallace's original organized rebellion against the English. You can explore any angle you'd like—did Marion exist? Was William Wallace on the run because of the slaughter of English men? How did the organized rebellion against Sir William Heselrig come about? Just make sure to start with a clear research question. Write your question down, and then explain what you found and how you found it, in a well-organized paragraph. Make sure you to cite your sources!

Section IV: Map Exercise

1. Trace the rectangular frame of Map 57.1 in black.

2. Using your blue pencil, trace the outline of the continent and of Wales, England, and Scotland. You do not need to include all the small islands around Scotland, but do include the Orkney Islands. Repeat until the contours are familiar.

3. Now using a new sheet of paper, trace the rectangular outline of the frame for Map 57.1 in black. Using your regular pencil, draw the line of the coast around the continent and the islands of Wales and England and Scotland, including the Orkney Islands. Erase and redraw until you are happy with your map. Then lay it over the original, and erase and redraw any lines which are more than ½" off of the original.

4. Now study carefully the locations of Scone, Lanark, Berwick, Montrose, Edinburgh, Dunbar, Stiling, Carlisle, Hawarden, Perfeddwlad, Gynedd, Irfon, Ceredigion, Deheubarth, Dyfed, Powys, Morgannwg, and London. When they are familiar for you, close the book. Mark and label each location on your map. Check your map against the original, and erase and re-mark any labels more than ½" off of the original.

5. Study the locations of the Battle of Stirling Bridge, Hadrian's Wall, and Offa's Dyke. Close the book, mark them on your map, and check your marks against the original.

Chapter Fifty-Eight

The Second Sultanate of Delhi

The student may use her text when answering the questions in sections I and II.

Section I: Who, What, Where

Write a one or two-sentence answer explaining the significance of each item listed below.

'Ala'-ud-Din

Bughra Khan

Duwa

Ghazan

Jalalu-d din Firu Khilji

Malik Kafur

Mu'izzu-d din

Nizamu-d din

Ulugh

Zafar

Section II: Comprehension

Write a two or three-sentence answer to each of the following questions.

1. How did Jalalu-d din Firu Khilji become Sultan of Delhi and the first Sultan of the Khilji dynasty?

2. Why did Jalalu-d din Firu Khilji rule from Kilu-ghari instead of from Delhi?

3. How did Jalalu-d din Firu Khilji deal with threats against him?

4. Explain how Jalalu-d din Firu Khilji's reign came to an end.

5. What gave the Chagatai an advantage in their battle for Khurasan? What were they able to do once they took hold of Khurasan?

6. Why did 'Ala'-ud-Din go against his councillors's advice to prepare for Delhi's siege by the approaching Mongol army in 1299? What was the result of the battle that followed?

7. How did 'Ala'-ud-Din want to commemorate his triumph over the Mongols?

Section III: Critical Thinking

The student may not use her text to answer this question.

As soon as Balban died and his court officials chose not his dead son's younger child to be sultan but rather Mu'izzu-d din, Delhi fell apart. There was no confidence in the stability of the kingdom, chiefs and nobles quarreled with each other, men were killed for no reason other than suspicion and doubt—the security of life in Delhi was lost. One man could tear a kingdom apart, and one man could put it back together. Write a paragraph explaining how 'Ala'-ud-Din was the latter kind of man, turning Delhi into one of the most efficient, tightly controlled, and aggressive empires in the world.

Chapter Fifty-Nine

The End of the Papal Monarchy

You may use your text when answering the questions in sections I and II.

Section I: Who, What, Where

Write a one or two-sentence answer explaining the significance of each item listed below.

Albert of Hapsburg

Babylonian Captivity

Benedict XI

Boniface VIII

Charles of Valois

Clement V

Dante Alighieri

Henry VII

Ghibelline

Guelph

Guillaume de Nogaret

Jacques de Molay

Philip V

Princess Joan of Navarre

Robert

Section II: **Comprehension**

Write a two or three-sentence answer to each of the following questions.

1. How did Pope Innocent IV undermine the power of the pope during his rule?

2. Why were the Ghibelline and Guelph parties still fighting a hundred years after their formation?

3. Why did Charles of Valois agree to help Pope Boniface VIII with the messy political situation in Italy? What was the result of his involvement?

4. Explain why Philip IV was on bad terms with Pope Boniface VIII, what the pope did about it, and how Philip IV responded.

5. How did Philip IV guard himself from the public backlash that would follow excommunication by Pope Boniface VIII?

6. What happened on July 11, 1302 when a large French army commanded by the distinguished Robert of Artois faced down a force of Flemish foot soldiers?

7. Why did Philip IV exile the Jews from France in 1306?

8. Why was Henry VII crowned Holy Roman Emperor outside of Rome?

9. Describe the deaths, birth, and invocation of obscure law that led to Philip V's coronation as king of France.

Section III: **Critical Thinking**

You may not use your text to answer this question.

The Knights Templar was a highly respected religious order of knights that protected Christianity. Why would Philip IV want to tear them apart? Write a paragraph explaining what happened between the Knights Templar and Philip IV in the early 14th century. Make sure to include what Philip IV got out of ruining the order in your answer.

Section IV: **Map Exercise**

1. Trace the rectangular outline of Map 59.1 in black.

2. Trace the coastal outline above France and Germany and through the Mediterranean. Include Sicily, but you do not need to include other islands. Also trace the line of the Seine. Repeat until the contours are familiar.

3. Using your black pencil, trace the different regions of France, Germany, Lombardy, the Papal States, the Kingdom of Naples, and Sicily. Trace the mountains with small peaks. Repeat until the contours are familiar.

4. Using a new sheet of paper, trace the rectangular outline of the frame for Map 59.1. Using your regular pencil, draw the coastline above France and Germany and through the Mediterranean, including Sicily. Then draw lines showing the regions of France, Germany, Lombardy, the Papal States, the Kingdom of Naples, and Sicily. Show the mountains with small peaks.When you are happy with your map, lay it over the original. Correct any lines which are more than ½″ off of the original.

5. Study closely the locations of Uzeste, Avignon, Bordeaux, Lyons, Paris, Courtrai, Brescia, Genoa, Lucca, Pisa, Volterra, Siena, Florence, Pistoia, Bologna, Venice, Rome, Anagni, and Naples. When you are familiar with them, close the book. Mark each one on your map. Then place your map over the original, and erase and re-mark any locations that more than ½″ off of the original.

6. Now study the regions of Gascony, Flanders, Bavarian, Austria, and the site of Fontainebleau. When you have learned them, close the book, mark each one, check your marks, and make any needed corrections.

Chapter Sixty

The Appearance of the Ottomans

The student may use her text when answering the questions in sections I and II.

Section I: Who, What, Where

Write a one or two-sentence answer explaining the significance of each item listed below.

Andronicus III

Catalan Company

Empress Anne

John Cantacuzenus

John V

Manuel

Michael IX

Oljeitu

Orhan

Osman

Roger de Flor

Stefan Dushan

Section II: **Comprehension**

Write a two or three-sentence answer to each of the following questions.

1. Who ruled over the Turkish sultanate of Rum? Why wasn't Ghazan bothered by the Turkish agitation in Asia Minor?

2. What happened that put Andronicus II on edge when the Catalan Company showed up to help the Byzantine army in September of 1302?

3. How did Andronicus II plan to stop Roger do Flor and the Catalan Company from their attack on Byzantine territory? Was he successful?

4. How did Andronicus III become emperor of Byzantium? What happened to Andronicus II?

5. Why was Orhan's territory called the Ottoman Empire?

6. Describe Orhan's advances on the Byzantine empire and how we know the Byzantine people were in a panic about this encroaching enemy.

7. Why was Stefan Dushan such a threat to Byzantium?

8. How did John Cantacuzenus manage to retake his place of power in Constantinople?

Section III: **Critical Thinking**

The student may not use her text to answer this question.

In this chapter we read about many different people's desire to rule Constantinople. Write a paragraph describing Osman's dream of conquering Constantinople, and explain how through his actions, and the actions of his son, his dream came closer and closer to being a reality.

Section IV: **Map Exercise**

1. Trace the rectangular outline of the map in black.

2. Trace the coastal outline around India, including the coastline of Sri Lanka. Also trace the lines of the Indus, the Ganges, and the Narmada. Repeat until the contours are familiar.

3. Using a contrasting color, trace the outline of the sultanate of Delhi. Using your black pencil, trace the mountains with small peaks. Repeat until the contours are familiar.

4. Using a new sheet of paper, trace the rectangular outline of the frame for Map 61.1. Then using your regular pencil, draw the coastline; the Indus, Ganges, and Narmada rivers; the mountain peaks; and the area of the Sultanate of Delhi. Erase and redraw as necessary. When you are happy with your map, lay it over the original. Erase and redraw any lines which are more than ¼" off of the original.

5. Now study carefully the Pandya, Hoysala, Kakatiya, Yadava, Gujarat, Mewar, Malwa, and Chuahan areas. When you are familiar with them, close the book. Mark each area on your map, and then check it against the original. Erase and re-mark any misplaced labels.

6. Now study carefully the locations of Delhi, Chittor, Devagiri, Warangal, and Dwarasamudra. When you are familiar with them, close the book, and mark and label each location on your map. Use the frame and geographical markers as a reference point. When you are happy with your map, lay it over the original. Erase and re-mark any labels which are more than ¼" off of the original.

7. Mark the location of Ranthambhore.

Chapter Sixty-One

The Fall of the Khilji

You may use your text when answering the questions in sections I and II.

Section I: Who, What, Where

Write a one or two-sentence answer explaining the significance of each item listed below.

Ghazi Malik Tughluq/ Sultan Ghiyas-ud-Din

Khusru Khan

Padmini

Qutb-ud-Din Mubarak Shah

Rajput kingdoms

Rana Ratan Singh

Section II: Comprehension

Write a two or three-sentence answer to each of the following questions.

1. Describe the conquests made in the later part of 'Ala'-ud-Din's reign.

2. Why did 'Ala'-ud-Din build a black pavilion in the middle of Delhi?

3. Why was Malik Kafur such a menace to the running of Delhi? How was the menace taken care of?

4. What did Qutb-ud-Din Mubarak Shah do during his rule as sultan?

5. How did Khusru Khan become sultan?

6. What did Khusru Khan do to lead to his beheading?

Section III: **Critical Thinking**

You may not use your text to answer this question.

'Ala'-ud-Din's biggest obstacle as he worked to destroy the Rajput kingdoms was Mewar. Gujarat, Malwa, and Ranthambhore fell to 'Ala'-ud-Din, but Mewar, the kingdom of the Guhlia, was harder to crack. Not only was the kingdom fierce, fighting successfully for five hundred years against Muslim invaders, but the fight was also personal: 'Ala'-ud-Din was supposedly enamored with the wife of the Mewar shah. Write a paragraph explaining the story of Rana Ratan Singh's capture, escape, and death. Then write a paragraph explaining why this story might not be true, and how the symbolic role 'Ala'-ud-Din was supposed to play in Jayasi's allegory matched his real-world actions as a conquering ruler.

Section IV: **Map Exercise**

1. Trace the rectangular outline of the map in black.

2. Trace the coastal outline around India, including the coastline of Sri Lanka. Also trace the lines of the Indus, the Ganges, and the Narmada. Repeat until the contours are familiar.

3. Using a contrasting color, trace the outline of the sultanate of Delhi. Using your black pencil, trace the mountains with small peaks. Repeat until the contours are familiar.

4. Using a new sheet of paper, trace the rectangular outline of the frame for Map 61.1. Then using your regular pencil, draw the coastline; the Indus, Ganges, and Narmada rivers; the mountain peaks; and the area of the Sultanate of Delhi. Erase and redraw as necessary. When you are happy with your map, lay it over the original. Erase and redraw any lines which are more than ¼" off of the original.

5. Now study carefully the Pandya, Hoysala, Kakatiya, Yadava, Gujarat, Mewar, Malwa, and Chuahan areas. When you are familiar with them, close the book. Mark each area on your map, and then check it against the original. Erase and re-mark any misplaced labels.

6. Now study carefully the locations of Delhi, Chittor, Devagiri, Warangal, and Dwarasamudra. When you are familiar with them, close the book, and mark and label each location on your map. Use the frame and geographical markers as a reference point. When you are happy with your map, lay it over the original. Erase and re-mark any labels which are more than ¼" off of the original.

7. Mark the location of Ranthambhore.

Chapter Sixty-Two

The Triumph of the Bruce

The student may use her text when answering the questions in sections I and II.

Section I: Who, What, Where

Write a one or two-sentence answer explaining the significance of each item listed below.

John Menteith

Piers Gaveston

Section II: Comprehension

Write a two or three-sentence answer to each of the following questions.

1. What is the significance of Edward I naming Edward II Prince of Wales?

2. What was the "War-wolf"? How was the "War-wolf" used to put a showy end to Scottish resistance in 1304?

3. How did William Wallace meet his end?

4. Why did Robert Bruce the Sixth decide to turn back on his alliance with the English?

5. What happened immediately after Robert Bruce the Sixth renewed the rebellion against England?

6. Why was Piers Gaveston banished to Gascony? How did Piers Gaveston later end up as regent of England?

7. For what reason did the English court hate Piers Gaveston? How did Edward II choose to deal with the situation?

8. Describe the circumstances that led to Piers Gaveston's death, and explain what happened to his body.

9. Who were the two enemies facing Edward II just before and after Piers Gaveston's death? How did he react to them?

10. What happened when Edward II decided to attack Robert Bruce the Sixth in Scotland during the summer of 1314?

11. How did Robert Bruce the Sixth become "King of Scotland" once again? What was Robert Bruce's first act as so-called king?

Section III: **Critical Thinking**

The student may not use her text to answer this question.

In this chapter we read more about the Scottish fight for independence. William Wallace was captured and killed, but Robert Bruce the Sixth took up the fight and soldiered on. This 14th century desire for independence still burns in the 21st century. Scotland has tried to declare its independence from England as recently as 2014. Write a paragraph explaining the Scottish Independence Referendum and what happened when voters were asked "Should Scotland be an independent country"?

Chapter Sixty-Three

The Great Famine

You may use your text when answering the questions in sections I and II.

Section I: Who, What, Where

Write a one or two-sentence answer explaining the significance of each item listed below.

Medieval Warm Period/ Medieval Climatic Anomaly

Murrains

Section II: Comprehension

Write a two or three-sentence answer to each of the following questions.

1. How did the Medieval Warm Period affect the quality and concentration of life in Europe?

2. What were the first signs that the the Medieval Warm Period was coming to an end?

3. How was England and the northwest of Europe affected by rain between the years 1314 and 1316?

4. What was the significance of the comet that was visible throughout most of Europe for a good portion of 1315 and 1316?

5. Describe how Europeans first dealt with the Great Famine, and then what hard choices they had to make.

6. How is the German folktale "Hansel and Gretel" related to the Great Famine?

7. Explain the erratic weather that hit Europe between the summer of 1317 and mid-March of 1321.

8. How did the Great Famine affect the population of Europe?

Section III: **Critical Thinking**

You may not use your text to answer this question.

The Medieval Climatic Anomaly has been used by politicians opposed to legislation to reduce carbon dioxide emissions as proof that climate change happens independent of human action. At the same time, those who say humans do affect the temperature of the earth have downplayed the warming period or deny that it happened at all in order to lay all the blame of climate change on people. Find one example of each side of the argument using the Medieval Climatic Anomaly as proof of their own stance on climate change. Write a paragraph that explains your findings. As always, make sure to cite your sources.

Section IV: **Map Exercise**

1. Trace the rectangular outline of Map 63.1 in black.

2. Using your blue pencil, trace the outline of the coast. Take your time, since there is a significant amount of coast on this map. Trace the coast of Greenland, Iceland, and all around Britain and the continent through the Mediterranean. You do not need to include all the small islands around Scotland and the Baltic Sea. Repeat until the contours are familiar.

3. Now using a new sheet of paper, trace the rectangular outline of the frame in black. Using your regular pencil, draw the coastline as you traced it before: around Greenland and Iceland around the continent and through the Mediterranean. As before, you need not include small islands around the Baltic Sea and Scotland. When you are happy with your map, lay it over the original. Erase and redraw any lines which are more than ½" off of the original.

4. Now study carefully the areas of Greenland, Iceland, Scotland, Germany, and France. Study carefully also the more local areas of the Pennine Moors, Dartmoor, Northumberland, Flanders. Also be sure you know the North Sea, the Baltic Sea, and the Mediterranean Sea. When they are familiar for you, close the book, and mark each. Then compare your map to the original, and make any needed corrections.

5. Now study carefully the locations of York, Ypres, Tournai, Cologne, Neustadt, and Salzburg. When they are familiar for you, close the book. Mark each on your map, using the frame and coastlines as reference. When you are happy with your map, lay it over the original. Erase and re-mark any labels which are more than ½" off of the original.

6. Mark the areas of famine and flood on your map. If you can replicate the skulls and water drops on the original map, feel free to do so! Otherwise, use a marker of your preference.

Chapter Sixty-Four

The Sultan and the Khan

The student may use her text when answering the questions in sections I and II.

Section I: Who, What, Where

Write a one or two-sentence answer explaining the significance of each item listed below.

Abu Sa'id Bahadur Khan

Al-Nasir Muhammad ibn Qalawun

Baybars

Chupan

George V

Ghiyath al-Din

Khatun

Uzbek

Section II: Comprehension

Write a two or three-sentence answer to each of the following questions.

1. What happened to Egypt in the years following the assassination of Khalil in 1293?

2. How did al-Nasir Muhammad ibn Qalawun survive the anarchic years following his older brother's death?

3. What were the circumstances that gave al-Nasir the confidence to seize the sultanate?

4. How did Oljeitu's attack on Egypt turn into a gain for al-Nasir?

5. Why did Abu Sa'id demand Chupan's daughter Khatun for himself?

6. Describe the circumstances that led to Chupan's death.

7. What happened to Chupan's family after his death?

8. How did Abu Sa'id's death change the Il-khanate kingdom?

Section III: **Critical Thinking**

The student may use her text to answer this question.

Al-Nasir Muhammad ibn Qalawun had a very successful time as sultan of Egypt. Explain how Egypt flourished under al-Nasir, and what circumstances allowed this flowering to happen.

Section IV: **Map Exercise**

1. Trace the rectangular outline of the frame for Map 64.1: The Collapse of the Il-khanate in black.

2. Using your blue pencil, trace the coastal outline through the Mediterranean, the Black Sea, the Red Sea, and the Persian Gulf. As usual, you need not include the small islands around Greece and Turkey. Include the lines of the Tigris and Euphrates from the Persian Gulf. Using your black pencil, trace the lines of the Spice Routes. Repeat until the contours are familiar.

3. Using contrasting colors, trace the outline of the Sultanate of Egypt and of the former Il-khanate. Repeat until the contours are familiar.

4. Using a new sheet of paper, trace the rectangular frame of the map in black. Then, using your regular pencil with an eraser, draw the coastline through the Mediterranean, the Black Sea, the Red Sea, and the Persian Gulf. As usual, you need not include the small islands around Greece and Turkey. Include the lines of the Tigris and Euphrates from the Persian Gulf. Draw the lines of the Spice Routes. Erase and redraw as necessary. When you are happy with your map, lay it over the original. Erase and redraw any lines which are more than ½" off of the original.

5. Now study carefully the locations of Cairo, Gaza, Jerusalem, Mecca, Medina, Damascus, Aleppo, Baghdad, Kahta, Gerger, Malatya, and Herat. When they are familiar to you, close the book. Mark each location on the map. Then lay your map back over the original, and erase and re-mark any labels which are more than ¼" off of the original.

6. Now mark each body of water, the location of Kerak, the Euphrates, and Georgia.

Chapter Sixty-Five

Mansa Musa of Mali

You may use your text when answering the questions in sections I and II.

Section I: Who, What, Where

Write a one or two-sentence answer explaining the significance of each item listed below.

Abubakari II

Cresques Abraham

Fomba

Ibn Amir Hajib

Maghan

Mansa Musa

Mansa Sulayman

Mari Diata II

Ndiadiane N'Diaye

Section II: Comprehension

Write a two or three-sentence answer to each of the following questions.

1. Who did Abubakari II first send out to explore the Atlantic Ocean? What happened to them?

2. What was the effect on Mansa Musa's treasury because of his distribution of gold in Cairo?

3. Why was Mansa Sulayman suspicious of Ibn Battuta?

4. What was Ibn Battuta's lasting impression of Mali?

5. How was Mansa Sulayman treated during his twenty-four years on the Mali throne?

6. What happened to the Mali government after Mansa Sulayman's death in 1359?

Section III: Critical Thinking

You may not use your text to answer this question.

Abubakari II went out to discover the world, but it was Mansa Musa that brought the world to Mali. When Mansa Musa first become king of Mali, he decided he wanted to go to Mecca, to make the *hajj*. Explain how Mansa Musa's pilgrimage to Mecca changed Mali's position in the world, for good and for bad.

Chapter Sixty-Six

After the Famine

The student may use her text when answering the questions in sections I and II.

Section I: **Who, What, Where**

Write a one or two-sentence answer explaining the significance of each item listed below.

Charles IV

Edward III

Hugh Despenser the Younger

Philip of Valois

Pope John XXII

Robert III ("the Lion of Flanders")

Roger Mortimer

Treaty of Edinburgh-Northampton

Section II: **Comprehension**

Write a two or three-sentence answer to each of the following questions.

1. When did Philip V of France try to start up a new crusade? How did the pope's living situation affect Philip V's power to rally excitement for a new crusade?

2. What obstacles did Philip V face as he tried to plan his next crusade?

3. How did the Pastoureaux come to murder over 150 Jewish people in Toulouse in a single day in 1320?

4. What did Pope John XXII do to end the Pastoureaux uprising?

5. Who did the English blame for their misfortune post-famine? Use part of the excerpt presented on page 463 from the protest poem "The Simonie" in your answer.

6. Describe the favors and gifts lavished on Hugh Despenser by Edward II, and what finally caused Isabella to leave England and seek refuge with her brother Charles IV, king of France.

7. How was Isabella able to raise an army against Edward II without her husband really noticing?

8. What happened to King Edward II and Hugh Despenser after Isabella arrived in England with an army behind her?

9. Describe the political decisions made by Edward III under the guidance of his mother and Roger Mortimer during the first four years of his reign.

10. What happened to Isabella and Roger Mortimer's power in England after Edward III came of age?

Section III: Critical Thinking

The student may not use her text to answer this question.

Section Three of *The History of the Renaissance World* is called "Catastrophes" and the first catastrophe we encountered was the Great Famine. In this chapter, we continue to see the effects of the Great Famine on Europe in the 14th century. Write a paragraph explaining how the treachery associated with the famine in France turned into a fear of lepers, and then a fear of lepers, Jews, and Muslims. Then explain why you think this fear exploded across France in 1321.

Section IV: Map Exercise

1. Trace the rectangular outline of the frame for Map 66.1 in black.

2. Trace the outline of the coast around Ireland, Scotland, England, the continent, and the visible portion of the Mediterranean. Also trace the lines of the Thames, the Seine, and the Loire. Repeat until the contours are familiar.

3. Now using contrasting colors, trace the outlines of the English Empire and France. Repeat until the contours are familiar. Show the mountains with small peaks. When you are happy with your map, lay it over the original. Erase and redraw any marks which are more than ½" off of the original.

4. Label the areas of Ireland, Scotland, Wales, England, Germany, France, Aragon, and Guienne. Then study carefully the areas of Flanders, Normandy, Brittany, and Anjou. Close the book, label each, and then check your work and make any needed corrections.

5. Study carefully the locations of Hereford, Berkeley, Winchester, London, Paris, Boudeaux, Castelsarrassin, Albi, Toulouse, Montclus, Avignon, and Aigues-Mortes. When you are familiar with them, close the book. Mark and label each one on your map. Lay your map over the original, and erase and redraw any lines that are more than ½" off of the original.

Chapter Sixty-Seven

The Southern and Northern Courts

You may use your text when answering the questions in sections I and II.

Section I: Who, What, Where

Write a one or two-sentence answer explaining the significance of each item listed below.

Ashikaga Takauji

Go-Daigo

Go-Uda

Hanazono

Hojo Takatoki

Kogon

Kuniyoshi

Muromachi bakafu

Nitta Yoshisada

Yutahito

Section II: Comprehension

Write a two or three-sentence answer to each of the following questions.

1. Explain how the succession of the Chrysanthemum Throne divided at the peak of the Mongol threat. Why were the two lines hostile to each other?

2. Describe the way *shikken* Hojo Tokimune and his successors ran the military government headquartered at Kamakura, and how the people of Japan reacted.

3. What compromise was made by the *shikken* in Kamakura to accommodate the junior line's desire to put Kuniyoshi on the throne?

4. How did Go-Daigo use his father to gain more power as emperor? How did he take advantage of Kuniyoshi's death to remain on the throne, and what did he do in an attempt to safeguard his power?

5. What was Hojo Takatoki doing while he should have been handling the succession quarrels in Kyoto caused by Go-Daigo?

6. What happened to Go-Daigo soon after he called for open rebellion against the corrupt and weakened *shikken*?

7. How did Go-Daigo raise an army against Takatoki from exile? What role did Ashikaga Takauji play in Go-Daigo's comeback?

8. Describe how Ashikaga Takauji and Nitta Yoshisada took down Emperor Kogon and Hojo Takatoki.

9. How did Go-Daigo and Ashikaga Takauji go from allies to enemies?

10. Explain how, by 1338, Japan had two imperial capitals, two emperors, two courts, one shogun, and no *shikken*.

11. When did the Ashikaga Shogunate begin? What was the Nambokucho era, and how did it coincide with the Ashikaga Shogunate?

Section III: **Critical Thinking**

You may not use your text to answer this question.

Japan's two-court arrangement may have involved a convoluted plan for the succession to the Chrysanthemum Throne, but it kept the imperial core of Japan stable. As political theorist Kitabatake Chikafusa wrote from his place at the Southern Court,

From the time of the heavenly founder, there has been no disruption in dynastic succession in Japan. Our country has been ruled without interruption by the sovereigns of a single dynastic line. . . . In our country alone, the imperial succession has followed in an unbroken line from the time when heaven and earth were divided until the present age. . . . This is entirely the result of the immutable mandate of Amaterasu, and is the reason why Japan differs from all other countries. The way of the gods is not readily revealed. Yet if the divine basis of things is not understood, such ignorance will surely give rise to disorder.

Explain how Ashikaga Takauji tried to comply with dynastic succession and to follow "the divine basis of things" but ultimately failed, throwing Japan into chaos.

Section IV: Map Exercise

1. Using your black pencil, trace the rectangular outline of the frame for Map 67.1: The Southern and Northern Courts.

2. Using your blue pencil, trace all the visible coastline (you do not need to include small islands). Repeat until the contours are familiar.

3. Using a new sheet of paper, trace the rectangular outline of the frame of the map in black. Then using your regular pencil, draw the coastline, using the frame of the map as a reference. Erase and redraw as necessary. When you are happy with your map, lay it over the original, and erase and re-draw any lines which are more than ¼″ off of the original.

4. Now study carefully the locations of Oki Island, Yasuki Harbor, Hoki, Kyoto, Mt. Hiei, Yoshino, and Kamakura. Also make sure you know the location of the Battle of the Minato River. When they are all familiar for you, close the book. Mark each location on your map, and then lay it over the original again. Erase and re-draw any labels which are more than ¼″ off of the original.

Chapter Sixty-Eight

Rebellions

The student may use her text when answering the questions in sections I and II.

Section I: Who, What, Where

Write a one or two-sentence answer explaining the significance of each item listed below.

Ahsan Shah

Firoz Shah

Harahara and Bukka

Hasan Gangu

Kapaya Nayaka

Malik Haji Ilyas

Pratapa Rudra

Ulugh Khan (Muhammad bin Tughluq)

Section II: Comprehension

Write a two or three-sentence answer to each of the following questions.

1. Why did general Malik Kafur give Pratapa Rudra a robe and a parasol? What did Pratapa Rudra do to subvert his acceptance of Malik Kafur's gifts?

2. Why did it take two sieges for Ulugh Khan to take Warangal? What happened to Warangal once the son of the sultan breached the city's walls?

3. Describe Ghiyas-ud-Din's reconquest of Bengal, and the tragedy that immediately followed.

4. How did Muhammad bin Tughluq deal with the numerous rebellions against his rule?

5. What happened to the regiments that were fighting with Muhammad bin Tughluq in the north after he died? How did they manage to get home?

6. How did Firoz Shah try to fix the damage done by Muhammad bin Tughluq? Did his actions bring India back together?

Section III: Critical Thinking

The student may use her text to answer this question.

When Ulugh Khan became sultan Muhammad bin Tughluq, he inherited rule at the height of India's expansion. Like the great rulers that came before him, he was energetic and ambitious. But he himself did not turn out to be a great ruler. Explain how Muhammad bin Tughluq's energy and ambition, rather than raising India up, ran India into the ground.

Chapter Sixty-Nine

Naming the Renaissance

You may use your text when answering the questions in sections I and II.

Section I: **Who, What, Where**

Write a one or two-sentence answer explaining the significance of each item listed below.

Benedict XII

Count of Märstetten

Defensor Pacis

Marsilius of Padua

Nicholas V

Siegfried Schweppermann

Section II: **Comprehension**

Write a two or three-sentence answer to each of the following questions.

1. How did the conflict over the German crown between Louis of Bavaria and Frederick of Hapsburg end?

2. Why did John XXII excommunicate Louis of Bavaria?

3. What was Louis of Bavaria's plan to garner more support from the German dukes after his excommunication from the pope-in-exile?

4. How did the German electors and Pope John XXII react to Louis of Bavaria's plan to split the German throne with Frederick of Hapsburg?

5. Why were John XXII's actions as pope questioned?

6. What was Dante Alighieri's view on the pope's right to confer the title of Holy Roman Emperor?

7. How did Marsilius of Padua build on Dante's ideas about man's power in the church? Who else shared views similar to those of Marsilius and Dante?

8. Explain how Louis of Bavaria finally became Holy Roman Emperor and how John XXII ended up deposed.

9. Why did Louis, now Holy Roman Emperor, leave Rome?

10. Describe John XXII's November 1, 1331 new interpretation of the Beatific Vision, and how this interpretation did harm to the pope.

Section III: Critical Thinking

You may not use your text to answer this question.

The Italian poet Petrarch revived the honor of the Poet Laureate. He was crowned on Easter Sunday, April 18, 1341, by the Roman Senate. Write a paragraph explaining why Petrarch chose Easter Sunday for his coronation.

Section IV: Map Exercise

1. Using your black pencil, trace the outline of the frame for Map 69.1: Lands Claimed by Louis of Bavaria.

2. Using your blue pencil, trace the outline of the coast through the Mediterranean. Include the islands of Sardinia, Corsica, and Sicily, but you need not include other islands. Also trace the line of the Rhine. Repeat until the contours are familiar.

3. Using a pencil in a contrasting color, trace the outline of the Holy Roman Empire claimed by Louis. Using your black pencil, show the mountains with small peaks. Repeat until the contours are familiar.

4. Using a new sheet of paper, trace the outline of the frame in black. Then using your regular pencil with an eraser, draw the outline of the coast through the Mediterranean. Include the islands of Sardinia, Corsica, and Sicily, but you need not include other islands. Also draw the line of the Rhine. Draw the mountains with small peaks. Erase and redraw as necessary, using the frame as a reference. When you are happy with your map, place it over the original. Erase and redraw any lines which are more than ½" off of the original.

5. Study the areas of Sardinia, Sicily, Apulia, the Papal States, Hapsburg, Bavaria, Lorraine, Märstetten, Carinthia, and Germany. When you are familiar with them, close the book and mark each area on your map. Then check your map against the book. Erase and re-mark any misplaced labels.

6. Now study closely the locations of Martirano, Rome, Viterbo, Florence, Mantua, Cremona, Milan, Avignon, Lyons, Ravenna, Ferrara, Padua, Verona, Mühldorf, Worms, Mainz, and Koblenz. When they are familiar for you, close the book. Mark each one on your map. Lay your map over the original, and erase and re-mark any locations which are more than ½″ off of the original.

7. Mark the site of Trausnitz.

Chapter Seventy

The Cities in the Lake

The student may use her text when answering the questions in sections I and II.

Section I: Who, What, Where

Write a one or two-sentence answer explaining the significance of each item listed below.

Acamapichtli

Achitometl

Cuacuauhpitzahuac

Huitzilopochtli

Lake Texcoco

Mexica

Tenochtitlán

Tlatelolco

Tezozomoc

Tizapan

Section II: Comprehension

Write a two or three-sentence answer to each of the following questions.

1. Describe the general journey story of the people moving south on the Central American land bridge.

2. How did the Mexica end up at Chapultepec? What happened once they arrived at Chapultepec?

3. What did the Mexica do to show their defiance against the king of Colhuacan?

4. How did the Mexica end up in Lake Texcoco? Why didn't the Colhuacan warriors follow the Mexica into Lake Texcoco?

5. What story did the Mexica tell about their journey to and settlement in Lake Texcoco? How did it help the Mexica deal with their situation?

6. How did the Aztecs come to be split between Tenochtitlán and Tlatelolco?

7. What tribute did Tezozomoc demand from Acamapichtli? Why did Acamapichtli decide to pay the tribute?

8. Why did the chieftains of Tlatelolco ask Tezozomoc to send them a royal son to be their ruler?

Section III: Critical Thinking

The student may not use her text to answer this question.

Before the Aztecs were known by that name, they were called the Mexica. The Mexica were driven out of Tizapan to their home of Tenochtitlán by Achitometl because the Mexica murdered his daughter, the princess of Colhuacan. Write a paragraph that connects the princess's murder to the later custom of human sacrifice practiced by the Aztecs. You will have to do some research to answer this question. As always, make sure to cite your sources.

Section IV: Map Exercise

1. Trace the rectangular outline of the frame for Map 70.1 in black.

2. Trace the outline of Lake Texcoco, including the small islands. Repeat until the contours are familiar.

3. Using a new sheet of paper, trace the rectangular outline of the map in black. Then draw the outline of Lake Texcoco, including the small islands. When you are happy with your map, lay it over the original, and erase and re-draw any lines which are more than ¼" off of the original.

4. Study the locations of Colhuacan, Chapultepec, Tenochtitlan, Tlatelolco, Azcapotzalco, and Texcoco. When they are familiar for you, close the book. Mark and label each one on the map, and then lay your map over the original. Erase and re-mark any labels which are more than ¼" off of the original.

Chapter Seventy-One

A Hundred Years of War

You may use your text when answering the questions in sections I and II.

Section I: **Who, What, Where**

Write a one or two-sentence answer explaining the significance of each item listed below.

Charles of Bohemia

David Bruce

Edward Balliol

Edward of Woodstock

Thomas Randolph

Section II: **Comprehension**

Write a two or three-sentence answer to each of the following questions.

1. What did Robert Bruce and the Early of Moray do to set David up for success as king of Scotland?

2. Who supported Edward Balliol's first attempt to take the Scottish throne? What happened when the invaders met the Scottish army?

3. Why did Edward III choose to support Edward Balliol instead of David Bruce? What was the result of Edward III's support?

4. How did the Holy Roman Empire end up entirely independent of the papacy?

5. What events led to the signing of the Treaty of Malestroit on January 19, 1343?

6. Explain how Edward III ended up knighting his sixteen-year-old son, Edward of Woodstock, on Norman soil on July 18, 1346.

7. How did Edward III direct his soldiers to behave once they reached Normandy? What actually happened?

8. Describe what happened when the French army, which outnumbered the English three to one, met its enemy at Crécy-en-Ponthieu.

9. How did David Bruce end up a prisoner of the English?

10. What happened after Philip VI lost Calais?

Section III: Critical Thinking

You may use your text to answer this question.

As we know from our reading, both in this chapter and previous ones, "War between England and France was nothing new." The reasoning behind the Hundred Years' War, however, is complicated, and is based on the crisscrossing of family lines and rightful claims to the throne. Write a paragraph explaining why English king Edward III claimed the right to the French throne and how he declared war on France. You may want to look back at chapters Fifty-Nine and Sixty-Six when working on your response.

Section IV: Map Exercise

1. Trace the rectangular outline of the frame for Map 71.1 in black.

2. Using your blue pencil, trace the outline of the coast around Ireland, Scotland, England, and the European continent. You do not need to include small islands. Also trace the line of the Seine and of the Loire. Repeat until the contours are familiar.

3. Using a new sheet of paper, trace the outline of the frame for Map 71.1 in black. Using your regular pencil with an eraser, draw the coastline around Ireland, Scotland, England, and the European continent. You do not need to include small islands. Also draw the line of the Seine and of the Loire. Remember to use the frame of the map as a reference. When you are happy with your map, lay it over the original. Erase and redraw any lines which are more than ½" off of the original.

4. Mark Ireland, Scotland, England, Normandy, Brittany, Poitou, Languedoc, and Gascony. Then study carefully the locations of Scone, Kinghorn, Berwick, Durham, York, London, Calais, Tournai, Crecy, Rouen, Paris, and Caen. When they are familiar for you, close the book. Mark and label each one on your map. Lay your map over the original, and erase and re-mark any labels that are more than ½" off of the original.

5. Study closely the locations of the Battle of Dupplin' Moor, the Battle of Sluys, and the castle of Aiguillon. When they are familiar, close the book. Mark and label each one on your map. Lay your map over the original, and erase and re-mark any labels that are more than ½" off of the original.

Chapter Seventy-Two

The End of the World

The student may use her text when answering the questions in sections I and II.

Section I: Who, What, Where

Write a one or two-sentence answer explaining the significance of each item listed below.

Toghon Temur

Section II: Comprehension

Write a two or three-sentence answer to each of the following questions.

1. Where did the plague start, and how do we know it started there? What caused the plague?

2. What tragedies did contemporary chroniclers record in the years after the deaths near Lake Issyk-Kul? Where and when did the plague make a reappearance?

3. Describe the particular mark of the plague that moved across the world in the 14th century.

4. How did the Golden Horde hope to break down Caffa, a Genoese-controlled trading port? How did this strategy spread the plague even further?

5. Explain some of the ways that the plague took its victims.

6. What did the poet Giovanni Boccaccio see in Florence that amazed him? What happened to the towns whose inhabitants were wiped out by the plague? How did Pope Clement VI react to the fast-spreading disease?

7. How did the plague affect England, Ireland, and Egypt?

8. What was the effect of the plague on Europe's economy after the spread of the disease began to slow?

9. How did survivors of the plague explain its existence?

Section III: **Critical Thinking**

The student may not use her text to answer this question.

The plague started its deadly creep across the world in 1338. It wasn't until 1346 that the Western world started to record the horrible death occurring the the East. One of the first accounts of the illness from an observer comes from the Arab scholar Abu Hafs 'Umar Ibn al-Wardi. He writes, "It began in the land of darkness [and] it has been current for fifteen years. . . . Plague sat like a king on a throne and swayed with power, killing daily one thousand or more and decimating the population. It destroyed mankind with its pustules. . . . How amazingly does it pursue the people of each house! One of them spits blood, and everyone in the household is certain of death." Write a paragraph or two that recounts another first-hand account of the plague. In your answer, attempt to pry some greater meaning from the account. What can you tell about the conditions at the time from the writer's description? A useful place to start your research would be with the list of books recommended in the footnote on page 505, but you do not have to use one of those texts as the source for your answer.

Chapter Seventy-Three

The Will to War

You may use your text when answering the questions in sections I and II.

Section I: Who, What, Where

Write a one or two-sentence answer explaining the significance of each item listed below.

Charles V

Charles of Navarre

Enrique of Trastámara

Estates-General

Etienne Marcel

Louis of Anjou

Jacques Bonhomme

John II

John of Gaunt

Pedro of Castile

Philip the Bold

Philip of Navarre

Section II: Comprehension

Write a two or three-sentence answer to each of the following questions.

1. Describe the deaths of Joan, queen of Navarre, Philip VI of France, and King Alfonso XI of León-Castile.

2. Why did Charles of Navarre think he had a shot at the French throne?

3. How did Charles of Navarre make himself an attractive candidate to replace the French king?

4. What were the terms of the truce made between Edward of England and John of France in April 1354? What happened to the truce?

5. How did John II's son and heir come to be called the "Dauphin Charles"?

6. What happened to Charles of Navarre's plot with the Dauphin Charles to overthrow King John of France?

7. How did King John of France and his son Philip end up as prisoners of the Black Prince?

8. How did the governing power in France shift while John II was held captive in England? How did this shift open up room for Charles of Navarre to, once again, make a bid for the French throne?

9. What caused the Jacques Bonhomme to come together in Saint-Leu-d'Esserent in armed revolt, the Jacquerie, against the French nobility in May 1358? What put an end to the revolt?

10. Describe Charles of Navarre's final attempt to take the French throne after John II's death.

11. How did Enrique of Trastámara become king of Castile?

Section III: Critical Thinking

You may not use your text to answer this question.

The idiom "a king's ransom" means a very large amount of money. In this chapter we read about literal cases of kings being held captive until a ransom was paid. For example, David of Scotland was able to free himself from his eleven-year imprisonment in England by finally agreeing to paying 100,000 marks. For this critical thinking question, explain why the Black Prince took King John of France prisoner. Then, explain what ransom was paid, and if that ransom did the job of not only releasing King John but guaranteeing peace between England and France.

Section IV: Map Exercise

1. Trace the rectangular outline of the frame for Map 73.1 in black.

2. Using your blue pencil, trace the coastline around England and the continent, up through and around the Mediterranean. Also trace the lines of the Oise, the Seine, the Loire. Repeat until the contours are familiar.

3. Using a pencil in a contrasting color, trace the English-held lands. Repeat until the contours are familiar. Use small peaks to trace the mountains.

4. Using a new sheet of paper, trace the rectangular outline of the map frame in black. Then using your regular pencil with an eraser, draw the coastline around England and the continent, up through and around the Mediterranean. Also draw the lines of the Oise, the Seine, the Loire. Remember to use the frame as a reference, erasing and re-drawing as necessary. When you are happy with your map, lay it over the original, and erase and re-draw any lines which are more than ½" off of the original.

5. Now label the areas of England, Normandy, Brittany, Touraine, Burgundy, Poitou, Aquitaine, Gascony, Languedoc, Navarre, Aragon, Portugal, and Granada.

6. Next, study carefully the locations of Calais, Rouen, Saint-Leu-d'Esserent, Paris, Evreux, Bretigny, Toulouse, Marseille, Granada, and Gibraltar. When you are familiar with them, close the book, and mark each one on your map. When you are done, lay your map over the original. Erase and re-mark any marks more than ½" off of the original.

7. Finally, study the locations of the Battle of Cocherel, the Battle of Poitiers, Arles, the Battle of Navarette, and the Battle of Campo de Montiel. When you are familiar with them, close the book, and mark each one on your map. When you are done, lay your map over the original. Erase and re-mark any marks more than ½" off of the original.

Chapter Seventy-Four

White Lotus, Red Turban

The student may use her text when answering the questions in sections I and II.

Section I: Who, What, Where

Write a one or two-sentence answer explaining the significance of each item listed below.

Amitabha

Ayushiridara

Chen Youliang

Corvée labor

Embroidered Uniform Guards

Fang Guozhen

Han Lin'er

Han Shantong

Hu Wei-yung

Mao Ziyuan

Toghto

White Lotus Society

Zhu Yuanzhang (the Hongwu Emperor)

Section II: **Comprehension**

Write a two or three-sentence answer to each of the following questions.

1. What are some causes for the drop in the Chinese population—forty million people—between the beginning and the end of the fourteenth century?

2. Why did Toghto have to direct a massive repair project in the center of the empire in 1351?

3. How did Han Shantong's rebellion end? What were the lasting effects of his uprising?

4. Why did Toghto lose his job as chancellor in 1354? How did he react to being fired?

5. What happened to Yuan China after the failed siege of Gaoyou?

6. How did Zhu Yuanzhang defeat Chen Youliang and the southern Red Turban movement?

7. What happened to Toghon Temur's holdings after Zhu Yuanzhang's success against Chen Youliang?

8. How did the Hongwu Emperor manage the aristocratic clans that lived on in Ming China?

Section III: **Critical Thinking**

The student may not use her text to answer this question.

At the end of the chapter we read that "the new Ming empire would be peaceful, and no price was too high to pay for peace." The Hongwu Emperor refused to eat meat, wore patched shirts, and ordered the crown prince to plant his own vegetable garden to save money. He acted with iron self-control and determination to keep his kingdom tranquil. But is tranquility the same as peace? Describe China under the first leader of the Ming dynasty, and then explain whether or not you think the kingdom was peaceful, or if its people were forced into submission by their ruler.

Section IV: **Map Exercise**

1. Trace the rectangular outline of map 74.1 in black.

2. Using your blue pencil, trace all the visible coastline. Include the line of the Yellow River, the Yangtze, and Lake Poyang. Repeat until the contours are familiar.

3. Using contrasting colors, trace the areas of Ming China and the Yuan Dynasty. Using contrasting colors, trace the alternate course of the Yellow River and the line of the Grand Canal. Repeat until the contours are familiar.

4. Using a new sheet of paper, trace the rectangular outline of the map in black. Using your regular pencil with an eraser, draw the coastline, the Yellow and Yangtze Rivers, Lake Poyang, and the separate areas of Ming China and the Yuan Dynasty. Use the frame as a reference, erasing and

redrawing as necessary. Draw the lines of the Grand Canal and the alternate course of the Yellow River. When you are happy with your map, lay it over the original, and erase and redraw any lines which are more than ½" off of the original.

5. Study carefully the locations of Shangdu Dadu, Gaoyou, Nanjing, Hangzhou, Nancheng, and Jiangzhou. When they are familiar for you, close the book. Mark each one on your map, and then lay your map over the original. Erase and re-mark any labels which are more than ½" off of the original.

6. Mark the Shandong Peninsula.

Chapter Seventy-Five

After the Mongols

You may use your text when answering the questions in sections I and II.

Section I: Who, What, Where

Write a one or two-sentence answer explaining the significance of each item listed below.

Borommaracha

Che Bong Nga of Champa (the Red King)

Jayavarmaparamesvara

Le Quy Ly

Prince An

Ramathibodi (U Thong)

Ramesuan

Syam

Thong Lan

Tran Due-tong

Tran Thuan Tong

Section II: Comprehension

Write a two or three-sentence answer to each of the following questions.

1. What happened to the Khmer after they became a vassal of the Mongols to buy peace?

2. Describe the rise of U Thong's power at Lopburi.

3. How did Borommaracha of Suphanburi take Ramesuan's throne?

4. Explain how the Khmer culture was already part of the Thai culture, and how Ramesuan continued that intermingling.

5. How did Che Bong Nga influence the abdication of the Dai Viet king?

6. Describe Le Quy Ly's final defeat of the Cham.

7. How did Le Quy Ly manage to usurp the Dai Viet throne? What royal heritage did he claim, and how was that reflected in his new name for the Dai Viet?

Section III: Critical Thinking

You may not use your text to answer this question.

The Champa were strong under the leadership of Che Bong Nga. They drove the Dai Viet back again and again. In 1389, Dai Viet general Le Quy Ly suffered the greatest defeat of his career. Fighting on the Luong river, his soldiers were massacred and he was forced to scramble away through the rough countryside with one of his surviving captains moaning "The enemy is stronger than we are, and resistance is impossible!" But as we found out, the traditional strength of the Champa was no match for the new technology used by Le Quy Ly. A single shot from a *huochong*, for all intents and purposes, ended the Champa's aggressive campaign against the Dai Viet. We learned just a little bit about *huochong* in this chapter. Do some research on your own and write a paragraph describing the evolution of the *huochong* from the fire lance. Make sure to cite your sources!

Chapter Seventy-Six

The Turks and the Desperate Emperor

The student may use her text when answering the questions in sections I and II.

Section I: Who, What, Where

Write a one or two-sentence answer explaining the significance of each item listed below.

Innocent VI

Manuel

Matthew

Murad

Suleyman Pasha

Urban V

Section II: Comprehension

Write a two or three-sentence answer to each of the following questions.

1. Why was John V frustrated by his co-rule with John VI?

2. How did John V end up as a prisoner of John VI?

3. Why did John VI grow unpopular after he made his own son Matthew co-emperor?

4. How did the Turks use the March 2, 1354 earthquake to their advantage?

5. What did John VI do to deal with the Turkish squatters, and what was the outcome of this approach?

6. What saved John V from the Serbians after he was given the throne by John VI?

7. How did John V attempt to deal with the Turks after he reclaimed the Byzantine throne?

8. Describe the return of the papacy to Italy.

9. What did Urban V do in exchange for John V's conversion to the Catholic faith?

10. How did John V manage to get home after he realized the Doge of Venice was not going to forgive the 30,000-ducat loan taken out by his mother Anne, back in the days of the civil war with John Cantacuzenus?

Section III: Critical Thinking

The student may not use her text to answer this question.

Many of us have heard a derivation of the verse from 2 Samuel 1:25, "How the mighty have fallen!" Write two or three paragraphs describing the decline of John V. In your answer, explain how John V started as the Orthodox co-emperor of Byzantium and ended up as a Catholic Turkish vassal.

Section IV: Map Exercise

1. Using your black pencil, trace the rectangular outline of the frame for Map 76.1: The Ottoman Empire.

2. Using your blue pencil, trace the outline of the coast around the Mediterranean Sea and the Black Sea. As usual, you need not include the very small islands around Greece. Also trace the line of the Danube. Repeat until the contours are familiar.

3. Now using contrasting colors, trace the outlines of the Byzantine Empire and the Ottoman Turks. Repeat until the contours are familiar.

4. Now using a new sheet of paper, trace the outline of the frame for Map 76.1 in black. Then using your regular pencil with an eraser, draw the coastline around the Mediterranean and the Black Sea. Draw the line of the Danube. Erase and redraw as necessary, using the frame of the map as a reference. Draw the separate areas of the Byzantine Empire and Ottoman Turks. When you are happy with your map, lay it over the original. Erase and re-draw any lines which are more than ½" off of the original.

5. Study closely the areas of Greece, Thessalonica, Serbia, Bulgaria, Thrace, and Asia Minor. When you are familiar with them, close the book. Mark and label each one on your map. Then check your map against the original, and erase and re-mark any misplaced labels.

6. Now study closely the locations of Thessalonica, Didymoteichon, Edirne, and Constantinople. When they are familiar for you, close the book. Mark and label each one on your map. Then lay your map over the original, and erase and re-draw any locations which are more than ½" off of the original.

7. Mark the location of the Battle of Marica River.

Chapter Seventy-Seven

The Disintegration of Delhi

You may use your text when answering the questions in sections I and II.

Section I: Who, What, Where

Write a one or two-sentence answer explaining the significance of each item listed below.

'Ali Hujwiri

Awliyâ'

Bahman Shah

Bukka Raya

Harihara Raya

Harihara Raya II

Muhammad Shah I

Shaikh 'Ala al-Haq

Sikandar

Sufism

Section II: Comprehension

Write a two or three-sentence answer to each of the following questions.

1. How did Firoz Shah Tughluq cultivate loyalty from his subjects in Delhi?

2. Describe the interpretation of Sufism given by the eleventh-century scholar 'Ali Hujwiri. Why was this version of Islam so appealing to the Muslim poor and the Hindu underclass?

3. Why did Shams-ud-Din embrace Sufism?

4. Explain what happened to the rule of Sri Lanka after the decay of Pandyan power.

5. Why was Firoz Shah a successful ruler even though is expeditions against neighboring kingdoms failed?

6. What happened to the sultanate of Delhi after Firoz Shah's death?

Section III: **Critical Thinking**

You may not use your text to answer this question.

Muhammad Shah I was known as a no-holds-barred warrior. He was the first to use gunpowder in his wars in the Deccan. As we learned in the chapter, "His gunpowder projectiles were inaccurate and unpredictable, valuable for noise and confusion more than for actual defense; they came from China, and the Indians called them hawai, 'rockets.'" Yet their use began to change the landscape. Write a paragraph that explains just how the hawai changed the landscape, and how military-mindedness has affected other landscapes. In order to complete this critical thinking question you must do some research. After you are done researching, pick one architectural or landscape change that came about as a result of military-mindedness.

Section IV: **Map Exercise**

1. Trace the rectangular outline of the frame for Map 77.1: Bahmani Expansion in black.

2. Using your blue pencil, trace the coastal outline, including Sri Lanka. Also trace the lines of the Kaveri, Tungabhadra, Wainganga, Narmada, and Indus. Repeat until the contours are familiar.

3. Now using contrasting colors, trace the outline of the Delhi, Bahmani, Vijayanagara, and Jaffna areas. Show the mountains with small peaks. Repeat until the contours are familiar.

4. Now using a new sheet of paper, trace the outline of the map in black. Then using your regular pencil with an eraser, draw the coastal outline, including Sri Lanka. Also draw the lines of the Kaveri, Tungabhadra, Wainganga, Narmada, and Indus, using the frame of the map as a reference. When you are happy with your map, lay it over the original. Erase and re-draw any lines that are more than ½″ off of the original. Mark each of the rivers.

5. Now study carefully the Punjab, Himalaya, Jaunpur, Bengal, Malwa, Jaunpur, Gujarat, Deccan, and Sri Lanka areas. Mark each on your map, check it against the original, and make any necessary corrections.

6. Next study carefully the locations of Ghazni, Lahore, Delhi, Chittor, Gaur, Daulatabad, Gulbarga, Vijayanagara, Jaffna, Dambadeniya, Gampola, and Kotte. When they are familiar for you, lay your map over the original. Erase and re-draw any locations that are more than ½″ off of the original.

7. Label Palk Strait.

Chapter Seventy-Eight

The Union of Krewo

The student may use her text when answering the questions in sections I and II.

Section I: Who, What, Where

Write a one or two-sentence answer explaining the significance of each item listed below.

Aldona

Casimir the Great

Charles II

Congress of Krakow

Hedwig

Jogaila

Mary

Privilege of Košice

Sigismund

Union of Krewo

Wladyslaw the Elbow-High

Section II: Comprehension

Write a two or three-sentence answer to each of the following questions.

1. How did Casimir create a unified Poland?

2. Describe Casimir the Great's funeral.

3. Explain how Louis of Anjou managed to become the Polish king. What arrangement did he make with the dukes of Poland in order to keep his place on the throne?

4. What happened to Mary's place on the Polish throne after her father's funeral?

5. How did Mary end up as a prisoner in Croatia, and how did she get out?

6. What happened between Sigismund and Mary after she returned to Hungary?

7. In what ways did the Teutonic Knights, invited into the Polish duchies to help conquer the Lithuanians, actually strengthen the Lithuanians and their relationship with Poland?

Section III: Critical Thinking

The student may not use her text to answer this question.

When Hedwig was made the ruling monarch of Poland on October 16, 1384, she was called "king" and not "queen." We only learn a little bit about Hedwig's life in this chapter. For this critical thinking question, explain why Hedwig was king, and not queen. In your answer, define the term "queen regnant." Then, after finding out at least three more facts about Hedwig's rule via your own research, write a paragraph that tells the reader more about the Polish "king." As always, make sure to cite your sources.

Chapter Seventy-Nine

The Rebirth of the Mongol Horde

You may use your text when answering the questions in sections I and II.

Section I: **Who, What, Where**

Write a one or two-sentence answer explaining the significance of each item listed below.

Amir Husayn

Kabil Shah

Nasiruddin Mahmud

Pir Muhammad

Timur-Leng (Timurlane)

Toktamish

Section II: **Comprehension**

Write a two or three-sentence answer to each of the following questions.

1. What kind of a fighter was Timur-Leng? Why were those that fought with him so loyal?

2. Describe Timur-Leng's treatment of his enemies and conquered subjects.

3. Why did Timur-Leng think he would be able to conquer the Golden Horde?

4. How did Toktamish assert his place as the Khan of the Golden Horde against Rus' resistance?

5. What happened the first time Timur-Leng attacked Toktamish? What did Timur-Leng do after the armies met in 1391 near the Volga river?

6. What happened the second time Timur-Leng attacked Toktamish? What happened to the Golden Horde after the attack?

7. How did Timur-Leng prepare for his invasion of Delhi?

8. Describe what happened to Delhi and its population after Timur-Leng defeated Nasiruddin Mahmud.

Section III: Critical Thinking

You may not use your text to answer this question.

Power does not always come from the person designated by a government to wield power. We can see this clearly when looking at Timur-Leng's pursuit of Mongol power. Write a paragraph that explains how power was distributed between the governors and the khan in the Chagatai realm. Then explain who Timur-Leng wanted to get rid of, and why.

Section IV: Map Exercise

1. Trace the rectangular outline of Map 79.1 in black.

2. Trace the coastal outline in blue, including the Persian Gulf and Caspian Sea. Trace the lines of the Oxus and Indus. Repeat until the contours are familiar.

3. Using contrasting colors, trace the areas of the Golden Horde and Chagatai Khanate. Show the mountains with small peaks. Repeat until the contours are familiar.

4. Using a new sheet of paper, trace the outline of the frame in black. Using your regular pencil with an eraser, draw the coastal outline, including the Persian Gulf and Caspian Sea. Draw the lines of the Oxus and Indus. Then draw the lines of the areas of the Golden Horde and the Chagatai Khanate. Draw the mountains with small peaks. When you are with happy your map, lay it over the original. Erase and re-draw any lines which are more than ½" off of the original.

5. Now study the areas of Sistan, Khwarezm, Transoxania, Mughulistan, Punjab, and Gujarat. When you are familiar with them, close the book. Mark each one on your map, and then check your map against the original. Make any needed corrections.

6. Now study the locations of Tabriz, Baghdad, Isfahan, Isfizar, Herat, Balkh, Samarkand, and Delhi. When you are familiar with them, close the book. Mark each one on your map, and then lay your map over the original. Erase and re-mark any locations more than ½" off of the original.

7. Mark the directions of Timur's campaigns.

Chapter Eighty

Compromises and Settlements

The student may use her text when answering the questions in sections I and II.

Section I: **Who, What, Where**

Write a one or two-sentence answer explaining the significance of each item listed below.

Ashikaga Yoshimitsu

Cheonsang yeolcha bunya jido

Go-Kameyama

Gongmin

Hosokawa Yoriyuki

Shin Ton

Wu

Yi In-im

Yi Seong-gye (Taejo)

Section II: **Comprehension**

Write a two or three-sentence answer to each of the following questions.

1. Explain Goryeo's relationship with the Yuan dynasty, and how King Gongmin started to reclaim his power after the coronation of the Hongwu emperor.

2. How do we know that the Mongol thread woven through Goryeo's life was a constant humiliation to Gongmin?

3. Why didn't all of Gongmin's subjects want to remove the Yuan influence from Goryeo culture?

4. Who was terrorizing Goryeo's shores and how did the people of Goryeo react?

5. Why didn't the Japanese government do anything to stop the *wokou*?

6. What did King Wu demand that led to his deposition as king?

7. How did Yi Seong-gye become Taejo and Goryeo become Joseon?

8. What did Taejo do during his transition into power to minimize bloodshed and show his own strength and purpose?

9. How did the Nambokucho era, the age of the "Southern and Northern Court," come to an end?

Section III: **Critical Thinking**

The student may not use her text to answer this question.

Diplomacy is the art and practice of conducting negotiations between nations. It is also the word we use when we talk about handling affairs with sensitivity, or without arousing hostility. To be duped is to be deceived or cheated. Write a paragraph explaining whether or not you think Taejo was acting diplomatically or he was being duped in his relations with the Ming. Then write a paragraph describing your thoughts on the end of the Nambokucho era: was Yoshimitsu being diplomatic, or was he duped? For both answers, make sure to explain your assertion fully with examples from the chapter.

Chapter Eighty-One

The House of Visconti and the Papal States

You may use your text when answering the questions in sections I and II.

Section I: Who, What, Where

Write a one or two-sentence answer explaining the significance of each item listed below.

Bernabò Visconti

Gian Galeazzo Visconti

Giovanni Visconti

Gregory XI

John Hawkwood

Matteo Visconti

Ottone Visconti

Robert of Geneva

Urban VI

Section II: Comprehension

Write a two or three-sentence answer to each of the following questions.

1. Describe the state of governance in Italy following Pope Urban V's return to Rome.

2. What kind of a person was Bernabò Visconti? How did he react when he was excommunicated by Pope Urban V?

3. What happened when Charles IV entered Italy in May of 1368 at the request of Urban V?

4. How did the Franciscan nun Birgitta of Vadstena react when she found out that Urban V wanted to return to Avignon? Was she right in her prophecy?

5. Explain how Gregory XI's plan to unify a league of Lombard cities against the Visconti went wrong.

6. What did Pope Urban V's death in Italy mean for the Roman cardinals? How did the French cardinals react?

7. How did the papacy end up divided, with one pope in Rome and another pope in Avignon?

8. What was going on in Italy while Urban VI was occupied with his cardinals after the split of the church?

Section III: **Critical Thinking**

You may not use your text to answer this question.

To this day, the symbol of Milan is a biscione, or giant snake. In the modern version, the snake is eating a child, though when the symbol was first introduced, during the days of the House of Visconti, the snake was eating something else. Find out what the snake was eating when the symbol was introduced, and then write a paragraph based on what you have learned about the House of Visconti in this chapter that explains why you think the Viscontis chose this particular symbol.

Section IV: **Map Exercise**

1. Trace the outline of the rectangular frame of Map 81.1: War in Italy in black.

2. Using your blue pencil, trace the coastal outline around France and through the Mediterranean around France, the Holy Roman Empire, and the visible coastline of Africa. Include the line of the Seine. Trace the mountains with small peaks. Repeat until the contours are familiar.

3. Using contrasting colors, trace the outlines of the Holy Roman Empire, France, the Papal States, the Kingdom of Naples, and Sicily. Repeat until the contour are familiar.

4. Using a new sheet of paper, trace the rectangular outline of the frame for Map 81.1. Using your regular pencil with an eraser, draw the coastal outline around France and through the Mediterranean around France, the Holy Roman Empire, and the visible coastline of Africa. Include the line of the Seine. Draw the mountains with small peaks. Then draw the outlines of the Holy Roman Empire, France, the Papal States, the Kingdom of Naples, and Sicily. When you are happy with your map, place it over the original. Erase and re-mark any lines which are more than ¼" off of the original.

5. Now study carefully the areas of Gascony, Flanders, France, Germany, and the regions you drew: the Holy Roman Empire, the Papal States, the Kingdom of Naples, and Sicily. When they are familiar, mark them on the map, and then make any needed corrections.

6. Now study the locations of Bourdeaux, Uzeste, Avignon, Paris, Geneva, Fonti, Milan, Pavia, Genoa, Lucca, Pisa, Siena, Rome, Anagni, Naples, Verona, Mantua, Bologna, Florence, Perugia, Assisi, Faenza, Cesena, Padua, and Venice. When they are familiar for you, close the book. Mark each one on your map, using the frame of the map as a reference. Erase and re-mark as necessary. When you are happy with your map, lay it over the original. Erase and re-mark any labels which are more than ¼″ off of the original.

7. Mark the site of the Battle of Chioggia.

Chapter Eighty-Two

Bad Beginnings

The student may use her text when answering the questions in sections I and II.

Section I: Who, What, Where

Write a one or two-sentence answer explaining the significance of each item listed below.

Bertrand du Guesclin

Charles VI

John Ball

John Wycliffe

Louis, the Duke of Anjou

Richard II

Wat Tyler

Section II: Comprehension

Write a two or three-sentence answer to each of the following questions.

1. How did the Black Prince react to the voluntary surrender of Limoges to the French? What is the most likely reason he reacted this way?

2. What led to the truce between Charles V of France and Edward III of England?

3. How was the death of Edward III good for Charles V? Why didn't Charles V take full advantage of his political good fortune?

4. What kind of bad advice did Charles VI get from his uncles after he lost the council of his regent Louis, the Duke of Anjou?

5. Describe Charles VI journey to Flanders and the battle that ensued near the village of Rosebecque.

6. Explain the three poll taxes imposed in England by Richard II based on the guidance of his governing council.

7. What happened as tax collection began in England in the spring of 1381?

8. How did the royal council at first deal with the tax revolt in England? What was the result of this plan?

9. What made Richard II agree to a parley with Wat Tyler?

10. Richard II agreed to a parley with Wat Tyler but what was his real purpose for meeting with the rebellious leader? What was his purpose in telling the rebellious English that he would be their captain and leader, and grant their requests?

Section III: Critical Thinking

The student may not use her text to answer this question.

When Charles VI became king of France, he was twelve. Richard II, who was already on the English throne, was thirteen at the time of Charles VI's coronation. Both young kings had to face considerable obstacles at the start of their reigns, most notably bad advisors and unruly citizens. Explain how both sovereigns used similar approaches to assert their power as young kings.

Section IV: Map Exercise

1. Trace the rectangular outline of Map 82.1 with your black pencil.

2. With your blue pencil, trace the coastline around Ireland, England, and the continent, through the visible Mediterranean. Also trace the line of the Loire. Repeat until the contours are familiar.

3. Using contrasting colors, trace the separate territories of the Empire of Richard II and the Kingdom of Charles VI. Repeat until the contours are familiar.

4. Using a new sheet of paper, trace the outline of the frame for Map 82.1 in black. Using a regular pencil, draw the lines of the coast around Ireland, England, and the continent, through the visible Mediterranean. Also draw the line of the Loire. Then draw the separate territories of the Empire of Richard II and the Kingdom of Charles VI. Erase and re-draw as necessary, using the map's frame as a reference. When you are happy with your map, lay it over the original. Erase and re-draw any lines which are more than ¼" off of the original.

5. Label the areas of Ireland, England, and France. Study carefully the areas of Wales, Devon, Essex, Sussex, Kent, Flanders, Anjou, Burgundy, Berry, Gironde, and Languedoc. When they are familiar

for you, close the book. Mark and label each one on your map. Check your map against the original, and make any needed corrections.

6. Now study carefully the locations of Plymouth, Dartmouth, Southampton, London, Brentwood, Rye, Dover, Calais, Meaux, Paris, Limoges, Bordeaux, and Bayonne. When they are familiar for you, close the book. Mark and label each one on your map. Then lay your map over the original, and erase and re-mark any labels which are more than ¼" off of the original.

7. Mark the sites of the Isle of Wight, the Battle of Rosebecque, and the Battle of La Rochelle.

Chapter Eighty-Three

Dislocation

You may use your text when answering the questions in sections I and II.

Section I: Who, What, Where

Write a one or two-sentence answer explaining the significance of each item listed below.

Bayajidda

Bornu

Bulala

'Umar ibn Idris

Section II: Comprehension

Write a two or three-sentence answer to each of the following questions.

1. Why was it so hard for Kanem to defend its borders?

2. On what did Kanem's prosperity depend?

3. Why did 'Umar ibn Idris move away from Njimi to Bornu?

4. Describe the Hausa kingdoms.

5. Explain the legend of Bayajidda and the foundation of the seven kingdoms.

6. What can we learn about the legend of Bayajidda and the ancestral development of the Hausa kingdoms?

Section III: Critical Thinking

You may not use your text to answer this question.

While oral traditions can sometimes be unreliable, looking at the details of legends can help us to learn about the development of a culture. Write a paragraph that explains what we can learn about Bornu's changing religion based on the legend of Bayajidda.

Section IV: Map Exercise

1. Trace the rectangular outline of Map 83.1 in black.

2. Using your blue pencil, trace the coastal outline around the Mediterranean and Africa. Include the each body of water visible on the map. Trace the line of the Nile. Repeat until the contours are familiar.

3. Using contrasting colors, trace the regions of the Empire of Kanem and the Kanem Influence. Repeat until the contours are familiar.

4. Using a new sheet of paper, trace the outline of the map in black. Using your regular pencil with an eraser, draw the coastal outline around the Mediterranean and Africa. Include the each body of water visible on the map. Draw the line of the Nile. When you are happy with your map, lay it over the origina. Erase and re-draw any lines which are more than ¼" off of the original.

5. Now study carefully the locations of Tunis, Tripoli, Zella, Bilma, Njimi, and Kaka. When you are familiar with the locations, close the book. Mark and label each one on your map. Lay your map over the original, and erase and re-mark any labels which are more than ¼" off of the original.

6. Mark the Sahara Desert, the Nile, the area of Bulala, and the location of Lake Chad.

Chapter Eighty-Four

Madness and Usurpation

The student may use her text when answering the questions in sections I and II.

Section I: Who, What, Where

Write a one or two-sentence answer explaining the significance of each item listed below.

Blanche of Lancaster

Constance of Castile

Henry Bolingbroke

Isabella

John of Aviz

John (of Castile)

Louis

Section II: Comprehension

Write a two or three-sentence answer to each of the following questions.

1. Why did John of Gaunt, Duke of Lancaster, make an urgent request from the king of England for money and ships?

2. How did John of Gaunt plan to get into Castile? Why did the king of Portugal agree to the plan?

3. What did John of Gaunt do after his first war with Castile proved fruitless? What did the king of Castile do in response?

4. How did the French prepare for the invasion of England? What happened to their planned attack?

6. When did negotiations for a peace treaty between England and France start? When did they end, and what were the terms of the treaty?

7. What did Richard II do to upset the period of peace that was supposed to follow the 1396 treaty with France and his marriage to Isabella?

8. Explain the circumstances of Richard II's abdication, and of his death.

9. Why was Henry IV's acceptance speech at his coronation significant, and how did his coronation mark a shift in the ruling house of England?

Section III: Critical Thinking

The student may not use her text to answer this question.

Just two chapters ago you wrote an explanation of how both Charles VI of France and Richard II of England asserted themselves by standing up to their own people. In this chapter, we see both kings, once again, having parallel experiences. In this critical thinking question, explain what similar experience the kings had, and how these separate but linked experiences cost each king his own power.

Chapter Eighty-Five

The Battle of Nicopolis

You may use your text when answering the questions in sections I and II.

Section I: Who, What, Where

Write a one or two-sentence answer explaining the significance of each item listed below.

Bayezid

Hannsen Greif

Helena

Lazar

Section II: Comprehension

Write a two or three-sentence answer to each of the following questions.

1. Describe the Ottomans' campaign of conquest through Murad's taking of Serbia and Bulgaria.

2. Give an overview of Bayezid's new policy regarding his place at the head of the Ottoman empire and his dealing with vassal rulers.

3. How did John V react to Bayezid's aggression? How was John V's death related to his reaction to Bayezid's aggression?

4. What happened between Manuel and Bayezid after John V's death?

5. How was Manuel's wedding to the Serbian princess Helena an example of his denial regarding the true state of Constantinople?

6. How did Constantinople survive the first siege laid upon it by Bayezid in 1394?

7. Why did Sigismund of Hungary agree to help Manuel? What happened when he tried to get a crusade going against the Turks?

8. How did Bayezid defeat the crusading force sent to attack him at Nicopolis in 1396?

9. Explain what Bayezid did with the prisoners taken at Nicopolis.

Section III: Critical Thinking

You may not use your text to answer this question.

Our chapter ends with Bayezid's triumph at Nicopolis. Bayezid did not treat his prisoners in a traditional manner, however. Write a paragraph that explains what Bayezid did with the prisoners that remained after his win at Nicopolis, making sure to include what Bayezid did that was off-script. Then write a paragraph that explains why you think the author of our text, Susan Wise Bauer, chose to include the story of Hannsen Greif's end alongside the story of Bayezid's treatment of his prisoners.

Chapter Eighty-Six

The Union and Disunion of Kalmar

The student may use her text when answering the questions in sections I and II.

Section I: Who, What, Where

Write a one or two-sentence answer explaining the significance of each item listed below.

Albert

Christian of Oldenburg

Christopher of Bavaria

Eric

Haakon

Karl Knutsson

Magnus Ericsson

Margaret

Olaf

Philippa

Valdemar IV of Denmark

Section II: Comprehension

Write a two or three-sentence answer to each of the following questions.

1. Describe the dispersal of the Scandinavians through the formation of the kingdoms of the Suetidi, the Dani, and the Hordar, and then describe the relationship of these three Scandinavian kingdoms.

2. In general, how did kings come to the throne in Scandinavia?

3. How did Margaret come to be known as "All-Powerful Lady and Mistress"?

4. What did Margaret do in order to become the ruler of Norway?

5. How did Margaret come to be known as "All-Powerful Lady and Rightful Mistress of Sweden"?

6. What happened to Albert after he added "Queen Breechless" to Margaret's list of monikers?

7. What did Margaret do to ensure the unity of Sweden, Denmark, and Norway?

8. Who challenged Margaret's rule of Scandinavia fifteen years after the death of Olaf? How did Margaret deal with the pretender?

9. What happened to rule of Norway after Christopher of Bavaria's death?

Section III: Critical Thinking

The student may not use her text to answer this question.

Over the course of our textbook we have read about the governing bodies of various countries not knowing how to address female sovereigns. Margaret of Denmark faced this dilemma herself, and eventually was given the appellation "All-Powerful Lady and Rightful Mistress of Sweden." Her enemy, Albert, gave her a different title, however. Write a paragraph that explains what name Albert gave Margaret, and why he gave her that name. If you do any research to answer this question, make sure to include citations in your paragraph.

Section IV: Map Exercise

1. Trace the rectangular outline of map 86.1 in black.

2. Using your blue pencil, trace the outline of the coast around Scandinavia and Europe. Try to include the islands and inlets as best you can. Repeat until the contours are familiar.

3. Using contrasting colors, trace the outlines of Norway, Sweden, Denmark, and Prussia. Repeat until the contours are familiar.

4. Using a new sheet of paper, trace the outline of the rectangular frame of the map in black. Then using your regular pencil with an eraser, draw the outlines of the coast around Scandinavia and Europe. Then draw the outlines of Norway, Sweden, Denmark, and Prussia. Erase and redraw as necessary. When you are happy with your map, lay it over the original. Erase and re-draw any lines which are more than ½" off of the original.

5. Label Norway, Sweden, Denmark, and Prussia. Then study the locations of Stockholm, Gottland, Kalmar, Lindholm, Scania, Danzig and Graudenz. When they are familiar for you, close the book. Mark each one on your map. Lay your map over the original, and erase and re-draw any labels which are more than ½" off of the original.

6. Mark the site of the Battle of Falköping.

Chapter Eighty-Seven

The Hussite Uprising

You may use your text when answering the questions in sections I and II.

Section I: Who, What, Where

Write a one or two-sentence answer explaining the significance of each item listed below.

Alexander V

Benedict XIII

Boniface IX

First Defenestration of Prague

Gregory XII

Hussites

Jan Hus

John XXIII

Lollards

Martin V

Wenceslaus IV

Rupert of Germany

Section II: Comprehension

Write a two or three-sentence answer to each of the following questions.

1. What were "imperial cities" *(Reichsstädte)*, and what did it mean to "mortgage" an imperial city?

2. How did Charles IV guarantee that his son Wenceslaus IV would be given his throne?

3. How did the Swabian city of Ulm challenge Wenceslaus IV's rule? What brought an end to the German king's war with the Swabian League?

4. Why did the German dukes continue to rebel against Wenceslaus IV?

5. How did Palatine Rupert come to be nominated by the German electors as Wenceslaus IV's replacement?

6. Why did John Wycliffe want to translate the Bible from Latin into English? Who opposed this project?

7. What other anticlerical beliefs did John Wycliffe hold, in addition to his belief that everyone should be able to study the bible without the help of the clergy?

8. Why did Wenceslaus IV reprimand the Archbishop of Prague? How was this action contradictory to his earlier support of Alexander V?

9. What did Sigismund hope to achieve at the Council of Constance? What was the setting like during the meeting?

10. How did the Hussites react to Wenceslaus IV's order that priests in Prague who had allowed laypeople to serve the Eucharist be arrested?

Section III: **Critical Thinking**

You may not use your text to answer this question.

Niccolò Machiavelli was a famous sixteenth-century political philosopher; his treatise *The Prince* is, arguably, his most well-known work. We met Machiavelli in this chapter; he described the condition of the German dukes and their relationship to Wenceslaus IV: "The cities of Germany enjoy a very extensive liberty. . . . [They] obey the emperor when they please, under no apprehension of being attacked either by him or by others, for the towns are defended by strong walls and deep ditches, and are provided with artillery and provisions for a year, so that the siege of these cities would be both long and painful." For this critical thinking question, write a short biography for Machiavelli. Then, give a brief description of his most famous work, *The Prince*. As always, make sure to cite your sources.

Chapter Eighty-Eight

The Taking of France

You may use your text when answering the questions in sections I and II.

Section I: **Who, What, Where**

Write a one or two-sentence answer explaining the significance of each item listed below.

Catherine (of France)

Catherine (of Wales)

Charles

Dauphin Louis·

Edmund Mortimer

Henry V

Henry Percy

Isabeau

Jehan Petit

John

Owain Glyndwr

Philip the Good

Section II: **Comprehension**

Write a two or three-sentence answer to each of the following questions.

1. How did Henry IV's putting down of the Welsh revolt turn into a civil war?

2. Why did the Duke of Burgundy flee Paris after the Feast of Saint Clement in 1407?

3. How did the Duke of Burgundy get away with murdering his cousin the Duke of Orleans?

4. What brought France to the brink of civil war in the early fifteenth century?

5. How did Henry V of England get involved in the French struggle between the Armagnac party and the Duke of Burgundy supporters? What was his reaction to the French internal conflict?

6. Describe the English siege of Harfleur.

7. What happened when the English army met the French army on October 25, 1415 near the wood of Agincourt?

Section III: Critical Thinking

You may not use your text to answer this question.

When French envoys arrived at the English court shortly after Henry V's coronation, Henry V gave the Armagnacs an offer they could refuse: he would defeat the Duke of Burgundy in exchange for the crown of France, marriage with the king's daughter Catherine, and a dowry of two million crowns. This was not so much an offer of support as an incitement to war. Explain how the inability of the Armagnacs and the Burgundy party to work together caused their crown, for all intents and purposes, to be turned over to the English king. In your answer, make sure to compare Henry V's original demands given to the Armagnac and Burgundian envoys to the terms of the Treaty of Troyes.

Section IV: Map Exercise

1. Trace the rectangular outline of the frame for Map 88.1 in black.

2. Using your blue pencil, trace the outline of all the visible coastline. Include the lines of the Thames in England and the Seine in France. Repeat until the contours are familiar.

3. Now using contrasting colors, trace the outlines of England and France. Repeat until the contours are familiar.

4. Using a new sheet of paper, trace the rectangular outline of the frame for Map 88.1: Agincourt in black. Then using your regular pencil with the eraser, draw the lines of the visible coast, including the Thames and Seine rivers. Then draw the outlines of France and England. Erase and re-draw as necessary, using the frame as a reference. When you are happy with your map, lay it over the original. Erase and re-draw any lines which are more than ¼" off of the original.

5. Now study carefully the locations of London, Dover, Calais, Harfleur, Paris, Meaux, and Troyes. When you are familiar with them, close the book. Mark each location on your map. Then lay your map over the original, and erase and re-mark any locations over ¼″ off of the original.

6. Mark the locations of the Battle of Shrewsbury, the Battle of Agincourt, and the castle of Rouen.

7. Label Normandy and Wales.

Chapter Eighty-Nine

After Timurlane

You may use your text when answering the questions in sections I and II.

Section I: Who, What, Where

Write a one or two-sentence answer explaining the significance of each item listed below.

Al-Zahir Barquq

Faraj

Firoz

George VI

Ibn Khaldun

John VII

Mehmed

Mircea the Elder

Musa

Qara Yusu

Shah Rukh

Suleyman

Threshold of Paradise

Vlad

Section II: **Comprehension**

Write a two or three-sentence answer to each of the following questions.

1. Describe Samarkand as it existed in Timur's lifetime.

2. How did Firoz of Bahmani benefit from becoming the supposed ruler of Malwa and Gujarat even though he did not actually rule over either kingdom?

3. How did the Burji dynasty come into existence, and where did they get their name from?

4. What did Timur do after Faraj's emirs declined to surrender Egypt's Syrian lands (and cut Timur's messenger in half at the waist)?

5. How did John VII get rid of the Ottomans without the help of the European kings?

6. Why did Timur help John VII protect Constantinople? What did the Mongol warrior really want?

7. How far did Timur get in achieving his goal of recreating the Mongol empire? What brought an end to his years of conquest?

8. Who took over the western reaches of Timur's empire after his death?

9. How did the Ottoman leader Mehmed come to make peace with Manuel?

10. Why did Manuel rebuild the Hexamilion Wall?

Section III: **Critical Thinking**

You may not use your text to answer this question.

Vlad the Impaler, son of Vlad Dracul, is well known as the inspiration for Bram Stoker's 1897 *Dracula*. Yet the violent and bloodthirsty Wallachian prince has, in reality, very little in common with Stoker's demonic vampire. Do some research and find out why Vlad the Impaler is often cited as the real Dracula, even if he really was nothing like the famous vampire. Write a paragraph explaining your findings, and make sure to give credit to your sources.

Section IV: **Map Exercise**

1. Trace the rectangular frame of map 89.1 in black.

2. Using your blue pencil, trace the outline of the coast through the Mediterranean and around the Middle East and Far East, including the Black Sea, Persian Gulf, and Caspian Sea. As usual, you need not include all the small islands around Greece. Trace the lines of the Indus and Sutlej. Repeat until the contours are familiar.

3. Using contrasting colors, trace the outlines of the regions of Byzantium, the Ottoman Turks, the Burji Dynasty, Georgia, and Timur's Empire. Trace the mountains with small peaks. Repeat until the contours are familiar.

4. Using a new sheet of paper, trace the outline of the map's frame in black. Then using your regular pencil with an eraser, draw the outline of the coast through the Mediterranean and around the Middle East and Far East, including the Black Sea, Persian Gulf, and Caspian Sea. Draw the lines of the Indus and Sutlej. Draw the outlines of the regions of Byzantium, the Ottoman Turks, the Burji Dynasty, Georgia, and Timur's Empire. Draw the mountains with small peaks. When you are happy with your map, lay it over the original. Erase and re-draw any lines more than ½″ off of the original.

5. Label each of the regions which you traced and drew. Then study carefully the areas of Hungary, Wallachia, Thessalonica, Caucasus, White Sheep, Black Sheep, the Sayyids, Kirman, Malwa, Gujarat, Deccan, Bahmani, and Vijayanagara. When they are familiar, close the book. Label each one on your map, and check your work against the original. Make any necessary corrections.

6. Study carefully the locations of Constantinople, Mardin, Edessa, Aleppo, Damascus, Cairo, Baghdad, Tabriz, Tbilisi, Isfahan, Yazd, Shiraz, Balkh, Utrar, Samarkand, Multan, Lahore, and Delhi. When they are familiar, close the book. Mark and label each one on your map. Lay your map over the original, and check your work. Correct any marks more than ¼″ off of the original.

7. Mark the Battle of Ankara, Khyber Pass, and Fort Bhatner.

Chapter Ninety

The Withdrawal of the Ming

The student may use her text when answering the questions in sections I and II.

Section I: Who, What, Where

Write a one or two-sentence answer explaining the significance of each item listed below.

Cheng Ho

Esen Tayisi

Fang Xia

Forbidden City

Hongxi

Jianwen

Le Loi/Binh Dinh Vuong

Nguyen Trai

Oirat

Ma-Huan

Wang Zhen

Xuande

Zhengtong

Zhu Di

Section II: **Comprehension**

Write a two or three-sentence answer to each of the following questions.

1. What happened to the Yuan dynasty after the Hongwu emperor came into power?

2. Why did the Hongwu emperor build a string of fortresses out into the steppe country?

3. How did Zhu Di try and establish legitimacy at the start of his rule?

4. Where were the naval expeditions ordered by Zhu Di heading, and what was the intention behind them?

5. How did the Dai Vet kingdom become known, once again, as the Jiaozhi?

6. What did Nguyen Trai do to make the uneducated villagers in Dai Viet believe that Le Loi was picked by the heavens to rule?

7. How did Emperor Xuande start his reign? How did his advisors react?

8. Describe the Oirat advance into Ming territory after the death of Xuande.

9. What happened to the Ming army after they decided to turn around from the Oirat front and head home?

10. Why did Esen Tayisi let Zhengtong go free? How was Zhengtong treated when he returned to Beijing?

Section III: **Critical Thinking**

The student may not use her text to answer this question.

Emperor Yongle was a big spender. When an ambassador from Baghdad visited the capital city Beijing in 1421, he was asked to attend a royal feast where a thousand different dishes were served: "geese, fowls, roasted meat, fresh and dry fruits . . . filberts, jujubes, walnuts, peeled chestnuts, lemons, garlics and onions pickled in vinegar . . . and various kinds of intoxicants." The diplomats present were required to perform eight prostrations in front of the emperor and in return they were loaded with lavish presents of silver, weapons, hawks, and horses. This is just one example of Yongle's lavish ruling style. While things looked good from the outside, the emperor's massive spending had severe consequences on Ming power. For this critical thinking question, write a paragraph that connects Emperor Yongle's expansiveness to later Ming isolationist policy.

Chapter Ninety-One

Failure

You may use your text when answering the questions in sections I and II.

Section I: Who, What, Where

Write a one or two-sentence answer explaining the significance of each item listed below.

Albert

Beatrice Lascaris

Compacts of Basel

Eugene IV

Facino Cane

Felix V

Filippo Maria Visconti

Francesco Carmagnola

Gian Maria

John VIII

John Zizka

Murad II

Prokop the Shaven

Section II: **Comprehension**

Write a two or three-sentence answer to each of the following questions.

1. Why did Filippo Maria Visconti marry Beatrice Lascaris? Why was the relationship between them so unhappy?

2. How did Filippo Maria Visconti's status change after he hired Francesco Carmagnola?

3. What demands were made by the Hussites in the Four Articles of Prague?

4. Why did the Hussites include serving the Eucharist "in both kinds" in the Four Articles of Prague?

5. How did the Hussites respond to Sigismund after he refused to grant the Four Articles of Prague?

6. Why did Sigismund have to negotiate with Filippo Maria Visconti in order to become Holy Roman Emperor? What were the terms of their negotiation?

7. How did Sigismund display his power after being crowned Holy Roman Emperor in 1433?

8. What terms did the Council of Basel agree upon regarding the Hussites? How did the Hussites react to the Council's recommendations?

9. Describe Sigismund's death.

10. How did the Council of Basel end up dividing and producing an antipope?

11. What was the "Decrees of Union," and why didn't John VIII publish the document in Constantinople?

Section III: **Critical Thinking**

You may not use your text to answer this question.

The Hussite rebellion was driven by the group's frustration with the entitlement and privilege of the Catholic clergy. Write a paragraph that explains how the behavior of the clergy at the Council of Florence, in particular during the time of John VIII's request for the Christian west to unify against the Ottomans, reinforced the complaints of the Hussites.

Section IV: **Map Exercise**

1. Trace the rectangular frame of the map in black.

2. Using your blue pencil, trace the outline of the coast around Italy and the surrounding coasts. Include all major islands and the small visible coast of Africa. Repeat until the contours are familiar.

3. Using contrasting colors, trace the areas of Naples and the Empire of Sigismund. Using your black pencil, trace the area of Bohemia within the Empire of Sigismund. Show the mountains with small peaks. Repeat until the contours are familiar.

4. Using a new sheet of paper, trace the rectangular outline of the frame in black. Using your regular pencil, draw all the coastline from Africa all around Italy, including the major islands. Use the frame of the map as a reference, erasing and re-drawing as necessary. Show the mountains with small peaks. When you are happy with your map, lay it over the original. Erase and re-draw any lines which are more than ¼" off of the original.

5. Now label the areas of Germany, Bohemia, Austria, Hungary, Naples, and Sicily. Study carefully the locations of Plzen, Prague, Lipany, Basel, Milan, Pavia, Piacenza, Venice, Genoa, Florence, and Rome. When they are familiar for you, close the book. Mark and label each one on your map. Then lay your map over the original, and erase and re-mark any locations which are more than ¼" off of the original.

Chapter Ninety-Two

Perpetual Slavery

The student may use her text when answering the questions in sections I and II.

Section I: **Who, What, Where**

Write a one or two-sentence answer explaining the significance of each item listed below.

Afonso V

Black Moors

Edward

Ferdinand

Gil Eannes

Guanches

Henry

Jean de Béthencourt

Peter of Coimbra

Nicholas V

The Cortes

Section II: **Comprehension**

Write a two or three-sentence answer to each of the following questions.

1. How did Castile take control of the Canary Islands? What happened to the Canary Islands after they became part of Castilian territory?

2. Why did John I of Portugal think he would be successful in taking over the port city of Ceuta?

3. Describe the Portuguese assault on Ceuta. What did John I have to do in order to keep control of the port?

/4. Why was Ceuta a disappointment to the Portuguese and how did Henry end up using the port? Why was this alternative use for the port also a disappointment at first?

5. What happened when Edward of Portugal and his brother Ferdinand attacked Tangiers?

6. How did Henry eventually get many captains to sail south of Cape Bojador?

7. Explain the purpose of the expeditions past Cape Bojador. What would happen if explorers did not find villagers?

8. What were some techniques used by the Portuguese to capture African slaves?

9. How did the chronicler Zurara comfort himself in the face of the suffering slaves at the Lisbon market?

10. What documents written by the pope gave approval for the enslavement of African captives?

Section III: Critical Thinking

The student may not use her text to answer this question.

For this critical thinking question, read Susan Wise Bauer's article "Spoiling for a Fight, Fighting for God" and then use Bauer's main point to explain the Portuguese justification for the slave trade.

"Spoiling for a Fight, Fighting for God" was first published on the website *Psychology Today* on June 2, 2016. You might remember some of the information covered if you also studied Susan Wise Bauer's *The History of the Medieval World: From the Conversion of Constantine to the First Crusade.*

Susan Wise Bauer, Ph.D.

"Spoiling for a Fight, Fighting for God"

Religious language doesn't create warriors—it just gives them permission.

In 1095, Pope Urban II asked the Christians of Europe to march to Jerusalem and take the Holy City away from its Muslim rulers.

And his appeal succeeded beyond his wildest hopes. Thousands upon thousands of warriors turned east, launching the First Crusade.

Urban's call certainly featured some good rhetoric. He hit on three themes that would pop up frequently, over the next millennium, in religious speech employed for political ends: a recounting of the dreadful deeds of those who hold other (or no) faiths ("the Turks and Arabs . . . have occupied more and more of the lands of those Christians . . . have killed and captured many, and have destroyed the churches and devastated the empire!"); an appeal to fear, warning that worse will inevitably follow ("If you permit them to continue thus . . . the faithful of God will be much more widely attacked by them!"); and, last but certainly not least, the certain claim to be speaking for God ("Moreover, Christ commands it!").

But the rhetoric itself doesn't necessarily account for Urban's success.

To find out why his call resonated so deeply with his listeners, you actually have to go back a century—to the death of the French king Louis the Sluggard, in 987. Louis had ruled for only a single year, and (as his name suggests) wasn't much of a king. He was important only because he was the last king of the Carolingian dynasty, the final royal descendent of Charlemagne.

The powerful Frankish noblemen Louis had attempted to rule rejected the idea of finding a distant Carolingian relation to elevate. Instead, they crowned a king from a new family: Hugh Capet, son of the count of Paris, one of their own. Without much royal authority to wield, Hugh Capet found himself trying to control a disorderly mass of competing dukes who were accustomed to carrying on vicious private feuds without interference. Private warfare between French dukes, private oppression of farmers by aristocrats, armed spats between men of different loyalties and languages: France was a sea of chaos from border to border.

In 989, Christian priests gathered at the Benedictine abbey of Charroux to look for a solution. If France were to survive, someone had to quench the flames of private war that had followed the disintegration of strong royal power. The priests had no army, no money, and no political power, but they had the authority to declare the gates of heaven shut. And so they began to wield it.

They announced that noncombatants—peasants and clergy, families and farmers—should be immune from ravages of battle. Any soldier who robbed a church would be excommunicated. Any soldier who stole livestock from the poor would be excommunicated. Anyone who attacked a priest would be excommunicated (as long as the priest wasn't carrying a sword or wearing armor).

This meeting at Charroux was the first step in a gathering Christian movement known as the Peace and Truce of God. Over the next fifty years, two church councils extended the conditions of the Peace and Truce. Merchants and their goods joined peasants, clergymen, and farmers as official noncombatants, immune from attack. Certain days were now completely off limits for fighting: under threat of excommunication, no one could wage war on Fridays, Sundays, church holidays, or any of the forty days of Lent.

In 1041, Henry III of Germany (which had its own troubles with feuding aristocrats) decreed that the Peace and Truce would be observed in Germany from Wednesday evening through Monday morning of every week of the year. Then, in 1063, priests in the northern German city of Terouanne put together another set of regulations for the Peace and Truce of God. "These are the conditions which you must observe during the time of the peace which is commonly called the truce of God," the document began. "During those four days and five nights no man or woman shall assault, wound, or slay another, or attack, seize, or destroy a castle, burg, or villa, by craft or by violence." Furthermore, the Peace would be observed during every day of Advent and Lent, as well as between the church feasts of Ascension and Pentecost—a schedule that made nearly three-quarters of the year off-limits for fighting.

The result? Scores and scores of German and French noblemen who were absolutely spoiling for a fight—and couldn't find one without risking excommunication. So when, in November of 1095, at the French town of Clermont, Urban II announced that it was time to recapture Jerusalem, he gave all those aristocrats who had been chafing under the restrictions of the Peace and Truce of God something useful to do with their energy.

"Let those who have been accustomed unjustly to wage private warfare against the faithful now go against the infidels," Urban II told his audience. "Let those who for a long time have been robbers, now become knights. Let those who have been fighting against their brothers and relatives now fight in a proper way against the barbarians. . . . Let those who go not put off the journey. . . . As soon as winter is over and spring comes, let them eagerly set out on the way with God as their guide." And those who eagerly set out would receive the greatest possible reward: "All who die by the way, whether by land or by sea, or in battle against the pagans, shall have immediate remission of sins," Urban promised.

And so they went. Then, just as today, religious rhetoric brought about political ends most efficiently—when it gave justification to something that the hearers already wanted, for entirely secular reasons, to do.

Chapter Ninety-Three

The Loss of France

You may use your text when answering the questions in sections I and II.

Section I: Who, What, Where

Write a one or two-sentence answer explaining the significance of each item listed below.

Duke of Bedford

Charles VII

Écorcheurs

Henry VI

Jeanne d'Arc

John Talbot

Pierre Cauchon

Treaty of Arras

Section II: Comprehension

Write a two or three-sentence answer to each of the following questions.

1. Explain Henry V's position as king of France through his sudden death from dysentery on August 30, 1422.

2. What important question did Charles VI's death raise? How was the question answered?

3. Describe the civil war in France through the appearance of Jeanne d'Arc.

4. What happened when Jeanne d'Arc met Charles VII at Chinon in March of 1429?

5. How did Charles VII's fortune change after Jeanne d'Arc started leading his army against the Burgundian-English forces?

6. What happened when Jeanne d'Arc and the royalist army attacked Paris?

7. How did Jeanne d'Arc plan to recapture the momentum of the royalist army? What happened instead?

8. How were women accused of heresy supposed to be treated by the court? Why was there a confusion of procedure at Jeanne d'Arc's trial?

9. Why was Jeanne d'Arc burned at the stake when she was originally supposed to be imprisoned for life?

10. What caused the relationship between the English-French alliance to fracture after Jeanne d'Arc's death?

11. How did Charles VII upset the dukes in France after reclaiming power in Paris?

12. Why did Charles VII go on the offensive against the English in June of 1449? What was the result of this turn?

13. Describe the illnesses faced by Charles VII and Henry VI.

Section III: Critical Thinking

You may not use your text to answer this question.

Jeanne d'Arc reignited the French army in the fight against the English, and she saved Charles VII from losing his throne. Yet, when she was captured by the English and tried for heresy, Charles VII did nothing to help her. Explain how, though devastating, Charles VII's refusal to help Jeanne d'Arc actually benefitted the French cause.

Section IV: Map Exercise

1. Trace the rectangular outline of frame of Map 93.1: The Dauphin against the English in black.

2. Using your blue pencil, trace the coastal outline around Ireland, England, and Europe, including the small visible portion of the Mediterranean. Also trace the line of the Loire. Repeat until the contours are familiar.

3. Using contrasting colors, trace the outlines of the areas loyal to England and loyal to France. Repeat until the contours are familiar.

4. Using a new sheet of paper, trace the rectangular outline of the map in black. Then using your regular pencil with an eraser, draw the coastal outline around Ireland, England, and Europe, including the small visible portion of the Mediterranean. Also draw the line of the Loire.Then draw

the outlines of the areas loyal to England and loyal to France. When you are happy with your map, lay it over the original. Erase and re-draw any lines which are more than ½" off of the original.

5. Label the areas of Ireland, England, Normandy, Brittany, and Gascony. Then study carefully the locations of Plymouth, Dartmouth, Southampton, London, Brentwood, Dover, Rye, the Isle of Wight, Calais, Guines, Arras, Tournelles, Compiegne, Coucy, Reims, Rouen, Meulan, St.-Denis, Paris, Rambouillet, Domremy, Troyes, Orleans, Meung, Mehun, Chinon, Poitiers, Bordeaux, and Bayonne. Then lay your map over the original. Erase and re-mark any locations which are more than ½: off of the original.

7. Mark the location of Mehun.

Chapter Ninety-Four

The Fall

You may use your text when answering the questions in sections I and II.

Section I: Who, What, Where

Write a one or two-sentence answer explaining the significance of each item listed below.

Aleddin

Casimir

Constantine XI Palaeologus

Frederick of Hapsburg

Halil Pasha

John Huniades

Ladislaus

Mehmet

The Battle at Varna

Urban

Wladyslaw III

Section II: Comprehension

Write a two or three-sentence answer to each of the following questions.

1. Describe Murad II's actions as Ottoman sultan through the destruction of the Hexamillion Wall.

2. What things did Albert II fail to do before his death on October 27, 1439?

3. How did Murad II plan to stop Hungary and Poland from unifying against him? Why did the plan fail?

4. Why did Murad II attack Belgrade? What happened when he attacked?

5. Explain how Belgrade and its defenders were able to hold off the Turks.

6. How did a papal legate convince Wladyslaw III and John Huniades to go on a Crusade against Murad II? What happened to the forces that were supposed to gather to fight the Ottoman sultan?

8. What was the purpose of Boğazkesen, "Cutter of the Strait?" How did it claim its first victim?

9. Describe the preparations Mehmet II made for his attack on Constantinople.

10. How did Mehmet II get around the massive chain that blocked the Golden Horn?

11. What finally caused the fall of Constantinople?

Section III: Critical Thinking

You may not use your text to answer this question.

The Turkish bombardment of Constantinople began on April 4, 1453. The weak forces inside of the city could barely defend themselves, and after the Golden Horn filled with enemy ships, and two more attempted invasions through the breaches in the walls took place on May 7 and May 18, Constantine asked Mehmet for terms on which the sultan would withdraw. Mehmet responded "Either I shall take this city, or the city will take me, dead or alive. . . . The city is all I want, even if it is empty." It was very important for Mehmet II to take Constantinople. Write a paragraph that connects his treatment by his father to his desire for conquest. How did his appointment to sultan, and then his demotion, relate to his burning desire to take the Christian Jewel on the Black Sea?

Maps to Accompany
The Study and Teaching Guide
for
the History of the Renaissance World

ALL MAPS DESIGNED BY SUSAN WISE BAUER AND SARAH PARK

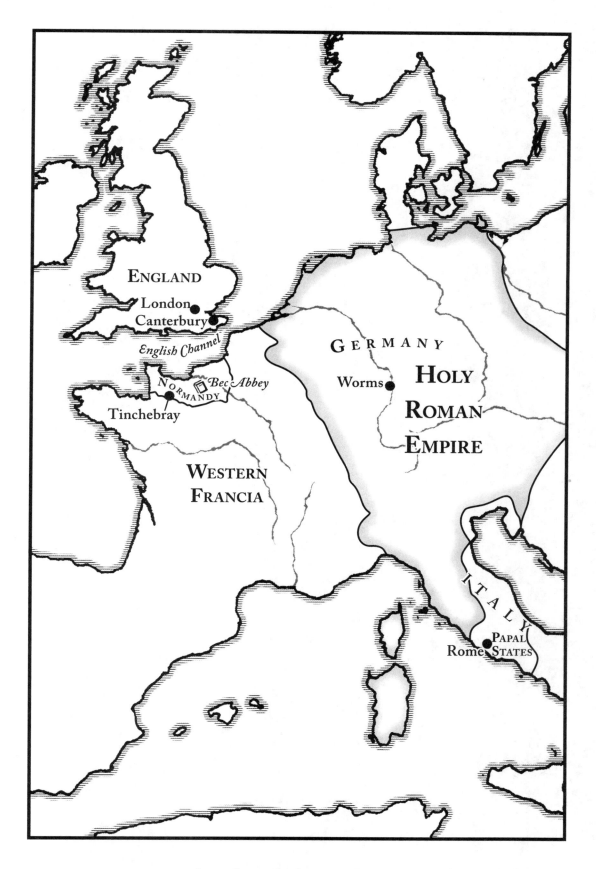

Map 1.1: England and the Holy Roman Empire

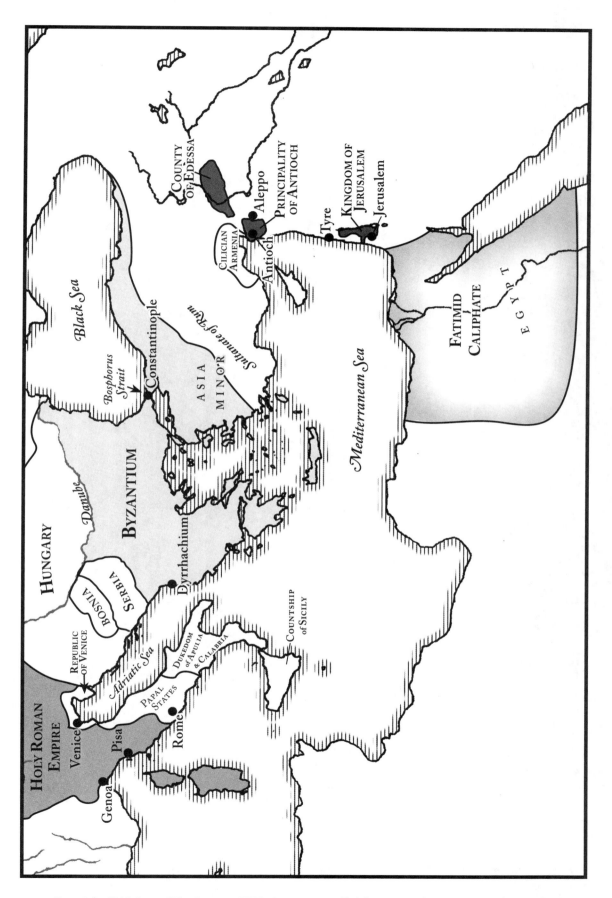

Map 2.1: The Lands of the Crusades

Map 4.1: The Kingdoms of China and Southeast Asia

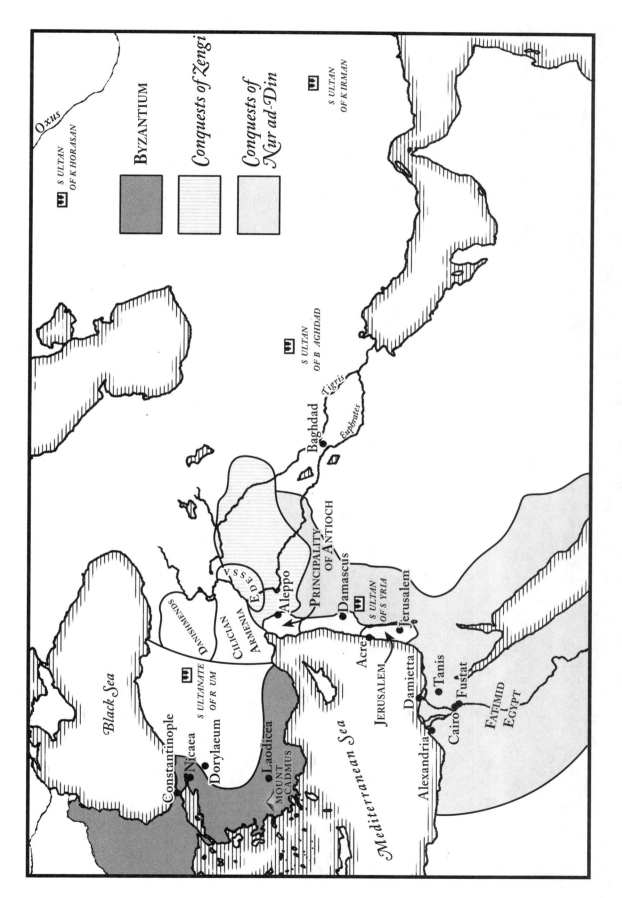

Map 5.3: The Conquests of Zengi and Nur ad-din

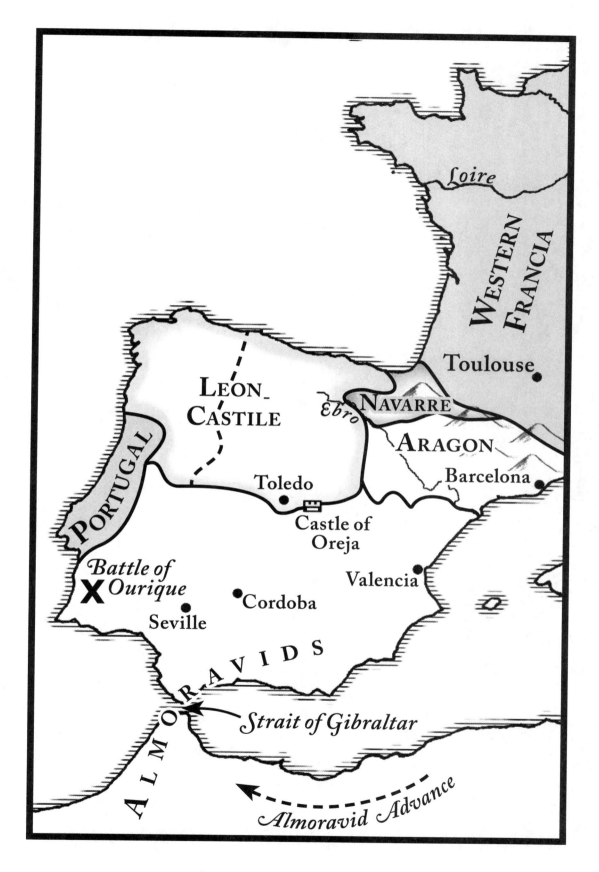

Map 6.1: The Spanish Peninsula, 1144

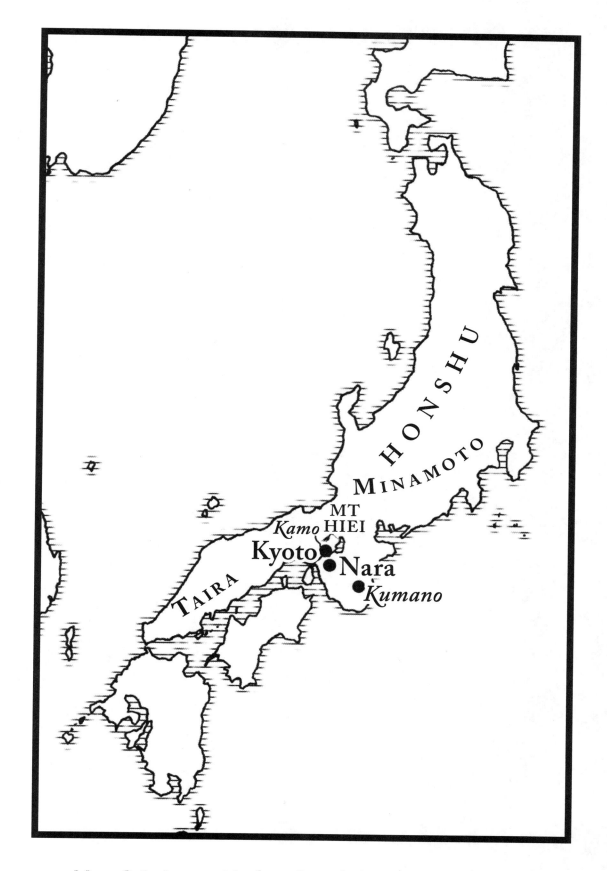

Map 9.1: **Japan Under the Cloistered Emperors**

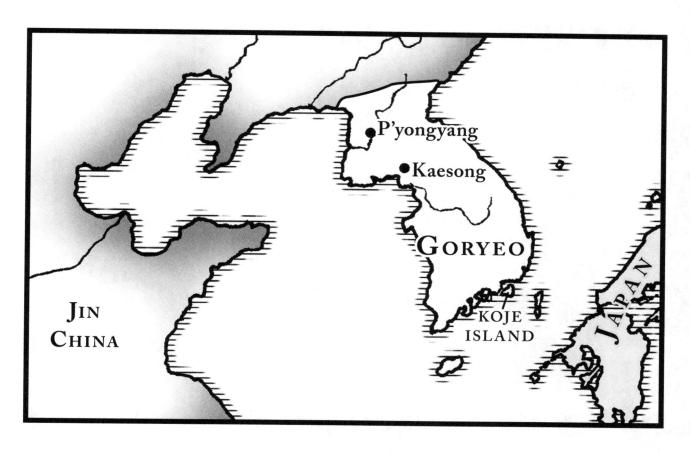

Map 10.1: **Goryeo**

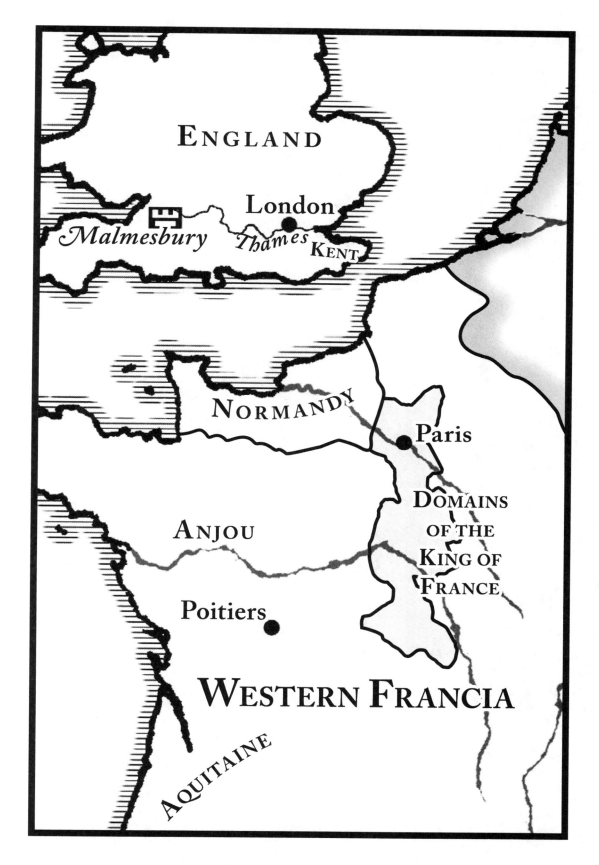

Map 11.1: Anjou, Normandy, and England

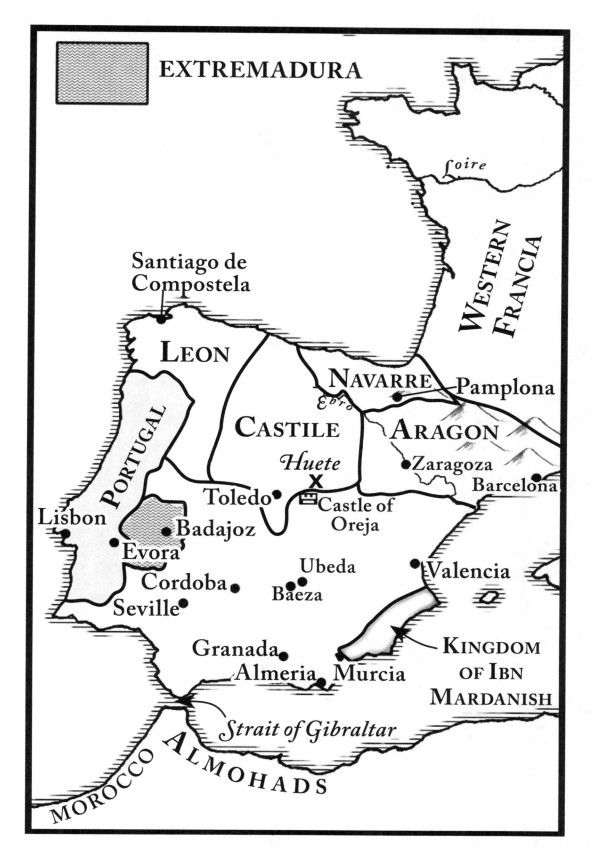

EXTREMADURA

Santiago de
Compostela

LEON

PORTUGAL

Lisbon

Evora

Badajoz

Cordoba

Seville

CASTILE

Huete
X
Castle of
Oreja

Toledo

Ubeda
Baeza

Ebro

NAVARRE Pamplona

ARAGON

Zaragoza
Barcelona

WESTERN
FRANCIA

Loire

Valencia

KINGDOM
OF IBN
MARDANISH

Granada
Almeria Murcia

Strait of Gibraltar

MOROCCO ALMOHADS

Map 13.1: The Kingdoms of Spain

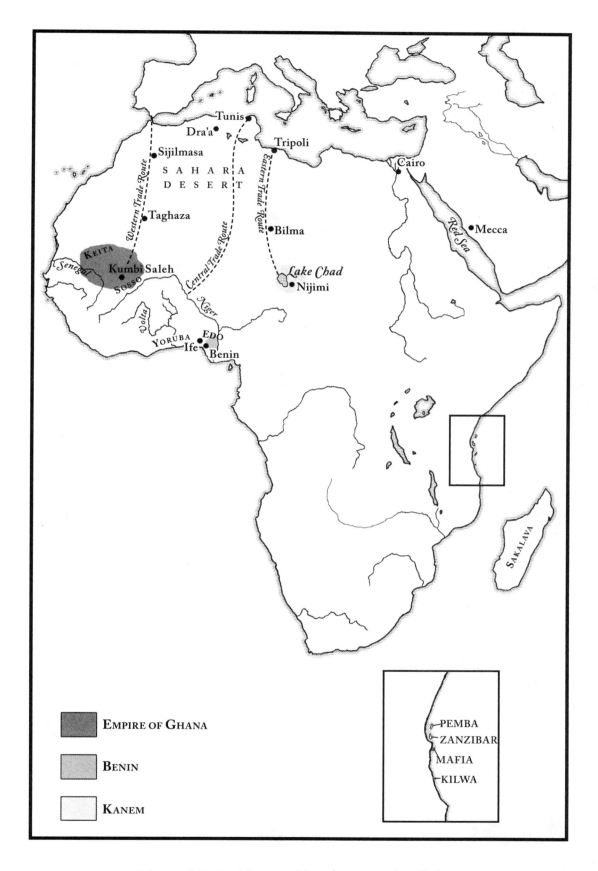

Map 14.1: **Many Nations of Africa**

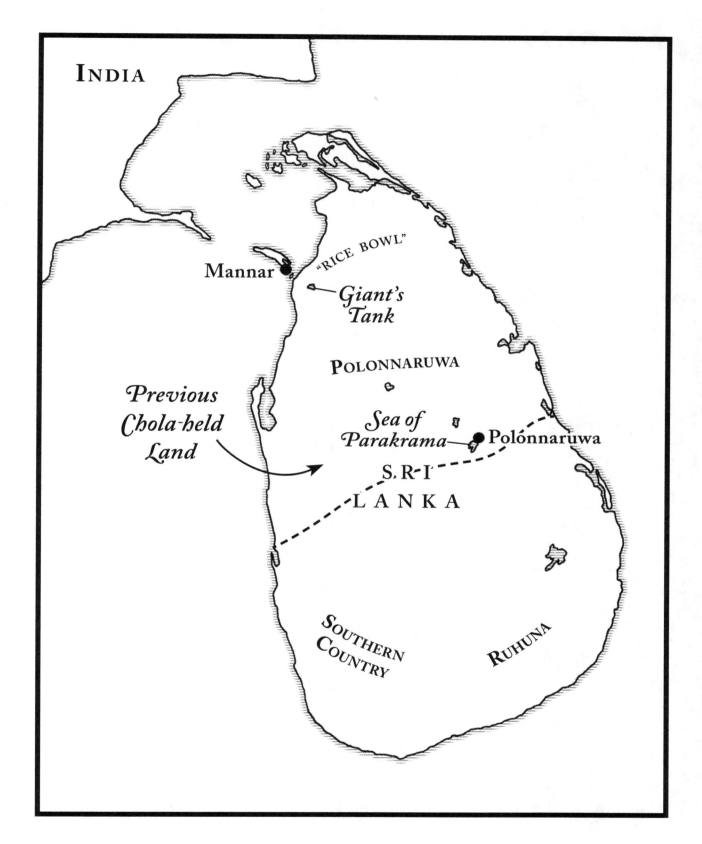

Map 16.1: The Island of Sri Lanka

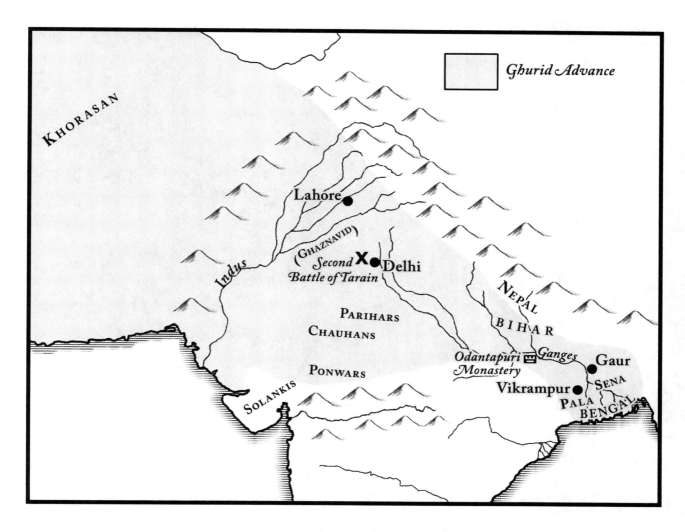

Map 17.1: The Ghurid Advance

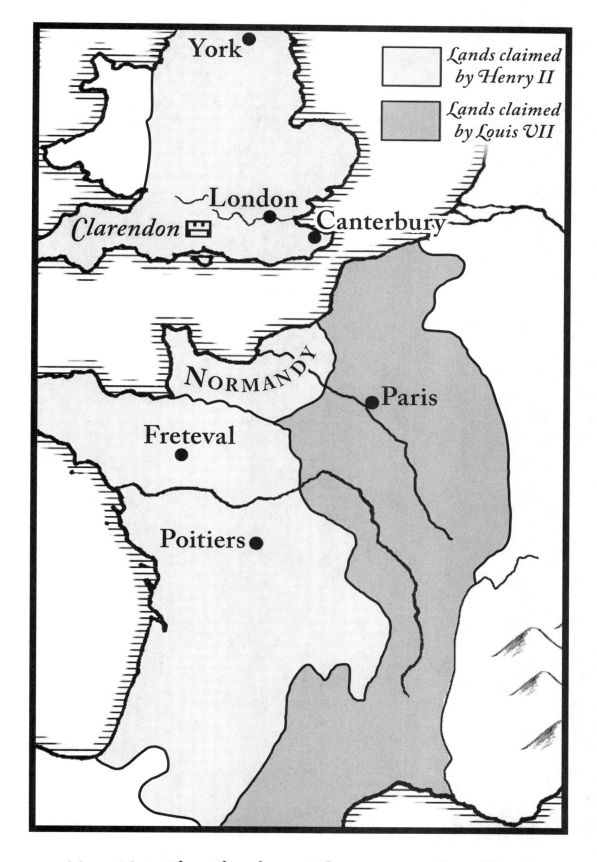

Map 18.1: The Kingdoms of France and England

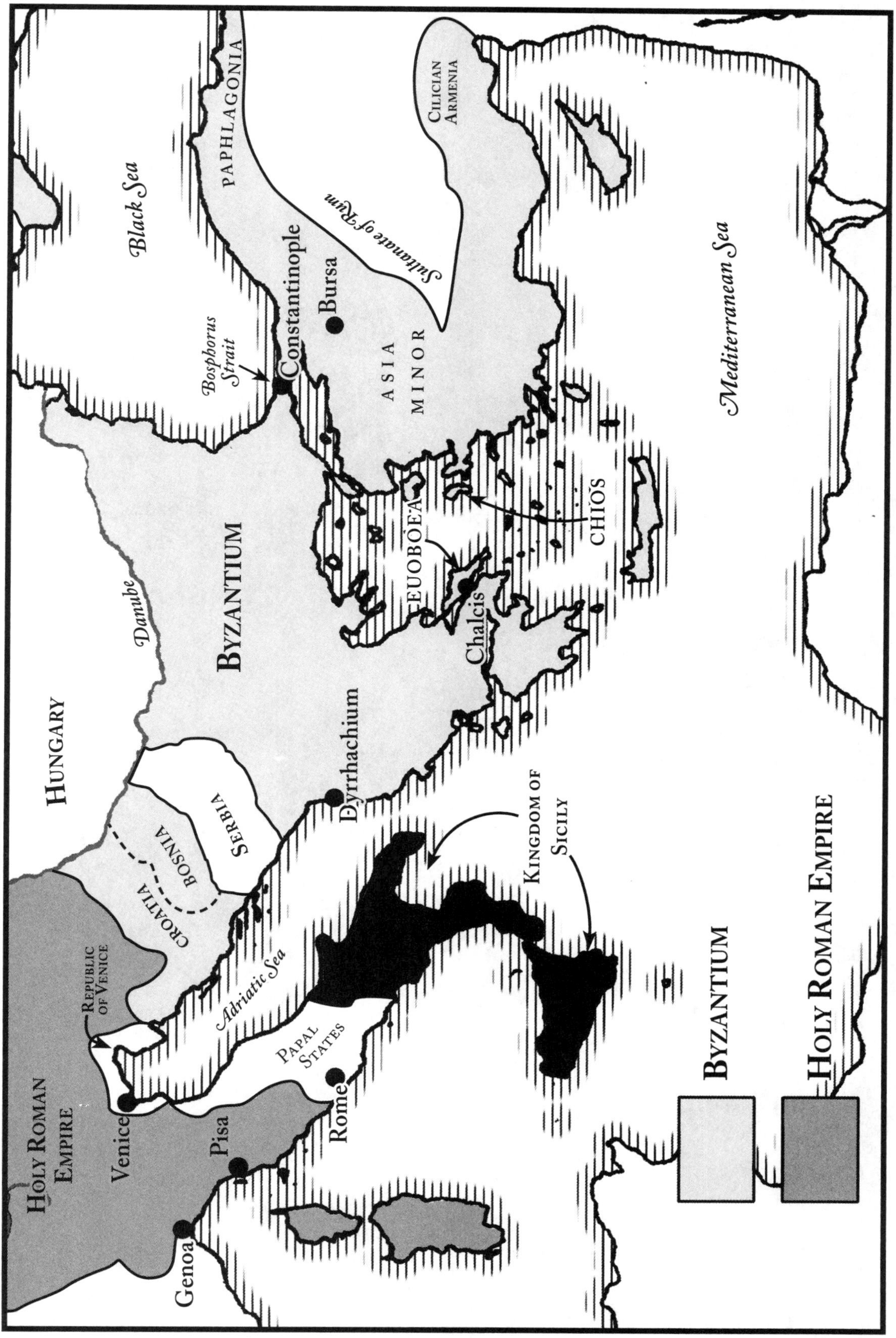

Map 20.1: Byzantium and Venice

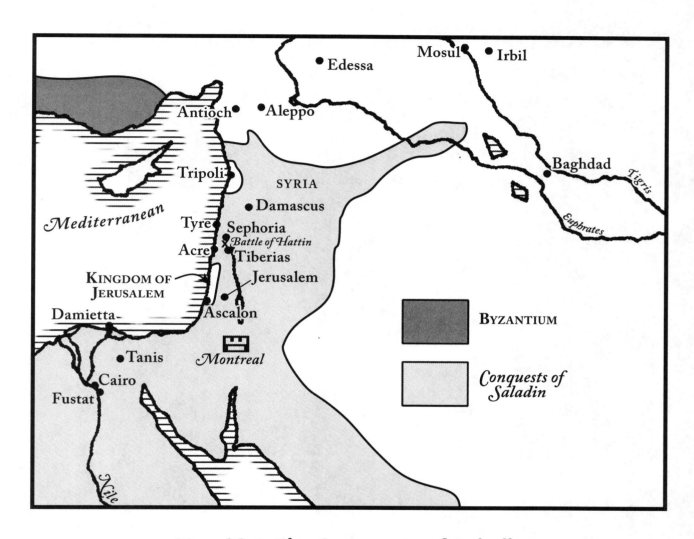

Map 22.1: **The Conquests of Saladin**

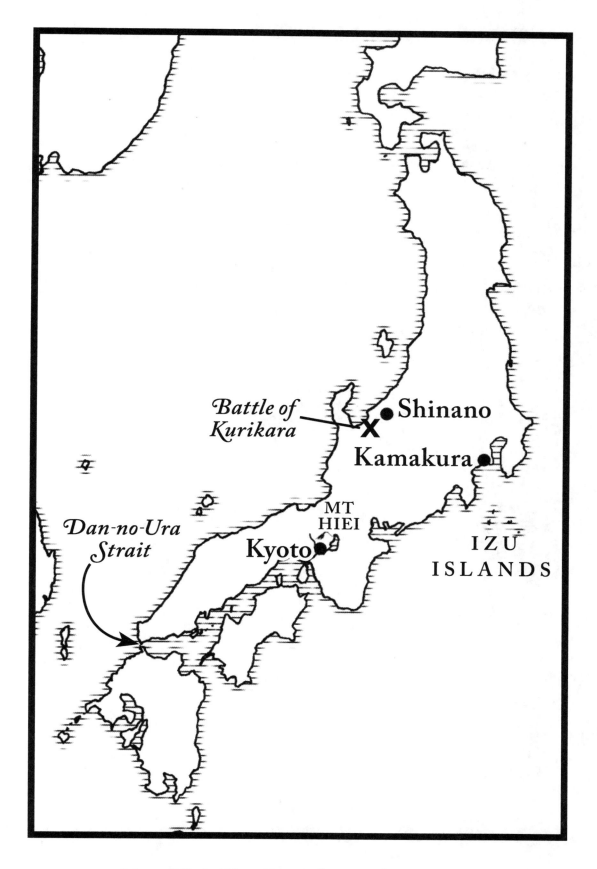

Map 23.1: The Kamakura Shogunate

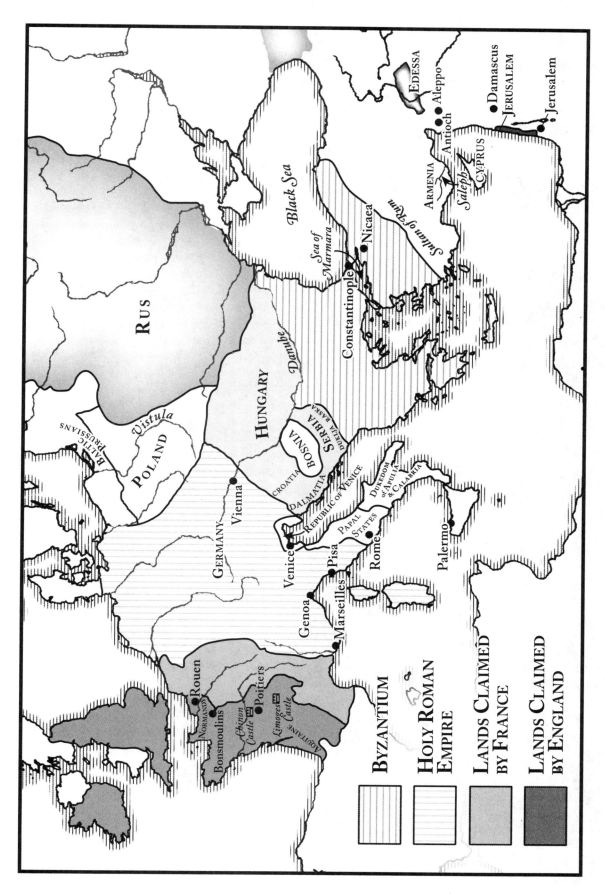

Map 24.1: The World of the Third Crusade

BYZANTIUM

HOLY ROMAN EMPIRE

LANDS CLAIMED BY FRANCE

LANDS CLAIMED BY ENGLAND

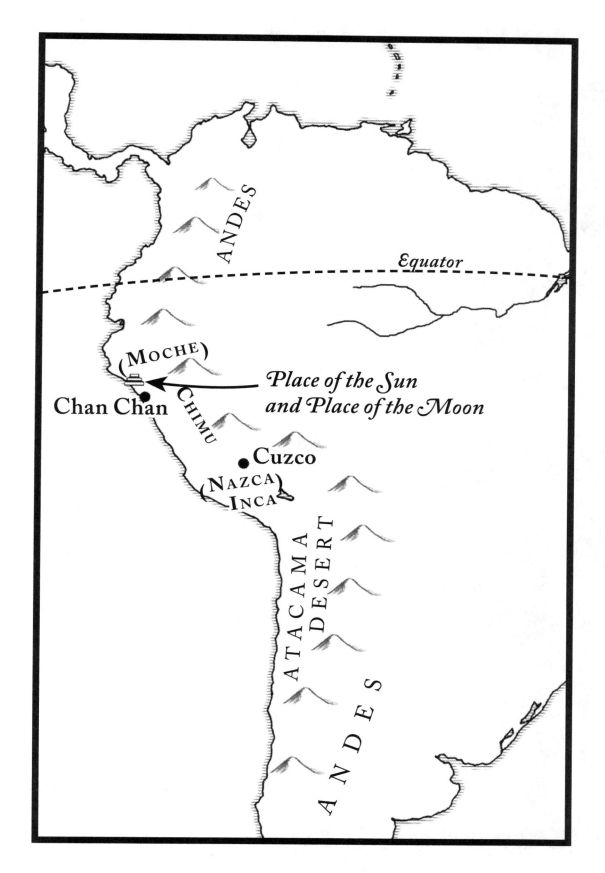

ANDES

Equator

(MOCHE)

CHIMU

Chan Chan

*Place of the Sun
and Place of the Moon*

Cuzco

NAZCA
INCA

ATACAMA DESERT

ANDES

Map 26.2: South America

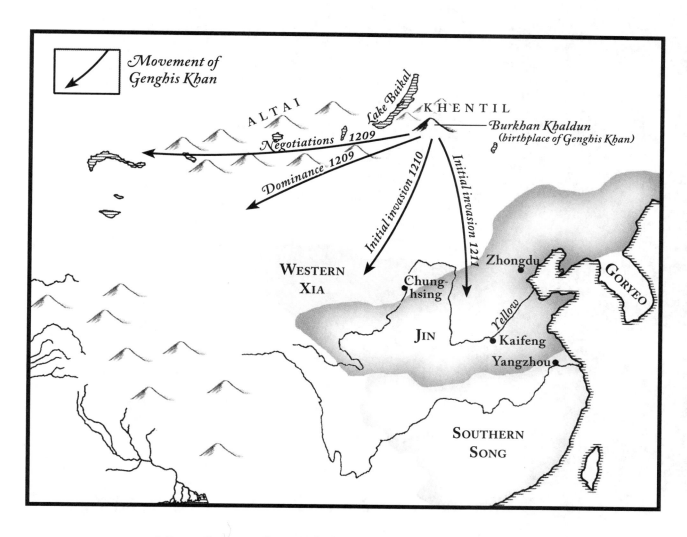

Map 27.1: The Advance of the Mongols

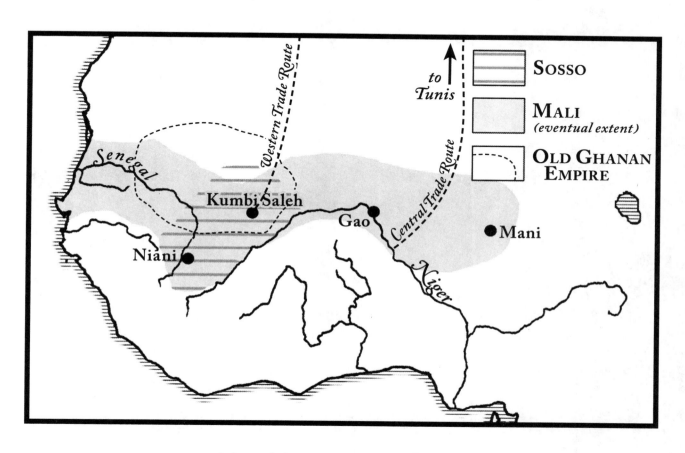

Map 29.1: **Sosso and Mali**

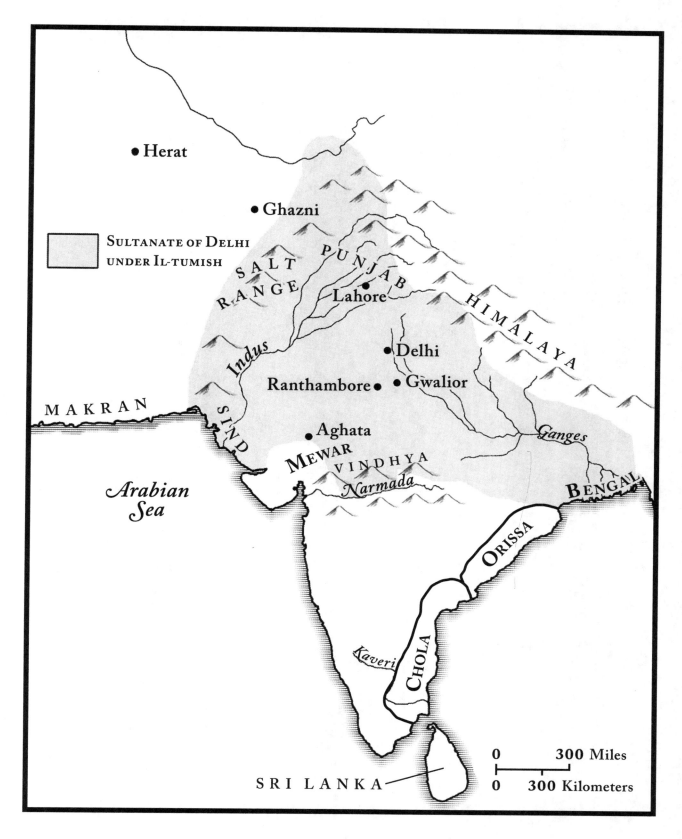

Map 32.2: Delhi Under Iltumish

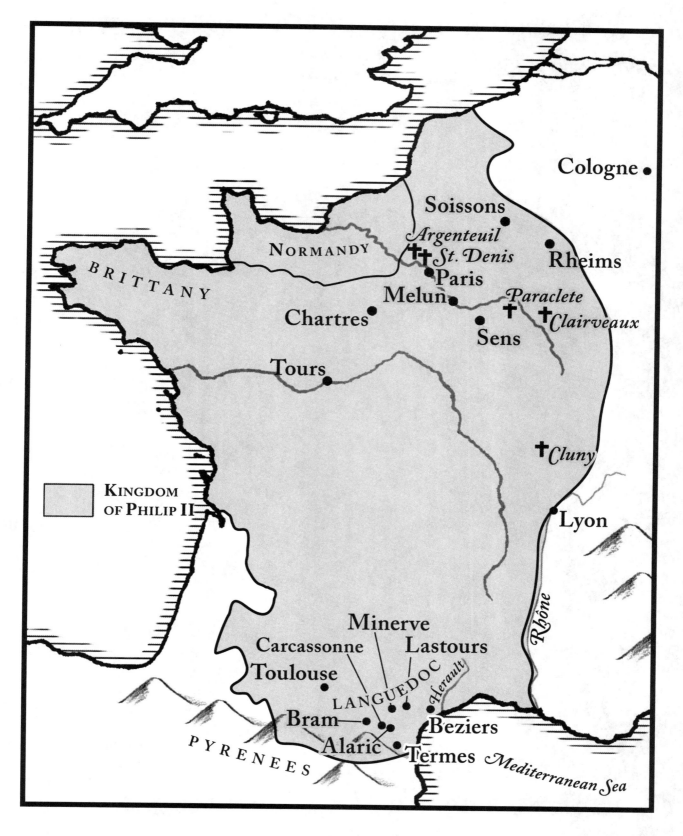

Map 33.1: The Albigensian Crusade

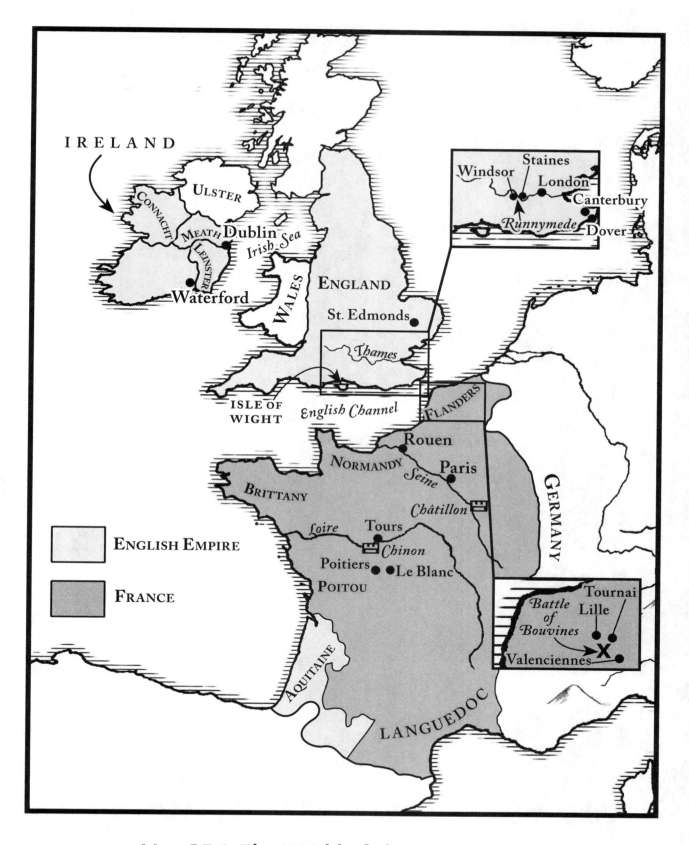

Map 35.1: The World of the Magna Carta

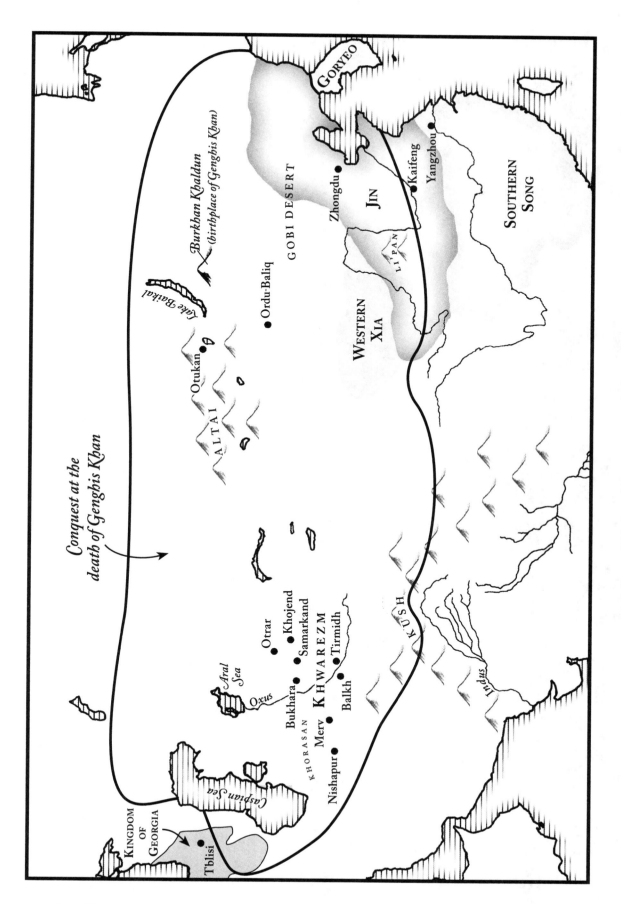

Map 37.1: The Mongol Empire

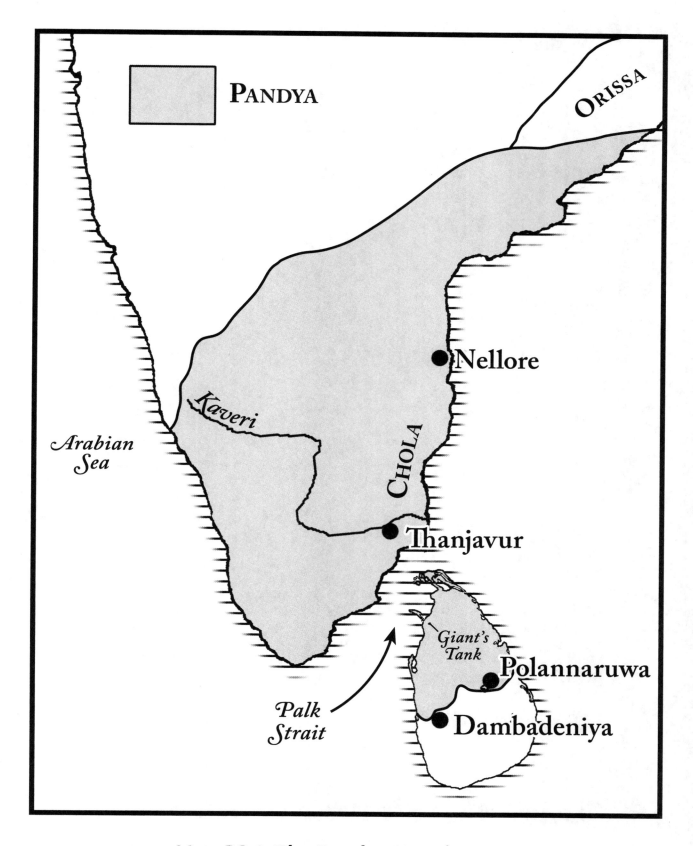

Map 38.1: The Pandya Renaissance

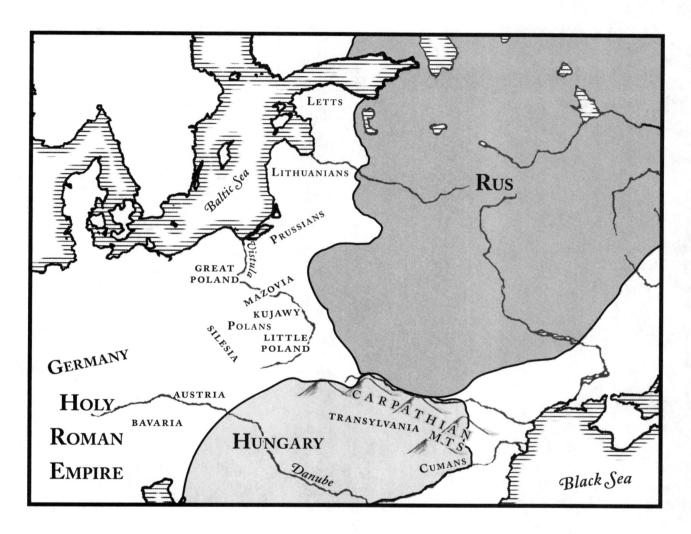

Map 40.1: **The Baltic Crusade**

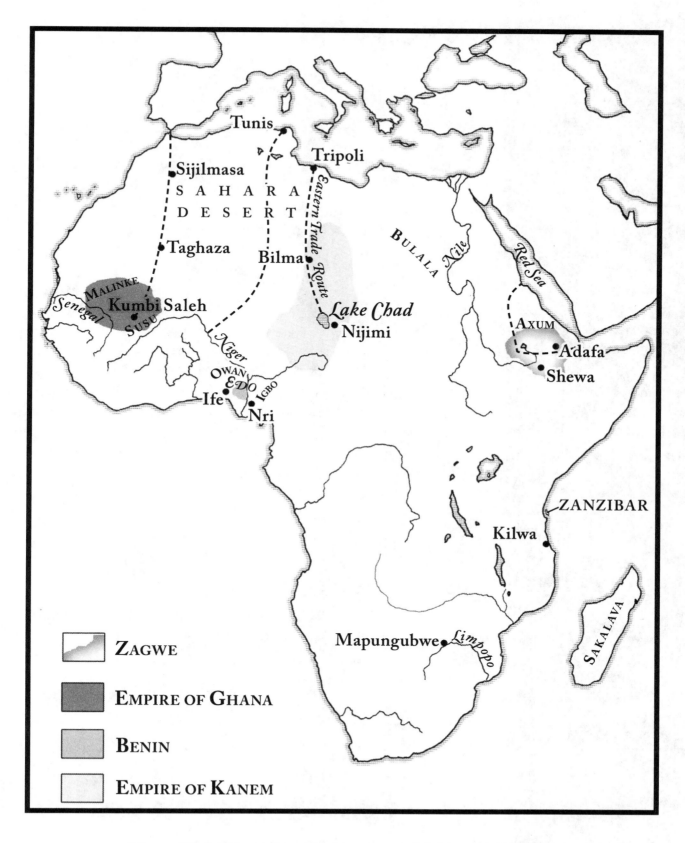

Map 41.1: **Zagwe, Kanem, and Mapungubwe**

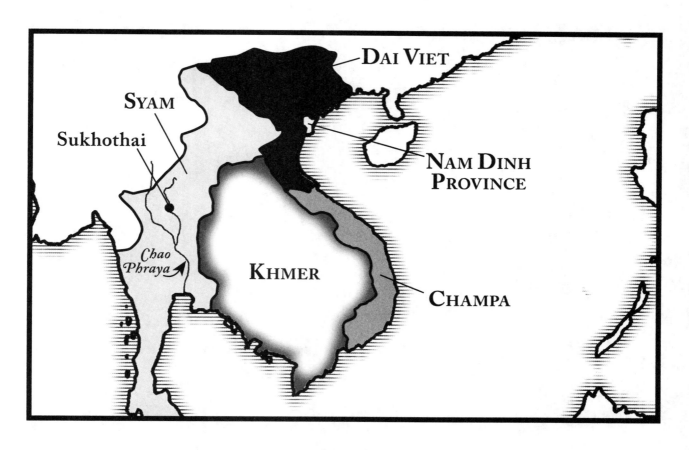

Map 43.1: The Four Kingdoms of Southeast Asia

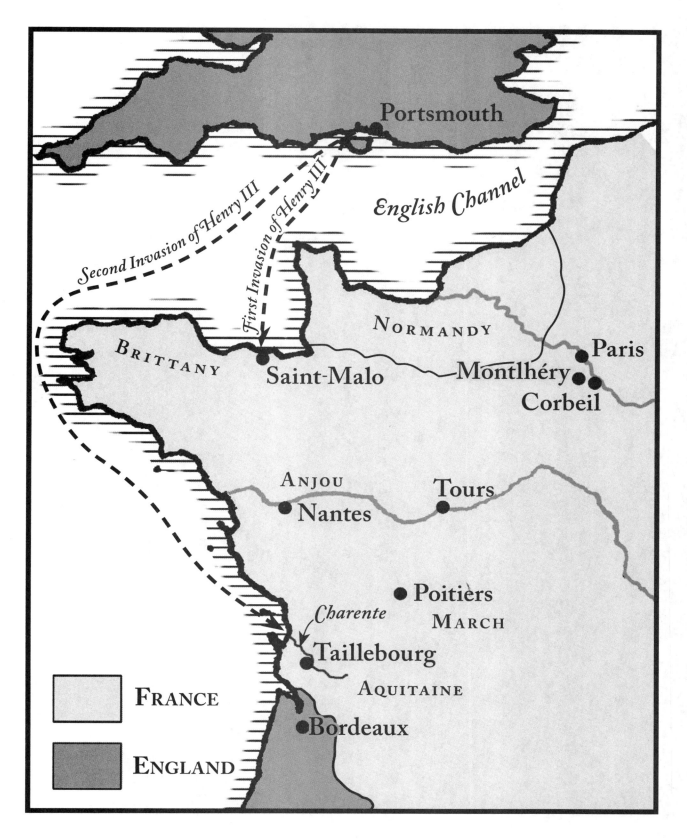

Map 44.1: **The Invasions of Henry III**

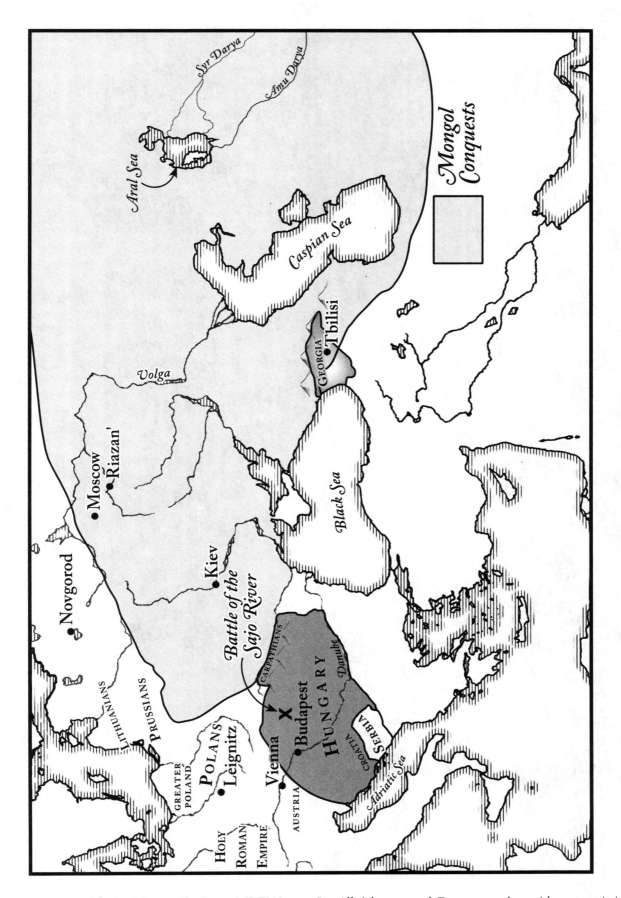

Map 45.2: Mongol Conquests in the West

Mongol Conquests

Syr Darya

Amu Darya

Aral Sea

Caspian Sea

Volga

GEORGIA · Tbilisi

Moscow ·
· Riazan'

Novgorod ·

Kiev ·

Black Sea

Battle of the Sajo River

LITHUANIANS

PRUSSIANS

CARPATHIANS

POLANS
· Leignitz

GREATER POLAND

Vienna ✕ · Budapest HUNGARY

Danube

HOLY ROMAN EMPIRE

AUSTRIA

CROATIA

SERBIA

Adriatic Sea

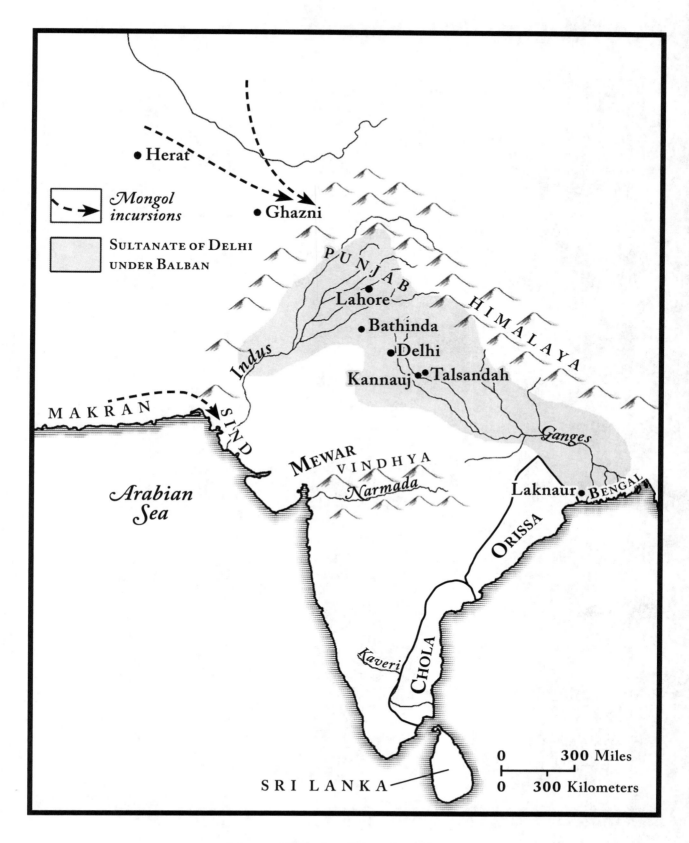

Map 47.1: **Balban's Wars**

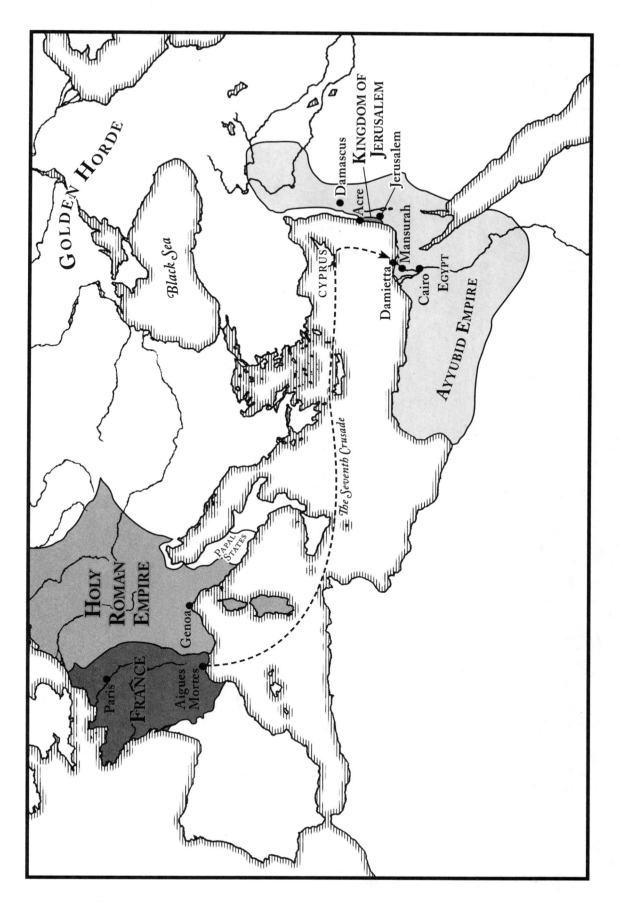

Map 48.1: The Seventh Crusade

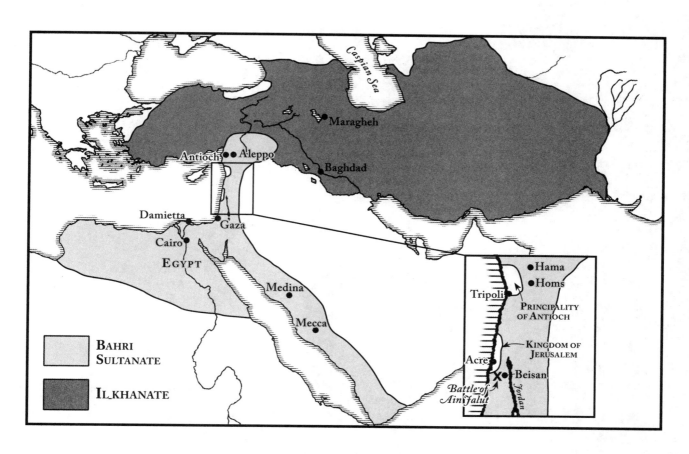

Map 50.1: **The Bahri Sultanate**

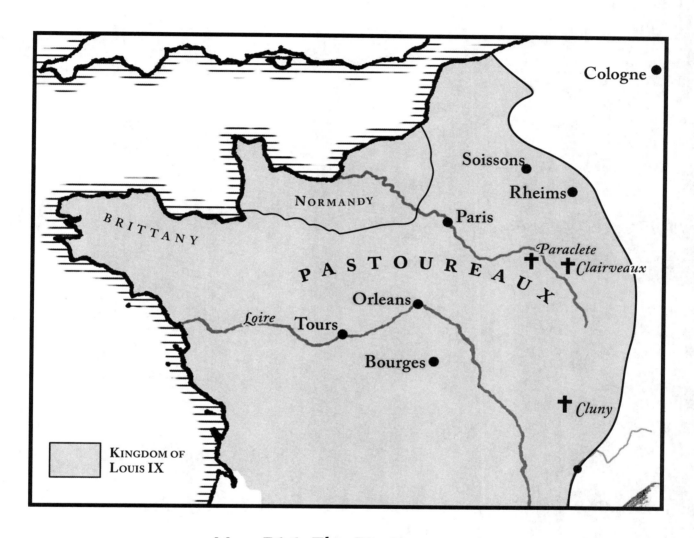

Map 51.1: The Pastoureaux

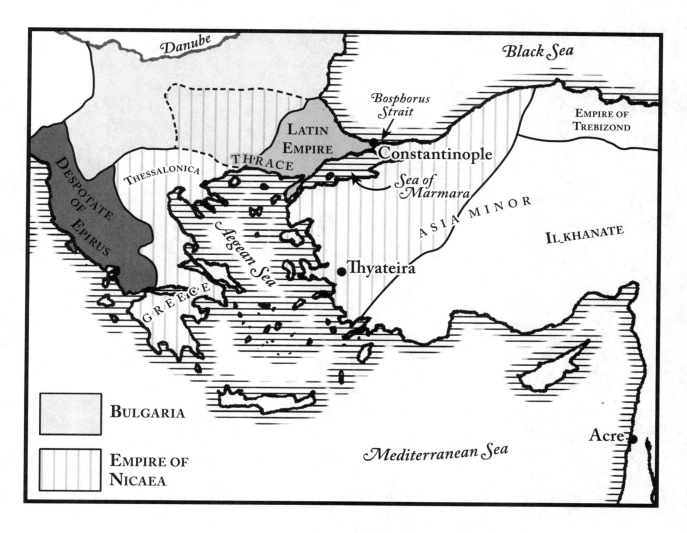

Map 53.1: **The Empire of Nicaea**

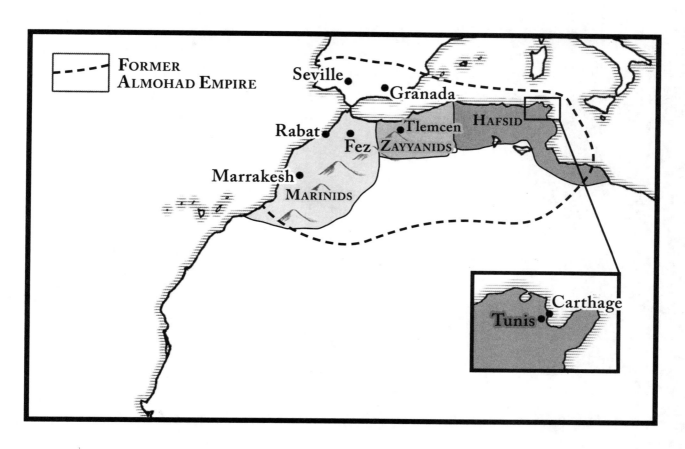

Map 54.1: After the Almohads

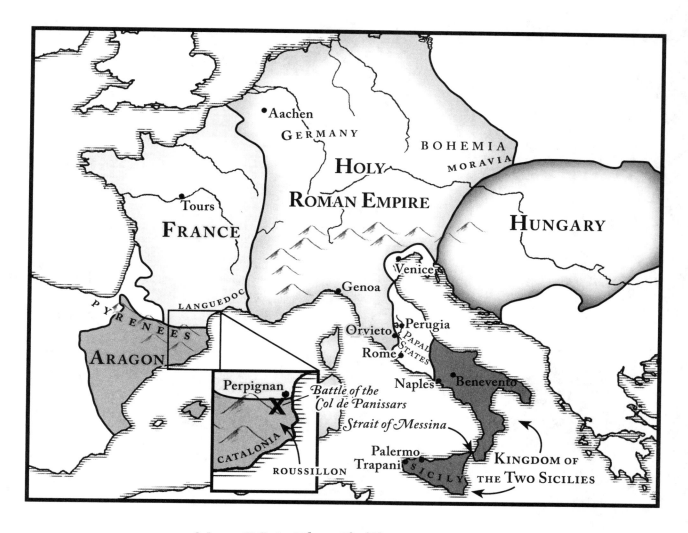

Map 56.1: The Sicilian Vespers

Map 57.1: Wars in Scotland and Wales

Map 59.1: The Empire, Divided

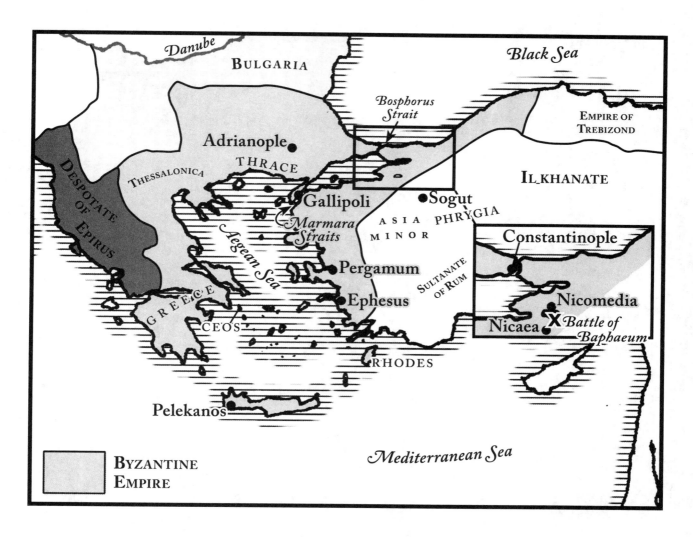

Map 60.1: **The Ottoman Invasion**

Map 63.1: Flood and Famine

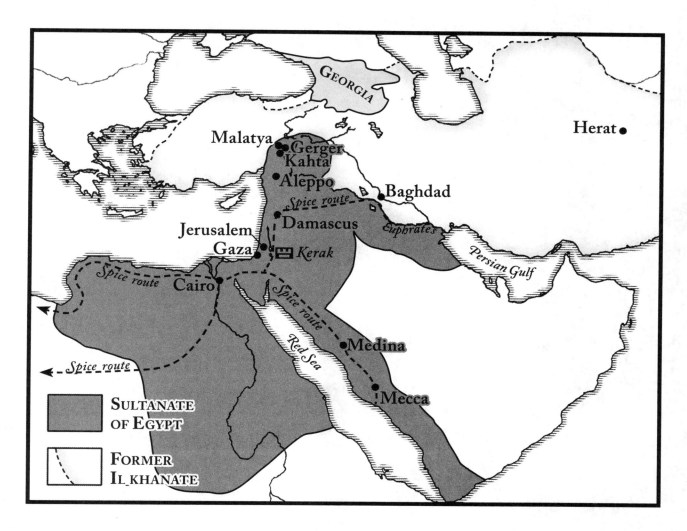

Map 64.1: **The Collapse of the Il-Khanate**

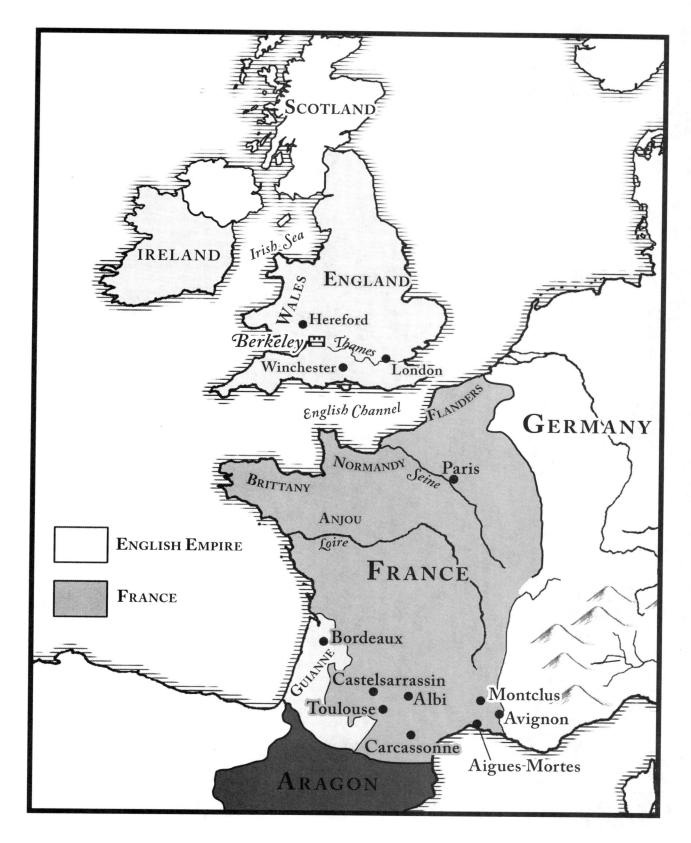

Map 66.1: Edward III and the Valois

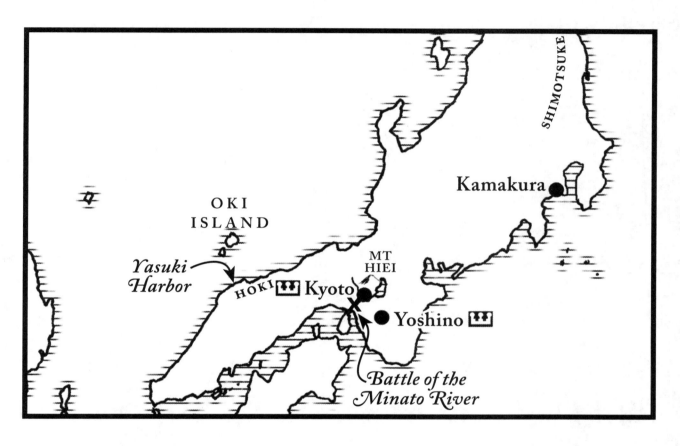

Map 67.1: The Southern and Northern Courts

Map 69.1: Lands Claimed by Louis of Bavaria

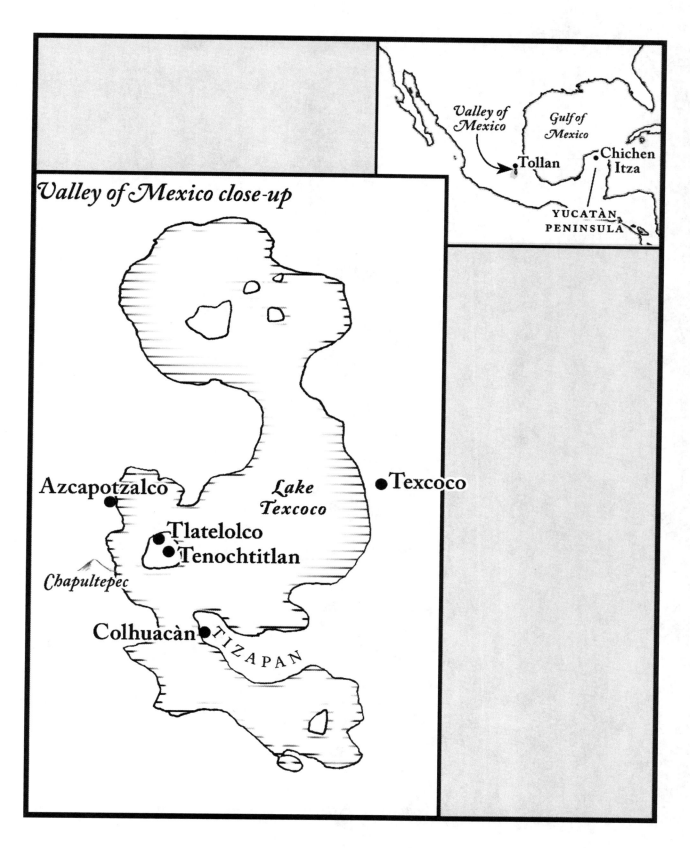

Map 70.1 The Aztecs

Valley of Mexico close-up

Azcapotzalco

Tlatelolco
Tenochtitlan

Chapultepec

Colhuacàn

TIZAPAN

Lake
Texcoco

Texcoco

Valley of
Mexico

Gulf of
Mexico

Tollan

Chichen
Itza

YUCATÀN
PENINSULA

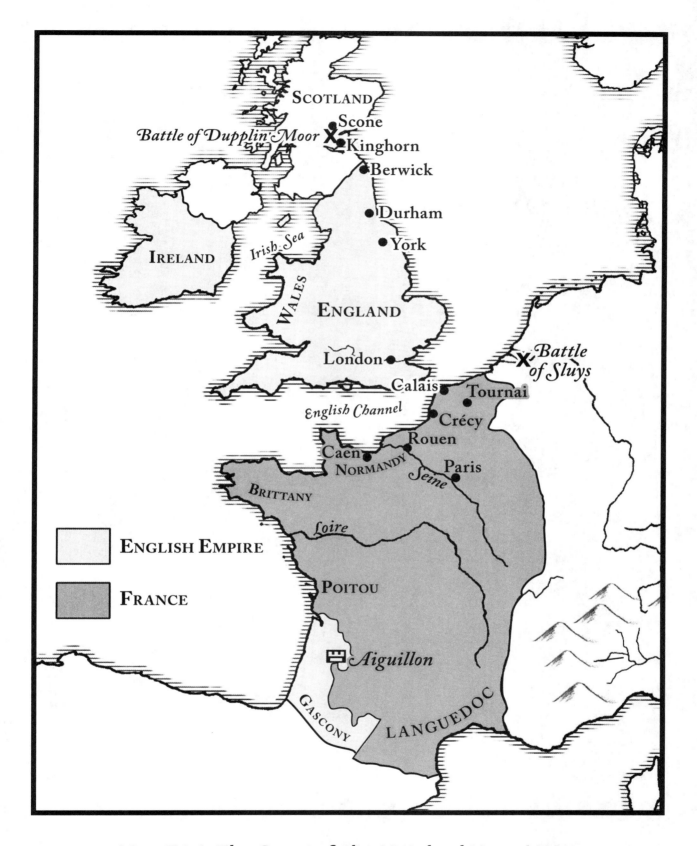

Map 71.1: The Start of the Hundred Years' War

SCOTLAND

Battle of Dupplin Moor ✗ Scone
Kinghorn
Berwick

Durham

York

IRELAND *Irish Sea*

WALES

ENGLAND

London
Calais
✗ *Battle of Sluys*
Tournai
English Channel
Crécy
Rouen
Caen
NORMANDY Paris
Seine

BRITTANY

Loire

ENGLISH EMPIRE

FRANCE

POITOU

Aiguillon

GASCONY LANGUEDOC

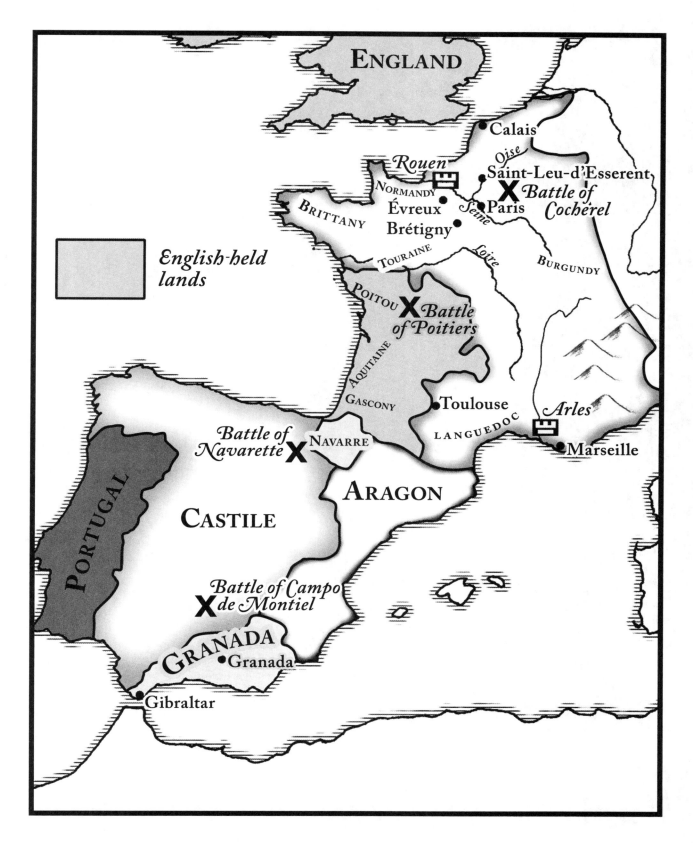

Map 73.1: French Defeats

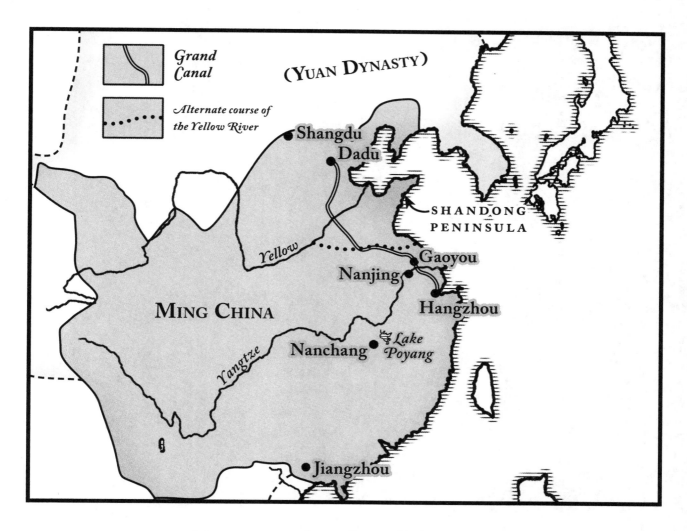

Map 74.1: The Rise of the Ming

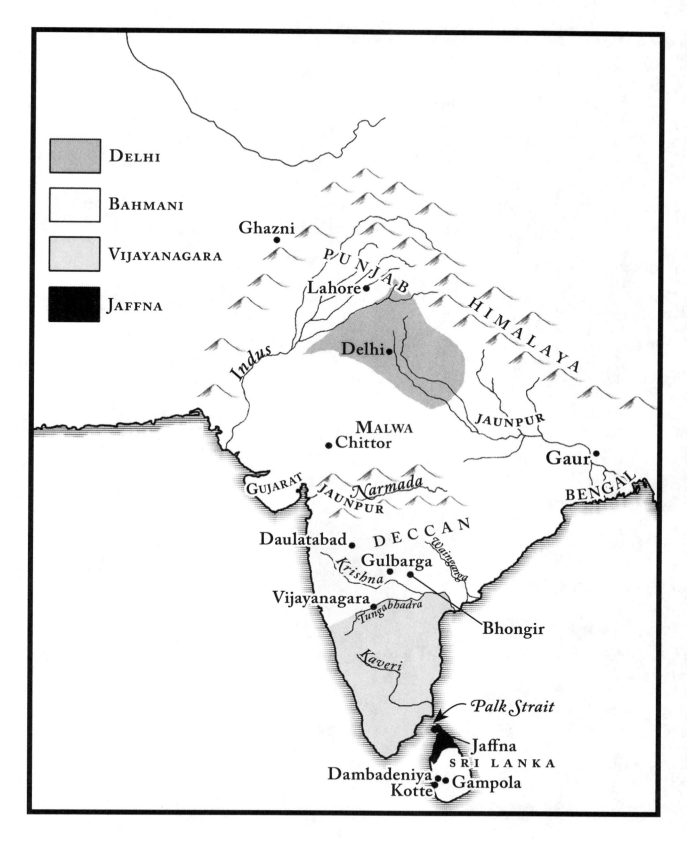

Map 77.1: Bahmani Expansion

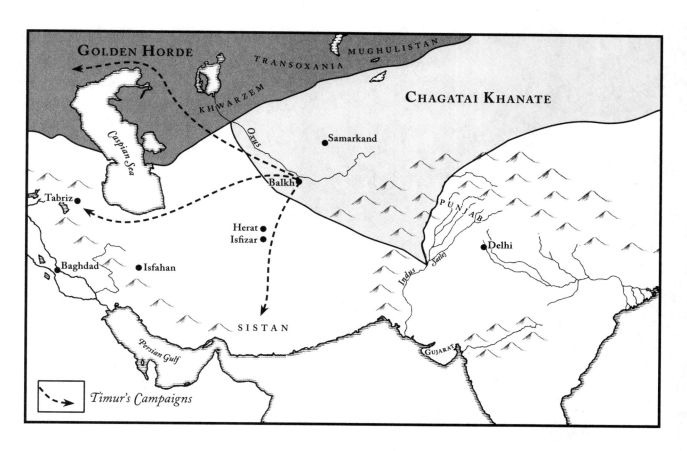

Map 79.1: **The Advance of Timur-Leng**

Map 81.1: War in Italy

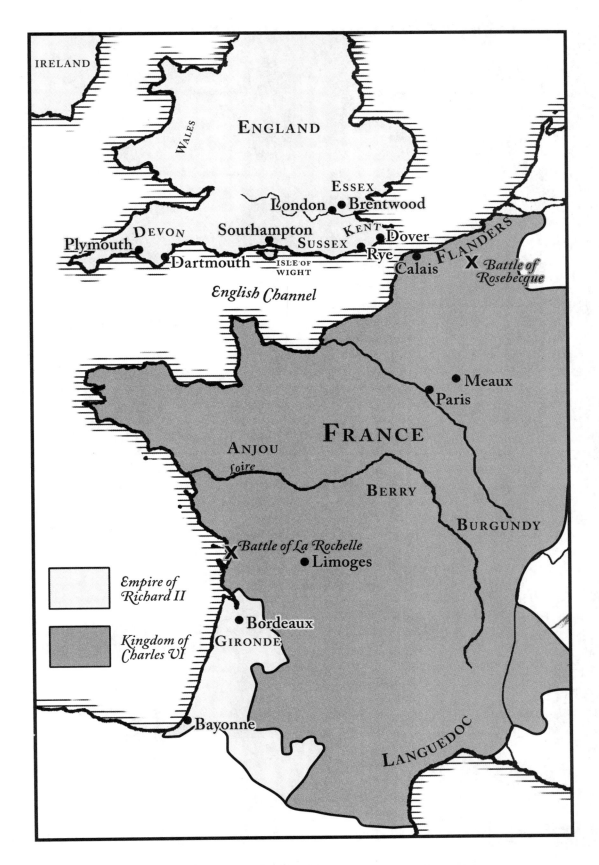

IRELAND

ENGLAND

WALES

ESSEX

London Brentwood

DEVON

Plymouth

Southampton KENT Dover

SUSSEX

Dartmouth ISLE OF Rye

WIGHT Calais FLANDERS

English Channel X *Battle of*
Rosebecque

Meaux

Paris

FRANCE

ANJOU

Loire

BERRY

BURGUNDY

X *Battle of La Rochelle*

Limoges

Empire of
Richard II

Bordeaux

GIRONDE

Kingdom of
Charles VI

Bayonne

LANGUEDOC

Map 82.1: Richard II and Charles VI

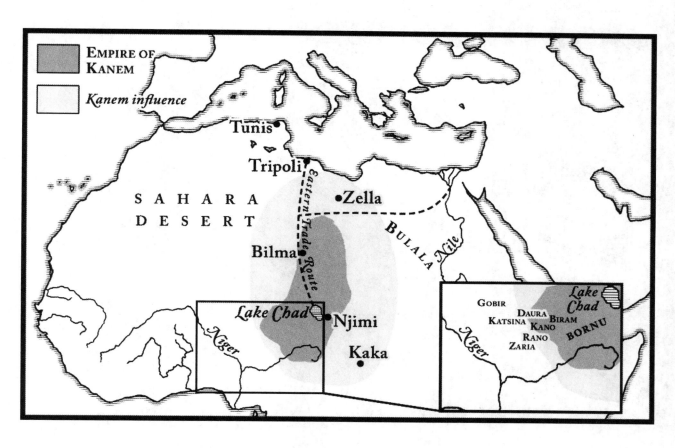

Map 83.1: The Hausa Kingdoms

Map 86.1: The Scandinavian Kingdoms

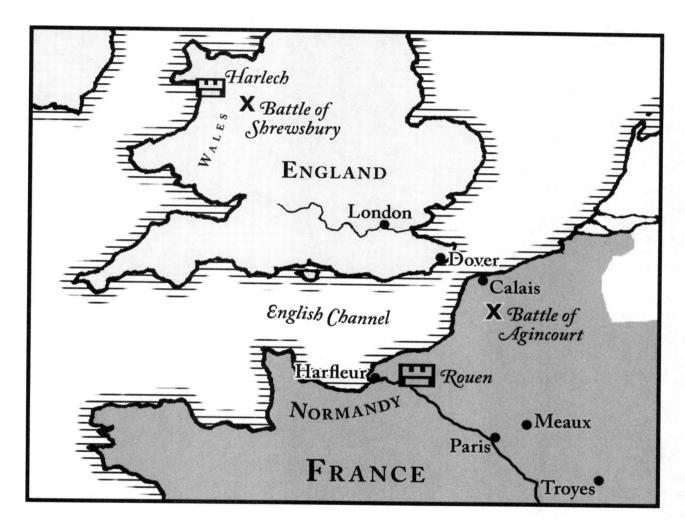

Map 88.1: The Battle of Agincourt

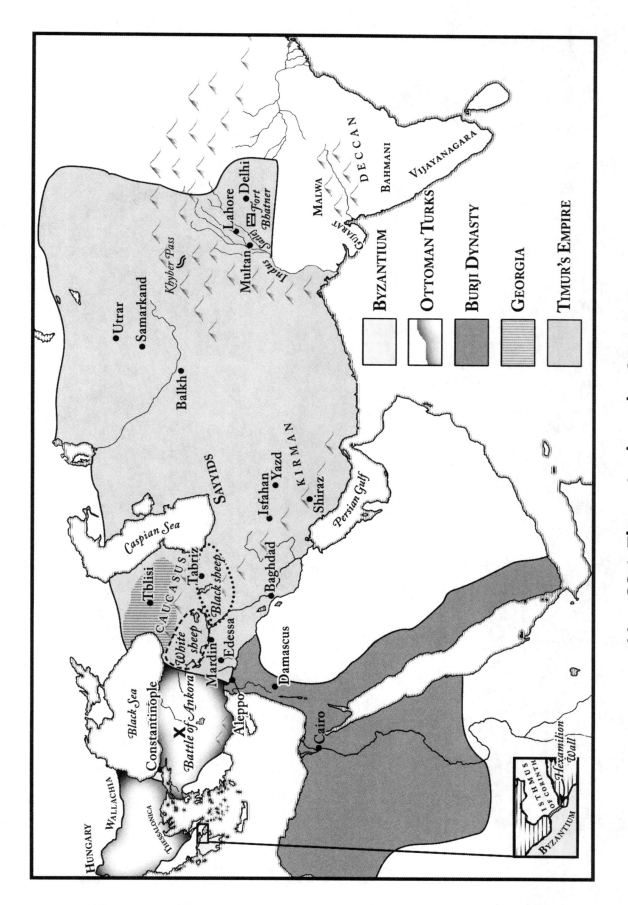

Map 89.1: Timur Against the Ottomans

BYZANTIUM
OTTOMAN TURKS
BURJI DYNASTY
GEORGIA
TIMUR'S EMPIRE

DECCAN
BAHMANI
VIJAYANAGARA
MALWA
GUJARAT

Delhi
Lahore
Fort Bhatner
Multan
Indus
Khyber Pass
Samarkand
Utrar
Balkh

KIRMAN
Yazd
Isfahan
Shiraz
Baghdad
SAYYIDS

Persian Gulf

Caspian Sea
Tblisi
CAUCASUS
Tabriz
Black sheep
White sheep
Mardin
Edessa
Damascus
Cairo
Aleppo
Battle of Ankora
Constantinople
Black Sea
Thessalonica
WALLACHIA
HUNGARY

ISTHMUS OF CORINTH
Hexamilion Wall
BYZANTIUM

Map 91.1: **The Empire of Sigismund**

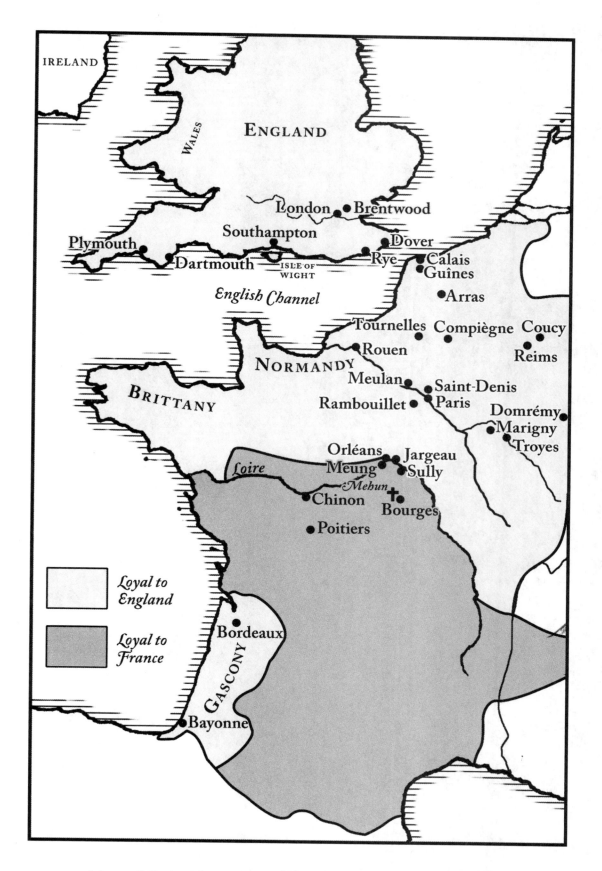

Map 93.1: **The Dauphin Against the English**